The Interior Design BUSINESS HANDBOOK

The Interior Design BUSINESS HANDBOOK

A Complete Guide to Profitability

FOURTH EDITION

Mary V. Knackstedt, FASID, FIIDA

WILEY

JOHN WILEY & SONS, INC.

Published by John Wiley & Sons, Inc., Hoboken, New Jersey
Published simultaneously in Canada

For general information about our other products and services, please contact our Customer Care Department within the United States at (800) 762-2974, outside the United States at (317) 572-3993, or fax (317) 572-4002.

Wiley also publishes its books in a variety of electronic formats. Some content that appears in print may not be available in electronic books. For more information about Wiley products, visit our Web site at www.wiley.com.

Library of Congress Cataloging-in-Publication Data:

Knackstedt, Mary V.
    The interior design business handbook : a complete guide to profitability /
Mary V. Knackstedt.— 4th ed.
        p. cm.
    Includes bibliographical references and index.
    ISBN 0-471-69698-6 (cloth)
    1. Interior decoration—Practice—Handbooks, manuals, etc. 2. Interior decoration firms—United States—Management—Handbooks, manuals, etc. 3. Interior decoration—United States—Marketing—Handbooks, manuals, etc. I. Title.
    NK2002.K57 2006
    747'.068—dc22
                                                                    2005017413

10 9 8 7 6 5 4 3

This book is dedicated to designers, those in our Forum and others who have shared concerns and information.

Together, we can continue to raise the standards for the field of interior design and increase our ability to serve our clients.

Contents

Preface

Today's designers are under great pressure to perform at a high level, often with greater speed than ever before. This means designers' business procedures must complement their creativity. I have revised this book extensively to make the business procedures as user-friendly as possible to the creative mind.

When we use the right procedures, the business portion of our organization can complement the creative process beautifully. As interior designers, we deal with business issues every day. We engage in business development when we seek new clients. We deal with finance every time we handle money. We sign contracts and letters of agreement, address personnel problems, and seek out new resources. We cope with masses of paperwork, including writing specifications and placing orders. Often we do these tasks without the background and advisors available to many other kinds of professionals.

To stay in business, we have to understand business. We don't have to earn business degrees or be personally capable of performing every business function, from accounting to devising retirement plans, but we do have to be able to talk with and understand the people who are specialists in these fields. If we are to pull our weight as members of financial planning teams and help our firms end the year with a profit, we cannot afford wearing blinders to financial matters.

Though business procedures are taught in design schools, they are not taught as extensively as they should be; the courses are usually scheduled for one semester or a year. Business procedures are the basis of communication we will use throughout our professional years. We must relate to other industries, including the financial and legal entities that are part of the business world. If handled properly, these relationships can ease and complement our own work practices. Moreover, a good basic understanding of specific business functions is necessary for everyone, not just the person running the design company. Staff members or anyone participating in the company, no matter in what capacity, will benefit from a good understanding of business practices.

Other professions establish strong liaisons and group activities through which they share business practices and solutions to common problems. The interior design profession needs to do the same. We can learn from each other, and by doing so, we can strengthen our individual firms and create a stronger and better-understood profession. We are fortunate to be able to perform business procedures at a higher level, because we are able to share and interact with other professionals in a way that was not possible in the past.

Awareness is the key. Just as we continue to learn about design throughout our lifetime, we need to keep current with other issues that affect the interior design field. Everything that affects business in general affects the interior design business. When insurance rates go up, or certain types of insurance become unavailable, we might have to modify the way we do business. The state of the stock market, the price of oil, and the value of real estate all affect our clients' attitudes toward buying design services; therefore, they affect our interior design businesses.

It's a chain reaction: If we are not operating our firms profitably, we all lose—our clients, because we don't have the same quality of interest in a job that is losing money and our staff and resources, because we don't have the funds to promptly meet our obligations. Consequently, we may not be able to attract the caliber of projects we enjoy working on and find most financially profitable.

When designers are comfortable dealing with money and with all the financial issues of our business, it gives us a tremendous sense of freedom and provides a good environment for creativity.

The *Interior Design Business Handbook* was written primarily for practicing interior designers, whether working independently or within large firms. It covers the full range of business activities and procedures for the life of a practice, from choosing a location and running a business on a daily basis to selling it when it's time to retire. It is also useful to students and as a training manual for support staff members.

The *Handbook* defines business procedures that work for interior design firms all over the country. It's a book to refer to just before meeting with business advisors. You may also want to give a copy to your bookkeeper and accountant, so they understand our field better.

This fourth edition of the *Interior Design Business Handbook* addresses many new issues not included in previous editions. My first book, *Interior Design for Profit*, was a very simple text. Since then, however, our work has become more complex, and each edition of the book has been progressively more extensive. Still, I was surprised at the number of changes that needed to be made in this edition. Banking, other financial issues, and many general procedures have changed significantly. Technology has been part of that change. Interior designers are also dealing more on an international basis. Even as I was finishing this book, I realized I wanted to keep going; there were so many more subjects I would like to present. But if I had included everything I would have liked, the book would have been so large it would be difficult to carry. Thus, it became necessary to address only the most important issues.

The *Handbook* establishes an excellent business foundation for your design firm. The information contained within has been researched and gathered in a very real, "hands-on" fashion during the many workshops, programs, and classes I have held with designers, architects, and others in related industries. At these meetings, many new questions surfaced. If I did not have a solution to them, I asked my consultants for their assistance in finding one. Once we found a solution, we asked the designers to try the particular procedure. If appropriate, we tested the procedure in our firm. After the procedure had been tried in a number of firms and polished, it was then presented in workshops, which became the basis of articles or books I have written. As a result, I can state with confidence that every procedure in this book works. These procedures are used daily in my own firm and other successful design firms throughout the United States.

In this edition of the *Handbook,* I have also added an extensive list of business terms designers frequently find in their various correspondence and documents.

I believe interior designers have a great contribution to make to the world. The creative process is very valuable in problem-solving situations. This book uses the design process to present and solve many business issues. You will find these procedures highly conducive to your creative style.

In working with many interior design firms—some near bankruptcy, others among the most profitable in the country—I have found that they have very specific problems. I've seen what goes wrong; even the most talented designers can lose money. But there are very easy ways of accomplishing our goals, and you will find many of those procedures here.

It is my hope that the *Interior Design Business Handbook* will enhance your creative energies by making the business end of interior design not only comprehensible but rewarding—in every sense of the word.

Interior design and architecture at one time were considered "gentlemen's professions," something people did because they loved doing it, not because they had a need for or interest in earning money. Today, however, though most of us love our work, we need to support ourselves and our families. To do that, we need the right business structure, one that enables us to be creative, to service our clients, *and* to earn appropriate income at the same time.

I would like to thank the many designers who have used and helped me develop this book. All of their input has been invaluable in helping me to determine its contents.

Acknowledgments

My goals in writing this book and in sharing business information have been to help create a professional standard for the interior design field and to try to ensure that there are rewards enough to keep all the bright and talented designers working in this field. Without the help and encouragement of many special people, I could never have completed a book of this scope and complexity.

Special thanks to the late Samuel Ledger, for teaching me to understand accounting procedures.

To Laura J. Haney, for teaching me to write and for developing and refining the earlier editions.

To Gary Harshbarger of Gunn-Mowery LLC, for updating me as to current insurance information and practices.

To Thomas Rozman, for updating legal information.

To Robert Rutz of PNC bank, for updating me as to current banking practices.

To Wendy Hyser, CPA, for research and review in a way that could only be done by a person with her education and experience.

To Alicia Walters, for assisting Wendy and me in typing the several reams of paper used in writing and revising the manuscript.

To Barbara Trainin Blank, for her assistance in editing the book.

To all my designer friends and fellow members of ASID, IIDA, IDEC, IDS, and IFDA, for posing questions that inspired research and for sharing their views on a variety of issues.

To the consultants and business friends, who helped develop ways to improve professional business practices for designers.

To my support staff, who helped me live, run a business, and write a book at the same time.

To all the designers in the Designers' Business Forum, for testing and proving these techniques work and add to the success of their businesses.

And to my friends, who thought I had deserted them.

CHAPTER 1

Finding Your Place in Interior Design

Interior design is a profession, a career, a vocation, and a lifestyle. It is not just a job. To practice it successfully, it is important to have a clear idea of what interior design involves, as well as an appreciation of its demands. It is just as important to know whether you have the combination of personal attributes and interests that a professional interior designer needs.

WHAT IT TAKES TO BE AN INTERIOR DESIGNER

Design expertise comes from exposure and experience, a combination of academic study and on-the-job learning. Every one of your experiences contributes to your design vocabulary. Design education stresses problem solving. The four to six years you spend in the formal study of interior design gives you the informational tools to use in your work, problem-solving skills being perhaps the most valuable tool of all. Interior design demands a tremendous amount of ongoing research. To be a responsible designer, you must study new technologies; new product specifications; new laws and regulations; and changes in building, fire, and safety codes. With each new project there is more to study and learn. Your education never ends. Learning is part of the designer's lifestyle.

Interior design work, by nature, requires that those who practice it learn to temper their innate idealism with the practical demands of reality. You design for real people in the real world. In every design project you undertake, you must be willing to strike a balance between what you envision as "the ideal" and what you can achieve within the project's practical constraints.

Interior design is creative work, and it attracts talented, creative people. In fact, without talent, you cannot go far in this field. Your challenge is to direct and focus your creativity. You will have no problem coming up with new ideas, but it is often difficult to determine which should have priority.

The days of sitting at a drafting table and drawing pretty pictures are over—if they ever existed. Designers have to make things happen. Social contacts are important in acquiring new projects. You must like people and be able to get along with all kinds of people and inspire their confidence. Take the personal inventory below to help determine whether you have what it takes to be an interior designer.

Personal Inventory for Prospective Interior Designers
1. How important is interior design to me?
2. What kind of lifestyle do I want to have?
3. Do I have the innate creative abilities to become a successful designer?
4. Am I willing to spend the time and money required for the necessary formal training?
5. How much time do I want to devote to my work?
6. In general, do I like the people in the field enough to work with them?
7. Do I have the personality to work with any kind of client?
8. Do I enjoy planning and organizing?
9. Am I self-disciplined?
10. Am I self-motivated?
11. Do I have better-than-average physical and emotional stamina?

An interior design career depends on organization. From beginning to end, every project involves myriad details; keeping on top of things is absolutely critical. Even if your firm has someone on staff whose job it is to expedite the projects, you will always have to deal with mountains of details.

Interior design demands high energy and passion. It is almost never a nine-to-five business; on occasion, it is a 24-hour-a-day profession. Interior designers need physical and emotional stamina to fuel their long hours and to cope with pressures of completing a job on schedule and to their client's satisfaction.

Most extremely successful designers—those with annual personal incomes of $200,000 to millions per year—are addicted to interior design. They live it, eat it, and sleep it. It is a passion they cannot live without. But design addiction can also be destructive, and the most successful designers are those who have managed to merge good business practices with their positive "addiction."

This book is about how you can integrate your love for the creative parts of interior design—and the way of life that comes with your career—with good business practices. It is about success with profitability.

FIVE TRADITIONAL DESIGNER-CLIENT RELATIONSHIPS

Today's world is different. It requires designers to specialize in subjects they have never heard of before or needed. The field is ever-changing and requires a creative mind as well as an understanding of business to properly position oneself in a profitable way. As you look through the traditional and basic ways to practice, you will find you will incorporate a number of them or grow from one to another. It is wise to look at the traditional standards to see the possibilities.

Designers may fill many different roles in their relationship with clients; the business structure established will reflect the roles accordingly. Traditional roles that designers have held in the past include pure designer, agent, merchant, employee, and contractor.

Pure Designer
In this capacity, the interior designer provides only professional design services: drawings, documents, and purchasing specifications for all required interior elements and furnishings. The scope of the work usually includes the preparation of the entire interior plan.

Agent
The designer can act as an agent on the client's behalf, placing the client's orders with manufacturers and showrooms. The monies go through the designer's firm or under his or her name. The designer is responsible for managing the project. In some cases, the contracts are written so that the designer does not assume responsibility for the merchandise and materials and the work performed.

Merchant
Many design firms will procure and sell merchandise. The designer becomes a merchant when selling merchandise. In some smaller communities, there is no choice for the designer but to act as a source of materials and to see them appropriately installed. The design firm may also charge a fee for the design of the space.

Employee
Some designers are employed by retail stores, where they are usually paid salary plus commission. When the client purchases items from that store, the designer's services may be included or offered at an extra fee. More and more often, firms of this type are charging some fee in addition to the retail or list price of items, depending on the individual financial structure of the company and its location.

Designers often work for companies that manufacture products for interior projects. They may assist in designing or selling these products. Since many products are unusual, a designer's input is often required to demonstrate the purpose and relationship of these products to the market of today.

Contractor

The designer may act as a contractor by employing the workers required to do construction, hang paper, finish surfaces, handle drapery and window treatments, and so on. In some states, the designer will have to carry a contractor's license to provide these services. In many instances, the craftspeople are directly employed by the design firm; in others, they work on a freelance or contractual basis.

WORKING STYLES

The arts tend to attract people who like to work alone, but interior design forces people to work together. This makes interior design almost as much a social science as an art.

Interior design touches many other disciplines. You will have constant interaction with all types of tradespeople, as well as with artisans from many different craft groups. A coordinated effort is essential to success.

Working Alone

If you work as an independent designer, you can do whatever you want at whatever speed you choose. If you want to work only one day a week, you can. If your forte is specialized work, perhaps you will need to work alone. If you are certain you have mastered your art to the point that you can perform every task within your specialty, and have the personality to work alone, an independent practice may be for you.

Apprenticeship

The value of an apprenticeship cannot be overestimated. Working with a firm or directly under a person of great talent can be a designer's way to the top. When designers see something done, they can usually replicate it. Often designers are limited in their career because they did not take the time to serve an apprenticeship or residency before beginning their own partnership or firm.

Teamwork

The trend now is to work in groups or teams. Designers who practice in groups do so because they see this as a better way to accomplish their goals. The group may not be part of a corporate structure, where all the designers work for the same firm, but design teams and design partnerships are working successfully, and there will be more of them in the future.

Interior designers are also realizing that by working together, as attorneys and physicians often do, they can share a business manager, an expediter, an accountant, an insurance consultant, legal services, and other professional management personnel. This gives them a better managed and more profitable firm, with opportunities for better retirement plans and many of the perks that are possible only in a team arrangement.

When designers work with other designers, they have the opportunity to test each other's designs to determine what will work. When three other people look at a design and all say, "I don't see any problems," obviously the chance of producing it successfully is much greater than if the design is done in isolation. This kind of trial process is important to quality design.

Increasingly, clients want one firm to control the entire project, even though their project may be complex enough to require several disciplines. Therefore, they tend to hire firms that can do it all. Obviously, a designer can team with other design professionals. Multidisciplinary design teams of architects, landscape architects, interior designers, and engineers have an advantage in bidding for larger projects. Clients usually prefer teams that have experience working together.

Government regulations require more recordkeeping than ever before. The nature of the work has changed, and clients are more likely to sue if the unforeseen occurs. Therefore, we need to become more professional and efficient and develop and maintain high administrative and production standards. We need access to more sophisticated tools, such as computerized equipment, which a small office may not be able to afford. But by working together, designers can afford this kind of equipment and enjoy the extra bonuses of other designers' professional knowledge, as well as the stimulation of their company.

Technology also permits designers to work where they want to work: at home, in the mountains, at the beach, or in any other locations where they feel most creative. Technology enables us to communicate, to share projects or administrative needs with others in any part of the country. I often work with specialists in other states, yet we work so closely, you would think we're in same office. Technology is a great research tool and a wonderful storage system; but, more important, it enables us to work with people who otherwise would be too far away. We can now design our companies to suit the type of work we are doing. Technology helps us to grow, and the opportunities are increasing constantly.

The key to developing a successful firm is to understand your firm's best capabilities, to realize its strengths and uniqueness, then seek work that is appropriate to your team. In certain circumstances, some functions might easily be filled by consultants, but the key areas of your firm should be managed by the principals. This gives you the type of control and positioning you need. Review your market. Understand the needs and the social dynamics of the community in which you are working. These two relationships put together will help you formulate a working structure within which you can develop new business in a natural and profitable way.

Design Associate

At one time, people became design associates because they didn't have funding to go off on their own or were not ready to start their own company. Today, many interior designers who have been practicing independently are associating with larger firms because the profitability is so much greater. In some interesting arrangements, profits are shared between the management company and the associate designer. In this way the associate is responsible for writing the orders to handle all the design issues. In some instances, the designers provide their own marketing and bring in their own jobs; in other cases, the firms bring them in.

Designers can work as hard as they want to. If the work or project is highly profitable, they profit accordingly. If they elect to do a project for little markup, perhaps as a marketing effort, this is also acceptable. Of course, certain overhead requirements must be met. If designers decide to take time off—for example, to study—this is their decision, because they are paid only for performance.

Experienced designers have found that being a design associate is one of the most profitable and most pleasurable ways to work. Let someone else handle the business problems; designers want to design. Also, if clients know there is a well-managed business and purchasing division, they are less likely to question pricing, billing, and other contract issues. In addition to high-quality management, the larger company atmosphere can also provide designers with the tools they could not afford on their own—high-tech environment, library, consultants, support staff, network of communication with other designers, and so forth.

This arrangement also permits the designer to work as an independent contractor. Designers cover all of their own expenses and are responsible for their own design work, but the managing company handles the actual processing of the project. The gross profits are usually split at different levels, depending on the varied responsibilities and levels of performance.

Today, we can arrange to work on the projects and parts of projects that use our best talents. There's no point in designers spending 75 to 90 percent of their day doing tasks they are not good at. Even when you practice alone, you don't have to do it all. You can have the best bookkeeper, the best specification writer, and the best lighting designer. You can build a team of professionals you can call on, and use the software programs they suggest. Whatever you need, it's there.

Design/Build Team

One of the major trends in our field is design/build, in which a team works together to produce a project. In this case, the designer may partner with an architect, civil engineer, contractor, and various other vendors to build a complete project with efficiency and cost-effectiveness.

SPECIALIZATION AND SPECIALTIES

At one time there were basically two specialties in interior design, residential and contract. Today there are many. Successful designers today generally specialize in a very small area. Thanks to technology, they are able to work easily throughout the world, assisting other designers, architects, and professionals.

Many designers will combine two or three specialties but usually have one as their lead. Then, as the market interest in the lead area fades, they can shift their primary focus to another of their specialties. It is fascinating to see how our background directs us to a specialty and positions us to meet many special needs.

This is definitely a time for specialization. Designers with the greatest name recognition and financial success are those who have specialized. (This could lead you to wonder if being multifaceted in accomplishments and abilities hurts more than it helps.) A review of design publications of the past 10 years shows that less-qualified design firms can and did take the market share from "better" firms just because they were very clear in stating that, for example, they only "do" offices, or medical facilities, or restaurants.

Specialization most often leads to better profit. Specialists know their work; it is easy because they have done it many times. The basics stay the same. You can vary certain facets of the design, but you do not have to relearn 80 percent of the process. This lowers the risk of error and speeds up design production.

In the past, interior design was a broad-based service profession—blanketing residential, contract, and industrial work. In the next decade, however, interior design will become more specialized than it has been, and some of the best and most interesting jobs will probably be in the specialties. The following sections offer brief looks at more than 100 areas of specialization.

Client demand can cause you to change your area of expertise. A designer in Ohio who specialized in education interiors found over time that although she had become a specialist and did some of the most up-to-date and innovative designs for education, the demand was no longer there. She was forced to change her orientation and began designing psychological and psychiatric spaces, working with many therapists to develop spaces to support their therapies. When interest in this dwindled, she found herself specializing in interiors that supported profit-making endeavors—professional services, manufacturing, general business, and spaces with a marketing or production component. In each circumstance, she was able to use some of what she had learned in the previous specialty. Still, she had to study, bring in many consultants, and do a lot of traveling to meet with other specialists in the course of mastering new areas.

Changes can be expensive, but they are often the best thing that can happen to creative people. Boredom is one of their greatest problems, so having a specialty developed out of another specialty is really the most productive and profitable way of making a change.

Acoustic Design

Hearing is one of the five senses, so sound is an integral part of every environment. As space becomes more expensive and people live and work more closely together, quiet has become a luxury. Specialists in acoustic design consult on projects ranging from concert halls, conference rooms, open offices, and restaurants to residential design. Controlling sound has become a science. In open landscape offices, there are sound-breaking panels and sound maskers. Teleconferencing rooms need the sound to be contained. In contrast, restaurants need a certain amount of noise to sell food. In any space, from residential to the most technologically demanding commercial environments, there are sounds we want to hear and sounds we don't want to hear.

Adaptive Reuse

Reusing old buildings for new purposes is a growing trend as the composition of cities changes and there is greater concern for ecology and protecting available resources. Factory lofts are converted into shopping malls and residential use. It is not always practical to maintain an older commercial structure as commercial real estate. For example, turning the Chrysler Building into a residential condominium building is being seriously considered. The building's construction will not accommodate the way computers are used today in business. Workstations can only be functional within so many feet of the main terminal. This makes many major landmark buildings obsolete as office space, while their location and the quality of construction argue that the building should be reused.

Administrative Headquarters Design

Every major company or organization has an administration building with needs and demands that require design. The demands change as the products change, and interior designers are called in to streamline and develop spaces to support workflow. At one time, designers just designed offices, but today social environments are also important. Sometimes, more important decisions are made over a cup of coffee than in the boardroom.

Airplane Design

This is a unique specialty. Airplanes range from a standard passenger carrier to a flying conference room or living space. Designers must consider design elements in terms of weight, fire safety, and psychological and environmental effects.

Amusement Park Design

Designers work on theme parks, developing the visual components that enhance rides and exhibits. These can incorporate animated figures and appeal to all the senses, even that of smell. These designers may develop unique signage for the park, design the fixtures, or be involved with the service areas: food service, restrooms, and souvenir shops. Park design has this in common with museums and community buildings. Safety, effectiveness, and efficiency are important. Profitability is determined by the effectiveness of the fantasy, and everything has to work so that the fantasy is maintained. Designing traffic patterns to keep people moving is an art in itself.

With the high level of technology available today, the amusement park experience has gone beyond anything anyone could have imagined. These designers are not just artistic; they are also very skilled in scientific thinking and computer knowledge and capabilities.

Apartment, Condominium, and Co-Op Design

With more multiple-housing developments in every part of the country, this specialty presents major opportunities. Some interior designers do only apartment layouts; others do only lobbies and corridors. Still others are responsible for the social rooms, which include function rooms, social areas, televideo conference centers, computer rooms, office and secretarial areas, and athletic areas.

Aquarium Design

This specialty is not limited to aquatic parks. There are designers who do large aquarium designs for homes, offices, and other businesses. There is a restaurant where one enters by walking over a sizable aquarium. Aquariums as a design element serve several purposes. Medical evidence suggests that gazing at an aquarium reduces blood pressure; and there is a social push toward using natural, earth-friendly materials in public spaces.

Art Consultant

Searching out existing art and contracting for the creation of art suitable to a specific interior environment is the function of art consultants, who usually work for the client. They provide the background to support the art investment. The specialist must have an extensive knowledge of fine-art disciplines as well as a practical and artistic understanding of interior design.

Art Dealing

Interior designers with an interest in fine art understand what people enjoy and will buy; they understand the space and know how to place art properly. This is a major asset for an art dealer, because art sells best when it can be envisioned or placed in an interior.

Audiovisual Center Design

Televisions, computers, videocassette recorders, and stereo equipment provide entertainment and worldwide communication for residential and commercial use. They are often clustered in the same area or room. The technical requirements of these devices demand knowledge of electronics, acoustics, and lighting disciplines.

Auditorium Design

This is a fascinating field, and very different from stage design. Acoustics and sight lines in theater design are vital and complex. Productions can be made or destroyed by very small design elements of the house. With today's multimedia opportunities, this field has become very complex.

Barrier-Free Design

Laws require that new commercial and public buildings, and renovations to existing buildings, make the space accessible to those in wheelchairs. Barrier-free design is increasingly desirable for all spaces. Probably more money has been invested in designing for the physically limited or orthopedically disabled than for any other group. Interior designers specialize in reviewing products and buildings to ensure that standards are met. This specialty is included in almost every project.

Bathroom Design

At one time a neglected and utilitarian room, today the bathroom joins the kitchen as a selling point for houses. Modern bathrooms may include spalike environments with whirlpool baths, saunas, and hot tubs. Public restrooms and bathrooms for commercial spaces demand state-of-the-art detailing. A new consciousness of human factors has greatly improved aesthetics, safety, and the adaptations needed to make the bathroom barrier-free. International bathing customs have had an influence as well, bringing us the European fixtures, the Oriental soaking tub, saunas, and steam rooms. Environmental concerns have brought new products and codes.

Beauty and Barbershop Design

Beauty and barbershops are often mixed-media salons. The designer may be asked to provide appropriate space for services such as waxing, massage, facials, manicures, and cosmetology, in addition to hair care. State regulations and requirements differ. Interior designers in the beauty field often work with or for suppliers, who may offer complete financing and turnkey projects.

CAD Specialist

A designer who is expert at computer-assisted drafting (CAD) and drawing is increasingly important today. Computers are instrumental in communicating with other design professionals. Designs created with CAD software may be used by the client as a basis for in-house space management. CAD's accuracy and capability to make quick changes is invaluable. Although there are still specialists, CAD has now become a basic tool of most designers.

Carpet and Rug Design

Who should know better how to design carpets and rugs than interior designers, who are responsible for a large volume of floor-covering sales? Interior designers working with textile specialists can develop the most suitable rugs for a given situation. Designing handwoven rugs is very different from designing for the technical demands of Axminster, Wilton, tufted, woven, or printed machines. A designer must either study at a textile-intensive school, such as the Philadelphia Textile School, or work extensively in the carpet field.

Ceramic Tile Design

This field encompasses foreign and domestic sources as well as artist-made and mass-produced tiles. Ceramic tiles are used for high-traffic, functional areas, as well as for decorative effect, including as murals and sculptures.

Closet Design

Space is at a premium today, and closet space especially so. Around the country, businesses that do only closets are designing storage components and new ways to store almost every item.

Code Safety Design Law Specialist

This person keeps up-to-date information on building, fire, and safety codes in all states. The specialist designer may consult with other designers, contractors, manufacturers, and owners.

Color Consultation

Color and its effects on people is a recognized science with well-documented results. Color is the most noticed of all the design elements. This specialty is used by all the design disciplines, as well as marketing firms, corporations, governments, and medical practices—anywhere encouraging specific reactions is desired.

Commercial Design

This specialty designs everything except residences, including retail space, businesses, offices, laboratories, factories, medical facilities, and other commercial space. Most commercial designers specialize further. Within the specialty of design for medicine, there are several subspecialties.

Computer Office Design

Designing to accommodate computer use is much in demand. Office requirements of computers have changed dramatically since computers first emerged in the workplace. In some ways, the requirements are less rigorous. In designing offices to accommodate computers, specialists usually work for the computer companies and may travel across the country to explain the requirements and conveniences of combining computer and staff functions.

Construction Supervision

Designers supervise, manage, and review the components of a project and advise on decision making. Interior designers are often hired to act as liaisons between the contractor and client. Sometimes they are responsible for hiring other consultants and contractors.

Corporate Campus Design

The designer creates a total environment. The corporate campus promotes efficiency and expresses the mission of the company through design tailored to meet the specific needs of that company. Campuses can include administration buildings, training centers, manufacturing or production facilities, and fitness centers. Some demand space that can be leased to support companies.

Corporate In-House Design

The staff interior designer for a corporation is responsible for maintaining the company's design identity. The designer may initiate and complete the design or hire design consultants on major design projects, as well as act as liaison between outside consultants and the firm.

Cosmetic Dentistry

The emergence of cosmetic dentistry has brought new challenges to the design of the dental office. The office must blend the professional medical requirements of dentistry with fashion and beauty to create effective, visually pleasing surroundings. The client who buys cosmetic dentistry services is very conscious of design and detail.

Country Club Design

These spaces combine aspects of residential and commercial design. The buildings must conform to area regulations and codes for fire, safety, labor, and industry. They must encourage proprietary feelings among the membership but also give the staff the tools to run programs with time and financial efficiency. Facilities may include indoor swimming pools, ball courts, gyms, locker rooms, restaurants, and areas for business meetings and socializing.

Dental Office Design

This is a highly engineered segment of the medical field; the design specialist must have an understanding of the mechanics as well as the antiseptic and medical aspects of the discipline. The dental profession has exerted the effort to develop business management techniques and to improve time use to make dentistry more efficient and professional. Space design for dental offices is an integral part of the new dentistry.

Design Coordinator

This person works directly with the client to define the client's wishes and takes the information to a design specialist. The design coordinator must be able to accommodate the artistic attitude and approaches of the design professional and understand and work closely with the client. With today's communication systems, this will become a great specialty because the design coordinator can network with design specialists all over the world. This person is responsible for bringing the specialist and the client together in a productive way. It takes extensive knowledge of the field to be able to create this bond.

Design for Children

Environment affects a child's behavior; there is a body of research indicating that what stimulates a child is not what stimulates an adult. Spaces for children must be adaptable, because children change and grow so rapidly. These spaces include every place a child might use—doctors' offices, libraries, schools, and retail spaces—not just bedrooms.

The children of today are very demanding clients. They are very aware of multimedia experiences and have high expectations. Many children are also well traveled and want to be in spaces that are very special.

Design for In-Home Medical Care

At one time, patients with chronic, debilitating illnesses were confined to hospital wards, but the trend today is toward in-home care. Not only do these patients enjoy the comforts of home, but they also have less risk of acquiring new infections while their immunities are low. This specialty means more than just installing a hospital bed. The residential space must be adapted to meet geriatric, orthopedic, or other medical requirements of both patient and caregivers.

Design for Vision or Hearing Impairments

The number of people affected with vision or hearing impairments grows each year in proportion to the aging of the population. More than 60 percent of people in the workforce today have some hearing loss, and probably a much larger percentage have some vision impairment. People are becoming more aware of the problems, as well as of the increased technology available to resolve them. There are successful applications for every situation, from residences to theaters.

Display and Exhibit Design

Retailers, wholesalers, specialty shops, museums, and all types of public spaces can use display and exhibit design to sell products as well as ideas. These displays may be permanent or built for travel. These exhibits must make an impact but also be easy to set up and take down.

Energy Conservation Design

An energy specialist advises on energy-efficient products and space planning for better use of energy. This may include solar design, adapting existing structures or developing new ones, or simply finding new uses for traditional products and appropriate uses for new ones.

Ergonomic Design

Ergonomic design is the science that relates people to the way they use things. It is an engineering science based on the physical needs of the human body. Factors considered are the measurements of the human body, human sensory capacities, comfort, body functions, safety, and emotional satisfaction.

Estate Manager

With the investment that owners make, they need a knowledgeable person to secure their investments and properly manage all activities of the property. A trained designer is usually part of the design team, acting as the owner's representative in procurement and handling issues with contractors and artisans.

After working on the property, estate managers are qualified to update and maintain the property, furnishings, art objects, and so on; prepare operations manuals; establish budgets; and handle all financial issues relating to the property.

Estate managers hire and train appropriate staff, oversee inventories, and do party planning. This position requires a person of background and sophistication.

Facility Management

The person or department responsible for the physical management of a facility coordinates purchasing, repairs, and maintenance. Facility managers plan and act as liaisons between the firm's executives and the consulting designers, architects, and engineers.

Factory and Production Consulting

This specialty includes traffic control and design to improve safety and to increase productivity. (See Ergonomic Design, page 13.) The emphasis is on keeping the environment stimulating so that workers stay alert, are productive, and are able to handle the machinery and equipment safely.

Faux Finishes and Stenciling

Faux finishes and stenciling have become vital and growing decorative elements since the 1980s. A fine arts or interior design degree is not essential for this type of work, but either helps in translating the client's desires into reality. Tools to create faux-finishing effects are available at every hardware store and in most hardware departments. Though books on these subjects are many—making the art understandable and desirable to the general public—most clients would rather hire a specialist than attempt faux finishing themselves.

Feng Shui

The ancient Chinese art of placement is considered the mother of natural sciences. Harmony and balance are the goals. A feng shui practitioner serves in the multiple roles of healer, psychologist, therapist, cleric, business consultant, financial advisor, and matchmaker. The concepts are drawn from Tibetan, Chinese Buddhist, and folk wisdom.

Forensic Consulting

This specialty was created by the litigious times we live in. When a product is made or used incorrectly and results in injury or death, a forensic designer may be consulted by attorneys. In addition to expertise in ergonomics and product construction, the forensic designer must also be familiar with court terminology and the correct way to testify. This field requires not only training but a special personality that holds up well under pressure.

Funeral Home Design

The funeral home must comfort and support people at an emotionally vulnerable time. It includes personal meeting areas for family viewing and chapel spaces that must be visually pleasing as well as practical. There are presentation and financial aspects to consider, as well as the appropriate physical supports for heavy objects and space for behind-the-scenes management.

Furniture Design

Interior and industrial design must be blended for good product design. The interior designer knows where the furniture goes and how it is used; the industrial-furniture designer knows construction techniques.

Furniture Manager

This is a person who handles all the purchasing documents, usually for a commercial project. The furniture manager handles all the bidding through to the final installation and is very much like a project manager on a construction project. This is a role many interior designers are very qualified to handle.

Geriatric Design

As our society grays, design for the mature market gains in recognition as a specialty. Retirement centers, nursing homes, even condominiums are designed to meet the physical, psychological, and cultural needs of older people. It's not just a case of dealing with illness and infirmity; rather, it means acknowledging the pleasures of life and the opportunities still available. Older people are no longer simply old; they act, hence like to be treated, as if they were young.

Graphic Design

These specialists can develop a corporate image or design graphics that define the space or movement of people through public-use facilities. A graphic designer develops the logos and icons used on everything from business cards and stationery to Web sites and Web pages.

Greenhouse Design

At one time, greenhouses were simply for plants. Now they are incorporated into residential and commercial spaces that also accommodate people. Depending on the climate, greenhouse design can involve controlling temperature, light, and humidity. Insulating elements and the design atmosphere are other factors. Manufacturers consult interior designers on the design of greenhouse components; some designers have made this their specialty.

Hard-Surface Flooring Design

Designing this type of flooring product demands knowledge of color trends, as well as a working knowledge of the properties of wood, ceramics, marble, vinyl, and other appropriate materials. In fact, there are so many hard-surfaced floors and flooring products that each one of them requires specialists.

Hardware Design

The work of interior and industrial designers enhances the functional and decorative effects of knobs, hinges, and handles, the hardware for use in buildings and on furniture. The demand is increasing for beautifully sculptured, handsomely crafted hardware.

Health and Fitness Club Design

Personal fitness became important in the 1980s. Health clubs are not just places to exercise but meeting spots for people with similar goals and interests. Athletic, aerobic, and recreational facilities of all sorts are proliferating. Keeping the facilities safe, convenient, and appropriate to their specific sports is involved enough that some designers have made it their specialty. Health and fitness club design has some aspects in common with country club design. As trends change, these spaces must be redesigned to meet the new needs.

Historic Preservation and Adaptive Reuse

Historic preservation demands technical and scientific knowledge and an ability and willingness to research small details. What were the colors, materials, and wallcoverings in use when the building was created? What hardware is appropriate? How historically accurate does the client want the building to be? Some people want the interiors to be absolutely authentic and will, for example, hide the electricity or do without it. They want everything exactly as it used to be, with no substitutions or modifications.

Technology has given designers the means to determine what the original colors were (and they are often garish when compared to the more subtle ones we are accustomed to seeing today). It is now possible to assign precise dates to furniture. The body of knowledge continues to grow.

Home Office Design

The home office is a space tailored to the way an individual works. Working with people who have been in the corporate scene for many years and who now want home offices can be exciting. The office may be small—and be incorporated into part of an apartment or bedroom—or it may be larger than any executive office in a corporate building. Quite often, the office contains all the bells and whistles of a commercial space, along with all the comforts of home, plus a few indulgences as well.

Home Theater Design

Home theater design is in great demand. This area of work demands extensive technical, audio, and visual knowledge. Home theater rooms require knowledge of many different aspects of design. Not only do these rooms need to be very luxurious and comfortable, but the client also expects their sound to be perfect and the pictures to be crisp and clear. In this room, the client expects to be able to access any cable or satellite system with the push of a button. This has become one of the highest-budget rooms of the residence.

Hospital Design

Today, some areas in a hospital have such complex technical requirements that hospital designers with a particular specialty have international practices. Specialties proliferate: Some designers do only emergency rooms and intensive care units, while others design patient and visitor areas; some designers combine both.

Hospitals are changing dramatically and quickly to support new systems of medicine, causing hospital designers to put aside most of their traditional systems and work with System Technology, a new and very demanding set of guidelines. Fortunately, as a result, hospitals are much more user-friendly. Insurance and legal requirements, along with cost-effectiveness, place demands and constraints on the design. It is highly unlikely that a specialist in hospital design would also work on a nursing home project; the demands are very different.

Hospitality Design

This field can range from the bed-and-breakfast to a large conference center. Some conference centers are practically cities in themselves. Hospitality design encompasses luxury spaces for community and celebration, as well as functional accommodations. Designers may specialize in restaurant dining halls, training centers and convention spaces, guest rooms, lobbies, and corridors.

Houseboat Design

Houseboats are, in essence, both residential and commercial structures. There is a tremendous amount of technical engineering required to keep them afloat, as well as to meet health and safety requirements. Houseboats can be three, four, or five stories high and provide sizable living and workspaces.

Human Factors

Human factors deal with all types of personal performance in work or personal spaces. Designers who specialize in this field often consult with owners and other design specialists to incorporate human concerns in standard and special-needs spaces.

Interior Landscaping

Plants add a natural quality to even the most static environment. This field requires knowledge of landscaping and botany to place plants where they are suitable. It may include contracting to provide maintenance and design changes for seasonal updates and plant health. Whereas greenhouses are primarily used to keep plants healthy and growing, interior "plantscaping" is an increasingly important component of a building's atmosphere. Design factors include temperature, light, and humidity control.

Journalism

Through writing, designers can expand the design field, making our work more understandable to people inside and outside the field. Designers can educate through columns and articles on design for newspapers and magazines, and more recently, on television as well. Writing is a special skill, as is the ability to relate on camera. Some people with design education have chosen design journalism but only after intensive efforts to learn these additional skills. If these skills do not come easily, designers who need to produce books and articles would do well to collaborate with a writer. This may be a more effective use of their time.

Kennel Design

In the competitive world of breeding pedigreed pets, space design for each species is a serious business. The designer must understand animals and their needs. In kennels, there are areas for grooming and training, food preparation and nutrition, as well as testing. Maintenance and health care are a prime concern.

Kitchen Design

The kitchen is often one of the most expensive parts of the house. Some equipment is unabashedly new. There are also historic designs infused with new technology. Scientific and artistic detail goes into the design and planning of components for residential and personal-use kitchens. The designer must have a complete knowledge of currently available products as well as the dietary requirements of the users.

The National Kitchen and Bath Association (NKBA) has created a curriculum that is offered by numerous design schools throughout the country. This program accredits designers in kitchen design.

Law Office Design

Law offices have many features in common with residences. A designer who is skilled in residential work will be excellent at designing them. Image, cost, and work efficiency are important considerations. An environment that supports legal professionals, visiting clients, and consultants provides visual and acoustical privacy. Law offices now incorporate highly technical equipment, as well as areas for specialized personal interaction.

Leadership in Energy and Environmental Design (LEED)

Clients not only are looking for long-lasting products but are concerned about buildings that will last many years. They want buildings to have flexibility so they aren't just suitable for today's purpose but for long-standing and environmentally friendly use. A sustainability or LEED person has to be knowledgeable in LEED and qualified as a LEED specialist. This individual must understand flexibility of use in building design.

Library Design

Libraries are individual and specialized, catering to local needs. A library in a county seat will be different from one on Wall Street. Libraries need space planning and marketing, with special attention to lighting and acoustics. Many libraries have exhibit areas or function rooms. They are true multimedia environments—lending books, videocassettes, art, and music. Electrical demands have increased greatly with the advent of computers, which are used for card catalogs, periodical indexes, and subject-dedicated databases. Spaces for extensive personal libraries are enjoying a comeback. Personal libraries are no longer just for English country homes.

Licensing

Many designers license their names to a product line. The designer can style or develop the product or merely endorse it. This is a growing field, encompassing wallcoverings, upholstery textiles, bed linens, tabletop china, and just about everything that can be used in interior spaces. Today, very fine designers design for inexpensive merchandise. Licensing fees are based on volume, and work on easily available consumer goods becomes very lucrative. Although some licensers are used principally for their names, most designers contribute to the design of products for widely divergent markets.

Lighting Design

Lighting, both natural and artificial, is a strong and important element, used for design, drama, ecology, and, of course, function. Scale, structure, engineering, and knowledge of the end use are critical components of good fixture design, as are the technical requirements and codes for specific projects.

Lighting Fixture Design

In any space, the human eye goes to the windows and the lighting fixtures. Scale, structure, engineering, and knowledge of the end use are critical components of good fixture design.

Liturgical Design

Churches, synagogues, and mosques are not just monuments but living centers that actively serve the community. Some offer recreation areas for children. These buildings are used for social events, theater productions, educational lectures, and community activities. Of course, each religion has its own design requirements, so the designer must know and understand the specific liturgy.

Manufacturer In-House Design

Manufacturers have staff designers who work not on design but on merchandising. To promote sales, many contract office furniture manufacturers offer interior design services at little or no cost to the end user. Designers, especially interior designers, work directly for manufacturers to help align products to the needs of today's design public.

Manufacturer Representation

This sales position is the link between the manufacturer and interior designer. Some of the best manufacturers' representatives are former interior designers or dealers.

They understand the product, know how to sell it, and appreciate what interior designers want. Within assigned territories, manufacturers' reps call on designers, providing catalogs, assisting in specification preparation, and writing purchase orders.

Marine Design

This specialty requires extensive knowledge of fire codes, marine standards and regulations, weights, and materials. Many products must be made specifically for marine use. Marine design encompasses all sizes of ships and boats, from working boats to cruise liners with the size and complexity of small villages. The design demands range from stripped-down—where every inch must have more than one use—to extravagant, with swimming pools, shops, ballrooms, and health spas. The designer deals with physical, psychological, and ergonomic issues as well. There are fewer restrictions—sometimes none at all—on smaller craft for personal use.

Marketing

Marketing specialists work in many parts of the market, including with the end user as well as designers. They develop and position design firms with appropriate clients. Some designers are better at design work than selling, so the need for and value of this specialty is well recognized and compensated.

Medical Center Design

Hospitals, clinics, rehabilitative-care centers, and nursing homes have requirements so specific and technologically complex that only a specialist could keep up with the constant changes in standards, codes, and equipment. This specialty includes emergency rooms, intensive-care units, lobbies, and administrative support. Examples of special-needs campuses are: medical complexes dedicated to heart care, birthing and women's care, and orthopedics.

Hospitals in many cities are being redesigned, and some doctors are designing centers to fit their own specialties. The medical field is changing so rapidly that some facilities are not even completed before major changes must be made. Outpatient care has expanded so dramatically that it has changed the profile of every medical institution. Medicine is advancing dramatically, so we can look forward to much more work in this area.

Medical Office Design

Every medical specialty requires special equipment, as well as appropriate space planning, traffic patterns, and storage management. Today's specialties use such an intensive array of high-tech equipment that offices require total replanning every few years. A complete understanding of the medical procedures and equipment, legal aspects, codes, and aseptic demands is needed. There are extreme challenges in this area, because the equipment in even the largest office is very imposing, and because the Health Insurance Portability and Accountability Act of 1996 (HIPAA) introduced regulations that force many offices to make major changes.

Medical Spa Specialist

Medical spas encompass plastic surgeons, dermatologists, and all types of skin treatments. These facilities require a considerable amount of equipment. The knowledge of both the processes used as well as the necessary equipment is essential for this design specialty. The medical spa may also include cosmetic dentistry, antiaging systems, hydrotherapy, and many other forms of massage and exercise treatments.

Model Home Furnishing

Model home furnishing may be handled by an independent designer who may also specify the architectural details of the interior to be purchased and installed by another contractor, or by companies dedicated to furnishing model homes. There are also companies that will "grant" all of the furniture, accessories, and appointments to builders for their use for several months or a year. At the end of that period, the companies retrieve the furniture to reuse in another project.

Model home design can be a promotional tool for design firms. In some areas, interior designers pay contractors or developers for the privilege of working on their models. The work may encompass all the interior architectural details, lighting, fixture specifications, and hard and soft furnishings. The furnishings are often sold with the home. In other instances, contractors consider this same work part of the presentation of the home and will hire designers, or lease furnishings, or both.

Modular Prefabricated Design

This area of the building industry is growing rapidly. It is cost-effective to build standard components in a factory-controlled situation. A high level of quality with skilled engineering can be accomplished by prefabricated design. Understanding requirements of building and delivery is critical. It's not just price, but quality, that is relevant here. It's more feasible to construct a much-better product under controlled conditions. Factory-built housing or modular complexes for other purposes also come with guarantees, something not available in on-site construction.

Modular prefab construction is usually most practical when building a hundred or more similar units. The designer creates a standard, builds a sample, checks all the details, confirms with the client, and analyzes the finished product. When all has been approved, several hundred units are built. These units ship well over water, which can be a construction advantage when placing large complexes on deserted islands, where there are very few construction trades.

Mural Painting

A number of mural artists are interior designers with fine-arts backgrounds. They first paint a miniature for the client, then execute the full-size product on canvas or directly on the wall. This art form has become very prominent. Demand is increasing and spilling over to create a new specialty, that of handpainted walls.

Museum Design

At one time, only people with backgrounds in history or art history worked in museums. Museums today offer many opportunities for interior designers, to design exhibits, promotions, and community projects. Because the preservation of artifacts is as important as the display, understanding the effects of humidity and lighting on artifacts is important. Interior designers may work directly for museums or be employed by consulting firms that specialize in museum work.

Nursing Home Design

As the levels of health care change, so do the codes, systems, regulations, and requirements. Nursing homes now cater not only to senior citizens but to young people who have short-term needs—those who live alone or have no one to care for them but require care for a limited time. Elements to consider in any design of nursing or convalescent homes include the probable length of the stay and the special equipment that patients will need. Changes in medicine make many facilities obsolete before they are five years old, so it is important to plan for change.

Office Design

While commercial and home offices have elements in common, the home office is usually for one or two people. Commercial office design requires knowledge of high-tech equipment, as well as an understanding of management and office production. The term "commercial office" today may still suggest open-plan offices. However, companies vary; hence they need different types of design. In general, these spaces are designed for large groups of people working together in a cooperative and productive fashion. The space must accommodate many different disciplines with varying needs.

Park Design

Amusement parks, municipal, and other parks need to be safe and efficient, and have effective traffic patterns and management systems. Designers may be called on to develop unique signage or to design fixtures or the service areas: food service, restrooms, and souvenir shops. Some designers work only on theme parks, where the emphasis is on getting people to come back often, especially if the park is for-profit. Parks are also hubs for many other environments, such as residential complexes, or campuses for education, medicine, or business.

Passenger Train and Bus Design

The interiors of passenger trains and buses must be designed for the comfort and safety of the traveler. They also need to be attractive. Passenger trains and buses of today are so different from those of the past. They incorporate much more technology and more pleasant environments.

Party and Ball Design

Designers organize and orchestrate parties and balls for corporations, charities, and other organizations. Entertainment and celebration require an appropriate atmosphere. It is not enough just to put people into a ballroom for so many hours; they want fantasies brought to life. The competition among charities is intense. The donors have been in every hotel many times. If the designer cannot show them something different, they are not interested.

Patio and Outdoor Room Design

Outdoor rooms are an important part of most buildings. Some can be used year-round, while others can be used only on a more limited basis. These rooms often have serious design considerations because of their structure and use. Interior designers are teaming with landscape architects to create exciting and functional spaces.

Photographic Set Design

This specialty works with manufacturers and advertising agencies to create settings designed to sell products. They maintain an inventory of props and backgrounds, spend weeks creating and building a set, then tear it down immediately after photographing it. Successful photographic set design requires an understanding of what photographs well and what does not, as well as what can be faked.

Photography Styling

Designers team with photographers to make interior spaces work better in photographs. This involves moving furniture to show the room to advantage and accessorizing the space. Very few interior designers and architects understand how to stage their own work for good photography.

Plumbing Fixture Design

To design sinks, lavatories, bathtubs, and spas, the designer must have training and a special interest in sculpture. Sometimes the specialist will be asked to recolor or redesign an existing line, but more often, the project means creating new forms. Fixtures manufacturers may revive the shapes of antique items or items from Asia, reworking them to meet today's plumbing standards. The day of strictly utilitarian bathroom fixtures is gone.

Prison Design

State and local governments are turning to private companies to help in constructing prisons, which are then leased back to the government. Some organizations, such as Volunteers of America, actually operate the prisons. Prison design is a specialty in the midst of change. Social scientists suggest that new prisons should not just house prisoners but help to rehabilitate them.

Privacy Design

Privacy is a major issue in almost every type of environment and design today, from public buildings to private residences. Privacy consultants have a design background, complemented with sound engineering training.

Product Design

Opportunities in the field of product design are as numerous as the products themselves. Designers can make vital contributions in helping manufacturers find and develop products that are wanted, function well, and suit the environments they will be used in. Designers have a hand in almost every product available today.

Product Display

Interior designers have traditionally designed store windows and product displays, but never has this type of design been brought to so refined and sophisticated an art form as recently. This strong merchandising approach often permits unlimited budgets, which encourage a free range of ideas.

Product Evaluation

Hiring designers to evaluate products for design quality, practicality, and marketability is a sound investment for manufacturers.

Product Marketing

Interior designers assist with marketing products by developing ways to use them. They are well qualified to assist in product design development, as a complement to the manufacturer's design staff. Consulting interior designers can help maintain a firm's position in the marketplace.

Professional or Promotional Organizations

Trade and professional organizations often hire interior designers as spokespersons or interpreters to build links between the product group and the designer or client. The designers' skill and knowledge can strengthen the relationship. Designers understand the needs of the end user as well as the multitude of design disciplines involved.

Project Management

Project management can be as simple as handling interior design development for one's own firm or as complex as running a project under a turnkey proposition. It requires complete understanding of various crafts.

Proxemics

Proxemics is the physical, psychological, and cultural impact of space on people. A consultant in this field evaluates any interior space that directs human behavior: educational; medical; business facilities, including work; production; or any space where there is social interaction. Private-use spaces, such as residences, can gain tremendously from this specialty.

Psychiatric Care Facility Design

While many of the codes in the psychiatric care facilities are the same as in other medical facilities, the type of therapy practice determines the design response. Use, practicality, safety, and ease of maintenance are prime concerns.

Public Relations

Interior designers with strong communications skills may choose to draw media attention to the work of other designers rather than run a design practice of their own. Some act as liaison between manufacturers, designers, and end users.

Purchasing

The designer may act as a purchasing agent for large companies, reviewing and testing products, then negotiating and ordering the furnishings. Purchasing agents or procurement companies can get better prices for the individual design firms that use them than they could get on their own.

Real Estate Development

A knowledge of space, its uses, and its potential for change has given many interior designers an edge in real estate sales and development. Some designers assist developers by restructuring and designing buildings for turnkey or development projects. In some states, interior designers need a realtor's license to be recognized and compensated for their contributions; in others, interior designers are part of a real estate development firm.

Real Estate Upgrading

Build a better home, please the client, and sell: These are the objectives in design upgrading for luxury development homes. Many experienced designers have moved into this specialty. There is opportunity for creative design, and it pays very well.

Rendering

CAD can do a lot, but there is nothing like a beautiful hand rendering. Rendering is a special art, requiring knowledge of graphics, fine art, and design. A good presentation is vital: Many design firms, even small ones, hire good renderers, either staff or freelance. Fees can run into the thousands of dollars.

Residential Design

At one time the most prevalent design specialty, residential design can also be the most lucrative. It requires a knowledge of human behavior within living spaces, an understanding of and ability to communicate with people, and a respect for the client. Generally, people hire residential designers whose tastes and communications skills are similar to their own.

Resort Design

Resorts are wonderful vacation places for hosting many types of activities, from the spa-type resort that is very luxurious and indulgent to the experiential resort that boasts everything from extreme sports to "tame" activities, such as music or other specialized interests. Resorts are found all over the country in many environments. They generally have many unique features. Resort designers are often experts in a particular specialty as well as in hospitality design. They are very aware of the unique issues of designing a space that has both living and activity areas.

Restaurant Design

There is room for design in every restaurant, from the fast-food stands in malls to local eateries to establishments for gracious dining. Knowledge of all design disciplines as well as of food management is essential.

Restaurant Kitchen Design

This requires knowledge of kitchen equipment and the know-how to adapt it to the preferences of individual restauranteurs. Kitchen specialists work independently or for equipment suppliers. Kitchens for country clubs, educational facilities, and large commercial restaurants are typical projects.

Retail and Specialty Selling

Selling is part of every design practice. Some designers have found it more lucrative to own, manage, or work for retail and specialty stores. Designers make good salespeople, especially in design-related areas, because they understand how to use a product and can show clients how. Interior designers may help develop a product mix for a specific store; this often means creating a design package to be sold by other people. It also can mean working with a group of artists to market their work.

Retail Store Design

This popular specialty requires skill in image development, marketing, traffic patterns, and security and concern for financial return on space. Custom fixturing is often part of the design. The designer may customize local spaces for national chains or work with individual store owners.

Security Consulting

Security must be built into every part of a building's design today; it is not just supplementary. Security incorporates many different types of systems, such as screening and the use of other cameras and devices that permit different types of monitoring. Security consultants are now so specialized that some deal only in educational institutions, others within federal and state buildings, others in office buildings, and yet others in residential spaces.

Set Design

Many interior designers started in set design; others expanded their practices to include set design. Although this is a unionized profession, there are still some opportunities. Set design for movies, theater, dance, and opera is a different world. The designer builds for show, not to last. Everything is designed to be seen from a certain perspective. The size and design of the theater—whether it is a proscenium or a theater-in-the-round—affect the placement of furniture and props. The director's vision of the production is critical to the choice of furnishings.

Shop-at-Home Services

At-home shopping is a powerful design field. There are extremely successful firms that specialize in shop-at-home service. Some stock a van or truck with a coordinated line of pictures, accessories, pillows, and draperies. They distribute their products to representatives or franchise owners. Even very sophisticated firms are finding ways to bring products to the home. If designers can show clients a product sample in their own space, very often they can sell it.

Shopping Mall Design

This is large-scale marketing. Each store in a mall must contribute to the total mall concept, which ranges from discount to luxury. Each mall promotes a different lifestyle or environment. Designers may work directly for the mall owners to coordinate all mall activities and designs or with individual retailers and in the common areas. The mall of today must allow space for entertainment and other activities. It must be an experience in itself, not just a place to shop.

Showroom Design

In Manhattan, Rome, Paris, London, and in every small city in the world, showroom designs and presentations account for an amazingly high-dollar figure. The primary job of the showroom is to sell a product. Whether the showroom is beautiful is a question of taste, but whether it works and produces can be measured.

Solar Design

Design for solar buildings is not just about solar collection but a matter of coordinating solar and environmental concerns with human needs. Energy efficiency, sun control, sunlight-resistant materials, and insulation are key.

Spa and Skin Clinic Design

This major trend requires many specific design considerations. Typically included are skin treatments, plastic surgery, dermatology, facials, and all forms of special treatments, ranging from therapeutic massage to cosmetics. The demands of this specialty are so great that many designers are working exclusively in this area.

Spaceship and Rocket Design

This is the ultimate challenge in ergonomic design—every inch must count. Many consumer products have been developed as a result of studies done for spaceship design. Designers who have worked for NASA have taught designers many things that they can use in general work.

Stadium and Arena Design

While architects and engineers are most often involved with shaping these spaces, interior designers are consulted on public areas, private salons, dining areas, kitchens, service areas, and even choice of seating. This specialty has aspects in common with theater, restaurant, and store design. Today's stadiums and arenas are expensive and luxurious, but they also must incorporate safety and security as primary concerns.

Storage Design

Planned storage is an essential design element. Storage specialists catalog the clients' storables, then plan for growth. Custom storage can range from making tiny drawers to accommodate contact lenses to developing automated filing areas for offices. Good storage means placing things in convenient locations near where they will be used, and putting lesser-used items in less accessible places. Since storage is generally an engineering process within each of design's different disciplines, a designer will usually specialize in a particular aspect of storage design, such as residential, legal offices, medical offices, or other types of commercial space.

Tabletop Display Design

Restaurants and department and specialty stores use tabletop display to sell food and other products. Clients today expect both drama and practicality.

Teleconference Center Design

Teleconference centers exist not only in large corporations but also in community centers and occasionally in apartment complexes. This discipline specifies the shape of the room, lighting, choice and placement of furnishings, and even the teleconference equipment. Sight lines, light and sound control, and audibility are prime concerns.

Television Design

There are presently 43 different television shows featuring interior design. This has become a major entertainment process. Television designers may do all of the preparation as well as the on-camera work. Many of these designers also have a background in theater.

Tenant Development Services

Interior designers work with landlords and developers to coordinate interior spaces for homes, apartments, and commercial offices. They may devise color schemes and layouts or may only ensure that the work of other designers coordinates with what exists in these buildings.

Textile Design

These interior designers have special knowledge of textiles, design rugs, fabrics, and wallcoverings. This combined discipline creates products that are appropriate, distinctive, and easy to use.

Training Center Design

Education takes place in more places than schools. Corporate training centers are found in office buildings; smaller firms use hotel meeting rooms or convention centers. Special demands include adaptable lighting, accommodating audiovisual equipment, and attention to acoustics and sight lines.

Transit Center Design

Airport, train, and bus terminals have become almost total-living environments for some people. Interior designers are called on to enhance people movement, entertain people, and accommodate their needs with airport shops, small conference areas, VIP clubs, and cocktail lounges. There is not much one cannot do in transit centers these days, from banking to seeing a podiatrist to hiring a secretary. Transit centers have become like cities in the range of services they offer the daily commuter, as well as the traveler who may have a layover of many hours. Chicago's O'Hare Airport has a laser show. Some centers offer college courses; others have educational displays. There is usually a church or chapel. Today's security demands have also changed many facets of transit centers. These areas will continue to reflect a significant demand for innovative design.

Turnkey Services

A team of designers, contractors, and vendors take a project from a client's desire to a completed, move-in, ready-to-use-building. The client deals only with one person or firm, agreeing to the terms and costs of the total project. This is a very efficient and cost-effective way of working. All the client needs to do is turn the key and open the door.

Underground Habitation Design

Because the temperature underground is a constant 55 degrees Fahrenheit, underground space has become a practical and appropriate area for living and working. Many computer centers, for example, are located underground. This field of designers is relatively underdeveloped.

Universal Design

Universal design is not just designing for the physically handicapped; it is intended to be useful for all. Spaces are often designed for multiple purposes, so they can function for many different people and reasons. Universal design is becoming standard among many building specifications today to ensure that the structure is user-friendly and convenient for all.

Vacation Home Design

Second homes are big business, but they often must be designed as turnkey projects because the clients are involved elsewhere. This market is growing. For some clients, the vacation home is a place to indulge in an opulence they would not feel comfortable expressing in other areas of their lives.

Vastu

Vastu is an ancient practice from India that has been in use for over 1,000 years. The objective is to achieve harmony, maximize the flow of energy, and make the home a retreat where people can recuperate from the stresses of the world. This uses a systematic approach to building and design. Practitioners believe that people's homes play an important part in helping them achieve their purpose and goals in life.

Wallcovering Design

Many interior designers design wallcoverings, drawing on their expertise with color, pattern direction, and scale. The field demands production and design expertise as well as an understanding of current trends.

Wall Finishes

Marbling, fresco, and textured finishes—some of which have not been seen for centuries—are again in demand. This specialty is no longer limited to historic restoration work; commercial and residential clients also request novel wall finishes.

Wayfinding

Wayfinding involves signage, but also many other aspects of the interior design discipline. It means designing a space, building, or complex that is easy for people to move around in. Finding one's way becomes natural rather than complicated and confusing. This specialty first became popular in hospitals, but it is now relevant to almost every large complex. People want to be able to find the things they are interested in easily, whether on a campus, in a conference center or hotel, or in any other complex.

Window Treatment Design

Draperies, shades, louver drapes, valances, cornices, and a broad spectrum of other treatments make up this specialty. Insulation, ventilation, light control, and energy conservation are all part of the specialty of today's window treatment design.

FINDING YOUR PLACE

With a plan, effort, and research, all designers have a reasonable chance to find their career niche within design—whether that means a general practice, specialized work, or working independently or in a firm.

Using this book, you will learn virtually everything you need to know to design your own successful independent career. That said, I admit I have a bias against starting to work independently too soon: It can be very risky, and for that reason, I strongly discourage it. If you want to give yourself the best chance for success in your career, find someone whose work you admire. Find a mentor and learn everything you can from that person. That usually means going into an established firm. But before you invest several years of your life in a firm, invest some time in learning as much as you can about the firm and its principals. Chances are that as a new member of the company, you will not be able to change it to suit yourself; you will have to work the way of the firm.

Find out exactly what kind of work the firm does. Look at its work in trade and design press magazines and books. Talk to the firm's clients; ask staff or contractors who have worked with the firm about the projects they worked on. And approach the firm directly. You do not have to say why you are interested in the firm; you can merely say you would like the opportunity to see more of their work because you admire it. Most design firms are proud of their work and will be happy to show and tell you about their projects. Visiting their installations will tell you quite a lot about the quality of the firm.

Find out as much as you can about the principals within the company—especially the person you have identified as the one you would like to have as your mentor. Know their educational and business backgrounds. Be familiar with their career histories: Where did they start, and how long has it taken them to reach their present status? That information may rest with former employers, clients, and other designers.

An interior design firm works as a team. When selecting a new job relationship, as when choosing a marriage partner, it is important to have a sense of how well the team works. You are going to spend a lot of time with these people, and you are going to share many different experiences and pressures. You want to learn as much as you can to ensure that you will be a complementary member of the team.

If you put the same care into planning your future as you put into your interior designs, you will most likely get what you want from your career. No one can expect to have the perfect job handed to them on a platter. Instead, plan for, plot, and go after the job you want and really should have. Do it in a professional manner, and you will find your place. You will probably also be successful.

I have conducted many seminars in which small groups of designers gather to define their best abilities and to examine what it will take to ensure that they can perform at their highest level. The group synergy, combined with the guidance of a business coach, has helped many individuals attain their twin goals of greater job satisfaction and higher profits.

After one of my lectures, a senior student at the Philadelphia Textile School asked for advice on how to get a job in textile arts in her home state of Colorado. She had found that most of the textile design positions were in the northeastern United States, around New York and Philadelphia. I asked what she meant by "no jobs." Wasn't there even one company?

Yes, she admitted, there was one firm specializing in fabrics for men's and women's ready-to-wear clothing, but she did not know much about them other than that they had a large factory, had been in the same location a number of years, and had said they had no openings when she had inquired.

The young woman's father was in insurance, so I pointed out that he would know a lot of people in the community and could find out about the major people in that firm—including their educational and work backgrounds. "You want to know about their families," I counseled, "whether they live within the community or commute from a distance—anything you can find out about how these people relate to this company."

I suggested that she use her Saturdays and free days to visit apparel specialty stores and department stores in big cities of neighboring states to research this firm. I told her she could talk to the buyers about how they felt about the fabrics made by that particular textile company, and she should create an outline of appropriate questions for every buyer: whether they liked the quality, which colors sold better, which year the line was best. I told her it would take about six months to accumulate the information she needed to put into a professional presentation.

After this was completed, I suggested that she test the presentation, polish it, refine it, and ask her professors to review it. Then, at my urging, she called the president of the firm when she went home for Christmas vacation. She told him she had spent six months doing research on his company, after which she asked for an appointment to review it with him. She got the appointment. He was surprised at her interest in his firm, and he was intrigued by some of the comments she made, which differed from what he had heard from his staff and marketing people. It is hard to know just what impressed him most, but the main thing is that he was impressed by the attention she had given his company. She told him of her textile arts training and that she intended to move back to Colorado and would like to work in his company.

Her tangible interest in his firm convinced the president that he wanted her to work with them. He did not know which job he was going to give her, but she was hired. He told her to come back in June, and he would have something for her then.

MEASURES OF SUCCESS

How is success measured in the interior design profession? Is a successful interior designer one whose name appears frequently in newspaper columns and in the popular design press? Or is a successful designer one who has achieved a reliable, steady income and some continuing creative satisfaction?

Public success and personal satisfaction go hand in hand. You do not have to be an Elsie de Wolfe or a Syrie Maugham to be successful today, because there are opportunities and alternatives open to you that did not exist when these two grande dames of the industry started their businesses on chutzpah, contacts, and not much else.

The truth is that many designers we see as successful do not take success for granted. In researching *Profitable Career Options for Designers* (1985), I discovered that successful people are always looking ahead to the next project or projects and that their favorite project is the one they are working on at the moment.

Being an interior designer today means making choices, developing an area of expertise, and being receptive to change. This is the mentality of successful designers. They are always looking for ways to improve. None of us should say, "There is only one correct solution, and it is mine." We should go out and find two or three or even a hundred ways of approaching a problem and use the one we feel best answers a client's needs.

Expect and plan for change. Designers are very creative people, and creative people need change. Most designers find they need to change the way they work in some major way at least every five to seven years because they have become bored. When they make these changes, their creativity rises, their excitement is fired up again, and they bring a higher level of performance to the field.

Many designers, successful in running their own businesses, find administration and management not their thing. They know they love to design, work with clients, and sell products. These designers find companies they can associate with in which they have the opportunity to be just designers. It is amazing to see how happy this makes them. Running a business requires you to create opportunities for other people, but it does not often allow for creativity, which is most important to the designer's creative spirit. Starting a business or having your own business may not be something you want to do.

It is not unusual or unexpected for designers to become bored with their work. Profitable businesses develop a good product and then repeat it. This is fine for a while, but as a creative person, you will understandably want to do something else eventually. There are ways to change your career and maintain your joy in your work, as well as to keep your business profitable. Sometimes, you will be able to redesign your career without outside help, but for the most part, it is better to do this as part of a group, with a business consultant as a coach.

ETHICS AND STANDARDS

When we speak of ethics, we quickly look at legal issues. Ethics are the things we cannot see or do as part of our general business practice. Ethics also includes issues of standards. Ethics and standards comprise an issue we must consider in every space we design. Many of us believe that if spaces are designed to be healthy, we will not use the particular materials that make the space unhealthy. There may be nothing wrong with the materials because they are being sold everywhere, but we do not believe they are appropriate based on professional standards and ethics.

We are seeing much more specialization in today's design world. Whether the designer is new to the field or has been in the business for many years, specialists have much more training and expertise in their particular area. Through technology, designers and clients can work with specialists, from all over the world. This brings a wonderful level of design, but does require more extensive coordination. So the position of "design coordinator" becomes key. Design coordinators must know how to get the best out of designers and clients.

The field demands a much higher level of expertise than ever before.

CHAPTER 2

Starting a Business

Many of us enjoy expanding our present businesses or creating new businesses, putting ideas together and making them work. This compulsion to forever do something new can be a strength, but it can also distract us from what should be our main focus: our interior design practice. Each year in our country there are many new businesses, and a number are very successful. This has become the era of the entrepreneur and small business. Still, many have failed.

Decide whether you want a business you can sell later or are really creating a professional job for yourself. These are two very different things. Business consultants emphasize that before starting a business you should plan how you will sell the business, if and when the time arises. If you want a business you can sell later, you must structure it in such a way that it can be turned over to and managed by another person. Many designers start their practice under their own name and design it around their own style. This may not be desirable to someone else. There are situations in which a designer working at a firm can grow with that firm and take it over one day. Before investing in your own business, decide whether you want a profitable business that can be run by others and will be saleable or whether you want to create a business strictly to use your design style. There are other considerations you should make to ensure adequate income and financial rewards when you decide to leave the business.

INITIAL CONSIDERATIONS

Before starting your own business, first look at how it might affect you. If you have been working for a company, you may have job tenure, a regular paycheck, paid holidays and vacation, sick leave, insurance plans, and the knowledge that when you have finished work each day you can leave it behind—it is ultimately someone else's responsibility. These benefits are not a part of a new business.

The idea of starting your own firm is exciting, but there is no point in starting it if you do not intend to make it a success. That takes an investment, in years, of time and effort. To start a business you will need to devote the first seven or eight years to the business, and running it well will probably require 80- to 120-hour workweeks. Is this a sacrifice you are willing to make? What about your personal needs? Will they mesh with the obligations entailed in starting a business? After all, you are establishing not just a job, but a lifestyle. Can you make this intense a commitment? If you are planning to start a primary personal relationship or a family, this may not be the best time in your life to also start a business.

Are you prepared to accept the responsibility of managing a business? A designer I know started a wonderful art gallery because his mother-in-law wanted something to do. This worked beautifully as long as the mother-in-law stayed interested. But after about two years, the fun wore off for her, and the designer was stuck with a gallery that had to be kept open 8 to 10 hours a day and that required a minimum of two people to staff. If you are considering investing in a business venture for a child or relative, give the venture a careful review. Is the relative committed to the project on a long-term basis? If not, would you be able to hire staff to continue it?

Personal Traits

Do you have the right personality to start a business? It takes a certain type of person to succeed in business. The following is a list of questions to ask yourself before starting your own business:

1. **Are you in good health?** You need to be in good shape to endure the physical and emotional rigors of starting and running a business.
2. **Do you really have all the energy it takes to make this project succeed?** Most people who succeed in their own businesses have boundless physical energy. If your physical energy is limited, perhaps you should consider teaming with another professional who can carry part of the burden.
3. **Are you a self-starter?** Are you the type of person who gets things done and starts projects on your own initiative? In your own business you will have to act without anybody else pushing you or reminding you.
4. **Do you enjoy other people?** Do you really like all kinds of people? You will find yourself working with people in a variety of professions and with diverse personality types—laborers, persons with limited education, high-level professionals, and eccentrics, among others.
5. **Are you a leader?** Your staff will be following your cues. You must be someone people are ready and willing to follow.
6. **Are you ready for the responsibilities of a business?** Do you understand exactly what this entails? Before deciding to start your own business, investigate

a number of other businesses to get a thorough knowledge of what you are facing.

7. **Are you a good worker?** Are you the kind of person who does not mind doing what it takes to get a job done and who will keep working as long and as hard as is necessary to complete a project well? Running your own business will demand your complete dedication.

8. **Are you well organized?** Interior design is a field that requires high organizational abilities.

9. **Are you a capable decision maker?** Do you enjoy making decisions? You will need to be ready to make them quickly and accurately without fear of failure.

10. **Do people have confidence in you?** Have you established a rapport with the people who have worked with you? For people to do business with you, they must have confidence that if they give you the job, it will get done.

11. **How committed are you to running your own business?** Too many designers start in business with the idea that it will be fun for a while. If that is your attitude, probably you should not consider starting in business. To develop a business always takes much longer and requires more energy than you might imagine.

12. **Do you have the excitement it takes to carry this through?** Your enthusiasm will inspire your staff to do its best. Are you enthused enough about the business and ready to handle whatever comes up?

13. **Are you a good communicator?** You must be able to express yourself clearly and speak with others at all levels; this is the only way to share ideas and work together.

14. **Do you know what you are doing?** Do you really know the interior design field or at least the specialty that you are selecting? It is much cheaper to learn in someone else's studio than to do it yourself. You must understand the field on a professional level. You are the last word; therefore, you must know everything about the work you are going to be doing, or where to get the answers. Know your field well before you start in business.

15. **Have you had any business training?** You have no idea how much you need to learn until you begin a business. Spend time reading and learning about any unfamiliar business processes. Talk with professionals such as accountants, attorneys, and other successful small business owners about the skills and resources it takes to run a business. Often, the local branch of the Small Business Association (SBA) or your community college holds programs on how to start and what to expect when starting a small business. Do not consider starting your own business until you have researched all aspects of it thoroughly.

Ask questions. What other problems can you foresee in starting your own business? What do you expect to get out of this business? List what you consider to be the assets and liabilities of starting the business.

PLANNING AHEAD

A successful business starts with a good plan. Too many designers enter business impulsively, without a plan. In today's business climate, a business without a good basic plan is not likely to succeed. Components of your plan should include:

1. **Written action plan that includes the following:**
   - When you expect to start.
   - Where your business will be located.
   - Your plan for earning profits.
   - What your areas of specialty, and potentially highest profit, will be.
   - How you will charge—fees, markup, or hourly rates (see Chapter 8, page 253).

   Every step of basic business planning (see Chapter 3) also applies. You should also prepare a forecast of expenses. Determine just how much money will be needed. See pages 64–70 for details on these business requirements.

2. **Clients.** Before you start your company or venture, make sure you have clients lined up. Review your present client load to see which clients you feel would come with you to a new business. It usually takes several years to develop a good client base. There is no point starting in business without a list of clients, because it is difficult and expensive to go out and find that first client. If you have your clients secured ahead of time, you automatically decrease the period it will take to start turning a profit.

3. **Staff.** Qualified, capable staff are your biggest asset, if you can put together the right people. You may make a plan with a particular person in mind and then find that person is not available. It is not realistic to expect people to work for you unless you can offer those individuals something that really holds their interest.

4. **Market.** Make sure there really is a market out there. Sometimes the fact that no one else is offering a service means there is no market for it. When you have a lot of other competitors, it may mean there's a tremendous market for your service, which you can top if you can find a better way of selling to that market. Do you know where your customers live? Are you in the correct geographic area? Interior designers work in very wide areas; however, it is most effective to work in an area that supports you. You can travel for a portion of your jobs, but it is usually too expensive to travel for every job.

5. **Production.** Do you have the ability to produce the products or items? Many businesses in the design field start with great ideas but have inadequate staff or production capabilities. There is no point selling something that can't be delivered. Plan in advance where your materials will come from and how your products will be manufactured. Having the ability to produce a few dozen items is not of much value if you need to sell thousands to make the business profitable.

6. **Resources.** Write a list of required resources—manufacturers, showrooms,

dealers, contractors—and spend time developing good rapport with them. Make sure that the people who serve as your resources get to know you and the quality of your work. Usually your resources will be sources you have used in the past—people you know think well of your design work.

7. **Finances.** All business ventures require money. Before you start a new business, have a source of more money than you need, preferably three to four times what you expect to spend. Find these funds before you start in business and before you are committed to expenditures for clients, staff, and so on. Too often businesses fail because they do not have enough capital.

    When considering your sources of capital, ask yourself:

    - How much money have you saved?
    - How much of your own funds are you ready to invest?
    - Do you have any equity in a residence or other properties that you could potentially use for borrowing collateral?
    - Do you have the ability to obtain a line of credit?
    - Do you have other sources of income?

    Generally there are few sources of financing for a new small business. Lending institutions will usually make loans for tangible property, such as buildings and equipment and perhaps some inventory, but not for "soft costs," such as salaries, advertising, and other day-to-day expenses. Usually you will need to use your own funds or those of individuals who are assisting you. Be prepared to make a financial investment in your new firm. If you need money and have to take in a partner, discuss with your attorneys ways of accepting either stockholders or partners. When you establish your business structure, build into your plans ways to adjust or change the agreement. In almost every instance, as a business develops, it becomes necessary to change the structure. Can yours be changed? Your attorney and accountant can advise you on this.

    Have you figured into your financial projection the amount of income you expect during these start-up years? What salary will you require? Can you live on less than what you have been making in order to permit your business to progress? Talk to your bankers, and be sure that they understand where you are going. Ask them to specify what borrowing ability you have. Specifically, ask them about various loans, such as long-term loans, short-term loans, lines of credit, and individual project borrowing.

    A break-even analysis is a valuable tool. It determines whether it is worth investing a stated amount of money and time in this project to reach a certain level of profit. For a new business, you should prepare a one- to three-year break-even analysis (see pages 387–388). An accountant or business consultant can help you prepare this analysis.

    After determining how much money you need to start your business, consider how much credit is available from your suppliers—what terms they will offer you. Also, determine what type of credit terms you are going to be able to work out with your potential clients. Often, interior designers can get retainers and deposits on items and can carry certain portions of their business. But it is foolhardy to think you can carry it all. Understand and outline your anticipated financial conditions, both on accounts receivable and accounts payable.

Today many designers are being paid on a cash before delivery (CBD) basis or even receiving the total amount of money before they purchase merchandise for clients. It is not appropriate to expect to run your business totally on your clients' money. Some types of work will not permit this; others may. However, you are still responsible for the work you are doing. You must have the revenue to cover all expenses on your projects without depending on your clients' money.

8. **Timeline.** How long will it take to make the venture work? Can you afford to take that time from your other endeavors? If you acquire sufficient business to keep you busy 30 or 40 hours a week and your time sells for $100 to $150 an hour, the new venture must be very good for you to be able to afford to pursue it. All business takes time, usually three to five times what you would estimate. This question refers not only to how long it takes to get started, but also how long it takes to get established. New clients and projects do not just walk in the door; they must be cultivated. As you do your break-even financial analysis, include an analysis of the time required to see how that compares with the time you are really willing to spend.

Almost any new business venture or project will take three to five years to get started. The initial planning requires a considerable amount of work, but it is nothing compared to the work of actually running a business. Time spent planning now is inexpensive—and it is absolutely essential in the total process of starting a business. The plan should include benchmarks, a point at which you stop, review, and reevaluate your plan to decide whether to forge ahead, stop, or veer off into a new direction.

Advantages

There are a number of advantages to running your own business:

1. **You have complete control.** You have the power to make the decisions. Therefore, you can direct the activities and control the design direction of the business.
2. **You have complete freedom to be as creative as you want.** You can do things your own way.
3. **You determine how great the profits will be.** You can make as much money as you like, depending on your ability, talents, ideas, and energy.
4. **You have the ultimate job security.** You can't be fired. If you do not bring in business, you are not going to have a company. Still, you cannot be forced to retire.

5. **There is great satisfaction in running a successful business.** Since it is your business, you can justifiably feel proud in taking all the credit.

Disadvantages

There are also some major disadvantages:

1. **Running the business will demand long hours.** Very few businesses run on a nine-to-five basis. Most independent designers work 12, 15, 16 hours a day. Often you will have to perform tasks that you would never have been asked to handle as an employee. When the job must be done, many times you are the person left to do it.

2. **There is the risk you will lose your investment.** If you make money, it is yours; but if you lose it, all your personal assets could be in jeopardy.

3. **Your income will fluctuate with the success of the business.** In the first years there is often a greater fluctuation than in later years; however, this is one of the risks of a small business. Your employees get paid, your suppliers get paid—and you get what is left.

4. **The responsibility for the business is all yours.** If something goes wrong, you are responsible.

5. **All of the pressures are basically yours to bear.** You must please all your clients. You must meet all your credit obligations, tax and insurance demands, and the payroll. This has to be done on a regular basis, not just when you feel like it.

6. **There are many federal, state, and local laws you must abide by, as well as all kinds of stipulations applied by your insurance companies.** It is amazing how many regulations there are to restrict business activities—and many are very expensive to comply with. It is wise to review your objectives with both your attorney and your accountant before you start your business.

GETTING FEEDBACK

It is important to find several advisors who will work with you on your project and will continue to advise you throughout your business career. You especially need a good accountant and a good attorney, as well as an insurance advisor and other consultants who will work on design projects when needed (see pages 120–129). Be sure you have these people lined up before starting your new venture. Confidentiality is important in starting a new business, so you may want to look outside your community for consultants if you cannot find people with whom you have developed a long-term rapport.

Accountant

Ask your accountant to prepare a financial projection (see Chapter 3) and a break-even analysis. Your accountant's thoughts may be different from those of a business consultant, as the two view business from different perspectives. You need to compare both points of view.

Bankers or Other Lending Institutions

Talk with professionals in the lending industry to understand what borrowing capacity you can expect.

- What type of loan can you obtain?
- How much can you borrow?
- What is the interest rate?
- What will be the repayment terms?
- What collateral will you need to secure the loan?

Business Consultant

Once you have prepared your plans, find a good business consultant—someone who is familiar with the interior design field—to validate any areas you may need to consider further.

Designer

Try your idea out on another designer or experienced person in your field whom you trust, someone with perhaps more experience and in a noncompetitive situation. We test every venture we plan with a few designer advisors before going any further. It is often surprising and exciting to see which additions or revisions they suggest. Additions are usually good at helping to build and mold a project.

Financial Advisor

The overall financial aspects of the venture should be reviewed by a financial advisor. This should be someone other than your accountant or attorney. The financial advisor's job is to really look at the financial development of your project, taking into consideration the resources of money available to you and your overall company potential.

Insurance Advisor

This person will advise on how you can properly cover your major risks with insurance. For example, a designer was interested in restoring downtown properties but found she could not purchase any kind of insurance on the project during construction or until the buildings were actually occupied. Because the restoration project would take two years in an underpoliced neighborhood, she and her insurance advisor decided it was much too heavy a risk.

Lawyer

An attorney will advise you whether you are putting your existing business or personal assets in undue jeopardy and help you to structure your business to minimize your risk.

Other Professionals

Talk with other people in businesses similar to yours to see what you can learn from them. What can you learn from their successes or failures? Develop a list of consultants and people you can call on and depend on.

BUYING AN EXISTING BUSINESS

Is it worth buying a business that someone has already started? Very often it is, because the business has an established clientele. If you can work in the business for a while, you can get an intimate knowledge of the condition of the firm and whether the practice is appropriate for you. Although it is more common for a design firm to be dissolved rather than sold on the retirement or death of its owners, many interior design businesses are sold and can be valuable to a young designer.

It is a sound idea to ease into the business. Work with the firm and develop a rapport with the clients and sources before committing to buying an established firm. There is one strong benefit: The structure is already established. However, do not shortchange yourself. Although the practice is established, you will still need the same business plan you would need if you were starting your own business.

Your business plan should include areas in which the existing business could be strengthened or revised to highlight your skills and minimize your weaknesses. Also include any processes, procedures, or structures in your plan to bring the business up to current standards. Talk with your attorney and financial advisors to determine the most desirable and practical overall plan to purchase the business. There are certain advantages in taking over an existing business, but there are also areas where the business could be strengthened or revised to take into account your own skills and weaknesses. The firm may need updating to present-day standards. You probably will want to shift some of the priorities. Talk with your legal and financial advisors to determine the best buyout plan for this business.

Advantages

The following are some of the advantages to buying an existing business.

1. **An established business generally has a greater potential for success.** The location of the business has been preselected; people know about it and are inclined to go there. Years of advance marketing have been done. If the business has been profitable, it should be much easier for you to continue to make a profit.
2. **The amount of planning necessary to start in business has been reduced.** Therefore, you can make your first sale that much sooner.
3. **Usually, the clientele is already established.** If proper introductions are made, you can continue with them and then start to build your own clientele.

4. **There may be some inventory available to get you started.** Office equipment and supplies are in place; these are items you do not have to buy and set up before making your first sale.

5. **Financing is usually easier to procure for the purchase of an existing business than for starting a new business.** Often, financing can be prearranged with the previous buyer. An exact figure is far easier to establish.

6. **You may be buying a business at a bargain price.** The sellers may need to sell. They may want to see their business continue and thus be willing to work with you and help you set up the situation to your advantage.

7. **You can call on the experience of a prior owner.** Even if you are not in complete agreement with the previous owner, at least you have a point of reference to check against. It is easier than doing everything yourself.

8. **Much of the original hard work of setting up has been eliminated.** Not that there is no work to be done or there are no adjustments to be made, but these can be handled gradually as you have time and money available. You do not have to do everything at once.

9. **Often, there is a group of experienced employees; you do not have to train them all.** If there are people you can work with, you begin with a tremendous advantage.

10. **There are many past business and client records available that can help you build and market for future business.** You will know which products clients have used before and, therefore, be better able to serve them than if you had just moved into an area with no records and no client background.

Disadvantages

There are also some clear disadvantages to buying existing businesses.

1. **If the business was poorly managed, the management problems can carry over into your business.** Bad habits often continue. Be sure the management system is what it should be. It's best to try and work within the business first, to evaluate its systems.

2. **If the employees who are working for the company are not appropriate, they can get in your way.** Sometimes you are better off not to have any employees than to have badly trained employees. Consider this and your obligations to the employees before committing to purchasing this business.

3. **Many policies established by the previous owners may no longer be appropriate and may be difficult to change—both with clients and employees.** Review these standards. (One reason it is wise to work in a firm for a period of time before determining whether you should buy is to get an idea of the situation that exists there.)

4. **Much of the inventory might not be appropriate to current-day sales.** While you may be able to sell off some of it for instant capital, you may find that a great deal of inventory people have in stock is just not currently saleable.

5. **If you put all of your monies into buying the business, you may be short of funds for extending and developing the business.** Allow for the fact that it takes a considerable amount of money to run a business effectively.

6. **The location and image of the firm may not be appropriate for your intended practice.** If this is the case, it is probably better to start your own business. But if the existing business has a blend of styling and background that relates to yours, it could be very worthwhile.

How can you find out about businesses that are available? Look for opportunities in:

- Design magazines or classified display ads.
- Realtor recommendations.
- Brokers' listings.
- Chamber of Commerce listings of businesses for sale.
- Trade sources.
- Professional referrals—accountants, attorneys, bankers. They can be of help in introducing you to businesses, but often they do not know the details or the background trade sources and other designers would have.
- Other designers. They usually know of people who have decided to retire or who for some reason want to get out of the business. If you start here, it is usually best to use other professionals to review the business before considering a purchase.

Evaluating an Existing Business

Buying an existing business is an excellent way not only to start in business but also to expand one's business. More and more designers are buying up other practices. Before making an offer, investigate whether the business is a good one to buy.

- Find out as much as you can about the business you are considering. Visit with people who work there. Talk to the owners of the firm and find out the names of their suppliers. When you learn their resources, talk to them to learn the quality of the company and the volume of its business. Very often sales representatives will give you a great deal of this information, although on an unofficial and confidential basis. Sometimes this information can give you leads to the direction and the success of a business.
- Visit some of the projects the firm has done and consider whether you would be proud to associate your name with this type of work.
- Have the company evaluated by other people in the field. Is the owner's asking price reasonable? It is usually best to have several people review this figure. Although the opinions of accountants, lawyers, and other professionals are worthwhile, you should also get an evaluation from someone knowledgeable in the design field, who can look at the business objectively. Also, try to get an independent appraisal of the business by a qualified business appraiser.

- Request to see the financial records, including the tax returns, of the business for at least the past three years. Have your accountant review the financial statements and tax returns to evaluate the financial health of the company. Have a business consultant, preferably one who specializes in the interior design field, review the records to evaluate the health of the business as compared with other similar firms in the industry. If possible, talk to some of the firm's clients. Find out how they perceive the work the firm does and how they would feel about the business continuing.

There are many ways of doing this type of investigation. The method chosen will vary according to the status of the current business. Is this a situation in which everyone knows the business is for sale, or is it more confidential? Either way, do a thorough investigation.

Determining a Firm's Dollar Value. There are many different formulas for estimating the dollar value of an existing company. You need to determine the floor and ceiling values so you can establish the range for negotiation.

The floor value of a design firm is the amount of cash that would be required to establish a comparable design firm, starting from scratch. To arrive at this figure, you should analyze the basic costs involved in starting and running a business.

1. **Initial fees.** Calculate the fees you would need to pay in the start-up years (legal and accounting, for example).
2. **Physical property.** An existing business usually has already paid for its facility, leasehold, and equipment. You should consider the time and money you would need to find and establish a new space.
3. **Cost of establishing a business.** Try to determine the cost of starting a business and the amount of money that might have been required to fund it up to this point. This would include covering the many losses usually incurred in the start-up years. This final cash figure could be considerable, as it generally takes a while for a design firm to become profitable. Usually, when you take over a firm, it is profitable from day one.
4. **Employee training.** Training employees to work effectively as a group requires a large financial investment. You will save considerably by starting out with a trained team ready to produce.
5. **Any promotion or advertising efforts already developed.** Generally, through promotion and advertising, the positioning of the firm has been established.

The ceiling value of a firm takes into account the firm's history and its potential for becoming more valuable than its current worth. To determine a business' ceiling value, research the following:

1. **Profits.** What is the firm's level of profits? Does the firm have the ability to continue at this level? While the balance sheet of a service organization is

generally easy to analyze, it is often difficult to determine the profitability factor and cash flow analysis.

2. **Goodwill.** Goodwill that can be transferred from an old ownership to a new one is a major factor in establishing a high ceiling value for a firm. However, the value of goodwill has to be determined on an individual basis. Generally, design businesses are highly personalized, and the owners are very involved in every part of the design service. If the owner is no longer there, how much of the goodwill of the firm will evaporate? Is the owner going to continue working with the company, or be willing to sign a noncompete agreement?

3. **Client base.** A firm's client base and the continuing projects you will inherit greatly influence the ceiling value. Most important is the ability of the firm to sustain its client base. Are the clients dedicated to the firm and willing to continue using the firm through the next ownership?

4. **Internal self-sustaining structure.** Is the management structured and well designed to continue into a new ownership?

5. **Location.** A firm's location plays a major role in establishing its ceiling value. For example, if a business is located in a progressive area or one with a pleasant climate, it will be significantly more valuable than one located in a less-desirable area. Is this location in a growing area where you can expect to meet clients in need of interior design services?

6. **Staff.** What are the general skills of the employees? In a design business that offers purely professional service, the assets are represented in the fees of services rendered. The inventory is, in essence, the staff, and the price charged for their design services.

7. **Special information.** Trade names, copyrights, patents, and other information, including customer lists and mailing lists, are assets you should consider in determining a firm's ceiling value.

8. **Long-term contracts.** Are there any long-term contracts in place that can be transferred to a new owner and generate an ongoing source of revenue? If so, this will generally make the purchase price of the business higher, but should provide the purchaser with a steady source of revenue, especially as the business transfers ownership.

The return expected from the investment of capital, taking into account changing economic conditions, is a determinant in calculating the ceiling value of a business. Buyers will normally pay a multiplier of approximately five times the firm's pretax income, which would be the firm's annual profits plus the salary of the owner. For example, if a company's profits per year are $200,000, and the owner draws a $175,000 salary, the pretax income would be $375,000. The firm's ceiling value would be five times $375,000, or $1,875,000. In determining the firm's pretax income, be sure to factor in any excessive travel and entertainment expenses and other fringe benefits. For example, if the owners received an additional 30 percent of their salary in the form of fringe benefits, this would raise the value considerably.

In the purchase or sale of a business, the buyer and seller usually have conflicting interests. For example, it is usually to the advantage of a seller of a corporate business to sell the stock, whereas it is usually to the advantage of the buyer to buy the assets. There are various provisions in the IRS code that, depending upon the structure of your business, may allow you to treat the sale of stock as an asset sale. Because the requirements of these code sections must be strictly adhered to in order to qualify for the tax benefits, it is imperative that you discuss the contemplated transaction with your tax accountant and lawyer before you enter into any negotiations.

There are generally three ways to evaluate a purchase:

1. **Adjusted net worth.** This is based on the historical value of the firm's earnings.
2. **Market value.** This method considers that past billings will remain relatively constant in the future and that no other significant financial changes are expected for the business or industry. A quick way to calculate this is to multiply the annual billings by .5.
3. **Earnings.** This method views earnings as increasing in the future and provides a premium purchase price. The quick calculation for this method is to multiply the pretax income (plus or minus any officer's salary or other owner's perks) by 5.

SELECTING THE RIGHT FORM OF OWNERSHIP FOR YOU

There are basically three forms of business ownership: sole proprietorship, partnership, and corporation. There are advantages and disadvantages to each form of ownership; you should discuss them with your accountant and attorney before deciding. Of course, the form can be changed in the future if circumstances demand it.

Sole Proprietorship

A sole proprietorship is the simplest form of ownership and the easiest to establish. An individual begins a firm and is automatically a sole proprietor. All profits earned by the business belong to the owner, who also bears all losses. The owner has total authority over the business operation. There are few legal restrictions with the sole proprietorship except for the general civil and criminal laws that apply to all forms of businesses. If you are a person who likes to take charge, this is a very attractive form of ownership.

Advantages. There are many advantages to a sole proprietorship. You are the boss. You have complete control over the size of the business and its direction. You can stop and start the business as you choose. You can simply make a decision and go from there. If you are looking for a situation in which you have maximum control and minimal government red tape, sole proprietorship may be your best choice.

A sole proprietorship is the easiest type of business to form legally, which also makes it the least expensive. You do not have the expense of setting up a corporation, and bookkeeping to meet government regulations is less expensive.

You keep all the profits. You can withdraw them for your personal use, consistent with business requirements or contractual obligations. It is your money.

A sole proprietorship, as an entity, does not pay income taxes. Rather, owners report the gain or loss on their individual income tax returns (whether filed singly or jointly with a spouse).

Disadvantages. While a sole proprietorship offers enormous freedom, with that freedom comes great responsibility and risk. One of the main disadvantages of a sole proprietorship is that you are totally responsible for everything that happens. In the event that you fail, your personal assets could be claimed by creditors. This may include your home, your automobile, and your savings. Unlimited liability is probably the worst feature of this type of business.

The owner must come up with the total capital required for the business. The amount of capital you are able to raise is limited by what you yourself have or are able to borrow. In a partnership or a corporation, you can draw on the resources of other people.

Because you have no co-owner to share the trials and tribulations of operating a business, you need to be the kind of person who is capable—and willing—to do everything.

A sole proprietorship may find it difficult to attract high-quality employees because the future of the firm may not appear as promising. However, an agreement might be made to arrange for an orderly transfer of part or all of the business under specified conditions. This would provide a greater incentive for top employees to join you.

Partnership

A partnership is an association of two or more persons, formed to operate a business for profit. Although a formal agreement is not legally required for partners, it's advisable that a legal document called the "Articles of Co-Partnership" be drawn up to establish the understanding between or among the partners.

Among the important issues that should be included in the partnership agreement are:

1. The contributions to the partnership that will be made by each party in terms of cash, property, or services.
2. How profits and losses are to be shared.
3. How authority is to be divided.
4. Whether the partners are to be paid a salary (in addition to the sharing of profits and losses).

5. Whether interest is to be paid to partners on their investment in the firm.
6. An understanding as to which withdrawals of funds may be made by the partners.
7. How disagreements are to be settled (perhaps by the appointment of an independent arbitrator).
8. How a new partner may be admitted to the business.
9. What happens upon the death or disability of a partner.
10. How assets and liabilities are to be divided in the event the partnership is terminated.

These are only a few of the items that should be included. A meeting of the partners, with their individual lawyers, should be held before a partnership is started to avoid misunderstandings later.

Types of Partnership

There are two types of partnership: general partnerships and limited partnerships. In a general partnership, all partners have unlimited liability for partnership debts. In a limited partnership, the partners are liable only to the extent of their investment in the partnership. A limited partnership must have at least one general partner (who will have unlimited liability). The general partner must be active in the operations of the business. A limited partner may or may not take active part in the management of the business.

Many types of relationships can be established within a partnership. This permits people of different talents and skills to establish a business. With designers, it can be a merging of different talents within the interior design field or a collaboration of individuals from various interconnected fields, such as architecture, landscape architecture, engineering, lighting, and business management.

Advantages of a Partnership as Compared with a Sole Proprietorship. Usually, two heads are better than one. One person may oversee the design functions, while another handles the bookkeeping or expediting. One can add tremendous strength to the other.

Partnerships are easy to start. There is very little additional expense, except writing up your partnership agreements and establishing the way you are going to work. More money and resources are available. Usually, all partners contribute capital to the firm. Also, they may be a source of additional capital, if necessary, or perhaps loans.

Partners can provide the business with a high-quality staff. A person who is willing to be your partner may be unwilling to be your employee. Sharing in the ownership and profits brings a high level of interest.

As with sole proprietorships, the business profit or loss is shown on each of the partner's individual tax returns, allocated according to the partnership agreement.

Advantages and Disadvantages of a Partnership as Compared with a Corporation. A partnership also has some advantages, as well as disadvantages, compared with a corporation. A major advantage is the absence of red tape. There are fewer governmental regulations and requirements.

On the other hand, a major disadvantage is that there are fewer perks and fringe benefits available. Also, as mentioned elsewhere, unlimited liability is a major disadvantage of a partnership.

Partnerships are less capable of acquiring capital than corporations. An individual who may be willing to invest in a corporation may, because of the unlimited liability, refuse to become a partner.

Corporation

A corporation is a legal entity formed under state laws. As such, a corporation is considered to be an "artificial person." Each state has its own requirements for incorporation. If you choose to incorporate, you should engage an attorney to handle the matter. A corporation is considered to be "domiciled" in the state of incorporation, but it may engage in business in any other state by registering with such state as a "foreign" corporation.

There are three forms of corporations:

- **C Corporation.** This is the traditional corporation in which the corporation, as a legal entity, is subject to federal corporation income taxes and to various taxes in each of the states in which it registers to do business. In addition, of course, it is subject to all taxes imposed on businesses generally, such as payroll and sales taxes.
- **S Corporation.** This corporation has the limited liability of a corporation, but the profits or losses of the business are passed through to the shareholders and taxed on the individual's personal tax return. The S Corporation itself does not pay any income taxes. There are restrictions and qualifications in order to establish an S corporation, so you should check with your tax advisor and attorney before settling on this form of business.
- **Limited Liability Corporation (LLC).** This corporation is similar to an S corporation, in which the shareholders have limited liability protection, and the profits/losses pass through to the shareholders individually. There are a couple of major differences. One is that an S Corporation may be formed by one person, but in many states an LLC requires at least two. Also, S Corporation profits/losses must be distributed according to each shareholder's percent of ownership, but those of an LLC may be distributed according to a different plan. Again, you should consult with your tax advisor and attorney to determine the right structure for you.

So many factors enter into the tax situation of a sole proprietorship, partnership, or corporation, that it cannot be said unequivocally that any one form of business operation is more tax-advantageous than another. You and your accountant must review each situation separately and make projections under each of the various assumptions before deciding which structure is right for you. There are factors other than taxes to be considered in deciding which business structure is advisable for your situation. The tax implications, in fact, may be one of the least-important considerations.

Some of the other advantages and disadvantages of a corporate form of business as compared with a proprietorship or partnership are as follows.

Advantages. The principal advantage is that a corporation has limited liability. Shareholders are liable for business debts only to the extent of their investments. There are more perks and fringe benefits available to the shareholder-employee. It is usually easier to transfer ownership. The shareholder needs only to assign stock certificate(s) to the new owner. This also facilitates the settlement of an estate upon the death of a shareholder. The business continues without being interrupted by the transfer of ownership.

It is easier to raise capital for a corporation, because a prospective investor may not be interested in a partnership, which would subject a partner to unlimited liability.

Disadvantages. As a creature of state law, a corporation involves more red tape to comply with the more numerous and sometimes complex regulations and requirements.

If your firm is a large organization, business arrangements sometimes become more cumbersome because of the formalities a corporation must observe but that a proprietorship or partnership can ignore.

Other Considerations. You should keep in mind that a business operation need not be confined entirely within a single corporation, partnership, or proprietorship. Often, for tax or other purposes, it is advantageous for real estate to be held separately by the individuals involved or by a second corporation. The first corporation, which operates the business, would then pay rent to the entity owning the real estate. Such arrangements have so many advantages that it is of utmost importance to review them at the time you are planning your business structure.

When you form a corporation, it is important to have a shareholder's agreement. If one of the shareholders dies, decides to retire, or does not want to be in the business any longer, without a shareholder's agreement, that individual can sell or bequeath stock to a stranger you might not want involved in the business. A shareholder's agreement should require, among other things, that the withdrawing shareholder first offer stock to the corporation or to the remaining shareholders for purchase at a specified or determinable price.

Most large interior design firms work under a corporate structure. Not nearly as many architectural firms do this, because in the past it was considered inappropriate for licensed professionals, such as doctors or lawyers, to practice under any kind of a limited-liability vehicle. Professional service corporations, commonly known as "PCs," came into existence to permit professionals to utilize the corporation for business and tax benefits without reducing their professional liability. In PCs, the licensed professional remains fully liable and accountable for any negligence committed by the professional or a staff member under the direction of that professional.

It is believed that licensing of interior designers probably would not affect these firms' working under a standard corporation, since there are many other licensed professional companies that have incorporated, such as insurance agents, stockbrokers, and many kinds of contractors.

Stockholders in a Corporation. Each person who owns stock in your corporation is a stockholder. This does not mean that every person who holds stock needs to be active in the company, but stock owners do have the right to vote for the corporation's board of directors and on certain corporate policies.

The board of directors represents the stockholders. The stockholders elect the members of the board annually, and their terms can vary according to the bylaws. Shareholders may vote for themselves to be members of the board, but it is not a requirement that a board member also be a shareholder.

The board of directors is responsible for setting corporate policies. Any major decisions affecting the corporate officers must be made by this board. The board must meet on a regular basis—at least annually—and keep records of its meetings and decisions.

Corporate Officers. The corporate officers have various, carefully delineated, functions.

1. **Chief executive officer.** The CEO is the officer of the firm responsible for the activities of the company. This position is usually held by the chairman of the board or the president.
2. **Chief financial officer.** The CFO is the executive officer responsible for handling the company's funds. This includes signing checks, keeping financial records, and supervising all financial planning. The CFO is usually a vice president in charge of finance, a treasurer, or, in some small companies, a controller. Many state laws require that a corporation have a treasurer, and therefore this person can have more than one title, such as vice president or treasurer.
3. **Chief operating officer.** The COO is the officer of the firm responsible for the day-to-day management of the corporation. Usually, it is the president or the executive vice president. The chief operating officer reports to the chief executive officer.
4. **Chairman of the board.** This person is the member of the corporation's board of directors who presides over board meetings and is the highest-ranking officer of the corporation. The position can carry either major or minor power, depending on the length of the term and the policies of the corporation. The position of chairman of the board is often reserved as a prestigious term for a past president, major stockholder, or family member.

5. **President.** This person is the highest officer of the corporation after the chairman of the board and sometimes titled the chief executive officer—in which case the president would outrank the chairman. The president is appointed by the board of directors and reports directly to the board. In a small corporation, the president and the chief executive officer are usually one and the same, having authority over all matters in the day-to-day management and policy-making decisions of the company.

6. **Outside director.** This person is a member of the company's board of directors who is not an employee of the company. Outside directors are usually paid a director's fee, which is a set amount for each board meeting or a certain annual fee. They become part of the decision-making process of the design firm and are often used for business development or increasing the company's operational knowledge.

> While business associations with relatives should not necessarily be discouraged, such relationships are usually much more sensitive than associations among nonrelated parties. In the event of a major disagreement, not only is the business relationship disturbed but the effect on family relationships can be traumatic.

Buy-Sell Agreements

In any business with another person, you need a buy-sell agreement. I cannot overemphasize the importance of such an agreement, which should be considered in the preplanning stage of the enterprise before the business association is effected. Your accountant should be consulted in planning the agreement, which your lawyer should draft.

There is usually a tendency when people engage in a business association to think there is no disagreement they would not be able to resolve amicably. Aside from the fact that such disagreements do occur, a more compelling reason for having a buy-sell agreement is to ensure, to the fullest extent possible, that no unwanted parties are brought into the business. Without a buy-sell agreement, one of the owners could sell or otherwise transfer all or part of that owner's interest to a person not acceptable to the other owners. This could happen, for example, if one of the owners dies and leaves interest in the business to a spouse, child, or any person not acceptable to the remaining owner or owners.

There are several ways by which a departing owner may dispose of interest. The remaining owner or owners may purchase the interest, or the business itself (usually in the case of a corporation) may purchase the interest in a "stock redemption" transaction. A word of caution with respect to the latter: Some states have laws that restrict stock redemptions under certain circumstances. If you are contemplating a redemption, check first to see whether your business may properly do so.

More often than not, a business itself is unable to purchase the interest without so depleting its capital that it would no longer be able to continue as a going concern. For this reason, it is important for a firm to have a means of funding the purchase. One way of providing these funds is for the firm to take out life insurance policies on the owners, with the company as the beneficiary. The insurance proceeds can then be used to fund the redemption without diminishing the firm's capital.

Life insurance policies can also be used to fund the purchase of interest by the remaining owners. In this case, each owner becomes a beneficiary in the policy on the life of the other owners.

An agreement must be reached as to how the costs of the insurance premiums are to be shared, since they may differ widely for each insured owner. Because the agreement is beneficial for the departing owner as well as the remaining ones, an equal sharing may be equitable. Whatever the case, the decision on this question should be included in the buy-sell agreement.

It is not uncommon for one or more owners to be uninsurable. In such a situation, the firm needs to provide other means of funding the buyout. The first right to purchase is meaningless if the required funds are not available.

The amount to be paid for shares in the firm should be fixed or determinable, and the entire buy-sell agreement should be reviewed periodically to update or amend it as the situation requires.

The IRS will accept for estate (death) tax purposes the value prescribed in bona fide buy-sell agreements, unless the value is clearly unrealistic. Accordingly, in a situation where estate taxes are an important factor for an owner, the IRS position may need to be considered when you are establishing the buyout price.

Taxes

Aside from the taxes peculiar to corporations, all businesses—whether conventional corporations, S Corporations, partnerships, or proprietorships—are subject to the regular taxes imposed on all subject taxpayers. Examples of some of the more common of these are:

- Payroll taxes (federal, state, and local)
- Mercantile taxes (local)
- Real estate taxes (local)
- Sales taxes (collected from customer)

See pages 422–429 for additional information.

Your accountant should be fully aware of the tax implications for your business in the jurisdictions in which it is located. (This is an additional reason to engage an accountant as soon as a business enterprise is contemplated.) The accountant can then see to it that all forms and applications are properly filed. Income taxes will vary, depending on your firm's structure.

Sole Proprietorships. Sole proprietors report the firm's profit or loss on their personal income tax returns. It is then taken into account with other elements in the return in determining tax liability.

Partnerships. A partnership does not pay income taxes as an entity. Rather, a partnership files a "Partnership Return of Income," which shows, among other things, the distributive share of the profit or loss for each partner. Each partner then includes this amount on individual income tax returns, and it is taken into account in the determination of the income taxes each partner must pay. It should be noted that a partner must report and pay income taxes on that person's entire share of the profit, even though it may not have been actually distributed that year. In other words, a partner reports the share of the income or loss in the year it is earned (or lost) by the partnership, regardless of when distribution is actually made. Distribution, in fact, is simply a withdrawal of capital from the partnership, and there is no tax implication for the partnership by reason of the withdrawal.

A partnership must also file a "Partnership Return of Income" in all states and some local jurisdictions where business is conducted, in addition to filing it with the Internal Revenue Service. As with the federal government, the partnership pays no income tax as an entity to the state or locality. The individual partners must report and pay tax as individuals on their distributive shares. The partners then may be subjected to income tax in a state or jurisdiction where they do not reside. There is little or no overlapping or double taxation, though, because the various taxing jurisdictions usually provide for a credit or offset for income taxes paid to other jurisdictions on the same reportable income.

Corporations. A corporation is a legal entity apart from the owners and, as such, is subject to corporation income taxes (not to be confused with income tax requirements of proprietorships or partnerships).

Corporations are subject to federal income taxes and to state or local income taxes in the jurisdictions where they engage in business. This is provided, of course, that the particular state or local jurisdiction imposes an income tax on corporations; most states and many localities do.

S Corporations. An S Corporation is a conventional corporation in every aspect except for income taxes. An S Corporation is one whose shareholders (as well as the corporation itself) have elected to be taxed much in the same manner as a partnership. As with a partnership, the S Corporation does not pay income taxes as an entity, but the shareholders report and pay taxes on their distributive shares.

A corporation must meet certain requirements in to be eligible to elect S Corporation status. Because these requirements have, at various times been changed, they are not listed here. If you are considering S Corporation status, consult with your tax advisor to see whether your corporation is eligible under the laws in effect.

S Corporation status is particularly advantageous to a new business that anticipates several years of losses before profits are generated. In an S Corporation, the owners can deduct the losses on their individual income tax returns. When the business becomes profitable, the owners can then elect to terminate the S Corporation status and revert to a conventional corporation (if a conventional corporation is considered at the time to be more desirable). After a revocation or termination, a corporation must wait five years before a new S Corporation election may be formed. S Corporation status can be elected effective with the inception of business; therefore, this is a matter to be considered in the preplanning stage of the enterprise.

In addition to income taxes, states (and some localities) impose various taxes peculiar to corporations. These taxes vary in each state and locality, so no generalizations can be made. State and local corporate tax implications should be considered at the time you are planning the business structure for your firm. Needless to say, you should select an accountant who is knowledgeable in the various tax areas, as well as competent in accounting matters.

Limited Liability Company. An LLC has a tax structure similar to a partnership in that its distribution of profits goes directly to owners. All owners report the profits on their individual tax returns. The major benefit is that an LLC has the liability protection of a corporation. This is a relatively new form of business that is available in most states (approximately 47) and is becoming more widely used than S Corporations, because LLCs have greater flexibility. Regulations do vary somewhat from state to state, which needs to be taken into consideration if you are operating in more than one state. Your attorney and accountant will explain the differences and determine whether an LLC is appropriate for your firm.

Ownership of an LLC is by the members, not necessarily by those owning shares of stock. The responsibilities of the members are defined by the operating agreement, which is similar to the bylaws or shareholder's agreement of a corporation.

Licenses

Many states now require licensing. If you practice in more than one state, you will need individual licensing in each state where you practice. Licensing also has CEU (continuing education unit) requirements in addition to those of the organizations to which you belong.

Other types of licenses or permits that may be required are:

- Zoning
- Building codes (including parking facilities)
- Safety standards

Fictitious Name Registration

To use any name other than your own for your business, you must file a fictitious name registration request. Your attorney can help you with this. First, a review (or search) is done by the office where the application is filed to determine that no one else has the same name registered in your state or geographic area. If the name is cleared, then various forms must be filed before the formal registration certificate is furnished. In certain states, this registration is good only for five years or so and then must be renewed. Check with your state to determine its requirements. If your registration needs to be renewed regularly, make sure to mark in your books when this has to be done. Many companies have run into problems because their registrations were not properly renewed.

Domain Name

If you are going to have a Web site, it is important to register a domain name in the beginning stages of your firm. The domain name should be directly related to the name of your business. It can be the designer's name or the name of the firm, for example. This will help easily direct potential clients to your Web site.

DEALERSHIPS

There is a tremendous change taking place in dealerships—along both residential and office furniture lines. In the past, through arrangements with residential and office furniture resources, larger design dealerships had many lines available. About 40 to 60 percent of the merchandise they sold was from the smaller lines. As long as the dealerships were able to meet a certain yearly volume and, in some cases, did not carry conflicting lines, they were given special privileges by the factories they represented. These privileges, which varied according to each furniture company, were usually better discounts, advertising reimbursements, exclusivity on certain items, and priority in deliveries.

Now, however, most well-known manufacturers are asking for exclusivity. They require interested dealerships not only to carry their line exclusively but also to meet their management standards. Moreover, companies such as Herman Miller have opened their own pavilions in the contract field, just as companies such as Henredon and Drexel Heritage are requiring showrooms to be exclusively devoted to their lines.

This changes the role of the interior designer. If a designer works for a company-directed dealership, he or she doesn't have the opportunity to use any other line. If a designer works for a company with diversified lines, then he or she usually doesn't have access to the major lines.

The purchasing options for the independent interior designer are also being strongly affected by these dealerships. In some cases, the dealerships refuse to sell to interior designers. In other instances, when the interior designers refer jobs to dealerships for processing, the dealership attempts to cut the interior designer out of the picture by suggesting that the client use the dealership's design department the next time.

Some of these dealerships are developing great management systems. They have transformed small businesses (in some cases, family businesses) into very attractive companies for others to buy. Some have started franchising dealerships and have a large corporate buying center. These companies use very sophisticated methods, are completely computerized with CAD, and have invested heavily in expensive equipment. They have hired strong marketing and image firms and play a significant role in the field. Their great advantage is that they know their line, and by working as a unit, they can afford the very best talent and equipment.

If a designer chooses to become part of one of the major dealerships, obviously there are advantages, because these firms do a lot of advertising. They offer special pricing and shipping and installation processes that would otherwise be unavailable to an independent design firm.

JOINT VENTURES AND ASSOCIATIONS

Joint ventures and associations are important vehicles that can help broaden your scope as an interior designer and that can be very profitable as well. A joint venture allows two firms to work together under the same contract, while each firm remains independent and is responsible for its own professional performances, legal positioning, expenses, and profits and losses. Joint ventures are similar to partnerships, both legally and financially, except that they are usually established to accomplish a single objective and then terminate, whereas a partnership is generally formed to operate indefinitely. Joint ventures can provide a new avenue to markets and can often give interior designers opportunities to work on larger projects—ones they would not be able to do independently because of the architectural, engineering, and other professional services these projects require.

In this industry we have the opportunity to easily communicate with specialists around the world. Global telecommunication is becoming a standard way of operating. Clients are demanding a high level of specialty. Since it is impossible to have a specialist in every design studio, joint ventures and associations are valuable.

Interior designers often form joint ventures or associate with other designers when one designer is doing a large project in a distant city and needs someone local to supervise it. This can help the management of the project considerably.

In a joint venture or association, you obviously want to form a relationship with a firm that you know or have worked with before and which you know will take responsibility for its portion of the work. A great deal of research is needed to determine whether a firm would make a good associate. When investigating a firm, check with other professionals they have worked with, as well as their past clients, to learn how their other joint-ventureship projects worked out.

It is also important to determine the structure of the project before developing the parameters of the venture or association. Many design firms find forming an association with another firm preferable to formal joint ventureships because associations do not require the legal paperwork necessary when setting up a joint venture. Clients, on the other hand, often prefer joint ventures, so they have one firm to relate to. In an association, each firm can point the finger at the other one if something goes wrong.

Before marketing for a project, it is best to have some form of a preliminary agreement that identifies the firms and the positions each will play on the project. Roles should be clearly defined, and all fees and administrative structures firmly established, before going after the project. Entering into these ventures casually can prove disastrous.

Creativity is the key to our business. Many firms find that producing very innovative, creative, and inventive projects often takes major financing and, therefore, large companies. I believe we will see a trend toward larger firms or small to midsize firms merging or bonding in ways to permit them to act as large firms to produce larger projects. It is not necessarily the size of the project, but the inventiveness that will bring our field to its next level. For this reason, firms with different skills need to come together to accomplish a high level of creative work.

CONSIDERATIONS

Today's design business demands are at a higher level than ever before. And because the field is so complex we are finding many more specialists. Our projects are changing—whether in general practice or in a specialty. With change comes the demand for different skills.

This causes the business structures to change often. Designers may move from individual practice to a be part of a larger firm or form a joint venture so they can work as expertly as possible on the project at hand. When you start your own firm, you must allow for this flexibility.

CHAPTER 3

Planning for Profit and Growth

Most of us work in interior design because we love it. Because we really love the field means we are willing to pour energy—no holds barred—into doing everything necessary to make each project absolutely great. We do not measure the effort that goes into our work, and there is no yardstick for what should be accomplished.

One Monday I asked my staff how many of them would come in to work if they were not getting paid, and most of them said they would. I asked some of my fellow interior designers the same question, and they all concurred, saying there was nothing they would rather do.

This kind of devotion is good for our clients, because they get outstanding projects. On the other hand, if we do it all for love, we may never finish a project or get paid. Designers need to measure their love of the design process against the time spent and money earned.

DEVELOPING A FIRM

The key to developing a firm is to understand its best abilities, realizing what we have to work with and going after work that is appropriate to your team. Yes, many times there are missing spots that can be filled in easily by consultants; but, still, the key areas should be covered by the primary principals of your firm. This permits you to have the type of control and positioning that you really want. Then you can fill in as required. Review your market to determine the needs. Consider the direction of the social dynamics of the community in which you work to formulate a working structure that will develop your business in a natural and profitable way.

PLANNING

"Vision without systems thinking ends up painting lovely pictures of the future with no deep understanding of the forces that must be mastered to move from here to there" (Peter M. Senge, *The Fifth Dimension,* New York: Doubleday, 1990, p. 12). Today, it is easier than ever to become just another firm offering design services. This underscores the value of planning.

Planning is establishing priorities. Planning provides a map and direction for the activities that lead us to achieve our goals. I find it a great help to draw a visual map of the processes needed to accomplish the goals at hand.

Planning makes decision making simpler, because it provides a yardstick to measure against. Without a plan, it is easy to fall into the habit of making no decisions or being pushed and pulled by events. Sometimes, we do not plan because we are afraid of failure. We do not want to measure the levels of success for fear it will show we have achieved none. But the only wrong decision is to make no decision. At least one day each year should be spent on planning. It is valuable to bring in a consultant skilled in this process or to attend a workshop to learn the best techniques.

SETTING GOALS

In planning your company, deal first with your personal goals—where you want to be as a professional—and then with the financial goals of the company. Remember, all planning is based on assumptions. That is why you should bring together the best possible people you can find to help you plan a program, based on their experiences as well as your own. Chances are good that your assumptions will become realities because they have direction and planning.

Personal Goals

Each of us has personal needs and desires. You cannot deny them if you are going to be happy and fulfilled. Personal goals are often dependent on meeting certain business objectives. It helps to correlate the two. Do your personal goals fit realistically within the interior design field?

We each know more about ourselves than anyone else in the world: what we like and dislike, what works best for us, and how we work best with other people. We know if we like to work alone or with other people. We know how much we value our profession. We also know our financial requirements—whether we want to live modestly or more comfortably, and whether we require a more than adequate income.

A good way to define your personal goals is to decide where you see yourself three years from now. Determine the lifestyle that is most comfortable for you and that best enhances your creativity.

Sit down and take stock of how you actually feel about the interior design field, even if you did not do so at the beginning of your career. How important is it to you now? Do you want to spend the rest of your life in design? Or do you just want to dabble in it for several years to gain experience before going into another field? It is important to put your private thoughts into perspective.

You can learn more about yourself by writing down these goals. This can be done alone or with another person. Sharing your goals and objectives with other professionals or friends is often enlightening. Other people can remind you of certain personal preferences you might not have considered.

As you list your goals, organize them in the order of their importance to you. List making and priority setting reinforce what you know and help you organize your thoughts so they are manageable. I begin each day with a list of goals and what I expect to get done. Lists help me accomplish more.

After listing your goals, make another list of the things that annoy you, the things that you really want to avoid. Do you feel good about your work? The people in your life? Yourself? List at least a half-dozen activities that you enjoy doing purely for fun, and the last time you had an opportunity to do any of them. All outstanding creative designers need balance in their lives to be able to continue to develop in their careers. To each person this is something different. We need to create safeguards to prevent burnout. If designers burn out, they are out of a job. Our career demands that we are always up and ready with new exciting ideas.

What should you be doing differently to make yourself happier? Less frustrated and bored? Finding the answers to these questions can prove to be an adventure in self-discovery. Review your problems of the past few years so you can eliminate as many of them as possible during the coming years.

It is a good idea to review your goals every three to six months to make sure they can be accomplished. You may find that you have the wrong sets of goals. My goals have been revised many times, but at least there is a goal pattern. It makes me feel more secure to think that I am ruling and running my life, rather than letting it run me.

Business Goals

What are your goals? To make a profit? Many interior design firms with beautifully designed offices are really not in business to make a profit. They do not have to be; they have income from other sources. But is that really a business? A business is an organized entity that manufactures a product or provides a service with the goal of making a profit.

Managing an interior design firm involves being a good planner and understanding the importance of setting overall business objectives. Possible goals might be growth, increased profit, increasing the rate of profit, or increasing your market share. Consider the big picture of your goals—where you want to be five years from now. At the same time, be flexible. We are creative in our work of interior design, so be creative in planning your business goals.

Your goals may change from year to year, depending on your financial situation and even different tax rulings. All business plans require testing. Often, some of the best master plans and strongest strategies on paper can prove unproductive during the testing period. This compels us to restructure and reestablish our business goals. Many companies never accomplish their goals because they have neither defined these goals nor organized their efforts to achieve them. Define your business goals very clearly to determine just how they fit with your personal goals, as well as those of your employees. The principals of the firm must agree on the firm's goals.

Are your goals simple? If they are too complex, they will be hard for your fellow workers to understand and help you to achieve.

Reaching Business Goals

Procrastination can keep you from reaching your business goals. Allow time in your regular schedule for planning and developing your goals effectively. Learn to balance large, important issues against the unimportant. Do not spend all your time putting out fires, and make sure you are working toward the goals you establish.

To plan my company's goals, I hire the very best business consultants I can find—professionals with different orientations—to help me. Planners often offer quite different input from that of your accountant or attorney. They usually show more creative ability and foresight within the business planning. It is also helpful to work with someone in interior design or a related field. These people can expose you to marketing objectives as well as to different trends they see developing. Be sure to also review your business goals with your accountant, business consultant, and attorney. On several occasions, I have had what I thought were very exciting business directions for my company, only to find after review with my accountant that some of these projects would require me to pay in taxes the money I thought I would be saving.

Review your business goals every few months. If you have not accomplished a portion of them, go back and reevaluate them. They might be the wrong goals for your company.

Mission Statement. It is often difficult for a firm to remain focused on its goals. Creating a mission statement and using it as a constant daily reference helps keep you on the right track. Determine your business direction—whom you expect to service and what your products will be—and put this into a mission statement. For example, our firm specializes in professional office design. This is our business direction. Our staff has a strong background in both medical and legal practices. This is what we do best. Do not let yourself flounder all over the design field trying to find the right spot. Select an area in which you excel and where there is a client demand, and service those clients.

Your mission statement needs to be constantly reviewed by you and all of your employees. I keep my mission statement inside a book I refer to daily.

FORMULATING A BUSINESS PLAN

Planning for the year is not something that can be done in an hour or so. Once a year, or anytime you are considering changing the structure or direction of your firm, you should take a week off to devote to planning and goal setting for the next year.

Write down your business plan. This helps you firm up your thinking and ensure that you have covered all of the essential issues before making actual changes in your business. The plan is also a useful reference later on; it enables you to compare your objectives, benchmarks, and levels of accomplishment over a given time period. After you create your plan, go through it with your tax advisor and attorney to be sure that it fits with your company's structure from a tax viewpoint as well as from a legal one.

Your plan should consider the following:

1. **Type of business.** The exact type of design services or design business you intend to establish or develop, as well as who your anticipated clients will be and how you will be charging, should head the elements in your business plan.
2. **Location.** Operating costs for a design firm can vary considerably, depending on the part of the country in which it is located. Generally, costs are highest in the larger cities in the Northeast or on the West Coast. Take location costs into account.
3. **Product.** Determine exactly what you are selling. Are you selling professional services only, or are you also selling merchandise? Designers in smaller communities must often provide additional services that firms in major cities do not need to offer, such as installation and follow-up and purchasing procedures. While these services can be profitable in some instances, the expense of maintaining divisions to coordinate them can be quite risky. Installation and purchasing services can destroy a firm's financial base.
4. **Facilities required.** What facilities will you require in order to provide your service? Will you need a showroom? An office? Can you work out of someone else's showroom for a while? Your residence? Write out exactly how you intend to present yourself.
5. **Marketing plans.** No matter what type of design business you enter, you will need to promote, market, and sell your product or services. How do you expect to carry this through?
6. **Your competition.** Are there other businesses in your area that you see as offering competition? Our field, at present, has considerable competition, not just from other design firms but from other professions and disciplines. Many kinds of specialists call themselves interior designers—big-box retail home supply stores, plumbing supply houses, kitchen cabinet salespeople, "decorating contractors," retail furniture salespeople, and others. Find out how strong your competitors are, what kind of people they are, and what their business

experience is. Make sure you know exactly who your competition is and what you can expect. If your specialty is office design, and there is already an office-equipment dealer in the area that gives away the service, you have a built-in problem.

7. **Available funds.** How much cash do you have on hand? How much more could you afford to invest in this project if necessary? You will need to have reserve funds available. Have you established credit with various resources? Do you have a line of credit at the bank? Set up a budget for your company so you know where the money is going over the next year.

8. **Revenue expectations.** How much do you expect to take in? From what resources? What percentage of your revenue do you expect to come from professional fees, and how much from other sources? Judging the expected revenue for an interior design firm is complex, because some firms work on a professional fee basis only, which makes all income "gross income." Other firms sell merchandise, and while their volume figures could be much larger, their gross income could be lower. The majority of highly profitable interior design firms have mixed sources of income, which may consist of professional service fees, extra purchasing fees, commissions, markups, and royalties, for example.

9. **Expense projections.** Write out your expected expenses for the next six months to a year. After enumerating these expenses, make additional allowances for the many unknowns. Please refer to Chapter 8, sidebar titled Establishing Your Overhead Costs.

10. **Administrative structure.** Good profitability comes from what you do on a daily and weekly basis, and you need an administrative structure for that.

11. **Support services and staff.** Make a list of the support services and staffing required to run your business successfully. Do you have these people in line? Do these people want to work with you, and are they able to work for you? Do you have backups available? Sometimes when you believe you have adequate personnel resources they become committed to something else. If you have backups in these situations, it will make your life a lot easier. On the whole, the most-profitable design firms are quite small (fewer than 5 members) or quite large (more than 50 members). Firms whose personnel number between 5 and 50 are hard to keep profitable, because they are not able to find the quality operational and financial management personnel they need to run effectively.

12. **Your time schedule.** If you are moving your firm in a new direction, consider how much time this will take and how the rest of your business will be affected.

PLANNING FOR PROFIT

Contrary to popular perception, the most profitable firms are well-run residential design firms with a high level of creative design. Specialty companies also show good profit, and firms that design very unusual work (described in the field as "fantasy work") generally tend to show excellent profit. Commercial work can also be very profitable, but the field is extremely competitive and requires high volume and repetition in order to show profit.

Very few interior design firms that charge purely on an hourly or per diem basis are outstandingly profitable. The most profitable firms base their charges on value, which means a certain fee base for a certain project. However, there is a degree of risk in this type of management. If you quote a price for a particular job, you are committed to that fee. Therefore, you need to know how to produce within a particular range. This is easier to do when you specialize.

Today, specialization is one of the most profitable ways for designers to operate. Because specialists have experience in one area, they know exactly how to handle and price their work. They know their precise profit factor.

Factors That Affect Your Profits

In the past, when design firms went out of business, it was usually because of poor financial management. Today, businesses are forced to close far more often because of lawsuits against them. Win or lose, a lawsuit generally costs the firm a considerable amount of time and money, not just in legal fees but in the stigma it creates. Liability insurance can reduce your cash losses, but it cannot retrieve your lost or damaged reputation.

Job processing strongly affects profitability. The faster a job can be completed, the more profitable it is. Because of internal as well as external issues, designers tend to have some jobs that drag on too long and decrease profits. You need to find a way to shorten this process.

Most firms expect their accounts receivable to be paid within 30 days. However, investigation shows that it is far more common for firms to be paid within 60 days; and sometimes accounts go uncollected for six to nine months, or even years.

Another trait that keeps many designers from achieving high profits is that we try to make each job extremely different—never repeating an item or a source. While creativity is part of good design, having too broad a range of projects can make profit projections difficult. Design firms that specialize tend to be the most profitable. Since the work is repetitious, they become experts, and so can work with ease and efficiency.

Ways to Increase Profits

There are two primary ways of increasing profit:

1. Increase the total sales or the amount of income secured by the design firm.
2. Increase the amount of profit or markup. It is important not to simply increase additional sales but to carefully and constantly keep track of the percentage of profit on each particular job. This is the basis of marketing, as much as it is of any other financial program.

Growth is really the key to profits for many business endeavors. The future of a company depends on its flexibility and willingness to grow. Determine whether you should get larger or smaller or stay the same size. Decide which will be the most profitable direction for your company to go.

Many people feel that doubling or tripling a firm's size overnight is the way growth is accomplished. That is simply not so. Growth is a gradual process, reached by improving the company's services—by increasing its opportunities to acquire more qualified personnel and additional technical knowledge. Management needs to anticipate the requirements for growth.

Management consultants can show you many sophisticated formulas for projecting your company's growth, but this is usually a quite involved and costly process. Designers can utilize a simple formula for business development by assessing the needs of clients they expect to service against the qualifications and background of the design firm. By matching the needs of clients to the firm's capabilities, designers can determine a profitable direction for their firm.

Analyzing Your Firm and Its Direction

In planning your firm's development, you will want to analyze the firm's experience by carefully looking at each of its activities and projects from the past 5 to 10 years. (Projects that were performed more than 10 years ago will have little relevance to today's market, unless they were particularly outstanding. Even then, their usefulness in marketing is limited.) Determine which areas have been the most profitable for you during the past five years. How can you use these projects as a base for acquiring new projects over the next five years? A marketing structure must be based on work to be done, building on the experience of work that has been done in the past.

For each project that the design firm has done, you will want to list the following:

1. **Name of the project.** The name of the project should be what you commonly call it, such as the particular name of the building, corporation, or the residential client.
2. **Name of the client.** The name of the client is the name of the person or entity for whom you worked on this particular job, whether it was a board of directors or the managing director of a project.
3. **Location of the project.** List the exact address. Also note whether the project was located in the same town in which you are (or were) located or was a distance from you. Include any information regarding difficulties in reaching the project or any communication problems.
4. **Type of construction.** Identify whether the project was new construction or remodeling. Also outline your involvement in the construction of this particular project—whether you, as the interior designer, were involved in part of the architectural planning or came into the project at a later date and were merely responsible for the furnishings.

Table 3.1 Design project analysis sheet. This sheet will help you plan your firm's development by determining which areas have been the most profitable. It can also serve as a basis for determining which jobs you want to consider in the future and how to price them.

DESIGN PROJECT ANALYSIS		
Client:	Project:	Staff:
Address:	Contact:	Date Started:
	Phone:	Completed:
Type of Construction: (new, renovations, etc.)	Size of Project:	
	Construction Budget:	
	Furnishings Budget:	
Type of Services the Firm Provided:	Design Accomplishments:	
Size of the Fee:	Source of the Job:	
Method of Charging:	Expected Referrals:	
Profit of the Project:	Percentage of Profit on Total Project:	

© *Design Business Monthly,* 1988.

5. **Size of the project.** Break this down as far as you think necessary. Depending on the size of your design firm, you may want to define specific areas, for example, carpeting, wall surface materials, drapery and window coverings, and so forth.

6. **Type of services the firm provided.** Outline all the services you provided, from the basic design to follow-through with construction inspections and feasibility studies to presenting various types of drawings.

7. **Design accomplishments.** List the objective of the job and whether it was accomplished from the owner's viewpoint as well as from the interior design firm's viewpoint. Include both the negative and positive aspects of the job, and determine whether the project is one you are pleased to have on your list of accomplishments.

8. **Size of the fee.** List the fee the firm received and the charging method used. Include details on how you were actually paid for the project—whether you were paid directly by the client or through an independent contractor or other source.

9. **Profit of the project.** List the firm's net profit on the job. This is calculated by computing all the costs—personnel time, materials, fees for supplying furnishings—and subtracting the overall income from the project.

10. **Percentage of profit on the total project.** The percentage of profit on the total project is the net profit divided by the total contract value for your services.

11. **Source of the job.** It is important to identify the source of the job so that additional marketing information can evolve. Under this category, list the components you feel contributed to your getting the job. List all the sources you feel were involved, whether the job was a referral from an individual who had used you on a previous project or the result of advertising, newsletters, or other media.

12. **Expected referrals.** After completing each job, review it from a marketing viewpoint to see just how this job can be used to secure future projects (see pages 132–133).

13. **Publicity potential.** After completion, you may want to interview the client and discuss other projects the client might want to offer you. You might ask whether the client would enjoy or consider magazine or publication exposure. It is important to review the client's attitudes before going further. Also, you might want the job to be considered for design competitions. Many designers have learned to take a single project and capitalize on it.

It is often helpful to complete this design project analysis form (Table 3.1, page 68) shortly after the project is completed, while the information is still fresh in your mind.

After you have made up a sheet like this for each of your projects, file them by year so you are able to judge how many projects you undertook during a particular year, what types of projects they were, and how successful they were. When the year is over, go through the file and summarize:

- Types of jobs done
- Number of jobs done
- Amount of costs for each job
- Percentage of profit for each job

These sheets will help you understand the trends of your company, as well as the trends of the marketing area around you.

Evaluating Your Team

Once you have defined your firm's direction, you must determine whether the staff or the team you now have is properly oriented to handle your objectives. Evaluate the ability of each and every member. You may have to replace certain members to achieve your goals.

Technology permits us to work together even though we are many miles, states, or countries apart. We can work very efficiently and offer our clients an extended palette of services we could never begin to offer within our own companies. As you look at your staff, consider what each member does on a regular basis and what must be kept within your own company. For a lot of high-level expertise it is advisable to use sources outside our own companies. Keep a list of who such sources are and how they work with you. The same applies to your staff. It is important to keep a list of their abilities. The form we have used (see pages 104–105) will assist you

An architectural firm I worked closely with had a problem in that its staff was not working at the level of the owner. After careful consideration, he decided to eliminate all but two people on his staff. The principal reviewed his projects and selected the people he wanted to work with. These were professionals who had different skills from his but worked at the same level or an even higher level. He created a joint venture agreement with these professionals, so when the next project came along he was ready to move on it.

He found this structure worked beautifully. He was sleeping at night because he didn't have to worry that others were not carrying their share of the project. After he developed this group, he brought in the appropriate support staff. Today, he has a most successful firm, producing a high level of work in an easy-to-manage and profitable manner.

with this task. You will learn who you are comfortable teaming with and who will help grow your company. We have all learned that some people work the same way we do, and we can expect to have projects returned promptly and appropriately. There are others who do not understand "our game," and therefore we do not want to get ourselves into a situation that involves them, because we will only get hurt.

Have every member of your staff and your out-of-house team complete the design staff questionnaire on pages 104–105. Since so much of our team is outsourced today, we must know as much about them as we would ordinarily know about any of the individuals under our direct employ. Analyzing the information on the forms will help you clarify your direction. The form should be updated annually by all staff employees. Then, when you are considering a new project, the staff's experience may help you sell your firm to a new client.

Outsourcing

Today, many of the top-level consultants we work with are not directly employed by us; we partner with them. It is advisable to perform an evaluation with consultants similar to the one you do with your staff (see Table 5.3, pages 104–105). Very often we do not know consultants as well as we should. They may be capable of participating with us in many other ways we may not be aware of. Knowing your consultants in depth is very valuable. This knowledge may lead to many more opportunities to work together efficiently.

SELLING YOUR BUSINESS

Businesspeople today believe that when you open a business, you should determine how long you are going to keep it and how you are going to sell it. Very few businesses have longevity in today's changing world.

What makes successful projects? Winston Churchill once said: "It's going from failure to failure, without the loss of enthusiasm, that counts." I think this is part of what makes a person successful—how one handles failure. If we concentrate exclusively on our failures, we diminish our self-confidence and lose much of the excitement that exists in any successful designer. I've heard everyone say—and I've heard it quoted many times—that failure can teach us a lot. But I do not believe failure can teach us as much as success can.

When you review design work and see something you like, be sure to accentuate the pluses. Of course, if there are problems, they should be acknowledged so they are not repeated. But promoting what is good within a staff, and within yourself, is the most important thing. At the end of every day, look at what you have done that you did well, and invest some time in examining the best parts of that activity. Ask yourself, How can I do it again? Can I make it even more polished?

Reexamine your design projects from time to time to see what you did best on each one. Do the same for each of your staff members to pinpoint their strengths. If their strengths are in areas they enjoy, try to let them concentrate on those areas. People are usually more successful in the areas they really like.

Today, it is considered good practice to plan how long you want a business to exist and to plan the process for selling it. If you are making the investment and going through the effort of establishing a working company, it should become something valuable. The type of company you design will determine whether the business will continue to exist or be just a short-term endeavor. Consider before you start what the company might be worth to someone else. How can you create a company that has value, could continue, and be saleable? Or are you establishing this company to provide you with a job? If the latter is the case, the business is not being established as a long-term investment. Designers start businesses for both reasons. Before you start, it is advisable to determine your intentions.

A very successful designer opened a business about three years ago and determined that her studio would be created to present her style of design. It would be designed just for her. She decided that everything that went into it and all the processes in running the business would be a reflection of the way she works. She decided in the beginning the income she needed to generate in the business to compensate herself and her staff appropriately. She had no intention of continuing the firm. Therefore, we planned so she would have the appropriate financial resources for emergencies and for her continuing life, after this business no longer existed. She does not plan on receiving any income from selling the business.

Others decide to form a business and grow it into a profitable firm that will be saleable. To profit from the sale, these owners must create a business someone else can take over. That decision is best made when you start the business. You may change your mind as you progress. There are ways of redesigning a business that was originally designed just for you to be turned over to another owner. However, it is extremely advisable to decide what you are aiming for in the beginning. That way you do not waste your energy and money.

If you plan to sell your business in the next few years, there are things you can do now to get the best possible price and establish the best situation for the sale.

- First, try to show as much profit on your books as possible. Interior designers tend to enjoy the perks their business can bring, rather than leaving them in the firm. Because you plan to sell the business, you want to increase the perceived value and leave as much in the company as possible.
- Spend time developing your clients, and try to establish as many contracts as possible for continuing projects. This is valuable to any prospective purchaser.
- Organize any copyrights or patents you might have. If you plan to sell them with the business, present them in a professional manner.
- Update your mailing lists and all of your contacts.
- Reexamine inventory with an eye toward eliminating what is not current. Can out-of-date items be turned into cash? If not, get rid of them. Make your studio appear as organized and attractive as possible.
- Hire a good appraiser to evaluate your building and the various advantages of your property location.
- Organize your business management system so it can be easily taken over by the new owner the day he or she walks in. Established procedures are very valuable to the next owner.
- Review your workforce and try to line up the best people possible. Employment contracts and noncompetitive agreements are also assets when selling a business.
- Take stock of your financial situation. Determine how much capital is required to run the business and how much is excess. Consult your accountant as to the best position. You may have $400,000 in working capital, but the business could be run well with only $200,000.

The price of a business is usually based on the amount of business it generates. The last 10 years of a business are the most pertinent in determining its value. Project sales over the next two to five years also contribute to a firm's value, which is why contracts or any other potential work are a tremendous asset.

CONSIDERATIONS

Planning and design are as much a part of the business as any of the work we do. Understanding who we are, what we are capable of, and how we can best perform within the business world is key. Our financial base is more important than ever before. We need to make allowances to have the funding and reserves to provide for our future needs. We need to look to experts and professionals in our business and other consulting fields to assist us in creating the right business structure for us to work together.

CHAPTER 4

Setting Up a Design Studio

The success of an interior design practice is greatly affected by the physical space in which it operates. Not only the building but its furnishings, equipment, and location are important to both clients and staff.

The first question to ask yourself in setting up a design studio is, Where do I want to work? What is an appropriate space in which you will be most productive? Where do you want to meet your clients? How do you want to work with your staff? These are some of the first questions that you must answer. Consider what is important to you. I have seen many designers give their staff great spaces, and they make sure their client interview area is well designed. But they neglect their own space. The principal, who is often the designer, is key to the operation of the firm, so make sure that individual's space is designed to allow great productivity.

THE RIGHT LOCATION

How much does location affect your business? It may not affect it at all. If you are going into a specialty and expect your range of clients to come from a wide geographic area, or if clients do not visit your office, you need not invest heavily in location. If, on the other hand, your design practice is dependent on the surrounding community, you must give location more consideration.

Market Proximity and Client Base
Is the area a practical base for you? If you specialize in residential design, for example, will you be accessible to your market? The location of a business can affect whether it succeeds or fails.

Are there clients in the area? Before you select an area in which to establish your design practice, determine whether the community is accustomed to using, or would like to use, interior design services. It may be an area where people really are not interested in design. They may feel that if their furniture has not fallen apart yet there is no need for them to buy anything new. Some people are just not stimulated by the design fashions of today. There are also certain areas where the financially well-to-do do not buy new things. These areas obviously are not good markets for interior design. The design business is based on change. If the community you are considering is staid or well established, it is probably not a good location for an interior design business.

Find an area with a broad customer base. It is better to be where there is a large number of clients, not just three or four. Very few interior designers can make a living from the projects of the same few clients.

Is there a high enough income base? If most of the people in the area earn a top salary of, say, $50,000 a year, they probably do not have money to spend on interior design services. Most interior design clients have income levels that start in the $100,000-a-year range.

If the community is prosperous, moving, and changing, it usually is a good environment for an interior designer. Any growing community has tremendous potential. If, on the other hand, the community is very quiet and retiring, it probably will not have the client base you need.

What is the median age of the people living in the area? As always, the amount of disposable income affects who becomes an interior design client. Today, some young people have extraordinarily high incomes. They buy multimillion-dollar homes and spend more millions furnishing them. The age range of design clients is changing, with the great surge in retirement homes and new condominium units. Older individuals are strong consumers of design services. Some senior citizens are ready to do things very differently from the way they did them in the past. Take a look at the social backgrounds and attitudes, as well as the ages of the people you are anticipating will be your clients.

Sizing Up the Competition

How much competition is there, and what does it offer? In any community you are considering, it is important to be aware of what your competitors are doing and how strong they are. Is the community economically vibrant enough to support both your competition and you? Why would members of the community buy from you?

Residential Suitability

Is this an area where you want to live? Where your employees will want to live? Can they afford to live in the area? It is very difficult to establish an interior design practice in an area where no one wants to be. You must consider your labor force.

The issue of residency has changed with the mobility of our society, thanks to technology of today. Many design firms have key staff members who contribute to their practice daily, yet live in other communities—and maybe even other states or countries. The location of your business very much depends upon the type of practice you have, the personnel you need, and whether you need to work together physically. Some designers today live on boats or islands, whereas years ago they had to live in major cities.

Some designers choose to live in an area because they believe it offers good business opportunities, but they do not like the environment or the people. This is a mismatch, and it is sad to discover it after you have invested 20 or 25 years in a location. I think it is extremely important to select a location that suits your personality and your family, as well as meets the other needs that affect everyday life.

Staff Availability

Affordability of support staff has become a major issue in selecting locations. Many firms in the affluent, elite Northeastern communities are moving into other areas, because they cannot get affordable support staff. If you are going to have to pay four times as much for a secretary in one community as in another, it might be worth considering living in a less expensive community to make your design practice succeed, particularly if your practice requires a large support staff.

Business Climate

Is the location one in which you can do business? Investigate the zoning restrictions or any community restrictions in the area. Zoning restrictions are often a major source of aggravation to a firm.

Some areas have more zoning restrictions than others. Find an area where you are wanted; it is less expensive and time-consuming than fighting zoning regulations. I know this from bitter experience. My firm survived, but I can easily imagine a new firm being destroyed by the battles we endured.

Can you have deliveries made or conduct retail business there? Some areas prohibit interior designers from doing business in typical office centers. Review the licensing requirements of the area before you select your location.

Location can also make a difference in your tax rates. Sometimes being just outside of a city's borders can change your tax rates. Carefully review what your taxes will be in any location you are considering.

You need easy access to suppliers and warehousing. While not all interior design firms sell merchandise, they all have to make sure that any merchandise they specify is in good condition. If you have to travel 50 or 60 miles to check merchandise every time you make a delivery, or if you are not checking it, then you are in trouble. Interior designers must be responsible for their work and, therefore, need to have these services conveniently located.

Visibility

In the early years of a design firm, it is usually best to be located somewhere you can be seen. In most cases, however, heavily trafficked areas, such as shopping centers or very busy streets, are not ideal. These locations require additional staff to handle the many people who will stop in just to visit. In the beginning, it is advisable to select a slightly less-trafficked area so that people entering your offices have

Questions for Evaluating a Location

1. Is it close to my market?
2. Are there sufficient potential clients with adequate income levels to support a design firm?
3. How much competition is there?
4. How do I feel about making this area my home for the next 10 years?
5. What is the quality of the area's schools and cultural resources?
6. Is there good police and fire protection?
7. Is there affordable housing available for both management and staff?
8. What is the quality and cost of the available staffing?
9. What is the quality of the business climate?
10. Does my business conform to the zoning within this area?
11. What are the taxes?
12. Are merchandise and materials readily available?
13. Can I get the contractors I need to perform the required tasks?
14. Am I able to get the warehousing I need, or can I supply it for myself?
15. How will I be able to process the jobs in this location?
16. Do I have the appropriate traffic flow?
17. Is this a good neighborhood for visibility?

to intentionally come to see you. The right type of traffic is far more important than the volume.

Try to select a safe, desirable area; the condition of the buildings surrounding yours can reflect on you. Be sure you are attracting the right type of client. Many practices do not need visibility. Designers well known in their specialties could live almost anywhere and work in almost any type of facility. Their clients may never see where they work.

A BUILDING FOR YOUR BUSINESS

Some design firms need a space that projects an image. Others could be located above a garage and it would not matter. Knowing your customers, needs, and budget will guide you in determining what the right space is for you. There are times when it is valuable to put together a good real estate package, but there are other times when one must keep major funds for the day-to-day business management.

Your firm's quarters must look professional. They must look like an interior designer's firm. However, you should not put so much money into a building that it leaves you without working capital.

If you expect clients to come to your office, it must be reasonably convenient for them. Whether your office is located in a rural or urban area, it must be accessible. If you expect your clients to arrive by car, make sure there is adequate parking for them. Too many firms allow only enough parking space for the design staff and none for clients. Think of the clients first. If there are not enough spaces for both clients and staff, arrange for your staff to park elsewhere.

Fortunately, interior designers tend to have a good sense of location. When I found my building, I asked several designer friends from other communities to come and look at it with me. This helped immeasurably, because they pointed out some major drawbacks but also some positive factors I might have missed. All of us have developed friends in other communities. This is a good time to use them as consultants.

What your interior space should look like is largely determined by the type of services you offer. If you are going to bring clients there, it must look like an organized working space. Interior designers are selling organization through design. If our offices are not organized, how can we recommend organization to our clients? My personal belief is that an interior design studio must be very well organized to conform to clients' expectations, if nothing else. Still, clients like to see action, so do not worry about showing that you are busy.

Leasing versus Buying

With both property and equipment, leasing should always be considered as an alternative to purchasing because it does not require a large capital outlay. This can be a real advantage. Leasing can be economical. It permits us to use our capital for working items, and there are often tax advantages. Sometimes, leasing property or equipment permits us to try before we buy.

Types of Real Estate Leases. The terms "leasing" and "renting" are often used interchangeably, but there are differences. Usually, renting refers to a short-term lease, and leasing to a long-term agreement. In addition, leasing often offers many additional financing benefits, sometimes permitting 100 percent financing. In other instances, leasing may also have considerable tax advantages.

There are many different leasing arrangements; each needs to be carefully reviewed to determine its appropriateness for your situation. Most leases fall into one of two categories: gross lease or net lease. Under a gross lease, the lessor is responsible for all the expenses, including maintenance, taxes, and insurance. Under a net lease agreement, the lessee (the person leasing the property) is responsible for these overhead expenses. This is becoming a more common type of lease.

Advantages and Disadvantages of Leasing. There are certain advantages to leasing:

1. With real estate, there are some locations that are not available for purchase.
2. You have the use of the building or equipment without a large initial cash outlay.

Questions for Evaluating a Building

1. Is the building physically suitable for a design business?
2. Does the exterior of the building reflect my design image? If not, can it be adjusted within a reasonable range to suit?
3. Is there an opportunity to use some type of display or image-attracting signage?
4. What is the cost of purchase or lease?
5. Can I design a space that is of value to our use, or am I paying for a lot of real estate that I will never be able to use?
6. How will the building hold up over the next 10 years?
7. Is the space flexible? Can we grow or shrink according to our needs?
8. What kind of history does the building have? What kind of business was there before? Did it do well?
9. Is it a pleasant place?
10. Is it a safe environment for both my employees and my customers? Am I going to have to worry about safety or provide a lot of extra security measures?
11. Is it in a stable neighborhood?
12. Is the building easily accessible for my clients? Can they find the location? If they will be driving, does it have parking?
13. Does the interior layout of the building correlate with the objectives of my design firm? Will it be easy to adapt into a productive space?
14. Is the lighting good?
15. What is the condition of the heating, ventilating, and air-conditioning (HVAC) system?

3. If you are taking a loan or mortgaging a property, you usually need a down payment. With many types of leasing, no down payment is required.
4. Your payments are spread out over a long period of time.
5. You are protected against being stuck with a building or equipment you do not want. If you determine that a location is not right for you, you can move. If equipment you have leased becomes obsolete, you can simply arrange to lease another type of equipment.
6. There are many tax benefits in leasing. In many instances, lease payments are totally deductible as operating expenses. However, the government carefully reviews leases to determine whether they are a disguised purchase rather than a true lease. Have your accountant review details of the contract.
7. The people who lease equipment to you generally service it, so if you have any problems, there is always someone to call.
8. Usually, flexible payment schedules can be arranged as required for your business situation. For example, if your cash flow is weaker at certain periods, normally you can arrange to make payments at times when you are in a better cash-flow position.

But there are also certain disadvantages to leasing:

1. There are some tax advantages of owning property or equipment that are not available to the person who leases them. However, you should check with your accountant to see whether leasing or owning is best in your particular tax situation.

2. At the end of the lease, the property or equipment still belongs to the lessor. If you had purchased it, you would have an asset, and could continue to use the piece of equipment or property.

3. Sometimes, tax benefits can make purchasing a property or piece of equipment considerably more affordable than it first appears. You need to do a cash analysis to determine whether it pays for you to purchase rather than lease.

4. Usually, a lease is for a specific term, and you must pay for the full term of the lease whether or not you need the space or equipment for the entire time. If you own property or equipment, you have the option of selling it when you no longer want it.

Before deciding to purchase a sizable item, whether it be real estate or an expensive piece of equipment, have your accountant do a cash flow evaluation of the cost of the lease.

Home Studios

It used to be considered unprofessional to work at home. This is definitely not the case today. Professionals in every field have home offices, and sometimes the home office is their only office. Whether you work at home or not depends upon how you work best. Some people find working at home distracting; others find they are much more productive there. You know your own style and your family. Many interior designers have adapted their apartments, turning the dining room or a second bedroom into a very effective design studio. Whether this would work for you depends completely upon the type of practice you have and how you use your studio.

If you work out of a home studio, you must be very careful to continue to maintain a professional appearance. If you have children or pets running around all day, your home might not provide the right atmosphere in which to meet with sales representatives or clients.

Another common practice designers find practical is to combine a design studio with living quarters for the designer. My design studio in Harrisburg, Pennsylvania, occupies a very large, 33-room house that I own. Part of the house is a small apartment, which I use as my home when I am in Harrisburg. This setup is both practical and convenient for me, because I usually work extended hours. I am often up and at my desk before the sun rises and sometimes work until very late at night. This had become a safety and security concern when I used to travel between my residence and my studio. In fact, the police suggested that I avoid coming and going at these hours because I had created a pattern that criminals could detect and exploit.

Working and living in the same building can be convenient. However, there is no privacy. When you live above your studio, you are, in a sense, working 24 hours a day. Everyone knows that if you are home, you are available if they need you. Weigh your lifestyle, your practice, and your preferences carefully when considering whether a design studio at home is appropriate. Generally, we all need to be able to get away from our work, at least at some point in our lives.

Many designers with home studios are also associated with larger firms under an associate or partnership arrangement. This allows their project management to be handled off the firm's premises.

Note, too, that the IRS has become less lenient than it used to be about offices at home. Under current laws, home office expenses are deductible only if that space is used exclusively for your business. If the IRS has reason to believe that the main part of your business is conducted at another location, and that your office at home is supplementary, the expense of maintaining the home office is not deductible. Ask your accountant for advice on this issue.

EQUIPPING YOUR OFFICE

Business equipment and supplies do not sell design, so keep your investment in these as minimal as possible. Your investment needs to be in producing the design project. Designers work in so many different styles that it is impossible to make a blanket statement about office needs. Equipping an office is highly personal. Having the right equipment can definitely make your design work a lot easier. Too many studios have a lot of equipment that staff really do not know how to use. Fortunately, CAD and other technologies are no longer very expensive. Almost anyone can afford them. Moreover, there are service companies that will do much of this work for us. You need to look at your practice and your staff's ability. Is it really practical to outsource, or should you keep the work in-house for reasons of convenience or confidentiality?

For every piece of equipment that you consider buying, do a break-even analysis first. Ask yourself if it is really appropriate for your practice right now, not two years from now. Remember, you are planning a growing business. Therefore, not everything needs to be done immediately.

Equipment

Electronic communication is the key to almost any system of documentation today. Whether with design consultants, architects, engineers, or specialists, or with contractors and clients, almost all communication we do is transmitted electronically. Computers and CAD are used for efficiency and extensive documentation. Therefore, most design studios require this type of equipment. Most designers know which equipment they are used to working with and which works best for them, given the type of projects they do. Most designers try to keep their offices as simple and efficient as possible. Some of our design work is done by hand because it has great client appeal.

The right piece of equipment is time-saving and can produce a much higher level of efficiency. Consider the way you work and the types of equipment you need. Many design offices have beautiful drafting tables because they still use them. Most offices require some form of a printer for everyday use. Often, finished documents are done with outside services, since there are so many beautiful processes available.

Keep your creative work away from your business work. When working on something creative, you do not want business issues distracting you. You need to completely separate the two areas. Many designers build a separate room for the sole purpose of the design aspects of the business. An area dedicated to creative thinking and design development is as important to a designer as an operating room is to a surgeon. If designers don't have the space for a separate area, many use drafting tables to lay out a project and build and work with it. Obviously, the size of the office space will determine how this area will be managed.

Designers can get creative ideas anywhere, but they need a space separate from the business end, where they can sit down and put it all together, and where they do not have to deal with the stress of other business issues.

Supplies. Stock whatever is convenient. You know what you use, how much of it you use, and how easy it is to obtain.

CAD System. CAD is a fairly standard tool for interior designers. Even a small CAD system will save you a great deal of time. If you want to change an interior plan or try something different, you can do it in a matter of seconds, rather than redrafting a whole plan. See page 84 for more detailed information.

Scanner. An optical scanner makes an exact replica of a picture or photograph. Designers use this device to trace an object, from either a freehand picture in a book or a floor plan. The tracing can then be translated directly onto their own drawings. This is a fast, inexpensive way of doing freehand sketches.

Large Monitor. Used with technology, a large monitor in your studio or a meeting room is excellent for reviewing the progress of drawings or designs. This eliminates printing them out and can be easily reviewed by the designers. Clients also love it.

Computers

For interior designers, it is no longer a question of whether or not to computerize, but how many computers to buy and for which functions. Computers expand a design business's range and permit the firm to handle a larger workload without adding staff or greatly increasing overhead. To survive and to get the competitive edge, interior designers need to work with present-day tools.

The role of the computer in interior design has changed radically over the past few years. The biggest difference is that the computer is no longer simply a tool for the support staff. At one time, only bookkeepers or secretaries worked with computers. Today, almost every executive not only has a computer but uses it to run the business. With computers, information such as a graphic representation of profits or time expenditures is at an executive's fingertips.

The best reasons for using a computer are:

1. **Accuracy.** It is difficult to do exacting work manually. The computer checks mathematics and prevents errors.
2. **Comparison.** It is to compare your work with that of other consultants, such as architects and electrical engineers.
3. **Fast and easy changes.** Changes that would have taken hours or days to redraw can be done in a matter of minutes.

Much of the work that once required the services of full-time secretaries or bookkeepers is now being done directly by designers themselves with computer software. Computers and software have not eliminated the need for support staff, but technology does change staff functions and the amount of time their work requires. Using computers and software allows us, for example, to employ a higher-level bookkeeper—perhaps for only one day a week. This gives a firm better control than we ever had in the past, even with full-time bookkeepers. Today, with technology, we are able to view the details of a project from many different angles. Also, your accountant can review your books each month by modem for a very low fee, saving you money.

You also need to look at how long it takes to learn to use a computer system. A number of software packages on the market are very hard to learn. They take anywhere from several weeks to six months to really understand, and that is a major investment in time. Other packages that are equally capable, but geared for computer novices, can be learned in several days or a week—a significant time-savings. Some programs are geared specifically to the interior design field, and many generic ones can be adapted to our special needs.

When selecting software, first consider how you work. There are programs that can be adapted to your system rather than forcing you to adapt to them.

The price of computers has come down so much that it is often much less expensive to buy a new one than to upgrade an existing one. At this point, you no longer have to buy the most advanced models just to be able to run business software.

It is a good idea to have a support person to call on when you have a problem. It does not really matter whether this is a staff person who is more computer-savvy than you or a person affiliated with one of the computer consulting firms.

Areas to Computerize. Routine management procedures such as bookkeeping and word processing are usually the best areas to computerize first. The next area would be drafting; programs such as a CAD system can greatly increase your business capacity.

In the typical design office, the bookkeeping and order-processing information is stored on one computer in the business office. However, the design office also needs access to information on delivery schedules and products. Your system could be networked to the design office. The idea is to be able to get the necessary information linked to as many sources as possible. If you need access to accounting functions, you should be able to get the information by using the computer at your workstation without having to go to the accounting room.

Computer Imaging. CAD systems as well as many graphic packages enable us to communicate very easily and accurately with other professionals, as well as our clients.

Many offices in the past had a CAD specialist. Today, designers usually have their own CAD workstations but share output devices such as printers and plotters. CAD is great for conceptual designing. Using CAD, designers can play with options to be sure they work, rather than having to do rough sketches and then asking a draftsperson to draw them up. Decisions can be made much faster when using CAD. However, some design offices keep a drafting table for quick drawings, as some designers still like to do their preliminary work manually.

Software. When setting up a computer system, find the software program most suitable to your firm before buying the hardware. Too many firms have bought computer hardware and then have not been able to find compatible software packages.

Interior design is a specialized field, so it is usually best to buy software from a firm whose programs are geared primarily to interior designers. That way you do not have to purchase capabilities you will never use. Training on how to run and use these programs is usually part of the package.

Some software packages eliminate a lot of the manual time designers once needed to take to specify furniture, fixtures, and equipment. Such software helps you to identify items on a floor plan and allows you to describe the item in as much detail as you need. It takes care of counting all the items and introducing them into the budget. The software also produces several types of documents that can be used for bidding or internal use and identifies what you may have omitted. If 100 types of furniture are identified but only 99 are specified, a person might never notice, but the computer will quickly alert you to the discrepancy.

Computer graphics packages sold for desktop publishing systems can give your proposals a more polished look. Besides the obvious advantages of formatting and error-free typing with these programs, you can also include illustrations and photographs in your proposals.

Catalogs from design industry suppliers now come on CDs or are Web-based. It may even be possible to research projects without ever leaving the computer. We can access individual items and catalog pages over the Internet at any time of day or night.

Telephone Systems

Landline telephone systems today offer so many options there is a lot to consider when deciding which system to buy or lease. Most of us are learning that some of the new technology is convenient for our design business programs. However, a lot of the offerings are in excess—items we do not use or do not really need.

When determining which system to buy, first list your needs. Determine how telephone-intensive your practice is. This will then help you decide just how many phones and what kind of services you need. In some design firms, every person needs a phone.

Define which type of equipment and features you need, and review the systems available to determine which best meets your demands.

If you use a modem or fax system, keep these lines separate. They should not tie into your phone system. See below for information on fax and modem technology.

Require your business or office manager, as well as one or two of your design staff, to review the different systems to determine whether they really supply the services appropriate for your firm. Very often, a management person will review the system from one viewpoint and the marketing department from another. Both points of view need to be considered before purchasing.

When considering a new phone system, get at least three quotes and then compare them, both in terms of price and features.

Check the service records of the individual companies you are considering. Consult other people who have used those companies' systems to determine whether they provide appropriate service.

Also review the teaching methods of the company. Does the company train the firms that purchase its systems to manage and get the most out of them? What kind of support will the firm provide? When you have a problem, you want a solution now. Your time is expensive, and the telephone is a vital tool. Whether you choose to purchase or lease your telephone system is a matter that should be reviewed by your accountant. The decision is generally determined by the cash-flow position of your company.

To purchase or lease a system requires a long-term contract, which makes it very difficult to change systems or alter the one you have. So take the time to be sure you have the appropriate system installed. Try to buy or lease a system with an approximately 30 percent growth potential, so as you need additional phones, the system will be able to accommodate them. However, technology today is changing rapidly, and you may find yourself changing your telephone system more frequently than that to obtain new features.

Fax Machine. It is hard to imagine a design firm today working without a fax machine. You can send drawings and details over the phone lines to factories. Most of our orders are faxed. The information is visible and date-stamped. Although it is possible to fax from a computer, or to install a machine that combines fax, scanner, and printer functions, it is also good to have a traditional fax machine. They are very inexpensive. Most offices today have both a computer with fax capability and a regular fax machine. Get one with good resolution (dots per inch, DPI), so that faxes are easy to read.

An Interior Design Library Collection

1. Computer with modem to access vendor Web sites
2. Vendor catalog compact disks (CDs)
3. Catalogs
4. Price lists
5. Textbooks and reference books
6. Directories and bibliographies
7. Professional journals and periodicals
8. Research and reference reports
9. Clippings and tear sheets
10. Fabric samples
11. Carpets
12. Wood and finish sample chips
13. Paint chips and wallcovering samples
14. Lighting samples
15. Other sample items, depending on the type of practice

Modem. A modem is a "modulator-demodulator" that codes information into audible frequencies for transmission through telephone or cable lines. New computers generally have at least one built-in modem. Now it is just a question of the type of linking you will use—telephone lines, cable, or other, depending on where you live and the connection speed you need.

Portable Phones. Whether cellular or digital, there are a number of portable phones that can travel with you wherever you go.

Fortunately, there are many sophisticated and inexpensive systems that can keep us in touch with our clients, contractors, and vendors, anytime we desire. The person on the other end of the phone has no idea whether you are at your desk, at home, or on the beach. With the proper phone systems, we can be in touch with almost anyone, anytime and anyplace. Design your system carefully so it supports you but does not drive you crazy.

Voice Mail. Voice mail has become common and has so many options. It is a wonderful way of leaving an exact message for the appropriate person. When managed properly, voice mail can be a great asset; when it is not, it is a great annoyance.

The Library

A library is a major tool of any design studio. Much information is available on the Web or on CDs. These systems are much less expensive to distribute and can easily be kept up to date. Designers still find they have to work with some catalogs and need actual samples of fabrics and other products. There still are some things we really want to see and touch.

Check the source of the information you find on the Internet. Some of it is intended for consumers and does not provide us with the level of detail we require. Furthermore, a lot of the material available over the Internet for general consumption is very inaccurate, so you must be wary of where the information is coming from. Unfortunately, some of our clients see this information, too, and this causes a lot of confusion in presenting professional design in our market.

If you do not have a great library, you cannot function in today's design world. The demands on the design library are increasing constantly, and individual library collections within studios may not be adequate for most practices. Fortunately, several new library systems are available: master research libraries, video libraries, computerized manufacturers' catalogs, and library update services.

In many major cities, large research libraries boasting 30,000 and more manufacturers' catalogs of materials for architectural and interior design projects are being developed in or near design centers. Maintaining a collection of this size requires professional management and can be expensive, making it impractical for the average design studio. However, master libraries for design research make membership available to professionals in the design field. Some charge membership fees; others do not.

In some larger cities, library specialists will set up a design library in your office or studio, customizing it to your specialty. The service includes weekly on-site updates and maintenance. Because this is their specialty, these professionals are able to keep your library up to date efficiently and cost-effectively all the time.

Several services extend to the studio design library. Large manufacturers now provide computerized library systems, including details needed for layout and specifications of their line. Weekly updates keep the systems current.

Video libraries are available from many manufacturers. These give us the opportunity to present products to clients in perspective. These images can be incorporated into our own video presentations for special clients. Designers who use this process make slides or videos of special items when visiting markets, showrooms, or factories. Videos are also used to show how products are made—answering the question of what makes one product different from a competing product. Another use of videos is training staff when no live trainer is available. Though not as effective as interactive training, these videos are certainly better than nothing.

At one time, it was enough to update your catalog library twice a year. Now, weekly or even daily updates are more appropriate. In this high-tech age, speed is a requirement.

In smaller cities, the opportunity to build a quality library is a good reason to develop a co-op or team group practice.

The Design Library. Although we can access many things over the Web, and we have catalogs on CDs, there is still a need for a good library. We and our clients want to be able to see and feel. Your design library will need to contain directories, catalogs, and an unwieldy collection of samples of carpets, fabrics, wallcoverings, laminates, paints, yarns, and wood finishes. Reference books, professional journals, new product brochures, tear sheets, and articles clipped from magazines and showhouse guides add to the incipient chaos.

In a design studio, it is important to allow space for a good working library. Because there is no convenient resource for the samples, product catalogs and directories, or even the specialized publications interior designers need, designers have to supply most of their own reference materials. The quality of your library strongly affects how well you are able to perform your services.

The first rule in establishing a design library is to define your studio's needs and then research the companies and sources to secure the appropriate products to fill those needs. Do not keep anything that is not useful.

Every collection that goes into your library needs an assigned position. Catalogs should be kept together, as should samples. You need open shelving for books, magazines, and catalogs, plus standard drawer files for smaller catalogs not kept in binders and for articles and pages torn from magazines. Product samples come in all shapes and sizes and should be filed according to their physical properties. Lucite trays and drawers are invaluable for carpet samples, as are standard metal file drawers. Within your catalog section, furniture for contract-office space should be kept together and separate from lighting fixtures or upholstered furniture.

A cross-referenced database is necessary for easy retrieval of information. Many product lines are apt to be classified in more than one category. An office furniture catalog might include desks and seating, as well as accessories and wallcoverings. Most companies supply more than one type of product, so the database should be organized both by company and product type. It is a simple matter to also note whether you have samples, if these are purchased or complimentary, and where they are kept.

Professional assistance in setting up an organized and easy-to-use library is available. Interior design and architectural libraries for both small and large firms are based on traditional library standards and coded according to the Construction Specifications Institute's (CSI) system. It may take 6 to 10 months for a professional to physically set up your system with complete documentation of every item used in the field.

Most libraries are dysfunctional because they have too much information. Regardless of your system, you should go through your library every year and get rid of old and inappropriate catalogs. Also keep a "tickler" file of the most recent products.

Although a design library is highly individual, there are basic categories we all handle:

1. **Your firm's standards file.** Each practice has certain standards it uses in most of its work. It may be a cabinet hinge detail, a carpet specification, or drawings of various details. Design studios that work efficiently do a lot of editing

rather than entirely creating every detail of each new project. They pull from past projects and edit and revise to suit the current project, rather than re-doing everything from scratch. The storage of this information can be on your computer or as a combination of paper and computer or Web-based resources. The important thing is to have a file available. This is an extremely efficient and time-saving element to any studio and, in most cases, one of its most valuable assets. We need easy access to our documents, the details that we have created through a lot of trial and error. When a project is finished, pull the items that can be reused before you put away the project. Store them so they are easily accessible for the next challenging project.

2. **Specifications.** There are excellent packages you can purchase from the American Institute of Architects (AIA) and other resources for standard specifications. There are many things designers have developed in their own standard practices that are particular to the way they work. These need to be accumulated in a way that can be easily duplicated and updated to meet current requirements.

3. **Catalogs from vendors.** These are a designer's primary source of specification information on all design projects. They are expensive, and space is increasingly valuable, so you should keep catalogs only for the product lines you use regularly. That means you must regularly review product lines. Catalogs are easiest to handle when placed on open shelves alphabetically by the manufacturer's name within product categories.

4. **Price lists.** Before filing these, you must carefully label them as to whether they are at-cost or at-list prices. Some are easy to identify, but others need careful scrutiny. Price lists are often filed directly with the catalogs. If the price list is at-cost, and this file is directly referenced by clients, studios occasionally will file it individually. Price lists for different categories should be kept separate; that is, fabric lines should be separated from furniture lines. Keep discount information either in the master file or with the price list. Some design firms code this information, so if customers see the price list, they will not be able to easily interpret the information.

5. **Textbooks and reference books.** These are invaluable for every designer.

6. **Directories and bibliographies.** These are important reference tools and should be grouped together, because they are constantly used for specification requirements. Duplicate copies are useful for your most often-used directories.

7. **Professional journals and periodicals.** These magazines are easiest to keep track of when one person is responsible for them, and when a distribution schedule is designated (see Table 10.6, page 340). You should be able to manage with a single subscription of each magazine, with an appropriate circulation schedule and filing system. A special section of the library should be devoted to the storage of publications. Periodical storage boxes can be used; but storing magazines on open shelves is more practical, as these publications are usually used as frequent reference materials for their first year or so.

8. **Research or reference reports.** These should be indexed for easy retrieval. This type of material is often used with individual proposals. They should be filed in manila folders and labeled according to the subject and date.

9. **Clippings and tear sheets from catalogs or magazines.** These should also be filed in folders. Some of the newest products and best photographs of products appear in magazines, and your clippings can be good selling tools.

10. **Fabric samples.** These may take up minimal space if your design firm is in a major market city where there is easy access to showrooms. In this case, samples can be borrowed at no charge for one week to 30 days. These are called memo samples, and there is no charge unless the designer fails to return them. Outside of these cities, design studios usually purchase samples at the beginning of each season, because the mailing time for memo samples would drastically increase the time it takes to develop a project.

    The samples themselves have a life of two to four years. Many studios tag and code the samples so the resources are not identifiable to the customer. Upholstery fabric samples are generally 27 by 27 inches, and other fabrics are a yard and a half or one full repeat. Designers need some fabric samples that can be cut and worked into presentation boards, so even a city practice has some outlay for samples. Firms that do not maintain a physical selection of fabrics use catalogs that describe the types of fabrics available from each supplier and have an appropriate collection of price lists.

11. **Carpets.** Carpet samples are normally presented in folders and are best filed on shelves alphabetically by company name and type of carpet. Additional three-by-five-inch samples are useful and should be filed according to color as an effective cross-reference; this size is also good to use on presentation boards. Larger carpet samples—usually 18 by 27 inches or larger—are kept on open shelves. Some design firms buy samples of the carpets they use frequently, but companies that do purely contract work quite commonly receive these samples on a complimentary basis.

Anything unusual—the rare fabric or catalog—is ordinarily purchased. Companies you work with in volume will give you samples, but in residential work and specialty fields, purchasing samples is the norm.

Storing samples of oddly shaped items is best done in shelves and drawers, according to size. These may be wood chips or larger items used for construction, depending on the type of projects you do. Keeping a room organized for these samples can be the most difficult part of maintaining a design studio.

The use of computers may decrease the physical space needed for catalogs. Any computer used for library purposes must be equipped with a modem, as manufacturers frequently update their catalogs online long before they send out their catalogs on compact disk.

Reference checks via computer allow a designer to get information about an unfamiliar source on a per-inquiry basis, and many reference materials are now available in software packages easily accessed by the computer.

Even when specification checks and catalog resources are completely computerized, however, design studios will still need product libraries. Clients want to feel a fabric, and designers want to test and see the quality of a carpet, wallcovering, fixture, or other product.

Keeping a library in good working condition is a challenge; a library is always growing and changing as you use it. Most designers have some special products they use over and over again. Then there are the new items you just saw at a market or design show and can hardly wait to use. When you arrange your system, whether it is highly organized or simply a special bin or section of your file drawers or part of your library shelves, it's advisable to keep these priority items separate. Give them some form of special identity marks so they are easy to find.

"Weed," "eliminate," and "throw away" are the most important verbs to apply to a design library. Whether you are in a specialty or a varied practice, things change. It is better to have a small and workable library than one that is so massive and jammed with information that you cannot find what you need when you need it. The key to interior design is organization.

CONSIDERATIONS

Specialty design studios can be anywhere. Technology gives us the privilege of a lifestyle we want in our preferred environment. We can blend our skills with a mixture of quality professionals, not just those from our own company, city, or state but throughout the world. Today's communication systems make this possible and practical. We are so fortunate in not having to accept inferior work—we can have and do the very best.

CHAPTER 5

Developing a Team of Staff and Consultants

Aside from you, the most valuable asset of your design firm is your staff and team. So much emphasis is put on buildings, properties, dealerships, and lines that what is sometimes forgotten is that the quality of your support team either contributes to your success or holds you back. When you begin your business, or consider any growth or restructuring, carefully review what part you plan to play in that growth and what kind of staffing you need to help you accomplish your goals. Staffing your business with the best-quality people should be your design firm's highest priority.

FORECASTING REQUIREMENTS

The nature of the projects your firm takes on determines what kind of personnel you will need in the future. This forecasting is easy when you keep an ongoing list of each project you have, the type of staffing required for each, and the hours of work you anticipate will be needed from your staff during the next 12 months. Keep this information on a form; an example is shown in Table 5.1, page 91. Use a separate form for your staff to list their individual projects, their estimated hours of work for the next month and the months to come, and any other job responsibilities they have, such as marketing. An example is shown in Table 5.2, page 95. Keeping these two forms up to date will help you analyze which jobs you can accomplish in a given period of time.

This information can be maintained either by hand on the forms shown or in a computer worksheet. What matters is that you institute a planning system you understand. You should be able to see at a glance the work to be done and the monies to be generated from that work. This is part of what makes a company profitable. In day-to-day business, it is easy to assign projects and then forget what a given person is doing and how much time it should take. Business is not static; in taking on additional priorities, you can sometimes forget about your staff's previous commitments. These forecasting sheets about the staff members and their projects tell you where they are going and how frantic their schedules are. You can see, at a glance, whether a project needs additional support or can be handled in-house by reapportioning the workloads.

Although you should try to plan for a 12-month period, realize you will have to make some adjustments to the plan. The plan is your guide. It should not be carved in stone. These sheets are effective for firms of all sizes, even a single-person firm. Employee scheduling sheets can also be valuable aids in forecasting income from current projects. They indicate which projects should be completed in a certain time and what the compensation from them should be.

Before considering hiring anyone, do an analysis of the project. Outline the direction in which you see your company going and determine what is financially practical for you to do. In analyzing the job, you should check the following:

- What is the work to be accomplished?
- Do I need additional help to do it, or can I use the staff that I have, working overtime?
- Is there any freelance staffing available?
- Could I hire a specialist to work this project, or outsource it?
- Am I going to need the kind of person who can do this work on a continuing basis?
- What kind of experience should the person I hire have?
- What type of skills are necessary to do this job?
- What is the labor market today?
- Can I get the type of person I want; if not, can I modify this job to fit the kind of person I am able to find?
- What am I able to pay?
- Will this job remain attractive in the future for the person I hire?
- Will the people I hire be able to develop their careers here and perhaps fit into other parts of my design firm?

STAFF POSITIONS

When planning your business, you need to consider not only how many staff members you should have but also what types of employees are necessary for your firm's size and goals.

Table 5.1 Forecasting labor requirements. This form will make it easy for you to determine what kind of personnel you will need in the future and which jobs you can accomplish in a given period of time.

FORECASTING LABOR REQUIREMENTS		Year:												
Project:	Type of Staff Required:	Hours of Work Required:												
		JAN.	FEB.	MAR.	APR.	MAY	JUNE	JULY	AUG.	SEP.	OCT.	NOV.	DEC.	

© *Design Business Monthly*, 1988.

Table 5.2 Monthly staff work plan. On this form staff members list their individual projects and responsibilities for the month, along with the estimated time they will need to perform them. This form can help remind you what a given person is doing so that you can utilize your staff most effectively.

MONTHLY STAFF WORK PLAN		Month:			
Person:	Project:	Estimated Time Required:			
		Week 1	Week 2	Week 3	Week 4
Other Responsibilities:		Time Required:			

© *Design Business Monthly*, 1988.

Chief Executive Officer (CEO)

The performance of the chief executive officer or the designer who starts the company or runs it plays a major role in the success of a design firm. A chief executive officer in a highly successful, rapidly growing firm of 10 works at least 65 to 100 hours a week. The CEO has a heavy investment in the firm, emotionally, physically, and financially. Working more than 65 hours per week is not recommended. It shortchanges your family and can kill your creativity.

Because the performance of the firm as a whole is so dependent on the CEO, there need to be some safeguards in place to keep that CEO stimulated and excited about the work. It is all too easy for a CEO to burn out because of the stress of various administrative problems. Therefore, efforts must be made to keep that person enthusiastic, if everyone else in the firm is to continue at a high-performance level.

In their book, *In Search of Excellence* (1982), Thomas Peters and Robert Waterman clearly state that the chief executive officer has a lot to do with the performance level of a corporation. I find this even more often the case in design firms. It is not just the CEO's design talent and excitement for design but also that individual's excitement for business, as well as his or her ability to use the tools of business that generate success.

Some of the most successful design firms do not have a formal structure. In these firms, CEOs have hands-on involvement with all of their key people. These firms work as a team, and the chief executive officer usually refers to the firm as "we." These designers have a vision they are able to share with their staff and clients. This intimate involvement and excitement of the CEO is what makes these companies successful.

Managing Director or Business Manager

The managing director or business manager is responsible for the management of the company, whether the firm has 3 or 4 people or as many as 75. In a small business, this individual is often a partner of the firm. The business manager is responsible for coordinating schedules, processing and expediting orders, managing finances, and handling any business management problems that may arise. This person usually has the authority to fire and to hire and deals with most of a company's consultants—such as accountants, attorneys, and other business professionals.

Although a business manager usually has very little to do with the design end of a business, that individual can assist in setting the management and financial requirements of the projects.

Usually, the business manager is a person with a business management background, rather than one in interior design. If we want to make a firm financially successful, we need different outlooks on a job. It is important for this person to be familiar with current business vocabulary, because most interior designers are short on business education.

Marketing Director or Manager of Business Development

Most design firms find it necessary to have a director in charge of developing business. Most successful design firms (running close to their total potential productivity) have one or more people doing marketing or business promotion for them.

Marketing and sales are usually part of every staff member's responsibilities. However, a good marketing program requires a primary person on the staff to devote his or her complete attention to this area. While marketing is done according to principles, someone has to keep the program on schedule and assign the tasks that do not have to be performed by the firm's principal. The marketing director has a great deal of control over the general direction of the company; therefore, the authority endowed in this person is considerable.

A marketing director should be a person who enjoys developing and creating business—a person who likes to sell. This kind of personality is of great benefit to any firm. Finding a good marketing director can be difficult. Most firms hire a person who has design experience but prefers to be out there selling and developing business. The salary or income of a marketing director is usually very high, which is why this position often attracts other individuals already on staff.

Human Resources Manager

The human resources manager was formerly known as the "personnel administrator." In a small firm, the human resources manager's job may be handled by the principal; but in a firm with 12 or more designers, this job requires a specific employee who may be either a staff member or a consultant.

Today, the position of human resources manager goes far beyond what the traditional personnel manager's job was: hiring and firing and establishing a personnel structure. The human resources manager is now asked to build a unified, productive workforce motivated to achieve the company's objectives. This person needs to be a results-oriented individual, willing and able to develop a workforce to fit the diversified needs of a design firm. Both small and large firms are realizing that staffing can greatly improve or inhibit the quality of a company's growth.

The functions of this position are basically staffing, personnel program administration, and planning for future staffing needs. Many firms cannot afford to have this type of person on staff full-time, but consultants or specialists are available to handle human resources management for you on an as-needed basis. You can add this requirement as part of your business development program. Sometimes, we are so close to people that we do not notice some of their unique abilities. Having someone else interact with your staff is often valuable to both you and the company in observing and capitalizing on these abilities.

Human resources managers are involved in many different areas, including the following:

- **Staffing.** Human resources managers ensure that positions are filled with qualified individuals who are trained appropriately and are able to meet the company's objectives.
- **Training and organizational development.** HR managers can devise programs, procedures, and a methodology to improve the performance of individual staff members. They can develop training programs, bring in consultants, and introduce new equipment that will elevate the staff's productive capabilities so the company can grow and be more profitable. The staff will have the opportunity to do better work, advance, and earn higher income.
- **Salary and benefits program administration.** HR managers organize the total compensation programs of the company as a whole, as well as individual salary situations.
- **Employee relations and communications.** HR managers create an environment that helps the company and the individual workers be more productive. They help with overall structuring and decision making to encourage a feeling of teamwork among the staff. They develop necessary communication programs for employees.

Receptionist

In many design firms, the receptionist and the person who answers the phone are one and the same person. This person represents you more than anyone else in your firm, and the quality of the receptionist's interaction with clients is very important in determining their attitude toward your company.

A good receptionist requires knowledge, control, grace, and courtesy. Find someone who knows all the people in your firm, what their strengths are, and how the firm operates. Then place that person in this key position and pay your receptionist well. Make sure that he or she is a "greeter"—someone who has courtesy and charm. It makes for very happy clients and helps keep your everyday schedule workable.

Other Staff Positions

Depending on the size of your design firm, you may want to hire various other types of staff members, including the following:

- **Assistant designer.** This is a trained designer who works with a more advanced design professional. Although an assistant director has a formal education in design, that individual may lack the necessary experience, creativity, or drive to be in a position with more responsibility.
- **Administrative assistant.** This position requires management, bookkeeping, and client communications skills. In general, this person must be a practical partner to the creative person.
- **Bookkeeper.** This person records business transactions in an orderly fashion. (See page 308 for additional information about this important position.)
- **Draftsperson.** This person does CAD or manual plans or sketches and usually has special training in architecture and design.
- **Installation specialist.** This person is responsible for all the details of actual installations. The installation specialist's skill and ability to handle problems on-site keep the work moving. An installation specialist also knows how to present a project with great showmanship. The closest analogy is a "magician."
- **Librarian.** This specialist manages a design firm's library and may have a formal design education or simply long-term experience with the firm. As more product information or resources are moving to Web-based materials, it is important that this person be computer- and Internet-savvy. It is as important to keep online libraries well organized as it is to keep paper-based materials organized, so information can be located with ease and accuracy.
- **Project manager.** This person manages the resources and activities necessary to achieve a set of objectives on a project within a specified time.
- **Renderer.** This is an interior designer or illustrator who creates drawings, called "renderings," of interior design or architectural work, usually while the work is still in the conceptual stages.
- **Salesperson.** This person sells design services or products.
- **Secretary.** This person handles correspondence and manages routine office work.

- **Staff designer.** This is a person with a design education who works for a design firm or department. The necessary qualifications and responsibilities for this position vary according to the designer's abilities and the firm's structure.

Short-Term Staff

If you have a special project you know is going to last only two or three months, you should consider either hiring a freelancer or "borrowing" a staff person from another firm.

Freelancers

The interior design field is full of freelancers, people who are available and want to work with you on specialized projects. In hiring a freelancer, it is important to define the parameters of the relationship. For example, when your project is confidential, freelancers should be asked to sign a statement to the effect that they understand it requires confidentiality. Freelancers are a very good resource. If you use these people regularly, you can relieve your firm of some overhead expenses and obtain skills you could not hire or be able to afford on a full-time basis.

Borrowing a Staff Person

We all know designers working in other communities. It is often possible to borrow a worker from another firm for a week or two to assist you with a special project. This is a good way of bringing an expert into your firm. You have the benefit of knowing the standards of the design studio the staff people come from, and they can gain new perspectives from being in your studio for a while. Design firms that work closely together can easily borrow and exchange staff members. This gives them the flexibility of being able to do large projects without the encumbrance of a larger staff.

Independent Contractors

Since we use so many outsourcers, it is important to define them as "independent contractors." Following are the general standards that are part of an independent contractor's process and agreement.

Today, the majority of design firms use as many independent contractors as possible. By hiring independent contractors, firms pay for services as they are rendered, saving on staffing costs. With the wide fluctuation in design work most firms experience, using independent contractors helps keep overhead down. Among the independent contractors a design firm might use are the following:

- **Artist.** A person trained and skilled in one of the many art processes, such as painting, that can carry out or develop the artistic portion of the design project.
- **Artisan.** A skilled mechanic in a manual occupation. This person is more highly skilled than a tradesperson or craftsperson.
- **Craftsperson.** One who practices a trade or manual occupation with a greater degree of skill than a tradesperson.

- **Contractor.** A person or company that undertakes to perform work, usually for a specific project at a specified price within a certain time frame.
- **Tradesperson.** A worker in a skilled trade, such as plumbing, carpentry, or electrical.

What are the differences between an independent contractor and an employee? The IRS scrutinizes this gray area carefully. You must take care in maintaining the records that prove the legitimacy of these independent contractors in case of a tax examination. Here are a few guidelines from tax experts that will help you to classify whether someone is an independent contractor or an employee.

Independent Contractor or Employee?

Independent Contractors

- Are paid for each individual project.
- Offer their services to other companies or people.
- Have their own tools and equipment.
- Earn a profit or suffer a loss from the activity.
- Establish, usually in conjunction with their employers, the scheduling of work to be done.
- May work in more than one location.
- Set their own hours.
- Hire and pay their own support people or assistants.

Employees

- Have a regular paying relationship.
- Work for one employer.
- Can be fired or may quit without any liability.
- Usually receive reimbursements for expenses.
- Are part of an organization.

Acknowledgment of Independent Contractor

If you are hiring an independent contractor and want to be sure you will not be responsible for taxes and other liability issues, it is important to acknowledge the independent contractor's status. Use the independent contractor's form shown in Figure 5.1, page 101. If additional conditions are required, have your attorney write a form for your specific situation. You will want to document the types of insurance your contractors have, noting any liability issues relating to your company. You need a document stating exactly what type of insurance they have. It is advisable to show this list to your insurance agent to be sure the coverage is appropriate.

FINDING THE RIGHT EMPLOYEES

The ability to attract and keep good workers is an extremely valuable asset. It is not easy to do. People work together for many reasons. In the design field, financial considerations are not always the major ones.

Figure 5.1 Acknowledgment of independent contractor. It is important to use an agreement such as this with each independent contractor you use to ensure that you will not be held responsible for the individual's taxes and other liability issues.

ACKNOWLEDGMENT OF INDEPENDENT CONTRACTOR

This document acknowledges that _____ has been retained for services (describe services here)

These services as stated above will be paid for in the following manner:

Amount:

Method of Payment:

It is acknowledged that:

A. The undersigned shall be deemed an independent contractor and is not an employee, partner, agent, or engaged in a joint venture with the Company.

B. Consistent with the foregoing, the Company shall not deduct withholding taxes, FICA, or any other taxes required to be deducted by an employee, as I acknowledge my responsibility to pay same as an independent contractor.

C. I further acknowledge that I shall not be entitled to any fringe benefits, pension, retirement, profit sharing, or any other benefits accruing to employees.

D. I further state that I have the following insurance to cover my work.

Type of Policy:

Limit:

Company:

How do design firms acquire new staff members? Two of the most common ways are through working together on a project and by learning about someone from a resource or individual who knows your firm. Other sources of recruitment for new staffers include design schools, other designers, the American Society of Interior Designers (ASID), International Interior Design Association (IIDA), International Furnishings and Design Association (IFDA), Interior Design Society (IDS), and any professional groups in which one has the chance to meet design professionals. Design firms today are looking for people who have specific skills. It makes no difference whether they are students or not. The important consideration is whether they can do the job as it needs to be done.

Writing a Job Description

Before hiring a new person, prepare a job description. This should include the approximate duties that will be performed, the responsibilities, and the specific skills, education, and experience required. For some jobs, we can train the staff member, but for others we need a competent individual who can perform the job immediately. Review your work objectives so they properly mesh with your staff selection.

A job description should include the following information:

- **Job title.** Make this as descriptive as possible.
- **Immediate supervisor.** To whom will the employee report? Is the new person to be an assistant to another designer or an assistant to your expediter? Whatever the position is, clearly spell out the chain of command.
- **Required background and experience.** Identify the educational background required for the position and any practical work experience desired. For example, "This person needs a degree in interior design and three years of experience working in the commercial office–related field." What experience would be ideal? Perhaps you would like the person to have worked with certain types of landscape panels. Or maybe the applicant should be familiar with all the components required in building and putting together a state-of-the-art office.
- **Job responsibilities.** List specifics, such as design layout work or assisting with presentation.
- **Special situations.** Are there special problems associated with this particular job? Will the job require working with other people with whom the new employee must be compatible?
- **Travel requirements.** Note whether the employee will be handling some out-of-town projects that will require travel to other locales. List the percentage of time you anticipate the employee will spend out of town.
- **Salary range.** Give the approximate range, dependent on qualifications. Identify whether there is a probation period and any review process.
- **Benefits.** Detail other compensation, such as health insurance, time off, and merchandise discounts.
- **Opportunities.** Does the job offer a chance for professional growth?

Trying Out a Person

If you can, it is a good idea to try out a prospective employee on a special project. If the person is unemployed, the prospective employee can come into your studio and work for a few weeks, on a weekend basis, or after hours. Trying a job is a great way for both the employee and the employer to test the situation.

INTERVIEWING A PROSPECTIVE EMPLOYEE

Every firm has a different interviewing procedure. I use an outline when I am interviewing a prospective employee to make sure I cover all of the important areas.

Interview Techniques

During the interview, compare the job requirements with the stated abilities and experience of the applicant. Discuss the requirements with the applicant and what you understand that person's background to be. You should ask to see a resume and a portfolio. And it does not hurt to have the person fill out a standard application form on the spot; it gives you some basis for your evaluation.

If the person is applying to be on your design team, it is valuable to have the applicant fill out the design staff questionnaire shown in Table 5.3, on pages 104–105. This questionnaire is good for the new employee, but it should also be updated regularly for your present staff. The more you know about your employees, the better. Sometimes, they have background and experience you may not realize or have forgotten. When you are planning a future project, review the staff questionnaires. It does not hurt to have this information for your consultants and other members of the team, as well.

Because most design firms are small, if a new person does not fit in, it can cause a lot of problems. Have applicants discuss their backgrounds.

Try to find out what their career goals are so that you can determine whether the job you can offer will fit their objectives. Take notes. When you are nearing the end of the interview, review these notes with your candidate. If you are seriously interested in the person, you may want to mention the fringe benefits and extra duties of the job.

Equal Opportunity Laws

There are a number of laws that prevent an employer from discriminating against an applicant on the basis of race, religion, marital status, political affiliation, gender, pregnancy, disability, national origin, or age. According to the Small Business Administration, you may not ask the questions listed in the sidebar on page 106 without risking being considered discriminatory against an employee or a prospective employee. Be warned.

Obviously, firms have preferences in design styles and qualifications, but you must be very cautious not to allow personal prejudices to enter into your selection criteria. It is too easy to be sued for discrimination. A firm can still select people it would like; however, it must be cautious that the applicants are judged for their professional merit and suitability only.

Legal Commitments

Be careful what you promise new employees. On paper, their qualifications may be excellent, but on the job, they may not perform to expectations. Nevertheless, in many instances, you can be held liable for commitments made to employees. Employees can also be held liable for their commitments to their employers. You must be cautious in the way you outline a position to a new employee. Many firms give a person a test or "probation" period of up to 90 days to evaluate his or her capabilities before making definite commitments.

Table 5.3 Design staff questionnaire. This questionnaire should be filled out by design staff applicants, and it should be updated annually by each member of your design team. This form will help you in planning your company's objectives, evaluating your staff, and matching projects with appropriate staff members.

DESIGN STAFF QUESTIONNAIRE		Page 1
Name:	Address:	Phone No.:
		Date:

Design School or College:

Degree Received:

Courses Studied:	From:	To:

Awards Received:

Other Education: (workshops, seminars, etc.)

Subject:	Dates Attended:

Employment Experience:

Company:	From:	To:
Your Title:		
Job Experience:		

Company:	From:	To:
Your Title:		
Job Experience:		

Company:	From:	To:
Your Title:		
Job Experience:		

Company:	From:	To:
Your Title:		
Job Experience:		

Professional organizations to which you belong and offices, committees, or posts that you have held in these organizations:

(continued)

Table 5.3   *(Continued)*

DESIGN STAFF QUESTIONNAIRE   Page 2

Any special abilities or knowledge that you feel would be of benefit to the firm, i.e., certain social acquaintances, fluency in foreign languages, knowledge within other disciplines, list of prospective clients with whom you are familiar or have had experience:

Design Project Experience:

Type: Date:

Client or Owner:

Cost of Total Project:

Cost of Work Done by Design Firm:

Services Rendered by Design Firm:

Your Responsibilities:

Accomplishments on This Project:

Type: Date:

Client or Owner:

Cost of Total Project:

Cost of Work Done by Design Firm:

Services Rendered by Design Firm:

Your Responsibilities:

Accomplishments on This Project:

Other Relative Information:

© *Design Business Monthly,* 1988.

Questions Not to Ask

In the past, employers often asked questions about the following topics, but today these are considered discriminatory:

- Marital status.
- Birthplace.
- Age.
- Religion.
- Disability.
- How or when citizenship was obtained.
- How skill in a foreign language was acquired.
- Extracurricular or nonprofessional affiliations or memberships in organizations.
- If female, if this is the applicant's married or maiden name.
- Any arrests for crimes. You may ask, however, if a person was ever convicted of a crime if the question is accompanied by a statement that the answer may not necessarily cause the loss of the job opportunity. (Note: It is illegal to refuse to hire employees for falsely answering a question about their arrest record.)
- If the applicant was ever refused bonding.
- Possessions: for example, whether the applicant owns a car or a home.
- Physical characteristics: It is illegal to ask questions about an applicant's weight or height, or to request a photograph of the applicant.
- Whether the candidate has children.
- Whether the applicant's spouse or parents work or any information about their jobs.

Getting References

When a prospective employee interviews with your firm, you may want to obtain information from previous employers. For legal reasons, it is desirable to receive written permission from the applicant authorizing the previous employer to release information about the applicant's work, so the previous employer will not be put in jeopardy. This will help you get a better quality of information. At the time of the interview, ask the prospective employee to sign a release form. Then send the release with your questions or the form you want filled out by the previous employer.

It is advisable to have an attorney prepare a release form to ensure that the statements are legally stated and the proper release of liability is included.

When sending an applicant's previous employer a request for information about the prospective employee, you need to include the authorization-to-release information letter signed by that person, so that the firm knows you have its former employee's permission to give out this information. A letter similar to the one shown in Figure 5.2 (page 107) could be used.

Hiring an Employee

When you decide to hire an employee, send that person a letter, such as the one shown in Figure 5.3 (page 108), defining the position, responsibilities, and the con-

Figure 5.2 Request for employment reference. A letter such as this should be sent to a prospective employee's former employer.

Date:

Re:

Dear (former employer):

We have received an application for employment from _____, seeking a position with our firm. We understand the applicant was previously employed by your firm. We would appreciate a reference on the individual, including confirmation of the dates of employment with you, a performance evaluation, and the reasons for termination. We have enclosed a release signed by the above-named person.

Please advise whether your reference should be held confidential.

Thank you for your anticipated cooperation.

Very truly,

_____

ditions of employment, to prevent this from becoming an issue later on. A special notation should be made that the association will be an *at-will relationship*; this means either the employer or the employee may decide to end the relationship at any time. Again, for legal purposes, it is good to have this documented.

Noncompete Agreements. It is becoming common in the design field to ask employees to sign noncompete agreements when you hire them. In signing such a statement, employees agree that if they leave your employment, they cannot work at the same type of business in that same geographic area for a period of time—which could be six months, a year, or longer. These agreements are very common, but our attorneys have advised us that they are difficult to support and expensive to fight. I have seen agreements restricting a designer from working in the field for as long as 10 years. Such an agreement would never stand up in court, because it is denying a person's livelihood.

If you are considering moving from a job where you have a noncompete agreement, review it with your attorney first. Clarify your position before negotiating a future job.

If you are considering hiring someone who has an agreement with another company, it would be best for you to run the agreement by your attorney. Your attorney can prepare a document to absolve your company of any responsibility, leaving all liability with the prospective employee. However, your attorney may recommend delaying the hiring until the situation has been legally clarified.

Figure 5.3 Employment letter. This letter should be sent to a person when you decide to hire him or her to be an employee. It defines the position and the conditions of the employment for future reference.

Date:

To: (employee)

Dear (employee):

We are pleased to confirm your employment by our design firm in the position of _____. You will report directly to _____, to start employment on _____, 20___.

Your salary shall be $_____ per _____. After successful completion of a probation period of 90 days, you will qualify to enroll in our health insurance plans and receive fringe benefits, as explained. For the first year, vacation time shall be prorated and you will be entitled to _____ days vacation this year.

It is understood and accepted that the employment relationship we have agreed to is an at-will relationship, and that it may be ended by either party, at any time, and for any reason.

If you agree this letter sets forth our understanding, please sign the enclosed copy and return it by _____ for our files.
                        (date)

We look forward to your joining the company.

Very truly,

_____

Agreed and accepted:

_____
(employee)

Figure 5.4 Sample letter of notification to unsuccessful applicants. Sending a letter such as this to applicants you will not be hiring is both courteous and kind.

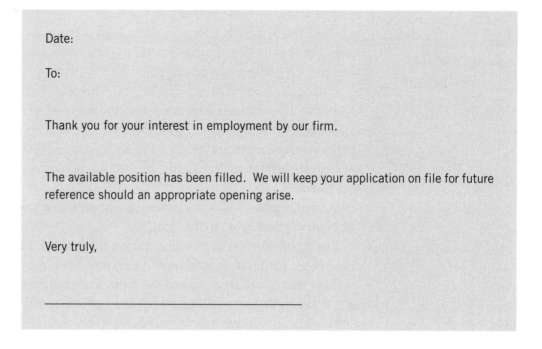

Date:

To:

Thank you for your interest in employment by our firm.

The available position has been filled. We will keep your application on file for future reference should an appropriate opening arise.

Very truly,

_____

Noncompete agreements are not legal in all states; but if they are legal within your state, you may find them helpful. It has been my experience that very few of these agreements hold up in court, but they sometimes encourage employees to be more focused during their time of employment. Although noncompete agreements are difficult to enforce, ask any prospective employee if he or she has signed one with a prior employer, and consult your attorney if such an agreement is in force.

Notifying Other Applicants

When you decide not to hire a person you interviewed, send a letter, such as the one shown in Figure 5.4 (above), or call the applicant promptly (or best, do both). Tell the person frankly that the position has been filled so the applicant can continue job hunting. It is kind, and creates goodwill, to give applicants some idea why they were not selected. However, be careful what you say, to avoid having your words construed as a form of discrimination. It does not hurt to stay on good terms with these applicants. At some time, they might fit another type of job with your firm. The design world is a small one; it usually pays to be friendly toward as many people as possible.

SALARIES AND BENEFITS

The salaries and compensations of interior design firms vary considerably from firm to firm and from town to town. Interior designers earn anywhere from very minimal to very high rates. The high rates are based almost completely on performance. Normally, designers begin at a starting rate and receive raises according to their productivity or the amount of work they are able to bring into a firm. In today's market, the designers who are able to bring in the work, or become part of the sales team, are generally the best paid. There are some high performers in different, unusual situations, but it is usually the designer who has proven ability to make things happen who gets the highest compensation.

A designer's performance can be easily measured. Designers' charges are usually based either on an hourly rate—for productivity—or on a flat rate, for value. Paying designers in terms of value can bring in higher revenues to the firm and therefore reap larger profits. In addition to salaries, many designers earn either a percentage of the firm's year-end profits or a percentage of the profits on the jobs they handled.

Many designers who work in sales are given a direct percentage compensation of the business they bring to the firm.

The higher a position is within a firm, the less fixed the salary or compensation tends to be. With higher-level jobs, the income is more apt to vary, based on individual productivity or the profits of the firm. Designers who hold the highest-paying jobs in firms may have as high a ratio as 10 percent fixed salary and 90 percent variable income. Designers in lower positions will receive either fixed salaries or salaries supplemented with small percentages of income based on productivity or profits.

Designers' income levels are not what they could be. In order for the level of income to be raised, however, higher levels of productivity need to be established. In almost every company I reviewed, I found that if the firm were able to get an additional 20 or 30 percent new business or to enlarge its projects to gain an additional 20 or 30 percent profit margin, it would be able to pay its employees considerably more. Today's interior designers need to determine exactly what makes them productive to learn how they might develop their salary potential.

Design Firm Benefits

Many of us work in the design field because we enjoy meeting people and like the work we do. But intangible benefits do not pay the rent. Today, everyone needs some form of financial benefits. The majority of design firms do not have as large a benefits package as is offered by other, larger businesses. But most are attempting to remedy this as best they can.

Health Benefits. A health insurance program that can give employees standard medical coverage is generally one of the primary benefits an employee expects. Whether the company or the employee pays the premiums depends on the individual contract. You should look for a package with the appropriate flexibility to meet your individual employees' needs. We are hoping that the laws will change to permit health coverage to move with employees should they leave your firm. At present, other than in situations that qualify under the Consolidated Omnibus Budget Reconciliation Act (COBRA), a person leaving the company cannot continue with that company's insurance and must find a new source of coverage.

There are ways for small firms to buy good health benefits at reasonable prices, such as through their local Chamber of Commerce or professional organization. At one time, good benefits were available only through larger firms, but this is not the case today. Individuals or small firms usually can find some way of aligning with an appropriate organization so they and their staff can receive benefits.

Vacations. Traditionally, design firms are not outstanding in terms of vacation benefits offered. Although larger firms will sometimes offer different vacation schedules, most firms give employees one to two weeks. Many design firms require the entire staff to take vacations at the same time, because they feel they cannot work with a short staff. Other companies do not permit more than one person to be gone from any one department at a time. Obviously, your individual production schedule must be considered, but it is the general rule that designers do not take vacations at prime contract periods, such as when a big contract is due or when there is a large installation. Most design firms are of moderate size, so work schedules have to take priority over personal ones, and vacation and off-time are arranged around contracts.

Insurance. A design firm is required by law to provide workmen's compensation insurance to its employees. Some firms also offer insurance coverage in case of illness or death.

Key Person Insurance. The death or disability of a primary person within a firm must be expected to cause major losses or heavy financial obligations to the company. This insurance not only protects the firm against such possible losses but also ensures that an appropriate person (beneficiary) will have funds to purchase the company from the heirs. This type of insurance can make a major contribution to the successful management of a company at a time of crisis by providing indemnification for the loss of services. This insurance can:

- Pay for the recruitment and training of a suitable replacement.
- Aid the company in maintaining its credit standing.
- Secure the business so it can continue, by providing working capital.
- Provide funds to redeem the key person's stock so the remaining staff can control the firm, rather than the deceased person's family or relatives.
- Provide benefits for the key person's family.
- Fund a deferred compensation plan for the key person's retirement.

Discounts. Usually, interior design firms try to make available to their staff any interior furnishings they have access to at reasonable or moderate terms. Sometimes, employees will be given a discount on the retail price; in other instances, they will be charged a small percentage over cost. It is usually appropriate for the firm to get some compensation for order processing and delivery. Buying privileges are one of the perks of working for a design firm.

Retirement Plans. In many situations, affording a proper retirement plan is difficult for small firms because the actuarial costs are so high. It costs a minimum of

$1,200 per year plus $200 per employee to meet the government requirements for a defined benefits plan. If you do not have a large enough group to have a retirement plan within your company, you might offer to match employee contributions to their existing retirement accounts. For example, you might offer to contribute up to 5 percent of their income, not to exceed $1,000. In this way, your employees are receiving some contribution, although not as much as they might be from a more accelerated plan.

Retirement plans must be set up according to government regulations, and they require constant updating. Check with your accountant and financial advisor regarding retirement plans, as revisions are being made almost daily. Bringing in special consultants to help you set up your firm's retirement planning is almost a must.

Tax-Deferred Qualified Retirement Plans. Today, most profitable design firms exert much effort to develop and maintain a well-trained team. In order to do so, appropriate compensation programs need to be in place. Fortunately, there have been many changes that make it practical and cost-effective for smaller companies to have good tax-deferred savings plans.

There are many advantages to tax-deferred plans. Because they are tax-deferred, a person is permitted to accrue a larger amount of savings than would be possible if taxes were paid at the time the monies were earned. Most often, we are in a higher tax bracket during these high-income years than when we retire.

This is an area in which it is best to consult your financial advisor. There are ways to design plans to dedicate greater funding to long-term, more valuable, or higher-paid staff members. There have been, and will continue to be, considerable changes in the rulings of qualified employee pension plans. In most cases, it is best to have a professional administer your plan.

Here are several types of plans that you might consider:

- **Defined contribution plan.** These plans have an individual account for each participant in the plan. Some common types of defined contribution plans are:
  - **401(k):** Eligible employees may contribute a percentage of their wages to their account, up to set limits annually, on a tax-deferred basis. Employers may provide matching contributions, if established in the plan documents.
  - **Profit-sharing plan:** An employer makes tax-deferred deposits, usually based on the business profits, to individual employee accounts. These contributions are discretionary and may vary from year to year.
  - **Employee stock ownership plan (ESOP):** In this plan, the company contributes its own stock into a retirement plan for the benefit of the employees. All eligible employees receive shares of the stock in their own individual accounts of the retirement plan.
- **Defined benefits plan.** Often these are established as Keoghs. Although not as popular as in the past, these plans are still used. They must be funded

A recent study by the National Center for Employment Ownership confirms that:

- Employee-owner companies enjoy increased rates of growth after installing a plan.
- Companies offering ownership to most or all of their employees have a median annual sales growth twice that of other companies.
- Employee-owned companies have greater operating margins and returns on equity than similar companies not sharing ownership.
- Over a 10-year period, most design firms provide substantial financial benefits to employees.

every year; contributions are not optional. An advantage is that if you are older and need to build your retirement quickly, you can contribute larger amounts in a shorter period of time. Employees cannot contribute to the plan, because actuaries are often needed to assist in determining the contribution and deduction limits. These plans can be more expensive to administer than some other plans.

Other plans that are less complex than the qualified plans are:

- **Simplified Employee Pension (SEP) plan.** In this plan, the employer makes contributions to a traditional individual retirement account (IRA) for each eligible employee. Employees generally cannot make contributions to this plan.
- **Savings Incentive Match Plan for Employees (SIMPLE):** There are two types of SIMPLE plans: SIMPLE IRA or SIMPLE 401(k). In both, employees make tax-deferred contributions to an individual account (IRA) or 401(k). The employer also makes matching or "nonelective" contributions to each employee's individual account. SIMPLE plans must be set up on a calendar-year basis only.

EMPLOYEE EVALUATIONS

It is traditional for a firm to give annual evaluations of employees. In a small design firm, however, it is better to evaluate staff performances as you finish a project. When the job is fresh in everyone's minds, the evaluation is more valuable and effective. You talk over the job with your staff. You might say, "This is what we did that we feel is great, and this is the part you played. Perhaps next time you would like to take on more responsibility or carry out certain tasks you did not do on this project."

As a firm grows larger, the evaluation process must become more formalized. In large firms, regular written employee evaluations are a good practice.

No matter when you perform an employee evaluation, there are a few key points to remember:

- Schedule the review in advance and dedicate adequate time to this conversation. This will help you and the employee be more relaxed about the meeting and allow you to plan for it appropriately.
- Keep the review objective and—where possible—the criteria for evaluation quantifiable and measurable.
- Be professional both in your conversation and in any written materials.

Employee review should not be a surprise. Keep communication open throughout the review period, and express compliments or indicate areas that need improvement as the circumstances occur.

Reviewing Goals

As you consider your firm's goals, first review your staff. Write down what is expected of your employees. Describe their jobs. Define all your employees' positions within the company and list their wages and responsibilities. Outline their benefits, working hours, pay schedule, and any overtime payment. This will help you later as you compare their capabilities with your plans for your firm.

As you evaluate your staff, you should also review their initial design staff questionnaires (see pages 104–105). The information on these questionnaires is useful in determining the value of an employee to the firm—both for reviewing current salary and marketing future projects.

In order for you to properly develop new and existing design staff members, you should have them update their design staff questionnaires every year. While some of the information will remain the same, education and employment experiences often change. Employee changes and additions should be recorded, along with a summary of their goals and objectives, so that when new opportunities arise within the firm, you can try to match them with the personal objectives of your staff.

Understanding the goals of each individual in your firm can help you in planning company objectives. When a staff member's objectives vary from the direction the design firm is taking, it is time to have a discussion with that employee. For instance, you might say, "This is where we see our company going. How do you feel about that?" Or, "I realize you would like to learn more about design trends, but I see your abilities as stronger in marketing. How would you feel about moving into the marketing area? I'd like it if you would try to relate to some clients directly to see if you enjoy it."

This ongoing, yet documented, interaction is important in long-term relationships. Once employees write down their objectives, you have a more reliable statement than casual conversation can provide. It is a good point of reference to be able to say, "Last year you felt the best thing you did was this particular job. Now I see you going in a completely different direction. How do you feel this compares with what you had planned at that time?"

How Much Do You Cost?

Do you know how much you and your employees cost? Figure out exactly what each employee costs your company, and then determine whether the employee is really earning what he or she is being paid. A person's cost is not just salary or take-home pay; it includes all the employee's fringe benefits—vacation, health insurance, sick leave, extra time off, business lunches, trips to conventions or shows, a car, and any other benefits, such as additional travel and attendance at meetings, that the individual is able to enjoy at company expense. You will find you are paying for a lot of extras.

Health insurance, vacations, and sick time are just part of it. Many corporations say a staff person costs them approximately 30 to 40 percent more than his or her salary. Within the design field, the cost is very similar.

You may discover, as I did, that your present staff is not really what you need. It is nice to have a well-known person who enhances the reputation of your studio, but you must ask whether that individual is really producing or is there just for "cosmetic" purposes. How much is having this person worth? Is this individual part of your image? Your advertising? You must evaluate your staff on a regular basis to be sure your employees continue to fit the business objectives of your company.

It is helpful to review your staff files at regular intervals so you can see how employees have progressed. Keeping these files current by updating the design staff questionnaire will help both you and your staff understand their development. Today, primary staff members expect to be part of the profit structure of a company. They need to have an understanding of how they are contributing to where the money is coming from.

Notice of Unsatisfactory Performance

When you have an employee who is performing at an unsatisfactory level, it is prudent to have a formal meeting with the employee. You should schedule this meeting with the associate and, if possible, with another management-level person such as your business manager. The management person will serve as a witness to the meeting and the discussion that takes place.

If you have an associate who is consistently underperforming or is moving toward termination due to discipline issues, you should document the situation in addition to having a meeting. Give the employee a memorandum outlining the unsatisfactory elements in his or her performance, the corrective action that must be taken, and the time frame in which this corrective action is to occur.

The purpose of issuing this notice of unsatisfactory performance is to protect the firm against any claims of discriminatory termination (a sample is shown in Figure 5.5, page 116). It is an excellent policy to have this memorandum for use as a support for any dismissal. To be safe, consult your attorney if you feel you are going to be dealing with any problems in this area.

Date:

To: (employee)

This memorandum confirms our meeting of _____, 20___, during which you were advised that your job performance has been unsatisfactory in the following respect(s):

You were advised that the deficiencies must be corrected if you are to remain an employee in good standing, and that you should take the following actions to correct the problem(s) described above:

We have every confidence that you can correct the problem(s), and you can become a productive employee.

Sincerely,

_____   _____
(employer)   (witness)

Receipt of the above notice is acknowledged:

_____
(employee)

TERMINATION OR RESIGNATION OF AN EMPLOYEE

Termination of an employee is probably one of the most difficult jobs any manager or business owner will ever have to perform. In our litigious society, it is important that this process be handled carefully and thoughtfully. By having a solid, consistent performance evaluation and review process in place, you can document more effectively any deficiencies an associate may have that may lead to termination.

Before you terminate an employee, review the documentation you have regarding the meetings you have held with the employee about the matter; also review the written warnings you have issued. Be sure the reason for termination is supported through

Figure 5.6 Notice of termination of employment. It is a good idea to provide a letter such as this to employees you are terminating. The employee should acknowledge receipt and return the acknowledged notice to the company. When terminating or firing someone, keep the meeting professional. Do not try to be nice or make it easier for the individual. State the exact reason(s). Be completely honest about termination decisions. But because there are so many lawsuits against employers today, it's a good idea to speak with your legal advisor in advance to seek direction in the matter before you take the action to terminate.

Date:

To: (employee)

Effective _____, 20____, your employment with the firm is terminated for the following reason(s):

Your severance pay and any fringe benefits due shall be according to company policy.

Please arrange for the return of any company property in your possession.

Very truly,

_____

(employer)

Receipt of the above notice is acknowledged:

_____

(employee)

previous notes and documentation. If the termination is for a substantial direct violation of a rule, such as carrying a gun to work, previous documentation is not as necessary. And by preparing and holding effective meetings with difficult employees, there should be no surprises. When outcomes are evaluated, employees will know they have either retained or lost their job by correcting or ignoring the action plan, respectively.

When you terminate an employee, it is often advisable to inform that person in writing, citing the specific reasons for termination. These reasons should have been substantiated in previous meetings with the employee. On receiving the notice of termination of employment (see Figure 5.6), the employee should acknowledge receipt and return the notice to the company. Severance and other benefits should

Figure 5.7 Formal resignation. When a corporate officer or director leaves the firm, he or she must submit a formal resignation such as this, which the firm must formally acknowledge.

Date:

To:

Management:

Please be advised that the undersigned hereby resigns as _____ of the corporation, effective upon acceptance.

Please acknowledge acceptance of said resignation on behalf of the corporation.

Very truly,

_____
(corporate member)

The foregoing has been accepted pursuant to vote of the directors/stockholders of the corporation, effective _____, 20___.

_____
(for the corporation)

not be paid until the acknowledged notice has been received. Have your attorney review all letters of termination.

Resignation with Formal Acknowledgment

A corporate officer or director who leaves the company must submit a formal resignation identifying his or her position as a corporate officer and stating that he or she is officially resigning from the corporation (see Figure 5.7). In that way corporate officers or directors ensure they will no longer be responsible for actions of the corporation or be involved in the corporation in any fashion. This resignation is then acknowledged by the board of directors.

Figure 5.8 Sample letter of resignation. When an employee resigns, he or she should submit a letter such as this to his or her employer. The employee may want to add certain details to this basic letter.

Date:

To: (employer)

I hereby tender my resignation from the firm, effective _____, 20___.

At that time I shall deliver all property of the firm in my possession.

Very truly,

_____

(resigning employee)

When an employee resigns, he or she should also submit a formal letter of resignation. This provides formal documentation for the employee file.

Exit Interview

It is important to remain on good terms with everyone you have worked with or for, whenever possible. It is a small world, and you never know when you will be working together again. To help with this, when employees resign, it is a good idea to hold an exit interview with them to learn the reasons they are leaving. This will help you evaluate what sort of person you need to hire as a replacement. You may find the job is not appropriately structured; in which case, you will want to revise the job before hiring a replacement. Or you may find that the qualifications of the departing employee did not fit the job. This is also an excellent time to learn about issues within your company that you may not have been aware of.

It is a good idea to write a report on each exit interview and add it to the employee's design staff questionnaire. State the name of the employee, the date of the exit interview, the date the employee was hired, and the employee's address, sex, marital status, age, and educational background. After an employee has worked with you for a while, you will know this information and have it in the individual's personnel file. Since interior design is a small field, you can be reasonably sure that you will work with this employee again. Having information about the person's lifestyle, interests, and skills can help us fit this particular person into the right relationship in your future business dealings.

You don't need a special form to record the exit interview. Generally, we use our regular staff evaluation form and just add the reason for the employee's leaving and the type of separation.

After the exit interview, you should determine the next action to take: to hire another person, ask another staff person to take on the additional work, or fill the absence in some other way.

Even if you wish the resigning employee were staying, you can make the most of the departure by using the occasion to learn information about your company that can help you with future direction.

HIRING CONSULTANTS

Every year American businesses spend billions of dollars on consultants to address specific problems their in-house staff may not have the expertise or time to handle. Smaller companies in particular find that consultants can make the difference between success and failure, profit and loss.

Appropriate consultants can help solve many types of problems for the design firm. They can also become part of a team on a design project. A good reference file and directory of consultants is valuable to the management structure of a firm. We need many types of consultants for many reasons.

When to Hire

You should hire consultants for one or more of the following reasons:

1. **To bring in additional expertise.** If you do not have a specialist on a particular subject on your staff, it is economical to hire a consultant with expertise in that area—whether the subject is accounting, law, computers, or design specialties such as lighting and hospitality.
2. **To make a design team stronger.** You can hire consultants to suit particular projects. In this way you can assemble a team of experts seldom found on any one person's staff. Consultants make a firm stronger.
3. **To review management or processing.** It is a good idea to bring in a consultant to determine whether your management is up to date or to recommend other processes more appropriate for managing your operation.
4. **To resolve conflict.** Design firms sometimes have conflicts regarding employees or staffing. Often these can be resolved more easily by bringing in an outside party to act as an impartial observer or mediator.
5. **To act as advisors to your staff.** You might hire consultants to train staff, act as their mentors, or help them develop their individual potential.
6. **To broaden the spectrum of information available to everyone within the company.** This can help you compete with very large specialized firms.

You should *not* hire a consultant under the following conditions:

1. **When your need is not defined.** There is no point in hiring a consultant unless you know exactly which areas you want that consultant to address.

2. **If your need will be very long term.** For a long-term need, you should consider hiring a person who will become part of your company.
3. **If the consultant is not experienced handling situations similar to yours.** If the consultant is extremely overqualified or has been dealing with very large companies, that consultant may not understand your small firm's issues.
4. **If the timing is not appropriate.** A consultant should be brought into your firm only when there is time for him or her to digest the information that is going to be reviewed. There is no point bringing in a consultant during a crisis. Unless the consultant can become directly involved in crisis management, you should resolve the crisis before bringing in that person. Make sure you have the time and are in the right mind-set to review the issues to be covered with this consultant.

Whom to Hire

There are two consultants every firm will need: an accountant and an attorney. At my firm, we also call on a number of other advisors for a variety of reasons. Generally, when I see a problem, I contact outside consultants for their review and opinion. They bring an objective viewpoint and management expertise we could not provide ourselves. Hiring a consultant gives us strength in areas outside our areas of major interest.

Your Accountant. You need the services of an accountant from the time you begin planning your business until the day you sell it. Too often, accountants are treated as postmortem people. To get maximum value, you must learn to use accountants in

When I was younger, I thought that if I wanted to learn something, I could take some courses, or enroll in college. As I developed my business, I found myself wanting additional knowledge in business and other specialized areas. I discussed this with a number of my business consultants, who told me the best way I could get the most appropriate, clearly defined, and up-to-date information on my subject was to hire a group of consultants. In essence, I was advised to look at my individual needs and find the best possible available consultant.

I have been using consultants extensively now for over 30 years. Rarely does a week go by when my firm does not use a consultant for some reason. Some of their fees have been startling, but usually they are more than worth it. When I have had a properly defined project and have been able to clearly state it to my consultants, their response has been amazingly quick and direct.

In short, consultants are part of our everyday vocabulary. We could not run our small firm without them. If you operated within a very large corporate structure, perhaps you would not need as many consultants. But for us it is one of the most rewarding methods of learning and conducting business. Consultants have also pointed me toward other specialists they believed I should know about or meet. They have also recommended lectures, people, courses, and books. When a consultant recommends that I review information, I know the time I spend doing so will be very worthwhile.

your planning stages as well as for your annual review. If the accountant becomes part of your company, you will get more from the relationship.

Your accountant can help you with your cash management systems and day-to-day operating techniques, enabling you to use your money to your best advantage. I do not like any accounting system that leaves room for question. I want to know ahead of time what we have done, where we stand, how our projects are developing financially, and how our time management is being handled. Any good accountant can set these systems up for you.

Invite your accountant to look over all your future business plans. Subtle flaws can result in unbelievable tax consequences or greatly affect your cash flow. Your accountant should also review your leases, loan agreements, contracts, and any long-term commitments before you are inextricably involved. You may want your accountant to review your insurance, as well, and to comment on the policies you have purchased. Because your accountant knows your financial needs, he or she is able to spot quickly whether your coverage is adequate. If it is not, your accountant can recommend what other insurance you should have. This can be exceptionally helpful.

The more your accountant is told about your operation, and the less your accountant has to discover by searching and probing, the more quickly he or she can start helping your firm. Accountants generally bill by the hour, so it pays to make their job easy. I recommend inviting your accountant and your attorney to regular meetings where you and they can discuss the advancement and structure of your company. Be sure they know each other and are familiar with what the other does on your behalf. Meet with your accountant several times a year; pick your accountant's brain about every financial aspect of your business.

One accountant worked with my firm from 1956 until he died in 1990. Mr. Samuel Ledger became our accountant because he was very easy for me to understand. He taught CPAs locally and was used to explaining financial matters in elementary language. Every time I considered an addition, a subtraction, opening another business, closing one, a move, or a change, Mr. Ledger was one of the first people I called in to see if my idea was economical. There were times I had projects I thought were extremely exciting, until he showed me how the taxes and additional accounting records required would make them impractical.

Before I met Mr. Ledger, I worked with a firm of many accountants, who insisted on doing it "their way" and really didn't care what I or my company wanted, only that it be done according to proper accounting principles. Those accountants could not communicate with me. It was important to me, when I started, to have someone who was able to relate to me in terms I could understand. The first work Mr. Ledger did for me was to prepare my annual taxes. I would take my little red book to him every year; he would prepare my taxes and charge me $25. The relationship grew considerably. He became a part of our company over 30 years, and I think he learned to enjoy us as much as we enjoyed him.

When it is time for your accountant to review your books, be sure the records are up to date and all the numbers are ready. To keep the accountant's professional fees reasonable, use your own bookkeeping staff to prepare the records. It is expensive for an outside person to come in and update your records. By having your books ready for your accountant on time, in clean, readable condition, you will not be paying an accountant's prices for clerical work.

Do not be afraid to ask your accountant questions, but remember that the orientation of accountants is to be conservative. If you have stated a plan of action, and your accountant suggests it is not financially feasible or does not recommend it, do not be afraid to ask for alternatives. It may be that only one phase of the project is inappropriate, and you can easily adjust the plan.

Learn to talk with your accountant. You should understand every form and report your accountant gives you. If you do not understand them, ask your accountant to explain them to you. If your accountant cannot explain it to your satisfaction, find someone who can.

Your Attorney. You need an attorney in the planning stages of starting a business, not after you have already launched it. Should it be a sole proprietorship, partnership, limited partnership, limited liability company, or a corporation? (These and other types of ownership are explained in Chapter 2.) You, your attorney, and your accountant should work together to tailor your business structure to fit your business and personal needs.

Other reasons to use attorneys are for contract interpretation, drafting, and review; for working out problems with clients who file suits; and for negotiating with employees.

Your attorney can also help you maintain your business structure, assist in preparing corporate minutes, corporate resolutions, and the documents required for tax and legal purposes.

I asked a number of attorneys how large a part they felt an attorney should play in a company structure. The answer was, in essence, "as large a part as the client requires." Some people need a person to talk to when they are testing ideas. An attorney is a good—albeit, expensive—person for this. Other people speak to an attorney only when they have a definite problem—a lawsuit or contract dispute, for instance.

I think there is a middle ground. For an attorney to give you the best service, you should bring that person in before the final die is cast, to help mold the manner in which issues are handled. Consult with an attorney if you think there is going to be a suit. Do not wait until someone sues you. Your attorney can help with the negotiations or preparations for a possible legal suit.

Selecting an attorney is often difficult. I think the best way to go about it is to compare notes with other businesspeople. Ask for recommendations from those who have used an attorney's services. Some attorneys do not want small business accounts. It is important to deal with an attorney who is interested in and handles issues you have or may encounter.

You can also find an attorney by consulting recognized law listings. Probably the best-known directory is the *Martindale-Hubbell Legal Directory*, available online at www.martindale.com or in many public libraries. It lists attorneys by area of practice, by location, and by firm. It also rates the attorneys for general ability and overall reputation.

The *Martindale-Hubbell Legal Directory* uses three ratings for general ability: A, B, and C. To be classified under any of these categories, an attorney must have been in practice for a particular period of time and must have been rated by fellow attorneys. While A is the highest rating, many good attorneys do not have an A rating simply because they have not been in practice long enough.

The directory also uses three ratings for overall reputation: V, AV, and BV. The V rating stands for a very high reputation; an attorney with an AV rating is well above average in reputation; and a person with a BV rating may be just as good. Reputation ratings tend to reflect an attorney's years of experience, rather than level of integrity. They do not reflect ability.

When you meet with the attorney you have chosen, discuss your business objectives and interests. Do not be put off if the attorney is not particularly enthusiastic. We hire attorneys for their skills and experience, not to have the same interests we have. From experience, an attorney knows that everything that crosses his or her desk is not necessarily going to succeed. The attorney may try to temper your enthusiasm to see if you have both feet on the ground and are aware of the realities. It is part of an attorney's orientation.

Ask whether the attorney will actually do your work or outsource to another lawyer. Very few lawyers today practice in a one-person office; most are in partnership or are part of a large company. If you expect your attorney to do all the work, make that clear at the outset. The attorney will price accordingly. If your work will be outsourced, get some idea who will perform the legal services and how they will be supervised, so that you are not disappointed with the outcome.

Judging the quality of an attorney's work can be just as difficult as selecting an attorney in the first place. Results are your best guide. Has using this attorney reduced or eliminated your firm's disputes and litigations? Are you in trouble with tax authorities or in other areas where the attorney represents you?

The lawyer-client privilege means your lawyer cannot be forced to reveal anything you tell him or her in preparation of any of your casework. However, you should be aware that this privilege does not apply to your accountant, your corporate treasurer, other employees, professional advisors, or board members.

Your Financial Planner. At one point, the financial planning of a firm was handled by its banker and accountant. Today, however, the financial world is much more complex, and many firms find that using a financial consultant can be valuable in planning their financial structure.

The financial planner will review all of your assets and liabilities, including your income tax returns; wills; and any settlements, contracts, deeds, mortgages, insurance policies, and other papers related to your financial position. With this information, the planner will calculate your net worth, give you a monthly cash flow statement (if your accountant has not already given you those), and recommend a plan for you that takes advantage of your best financial opportunities.

A financial planner will review everything, from your types of mortgages to your kinds of investments, retirement plans, and company structures. The planner will look at your total financial position, not just your company's—a different viewpoint from that of your accountant.

Financial planners can come from many different backgrounds. Anyone can claim to be a financial planner, so you must use caution in selecting one. Look at the person's credentials. The planner should belong to the Financial Planning Association. Many colleges and business schools offer programs in financial planning, and though people who have attended these classes may have certificates or a degree, this in no way guarantees their expertise.

An excellent way to find a financial planner is through a reference from a personal friend or your banker, accountant, lawyer, or someone else who normally works with planners. When interviewing a financial planner, ask to see the kinds of plans he or she has prepared for other people. Also ask what types of firms have used the planner. Some planners will take only very large accounts; others will take reasonably small ones.

Planners usually cost anywhere from $1,000 and up, depending on the area they are in and the type of services they offer. Many charge a fee (flat or hourly). This is the only type of planner I would recommend. I feel that someone who earns a commission on whatever that individual sells you cannot have an objective viewpoint. It is usually worthwhile to review your program every year with a financial planner.

Other Consultants. You should also consider hiring the following professionals:

- **Advertising and promotion consultants.** When making large investments, you want the best results. These specialists know the market and the many issues that affect the results of your expenditure.
- **Architects.** If a designer initiates the project, it is common for the designer to hire an architect as a consultant.
- **Business development consultants or business coaches.** It can be a real help to have someone outside your firm assist you in analyzing your opportunities and the development of your company. This person knows a lot about the current happenings in the field and can help review your options. It is also very valuable to hear about the different systems and processes that work in other firms. There are coaches and programs for most needs, from a hands-on examination of your particular firm to a more general course that gives you guidelines. In the Designers' Business Forum, we bring designers together in groups so they not only see what others are doing but hear about their goals, roadblocks, and successes. Interior design can be a very lonely business. A good program such as the Designers' Business Forum will put you in the company of noncompeting designers, so you can speak freely and gain true support.

- **Collection agencies.** They usually work on a contingency basis—paid based on results. It is best to find a firm that is effective in getting results from your type of client.

- **Design consultants.** Without the input from other designers, I am sure that I would have made many more mistakes than I have. When we are doing something unusual or have concerns about an issue, we have another designer review it. When I purchased the building I am in, I asked two other designers to review my plans for the building to see if they could find any ways of improving on our plans. It was amazing how much they found. They immediately suggested doing several things that saved expenses and disruption later. It is so stimulating to have another viewpoint. It is a very enriching experience and a great contribution to almost any project.

- **Engineers.** There are many types of engineering services our projects require—structural, civil, acoustical, and lighting. With all the high-tech work we do today, the list is very extensive. Designers require engineers not just to ensure liability issues, but also to bring designers' projects to a higher level than their firms can do in-house.

- **Educational consultants.** Usually, these are experienced educators who are familiar with the many programs offered by various institutions. They also have current knowledge of the field, so they are able to advise on programs that would be suitable to a particular designer's needs. Today, there are many courses available, but they are on different levels. Consultants will help you find the ones that are best for you. They recommend the different kinds of educational programs that might be appropriate for your staff, either on an in-house basis or on a special basis. Ideally, the interior design school you attended will keep in touch with you throughout your career. An educational consultant affiliated with your school would enable you to pay the school a fee that allows the school to monitor your curriculum vitae, keep you up to date, and assist you in a career change. This process is explained more extensively in my book *Interior Design and Beyond* (1995).

- **Employee benefits consultants.** There are many companies that can review your benefits package plan. They can also create a package for you, show you how to manage it, and present it to your employees. Most of these consultants cater to larger firms; however, some are available to small design firms.

- **Human resources consultants.** There are firms dedicated solely to the development and implementation of employee relations strategies. These firms specialize in compensation training, development, communication, and management effectiveness. They will create policy manuals, handbooks, and supervisory training procedures. However, these firms usually work with larger firms of a hundred or more.

- **Import and export specialists.** If you plan to do work abroad, you should consult this kind of specialist, who can help determine how you should handle your work abroad—addressing such issues as government regulations, legal permits, representatives, shipping, joint venture involvement, and anything else related to working in a foreign country.

- **Insurance specialists.** Whether you have an agent, broker, or consultant, you should have your insurance policies reviewed periodically to ensure appropriate coverage.
- **Leadership consultants.** There are many consultants who train and consult on leadership. Every chief executive officer and manager understands there are many problems in leadership. These consultants can train you in techniques that will help you lead your firm.
- **Management consultants.** These consultants will review your management procedures to determine what can be done to improve the individual management of your firm. Many design firms use some management consulting, because an outsider has the necessary distance from the day-to-day operations to provide an objective overview of a management system.
- **Marketing consultants.** Marketing consultants specialize in setting up marketing programs and in showing firms how to develop them.
- **Mergers and acquisitions consultants.** These consultants are very useful if you are considering merging with or acquiring another company. They will help you explore and evaluate the different options available to your company and provide assistance in staff evaluation.
- **Productive systems analysts.** Any firm that has production scheduling or any kind of production system can use productivity systems analysts. These specialists review manufacturing and professional service organizations to determine their individual productivity.
- **Recruitment specialists.** It is often difficult to know how to locate and attract the particular consultant or part- or full-time employees you need. Professional recruiters can help set up the structure and procedures for you.
- **Technology consultants.** Specialists in technology can determine what would best suit your needs. From analyzing your telephone, your computer, and its software to evaluating your mobile technical needs, such as laptops, PDAs, phones, and any infrastructure to support the products or networks, using a consultant to provide guidance before investing is advisable. Technology is changing rapidly, and you'll want to invest in support systems that will take you into the future, not just work today.
- **Training consultants.** These are specialists who can be brought in to train your staff, depending on your needs. They can also be hired on a per-assignment or per-project basis to help bring your staffing up to date. Using training consultants is often less expensive than sending your employees to school.

Consultant Contracts

The contract you have with your consultants can be ongoing or single-purpose, depending on your requirements. Before you hire a consultant, it is a good idea to:

- Draft a contract or a letter of agreement. (Your consultant may also give you a letter of agreement.)
- Define your service requirements so your goals will be based on reality. Your goal may be to train a designer in the use of CAD. If so, explain to the consultant the type of work you expect the designer to be doing so that the consultant

can set priorities on what to teach. It may be more important to teach space planning than other types of drafting to this designer. By carefully defining your goals you will save a tremendous amount of your consultant's time—and your money.

■ State the starting and completion dates of the project. Every project has time limits. You should know how many hours the consultant will be working in order to plan your schedule and estimate your costs for the project.

■ Include a clause to cover any additional work or modifications that might be needed. For example, if the consultants are going to continue to advise on a weekly or monthly basis, or be available for telephone consulting, what will your costs be?

■ Outline what support the consultant will require. If the consultant works on-site, will an individual office be required? Determine the time, personnel, and physical requirements that will be necessary for the consultant to do the job.

■ Include a definition of termination. If you find that you are not happy with the consultant's handling of the project, you need to know how you can terminate the relationship. This should be defined before you start working together.

■ Spell out financial arrangements: the fee per hour or day, set fee for the assignment, or the reward in the case of negotiating a contract. If the consultants help get a contract for you, they might be paid on a percentage basis. Outline the payment schedule, listing exactly when the fee will be paid and what your obligations are so you can be prepared. Spell out which expenses and other items you will cover. These might include travel expenses and others incurred in relation to the job.

■ Be sure you have a confidentiality clause in your document. You are hiring a consultant because you want top-quality, up-to-date information and the best-caliber work. The products of your cooperative effort should be used only for your firm and not by competitors.

■ Determine up front the right of ownership of information or any products or sales developed from your relationship with a consultant. I make it understood from the beginning that when I use a consultant, this is my project, done for my client. I do the billing, and my consultant has no right to work for the client independently of my corporation.

■ Include in your agreement a right-to-advertise clause to prevent the consultant from using your company's name for promotional purposes without written approval. The consultant is usually permitted to list your name on a resume without consent, but this should be clearly documented in your agreement.

■ Include a statement regarding the legal process. It should be clearly stated that in the case of any litigation, the consultant is required to cooperate with your company. A consultant will usually want to put some kind of stop-work clause into the agreement, which means that if you do not pay at a given prescribed time, the consultant has the right to stop working. An appropriate up-front agreement is crucial with consultants. It makes for a better working relationship and helps eliminate problems later on. Even though you expect never to disagree, formulating the process in advance by which to disagree is always advisable. Considerations as to legal responsibility must be considered in each and every relationship we have. (Refer to issues relating to construction law in Chapter 11, pages 408–409).

CONSIDERATIONS

Find the best people, no matter where they are, to be a part of your team. You do not need to hire them as employees. You may engage them as needed.

There is a very strong trend toward larger firms that can move and perform quickly. You will see not only traditional firms but also virtual firms that are blends of professionals from all over the world. Technology permits us to work in this manner, and we will see more and more of it. You must be the best, and you must hire the best.

CHAPTER 6

Marketing and Selling

Marketing is the process of getting goods and services to a client. It can be divided into three major areas: market development, advertising and public relations, and sales.

Just as McDonald's has learned to sell hamburgers and hospitals have learned to sell medicine, interior designers need to learn to market and sell design services. We need to develop the communication techniques that work with the particular client group we seek, because it is the person who knows how to market and how to sell who gets the business.

A designer's business is to create interiors that are far above the levels the clients could accomplish themselves. Clients expect us to solve the problems they cannot or do not want to solve on their own. It is the designer's job to identify the problem, and through knowledge, technical skill, and experience, show the client how to solve and expedite the situation. To sell their services, interior designers must show that they are businesspeople who understand construction and appropriate schedules and budgets. Only an informed consumer can differentiate between partial service and full service, unqualified and qualified designers; and it is up to us to educate the consumer through marketing. The longstanding method of obtaining new clients through word of mouth is no longer adequate, even for firms that have been in business for decades. The majority of design firms rely on referrals as their major marketing tool, but referrals are usually not enough to keep firms working to their full potential.

Marketing and selling is the process of building a relationship between the right client and the right firm. It is important that the type of marketing you do represents the type and quality of work you are looking for.

MARKET DEVELOPMENT

To maintain your business activity and required growth three years into the future, you have to seek new business now. Marketing is an effective tool for controlling short-, middle-, and long-term development.

The first and most important part of marketing is establishing your company's overall goals and defining its strengths and capabilities. You can then identify which strategies you need to achieve your objectives.

Before beginning your marketing program, answer the following questions:

1. What is the size of your firm, and what is its general organization?
2. What types of employees do you have, and what are their areas of expertise?
3. Who is the person in your firm responsible for your marketing efforts?
4. What are your firm's strengths?
5. What are your firm's weaknesses?
6. How do you expect to overcome these weaknesses?
7. Who will carry out your firm's marketing efforts? List what is to be done and who will handle it.
8. Which selling tools are available to you, and which ones will you need to acquire?

The most costly mistake marketers can make is to place their entire emphasis on existing or prospective clients and overlook their firm's capabilities. Review the work you have done. Which parts are very easy for you to do with excellence? Do you have the right team and resources to do the work profitably?

Finally, for market development to be effective, it must be a highly systemized, structured process, with exact schedules and reviews of each part of the client interaction—from the first contact through proposal writing and follow-up.

Market Research

Your market is your actual and potential clients. Today, most interior designers need to develop business, and a prime tool for doing this is market research. The purpose of market research is to identify additional business areas and evaluate effective ways to secure business in these areas. The effectiveness of basic market research can be quite significant in proportion to the time and effort put into it. The business activities that make up market research include analyzing and understanding consumer circumstances, economics, and attitudes; it is also knowing the competition and being aware of relevant government regulations. The ability to recognize early trends is as important as knowing the current situation.

All marketing is guesswork. However, the more information you can acquire in your research, the more scientific and profitable your marketing becomes. It is possible to hire someone to do all or part of your market research, but very few interior design firms are large enough to afford this luxury. Those that are large enough may wish to consult *Bradford's Directory of Marketing Research Agencies*, which lists market research firms, their principals, number of employees, and the type of market research they do.

Investigating the Competition. To exist in the marketplace, you need to know your competition. It is relatively easy to find out what your competition is doing just by being observant. As interior designers, we have the ability to know what was done on a project and how just by looking at it. In addition, many times clients, friends, and other people will give you information.

Competition for the interior-design dollar has become increasingly aggressive. Published surveys rate interior design as the highest paying of the design professions, over architecture, landscape architecture, and engineering.

The competition comes from all directions—from large architectural firms with small interior design departments to spouses of the CEO and the office supply distributors that suddenly announce they have a design department. Even the manufacturers themselves offer competition. Some are qualified; others are not.

Often, designers are not competing with their peers, but with people who may have minimal, if any, design training. Many of these newcomers are unaware of the scope of interior design, do not provide full service, and can undercut professional interior designers' prices as a result.

We need to maintain rapport with our design competition and to work with them, if possible. It is usually best not to talk down a competitor; instead, show a potential client how your design services are exceptional.

Identifying the Client. At one time, marketing was considered selling a product to a client. Today, marketing is determining who needs what you have to sell. Is the product or service saleable? Is the client ready for this product or service at this particular time? Professional designers should pinpoint their marketing area. It is quite costly to blanket the field; even a large design firm cannot afford to do this.

Set geographic limits for your marketing efforts. Ask yourself the same questions you would ask yourself in deciding on a location for a new business (see pages 74–77). Being where you are visible and where there is work makes marketing easier.

Identify the kind of person you want to attract as your potential client. If your focus is hospitals, it would be foolish for you to allocate research funds or marketing energy in residential areas.

Sources for Jobs

Every interior designer has many sources for potential clients. The following list of prospects should always be considered.

Referrals. Be referable—do quality work, and establish client-friend relationships so you become a firm clients will be happy to refer to. The best source for new clients is referrals. Because design is a sizable investment, prospective clients are wary of hiring interior designers without knowing something about them.

One of the best prospecting methods is to review your present work to see if there are contacts from these jobs who can help you to get more work. No job stands alone. There are always other jobs that can come from every completed job. The clients for whom you have done satisfactory work are excellent referral sources—if you keep in touch with them. Ask them if they would be willing to write testimonials for you or case studies based on their projects. These can often be published or mailed to prospective clients. Call clients and ask them to give you an overview, either through an interview or a written comment, or just ask what they thought of your job.

Anyone who uses an interior designer creates a demand among friends and acquaintances for design work. These people probably do not want exactly what the others have; they are potential clients.

1. **Friends.** Some people work well with friends, while others prefer an arm's-length relationship. You alone can determine whether you wish to work with friends, but many designers begin their careers this way.
2. **Interprofessionals.** Engineers, architects, and other professionals in design-related fields are excellent sources for clients. They often have jobs that need interior design services.
3. **Contractors.** Interview both general contractors and subcontractors to find out the type of projects they are working on and whether there are any opportunities for a design professional.
4. **Manufacturers, representatives, wholesalers, supplies, distributors.** All have salespeople in the field and are aware of future projects. These groups can be excellent sources for the interior designer to develop.
5. **Business development organizations.** Every region has several organizations dedicated to business development. The Chamber of Commerce is a traditional one, but there are many more. Some handle only business development for special groups, such as minority-owned firms.
6. **Government.** A major purchaser of design services and products today, the government is a special type of client with specific communication requirements, both in qualifying for a project and in documenting the job. In order to formulate the appropriate approach, you may want to attend one of the courses given by the Small Business Administration or other localized business development organizations. These organizations have prepared up-to-date guides and contact lists.
7. **Government officials.** Often, the officials within a community are aware of new building projects and new industries coming into the area.
8. **Owners.** Owners of any large project, such as an apartment building or an office building, are excellent sources for learning about new tenants. Normally, the owners are interested in maintaining a good standard within their building and so are happy to share this information.

Networking. It is often said that what counts in business is not what you know but who you know and how you use those contacts. The process of developing and using your contacts for informal advice and moral support as you pursue your career is called "networking." It is a popular and valuable tool for interior designers, because, through networking, you can learn about jobs, people, and situations that credit reports don't cover. With a good networking system, it's easier to find the right type of client.

Some networking relationships may be quite profitable, but not all are effective. Time spent networking is an investment. Is the return adequate? If it is not, perhaps you have the wrong networking group.

People tend to label almost any interaction as "networking." However, effective networking must have a goal, a strategy, and a direction. Set as your goal that in the next month you will meet a certain number of people: prospective clients, suppliers, contractors, competitors, and perhaps a few masters in the field. Allow yourself a specific amount of time to make these contacts and then make use of mealtimes, or even exercise periods, to interact with these people. Then write out a networking program for the next 12 months.

The basis for a good networking system is your list of friends, your telephone book, your correspondence files, and even your address book. This is your current group for normal interaction. If you can, separate these lists into personal and business acquaintances.

For networking to be successful, you should follow these guidelines:

1. **Meet business contacts on a regular basis.** To do so, plan events and situations to occur on an average of once every four to six weeks throughout the year. In addition, go to events, either alone or with someone from your group. Go to seminars, workshops, meetings—any kind of an organized program. You will find that at almost any community meeting you end up speaking with new people or renewing an acquaintance. Exchanging updates on what each of you has been doing paves the way for more useful conversation.

2. **Make the first contact.** Do not be afraid to say hello to someone or call a person about a situation. People are usually flattered that you have taken the time to call them.

3. **Ask the right questions.** You can probably acquire some information about anything just by contacting four or five people. Just ask: "Who do you know that could do this particular craft?" or "Where can I find this item?" People like to be asked questions. They enjoy being considered authorities.

4. **Network with your competitors.** Many designers see other designers solely as competitors. I do not. Other designers help us get jobs because they create an audience of people who want design services. No one's services are appropriate in all situations. Talk to your competitors. There are many ways to share information without jeopardizing your business. Good relationships with your fellow designers can save you a lot of aggravation and money, just in shared tips.

5. **Stay in touch.** You must keep in regular contact with anyone with whom you want to build a networking relationship. Sometimes it is better not to start a

relationship if you cannot keep it up. Keep in contact with people on a once-every-four-to-six-week basis. Often, a short note or a phone call is all that is needed. If they are not available, leave a message. Just make sure there is some kind of contact on a regular basis so that when you do need special information from these people, they remember who you are. Then they are usually happy to respond.

6. **Send birthday and anniversary cards.** If you can, learn the dates of your contacts' birthdays and anniversaries and send them cards. A number of professionals organize these mailings on a yearly basis, with all the cards addressed and ready to go on January 1. Their assistants then put the cards in the mail on specific dates to ensure that they reach their destination at the proper time. If you cannot organize these mailings on an annual basis, do it at least on a monthly basis. Keep a book with these special dates and names in it. Many well-known businesspeople seldom get a birthday card, so when they do get a special card, a few flowers, or a small gift beautifully wrapped, this makes a great impression. They will remember you, sometimes years later.

7. **Send thank-you notes.** When people do a favor for you, send a note thanking them. Saying thank you is important, but you will make more of an impact if you also send a handwritten card. All it has to say is something like, "Thank you for the favor you did for me last Tuesday."

8. **Promote others.** In introducing people to other people and recommending them for projects, you accumulate goodwill. It is always good to be owed a favor. When I meet people who are good in specific disciplines, I make a point of trying to help them progress as far as possible within their given field. I try to have them meet the right people in the right situations—and I expect them to recommend me in return.

   Reciprocity is expected when you give a person a reference. A designer I know in Arizona recommended a landscape architectural firm so successfully that the firm received 20 jobs at one time as a result, but he got no client referrals in return from the firm. When he mentioned this to the principal of the firm, the principal was supportive, but still no jobs resulted. As it turned out, the landscape firm simply did not understand enough about interior design to be able to promote any designer. So the designer started looking for a more reciprocal situation. Sometimes, it's not that the firm does not recommend you; it is that the firm is not capable of selling you.

9. **Try to enlarge your networking system.** Usually, everyone you can introduce to your network makes the system a stronger and more valuable marketing tool.

Getting the Right Jobs

You must determine which clients are worth approaching and how much is appropriate to invest in each individual project.

Larger projects and continuing commissions are the most financially desirable; but, remember, many firms are going after those jobs. Sometimes the most lucrative projects come from smaller clients, with whom the principal of your firm has taken the time to develop rapport. These clients appreciate the attention and are often willing to reward the designer, both financially and with good design opportunities.

Review your success in getting jobs. If you are trying for jobs in a certain area, and you have lost the last six or eight, you are either going after the wrong jobs or you need to review your whole marketing presentation.

> Taking the wrong job can destroy your firm. There is no faster way to ruin a project and diminish your reputation than by taking on a project that is beyond the capability of your firm or is inappropriate for your firm. It is exciting to move into a new area, but do not jump into it before you are ready to handle it.

Source of Market Information. A lot of market research can be done from the materials available from the government. Look in "Government Publications and Their Use," available from Brookings Institute, 1775 Massachusetts Ave. NW, Washington, DC, 20036; or go to www.brook.edu. Another popular source is the "Guide to U.S. Publications." To order government publications, write to the Federal Consumer Information Center, Pueblo, CO, 81009; or go to www.Pueblo.gsa.gov. All publications of the Government Printing Office (GPO) are on sale through the FCIC in Pueblo. The GPO Web site at www.access.gpo.gov/index.html can tell you what is available. The Small Business Administration and the Department of Commerce Field Office are other good sources of information.

For the most specific information, define your market group. If your specialty is residential design for the highly affluent, you should read the social columns and announcements in many publications to watch the social movement of your potential clients. Designers who specialize in space planning for large offices might want to add *Commerce Business Daily* to their reading lists. This publication lists government jobs being put out for bid.

It is important for the interior designer to be aware of general economic trends, as well as specific developments and directions of the organizations that may require design services. Publications that are helpful include:

- *Wall Street Journal*
- *Barron's*
- *BusinessWeek*
- *Forbes*
- *Time*
- *The New York Times*
- *The National Observer*

Other local papers published by statewide business organizations, such as *Business Magazine* and *Banking Magazine*, and magazines related to each individual dis-

Qualifying the Job and the Client

There are several key items you should look at in qualifying a job from a potential client:

1. Is it the right type of job for you?
2. Is it the right-size job?
3. Is there opportunity for professional growth? Does the job offer new challenges?
4. Is the prospective client accustomed to making decisions?
5. Is the client reasonable—or overly demanding? Check with a number of other designers or contractors who have worked with this client to get a feel for what the client is like. If the person has an ego problem and needs boundless support, the job may become too time-consuming and difficult to handle.
6. Is the timing right, or will you have to rush to prepare your proposal? Usually, a poor proposal is worse than no proposal.
7. Does the client pay bills promptly? Does the client have a good credit rating, and is the client willing to meet the requirements?
8. Is this particular prospective client connected with any special competitor of yours? If prospects have a relative or friend in the design business to whom they have given previous business, it is probably not worth pursuing this client to any great extent.
9. What will it cost you to develop this particular client? Is it worth it in relation to the payoff of the potential project?

cipline in which you are working can also be valuable. Newspapers and magazines should not be underestimated as information sources, for they are media to which our clients are constantly exposed.

Read what your prospective clients read. If you are to work in a specialty, you must have an understanding of the current issues and changes within that specialty.

Two other publications you should read are *Standard & Poor's Industrial Surveys* and the *Dodge Reports. Standard & Poor's Industrial Surveys* analyzes trends in construction, utilities, retailing, and transportation.

McGraw-Hill publishes the *Dodge Reports,* which are available for specific geographic areas. This is an excellent outline of the buildings under construction within a given area, the firms that are designing them, the details of the contracts, and the other professionals involved in the projects.

Most of these publications are available online or in your local library's business section.

Your Marketing Staff. Traditionally, most market development was done by the principals of the firm; today, however, the client development process has become so extensive that it is impossible for the principals to be active in the design process and handle all the market development as well. These are really two completely different functions. It is better to have someone specifically devoted to the marketing function. The person handling the marketing division must have both a good knowledge of the design field as well as excellent interpersonal skills. This combination is very difficult to find. The person responsible for marketing often influences the design decisions because of his or her liaison with the client.

Small firms that cannot afford a full-time marketing employee may choose to use a part-time person to keep the program on target. The most important function of the marketing person is to have a consistent program and to work at it regularly. This is not something you can do only when you need new business. By then, it is usually too late.

PUBLIC RELATIONS

The field of public relations comprises those business functions concerned with informing the public of your abilities, activities, and policies, and attempting to create a favorable public opinion. Public relations can include hiring a publicist, but for most interior designers it consists of personal interaction, such as attending community functions and inviting the public to see their work.

Public relations has three purposes:

1. To make you known to your resources.
2. To make you known to your peers.
3. To make you known to potential clients.

You tell people about your firm with your studio, your personal appearance, your business card, your stationery, the community meetings you choose to attend, your portfolio, and in many other ways. Public relations is not orchestrated for you; you engage in public relations with each client contact—even with the way your telephone is answered. The goal is to present yourself in a favorable light. Research shows it takes a minimum of 7 to 10 contacts to build enough rapport with a prospective client to be able to sell to that person.

A professional publicist directs a public relations campaign from a palette of resources and techniques, choosing those that best suit the client. Public relations is labor-intensive. Choose activities that suit your skills and personality, and they will become part of the way you do business.

Fundamental Public Relations

You can contribute tremendously toward improving your firm's public relations through the following activities—which demand only time:

1. **Provide the best service possible.** Clients will usually return to you and give you good recommendations.
2. **Call on potential clients.** Visit developers and other people you know who may have contracts available.

3. **Talk to current clients.** See if they will introduce you to other people who could be good prospective clients.

4. **Attend every event possible within your community.** Try to be very visible within the community where you want to develop business. Be seen at places where you feel your clients will be. If you are interested in a sport or cultural activity, be a regular supporter and meet everyone there. Taking part in community affairs is an excellent way to show your future clients you are interested in their lifestyle—that you not only approve of it but are a part of it. Many designers have acquired their total client list by being active in community affairs. It is important, however, to become active in an area in which you are really interested, as well as one that offers a good source of clients. One word of caution: Watch your position on controversial issues. As a general rule, it is not good marketing for an interior designer to take sides in public. Some people are very active in political and highly controversial social issues, and they will judge you by your position on these issues.

5. **Go to various conferences or seminars and sit with your prospective clients.** Do not sit with other designers or professional people; you want to appear accessible to your clients, not exclusive.

6. **Meet people. Schedule lunch meetings.** Some designers have breakfast, lunch, or dinner with a different prospective client every day. Getting out there and meeting clients is very important.

7. **Be aware of your personal appearance.** People may make a decision whether or not to retain you as a professional designer based on your personal appearance. You should try to develop a personal style that will be attractive to the types of clients for whom you will be working.

8. **Learn to advertise yourself.** It is easy to forget how important it is to be visible. Become an authority on something. A number of designers I know have developed a personal interest and become world experts. One expanded her expertise in Art Deco at a time when few people shared this interest. Through her lectures on this subject she was able to get jobs in other parts of the United States, as well as other parts of the world. Without that special interest, those exposures and opportunities would never have been available to her.

Many designers donate their services to charitable organizations. I think it is important to submit a bill with your donation for one principle reason: to let the client realize the value of the services that you are donating. Very often, designers will donate many hours or weeks of their time to a community organization, and the organization will feel it is getting something that took no effort or was of no financial value. If these organizations get a bill, and perhaps even a quotation ahead of time stating, in effect, that you are donating so many thousands of dollars worth of your services, you will receive proper recognition for your contribution to the project.

The Tools of Public Relations
Good public relations require you to spend at least a modest amount of money on certain promotional tools. Your public relations budget should be a predetermined

amount. The figure generally budgeted for promotion is 3 to 5 percent of gross income (not gross sales), although some consultants suggest 5 to 10 percent. I suggest you put this money aside specifically for promotion to ensure that you have future jobs. New businesses usually need the largest budgets.

Your Business Card. One of the first things each client sees is your business or calling card. This should be regular in size and include the basics of all business cards: name and title; telephone numbers (with area code); e-mail address; Web site address; company name; type of business; and logo (if you have established one). To eliminate any one of these items may cause problems at a later date. Your business card is your insurance that you are represented properly when you or your staff cannot be there in person. Great care should be taken to make sure it is accurate.

Your Stationery. Your stationery should be of a standard quality and color. Use reasonably well-designed stationery and business cards; it is attractive when the two coordinate. Note: It is important to use someone who is qualified in graphic design for designing both your stationery and your business card.

Letters of Interest. Sales letters are an important medium for everyone. Since every firm has stationery, these letters are a personal way of directing your particular business to the attention of good prospective clients. Your letter should:

1. Suggest that you understand the client's problem.
2. State your standard practice of working.
3. Set a date for a follow-up call. Be sure to follow up on the letter; otherwise, there is no point in sending it out.

Figure 6.1 (page 141) shows a sample letter of interest.

Your Portfolio. Whether you are a beginning designer or an established professional, your portfolio is an important part of your professional presentation and must be updated constantly. This does not mean some of your older designs cannot be included; it means you must have the portfolio in readiness at all times, and it must be reasonably representative of your work. Initially, it might be the portfolio you created in art school.

Your portfolio or design presentation may include slides, photographs, and brochures. Its style and presentation will vary according to your design specialty. Ideally, you should be able to adapt your presentation to your client's needs.

Your Web Site. Today, one of the most widely used and often very cost-effective methods for presenting portfolios and promotions is via the Internet. Some designers have elaborate Web sites, incorporating audio and video presentations to entice viewers and potential customers. Other designers use more basic, streamlined Web pages to gain a presence on the World Wide Web.

Figure 6.1   Sample letter of interest. A letter such as this can be an excellent way to bring your business to the attention of good prospective clients.

Dear Mr. Cross:

We understand that you will be interviewing design firms to help you renovate your health care facility. Our firm is interested in being retained for this project.

We have had a general interior design and space planning practice in Home City since 1982. During this time we have been responsible for a number of projects similar to yours, including the space planning and specification of furnishings for over 200 patient rooms and adjacent lobbies in two area hospitals, dental and optometric offices, and dormitories for 2,000 students at a residential college.

On most of these projects, in addition to providing the traditional design services, we also analyzed the space, developed the project jointly with the client, and supervised the contractors as well as the installations.

You will be particularly interested to know that on the hospital projects we worked with Stevenson Bros., a highly skilled general contracting firm with an excellent record in this state. We and Stevenson Bros. are prepared to collaborate again on your project.

Our staff includes specialists in planning and design, both of spaces and of furniture. In addition, we also have longstanding working relationships with several local structural and electrical engineering firms and the well-known architectural firm of Tower & Stone.

To tell you more about our firm we have enclosed a brochure, project fact sheets, and a magazine article about one of our past projects.

We look forward to meeting with you to discuss our qualifications in more detail.

Sincerely,

James Doe
President
Doe Design, Inc.

No matter what the Web site includes, be sure it provides at least core information about the business: firm name, studio or mailing address, telephone number(s), fax number, e-mail address, and the name of a contact person in the firm. Also remember the Web site provides the viewer with an image or impression of the designer and the designer's firm. A Web site does not need to be expensive and multimedia, but it should appear polished and professional.

When planning a Web site, be sure the Web address is easy for people to find and remember. Web addresses are unique to each entity and are registered as "domain names": A Web address for a designer may be as individual as the designer's name or the name of the firm. Keep the domain name short, simple, and yet reflective of the firm.

Mailings. Mailings are valuable to keep your name in front of the client. Anytime you have good information, send it out—let your clients hear from you. Send out a report and perhaps some photographs of the work you are doing.

Postcards are great. They are visual, and the client does not have to open an envelope. Postcards permit everyone to see your work as they pass through the family or organization.

Brochures. Folders and brochures are good advertisements. The formal brochure on heavy, coated stock paper is becoming increasingly rare. Technology permits you to create some very attractive and practical brochures in-house. Creating it in-house gives you the flexibility to produce only what you need, to design various brochures for different groups of clients or a specific brochure for a special client. Unless you are a very big firm, it probably does not pay to print a large quantity of brochures that may be obsolete by the time they are printed. Create a folder that coordinates with the graphics on your stationery. Into this folder, insert your card, a sheet of general statistics on what interior design is, and another sheet of information specific to the type of project and client you seek.

There are great advantages to being able to print things in-house. The key is to have a professional format to work with. There are graphic specialists today who will do this for you. Graphic artists realize they are not the sole producers of printing today. Many of them specialize in programs that are a cooperative effort, in which they create the "master," which you are then able to alter on an individual basis to fit your particular situation.

We are in the design business; therefore, clients expect everything we do to be well designed. We see so many in-house-generated graphics today that are poorly done and do not properly represent professional design. Have a professional graphic designer coordinate your brochures. He or she will do it in such a way that you will have the flexibility to switch photographs and add basic information that may be required for a particular client. Be sure all of your materials are appropriately coordinated and are representative of today's design world. Graphics have style, the same as fashion, and must be updated on a regular basis.

Letters of Commendation. When you receive letters of commendation from outstanding clients, ask them permission to copy the letter and send them to other prospective clients.

Some designers and architects send out letters of commendation as a regular mailing to prospective clients and past clients. Figure 6.2 and 6.3 (pages 143 and 144) show sample commendation letters.

Figure 6.2 Sample letter of commendation. A satisfied client will usually be happy to write you a letter such as this.

Professional Administrative Service
123 North Broadway
Stamford, CT 06900

Prospective Clients:

We chose the architectural and interior design firm of I. B. Designer and Association to design our office space and all public areas, as well as for the entrance to our new corporate storage facilities in Connecticut.

Our choice, we feel, was excellent. Mr. Designer's unique solutions to the almost overwhelmingly large spaces are pleasing to everyone who is working in these areas—a factor most important to me and my firm.

We are all very proud of our various new facilities, as is Mr. Designer. We would definitely recommend this firm to others for any project whatsoever.

Sincerely,

J. A. Smith
President

Public Relations as an Investment

There are certain public relations activities that can help bring your firm to the attention of potential clients.

Entertaining. Business entertaining is a very valuable marketing tool for designers. It is important to have a space to entertain in that represents your design style. If you cannot entertain in your own space, you should consider using your client's. I know several designers who make a point of entertaining in their client's spaces as soon as they complete a project. They feel this both compliments their client and shows pride in the project; it also shows potential clients the quality of work the designers do. It has brought them a gratifying number of new projects.

When selecting the place to do your entertaining, determine whether it reflects the image you want to present. We are in the image business. Make sure your space makes a positive statement about you.

Most entertainment expenses are tax-deductible, subject to some limitations, when the goal of the entertaining is to make a sale or achieve a definite business objective. You do not need to get the job in order to take the tax deduction, but you must prove you are working toward a specific job.

Entertaining has many advantages. Very often you and your guests feel more at

Figure 6.3 Another sample letter of commendation.

John and Elizabeth Jones
112 Country Club Road
Cincinnati, OH 19475

Professional Interior Design, Inc.
123 Front Street
Cincinnati, OH 19475

Dear Designer:

Elizabeth and I have been meaning to formally write and thank you for the wonderful contribution you have made to our family over the last three years.

Your talent, incorporated with your guidance and support, has provided us with two wonderful residences. Both are very different. Our city home, more formal, is easy and satisfying for our many activities, which include a considerable amount of entertaining. It's hard to believe, but we had more than 900 people here during the month of December. After all that "wear and tear," things still look great.
We love our mountain house as well. It is warm and so relaxing! We always feel equally at home here in the country. The personal touches you suggested give us the comfort we desire.

We both want to thank you particularly for the education we gained and the pleasure we experienced during the work process. We came to appreciate many of the skills and beautiful products you brought to us, since we understand their value.

You and your staff were very dependable, and their assistance was greatly appreciated. It was exciting and fun, and we now have two lovely residences we are happy to call "our homes."

We look forward to your continuing to work with us when we have needs for updates and changes.

With pleasure,

John P. Jones

ease. There is time to discuss design ideas and develop concepts. Telephone interruptions and other day-to-day problems can be put aside.

For a profit-oriented evening, limit your party to 8 to 10 people. When gatherings get too large, you do not have the opportunity to interact with your clients. Some designers entertain in a client's space before beginning a project. Other designers gain permission to give a party in a completed client space. Use your creativity in entertaining, but document what you spend so you have no problems with the IRS.

Estimates are no longer accepted; you must have receipts, and your program for the evening must be clearly defined.

Entertaining in your studio can bring positive results. Most interior designers have reasonably attractive studios; even small studios usually have one or two nice spaces or a conference room where people can gather. Try to bring clients and prospective clients into your space.

Having groups of people in for lunch or an early cocktail party is a low-stress way of marketing yourself and your firm. Invite people who might enjoy seeing what you are doing. Of course, you cannot expect people to take three hours to see everything you are doing or have done, but most people can spare an hour for lunch. Plan to keep your presentation or program short and to the point.

I try to have different groups of people in at least once a month. At times, we'll ask a former client to come as a catalyst or to bring along anyone else who might be interested in the kinds of projects we've developed.

When these groups are visiting, invite them to see any items you think might be of interest to them—a special book you have in your library, your new CAD system, or some new products you are trying.

Make sure they pass by a few samples of your work, either photographs or drawings, as they walk into the conference room; this stimulates interest. These informal gatherings introduce design services in almost a museumlike atmosphere—there is no perceived pressure to buy, only an effort to acquaint potential clients with a range of design services.

Show Houses. Show houses give you an opportunity to present your talents. They are a good way to expose your work to the many people who are interested in seeing quality furnishings or retaining a good designer.

Before you commit your firm to participating in a show house, find out which rules and regulations apply. Also check on the coordinators. Have they run a show house before? What are their responsibilities? Some show houses allow you to staff the rooms. Others insist your work speak for itself.

Show houses are expensive, which can be a major drawback to using this method of advertising. If you elect to participate in a show house, take the time to do it well to represent your design talent properly.

In metropolitan areas, many wholesale sources will supply designers with products to use in show house displays. This reduces the cost of doing the show house. The show house staff will have a list available of sources willing to supply paint, carpeting, furnishings, electrical fixtures, as well as many services such as paperhanging and carpentry. This list should be made available to you when you are negotiating to design a room within a show house. In small towns, these arrangements are not generally available, which makes the cost of participating in show houses considerably higher.

Show-house projects should be designed so they can be favorably photographed. When selecting your room, consider both the exposure to visitors and the photographic qualities of the space.

Contests. One of the easiest, least expensive public relations efforts is to enter the contests sponsored by design resources. Very often, you will be competing with fewer people than you might expect.

Most contests want photographs and drawings of actual installations, as opposed to conceptual drawings. In a competition, the quality of your photography can be as important as the quality of your design; you may want to take new photographs of a job. Even if you do not win, your work will have been exposed to magazine and newspaper editors, and may be published.

Publication. Get your work published, if at all possible, in local papers and consumer-oriented magazines. Publication in professional journals and magazines is not usually as worthwhile; these are read primarily by your peers and do not bring you work. Publication is only useful when your work is seen by prospective clients.

If you can, write articles for magazines; again, consumer-oriented magazines are the most valuable. Send your clients and prospective clients reprints of your articles or press releases that feature your studio.

Publicists

Is it worthwhile to hire a professional publicist? Yes, if you can afford to support a long-term campaign. Most publications have anywhere from a week- to a nine-month lead time, and people rarely act immediately on what they read. They may carry a clipping around for years before they can afford to hire a designer. Public relations is an investment in time as well as money.

Publicists are most useful when you consistently do spectacular work or have new products and ideas to sell throughout the year. When the requests for information and photography you receive from magazines and newspapers become so numerous that they interfere with your ability to run your studio, you need a publicist to sort out which requests deserve your personal attention. Most interior designers need a publicist on a one-shot basis, but publicists rarely work this way. They need a consistent flow of information to maintain credibility with their editorial contacts. Interior designers can rarely supply this, but their resources can.

Any large or national product manufacturer normally has a public relations program, for which they need examples of products in use. Carpeting, laminate, wallcovering, and tile manufacturers usually have their own programs. Sometimes the manufacturer of a fiber used in carpeting has a publicist. There are also associations of manufacturers with public relations programs, such as the National Association of Mirror Manufacturers, the Marble Institute of America, the International Linen Promotion Commission, and the Wool Bureau.

When a product manufacturer photographs a design project, it is usually because that product is predominant, if not exclusive. Some designers even specify their projects with this in mind. If your project meets the product manufacturers' standards and fills a need, they may offer photographs of it to a magazine, or include it in publicity packets going to newspapers and news syndicates. These publications will often then contact you for more information.

Designer friends of mine have seen photographs of their work appear on full pages in 10 or 12 magazines in a single month—and the publicity has cost them nothing except their time and effort. By working with your resources, it is possible to get the kind of exposure no interior design firm could afford.

If specific product manufacturers do not choose to publicize your work, and if your work does not fit any of the categories of available design competitions, this does not mean it cannot get publicized. However, you may have to hire the photographer and place the work with a magazine yourself.

Find out which magazines are appropriate for your special project and what their requirements are for publication. The American Society of Interior Designers (ASID) pamphlet "How to Get Your Work Published" (available on the ASID Web site at: www.asid.org/ASID2/resource/research.asp) includes a list of magazines that publish design work, along with their addresses, editors' names, and requirements. In all cases, it helps to double-check the editor's name with a phone call. A correctly addressed, well-photographed project will influence an editor in your favor.

Some magazines prefer to be approached by a designer rather than by a publicist. The editor can then contact the designer directly with questions and get specific answers in the designer's own words. This avoids having both questions and answers filtered through a third party.

ADVERTISING

At one time, it was considered unprofessional for interior designers and other professionals to advertise. The only advertising materials considered professionally appropriate were announcements and formal statements. Today, the stigma is gone, and everyone advertises. Designers have always placed courtesy ads in the printed programs of arts and other cultural events in their community, but today they also advertise to keep the firm's name in the public eye. People should be aware of your firm, beyond the fact that it exists. Ideally, your firm will be seen as prosperous, involved in exciting things, and obviously interested in the next big project.

Clients and prospects may remember your name but often not where they heard or saw it. It does not matter if it was in an ad, editorial, or some combination. With advertising, you have some control. You decide how the ad should look and where to place it.

Repetition is an important factor. Usually, it is more effective to run a smaller ad four times a year than a single large ad once a year. You should devise a plan that includes a budget, as well as a rough idea of what your ad will look like and what it will say about your firm. To get the most for your money, enlist the help of an advertising agency or someone who is familiar with media buying. An agency will help you develop and maintain a professional style. Interior design is a visual business, and potential clients expect us to look good in all our undertakings.

The Keys to Advertising

The goal of advertising is to create a clear awareness of your company and its unique selling proposition. But be aware that advertising probably will not produce immediate results, and this can be frustrating.

There is no perfect formula for effective advertising, but using the following tried-and-true methods will increase the odds in your favor:

- **Be consistent.** If you change the message, keep the look the same.
- **Be constant.** Repeat the same message.
- **Create a need.** Strike an emotional chord to sell what clients do not know they need yet—peace, tranquility, romance.
- **Be clear.** Say what you mean, and mean what you say.
- **Be different.** Promising friendly service or the best prices is overused.
- **Do not assume.** Do not make the mistake of assuming the public has knowledge of industry terms or services. Educate them.
- **Create campaigns instead of ads.** Emphasize a single point—powerfully.

Choosing the Right Publications

The market research you did for your business (see pages 64–70) defined what services you provide, your geographic area, and the type of customer you wish to attract. You will need this information to determine in which publications to advertise.

Although we see some very expensive and opulent ads for design firms in the *Architectural Digest,* the *New York Times Magazine,* and professional design publications that are also available to outsiders, these ads are not appropriate for all firms. Unless you have an international or national clientele, national advertising is not advisable. Your advertising campaign should reach the customers you want and can service. For most interior designers, advertising in regional and local publications is more effective. There are many regional design magazines. A trip to your local newsstand should produce at least two possible target publications. An added benefit is that the cost of advertising in regional magazines is much less than in national publications.

Repeating a full-page ad three or four times a year will usually give you sufficient exposure. A quarter-page (or smaller) ad should be run more often. If your business is largely residential, a national full-color ad in *Architectural Digest* will undoubtedly give you prestige; but unless you can afford to repeat the ad several times during the year, it is a long shot.

The Design of Advertisements

Regional and local publications will often help you design an ad at little or no cost above the price of typesetting. They will often incorporate elements from your stationery or brochure design.

While line drawings dress up an ad, using photography can be tricky. Only high-quality or professional photography will serve your purposes. In photographs, small imperfections can become major ones when the publication has a high print run.

An advertising agency can usually create the best looking and most effective ad for you. This is important, because interior design is a visual profession. Ad agencies are skilled in creating ads to meet the individual requirements of magazines and other publications. They keep information on file regarding ad sizes, type sizes, screen requirements for black-and-white photography, and separation requirements for color photography. They also keep a record of the circulation, demographics, and prices for ads in specific publications.

Do not go to anyone until you have worked out your marketing plan and have determined what you want to accomplish. The more specific you are, the better your advertising can be directed to meet this market. You will have to educate the agency or advertising consultant about the design industry and what makes your firm special. If you have not outlined what you want in advance, the education process can be lengthy and expensive. Mishaps include ads placed in the wrong publications, ads that do not fit the nature of the business, or ads that showcase the wrong aspect of your business.

Having a relationship with someone in advertising—the right agency—can be very valuable to you. You get the best value when you form a long-term relationship. An agency that sees what works, knows how you are progressing, and understands the idiosyncrasies of your business will become a valuable member of your team. And advertising will become part of your business process. As you work together, you will learn how many of your general activities can complement a good marketing and development program.

A 2004 survey by ASID of small and medium-size firms stated that designers who want to increase their business need to do a better job defining their place in the market and actively promote their sources. Most firms did very little or nothing to promote their business. The research indicated that the two most effective ways of marketing were:

1. *Internet and Yellow Pages. They generate a greater return than newspaper or magazine ads.*
2. *Networking. Maintaining contact with former clients and developing new clients to build testimony and referrals.*

In addition, designers need to provide consumers with better information on what they do as there is a lot of confusion about the role and work performed by interior designers.

Photography

How should you photograph your work? If all you need, say, is a visual record of contents to accompany an inventory for insurance purposes, a competent amateur can do the work for you. Camera technology has changed, making it easier for amateurs to take better photos. Digital cameras allow you to see your results immediately. If you do not like the photo, delete it and take another. On the other hand, a good photograph, which may be timeless, can take a lot of time to achieve. Record shots are usually taken using a 35mm camera, slow film, a wide-angle lens, and a tripod. Slow film will give definition and clarity to the photo; the tripod is a must with slow film.

The better the quality of the photography, the better your work appears to be. Take the time to analyze the quality of the work shown in national and regional magazines.

Keep a good picture story of your projects. With today's technology, even simple working prints can be made into a good before-and-after story. Your camera equipment does not have to be expensive or the latest thing in digital technology. Most photography can be digitized. Every day there are new possibilities in photography. The point is, you cannot go back and take a before picture when the project is finished. Sometimes, a detail of a project in the works can tell a great story about how designers work, as well as the part played by various craftspeople.

Excellent photography has an arresting quality. It takes hold of you and elicits a reaction on an elemental level. Good photography can manipulate the way you feel about a subject by changing the way you perceive it. The magic of photography is achieved with angles, lights, and the photographer's skill. An excellent source of information on the photography of interiors is Norman McGrath's book, *Photographing Buildings Inside and Out* (1993).

Cost. Photography of the type found in national shelter magazines and advertising requires an investment of several thousand dollars. Not all of your work merits, or even requires, this elaborate and precise a visual record.

You might try to get your client to agree to pay half your photography fee. Clients may be interested in having these photographs for many reasons: for their personal records; for insurance purposes; or, if the clients are a business or professional account, for use in their own marketing program.

Publication Requirements. Be sure to consider the final use of your photographs in determining whether you need transparencies, black-and-white shots, or color prints.

If you plan to submit photographs to a magazine for editorial use or advertising, you should first check with the publication in which you hope to be published to find out their particular requirements and standards for photography. Do not invest in a form of photography the particular publication you are targeting cannot use.

Creativity in photography is exceptionally important. If you are using a photograph for a magazine or publication, be sure it is properly laid out and well designed.

Magazines want something attractive. Even if you are forced to move furniture or alter your design, be adaptable when working with the photographer.

Photographers. I recommend you use professional photographers who are familiar with interior design work. These special photographers are available in most areas; their costs vary according to the locale.

Interior photography is an art form, an area of photography so specialized that books on photography rarely devote more than two pages to it.

How good a photo is depends on the photographer's eye for composition and knowledge of film, cameras, and lighting. An error in choosing film, lighting, or filters for a job can result in colors that are not true. Almost as important is the skill of the film lab. Sloppy processing in the film lab can give your colors unwanted casts.

The interiors photographer must compensate for unique problems. What you see when you look into a room is not what the camera sees. A camera's distortion of small spaces is so extreme that what is seen through the viewfinder as perfectly centered is, in fact, off to one side. This distortion can vary in degree from camera to camera (it is most problematic with point-and-shoot cameras) and in accordance with the distance between the subject and the camera. Skilled photographers know their camera and have learned to compensate.

You do not have to be a photographer yourself to get good results from a photographer, but you must provide some basic information. No matter how brilliant photographers are, they are not mind readers. If you do not tell them what you expect, do not be surprised when you do not get it. On rare occasions photographers are so experienced they will be able to tell you what is important about your space. But don't take the photographer's knowledge for granted; discuss what your needs are by answering the following questions.

1. Which spaces are the most important?
2. Does the room have a focal point?
3. What qualities do you wish to capture? Is there a mood you feel your work evokes? The photography can enhance or diminish this mood.
4. Do you need a photograph of the whole room, or will shots of certain areas be more effective? If you designed a table specifically to enhance a sculpture, for example, tell the photographer. If what you are selling is efficient use of space, tell the photographer. Otherwise, you may get photographs that do not help sell your work.

Interiors are not static works of art. They change with use; they weather and acquire marks of wear. A carefully placed display of collectibles may be shoved aside to make room for a stack of work brought home from the office.

Interiors are at their best during the first month after installation. Be sure your work is photographed correctly the first time; you are probably not going to get a second chance. If the work is being photographed for possible publication in a national magazine, bear in mind that it may take several days for the photographer to fine-tune the lighting and the angles.

Video

Video recording is an excellent and inexpensive tool. It is an effective way to document projects from beginning to end. With the help of technology, you can prepare a great presentation. People like to see not only the before-and-after shots but the process of accomplishing the project.

Clients enjoy seeing design videos and prefer video presentations to slide shows. Almost every household in the United States now owns a computer or DVD player, so sending your CD or video home with someone to review, or passing it around among a group of potential clients, can save you time in your initial sales efforts.

A collection of slides can also be worked into a video presentation. As with any brochure or marketing presentation, videos must be kept up to date. Video presentations are useful for approximately two years, after which time they need to be reworked to incorporate newer work.

Videos are inexpensive and really do sell. They can tell the design story like nothing else. You can include project before-and-after shots, collect material from a variety of projects, and include photos taken from design centers, showrooms, or the Internet. If you are doing a promotional video, keep it short—five to eight minutes in length—and have someone do the voiceover for you. You will have a more professional product, since a narrator can say things about your firm that would sound like bragging coming from you. Videos can be styled to fit your particular client's interest.

SELLING

The word "selling" has negative connotations to many people. No one wants to be sold to. We enjoy the process of acquiring. We love to own things with special value. Good selling involves the ability to create romance, to explain the special potential of a product. Selling interior design services requires finding a prospect with a problem, convincing the prospect you have the ability and experience to solve that problem, and converting that prospect into a client. Selling is building a relationship. Everyone, including physicians and attorneys, must sell. The best designer-client relationships are lifelong, so it is worth spending a lot of care and effort finding the right client and building the right relationship.

Although your portfolio and photographs can support your sales effort, what sells a job is your skill at communicating to the client the abilities of your firm to do the project.

Most people come to us with a need, or something they think they need, just as a person might go to a doctor and complain of a cold or the flu. It is up to the designer to learn enough about the client to make a good diagnosis.

How to Sell

Some interior designers are excellent salespeople. In the past, they might have been called "hucksters," but now we realize marketing and professional sales abilities are needed to get the right projects. Salespeople have to be very positive, enthusiastic, and proud to work for their firm. They know and respect the competition but believe that their firm will do a better job for the client. Most good salespeople are able to see a situation as the client sees it. They can understand and respect the client's opinions and work with that person without necessarily having to agree with him or her. Salespeople help develop rapport between a firm and a client. Because of their sensitivity to the client, they create an atmosphere in which good decisions can be made.

Good salespeople have a lot of drive. They must be willing to do whatever it takes to get a job. They have to be able to keep their enthusiasm level high; they can't allow themselves to be discouraged. Even after they have lost a job, they have to keep right on going, to try and win the next one.

A number of successful salespeople operate along the K.I.S.S. principle: Keep It Short and Simple. Good presentations are prepared with precision, but they are delivered in a very short, simple, and direct fashion.

There should be no surprises when you are trying to sell to a client. Make it easy and comfortable for your client. Encourage the client to ask questions. The more the client talks and the less you talk, the better it is. In a sales conversation, the client should talk 70 to 80 percent of the time, and the salesperson 20 to 30 percent of the time; this is the perfect balance. Try to encourage your clients to give you information, to tell you what they think is important. During a sales conversation, your ability and willingness to listen are crucial. So are your skills of observation. You can often pick up visual cues from the surroundings, from what the client wears, and from the client's body language.

Cold Calls. For many people, the idea of making cold calls is terrifying. That may be because they do not know how to do it. The trick is to make them warm, to find out about clients in advance, to get an understanding of who they are and what they want. There are so many ways of doing this. The theory of six degrees of separation—that you are only six people away from anyone you want to meet in the world—is true.

One Florida design firm specializing in banks has a remarkably high cold-call success rate. When the chief designer completes the design of a bank in a given town, he makes a point of visiting every other bank in the region and introducing himself. He will tell them about the bank he has just completed and suggest they stop by and visit it. He will also ask them when they will be ready to update. While visiting these other banks he is usually able to tell, just by looking around, what could be done in their spaces and what styles would be most suitable. For those banks he feels are his most likely prospects, he actually does the design preparation and budgeting without further contact or expression of interest. He then returns with the completed design and contract and generally sells the project in the same visit.

At one time, making cold calls was a viable way to get new business, but the process has been overused and abused, and today you have to tread carefully. In my book *Marketing and Selling Design Services: The Designer-Client Relationship* (1993), you'll find many systems of bridging and building a relationship between the designer and a prospective client. It is also worthwhile to spend some time attending a class or two on this subject. Seeing a good cold-caller in action will make it much easier to learn to do it yourself. Clients really want to know designers, but they also want to know you understand them and have respect for them.

The Emissary Method. When the principals of a firm are not able to do all of the market development, it can be effective to hire someone to act as an emissary. This person will preinterview prospective clients and size up the project and its general qualifications. The emissary will describe the design firm in glowing detail, telling the potential client about the principals in charge, the design staff, and the management group. Then the emissary sets up a time for a formal presentation, at which the emissary is present. By the time of the presentation, the emissary will have developed a friendship with the prospective client. An emissary will also assist in the communication between the client and the design team, will bring business to a firm, and will continue to look out for the interests of the prospective clients that he or she brought to the firm.

Client Attitudes in Buying Design. Some design jobs are sold purely on emotion, but the majority are sold to management-oriented decision makers.

What clients wanted in an interior designer 15 or 20 years ago is different from what they are looking for today. In 1980, most clients were looking for a total service organization with a lot of design know-how and high creativity. They looked at past projects, your availability to do the job, and, lastly, your prestige. Today, clients are not just looking for a designer. They are looking for a person they can relate to who happens to be a designer. This is the key to building that all-important designer-client relationship: Who are you, what is your value system, and how is it similar to theirs? They want to know why you are a good person to be around, because you will become a part of their life; therefore, it is necessary for the designer be a complementary personality.

After clients are confident you are the kind of person they want to be around, they look at your experience with their type of project, then at your experience with their firm. They next evaluate your ability to complete a project on time and within budget, and your accuracy in making estimates and specifications. Further down the list of their considerations is the kind of design work your firm does, the firm's quality of management, your enthusiasm, the size of the firm, and its in-house capabilities.

The Initial Interview

The initial interview is your client's first opportunity to see you as a person. Sometimes it can even be the client's first real contact with the interior design profession. It is also your first chance to evaluate the client. Ask yourself if you think it will be possible to establish the rapport needed for the duration of the project. Or does this person have personality traits that spell trouble?

Advance Research. Before the initial interview, try to find out as much about the prospective client as possible. If the client was referred to you, check with the person who gave the referral. You can find out a great deal about almost anyone. If you are going to invest your time in a project that may take many months or even years, you should research the client before the initial interview. Talk with the other professionals on the job: the architect, engineers, and contractors. You may have worked with some of them before. All this preparation helps you with the initial interview. You will know what questions to ask and, conversely, which subjects you should avoid.

Defining the experience level of a client is helpful. You may want to call a designer who has worked with the client before to find out how that collaboration went. A designer can tell you a lot with just a few sentences.

One of the most difficult things to do is to "qualify" clients. Too many designers continue to solicit business from clients who are impossible—either they do not pay or they are too demanding. Why not leave those clients for your competitors and spend your time and effort in finding clients who are the type of people for whom and with whom you want to work? Too many designers continue to solicit business from clients who are inappropriate to their practices.

Whether a project is residential or contract, do a credit check on the client (see page 356), and do it now. At first glance, most clients appear wonderful, but there may be hidden issues. Now is the time to find out about their credit history. You will also want to learn what the client firm's objectives are and who the other professionals involved in the project are. Who are the principals of the firm? Who will be in charge, and what are that individual's accomplishments and interests? Sources for this information include *Dun & Bradstreet* reports (see pages 406–407), conversations with contractors, and building reports (these list the contracts let on a building for construction, electrical wiring, and plumbing, and the budget for each). From this information you can get a working idea of the possible design budget.

The Prospective Client Report. When you are interviewing a new prospective client, there is some basic information you need to document. The prospective client report shown in Table 6.1 (page 156) is an outline for your initial interview. It includes a space to record the necessary basic information, such as name, address, and contact person. The report also provides space to list a definition of the project, the client's objective, and the results of the meeting. At the end of the form is a section in which to note the research or information you will need for the next meeting, the date of the next contact, and the general financial arrangements. Taking some notes during the interview is seen as professional, but writing all the time can be distracting to the client. Fill out the prospective client report as soon as you leave the client.

At the end of an interview or any business conference, I find it helpful to take out my tape recorder and explain to the client that I am going to summarize the meet-

PROSPECTIVE CLIENT REPORT	Referred By:
Client:	Contact Person:
	Position:
Address:	Phone No.:
New Address (if moving):	Directions:
Project:	
Objective:	
Result of Meeting:	
Research or Information Needed for Next Meeting:	
Date of Next Contact:	
Financial Arrangements:	

© *Design Business Monthly*, 1988.

ing. This is so my staff and all others working on the project will have the full details of the meeting. At that point, I review my notes and dictate a detailed summary, which the client may correct or add to. This has proven very helpful through the years. It also gives me the basis for my next meeting.

Planning the Interview. The next step is to write out your objectives for this meeting. In an initial interview, you need to determine the scope of the project, the client's needs, the scheduling, the financial expectations, and any constraints. Before this meeting you should review the design service outline and meeting forms shown in Figures 6.4 through 6.12 (pages 211–224).

The location of the initial interview is a matter of personal preference. I hold my initial interviews on the job site so I can see some of the particulars and assess the client's experience. Seeing where and how clients live and work helps me determine their design standards. I gather all the visual clues possible. If clients say they want to redo an office inexpensively, I have no idea what they mean until I see the space.

If the room is done in one-of-a-kind pieces, and the clients say they want to scale down, I know I still have a workable budget.

Plan what you will wear to the interview. The way you look and dress is critical. If you appear to come from a different world, your clients may find it difficult to relate to you. You are there to create a connection, and the way you look is part of your presentation. Some of us are more comfortable in simple fashions; others prefer flamboyance. Your appearance must fit your personality and design tastes.

Leave nothing to chance. Make a checklist of topics you need to discuss, and take notes during the meeting. The design service outline (Table 8.1, page 255) is designed for this purpose. You may want to make some adjustments to fit your own practice (see pages 255–260). Not only does this save time but it also reinforces clients' belief that they are dealing with a professional. Your topic checklist must include carefully researched written cost estimates and a time schedule. If costs are revised later because of a substantial design change, put your financial expectations in writing. Most money problems between client and designer occur because the project has not been adequately defined. You build the designer-client relationship through careful observation, listening to clients, and stopping every so often to paraphrase what they have said and to ask for confirmation. It is critical to take in every bit of information, to review, question, and confirm. This is the foundation for a serious relationship.

Interview Techniques. The initial interview can tell you a great deal. Ask questions about the client, as well as what the client needs, wants, and can afford. Listen carefully to the answers; note the client's body language. At first, it is usually best not to offer an opinion or make a judgment; try to be neutral. Smile or nod, and use short answers such as: "Yes," "Sure," "Right," and "Of course."

- Has the prospective client ever used an interior designer before, or is the client acquainted with someone who has?
- Where did the client hear of your firm, and what does the client know about you?
- Has the client seen a space you designed, or spoken to a former client? If not, arrange for the client to speak to a former client in the same business the new client is in. Each profession has its own jargon and subject matter. It is important for clients to understand something about the design business and the scope of services available, and they will understand better if information is put in terms they use every day.

Observe. Question. Probe. Use state-of-mind probes, questions such as "How do you feel?" and "What do you think about this?" to draw out the prospective client. Use echo probes; that is, repeat what the client says to encourage him or her to expand on a theme. Or return to an issue you have already discussed, and ask a reflective question.

Does your language say what you mean, or is it open to interpretation? A single comment can influence or color the whole job. You should aim for simplicity and clarity in everything you do and say in an initial interview. Many clients do not understand the design field or its vocabulary. When discussing sizes, always relate them to an item the potential client has at home or in the office, something familiar the person can visualize.

If, during the interview, it becomes apparent the prospective client is not appropriate for your firm, bow out as gracefully as possible. No amount of money can compensate for the emotional and professional strain and physical upsets some people seem to generate.

The following interviewing techniques can help you to determine the acceptability of a client.

1. **Trust your gut reaction.** It is not always easy to spot the potential problem client, but the first rule of interviewing is to trust your gut reaction. Our initial responses to people are based on nonverbal clues. You can often sense a problem without being aware of the source or reasons.

2. **Probe the humor index.** What amuses us taps our deepest biases and values. Arm yourself with a few quips and funny stories. If your prospective client reacts blandly, the prognosis for a good rapport between the two of you is not good. If the prospective client responds negatively, it is definitely not good.

3. **Assess the empathy level.** Every designer has a story or two about something that went wrong on a job, whether through an "act of God," personal miscalculation, or factory error. Test the potential client's reaction to one of these stories. A person who says, "That had better not happen on my job!" or is overly critical of the event is probably a client you would want to send to a competitor of whom you are not too fond. Look for some expressions of sympathy or understanding—a viewpoint that reflects tolerance.

4. **Use the what-if probe.** This strategy is intended to determine the potential client's reactions to frustrations and disappointments. You might believe you can meet your client's expressed deadline, but you also know that things can go wrong. Using the what-if probe, you might say, "I'm pretty sure everything will be finished by Christmas, but I do not have control of every link in the chain. All sorts of things can go wrong—strikes, floods, factory errors—

One designer described a dream job he had turned down. The potential client lived in a well-appointed residence that was to be remodeled in a way that perfectly fit that designer's particular style. However, his initial interview at the prospect's home was interrupted by two phone calls, which the client took in the kitchen. He overhead her saying, "Sue him!" and "Do not take anything from him!" After he heard, "Take him to court!" two times, the designer knew he had to tread carefully because he was obviously dealing with a very litigious person. There was no guarantee he would not be the next person she sued that month. He learned later the designer who had accepted the work wound up embroiled in a lawsuit.

and these could delay completion. Being optimistic, I do not think they will. But what if they do?" Assess your client's reaction to predict how he or she might behave if a problem does arise.

5. **Listen to the prospective client's words.** The words you need to be most aware of are "should," "ought," "must," and "have to." The "must" and "should" types betray a lack of flexibility and a penchant for rage and unreasonable demands. Quite often, inflexible people have learned to mask their aggressive feelings with a façade of cordiality and superficial approval. But they cannot hide the manner in which their underlying hostilities slip out in their conversation. For example, "You must be sure that the project is completed by the fourteenth." The sentence may be said pleasantly, with a warm, friendly smile, but it contains the giveaway "must." Take notice.

There are many, many individual interview techniques. No matter which one you use, it helps to keep a list of the techniques that work for you on your interviewing sheet, with an outline of the questions you want answered.

Charging for the Initial Interview. Should you charge for the initial interview? In larger cities, designers will not consider going out to see a project without arranging for a fee. The amount of that fee depends on the part of the country. They have learned that clients will call four, five, or six designers and pick their brains and never do any serious work. Therefore, the policy of some designers is to charge in advance for a review of the project. There are other designers who say they would not walk out of the studio without being paid for their time. My usual policy is not to charge for the first interview, as this interview gives me an opportunity to look over the space and the situation and to determine whether I want the job. I have walked into a number of situations I felt were inappropriate to my practice. Because I did not charge, I felt free to walk out.

If you are going to charge, notify the client *before* you go out to the project site and clarify exactly what the charge will be. Some designers regard the initial interview as part of their marketing effort and do not charge—or charge a very small fee. If some-

As a consultant to design firms, I receive many phone calls on the question of charging for initial interviews. Designers say, "What do I do? I sent my assistant out there, and the clients were very nice. But then when I sent them the bill, they didn't want to pay it. Is my assistant not handling it properly?" I find these problems most likely stem from the fact that the management has not structured the situation properly. If getting paid for initial interviews is a problem, and you do not want to consider these interviews part of your marketing efforts, then state your fee in advance over the phone and in a written letter of agreement. This will save you a lot of aggravation. Remember that many of our clients have never purchased design services of any kind before and really do not know the customary procedures. Help them by giving them the price tag in advance.

one just wants a simple answer, you may be providing more of an on-site consultation. Make your policy clear before the interview. One way is to send out a written agreement stating, for example, "We will review your reception room for the change of wall color. Our consultation fee for that interview will be $600." Have the prospect sign the agreement and return it to you before the two of you meet.

The Presentation

When you make a presentation for a business or commercial organization, who should attend the interview? The principal of the firm usually needs to attend, as well as the person who will be responsible for the project itself—the project manager or the person who will be dealing with the client on a day-to-day basis. You might also consider including several expert consultants or other in-house staff members. If the presentation is for a small job, take two or three people. If it is for a larger job, you may take four or more people. However, be careful not to take along too many people; it is a general rule that you do not ever want to have more people on your team than the client has on the selection committee.

Usually, the client establishes the time and duration of the interview, allotting each presenter a half-hour, an hour, or two hours, depending on the issues to be covered. Then the client introduces the first design firm's chief executive officer or principal in charge, who then introduces the team and outlines the presentation.

Sometimes you will be given an opportunity to choose the order in which you fall in the presentation scheduling. The last position is ordinarily the best, and the next best would be the first position. The middle presentation position is usually the weakest spot.

At a team presentation, the principal generally makes the introduction and then immediately turns over the presentation of the project to the person who will be in charge of the project—the project manager—because this is person who will have the strongest and most direct relationship with the client. After that presentation, both the project manager and the principal answer questions. If the presentation is held in the design office, the principal might then give a tour of the offices, or the principal and project manager might take the clients on a tour of other similar projects.

The Agenda. Make enough copies of the agenda so that each member of the client firm who attends has one. Handing out copies of your proposal precludes members having to write down every detail; they will have the names and positions of each of the presenters, and some of the main items will be listed on the agenda as well. Leave space on the copies in case they want to take notes. The agenda usually should be bound or presented in a formal, attractive way.

Make sure the agenda has your company's name prominently displayed. The clients usually see many people during a proposal period; you do not want them to confuse you with some other design firm.

With your agenda, or after your presentation, you may want to pass out additional information on your group, such as magazine articles, newspaper articles, or brochures.

Should visual aids be used and, if so, what kind? A lot of people feel that the most deadly presentation is a slide show or PowerPoint display in a dark room. If you are going to use slides in presentations to very large groups, make sure any text on the slides is readable from at least 20 feet away.

Where should the interview be held? It can be held in the client's space, in your office, on the site of the potential project, or, if you can arrange it, at a completed project of yours similar to the one you hope to design for this prospective client. This can be an excellent way of showing off your work.

Presentation Techniques. Clients basically want to know who you are, what your firm does, how long you have been in business, where your office is located, what kind of services you are able to provide, and what types of consultants and other professionals you would be bringing to the project. They will want to know about recent jobs you have done that are similar to their project—and, if the projects were particularly successful, why? All new clients have some unique needs. First, they need to be sure they can work with you and you are the kind of person they want on their team. Then they are interested in quality, scheduling, and budget.

When making a presentation, you should try to relate whatever you present to the client's project. Clients are only interested in your past projects as they relate to their current project. In some of the most outstanding presentations I have seen, the designers have said, "Here is your problem, and this is our solution."

Clients like a designer who is on *their* team, who shows understanding for *their* viewpoint. Designers who have a similar background to that of their clients can do this more easily. Clients need encouragement from their designers. And often they need help understanding just how products work and how they will fit into their lifestyle—whether it is at their business, factory, or residence.

When you use any technology—be it fiber-optic lighting or ergonomic seating—you need to reduce the complexity of the technical data in your presentation so it is easier for your clients to understand.

It is not enough just to show clients how products work and how simply they can be operated; you must relate a product to the client's problem. Do not just tell a client a low-voltage lighting system is the solution; go through the system with the client: explain how it works, and then show it in actual use on a job site. Letting clients see the real-life applications of a product allows them to become comfortable with the new technology.

As designers, we often become so involved with new products and design ideas we think everyone understands what we do. This is not true. Take your cue from clients' space as to how much background and understanding they have about what you are presenting. Then find an easy way to present it. Use words your clients will understand; do not feel you have to use a professional design vocabulary.

You never endear yourself to people by embarrassing them, nor do you develop clients by embarrassing them. Make it easy for them to understand what you are doing. Make them feel comfortable, and you will never want for clients.

Do Not Embarrass Your Clients

This is something I learned early in my career. I was working on a large corporate project, and one of my client liaisons asked me to make a private presentation to him several days before I was scheduled to give my presentation to the board of directors. The project was a historic restoration, and my presentation showed I had done my homework. I described certain types of credenzas and cornices, and made liberal use of other design terms. After I used one such term, my client liaison stopped me and asked, "What does that mean?" So I explained. He gave this valuable advice: "Do not embarrass your clients. Do not make them have to ask you what you mean." I later read that only the smartest people explain things in the simplest terms. People who lack confidence are the ones who are most apt to use words others might not understand.

Should you show enthusiasm? There is a saying that enthusiasm indicates you will accept a low fee. Show you are interested in doing the job, that you want the job, but not that you do need the work. Generally, if you are too enthusiastic, prospective clients will worry you haven't been getting business, and they will wonder why.

Here are some tips to help you sell a project.

1. Make sure your presentation is thorough, very organized, and exciting. You will put the client to sleep with a dull professional presentation. You should appear intelligent, aggressive, and talented. Let the potential client realize you are accustomed to winning jobs.

2. Check with the client in advance as to how much time is available for your presentation; then structure it accordingly. There is nothing worse than preparing a presentation that takes three hours, only to find you have 30 minutes in which to give it. Such a situation can cause you to lose your orientation and give a poor presentation.

3. In making your presentation, say why a client's project is of interest to you, and show how many elements of the project are similar to ones you have handled before. Describe the expertise and knowledge of your staff, and explain how they will interact on the project. If other staff members are going to occupy a primary position on the project, it is important for you to have those people take part in your presentation. When the principal makes the presentation and then vanishes, leaving the job to be handled by staff members, clients feel neglected. They want to feel their project is important and in the hands of the best possible people. If you, as the principal, are going to be involved personally in the project, say so, and explain what your dedication will mean to the project.

4. Provide references from previous clients who have used you for similar jobs. Before going to an interview, I will often send my prospective clients a list of

previous clients and suggest that they speak to those clients before we come for our presentation.

5. Explain how your design firm is different from competitors. What are your strong points? What can you offer the client that other studios cannot?

6. Put your most important information on the first page of your agenda, and make it very easy to read and understand. Remember that what you write will be read by every person on the selection committee. Is it clearly stated? Have you presented your company as you had intended? Have a capable person review your proposal to make sure it is stated in an appropriate fashion and that there is nothing that might be misunderstood.

7. When making a presentation, speak up so everyone in the room can hear you.

8. Dress in businesslike clothing. Generally it is better to be a bit on the professionally neutral side than to seem too artistic. However, what is appropriate depends on the type of design that you are presenting. Not everyone expects to see you in a banker's suit.

9. Go over your presentation; rehearse it; and try it out on everyone you can before the actual presentation day. Practice until you feel very comfortable with the presentation. If you have the opportunity, videotape yourself, and see how you are coming across.

10. Be aware there is almost always someone in the selection group who does not want to hire you, someone who really has it in for you. All you can do is present your team in the best way possible.

11. Give the client something in advance. Prepare an analysis, build a model, draw some sketches, or take some photographs. Try to give the client something that shows you have put in effort already. In many states in this country, as well as in Europe, architects and designers often completely design a space before being awarded the job. I am not sure how they can afford to do this, but it happens. Even if you are not doing a full presentation, try to make the client feel that you have taken time on the project.

Presentation Costs. Generally, interior designers will spend about 4 to 10 percent of their fee to get a job. This figure includes money spent on general promotion, plus the direct marketing expenses for special projects. Established firms usually spend approximately 4 percent of their fee. However, with new firms, this percentage is often as high as 10, 15, and even 20 percent. The newer the firm, the more it costs to get projects.

Negotiating

When situations come up that require special negotiating—such as a client who wants special handling on a project, a better price, or an adjustment in a quotation—it is best to turn the negotiation over to someone else within your company. Should a situation arise that cannot be amicably handled, it is a good idea not to have a salesperson in a position to be blamed. It is best to let the salesperson continue to be the good guy. Do not have the salesperson deal with the problems of the client to whom he or she is attempting to sell.

Sharing these responsibilities, even within a small firm, works to your advantage. The client realizes there is another administrative person handling decisions, which makes your design firm appear to be much more professional. Even if you are making the decision yourself, and you are one of the chief executive officers, it is best to turn this kind of interaction over to someone else in the firm.

Closing the Sale

One of the most difficult parts of selling is to know when and how to close. Have a list of leading questions ready. Prepare questions that cannot be answered with a yes or no; this will require the client to give an extended answer.

You might say: "Now that we've reviewed your plans, what other questions do you need answered before you are prepared to make a decision on the project?" Or: "If we are the selected designers, when would you like us to start work?" Other good questions are: "What are your scheduling plans, so we can alert our studio to reserve time for the appropriate people required for this job?" "When will you need your plans and specifications?" "Shall we start working on the final designs for you?"

If you do not get a positive response to these questions, go back over the preliminary portion of your presentation to make sure they understand your position. Attempt to reorient or resell the project.

It is important to keep an itemized list of every point you have discussed on a project, as well as the results you have achieved. If you have been summarizing on tape in the client's presence at the end of each meeting, you are using a good closing tool. That confirms where you are and what their goals are. File this list so you can refer to it during future contacts.

Sometimes designers lose a project because they oversell. The client is ready to buy, and the designer talks the client out of it. Losing a sale can sometimes happen simply because the designer neglected to ask for the job.

It takes an average of 7 to 10 calls to develop a client, and some designers stop too soon. You should try to establish a date for calling a client before you leave the person's office. You might say: "I will call you at the end of the month, and I will have these other details ready for you at that time." On the prospective client report shown earlier in Table 6.1 (page 156), there is space for information or research to be done before you see a potential client again. You may want to use a "tickler" file to remind you to call people at the appropriate times.

Debriefing

Debriefing should be done whether you get the job or not. Do it while everything is fresh in your mind. One of the best ways you can develop your firm's standards is to understand why you lost a job. This review is probably one of the most effective learning methods there is. If you have made a presentation on a project, and you suspect or know someone else got the project, follow up. Call the client and find out why your firm was not chosen. Before you call or speak with the client, however, prepare a list of questions you want answered, so that you can keep the conversation short—only a few minutes long. Reading from a predetermined list also lets the client know the call is a standard procedural one used to evaluate your position in the field.

First of all, ask how the client made the decision, and who was selected for the project. Then ask how your presentation compared with the others and what the client thought of it. Finally, ask the client whether your firm could be considered for any other projects the client has planned.

It creates goodwill to talk to the prospective client who decided against using your firm, to say you are pleased the person made a decision. You congratulate the client, and add that you would like to work with the person in the future should the opportunity present itself. Your goal is to leave the client with a pleasant and positive impression of you and your firm. You are disappointed professionally but not angry you did not get the project. You will not let losing this project stand in the way of your being considered for another project.

CONTRACTS AND LETTERS OF AGREEMENT

A contract is one of the most critical documents to an interior design firm, as it can either make or break a project. It must be written in appropriate legal terms, although most designers prefer to see it written as simply as possible. To ensure that your contract is appropriately designed for both your firm and your client requires a cooperative effort between the management of your firm and your legal consultant. Each client is different. Whether the agreement is formal or informal in style is not the issue. You need to clearly state what you mean, whether in technical terms or using other terminology.

Before accepting contracts from large corporations, where the client writes the contract, your attorney needs to review both the client's contract and your contract to ensure they are in harmony. I have seen contracts written by clients that are over 150 pages long. The costs of properly reviewing these may be more than the contract is worth, and it is important to choose an attorney to review this type of document who is familiar with the type of work the firm does.

At least once a year you should review your projected design ambitions and your legal positioning to be sure your contracts reflect where you stand.

When you determine the services your firm will offer a client, review your contract carefully to be sure your firm is able—both practically and legally—to provide the services for which you are negotiating. It is more prudent for a design firm to offer fewer services—but ones it can confidently perform—than to offer services that may put the firm in jeopardy.

General Provisions

When preparing a contract or letter of agreement, be sure to include the methods for completing the project—how it is going to be contracted. Make it clear in your contract whether you will be responsible only for the design and the specifications writing, the supervision of the project, or the coordination of the complete turnkey project. The financial formats also need to be included.

Also, review and define exactly which areas are to be designed. If you have agreed to do three offices and the client has decided to add three more, you will need to prepare a different contract or proposal or include an addendum to the first.

When preparing a contract, carefully review with the client the exact scope of the project, to identify your responsibilities when there are other design professionals involved. Define their precise responsibilities, as well, and clarify how any overlapping responsibilities will be handled.

A contract that is going to involve other architects or contractors should clarify exactly which items are included in your fee. For example, a phrase in your contract could state that you are involved with the selection and detailing of items—including lighting fixtures, wallcoverings and paints, floor coverings and finishes, custom hardware (whether it be plumbing or other decorative hardware)—therefore, all cabinetwork that is included for any areas, built-in or other custom woodworking or doors, will be covered under the fee for interior design services. It should also state that, although these items may be purchased by the contractor, the percentage-of-fee billing does apply to them.

State your firm's position regarding purchasing and fee schedules. For example, if a client of ours purchases items involved in the implementation of the interior design, which is part of the design, our office will assist in any way possible with these purchases. But it is understood that our standard design fee will apply to these purchases as well as to the items purchased through our studio. This includes items purchased through other contractors or individually, as they are specified, and items purchased for the room at a later date.

It is important that proposals state a time limit through which the prices are good, usually 10 to 30 days. If the client does not make a decision and sign the contract within this period, the project will be delayed. Since prices and terms are constantly changing, the designer will need to review the items again for pricing and availability. This may take considerable time. Include in your contract the fee to be charged for additional time if the contract is not accepted within the time limit.

Ways to Prevent Lawsuits

Major disagreements between client and designer usually arise from a breakdown of communications; unfortunately, that can lead to lawsuits. To prevent lawsuits, assume nothing and document everything, in contracts or letters of agreement. Here are a few suggestions:

1. A design contract should clearly describe the services to be rendered and the extent of the designer's responsibility. Generally when a contract document

Are Letters of Agreement Really Binding?

Do we really need to use contracts like those of AIA and ASID, or is there another, more valid form? Several attorneys have said there is no contract written that guarantees against disputes and misunderstandings. However, contracts are valuable, because they spell out some of the areas of possible dispute and litigation. They define, and make the client aware of potential problems. They acquaint clients with trade terms and familiarize them with the ways interior designers charge and calculate their fees. So I feel a contract is valuable in clarifying your communications and minimizing the potential for misunderstandings. By law, it is necessary to have a written agreement for anything more than $500.

It is not necessary to use a contract, but if you choose not to use one and something goes wrong, you are the person who did not take the initiative or the time to clarify to your client your position and services.

is ambiguous or incomplete and there is a lawsuit, the ruling is against the author of the document. Declare exactly what you will do—and live up to your contract.

2. List the amount of compensation you expect and explain how this will be computed. State how billing is to be done—on an hourly basis, specified total-project-cost basis, daily basis, or percentage basis—and include a payment schedule. Make reference to all of your billing and collection requirements. State in your contracts that work will not continue if these conditions are not met.

3. Watch your time commitments. If you commit your firm to a schedule in which the project will take six months for design ordering and installation, it is safer to say your firm will finish the project three months after the completion of the construction program, when the building is available for interior work. If the construction is delayed, your project will be delayed, too. Committing to a date over which you have no control can be disastrous. Do not assume responsibility for anything you cannot control.

4. Stipulate who owns the drawings and specifications. You may be liable for design or material failures if a client uses your documents for a different project subject to different requirements. Copyright your drawings and your specifications. If you own the copyright, it is nontransferable to another owner. If your client needs to own your specifications or documents, you should retain ownership of the copyright.

5. Retain the right to use your designs and documents as you choose. You should be free to adapt the details to other projects, publish the designs, or use them in any way.

6. Consider the possibility of licensing the documents. You may want to negotiate for the client to have the nonexclusive rights to copy and reproduce the documents for a specific project; however, make sure this license is not transferable to any other project.

7. Thoroughly delineate the duties and obligations of each party involved in the project. When using consultants, be sure they provide documentation of their responsibilities and positions in respect to the project so you are not liable for their responsibilities. Make it clear when you require support documents on the project, without which you will not be able to continue. For example, you might need the engineering documents, architectural documents, and specifications that affect your design. Make delivery of these documents part of the contract, since the absence of such documents could delay the project or add to your liabilities.

8. Be careful how your contract lists the prices that are to be charged. You cannot be responsible for your suppliers' price increases. Unless you have total control of the project, do not let your contract tie in with these financial obligations in any way.

9. Note that your design detailing relies on the work of other people. Specify that you are using information from particular data, and document their source—whether architectural prints, for example, or the client's specifications. If a problem arises from an error based on faulty information, this documentation can give you a legal out.

10. If the project requires certifications, such as for flameproofing, fire retardants, and so on, have these prepared by the appropriate agencies and addressed directly to the client's projects so the organization doing the documentation is responsible, not you. Also, any guarantees appropriate to the project should be sent directly to the client, so if any problems should occur, the guarantors are responsible.

11. Spell out exactly how changes will be handled. In the precontract phase, determine how additions or deletions will reflect on your fee or charges. It is important to document this process early in the job, when it is easy to negotiate; after you have started a project, it becomes far more difficult.

12. Disclaim responsibility for changes made by anyone but yourself. That way, the minute the owner makes any changes in the design, you automatically are no longer responsible for the total project. Even if the change the client makes is small, you must relieve yourself of responsibility. Small changes can affect the quality and safety of the design.

13. Try to put all documents in clear, simple, and plain language. Avoid words that suggest excellence or any form of perfection. These are not clearly defined and can create unreal expectations, which may lead to lawsuits.

Types of Contracts and Letters of Agreement

Designers work with many types of contracts. Many prefer to use ASID documents or a preprinted contract because they feel these are more easily accepted by the client. These forms are very adaptable, although they are designed for the interior design profession. No two firms are alike, and there are many state and local laws that affect our practices, so it is imperative that your lawyer, accountant, and insurance advisor review these agreements. There are also specific terms and conditions that may be part of your business practice that need to be added.

Many firms have their own standard printed contract that merely requires filling in several blank spaces. Each interior design studio has its own preferences. We have included seven ASID documents for Residential Interior Design Services Agreements for your review, shown as Forms 6.1 to 6.7 (pages 170–209). I suggest you purchase a complete set from ASID, then review them with your advisor. Doing so will help you recognize the many issues to be considered. Then review the way you work: What are your issues and problems? After considering these, determine which type of agreement is best for your firm.

ASID Documents. ASID has prepared contract documents suitable for various design services (see pages 170–209). A careful review of these will assist a design firm both in defining services to be rendered and in understanding the appropriate legal terms for presenting them. The legal advisors of many firms suggest the firms use these ASID documents, because they are generally accepted documents; hence, they stand a better chance of holding up in court. Other firms find these forms forbidding and have their legal counsel prepare special documents suitable to their practice. Whether your firm elects to use a formal contract or a simple letter of agreement, these contracts represent the best source of information for reference in preparing your documents. ASID contracts may be used by any interior designers, but interior designers may not use the AIA contracts unless they are also registered architects. Contracts are an excellent reference for interior designers, to make them aware of what architects have traditionally included in their contracts. There currently is no official contract document for commercial projects through ASID for interior designers.

Some very large jobs are done with simple letters of agreement. But in more litigious areas, doing even a small project without an extensive contract could be risky. Contracts or letters of agreement must be authored to suit you, your firm, and your client.

Letters of Agreement. As noted above, some design firms prefer to work with a simple letter of agreement. However, these are often more difficult to write than a 10- or 12-page contract. Since your attorney determines your legal positioning, he or she needs to write or approve these documents. Each state and each local area has specific restrictions that may require a change in these documents.

As you move from one specialty to another, you will need to alter these documents to fit your new needs.

In reviewing various letters of agreement from the past 20 years, I noticed that recently the quantity of disclaimers is increasing at an unbelievable rate. Obviously, designers have had many problems, or they would not be so cautious in their legal documentation.

Unfortunately, when there is a problem during a project, it affects not only the financial and legal aspects of a project but very often your opportunity to complete a quality design project.

ASID Document ID120

RESIDENTIAL INTERIOR DESIGN
SERVICES AGREEMENT

This **AGREEMENT** is

made this _____ day of _____ in the year of Two Thousand and _____

BETWEEN the **CLIENT:**
(name and address)

and the **DESIGNER:**
(name and address)

The **CLIENT** and the **DESIGNER** agree as follows:

The Project pertains to the following areas within Client's residence located at

_____ :

(List areas below:)

1. INTERIOR DESIGN SERVICES

Designer shall perform the following interior design services:

(Describe the interior design services to be performed by Designer)

2. DESIGNER'S COMPENSATION

(Describe the methods of Designer's compensation and the services to which each compensation method applies if more than one compensation method is used)

3.   MISCELLANEOUS

3.1   Should Designer agree to perform any design service not described above, such "Additional Service" will be invoiced to Client at the following hourly rates:

Design Principal	$_____
Project Designer	$_____
Staff Designer	$_____
Draftsman	$_____
Other employees	$_____

Hourly charges will be invoiced to Client _____ and are payable upon receipt of invoice.

3.2   Disbursements incurred by Designer in the interest of the Project shall be reimbursed by Client to Designer upon receipt of Designer's invoices, which are rendered _____. Reimbursements shall include, among other things, costs of local and long distance travel, long distance telephone calls, duplication of plans, drawings and specifications, messenger services and the like.

3.3   Designer's drawings and specifications are conceptual in nature and intended to set forth design intent only. They are not to be used for architectural or engineering purposes. Designer does not provide architectural or engineering services.

3.4   Designer's services shall not include undertaking any responsibility for the design or modification of the design of any structural, heating, air-conditioning, plumbing, electrical, ventilation or other mechanical systems installed or to be installed at the Project.

3.5   Should the nature of Designer's design concepts require the services of any other design professional, such professional shall be engaged directly by Client pursuant to separate agreement as may be mutually acceptable to Client and such other design professional.

3.6   As Designer requires a record of Designer's design projects, Client will permit Designer or Designer's representatives to photograph the Project upon completion of the Project. Designer will be entitled to use photographs for Designer's business purposes but shall not disclose Project location or Client's name without Client's prior written consent.

3.7   All concepts, drawings and specifications prepared by Designer's firm ("Project Documents") and all copyrights and other proprietary rights applicable thereto remain at all times Designer's property. Project Documents may not be used by Client for any purpose other than completion of Project by Designer.

3.8   Designer cannot guarantee that actual prices for merchandise and/or interior installations or other costs or services as presented to Client will not vary either by item or in the aggregate from any Client proposed budget.

3.9   This Agreement may be terminated by either party upon the other party's default in performance, provided that termination may not be effected unless written notice specifying nature and extent of default is given to the concerned party and such party fails to cure such default in performance within _____ (____) days from date of receipt of such notice. Termination shall be without prejudice to any and all other rights and remedies of Designer, and Client shall remain liable for all outstanding obligations owed by Client to Designer and for all items of merchandise, interior installations and other services on order as of the termination date.

3.10   In addition to all other legal rights, Designer shall be entitled to withhold delivery of any item of merchandise or the further performance of interior installations or any other services, should Client fail to timely make any payments due Designer.

3.11   Any controversy or claim arising out of or relating to this Agreement, or the breach thereof, shall be decided by arbitration only in the _____ in accordance with the Commercial Arbitration Rules of the American Arbitration Association then in effect, and judgment upon the award rendered by the arbitrator(s) may be entered in any court having jurisdiction thereof.

3.12   Client will provide Designer with access to the Project and all information Designer may need to complete the Project. It is Client's responsibility to obtain all approvals required by any governmental agency or otherwise in connection with this Project.

3.13   Any sales tax applicable to Design Fees, and/or merchandise purchased from Designer, and/or interior installations completed by Designer shall be the responsibility of Client.

3.14   Neither Client nor Designer may assign their respective interests in this Agreement without the written consent of the other.

3.15   The laws of the State of _____ shall govern this Agreement.

3.16   Any provision of this Agreement held to be void or unenforceable under any law shall be deemed stricken, and all remaining provisions shall continue to be valid and binding upon both Designer and Client.

3.17   This Agreement is a complete statement of Designer's and Client's understanding. No representations or agreements have been made other than those contained in this Agreement. This Agreement can be modified only by a writing signed by both Designer and Client.

4. ADDITIONAL TERMS

CLIENT:

_____

_____

DESIGNER:

_____

_____

ASID Document ID121

RESIDENTIAL INTERIOR DESIGN
SERVICES AGREEMENT

SPECIAL INSTRUCTIONS REGARDING PAGE 3

Note that this Agreement contains two alternative paragraphs 2.3. Each alternative appears on a separate "Page 3." Except for Paragraph 2.3, the remaining language on each alternative "Page 3" is identical.

If Designer does not intend to charge a fee for Merchandise and Interior Installations purchased by Client through Designer, then (1) carefully remove and discard the second "Page 3"; and (2) use the first "Page 3" which contains the following language in Paragraph 2.3:

> *Merchandise and Interior Installations to be purchased through Designer will be specified in a written "Proposal" prepared by Designer and submitted in each instance for Client's written approval. Each Proposal will describe the item and its price to Client (F.O.B. point of origin). The price of each item shall be the amount charged to Designer by the supplier of such item ("Client Price").*

If Designer intends to charge a fee for Merchandise and Interior Installations purchased by Client through Designer, then (1) carefully remove and discard the first "Page 3"; and (2) use the second "Page 3" which contains the following language in Paragraph 2.3:

> *Merchandise and Interior Installations to be purchased through Designer will be specified in a written "Proposal" prepared by Designer and submitted in each instance for Client's written approval. Each Proposal will describe the item and its price to Client (F.O.B. point of origin). The price of each item to Client ("Client Price") shall be the amount charged to Designer by the supplier of such item ("Supplier Price"), plus Designer's purchase fee equal to _____ percent (____%) of the Supplier Price (exclusive of any freight, delivery or like charges or applicable tax). The fee is in addition to the hourly fees payable to Designer for its Interior Design Services.*

ASID Document ID121

RESIDENTIAL INTERIOR DESIGN
SERVICES AGREEMENT

This **AGREEMENT** is

made this _____ day of _____ in the year of Two Thousand and _____

_____

BETWEEN the **CLIENT**:
(name and address)

_____

and the **DESIGNER**:
(name and address)

The **CLIENT** and the **DESIGNER** agree as follows:

The Project pertains to the following areas within Client's residence located at

_____ :

(List areas below:)

_____

INTERIOR DESIGN SERVICES

1. Design Concept Services

1.1 In this phase of the Project, Designer shall, as and where appropriate, perform the following:

    A. Determine Client's design preferences and requirements.

    B. Conduct an initial design study.

C. Prepare drawings and other materials to generally illustrate Designer's suggested interior design concepts, to include color schemes, interior finishes, wall coverings, floor coverings, ceiling treatments, lighting treatments and window treatments.

D. Prepare layout showing location of movable furniture and furnishings.

E. Prepare schematic plans for recommended cabinet work, interior built-ins and other interior decorative details ("Interior Installations").

1.2 Prior to commencing Design Concept Services, Designer shall receive an Initial Design Fee of _____ dollars ($_____). This non-refundable Design Fee is payable upon signing this Agreement and is in addition to all other compensation payable to Designer under this Agreement.

2. Interior Specifications and Purchasing Services

2.1 Upon Client's approval of the Design Concepts, Designer will, as and where appropriate:

A. Select and/or specially design required Interior Installations and all required items of movable furniture, furnishings, light fixtures, hardware, fixtures, accessories and the like ("Merchandise").

B. Prepare and submit for Client's approval Proposals for completion of Interior Installations and purchase of Merchandise.

2.2 Designer may, at times, request Client to engage others to provide Interior Installations, pursuant to the arrangements set forth in the Project Review services described in paragraph 3 of this Agreement.

2.3 Merchandise and Interior Installations to be purchased through Designer will be specified in a written "Proposal" prepared by Designer and submitted in each instance for Client's written approval. Each Proposal will describe the item and its price to Client (F.O.B. point of origin). The price of each item to Client ("Client Price") shall be the amount charged to Designer by the supplier of such item ("Supplier Price"), plus Designer's purchase fee equal to _____ percent (___%) of the Supplier Price (exclusive of any freight, delivery or like charges or applicable tax). The fee is in addition to the hourly fees payable to Designer for its Interior Design Services.

2.4 No item can be ordered by Designer until the Proposal has been approved by Client, in writing, and returned to Designer with Designer's required initial payment equal to _____ percent (_____%) of the Client Price. The balance of the Client Price, together with delivery, shipping, handling charges and applicable taxes, is payable when the item is ready for delivery to and/or installation at Client's residence, or to a subsequent supplier for further work upon rendition of Designer's invoice. Proposals for fabrics, wall coverings, accessories, antiques, and items purchased at auction or at retail stores require full payment at time of signed Proposal.

3. Project Review

3.1 If the nature of the Project requires engagement by Client of any contractors to perform work based upon Designer's concepts, drawings or interior design specifications not otherwise provided for in the Interior Specifications and Purchasing Services, Client will enter into contracts directly with the concerned contractor.

3.2 Designer will make periodic visits to the Project site as Designer may consider appropriate to observe the work of these contractors to determine whether the contractors' work is proceeding in general conformity with Designer's concepts. Constant observation of work at the Project site is not a part of Designer's duties. Designer is not responsible for the performance, quality, timely completion or delivery of any work, materials or equipment furnished by contractors pursuant to direct contracts with Client.

4. COMPENSATION

4.1 For all Interior Design Services provided by Designer pursuant to this Agreement, Designer shall be compensated by Design Fees computed on the following hourly basis:

Design Principal	$_____
Project Designer	$_____
Staff Designer	$_____
Draftsman	$_____
Other employees	$_____

4.2 Hourly charges will be invoiced to Client _____ and are payable upon receipt of invoice.

5. MISCELLANEOUS

5.1 Should Designer agree to perform any design service not described above, such "Additional Service" will be invoiced to Client at the following hourly rates:

Design Principal	$_____
Project Designer	$_____
Staff Designer	$_____
Draftsman	$_____
Other employees	$_____

Hourly charges will be invoiced to Client _____ and are payable upon receipt of invoice.

5.2 Disbursements incurred by Designer in the interest of the Project shall be reimbursed by Client to Designer upon receipt of Designer's invoices, which are rendered _____. Reimbursements shall include, among other things, costs of local and long distance travel, long distance telephone calls, duplication of plans, drawings and specifications, messenger services and the like.

5.3 Designer's drawings and specifications are conceptual in nature and intended to set forth design intent only. They are not to be used for architectural or engineering purposes. Designer does not provide architectural or engineering services.

5.4 Designer's services shall not include undertaking any responsibility for the design or modification of the design of any structural, heating, air-conditioning, plumbing, electrical, ventilation or other mechanical systems installed or to be installed at the Project.

5.5 Should the nature of Designer's design concepts require the services of any other design professional, such professional shall be engaged directly by Client pursuant to separate agreement as may be mutually acceptable to Client and such other design professional.

5.6 As Designer requires a record of Designer's design projects, Client will permit Designer or Designer's representatives to photograph the Project upon completion of the Project. Designer will be entitled to use photographs for Designer's business purposes but shall not disclose Project location or Client's name without Client's prior written consent.

5.7 All concepts, drawings and specifications prepared by Designer's firm ("Project Documents") and all copyrights and other proprietary rights applicable thereto remain at all times Designer's property. Project Documents may not be used by Client for any purpose other than completion of Project by Designer.

5.8 Designer cannot guarantee that actual prices for Merchandise and/or Interior Installations or other costs or services as presented to Client will not vary either by item or in the aggregate from any Client proposed budget.

5.9 This Agreement may be terminated by either party upon the other party's default in performance, provided that termination may not be effected unless written notice specifying nature and extent of default is given to the concerned party and such party fails to cure such default in performance within _____ (____) days from date of receipt of such notice. Termination shall be without prejudice to any and all other rights and remedies of Designer, and Client shall remain liable for all outstanding obligations owed by Client to Designer and for all items of Merchandise, Interior Installations and other services on order as of the termination date.

5.10 In addition to all other legal rights, Designer shall be entitled to withhold delivery of any item of Merchandise or the further performance of Interior Installations or any other services, should Client fail to timely make any payments due Designer.

5.11 Any controversy or claim arising out of or relating to this Agreement, or the breach thereof, shall be decided by arbitration only in the _____ in accordance with the Commercial Arbitration Rules of the American Arbitration Association then in effect, and judgment upon the award rendered by the arbitrator(s) may be entered in any court having jurisdiction thereof.

5.12 Client will provide Designer with access to the Project and all information Designer may need to complete the Project. It is Client's responsibility to obtain all approvals required by any governmental agency or otherwise in connection with this Project.

5.13 Any sales tax applicable to Design Fees, and/or Merchandise purchased from Designer, and/or Interior Installations completed by Designer shall be the responsibility of Client.

5.14 Neither Client nor Designer may assign their respective interests in this Agreement without the written consent of the other.

5.15 The laws of the State of _____ shall govern this Agreement.

5.16 Any provision of this Agreement held to be void or unenforceable under any law shall be deemed stricken, and all remaining provisions shall continue to be valid and binding upon both Designer and Client.

5.17 This Agreement is a complete statement of Designer's and Client's understanding. No representations or agreements have been made other than those contained in this Agreement. This Agreement can be modified only by a writing signed by both Designer and Client.

6. ADDITIONAL TERMS

CLIENT:

_____

_____

DESIGNER:

_____

_____

ASID Document ID122

RESIDENTIAL INTERIOR DESIGN
SERVICES AGREEMENT

This **AGREEMENT** is

made this _____ day of _____, in the year of Two Thousand and _____

BETWEEN the **CLIENT:**
(name and address)

and the **DESIGNER:**
(name and address)

The **CLIENT** and the **DESIGNER** agree as follows:

The Project pertains to the following areas within Client's residence located at

_____:

(List areas below:)

INTERIOR DESIGN SERVICES

1. <u>**Design Concept Services**</u>

1.1 In this phase of the Project, Designer shall, as and where appropriate, perform the following:

A. Determine Client's design preferences and requirements.

B. Conduct an initial design study.

C. Prepare drawings and other materials to generally illustrate Designer's suggested interior design concepts, to include color schemes, interior finishes, wall coverings, floor coverings, ceiling treatments, lighting treatments and window treatments.

D. Prepare layout showing location of movable furniture and furnishings.

E. Prepare schematic plans for recommended cabinet work, interior built-ins and other interior decorative details ("Interior Installations").

1.2 Not more than _____ (_____) revisions to the Design Concept will be prepared by Designer without additional charges. Additional revisions will be billed to Client as Additional Services.

2. Interior Specifications and Purchasing Services

2.1 Upon Client's approval of the Design Concepts, Designer will, as and where appropriate:

A. Select and/or specially design required Interior Installations and all required items of movable furniture, furnishings, light fixtures, hardware, fixtures, accessories and the like ("Merchandise").

B. Prepare and submit for Client's approval Proposals for completion of Interior Installations and purchase of Merchandise.

2.2 Designer may, at times, request Client to engage others to provide Interior Installations, pursuant to the arrangements set forth in the Project Review services described in paragraph 3 of this Agreement.

2.3 Merchandise and Interior Installations to be purchased through Designer will be specified in a written "Proposal" prepared by Designer and submitted in each instance for Client's written approval. Each Proposal will describe the item and its price to Client (F.O.B. point of origin). The price of each item shall be the amount charged to Designer by the supplier of such item ("Client Price").

2.4 No item can be ordered by Designer until the Proposal has been approved by Client, in writing, and returned to Designer with Designer's required initial payment equal to _____ percent (____%) of the Client Price. The balance of the Client Price, together with delivery, shipping, handling charges and applicable taxes, is payable when the item is ready for delivery to and/or installation at Client's residence, or to a subsequent supplier for further work upon rendition of Designer's invoice. Proposals for fabrics, wall coverings, accessories, antiques, and items purchased at auction or at retail stores require full payment at time of signed Proposal.

3. Project Review

3.1 If the nature of the Project requires engagement by Client of any contractors to perform work based upon Designer's concepts, drawings or interior design specifications not otherwise provided for in the Interior Specifications and Purchasing Services, Client will enter into contracts directly with the concerned contractor.

3.2 Designer will make periodic visits to the Project site as Designer may consider appropriate to observe the work of these contractors to determine whether the contractors' work is proceeding in general conformity with Designer's concepts. Constant observation of work at the Project site is not a part of Designer's duties. Designer is not responsible for the performance, quality, timely completion or delivery of any work, materials or equipment furnished by contractors pursuant to direct contracts with Client.

4. COMPENSATION

4.1 Designer's compensation for the Interior Design Services described above shall be a fixed fee of _____ dollars ($_____) payable as follows:

4.2 Designer's compensation shall be subject to renegotiation if:

    A. The scope of the Project changes materially; or

    B. Through no fault of Designer, its Interior Design Services are not substantially completed within _____ (___) months of the date of signing this Agreement.

5. MISCELLANEOUS

5.1 Should Designer agree to perform any design service not described above, such "Additional Service" will be invoiced to Client at the following hourly rates:

Design Principal	$_____
Project Designer	$_____
Staff Designer	$_____
Draftsman	$_____
Other employees	$_____

Hourly charges will be invoiced to Client _____ and are payable upon receipt of invoice.

5.2 Disbursements incurred by Designer in the interest of the Project shall be reimbursed by Client to Designer upon receipt of Designer's invoices, which are rendered _____. Reimbursements shall include, among other things, costs of local and long distance travel, long distance telephone calls, duplication of plans, drawings and specifications, messenger services and the like.

5.3 Designer's drawings and specifications are conceptual in nature and intended to set forth design intent only. They are not to be used for architectural or engineering purposes. Designer does not provide architectural or engineering services.

5.4 Designer's services shall not include undertaking any responsibility for the design or modification of the design of any structural, heating, air-conditioning, plumbing, electrical, ventilation or other mechanical systems installed or to be installed at the Project.

5.5 Should the nature of Designer's design concepts require the services of any other design professional, such professional shall be engaged directly by Client pursuant to separate agreement as may be mutually acceptable to Client and such other design professional.

5.6 As Designer requires a record of Designer's design projects, Client will permit Designer or Designer's representatives to photograph the Project upon completion of the Project. Designer will be entitled to use photographs for Designer's business purposes but shall not disclose Project location or Client's name without Client's prior written consent.

5.7 All concepts, drawings and specifications prepared by Designer's firm ("Project Documents") and all copyrights and other proprietary rights applicable thereto remain at all times Designer's property. Project Documents may not be used by Client for any purpose other than completion of Project by Designer.

5.8 Designer cannot guarantee that actual prices for Merchandise and/or Interior Installations or other costs or services as presented to Client will not vary either by item or in the aggregate from any Client proposed budget.

5.9 This Agreement may be terminated by either party upon the other party's default in performance, provided that termination may not be effected unless written notice specifying nature and extent of default is given to the concerned party and such party fails to cure such default in performance within _____ (____) days from date of receipt of such notice. Termination shall be without prejudice to any and all other rights and remedies of Designer, and Client shall remain liable for all outstanding obligations owed by Client to Designer and for all items of Merchandise, Interior Installations and other services on order as of the termination date.

5.10 In addition to all other legal rights, Designer shall be entitled to withhold delivery of any item of Merchandise or the further performance of Interior Installations or any other services, should Client fail to timely make any payments due Designer.

5.11 Any controversy or claim arising out of or relating to this Agreement, or the breach thereof, shall be decided by arbitration only in the _____ in accordance with the Commercial Arbitration Rules of the American Arbitration Association then in effect, and judgment upon the award rendered by the arbitrator(s) may be entered in any court having jurisdiction thereof.

5.12 Client will provide Designer with access to the Project and all information Designer may need to complete the Project. It is Client's responsibility to obtain all approvals required by any governmental agency or otherwise in connection with this Project.

5.13 Any sales tax applicable to Design Fees, and/or Merchandise purchased from Designer, and/or Interior Installations completed by Designer shall be the responsibility of Client.

5.14 Neither Client nor Designer may assign their respective interests in this Agreement without the written consent of the other.

5.15 The laws of the State of _____ shall govern this Agreement.

5.16 Any provision of this Agreement held to be void or unenforceable under any law shall be deemed stricken, and all remaining provisions shall continue to be valid and binding upon both Designer and Client.

5.17 This Agreement is a complete statement of Designer's and Client's understanding. No representations or agreements have been made other than those contained in this Agreement. This Agreement can be modified only by a writing signed by both Designer and Client.

6. ADDITIONAL TERMS

CLIENT:

_____

_____

DESIGNER:

_____

_____

ASID Document ID123

RESIDENTIAL INTERIOR DESIGN SERVICES AGREEMENT

<u>SPECIAL INSTRUCTIONS REGARDING PAGE 2</u>

Note that this Agreement contains two alternative paragraphs 1.2. Each alternative appears on a separate "Page 2." Except for Paragraph 1.2, the remaining language on each alternative "Page 2" is identical.

If Designer intends to charge a fixed fee for Design Concept Services, then (1) <u>carefully remove and discard the second "Page 2"</u>; and (2) <u>use the first "Page 2"</u> which contains the following language in Paragraph 1.2:

> *Prior to commencing Design Concept Services, Designer shall receive an Initial Design Fee of _____ dollars ($_____). This non-refundable Design Fee is payable upon signing this Agreement and is in addition to all other compensation payable to Designer under this Agreement. Not more than _____(_____) revisions to the Design Concept will be prepared by Designer without additional charges. Additional revisions will be billed to Client as Additional Services.*

If Designer intends to charge hourly fees for Design Concept Services, then (1) <u>carefully remove and discard the first "Page 2"</u>; and (2) <u>use the second "Page 2"</u> which contains the following language in Paragraph 1.2:

> *Designer shall be compensated for its Design Concept Services on an hourly basis at the rates set forth in paragraph 4.1 of this Agreement. Hourly charges will be invoiced to Client _____ and are payable by Client upon receipt of invoice. Upon signing this Agreement, Designer shall receive a non-refundable initial advance of _____ dollars ($_____), which constitutes the minimum fee due Designer for Design Concept Services. This advance will be credited against hourly charges otherwise payable by Client to Designer for Design Concept Services.*

ASID Document ID123

RESIDENTIAL INTERIOR DESIGN
SERVICES AGREEMENT

This **AGREEMENT** is

made this _____day of_____ in the year of Two Thousand and _____

BETWEEN the **CLIENT**:
(name and address)

and the **DESIGNER**:
(name and address)

The **CLIENT** and the **DESIGNER** agree as follows:

The Project pertains to the following areas within Client's residence located at

_____:

(List areas below:)

INTERIOR DESIGN SERVICES

   1. <u>Design Concept Services</u>

  1.1 In this phase of the Project, Designer shall, as and where appropriate, perform the following:

      A. Determine Client's design preferences and requirements.

      B. Conduct an initial design study.

C. Prepare drawings and other materials to generally illustrate
    Designer's suggested interior design concepts, to include color
    schemes, interior finishes, wall coverings, floor coverings, ceiling
    treatments, lighting treatments and window treatments.

D. Prepare layout showing location of movable furniture and
    furnishings.

E. Prepare schematic plans for recommended cabinet work, interior
    built-ins and other interior decorative details ("Interior Installations").

1.2 Prior to commencing Design Concept Services, Designer shall receive an Initial Design
     Fee of _____ dollars ($_____). This non-refundable
     Design Fee is payable upon signing this Agreement and is in addition to all other
     compensation payable to Designer under this Agreement. Not more than_____
     (____) revisions to the Design Concept will be prepared by Designer without
     additional charges. Additional revisions will be billed to Client as Additional Services.

2. <u>Interior Specifications and Purchasing Services</u>

2.1 Upon Client's approval of the Design Concepts, Designer will, as and
     where appropriate:

A. Select and/or specially design required Interior Installations and
    all required items of movable furniture, furnishings, light fixtures,
    hardware, fixtures, accessories and the like ("Merchandise").

B. Prepare and submit for Client's approval Proposals for completion
    of Interior Installations and purchase of Merchandise.

2.2 Merchandise and Interior Installations specified by Designer shall, if Client wishes to
     purchase them, be purchased solely through Designer. Designer may, at times,
     request Client to engage others to provide Interior Installations, pursuant to the
     arrangements set forth in the Project Review services described in paragraph 3 of this
     Agreement.

2.3 Merchandise and Interior Installations to be purchased through Designer will be
     specified in a written "Proposal" prepared by Designer and submitted in each
     instance for Client's written approval.   Each Proposal will describe the item and its
     price to Client (F.O.B. point of origin). The price of each item to Client ("Client
     Price") shall be the amount charged to Designer by the supplier of such item
     ("Supplier Price"), plus Designer's fee equal to _____ percent (____%) of the
     Supplier Price (exclusive of any freight, delivery or like charges or applicable tax).

2.4 No item can be ordered by Designer until the Proposal has been approved by Client, in writing, and returned to Designer with Designer's required initial payment equal to _____ percent (____%) of the Client Price. The balance of the Client Price, together with delivery, shipping, handling charges and applicable taxes, is payable when the item is ready for delivery to and/or installation at Client's residence, or to a subsequent supplier for further work upon rendition of Designer's invoice. Proposals for fabrics, wall coverings, accessories, antiques, and items purchased at auction or at retail stores require full payment at time of signed Proposal.

3. Project Review

3.1 If the nature of the Project requires engagement by Client of any contractors to perform work based upon Designer's concepts, drawings or interior design specifications not otherwise provided for in the Interior Specifications and Purchasing Services, Client will enter into contracts directly with the concerned contractor. Client shall provide Designer with copies of all contracts and invoices submitted to Client by the contractors.

3.2 Designer will make periodic visits to the Project site as Designer may consider appropriate to observe the work of these contractors to determine whether the contractors' work is proceeding in general conformity with Designer's concepts. Constant observation of work at the Project site is not a part of Designer's duties. Designer is not responsible for the performance, quality, timely completion or delivery of any work, materials or equipment furnished by contractors pursuant to direct contracts with Client.

3.3 Designer shall be entitled to receive a fee equal to _____ percent (___%) of the amount to be paid by Client to each contractor performing any work based upon Designer's concepts, drawings, specifications ("Project Review Fees").

3.4 The Project Review Fees shall be payable by Client to Designer as follows:

4. MISCELLANEOUS

4.1 Should Designer agree to perform any design service not described above, such "Additional Service" will be invoiced to Client at the following hourly rates:

Design Principal	$_____
Project Designer	$_____
Staff Designer	$_____
Draftsman	$_____
Other employees	$_____

Hourly charges will be invoiced to Client _____ and are payable upon receipt of invoice.

4.2 Disbursements incurred by Designer in the interest of the Project shall be reimbursed by Client to Designer upon receipt of Designer's invoices, which are rendered _____. Reimbursements shall include, among other things, costs of local and long distance travel, long distance telephone calls, duplication of plans, drawings and specifications, messenger services and the like.

4.3 Designer's drawings and specifications are conceptual in nature and intended to set forth design intent only. They are not to be used for architectural or engineering purposes. Designer does not provide architectural or engineering services.

4.4 Designer's services shall not include undertaking any responsibility for the design or modification of the design of any structural, heating, air-conditioning, plumbing, electrical, ventilation or other mechanical systems installed or to be installed at the Project.

4.5 Should the nature of Designer's design concepts require the services of any other design professional, such professional shall be engaged directly by Client pursuant to separate agreement as may be mutually acceptable to Client and such other design professional.

4.6 As Designer requires a record of Designer's design projects, Client will permit Designer or Designer's representatives to photograph the Project upon completion of the Project. Designer will be entitled to use photographs for Designer's business purposes but shall not disclose Project location or Client's name without Client's prior written consent.

4.7 All concepts, drawings and specifications prepared by Designer's firm ("Project Documents") and all copyrights and other proprietary rights applicable thereto remain at all times Designer's property. Project Documents may not be used by Client for any purpose other than completion of Project by Designer.

4.8 Designer cannot guarantee that actual prices for Merchandise and/or Interior Installations or other costs or services as presented to Client will not vary either by item or in the aggregate from any Client proposed budget.

4.9 This Agreement may be terminated by either party upon the other party's default in performance, provided that termination may not be effected unless written notice specifying nature and extent of default is given to the concerned party and such party fails to cure such default in performance within _____ (____) days from date of receipt of such notice. Termination shall be without prejudice to any and all other rights and remedies of Designer, and Client shall remain liable for all outstanding obligations owed by Client to Designer and for all items of Merchandise, Interior Installations and other services on order as of the termination date.

4.10 In addition to all other legal rights, Designer shall be entitled to withhold delivery of any item of Merchandise or the further performance of Interior Installations or any other services, should Client fail to timely make any payments due Designer.

4.11   Any controversy or claim arising out of or relating to this Agreement, or the breach thereof, shall be decided by arbitration only in the _____ in accordance with the Commercial Arbitration Rules of the American Arbitration Association then in effect, and judgment upon the award rendered by the arbitrator(s) may be entered in any court having jurisdiction thereof.

4.12   Client will provide Designer with access to the Project and all information Designer may need to complete the Project. It is Client's responsibility to obtain all approvals required by any governmental agency or otherwise in connection with this Project.

4.13   Any sales tax applicable to Design Fees, and/or Merchandise purchased from Designer, and/or Interior Installations completed by Designer shall be the responsibility of Client.

4.14   Neither Client nor Designer may assign their respective interests in this Agreement without the written consent of the other.

4.15   The laws of the State of _____ shall govern this Agreement.

4.16   Any provision of this Agreement held to be void or unenforceable under any law shall be deemed stricken, and all remaining provisions shall continue to be valid and binding upon both Designer and Client.

4.17   This Agreement is a complete statement of Designer's and Client's understanding. No representations or agreements have been made other than those contained in this Agreement. This Agreement can be modified only by a writing signed by both Designer and Client.

5. ADDITIONAL TERMS

CLIENT:

_____

_____

DESIGNER:

_____

_____

ASID Document ID124

RESIDENTIAL INTERIOR DESIGN SERVICES AGREEMENT

SPECIAL INSTRUCTIONS REGARDING PAGE 2

Note that this Agreement contains two alternative paragraphs 1.2. Each alternative appears on a separate "Page 2." Except for Paragraph 1.2, the remaining language on each alternative "Page 2" is identical.

If Designer intends to charge a fixed fee for Design Concept Services, then (1) <u>carefully remove and discard the second "Page 2"</u>; and (2) <u>use the first "Page 2"</u> which contains the following language in Paragraph 1.2:

> *Prior to commencing Design Concept Services, Designer shall receive an Initial Design Fee of _____ dollars ($_____). This non-refundable Design Fee is payable upon signing this Agreement and is in addition to all other compensation payable to Designer under this Agreement. Not more than _____(_____) revisions to the Design Concept will be prepared by Designer without additional charges. Additional revisions will be billed to Client as Additional Services.*

If Designer intends to charge hourly fees for Design Concept Services, then (1) <u>carefully remove and discard the first "Page 2"</u>; and (2) <u>use the second "Page 2"</u> which contains the following language in Paragraph 1.2:

> *Designer shall be compensated for its Design Concept Services on an hourly basis at the rates set forth in paragraph 4.1 of this Agreement. Hourly charges will be invoiced to Client _____ and are payable by Client upon receipt of invoice. Upon signing this Agreement, Designer shall receive a non-refundable initial advance of _____ dollars ($_____), which constitutes the minimum fee due Designer for Design Concept Services. This advance will be credited against hourly charges otherwise payable by Client to Designer for Design Concept Services.*

ID124-1996

ASID Document ID124

RESIDENTIAL INTERIOR DESIGN SERVICES AGREEMENT

This **AGREEMENT** is

made this _____ day of _____ in the year of Two Thousand and _____

BETWEEN the **CLIENT**:
(name and address)

---

and the **DESIGNER**:
(name and address)

The **CLIENT** and the **DESIGNER** agree as follows:

The Project pertains to the following areas within Client's residence located at

_____:

(List areas below:)

INTERIOR DESIGN SERVICES

1. <u>Design Concept Services</u>

1.1 In this phase of the Project, Designer shall, as and where appropriate, perform the following:

A. Determine Client's design preferences and requirements.

B. Conduct an initial design study.

C. Prepare drawings and other materials to generally illustrate Designer's suggested interior design concepts, to include color schemes, interior finishes, wall coverings, floor coverings, ceiling treatments, lighting treatments and window treatments.

D. Prepare layout showing location of movable furniture and furnishings.

E. Prepare schematic plans for recommended cabinet work, interior built-ins and other interior decorative details ("Interior Installations").

1.2 Prior to commencing Design Concept Services, Designer shall receive an Initial Design Fee of _____ dollars ($_____). This non-refundable Design Fee is payable upon signing this Agreement and is in addition to all other compensation payable to Designer under this Agreement. Not more than_____ (____) revisions to the Design Concept will be prepared by Designer without additional charges. Additional revisions will be billed to Client as Additional Services.

2. Interior Specifications and Purchasing Services

2.1 Upon Client's approval of the Design Concepts, Designer will, as and where appropriate:

A. Select and/or specially design required Interior Installations and all required items of movable furniture, furnishings, light fixtures, hardware, fixtures, accessories and the like ("Merchandise").

B. Prepare and submit for Client's approval Proposals for completion of Interior Installations and purchase of Merchandise.

2.2 Merchandise and Interior Installations specified by Designer shall, if Client wishes to purchase them, be purchased solely through Designer. Designer may, at times, request Client to engage others to provide Interior Installations, pursuant to the arrangements set forth in the Project Review services described in paragraph 3 of this Agreement.

2.3 Merchandise and Interior Installations to be purchased through Designer will be specified in a written "Proposal" prepared by Designer and submitted in each instance for Client's written approval.   Each Proposal will describe the item and its price to Client (F.O.B. point of origin). The price of each item to Client ("Client Price") shall be the amount charged to Designer by the supplier of such item ("Supplier Price"), plus Designer's fee equal to _____ percent (____%) of the Supplier Price (exclusive of any freight, delivery or like charges or applicable tax).

2.4 No item can be ordered by Designer until the Proposal has been approved by Client, in writing, and returned to Designer with Designer's required initial payment equal to _____ percent (____%) of the Client Price. The balance of the Client Price, together with delivery, shipping, handling charges and applicable taxes, is payable when the item is ready for delivery to and/or installation at Client's residence, or to a subsequent supplier for further work upon rendition of Designer's invoice. Proposals for fabrics, wall coverings, accessories, antiques, and items purchased at auction or at retail stores require full payment at time of signed Proposal.

3. Project Review

3.1 If the nature of the Project requires engagement by Client of any contractors to perform work based upon Designer's concepts, drawings or interior design specifications not otherwise provided for in the Interior Specifications and Purchasing Services, Client will enter into contracts directly with the concerned contractor.

3.2 Designer will make periodic visits to the Project site as Designer may consider appropriate to observe the work of these contractors to determine whether the contractors' work is proceeding in general conformity with Designer's concepts. Constant observation of work at the Project site is not a part of Designer's duties. Designer is not responsible for the performance, quality, timely completion or delivery of any work, materials or equipment furnished by contractors pursuant to direct contracts with Client.

3.3 Time expended by Designer for all Project Review services will be charged to Client on an hourly basis at the rates set forth in paragraph 4.1 of the Agreement.

4. MISCELLANEOUS

4.1 Should Designer agree to perform any design service not described above, such "Additional Service" will be invoiced to Client at the following hourly rates:

Design Principal	$_____
Project Designer	$_____
Staff Designer	$_____
Draftsman	$_____
Other employees	$_____

Hourly charges will be invoiced to Client _____ and are payable upon receipt of invoice.

4.2 Disbursements incurred by Designer in the interest of the Project shall be reimbursed by Client to Designer upon receipt of Designer's invoices, which are rendered _____. Reimbursements shall include, among other things, costs of local and long distance travel, long distance telephone calls, duplication of plans, drawings and specifications, messenger services and the like.

4.3 Designer's drawings and specifications are conceptual in nature and intended to set forth design intent only. They are not to be used for architectural or engineering purposes. Designer does not provide architectural or engineering services.

4.4 Designer's services shall not include undertaking any responsibility for the design or modification of the design of any structural, heating, air-conditioning, plumbing, electrical, ventilation or other mechanical systems installed or to be installed at the Project.

4.5 Should the nature of Designer's design concepts require the services of any other design professional, such professional shall be engaged directly by Client pursuant to separate agreement as may be mutually acceptable to Client and such other design professional.

4.6 As Designer requires a record of Designer's design projects, Client will permit Designer or Designer's representatives to photograph the Project upon completion of the Project. Designer will be entitled to use photographs for Designer's business purposes but shall not disclose Project location or Client's name without Client's prior written consent.

4.7 All concepts, drawings and specifications prepared by Designer's firm ("Project Documents") and all copyrights and other proprietary rights applicable thereto remain at all times Designer's property. Project Documents may not be used by Client for any purpose other than completion of Project by Designer.

4.8 Designer cannot guarantee that actual prices for Merchandise and/or Interior Installations or other costs or services as presented to Client will not vary either by item or in the aggregate from any Client proposed budget.

4.9 This Agreement may be terminated by either party upon the other party's default in performance, provided that termination may not be effected unless written notice specifying nature and extent of default is given to the concerned party and such party fails to cure such default in performance within _____ (____) days from date of receipt of such notice. Termination shall be without prejudice to any and all other rights and remedies of Designer, and Client shall remain liable for all outstanding obligations owed by Client to Designer and for all items of Merchandise, Interior Installations and other services on order as of the termination date.

4.10 In addition to all other legal rights, Designer shall be entitled to withhold delivery of any item of Merchandise or the further performance of Interior Installations or any other services, should Client fail to timely make any payments due Designer.

4.11 Any controversy or claim arising out of or relating to this Agreement, or the breach thereof, shall be decided by arbitration only in the _____ in accordance with the Commercial Arbitration Rules of the American Arbitration Association then in effect, and judgment upon the award rendered by the arbitrator(s) may be entered in any court having jurisdiction thereof.

4.12 Client will provide Designer with access to the Project and all information Designer may need to complete the Project. It is Client's responsibility to obtain all approvals required by any governmental agency or otherwise in connection with this Project.

4.13 Any sales tax applicable to Design Fees, and/or Merchandise purchased from Designer, and/or Interior Installations completed by Designer shall be the responsibility of Client.

4.14 Neither Client nor Designer may assign their respective interests in this Agreement without the written consent of the other.

4.15 The laws of the State of _____ shall govern this Agreement.

4.16 Any provision of this Agreement held to be void or unenforceable under any law shall be deemed stricken, and all remaining provisions shall continue to be valid and binding upon both Designer and Client.

4.17 This Agreement is a complete statement of Designer's and Client's understanding. No representations or agreements have been made other than those contained in this Agreement. This Agreement can be modified only by a writing signed by both Designer and Client.

5. ADDITIONAL TERMS

CLIENT:

_____

_____

DESIGNER:

_____

_____

ASID Document ID125

RESIDENTIAL INTERIOR DESIGN SERVICES AGREEMENT

SPECIAL INSTRUCTIONS REGARDING PAGE 2

Note that this Agreement contains two alternative paragraphs 1.2. Each alternative appears on a separate "Page 2." Except for Paragraph 1.2, the remaining language on each alternative "Page 2" is identical.

If Designer intends to charge a fixed fee for Design Concept Services, then (1) <u>carefully remove and discard the second "Page 2"</u>; and (2) <u>use the first "Page 2"</u> which contains the following language in Paragraph 1.2:

> *Prior to commencing Design Concept Services, Designer shall receive an Initial Design Fee of _____ dollars ($_____). This non-refundable Design Fee is payable upon signing this Agreement and is in addition to all other compensation payable to Designer under this Agreement. Not more than _____(____) revisions to the Design Concept will be prepared by Designer without additional charges. Additional revisions will be billed to Client as Additional Services.*

If Designer intends to charge hourly fees for Design Concept Services, then (1) <u>carefully remove and discard the first "Page 2"</u>; and (2) <u>use the second "Page 2"</u> which contains the following language in Paragraph 1.2:

> *Designer shall be compensated for its Design Concept Services on an hourly basis at the rates set forth in paragraph 4.1 of this Agreement. Hourly charges will be invoiced to Client _____ and are payable by Client upon receipt of invoice. Upon signing this Agreement, Designer shall receive a non-refundable initial advance of _____ dollars ($_____), which constitutes the minimum fee due Designer for Design Concept Services. This advance will be credited against hourly charges otherwise payable by Client to Designer for Design Concept Services.*

ASID Document ID125

RESIDENTIAL INTERIOR DESIGN
SERVICES AGREEMENT

This **AGREEMENT** is

made this _____ day of _____ in the year of Two Thousand and _____

BETWEEN the **CLIENT**:
(name and address)

and the **DESIGNER**:
(name and address)

The **CLIENT** and the **DESIGNER** agree as follows:

The Project pertains to the following areas within Client's residence located at

_____:

(List areas below:)

INTERIOR DESIGN SERVICES

1. Design Concept Services

1.1 In this phase of the Project, Designer shall, as and where appropriate, perform the following:

A. Determine Client's design preferences and requirements.

B. Conduct an initial design study.

C. Prepare drawings and other materials to generally illustrate Designer's suggested interior design concepts, to include color schemes, interior finishes, wall coverings, floor coverings, ceiling treatments, lighting treatments and window treatments.

D. Prepare layout showing location of movable furniture and furnishings.

E. Prepare schematic plans for recommended cabinet work, interior built-ins and other interior decorative details ("Interior Installations").

1.2 Prior to commencing Design Concept Services, Designer shall receive an Initial Design Fee of _____ dollars ($_____). This non-refundable Design Fee is payable upon signing this Agreement and is in addition to all other compensation payable to Designer under this Agreement. Not more than_____ (____) revisions to the Design Concept will be prepared by Designer without additional charges. Additional revisions will be billed to Client as Additional Services.

2. Interior Specifications and Purchasing Services

2.1 Upon Client's approval of the Design Concepts, Designer will, as and where appropriate:

A. Select and/or specially design required Interior Installations and all required items of movable furniture, furnishings, light fixtures, hardware, fixtures, accessories and the like ("Merchandise").

B. Prepare and submit for Client's approval Proposals for completion of Interior Installations and purchase of Merchandise.

2.2 Merchandise and Interior Installations specified by Designer shall, if Client wishes to purchase them, be purchased solely through Designer. Designer may, at times, request Client to engage others to provide Interior Installations, pursuant to the arrangements set forth in the Project Review services described in paragraph 3 of this Agreement.

2.3 Merchandise and Interior Installations to be purchased through Designer will be specified in a written "Proposal" prepared by Designer and submitted in each instance for Client's written approval. Each Proposal will describe the item and its price to Client (F.O.B. point of origin) ("Client Price"). The Client Price for each item of Merchandise and Interior Installations includes a fee for services rendered in this phase of the Project.

2.4 No item can be ordered by Designer until the Proposal has been approved by Client, in writing, and returned to Designer with Designer's required initial payment equal to _____ percent (____%) of the Client Price. The balance of the Client Price, together with delivery, shipping, handling charges and applicable taxes, is payable when the item is ready for delivery to and/or installation at Client's residence, or to a subsequent supplier for further work upon rendition of Designer's invoice. Proposals for fabrics, wall coverings, accessories, antiques, and items purchased at auction or at retail stores require full payment at time of signed Proposal.

3. <u>Project Review</u>

3.1 If the nature of the Project requires engagement by Client of any contractors to perform work based upon Designer's concepts, drawings or interior design specifications not otherwise provided for in the Interior Specifications and Purchasing Services, Client will enter into contracts directly with the concerned contractor. Client shall provide Designer with copies of all contracts and invoices submitted to Client by the contractors.

3.2 Designer will make periodic visits to the Project site as Designer may consider appropriate to observe the work of these contractors to determine whether the contractors' work is proceeding in general conformity with Designer's concepts. Constant observation of work at the Project site is not a part of Designer's duties. Designer is not responsible for the performance, quality, timely completion or delivery of any work, materials or equipment furnished by contractors pursuant to direct contracts with Client.

3.3 Designer shall be entitled to receive a fee equal to _____ percent (___%) of the amount to be paid by Client to each contractor performing any work based upon Designer's concepts, drawings or specifications ("Project Review Fees").

4. MISCELLANEOUS

4.1 Should Designer agree to perform any design service not described above, such "Additional Service" will be invoiced to Client at the following hourly rates:

Design Principal	$_____
Project Designer	$_____
Staff Designer	$_____
Draftsman	$_____
Other employees	$_____

Hourly charges will be invoiced to Client _____ and are payable upon receipt of invoice.

4.2 Disbursements incurred by Designer in the interest of the Project shall be reimbursed by Client to Designer upon receipt of Designer's invoices, which are rendered _____. Reimbursements shall include, among other things, costs of local and long distance travel, long distance telephone calls, duplication of plans, drawings and specifications, messenger services and the like.

4.3 Designer's drawings and specifications are conceptual in nature and intended to set forth design intent only. They are not to be used for architectural or engineering purposes. Designer does not provide architectural or engineering services.

4.4 Designer's services shall not include undertaking any responsibility for the design or modification of the design of any structural, heating, air-conditioning, plumbing, electrical, ventilation or other mechanical systems installed or to be installed at the Project.

4.5 Should the nature of Designer's design concepts require the services of any other design professional, such professional shall be engaged directly by Client pursuant to separate agreement as may be mutually acceptable to Client and such other design professional.

4.6 As Designer requires a record of Designer's design projects, Client will permit Designer or Designer's representatives to photograph the Project upon completion of the Project. Designer will be entitled to use photographs for Designer's business purposes but shall not disclose Project location or Client's name without Client's prior written consent.

4.7 All concepts, drawings and specifications prepared by Designer's firm ("Project Documents") and all copyrights and other proprietary rights applicable thereto remain at all times Designer's property. Project Documents may not be used by Client for any purpose other than completion of Project by Designer.

4.8 Designer cannot guarantee that actual prices for Merchandise and/or Interior Installations or other costs or services as presented to Client will not vary either by item or in the aggregate from any Client proposed budget.

4.9 This Agreement may be terminated by either party upon the other party's default in performance, provided that termination may not be effected unless written notice specifying nature and extent of default is given to the concerned party and such party fails to cure such default in performance within _____ (____) days from date of receipt of such notice. Termination shall be without prejudice to any and all other rights and remedies of Designer, and Client shall remain liable for all outstanding obligations owed by Client to Designer and for all items of Merchandise, Interior Installations and other services on order as of the termination date.

4.10 In addition to all other legal rights, Designer shall be entitled to withhold delivery of any item of Merchandise or the further performance of Interior Installations or any other services, should Client fail to timely make any payments due Designer.

4.11 Any controversy or claim arising out of or relating to this Agreement, or the breach thereof, shall be decided by arbitration only in the _____ in accordance with the Commercial Arbitration Rules of the American Arbitration Association then in effect, and judgment upon the award rendered by the arbitrator(s) may be entered in any court having jurisdiction thereof.

4.12 Client will provide Designer with access to the Project and all information Designer may need to complete the Project. It is Client's responsibility to obtain all approvals required by any governmental agency or otherwise in connection with this Project.

4.13 Any sales tax applicable to Design Fees, and/or Merchandise purchased from Designer, and/or Interior Installations completed by Designer shall be the responsibility of Client.

4.14 Neither Client nor Designer may assign their respective interests in this Agreement without the written consent of the other.

4.15 The laws of the State of _____ shall govern this Agreement.

ID125-1996 **4**

4.16   Any provision of this Agreement held to be void or unenforceable under
        any law shall be deemed stricken, and all remaining provisions shall continue to be
        valid and binding upon both Designer and Client.

4.17   This Agreement is a complete statement of Designer's and Client's understanding.
        No representations or agreements have been made other than those contained in this
        Agreement. This Agreement can be modified only by a writing signed by both
        Designer and Client.

5. ADDITIONAL TERMS

CLIENT:

_____

_____

DESIGNER:

_____

_____

ASID Document ID126

RESIDENTIAL INTERIOR DESIGN SERVICES AGREEMENT

SPECIAL INSTRUCTIONS REGARDING PAGE 2

Note that this Agreement contains two alternative paragraphs 1.2. Each alternative appears on a separate "Page 2." Except for Paragraph 1.2, the remaining language on each alternative "Page 2" is identical.

If Designer intends to charge a fixed fee for Design Concept Services, then (1) <u>carefully remove and discard the second "Page 2"</u>; and (2) <u>use the first "Page 2"</u> which contains the following language in Paragraph 1.2:

> *Prior to commencing Design Concept Services, Designer shall receive an Initial Design Fee of _____ dollars ($_____). This non-refundable Design Fee is payable upon signing this Agreement and is in addition to all other compensation payable to Designer under this Agreement. Not more than _____(_____) revisions to the Design Concept will be prepared by Designer without additional charges. Additional revisions will be billed to Client as Additional Services.*

If Designer intends to charge hourly fees for Design Concept Services, then (1) <u>carefully remove and discard the first "Page 2"</u>; and (2) <u>use the second "Page 2"</u> which contains the following language in Paragraph 1.2:

> *Designer shall be compensated for its Design Concept Services on an hourly basis at the rates set forth in paragraph 4.1 of this Agreement. Hourly charges will be invoiced to Client _____ and are payable by Client upon receipt of invoice. Upon signing this Agreement, Designer shall receive a non-refundable initial advance of _____ dollars ($_____), which constitutes the minimum fee due Designer for Design Concept Services. This advance will be credited against hourly charges otherwise payable by Client to Designer for Design Concept Services.*

ID126-1996

ASID Document ID126

RESIDENTIAL INTERIOR DESIGN SERVICES AGREEMENT

This **AGREEMENT** is

made this _____ day of _____ in the year of Two Thousand and _____

BETWEEN the **CLIENT**:
(name and address)

and the **DESIGNER**:
(name and address)

The **CLIENT** and the **DESIGNER** agree as follows:

The Project pertains to the following areas within Client's residence located at

_____ :

(List areas below:)

INTERIOR DESIGN SERVICES

1. Design Concept Services

1.1 In this phase of the Project, Designer shall, as and where appropriate, perform the following:

A. Determine Client's design preferences and requirements.

B. Conduct an initial design study.

C. Prepare drawings and other materials to generally illustrate Designer's suggested interior design concepts, to include color schemes, interior finishes, wall coverings, floor coverings, ceiling treatments, lighting treatments and window treatments.

D. Prepare layout showing location of movable furniture and furnishings.

E. Prepare schematic plans for recommended cabinet work, interior built-ins and other interior decorative details ("Interior Installations").

1.2 Prior to commencing Design Concept Services, Designer shall receive an Initial Design Fee of·_____ dollars ($_____). This non-refundable Design Fee is payable upon signing this Agreement and is in addition to all other compensation payable to Designer under this Agreement. Not more than_____ (____) revisions to the Design Concept will be prepared by Designer without additional charges. Additional revisions will be billed to Client as Additional Services.

2. Interior Specifications and Purchasing Services

2.1 Upon Client's approval of the Design Concepts, Designer will, as and where appropriate:

A. Select and/or specially design required Interior Installations and all required items of movable furniture, furnishings, light fixtures, hardware, fixtures, accessories and the like ("Merchandise").

B. Prepare and submit for Client's approval Proposals for completion of Interior Installations and purchase of Merchandise.

2.2 Merchandise and Interior Installations specified by Designer shall, if Client wishes to purchase them, be purchased solely through Designer. Designer may, at times, request Client to engage others to provide Interior Installations, pursuant to the arrangements set forth in the Project Review services described in paragraph 3 of this Agreement.

INTERIOR DESIGN SERVICES

1. Design Concept Services

1.1 In this phase of the Project, Designer shall, as and where appropriate, perform the following:

A. Determine Client's design preferences and requirements.

B. Conduct an initial design study.

C. Prepare drawings and other materials to generally illustrate Designer's suggested interior design concepts, to include color schemes, interior finishes, wall coverings, floor coverings, ceiling treatments, lighting treatments and window treatments.

D. Prepare layout showing location of movable furniture and furnishings.

E. Prepare schematic plans for recommended cabinet work, interior built-ins and other interior decorative details ("Interior Installations").

1.2 Designer shall be compensated for its Design Concept Services on an hourly basis at the rates set forth in paragraph 4.1 of this Agreement. Hourly charges will be invoiced to Client _____ and are payable by Client upon receipt of invoice. Upon signing this Agreement, Designer shall receive a non-refundable initial advance of _____ dollars ($_____), which constitutes the minimum fee due Designer for Design Concept Services. This advance will be credited against hourly charges otherwise payable by Client to Designer for Design Concept Services.

2. Interior Specifications and Purchasing Services

2.1 Upon Client's approval of the Design Concepts, Designer will, as and where appropriate:

A. Select and/or specially design required Interior Installations and all required items of movable furniture, furnishings, light fixtures, hardware, fixtures, accessories and the like ("Merchandise").

B. Prepare and submit for Client's approval Proposals for completion of Interior Installations and purchase of Merchandise.

2.2 Merchandise and Interior Installations specified by Designer shall, if Client wishes to purchase them, be purchased solely through Designer. Designer may, at times, request Client to engage others to provide Interior Installations, pursuant to the arrangements set forth in the Project Review services described in paragraph 3 of this Agreement.

2.3 Merchandise and Interior Installations to be purchased through Designer will be specified in a written "Proposal" prepared by Designer and submitted in each instance for Client's written approval. Each Proposal will describe the item and its price to Client (F.O.B. point of origin) ("Client Price"). The Client price for each item of Merchandise and Interior Installations includes a fee for services rendered in this phase of the Project.

2.4 No item can be ordered by Designer until the Proposal has been approved by Client, in writing, and returned to Designer with Designer's required initial payment equal to _____ percent (____%) of the Client Price. The balance of the Client Price, together with delivery, shipping, handling charges and applicable taxes, is payable when the item is ready for delivery to and/or installation at Client's residence, or to a subsequent supplier for further work upon rendition of Designer's invoice. Proposals for fabrics, wall coverings, accessories, antiques, and items purchased at auction or at retail stores require full payment at time of signed Proposal.

3. Project Review

3.1 If the nature of the Project requires engagement by Client of any contractors to perform work based upon Designer's concepts, drawings or interior design specifications not otherwise provided for in the Interior Specifications and Purchasing Services, Client will enter into contracts directly with the concerned contractor.

3.2 Designer will make periodic visits to the Project site as Designer may consider appropriate to observe the work of these contractors to determine whether the contractors' work is proceeding in general conformity with Designer's concepts. Constant observation of work at the Project site is not a part of Designer's duties. Designer is not responsible for the performance, quality, timely completion or delivery of any work, materials or equipment furnished by contractors pursuant to direct contracts with Client.

3.3 Time expended by Designer for all Project Review services will be charged to Client on an hourly basis at the rates set forth in paragraph 4.1 of the Agreement.

4. MISCELLANEOUS

4.1 Should Designer agree to perform any design service not described above, such "Additional Service" will be invoiced to Client at the following hourly rates:

Design Principal	$_____
Project Designer	$_____
Staff Designer	$_____
Draftsman	$_____
Other employees	$_____

Hourly charges will be invoiced to Client _____ and are payable upon receipt of invoice.

4.2 Disbursements incurred by Designer in the interest of the Project shall be reimbursed by Client to Designer upon receipt of Designer's invoices, which are rendered _____. Reimbursements shall include, among other things, costs of local and long distance travel, long distance telephone calls, duplication of plans, drawings and specifications, messenger services and the like.

4.3 Designer's drawings and specifications are conceptual in nature and intended to set forth design intent only. They are not to be used for architectural or engineering purposes. Designer does not provide architectural or engineering services.

4.4 Designer's services shall not include undertaking any responsibility for the design or modification of the design of any structural, heating, air-conditioning, plumbing, electrical, ventilation or other mechanical systems installed or to be installed at the Project.

4.5 Should the nature of Designer's design concepts require the services of any other design professional, such professional shall be engaged directly by Client pursuant to separate agreement as may be mutually acceptable to Client and such other design professional.

4.6 As Designer requires a record of Designer's design projects, Client will permit Designer or Designer's representatives to photograph the Project upon completion of the Project. Designer will be entitled to use photographs for Designer's business purposes but shall not disclose Project location or Client's name without Client's prior written consent.

4.7 All concepts, drawings and specifications prepared by Designer's firm ("Project Documents") and all copyrights and other proprietary rights applicable thereto remain at all times Designer's property. Project Documents may not be used by Client for any purpose other than completion of Project by Designer.

4.8 Designer cannot guarantee that actual prices for Merchandise and/or Interior Installations or other costs or services as presented to Client will not vary either by item or in the aggregate from any Client proposed budget.

4.9 This Agreement may be terminated by either party upon the other party's default in performance, provided that termination may not be effected unless written notice specifying nature and extent of default is given to the concerned party and such party fails to cure such default in performance within _____ (____) days from date of receipt of such notice. Termination shall be without prejudice to any and all other rights and remedies of Designer, and Client shall remain liable for all outstanding obligations owed by Client to Designer and for all items of Merchandise, Interior Installations and other services on order as of the termination date.

4.10 In addition to all other legal rights, Designer shall be entitled to withhold delivery of any item of Merchandise or the further performance of Interior Installations or any other services, should Client fail to timely make any payments due Designer.

4.11 Any controversy or claim arising out of or relating to this Agreement, or the breach thereof, shall be decided by arbitration only in the _____ in accordance with the Commercial Arbitration Rules of the American Arbitration Association then in effect, and judgment upon the award rendered by the arbitrator(s) may be entered in any court having jurisdiction thereof.

4.12 Client will provide Designer with access to the Project and all information Designer may need to complete the Project. It is Client's responsibility to obtain all approvals required by any governmental agency or otherwise in connection with this Project.

4.13 Any sales tax applicable to Design Fees, and/or Merchandise purchased from Designer, and/or Interior Installations completed by Designer shall be the responsibility of Client.

4.14 Neither Client nor Designer may assign their respective interests in this Agreement without the written consent of the other.

4.15 The laws of the State of _____ shall govern this Agreement.

4.16 Any provision of this Agreement held to be void or unenforceable under any law shall be deemed stricken, and all remaining provisions shall continue to be valid and binding upon both Designer and Client.

4.17 This Agreement is a complete statement of Designer's and Client's understanding. No representations or agreements have been made other than those contained in this Agreement. This Agreement can be modified only by a writing signed by both Designer and Client.

5. ADDITIONAL TERMS

CLIENT:

_____

_____

DESIGNER:

_____

_____

Figures 6.4 to 6.12 (pages 211–224) contain examples of nine letters of agreement design firms use. You may be able to adapt them to your firm and situation; but, again, before you do, review them first with your legal consultants.

When to Present a Letter of Agreement or Contract

In some situations, it is to your advantage to have a simple letter of agreement or contract that can be filled in very quickly. These documents can be used on those occasions when you approach a client with a small project; the agreement can be presented on the spot. Often it will be signed, and you will be given your retainer right then and there. Figure 6.4 (page 211) shows a sample of such a form.

In most cases, you should see and review the project before presenting a letter of agreement or a contract. Talk with the clients and investigate the situation carefully by doing some of the recommended precontract checks (see Figure 6.5, page 212). The more you know about the project, the better the contract you will be able to write. If you have properly outlined the contract, it can serve as an outline of the work to be done, making it very easy to coordinate the schedule and process the plan. Before presenting a contract, you usually will have had an initial interview and will have spent time doing research and preparation. Often you will not present your contract until after a second or third interview. The second interview is often used by designers to review their outline of what is to be included and to check other details they feel should be worked into the contract proposal. The proposal should then be mailed or given to the client at the next meeting.

Do not become so excited about starting a new project that you forget about some of the legal ramifications. In today's business climate, you must be extremely cautious. Take extra time to define each project; be sure you and your client understand the services to be rendered and the accompanying responsibilities. The obligations of the client need to be as carefully defined as those of the design firm.

In reviewing letters of agreements and contracts, you must be as specific as you can. In your documents, include your expectations, exactly what services you are providing, the rooms you are working on, the products you are purchasing, the number of meetings that will be included, and how many months the contract is valid.

CONSIDERATIONS

Communication is the key to good contracts, whether in written or verbal form. A designer who has an understanding of the field, is able to see a project from a client's view, and then to work with the artistry that defines our profession will have a great position in this new market. A lot of marketing and selling will be done quickly. Clients want things done with speed, but they also want excellent rapport with designers. If you can sell a job, you will have the key position. Specialists will be strong in selling and marketing and will make a huge difference in the way our field is presented.

Figure 6.4 Sample letter of agreement. This letter of agreement would be used with a cover page describing the project. Or a space could be left above "Design Fee" for the project definition. It is suitable for either a small contract or residential use.

This agreement made this _____ day of _____, 20_____ between _____(firm's name) (hereafter called _____(firm's name) and _____(client's name) (hereafter called CLIENT).

1. _____(firm's name) agrees to perform the following services for CLIENT in connection with Premises at _____:
(a) DESIGN FEE

Please sign and return copy.

2. In consideration for the services to be performed by _____(firm's name), CLIENT agrees to pay _____(firm's name) AS FOLLOWS:
   (a) One-third of design fee when signing of contract.
   (b) One-third at first presentation of design.
   (c) Balance upon completion of contract.

3. In the event CLIENT should cancel this contract, then all funds paid hereunder shall be retained by _____(firm's name) and, in addition, CLIENT shall pay any cost incurred by _____(firm's name).

4. Sales tax or any other taxes are not included in contract.

5. Prices subject to change 30 days after the above date.

IN WITNESS WHEREOF the parties hereto have set their hand and seal the day and year above written.

_____ _____ _____ _____
(for firm)   (date)   (client signature)   (date)

_____   _____
(firm name)   (client print name)

Figure 6.5 Sample letter of agreement. This letter of agreement for design services is for a firm charging an hourly fee as well as offering purchasing and expediting services.

This Letter of Agreement will serve as our agreement in outlining the services to be rendered by _____ in connection with the interiors of _____.

As Designer, I agree to do the following: consult, evaluate, plan, design, shop, budget, and supervise all contract and subcontract work that comes under my direction. For all Designing Services rendered by my firm, the following fee schedule will be used:

$_____ per hour for my services, not to exceed $_____ per day. My assistant designer and draftsman will be billed at $_____ per hour. Charges will be made for all out-of-pocket expenses such as travel (other than normal commuting expenses), telephone calls, and any necessary blueprinting or professional rendering made at your request.

A time sheet and record of all out-of-pocket expenses will be kept by my offices. These records will be available for your inspection. All purchases will be billed to you at prices quoted.

All purchases, design plans, or work to be ordered by my firm will be submitted for your approval in the form of estimates. Each estimate will require your signature and a 50 percent retainer to authorize the placement of any orders or the execution of any design plans. An additional 25 percent will be due at the end of three months if merchandise is ready but cannot be installed. The final payment will be due upon delivery.

There are no sales taxes added to the Design Fee; only to product purchases. All freight charges or extra insurance ordered by you will be payable by you. I can assume no responsibility for delays occasioned by failure of others to meet commitments beyond my control. You shall have the benefit of all guarantees and warranties possessed by me against any manufacturer. Any items purchased that have been approved by you on the signed estimate cannot be canceled or returned without additional expense to you.

At this time, I am requesting a retainer fee of $_____. This retainer fee will be deducted from your financial statement at the completion of this assignment. The signing of this Letter of Agreement and the receipt of the retainer fee authorizes me to proceed with this project. In the event this project is terminated before completion, the retainer fee will be applied as a compensation for services rendered based upon my hourly Design Fee.

If you consent to this Letter of Agreement, please sign and return one copy of the letter to me together with the retainer fee.

I am looking forward to being of service to you.

For Firm:

_____   _____
(firm name)   (date)

Agreed and Accepted by:

_____   _____
(client signature)   (date)

_____
(client name)

Figure 6.6 Sample letter of agreement. This is a simple contract for professional services from design through completion, including supervision.

CONTRACT FOR PROFESSIONAL SERVICES

This contract is made between the Designer:

and the Client:

for the following project:

1. The Designer's professional services shall consist of consulting with the Client to determine the scope of work; preparing the necessary preliminary studies; making preliminary estimates; preparing working drawings and specifications; and consulting with architects, engineers, or other special consultants.

2. The Designer will perform or procure such periodic inspections as the designer may consider appropriate. The Designer will endeavor to warn the client against defects and deficiencies in the work of the contractor(s) but shall not have responsibility for the failure of the contractor to comply with drawings or specifications or any latent defect in the work of the contractors(s).

3. The Client has the assurances of the Designer that the Designer's service shall be rendered in good faith and in a professional manner; but the designer cannot be responsible for the performance, quality, or timely completion of work by the contractor(s). Nor can the Designer be responsible for the guarantee of any fabric, material, or product against wearing, fading, soiling, or latent defect.

4. All drawings, specifications, and documents prepared by the Designer are instruments of service for the execution of the work on the project and are the exclusive property of the Designer, whether the work on the project is executed or not; and the Designer reserves the plan copyright, whether the work on the project is executed or not, and said plan shall not be used on any other project without the Designer's prior written consent.

5. The Client shall pay the Designer for his or her services, a fee based upon time dedicated by the Designer at the following rates:

        Principal

        Designer

        Design Assistant

        Administration

(continued)

Figure 6.6 *(Continued)*

In addition, extensive travel expenses, long-distance telephone costs, extensive printing or reproduction charges, or other out-of-pocket expenses will be billed at the Designer's cost. The Designer will bill the Client following the fifteenth of and last day of each month for the fees payable to that point. The amount is due and payable within 10 days following receipt of statement.

6. Additional terms:

The parties agree to the foregoing conditions.

For Designer:

_____

For Client:

_____

Date: _____

Figure 6.7 Sample letter of agreement. This letter of agreement is used for a straight-fee or lump-sum professional service contract. It is suitable for residential or contract use.

AGREEMENT FOR PROFESSIONAL DESIGN SERVICES

BETWEEN: (designer)
AND: (client name and address)
FOR: (project)

A. PROFESSIONAL SERVICES
The designer's professional services during the course of the project consist generally of the following:
1. Consulting with the client to determine the scope of the work and preparation of cost estimates.
2. Preparing the necessary preliminary studies.
3. Planning room layouts and selecting necessary wall and floor coverings, draperies, furniture, and accessories for client approval.
4. Making preliminary estimates.
5. Consulting with architects, engineers, or other special advisors.
6. Preparing working drawings and specifications as needed.
7. Securing contractors needed to provide services for the completion of the design project, including specification of work to be done and appropriate supervision of those contractors.

B. FEES AND PAYMENT PROVISIONS
The client agrees to pay a fee of $ (fee or fee range) to the designer for the services outlined above. In addition, the following expenses by or on behalf of the designer for this project will be paid by the client at the designer's cost.
1. Extensive travel (more than _____ miles monthly at a rate of _____ ¢/mile) above _____ miles.
2. Long-distance telephone expenses.
3. Blueprinting or reproduction expenses.
4. Renderings.

If the designer arranges for other contractors to perform specific services as part of the project, the client will pay a supervision fee to the designer of 25% of each contractors' billed cost.

Payment of the fee will be as follows:
1. Initial retainer of 50 percent of the fee as authorization to proceed.
2. Supervision fees upon completion of contractor's work and billing.
3. Balance of fee and other expenses upon completion of project.

Invoices are payable within 10 days of receipt. Balances unpaid after 30 days are subject to an interest charge of 1.25 percent per month. Interest will continue to be charged on unpaid balances after 30 days even though a partial payment has been received.

(continued)

Figure 6.7 *(Continued)*

C. <u>TERMS AND CONDITIONS</u>

1. Designs, drawings, and scale models will remain in the property of the designer unless a written agreement has been issued to the contrary.
2. Periodic inspections and observations of work on a project will be made as we consider appropriate. We do not have responsibility for the failure of contractors to comply with drawings or specifications prepared by us, nor for latent defects in their work.
3. If, after a definite scheme has been approved, the client makes a decision which, for its proper execution, involves extra services or expenses for changes in or additions to the studies, drawings, specifications, etc., the client will pay the designer for such extra services on a design time fee basis of $_____/hour.

We agree to the services as outlined, the fees and payment provisions, and the terms and conditions.

Designer: _____   Date: _____

Client: _____   Date: _____

Figure 6.8 Sample letter of agreement. This letter of agreement is suitable for a residential or small contract project that is based on retail pricing.

This letter will confirm that you are retaining our firm to assist you in the interior design of your home in _____.

Our services include the following: preparing furniture plans; shopping for and selecting all furnishings to be purchased from our sources and workrooms; assisting in paint selection and overseeing painting; and placing furniture, accessories, and art.

All merchandise purchased by you, including custom-designed furniture and cabinetry, will be sold on a showroom list basis. Miscellaneous charges for freight, delivery, packing, and sales tax will be additional. A written estimate reflecting the specified price will be sent to you after selection of merchandise.

A signed estimate and 50 percent initial payment are necessary before merchandise is ordered. However, pro forma merchandise, inventory items, and immediately deliverable items must be paid in advance of delivery. We have been advised by our suppliers that all prices are subject to change without notice. Should this happen, we will obtain your approval before proceeding with the order.

Contracts for the work of carpenters, electricians, plumbing contractors, and similar tradespeople will be entered into directly between you and the contractor. We will be available for consulting with regard to architectural changes and additions, and for the review of the work of the above-mentioned tradespeople to ensure adherence to plans and specifications.

You will be invoiced for this consultation or review at the rates of $130.00 per hour for my time, $90.00 per hour for any architect engaged by our firm, $50.00 per hour for project designers and senior CAD personnel, and $40.00 per hour for junior CAD personnel and staff.

We request that clients sign working drawings as a confirmation of their agreement with the designs. Should you decide not to proceed with any custom furniture or cabinetry that we design for you, you will be billed at our hourly consultation rates for design time. Blueprinting charges will be additional.

Should you decide not to proceed with interior design selections that we have made in consultation with you and that you purchase directly from others, you will be billed at our hourly consultation rates for design time.

Should you terminate our business relationship, all time spent by me or my personnel (including preparation of furniture plans, selection of furnishings, and all other services described in the second paragraph of this letter) will be billed at the appropriate hourly charges. Should there be any cancellation charges, they will be billed in addition. The balance in your account will be refunded to you after the above charges have been deducted.

(continued)

Figure 6.8 *(Continued)*

An authorized signature on a copy of this letter, along with a $_____ retainer, will constitute authority for us to begin the project. This retainer will be applied to final billing.

If you have any questions concerning this letter, please share them with me. I look forward to working with you.

Very truly yours,

Mary V. Knackstedt

Client Approval: _____

Date: _____

We request your permission to photograph and publish our design work. Your signature below is our authorization.

Client Approval: _____

Figure 6.9 Sample letter of agreement. This letter of agreement would be used for the purchasing of furnishings and services relating to a residential or small contract job, most likely during the order-placing phase.

This Agreement made this _____ day of _____, 20_____ between _____ (firm's full name) (hereafter called _____ (firm's name) and _____ (client's name) (hereafter called Client).

1. _____ (firm's name) agrees to perform the following services for Client in connection with premises:

2. In consideration for the services to be performed by _____ (firm's name), Client agrees to pay as follows;
   (a) One-half costs to _____ (firm's name) of total contract to be ordered when signing of contract.
   (b) Remainder of costs to be billed as installed.
   (c) Balance upon completion.

3. In the event Client should cancel this contract, then all funds paid hereunder shall be retained by _____ (firm's name) and, in addition, Client shall pay any costs incurred by _____ (firm's name) for merchandise or goods ordered.

4. All merchandise required to be purchased or services to be rendered under this contract shall be procured by _____ (firm's name) through its own facilities or sources, unless it is specifically specified to the contrary herein. _____ (firm's name) will not be responsible for the quality of merchandise ordered or services preformed through Client's sources.

5. _____ (firm's name) cannot and does not guarantee the merchandise installed or used under this contract from ordinary wear and tear, fading, or latent defects not apparent at the time of installation.

6. All drawings, photographs, renderings, materials, and samples supplied by _____ (firm's name) shall remain its property and shall be retained by it after the completion of this contract.

7. _____ (firm's name) shall not be responsible for any delays in the performance of its services caused by third parties or by any other reason or cause beyond its control.

(continued)

Figure 6.9 *(Continued)*

8. Client authorizes _____ (firm's name) to make photographs or other reproductions of the work performed by _____ (firm's name) and to thereafter publicly display the same through a new medium or otherwise, provided only that the Client's name is not to be used in connection therewith without the express consent and permission of the Client.
    _____ (firm's name) is hereby given permission, after completion of the work, to enter Client's premises for the purpose of making such photographs or other reproductions, which photographs or reproductions shall become the exclusive property of _____ (firm's name).

9. In the event any dispute shall arise between _____ (firm's name) and Client in connection with this contract, it is hereby agreed that such dispute shall be referred to three arbitrators, one to be appointed by the first two named arbitrators. An award in writing signed by any two of the three arbitrators shall be final and conclusive and binding upon the parties hereto. The procedure to be followed by the arbitrators, and all other questions concerning the scope and method of arbitration, shall be as provided under _____ (your State's arbitration act).

10. Sales tax or any other taxes are not included in contract.

11. Prices subject to change if contract is not signed and returned within 30 days of above date.

IN WITNESS WHEREOF the parties hereto have set their hands and seals the day and year first above written.

For Firm:

_____   _____
(signature)   (printed name)

For Client:

_____   _____
(signature)   (printed name)

Figure 6.10 Sample letter of agreement. This letter of agreement is for designers working on a percentage- or commission-compensation method, where no hourly rate or other design fee is charged.

Dear:

This letter will confirm our method of operation in connection with the work we have discussed for the project at the above address.

All furniture and furnishings, as well as services provided through this office, will be sold to you at our net cost plus a 30 percent commission. There will be no additional charge for our design services. Travel expenses, toll telephone calls, sales taxes, shipping charges, and other such out-of-pocket expenses directly applicable to the project will be rebilled to you at our net costs on a monthly basis.

We request a $_____ retainer, which will be credited to your account at a time of the final billing. Each purchase will be covered by an invoice describing the item and requesting a 50 percent retainer and your signed approval. The balance is due upon delivery. For antiques, we request payment in full when the invoice is approved. This schedule is for each invoice submitted.

If the above meets with your approval, please sign at the bottom of the letter and return one copy to us along with the initial retainer.

Cordially,

_____
(signature for firm)

Accepted and Approved:

_____
(client signature)

Date: _____

Figure 6.11 Sample letter of agreement. This proposal was for a small office project. A similar proposal could be used for a simple residential project, where a more formal contract might seem inappropriate.

PROPOSAL FOR PROFESSIONAL DESIGN SERVICES

TO:

RE:

This proposal for interior design planning of the first floor of the newly purchased building at this address will consist generally of the following.

1. Review of existing furnishings and equipment in present office.
2. Review of space and task requirements for the new facilities.
3. Space Planning: Review of the existing building conditions and preparation of a plan to accommodate the needs as specified, i.e., partitioning, general layout, etc.
4. Specifications for types of materials that would be required to implement the study, as well as furnishings.
5. Preparation of a master color scheme.

Specific services during the study include:
1. Presentation of the design plan to the client for review, with changes as needed to accommodate the client's preferences.
2. Preparation of the final budget estimate and design plan for client approval.

The fee to provide the services described in this proposal will be in the range of $_____ with a retainer of $_____ required to begin this project.

The client will provide floor plans, measurements, and prints as needed.

Designer submitting proposal and responsible for this project:

_____   _____
(date)   (signature)

I agree to the services outlined in this proposal and authorize the designer named above to proceed upon receipt of this signed agreement and my check in the amount of: $_____

_____   _____
(date)   (signature)

Figure 6.12 Sample letter of agreement. This letter of agreement is for a firm requiring a design fee by the hour and a percentage fee on items purchased for the project (both contracted items and furniture).

Dear :

After meeting with you and discussing the design and space planning of your residence, we are ready to begin making definite plans.

This proposal outlines our firm's financial requirements and defines our services and responsibilities, as well as our role in relation to any other design professionals you may involve in this project. If you approve this proposal, by signing it and returning it to us with the initial payment, our firm will send a comprehensive letter of agreement.

Design Areas: The scope of the project encompasses your entire residence.

Design Services: For the design work of your residence, our firm will perform the following services:

1. Initial design study. The initial floor plans you provided will probably undergo some revision based on your needs and desires. Further consultation with you will clarify the extent of these revisions before we prepare the preliminary architectural and interior design concept.

2. Preliminary architectural and interior design concept. A complete design presentation shall be prepared for your approval and will include:

   a. Architectural drawings and documents. We will detail all interior and exterior architectural changes for your project.

   b. Preparation of complete floor plans. These will be drawn to scale and will include a proposed furniture layout.

   c. Finalization of all architectural and working drawings. All working drawings shall be submitted to you for your approval and for consultation with other design professionals involved with the project. Any necessary revisions will be made and final approval will be acknowledged by you in writing.

   d. Preliminary design concept. After you have approved our layout drawings, we will make a complete presentation, including furniture selection, material selection (fabrics, wallcoverings, curtain design, floor design, a color selections, lighting, etc.), and other visual aids we deem necessary to illustrate our design plan.

Purchases: All purchases will be made available to you at wholesale, or "net," cost. Our firm will act as your purchasing agent and all bills from vendors will be forwarded to our office for payment. We will prepare all specifications and purchase orders, which specify payment terms with which you must comply; however, our firm will deal with all vendors on a financial basis.

(continued)

Figure 6.12 *(Continued)*

Compensation: Our firm will bill on an hourly basis for our design and planning services as specified by the description of design services. The rates are:

Firm Principal	$____ per hour
Senior Designer	$____ per hour
Drafting	$____ per hour

Furthermore, the fees for selecting and specifying all purchases of furniture and furnishings shall be based on certain percentages of the furniture and furnishings budget, which are:

35 percent on the initial $100,000 of the "F&F" budget
30 percent on the "F&F" budget above $100,000

If the above meets with your approval, your signature below will indicate your acceptance of the basic terms of our agreement. Please return one signed copy and a retainer of $_____. We will present a more detailed agreement for your acceptance within several weeks. Of course, please call if you have any questions.

Sincerely,

Interior Design Firm
By: _____
(president)

Accepted and Approved:

_____

_____

CHAPTER 7

Succeeding in Project Management

Interior design is a creative discipline, whether you are doing the design work or producing the project. The process requires *managed* systems, as it takes many creative professionals, as well as craftspeople and many vendors, to complete a project.

Project management has several separate and distinct stages:

- Programming
- Schematic design
- Design development
- Contract, placing orders, contract administration, installation supervision, postoccupancy evaluation, client retention, and client loyalty

These are the terms traditionally used to refer to various aspects of the interior design project process; however, that is changing. Today, we may perform various tasks at different stages; and the systems can vary and the phases may be called by different names. We have to examine our projects and responsibilities, then determine the best process to complete a particular project.

The size and type of project determines the client-designer relationship in each of these stages; however, the basic purpose of each step of the process remains the same.

The programming phase will define the project and the initial contractual agreement between the client and designer. The schematic design phase is for preliminary designing of space allocation and determining locations for partitions, furnishings, and equipment; establishing concepts of `types and qualities of finishes and materials; and preparing a budget and estimated schedule for project completion. This phase is meant to define for the client all major decisions concerning the parameters of space, layout, quality of products, and probable costs of the project—as well as the relationships and scope of work and products to be provided by the designer or other professionals—prior to the next step, finalizing and detailing all aspects of the project. Client review and approval is essential prior to the next phase.

The design development phase includes finalizing all design layouts; details of all interior construction; specifications for all products, materials, and equipment; and work methods and standards, in addition to any other document preparation needed before the owner's review and approval of this stage.

During the contract documents phase, decisions must be finalized for the execution and installation of the project. How the work will be managed by the design firm or the client, and the types and numbers of contracts or purchase orders issued between the owner and contractor or supplier for products, must be determined and mutually agreed on. It is a time of preparing and executing the bidding, contracting, and procurement documents in preparation for the next step of the process.

The contract administration and installation phases commence with the award of one or more contracts or the issuance of purchase orders; they formally terminate when the final payments to the contractors or suppliers have been certified. It is the step in the process that includes the actual procurement, construction, installation, and final finishing and placement of all elements of the total project.

THE PROGRAMMING PHASE

Data Collection

Forms such as the ones shown in the tables throughout this chapter are often valuable in collecting information. Having a list to check off will prevent you from forgetting different phases. It is also an excellent reference for the staff working in your studio, because they will know exactly where to go in your file for particular information. Depending on the type of work you do, you may want to create a file of forms useful to your practice. Much of this work is now done on the computer, but the key is to have a standard and a list of reminders, rather than having to begin from scratch on every project.

Your initial discussions with a client establish the parameters of the job. You will learn what type of work is required, the client's preferences and direction, the budget, contract terms, the previous work done on the project by others, and the availability of other plans or blueprints. You will also discover which other professionals and design consultants will be involved in the project. (See pages 156–157 for a more detailed discussion of the initial interview.)

While the initial discussions are under way, your business or financial personnel or consultant will obtain credit information about the client from a credit bureau or other appropriate resources (see page 405).

After your initial review, when you have decided to proceed with a particular client, you prepare a contract or letter of agreement based on a review, analysis, and evaluation of the client's objectives, the services the client needs, and the site requirements—all of which are included in the written proposal. The contract letter of agreement also includes the proposed contract terms for work and the schedule of payments; when signed by the client, this becomes the initial contract between the client and the designer. This first contract is usually for all services to be performed by the designer's firm through the schematic design phase or preliminary design phase and the design development phase.

THE SCHEMATIC DESIGN PHASE

After the client has signed your contract or letter of agreement, you then proceed to the preliminary design phase. This starts with an examination of the client's plans, or premises, to determine existing conditions and material and to evaluate aspects of the facilities that would affect delivery or accessibility to the project site.

You will also review the requirements for protection of property and any removal of existing furniture, fixtures, and equipment. The existing conditions of the site are spelled out (see Table 7.1, page 228). Your design firm should make an inventory of the client's existing furniture to describe its condition, dimensions, sizes, details, and history.

Next, prepare evaluations. This is the *concept* stage of the design. You will consider all details affecting the interior space, including furniture, layouts, traffic patterns, existing interiors, any built-in cabinetry, lighting, special HVAC requirements, doors, and windows. This is the time to interview all parties involved, starting with the client and all those leasing or using the spaces. Your design service outline creates a base for an even more extensive review.

At this stage, you also should meet with the architect and other design professionals associated with the job to exchange any special technical data, as well as to establish the position and responsibilities of your design firm in relation to them.

During this stage, you will do your product research, which involves finding furnishings, equipment, fabrics, and materials appropriate to the specifications and requirements of the project. You will also prepare preliminary drawings, sketches, displays, and estimates of probable project costs for presentation to the client for the client's review and approval.

THE DESIGN DEVELOPMENT PHASE

Once your preliminary work has been approved by the client, you can move it into the final design development phase, in which you prepare detailed drawings and specifications based on all decisions and data collected in earlier phases. You also

Table 7.1 Existing conditions sheet. This is helpful in documenting the preliminary design phase.

EXISTING CONDITIONS								
Client:		Room:				Photo No.	Date:	Page __ of __
Floor:								
Walls:	N	S	E	W	Color:			
Block								
Brick								
Glass								
Plaster/Drywall								
Wood/Paneling								
Paint								
Accent Paint								
Vinyl								
Ceramic Tile								
Wainscot/Chair Rail								
Thermostat								
Telephone								
Other								
OUTLETS								
Ceiling:								
Lighting:								
Cabinetwork:								
Other:								

© *Design Business Monthly,* 1988.

write detailed specifications for all items to be purchased and prepare workroom or subcontractor specs.

You prepare a detailed statement of probable project costs, including the cost of furnishings, finishes, contracting, and materials. Then you review their availability. At this point, you may want to establish an allowance for accessories and any other items required to complete the project. You will also prepare a review of shipping

WORKSTATION SUMMARY				Client:
				Date:
Position:	Name:	Location:	Needs:	Notes:

© *Design Business Monthly,* 1988.

and other installation expenses and terms and review and update your payment
terms. Before continuing on to the next process, you must receive and document
formal approval of the proposal by the client.

THE CONTRACT PHASE

After receiving the approvals of the design development phase, the design firm
makes any further necessary adjustments. It then prepares construction documents
and the specifications required for the construction work on the project. The design
firm also may recommend contractors appropriate for the project, and prepare,
request, receive, and review bids.

Appropriate purchase documents with detailed specifications are also prepared
at this stage—including requirements for fabrication procurement; shipment; and
delivery and installation of all furniture, furnishings, and equipment required for
the project. The design firm may assume the responsibility for purchasing and project management of the installation or may merely supervise or assist, depending on
the contract.

Most documentation is done by computer. Many designers use Pilot and Excel;
others use standardized forms with extensive detail that can simply be filled in with
preferences. A paper system is used here for illustration purposes only. Any system

Table 7.3 Design master sheet. This sheet documents in one place all the details for each room you are designing. It is prepared at the design development phase, after the preliminary work has been approved by the client. You may wish to write the details in pencil in case changes are made. Keeping this single record can help you in many ways when you make additions, revisions, or even redo a project many years later. Have it printed on heavier stock paper so it is easy to find in the file and can stand up to the wear and tear of continuous or long-term use.

DESIGN MASTER SHEET		
Client:	**Room:**	**Date:**

Floor:

Wall:

Woodwork:

Ceiling:

Window Treatment:

Feature:

Lighting:

Furniture:

Lamps:

Accessory Items:

© *Design Business Monthly,* 1988.

Table 7.4 Room specification sheet. In the concept stage of the design, you prepare detailed descriptions. A sheet such as this will facilitate review and approval of your room specifications by the client and contractor. The detailed descriptions in this worksheet are useful for the owner's records and for working with contractors. A copy can be posted in the room itself so that all the contractors and vendors have the information they need. On this worksheet, the objective is to keep information simple and easy to read, so that everyone can understand it. The approval sections should be visible, so the contractors can confirm that the appropriate authorities have given their approval.

ROOM SPECIFICATION				
Client:		Room No.:	Name:	Date:

Carpet:

Walls:

Ceiling:

Window Treatment:

Built-ins:

Furniture:

Room Layout:	Approval:	Moving Schedule:
	Contr.:	From:
	Owner:	To:
		To:

© *Design Business Monthly,* 1988.

PROJECT MASTER SHEET								Date:	
Client:				Contact:				Designer:	
Address:				Phone No. Home:				Start Date:	
				Work:					
								Completion Date:	
Date:	Order No.:	Supplier:	Item:	Area:	Quoted:	Exp. Ship. Week of:	Rec'd.:	Del'd.:	Billed:

you devise should be easy to read; keep certain items in the same locations on the pages. The goal is to have a system that makes it easy for anyone who picks up the document to understand what has been done and what still needs to be done. Document in whatever form is best for your type of business. The key is to keep the documents up to date. Much effort goes into creating the basic forms. Once you have established a procedure, a support person can fill in the details. This master record is the one we refer to when making client calls and holding project meetings. The project master sheet makes everything easy to find and has the most updated information.

Clear communication is critical throughout the project. Many unexpected issues and questions come up, even on the best-planned projects. Designers work on many projects at one time: therefore, things can get confusing.

A standard form listing the items for each project lets the designer see the issues affecting the project easily as they occur. This allows problems to be dealt with early, when it is easy for the designer to make adjustments. The delay of even one item affects many other parts of a job.

Organization is a major part of the interior design profession. It is said that design is 10 percent of the job and making it happen is 90 percent. There are so many small details that can make or break a project. We must have a way to stay on top of those details throughout the project.

PLACING ORDERS

After the client accepts the proposals, your firm places all orders and finalizes subcontracts. You will meet with contractors to determine scheduling and organize delivery installations. Any additional necessary detailed drawings will be prepared and reviewed. You will also review your insurance coverage to confirm that all the items are covered appropriately.

With all the details carefully defined as you progress through the design process, the orders are ready for a final review. Many firms require orders to be placed within 24 hours of the client's approval. If the client requests any revisions at this stage, you should determine how they will affect the schedule and budget. Before making any changes in your orders, get approval from both the client and the contractor to determine the correct costs and whether the change will affect the schedule. All changes should be in writing and faxed or e-mailed to the client, the contractor, and others, as required.

Shown on the next several pages, in Tables 7.6, 7.7, 7.8, and 7.9 (pages 234–237) are documents used by my firm to assist the staff in placing orders and tracking the progress. These forms allow a comprehensive summary of a particular piece of a project to be maintained in one place.

THE CONTRACT ADMINISTRATION PHASE

After the contract development phase has been completed, the contract administration phase begins. This phase encompasses the follow-through period, installation, and postoccupancy evaluation. The importance of this phase is often underestimated. There is a very delicate balance required in both keeping the client well informed and

Table 7.6 Reupholstery checklist. This checklist outlines all project details involving reupholstery. It is useful to include a photograph of the existing furniture for appropriate documentation (a second photograph should go to the workroom). It is easy to put the wrong fabric on furniture. This worksheet, with its accompanying photo of the piece and fabric sample—with the correct side up, clarifies your instructions.

REUPHOLSTERY CHECKLIST			
Client:	Purchase Order No.:		Date:
Workroom Time Required:	Pick-up Date:		Expected Completion:
Description of Furniture:		Fabric:	
		Source:	
		Number:	
		Color:	
Style and Approximate Size:		Description:	
		Width:	
		Repeat:	
Instructions to Workroom:		Sample:	
Changes in Construction:			
Frame to Be Tightened:			
		Sketch or Photo:	
Wood to Be Refinished:			
Cushion Fill:			
Arm Hoods:			
Others:			
Special Instructions:			

© *Design Business Monthly,* 1988.

comfortable and supporting the various vendors and craftspeople. We are putting together many different personalities, and although we may feel they are the best people available to do the job, and we have taken great care during the designing and planning phases, there are always unexpected situations and problems.

The "Twilight Zone"

The follow-through period is often called the "twilight zone." The twilight zone actually begins the moment a client signs a contract or places an order and ends when the merchandise is delivered or an installation is completed. During this period, all of a client's worries and insecurities about the project come into full flower, and, if left unchecked, cause difficulty on installation day. Maintaining communication with the client for the duration of the project is the way to avoid problems.

Client Updates. Establish a regular day and time with the client for a weekly update call from your office on the stage of completion of the project. Early in the job there is often not much to report. The report may consist of saying: "We are working on

Table 7.7 Window treatment checklist. This is a good checklist to use when preparing specifications for any type of window treatment, including draperies, shades, and shutters. It also provides space for a sketch or photograph of the existing window or treatment.

WINDOW TREATMENT CHECKLIST		
Client:	Purchase Order No.:	Date:
Room Location:	Workroom Time Required:	Expected Installation:
Type of Treatment:		Fabric or Product Used:
		Source:
Type of Valance:		Number:
		Color:
		Description:
		Width:
		Repeat:
		Sample:
Measurements and Specifications:		Sketch or Photo:
Hardware/Rod Location:		
Length:		
Width:		
Extension:		
Overlap:		
Other:		
Accessories: (tie-backs, finials)		

© *Design Business Monthly*, 1988.

your preliminary design, have completed all the data collection, and are doing research on some of the materials required."

When clients know they will hear from you once a week, on a given day, you can avoid many calls from them throughout the week. You also will be better prepared. Before speaking to your clients, you can consult their file for up-to-date information, and you will be able to speak intelligently about their jobs.

In our studio, each project has a master sheet (see Table 7.5, page 232). This is produced on a computer so that it is available to all staff involved. Some designers prefer a paper copy for review and comments. The information noted on this form is then transferred into the electronic document—where we outline the components of the job at any particular time. We call our clients with the master sheet in front of us. On the back of the master sheet we keep simple records. Our managing director notes any comments the clients may have during the telephone conversation. This means, in addition to having a master file with all the original specifications for a job, we have a complete rundown on exactly what is being done as well as a record of all conversations and important data. If the designer wants to know what the managing director has said to a client, the designer refers to the master sheet. When this is done on computer you also have the advantage of being able to network it so that everyone in your firm has the most up-to-date information at all times.

When we make a presentation, we give the client a copy of the project schedule,

Table 7.8 Furniture, furnishings, and equipment (FF&E) specifications sheet. This type of specification sheet is appropriate for use when you are sending a project out for bids. These sheets, which normally have the design firm's name on them, can become part of a large purchasing document. All you need is an easy-to-understand reference sheet, whether it is drawn up by hand or on a computer. Keep it simple.

FURNITURE, FURNISHINGS, AND EQUIPMENT SPECIFICATIONS				
Project:			Date:	
Spec. No.:	Quan.:	Description: (manufacturer, catalog no., finish)	Unit Cost:	Ext. Cost:

© *Design Business Monthly,* 1988.

stating when the materials are expected, as well as when the different craftspeople will be working in the client's space. If revisions are required, or a final date is set, we tell the client during our weekly report. We will also send the client an updated outline of the schedule, so they will have the space ready for the arrival of the craftspeople.

You should talk weekly to the other professionals involved on the job, such as architects, engineers, or job coordinators. Neglecting this communication destroys cooperation and can undermine the project. This regular interaction not only serves to support professionalism but is an excellent marketing tool. If clients know you are on top of their job, they feel they are receiving very special personal care and are quick to recommend you to their friends.

This weekly communication can also spur clients to enlarge their project. Knowing the original work is moving along smoothly and not causing any major discom-

Table 7.9 Letter of transmittal. Transmittal sheets are used for all correspondence between the designer, other consultants, and contractors. A transmittal sheet such as this should be attached to shop drawings, letters, prints, change orders, plans, and samples—anything that would require a comment, approval, or request. Any change in work orders should be documented with a letter of transmittal. The fax has changed the way these forms look. What is important is that there are areas to check and return.

YOUR FIRM NAME HERE
123 Main Street
YOUR TOWN, STATE and ZIP

LETTER OF TRANSMITTAL

Phone 123-4567

TO:

DATE:	JOB NO.
ATTENTION:	
RE:	

WE ARE SENDING YOU ☐ Attached ☐ Under separate cover via _____ the following items:

☐ Shop drawings   ☐ Prints   ☐ Plans   ☐ Samples   ☐ Specifications
☐ Copy of letter   ☐ Change order ☐ _____

COPIES	DATE	NO.	DESCRIPTION

THESE ARE TRANSMITTED as checked below:

☐ For approval   ☐ Approved as submitted   ☐ Resubmit ___ copies for approval
☐ For your use   ☐ Approved as noted   ☐ Submit ___ copies for distribution
☐ As requested   ☐ Returned for corrections   ☐ Return ___ corrected prints
☐ For review and comment ☐ _____
☐ FOR BIDS DUE _____ 20___ ☐ PRINTS RETURNED AFTER LOAN TO YOU
REMARKS

COPY TO: _____ SIGNED: _____
If enclosures are not as noted, kindly notify us at once.

© *Design Business Monthly,* 1988.

fort or interference in their lives seems to make clients feel secure about buying design services.

When a delay or problem arises, inform the client. But before you present the issue, find a solution or alternate selection. Give the client the options you have worked out, and ask for input. It is usually best to offer no more than two possible solutions unless you are sure of the client. Offering more only tends to confuse the issue.

Purchasing and Follow-Up. What happens to an order from the time it is placed until the product is delivered? During this period, small developments can either make or break an order, as well as a client relationship. Again, regular communication with your suppliers and your client is essential.

Getting the job completed as scheduled depends on the designer's ability to create a project that is practical to produce within the defined budget and medium. It must be within the range of abilities of your staff and craftspeople.

Most orders today are placed by fax. But in addition to placing a written order for merchandise, you should also phone it in to see if any items have been discontinued or if there is anything incorrect or incomplete about your purchase order. This follow-up phone call ensures changes can be handled immediately, not three weeks down the road, when they could affect a larger body of work. After making this call, tell your client the orders have been placed with no problem or, for example, that one fabric has been discontinued and will require another selection. Ask when it would be convenient for your client to arrange an appointment to make that selection.

You must carefully consider the project schedule when you choose which materials to specify. Determine, for example, whether you can afford to specify materials from all parts of the world when you have only 90 days to complete a job.

When an order is submitted to the person processing the job (the expeditor), the design has been completed and there is an expected delivery date on the project. This date has been established by the designer and the client. The expeditor knows by seeing this date that the client is expecting the order in a set period of time, ranging from two weeks to a year or longer. (Few orders are done in a period of two weeks.)

Everything you consider for a project is based on the date of completion. One item may have 20 to 30 parts. For example, fabric, finish, trimmings, several different crafts—may be part of a chair. Your expeditor places the orders for each and every process or material you specify, then attaches one copy of the purchase order marked with the date the order is required to the initial work order. Another copy of the purchase order is placed in your On Order file—an alphabetical file of each and every company with which you have orders. When you get an invoice in from Fabric Company A, for example, you can go to your On Order file and match the invoice with the order.

On your purchase order, you should include the name of the client and a purchase order number. In our firm, the work order number we start out with follows through on all the subsequent purchase orders. This means if a work order number is 9046, the purchase order numbers would be 9046A, 9046B, and so forth.

After an order has been placed with a company, expect an acknowledgment or some confirmation from them within a few days. Review the details of this acknowledgment carefully to be sure it agrees with your order. This will tell you if the product is available, in which case you may receive an invoice for it. If the product is not available, the company will let you know how long it will be before it is available or if the product has been discontinued.

You should immediately compare all acknowledgments with your delivery expectations. If you have a year in which to deliver a sofa, for example, and there is a three-month delay in the fabric shipment, it really will not matter, since you know it only takes another 30 to 60 days to produce the sofa after you have the fabric. But if the acknowledgment says the delivery of this fabric will be in 60 days, and the client is expecting delivery in 90 days, you know you have to do some checking. Even though you have a 30-day cushion, you really cannot count on that, because it means the fabric is expected from the mill on that date, not that it will be delivered to you on that date. The fabric may be coming from England or Italy. This could cause additional shipping delays before it is sent from the factory to you.

At this point, it is important to bring the delay to the attention of the designer in charge. The designer may say: "There is a fabric almost identical to that from another firm. Let's consider using the fabric from Fabric Company B instead of from Fabric Company A." The designer will then compare the two fabrics and decide whether this is a reasonable option. Your firm will then check with Fabric Company B to ensure availability of this fabric and put a reserve on the fabric. At that point, you check with the client for approval. If the client approves the change, you call both fabric companies to change the fabric to be used from Fabric Company A's to Fabric Company B's.

When you change an order, you must notify all affected vendors. In the case of a sofa, which is to be made by an upholsterer, the upholsterer is expecting a fabric from Fabric Company A with a certain identifying number. You must inform the upholsterer that this particular fabric is not available and the upholsterer will be receiving fabric from Fabric Company B instead.

Suppose your client decides there is no substitute for the fabric selection, and you, as the designer, agree. If a major change of fabric must be made, adjustments on deliveries of all the other items will have to be made to coordinate deliveries. It may not be a matter of just changing sofa fabrics; it may mean changing the draperies, accent pillows, or three or four other items that go with the different fabric.

Understanding the situation, your client may be prepared to wait and to adjust the job completion date accordingly. When the client is given a choice, it makes for much better rapport.

Weekly Merchandise Checks. Another important follow-up procedure is to check, on a weekly basis, every client order and merchandise order to see if there are any acknowledgments pending and if anything has not arrived by your expected delivery dates. When there is a discrepancy, contact the involved suppliers by telephone, fax, e-mail, or letter to determine why the item is delayed or what the problem is. They may never have received your order. These weekly checks allow you to catch problems quickly, not three weeks later, when you are expecting an item on your loading dock.

A record of all the activities is kept on the master sheet for easy reference. Today, there are several computer programs that can handle your design firm's source communications and documentation (see pages 361–363).

Merchandise Inspection. Always inspect merchandise before it arrives on-site. If you have an installation scheduled, check with the warehouse to be sure the merchandise has arrived and that it is the proper color, size, and shape. Regardless of the supplier, it is advisable to visit the warehouse and see the merchandise yourself. There are ways you can open and repack cartons without adversely affecting your scheduling. It is easier to check merchandise when it is in a warehouse facility than later. Someone who knows what was ordered and the details of the piece must see the item before it is delivered to the client. It is time-consuming and expensive to do this, yes, but it is also a mark of professionalism.

By inspecting the items, you can also determine in advance how complex assembling the pieces will be. If you have installers who are not familiar with assembling an intricate item, a trip to the factory for training or to request a factory person to assist with the installation can save time in the long run. Do not get involved in an installation unless you have experts available.

Assemble any item that can be preassembled in your own warehouse or workroom so you spend as little time as possible at the client's space. Also, if there is a problem during assembly, preassembly lets you know about it before you reach the client's. Even if you must take the product apart again and repack it, be sure it fits together and you have all the pieces.

If you are unfamiliar with the installation assembly process, ask the product manufacturer if you can visit another installation site so you can see just how this assembly is performed. It is unprofessional to deliver a product your staff cannot professionally assemble.

Organizing the Workers. Depending on the craft, the designer should review the project with the contractors and craftspeople and their management. Explain the project. Show them the completed design, so they understand why their part of it is being executed in a certain fashion. If the plumbers realize what the next three steps in a job are, for example, they will better understand their limitations and why they cannot take three feet when only one foot has been allotted.

Explaining the overall project to the craftspeople involved serves two functions. First, it helps them understand how they fit into the total process. Second, it gives them a sense of pride—they understand what they are working on and that you respect them enough to make them a part of this outstanding project.

During the installation, you will have a large number of different contractors and craftspeople to coordinate. To make sure they work well together, you should understand the exact processes required for them to do their jobs, and program exactly how they are to coordinate. Go over the project with each craftsperson or delivery person approximately three weeks prior to the installation, and again within about four days of the installation to be sure everything is ready. If everything is not complete and ready, it is better to change the installation date. When scheduling an installation by any contractor or craftsperson, visit that person's warehouse and go over the list of plumbing and lighting fixtures and other items required for the project. Often, contractors will start a project thinking they have everything they need when they only have 90 percent of it. The last 10 percent will hold up the job.

You must determine whether the contractor or craftsperson should go into the client's space without all the equipment or collect the rest of the materials—and make any substitutions—before they start.

Plan the job so that each craftsperson or contractor can perform the installation easily and with the least likelihood of damaging other parts of the project. When you do a project on a tight schedule, even though it requires a lot of give-and-take from the subcontractors, efficient coordination makes the project appear perfectly orchestrated. The client can usually afford to have a highly paid project manager on-site for such a short period of time. If a project is done over a long, spread-out period, supervision by a top-quality person is often cost-prohibitive.

INSTALLATION SUPERVISION

Installations require supervision. Work closely with your installation people, because they can make or break a job. The better the installers understand a project, the better job they do. Larger firms have specialists who do only installation work. In smaller firms, the project manager will supervise the project throughout the process. The art of installation is becoming quite respected as a specialty, as the quality of the project is at great risk if installation is not done properly. Whether the supervisor is an installation specialist or project manager, that person should be involved with the project from the concept phase throughout completion. If a design passes this person's approval, you know it will work and can be installed without extreme difficulty.

The person who supervises the complete installation should understand the job and its composition. The supervisor should review the design concept in the initial stages to determine any areas in which the project might be adjusted to save money or to make the installation go smoother.

An on-site project manager has to make many decisions and adjustments on the design project. Seldom is the existing facility identical to what is expected. The project manager should be included in the overall design program so he or she can understand exactly which adjustments are negotiable and which are not. If the installation manager is familiar with the project and has checked all items delivered to the warehouses, he or she will be prepared for anything that arises. A well-prepared project manager, often one of the best-paid people on a design team, can make an installation look professional—and the design team look great.

Whoever supervises the installation must not only know the project but must also be willing to make the necessary adjustments to keep other people working effectively. If a supply item is required and is not on-site, the supervisor takes care of getting what is needed so nothing stops the workers from continuing their job. The supervisor must be willing to be inconvenienced if necessary to keep the rest of the job running.

Project managers are often outsourced, but it is best if you use certain people on a regular basis so they become accustomed to the various standards of your company. It is very difficult to give someone not closely related to your firm a project management job.

If you are doing installation in a building, there are requirements for anyone working there. You will need insurance forms and other documents to be completed in advance of your installation. This process can often take several weeks or even a month.

Preparing the Site

The day before the installation, the building management needs to be informed of the requirements of the installation team. Parking allowances, street closings, and other preparations may need to be arranged. This is all part of your preparation. Making the extra effort to clear a parking lot and hire a person to direct traffic onto the lot is often one of the cheapest and best expenditures you can make. The traffic coordinator can control the arrivals of various pieces so one person does not arrive a half-hour early to install that part before its base arrives.

Although previous scheduling and planning has been done, always check the job site the day before the installation. Be sure the space is clean and ready for you. Make sure proper temperatures have been maintained for carpeting and other types of installation. Check that the HVAC system is under proper control and is clean and properly functioning so dust does not become a contaminant.

It is usually wise to ask clients to be away from the site during the day of installation. If clients feel they must be part of the installation, you should select the appropriate times in the day for them to come for comments and approval. Typically, when clients are on-site, they become concerned with inappropriate details, and the continuity of the installation is affected.

Taking Charge

Sometimes clients say their office can handle the installations; this should be discouraged. Rarely does a client understand installation procedures, and it takes only one careless installer to mar a project that took months or perhaps years of careful design and development.

If at all possible, designate a member of your staff to be on-site throughout the installation, or at least to make periodic checks to ensure your standards are met by the craftspeople.

Typically, an unsupervised delivery team will drop dirty cartons in the middle of the space. You can end up with grease on the carpet, or worse. Make sure this never happens. What the client remembers most is the last impression of your installation process.

Installation of Furnishings

The installation is one of the strongest selling aspects of the job. You constantly resell a project to a client by the way you manage the job—not just in the initial interview or presentation, but the whole way, through the "twilight zone" and into the installation itself. Your performance and the way your craftspeople work in a client's facility can either create confidence or destroy it.

The way you handle an installation affects not only that project but your future relationship with those clients and their associates.

Planning for Problems

In order to orchestrate a polished installation, you must be prepared in advance for any problems. Have on hand the tools and equipment you will need to take care of problems. Planning for mishaps prevents them.

With advance planning, a great deal of difficulty and expense can be avoided at the end of the project. When you begin a project, check out the delivery procedures for your client's building. It is important know sizes of openings, elevator capacity, and hours of access to the elevators. Some furniture simply cannot be installed in some spaces. We have all heard about the 10-foot sofa that couldn't be delivered to the thirty-fourth floor of a penthouse, or the boardroom table that would not fit up the elevator shaft. When considering a design project, obviously, the access to the space has to be considered. Many corridors and entrances in buildings are much narrower and smaller than one would expect; these are limitations you must take into account in the planning stages.

If you are having several sofas made, order sufficient fabric to replace the back or the seat (normally two to three yards). If you are ordering a chair, order one yard of extra fabric to replace the back or the seat cushion. By ordering extra fabric in advance, if there is a problem during the course of delivery, you are ready to take care of it immediately. If there is no problem, you can give the extra fabric to the client and say: "We are including this piece of matching fabric as insurance against a cigarette burn or small tear. Put it away and keep it just in case." Or, if you have storage space, you can keep the fabric in your warehouse with your client's name on it. It is amazing how often this extra material gets used; and even if it does not get used, it has still been a great backup. It is always better to have an extra yard of material on hand than to have to call and try to match a yard or two of fabric at the time of the installation.

When ordering carpeting, order a few extra feet. This lets you cut around an unexpected flaw or finish a closet that the carpenter created from hidden space. It gives you the chance to make your installations what they should be. A little extra carpeting can be used to repair minor damage without requiring the whole carpet to be replaced.

Always be prepared to handle touch-ups and minor repairs. If your installation people do not have a trained repair staff, schedule a standby for that particular project to take care of any little repairs so they are handled immediately—not three months later.

A stain-removal kit and cleaning supplies should be part of your equipment for all installations. Insist that every delivery truck servicing you has the equipment to vacuum, dust, and clean every interior item. Any cleaning supplies needed for new textiles or other items that will be handled should be included.

It is unusual for every item to arrive at an installation in perfect condition and in perfect sequence. There are usually some adjustments required during installation. Today, there are specialists who know how to touch up finishes and make minor repairs or adjustments to make an installation seem perfect. These specialists can eliminate a lot of problems and complaints.

Installer's Records

On any project requiring work at a client's premises, whether it involves installation, delivery, or another type of work, use an installation sheet with the client's name at the top to help control each phase (see Table 7.10, page 245). It lists the various items ready to be delivered or work to be done at that particular site, whether it is a residence or a contract space. The number of assignment sheets you will need depends on the number of stages the project has. For example, the first phase may include removing the old furnishings and preparing the space for painting, wallcovering, or carpet installation.

An installation sheet must define the tasks that are to be done, and it should include space for the installer's comments. Comments may be about missing pieces or other problems or the fact that the client is so delighted they want to continue and do another project with you.

An installation may be done at one time or in many phases. It is important that everything that must be accomplished in each phase is listed. You must verify that all the necessary materials are on hand and ready for the installation. With an installation sheet you will avoid forgetting items or having three parts of an item but not the other two.

The system the designer uses to manage the installation greatly influences the quality of the installation work. Keep the following issues in mind:

1. The firm's work is very creative. The installers are not doing routine work; much of the project has not been done before.
2. A productive project manager gives the installers a second or third way of doing the project in the event a problem occurs. The installers are then prepared to continue with the installation even if something unexpected arises.
3. An experienced and skilled manager does not want his or her staff to appear unprofessional; therefore, every part of the job is carefully staged and rehearsed.

When the installers arrive at the client's property, even if a designer or assigned supervisor is there, they should call the designer's office to confirm they are on location. (Later, the time marked on the installers' time sheet is verified at the office against the master phone schedule.) In addition, when the installers arrive, they should give the office a status report on the site. Even with the best of checking and planning, problems can arise. The office must be made aware of any difficulties. The installer might say, for example, "The paper hanger is not finished with the wallcovering, and we can only do a little more work until this is completed. He should be

Table 7.10 Installation sheet. This sheet includes all the items you want delivered or completed on the date noted. It is a checklist for the installer and everyone involved so they know what they have to do and in what order. This list can ensure that the installer and other workers complete all the appropriate items during their visit. The bottom part of the page is to note problems and issues that arise. This enables the installers and workers to give you feedback and apprise you of any situation that might affect their completion of the job or other items that need to be done. This sheet should be prepared by the project manager or managing director; it is later returned to that person after the installer has noted the amount of time spent, the items completed, and their history and results. This simple form helps tremendously both with billing and with scheduling any follow-up work.

INSTALLATION				
Client:		Staff:	Date:	From: To:
Items to be Completed Today:				

Items to be Done for Next Appointment:

© *Design Business Monthly*, 1988.

finished by this afternoon. What do you want us to do?" The person who manages the time scheduling in the office will then know the movement of each person on staff. If a client has a question regarding additional scheduling, or an adjustment to the schedule, it should be handled in the main office—not by the installers, who may not understand the full planning process. When the installers are finished for the day, they should call the office again to say, for example, "We have completed this project and are returning to the studio," or "We are going on to the next client's job." At the end of the day, the installers will return the installation sheet to the office, marking off everything they completed, time spent, and any additional work requiring extra charges. On the bottom of this sheet the installers or project supervisor note any comments made by the client, such as, "I like the way we have done the office, but I would really like to add three extra chairs to the conference room." These notes are important reference tools that can alert the designer to additional sales opportunities on that project. These records are kept in the client's master file and used for billing purposes. Whether the billing is done through a computer system or manually, the process is similar.

Every project needs to be managed by the office, because a firm always appears more professional when control is centered there. Installers should not say to a client, "I'll be back tomorrow with these items," if they do not know where the items are. They should say instead, for example, "I'll go back to the office to get the three or four items I need to complete your project. As soon as I have them, our staff person will call you and arrange for me to come out again and finish up." This helps the installers by not putting them in the position of having to answer such questions as, "Will you be back tomorrow to finish this?" Sometimes, the installers do not know the answer, and this process lets them off the hook.

Installation Day

You need a script and choreography to ensure a well-planned, professional installation day. It is more than just showmanship; time equals money. There may be clauses in the contract that require a penalty for each day the project is late. If you can shorten the installation time, your profits will be greater. If you spend too much time on one project, when you should be working on others, it costs you business.

When installation people arrive in a space, the designer or project manager must impress on them that this is a new, finely finished space. It must be treated with the utmost care, as if it were a fine piece of crystal or a lovely couture garment.

How the installers are dressed and how they treat the site are critical. Clients feel their furniture deserves special handling. Insist that anyone who touches or goes near the furniture understands it is expensive and must be handled carefully. The best people working for you should be the people doing the installation, but so often firms use their lowest-paid and newest staff members. Novices should be kept in-house; do your training where clients cannot see it.

Inform your installation people that playing loud music, eating, drinking, and smoking in the installation area are all forbidden. On a large installation project, you should create a break area for the workers, where they can go to drink sodas and smoke, but be sure they realize they may not drink or smoke in any other part of the space. The break area must be clean when you leave, even if the installation supervisor has to do it.

You can save time and money by having coffee or sodas on hand and arranging for lunches to be delivered. It is usually a good investment to pay for and bring in the installers' lunches, just to keep them working and on the job.

When making a delivery, it is advisable to put walk-off mats down from the truck into the space. You should also cover carpeting as appropriate; brown carpenter's paper is usually better than plastic runners because it is less slippery. The paper also gives the area the appearance of work in progress.

The "white glove and bootie treatment" requires installation people to wear clean white gloves; it requires those walking into a clean space with clean carpets to put on fabric booties over their shoes so they do not get any outside soil on the carpet. This obsessive concern for a project is greatly appreciated by clients, who usually have made a large investment in the space and want it perfect. Great care should be taken on installation day to assure the client that everything about their project is special. With this kind of emphasis, you can build lasting rapport with clients.

The way furniture is wrapped when it goes into a space is also important. If it is covered with clean brown paper and nicely taped, that is fine. If the paper or plastic is soiled or in any way torn, do something about it. Furniture delivered blanket-covered is well protected. When you arrive in a client's space, the blankets are lifted off so the client can see the special piece of furniture. This is good show-manship. Today, plastic has replaced blankets (which is great, because plastic keeps items clean and dry), but the showmanship is still considered your signature of quality.

If you are merchandising or selling products, your company will make the deliveries. Again, the way your trucking and delivery processes are handled strongly reflects the quality of your overall product. Designers deliver their furnishings in many different ways. One firm in California uses women to make the deliveries in attractive, nicely painted vans. The women wear black slacks and white, tailored blouses that are neatly ironed. They deliver almost all of the furniture the firm supplies. This is showmanship. All the clients talk about the way their deliveries are made.

Never leave a job site until it presents the very best effect it can for this stage of the project. If you have not yet completed the project when you leave for the day, be sure the area is thoroughly vacuumed and cleaned. Pay attention to details so the area looks organized; many times the client will sneak a peak.

Check your insurance coverage regarding your liability position while supervising or installing a project. In Chapter 11, care, custody, and control are discussed (see pages 417–419). Obviously, the responsibilities of the design firm need to be defined and addressed prior to an installation.

At the completion of the installation, go through the project and prepare a punch list of problems, then make an appointment with the client several days later to go through this list. Point out to the client any flaws or imperfections and explain which are going to be corrected. Show clients before they show you.

Design Review

A design review should not be done just at the end but throughout the project. During a design review, staff members meet not just to review the design but also to review the scheduling, budget, and client's expectations. A regular ongoing review throughout the project will strengthen it and keep everyone on target. Firms often wait too long before the first design review and concern themselves more with design quality than with other issues that are perhaps even more important to the project's success, such as whether they are really accomplishing their communication objectives with the client.

The Maintenance Manual

You should supply a maintenance manual to the client at installation time or immediately thereafter. This manual lists each and every piece of furniture, equipment, furnishings, and material incorporated into their project—including carpeting, wallcoverings, draperies, window treatments, furnishings, textiles, and lamps. The manual also explains everything needed to keep this installation in as fine a condition as possible. It lists handling precautions and cleaning and maintenance instructions, as well as the right wattage for the lamping. The manual includes the addresses and phone numbers of other companies that should be called for various services and additional instructions for adequate maintenance.

A maintenance manual is supplied to both residential and contract clients and is part of every design package. This manual also includes all of the guarantees, warranties, and any special instructions for the products you have supplied. These warranties are automatically passed on to the client. Any certificates for flameproofing or special finishes should be made in the client's name rather than that of the design studio. Then, if there is a claim, it will be handled directly by your client and the manufacture; you will not be legally or financially responsible.

The maintenance manual is not only an important service to the client; it may also protect the design firm. The manual clearly states the appropriate care each piece of furniture should have, as endorsed or prescribed by the manufacturer. Last, but definitely not least, the maintenance manual is a great marketing tool. It keeps your name in front of clients, identifying you as a continuing part of their interior design projects.

POSTOCCUPANCY EVALUATION

After the installation is complete, evaluate your performance. Discuss the project with the clients to determine whether their expectations have been met. In addition ascertain if you can expect referrals.

A postoccupancy evaluation should be made at certain periods after the job is completed—usually at three months, six months, and a year. This is a good way for you to keep in touch with your clients and to evaluate your own work. It also gives you an understanding of how the clients see the performance of your design organization. The past client follow-up summary form shown in Table 7.11 (page 249) will help you organize these evaluations.

If there are problems, a postoccupancy evaluation positions you as a part of the problem-solving team rather than as the adversary. You are usually able to determine just what needs to be done, which makes the client appreciate you. Taking care of problems is a normal and required part of every design project. If possible, try to find a problem the client has not noticed and have it corrected. This shows your service ability.

Evaluations of this sort will also help you define your future market. If the project moved ahead smoothly, meeting your project objectives and design expectations

Table 7.11 Past client follow-up summary. After you have completed a job, you need to stay in contact with the client. This summary sheet works very well for postoccupancy review and additional follow-ups. Normally, it is advisable to talk with clients every three to six months. This type of reference sheet appropriately filled out will help manage that process.

PAST CLIENT FOLLOW-UP SUMMARY

Client:			Contact Person: Position:
Address:			Phone No.:

Finish Date:	Job:	Type: (room or building)	Size:

Last Contact Date:	Client's Comments:	Follow-through:

© *Design Business Monthly,* 1988.

as well as the client's needs, your firm is capable of handling more of this kind of work and should continue to market for this type of project.

Handling Complaints

How you handle complaints can be an important part of marketing and sales development, because it strongly affects the way clients relate to your firm in the future.

The fact that the client called you at all is positive. It means the client is interested in your firm and may plan to use you again. If this were not so, the clients would not bother to call; they would simply go to someone else. Look at a complaint as a positive response.

In most complaints, emotion and facts get mixed. To get to the facts, acknowledge the emotion, but do not respond to it. Since most complaints are made by phone, responding to them is discussed more fully in the section on telephone communication (see page 348).

Give your clients attention; let them know you are concerned, that you are on their side, and that you will find a way to solve the problem. Try to make clients part of your team in solving problems, and let them know the problem is a priority issue with your firm.

It is best to have a scheduled program for handling complaints. Many firms require complaints to be handled within 24 hours of receipt, and sooner if possible. The faster you can get back to clients, the less time they have to worry about the issue. Prompt handling of complaints is a very important strategy. There are some clients you can never please, but if you have gone through the whole project with the clients, and they are generally pleased with it, usually complaints can be easily managed.

Give complaints priority handling, and make every effort to leave the client with a positive impression of your firm. It takes too long to develop a client to let some small item become a major issue. The better your management of a project, and the more you know about the contractors, various installation people, and other people who are interacting with the client, the easier it is to avoid complaints.

Privacy

With today's concern about identity theft as well as privacy in all issues, confidentiality has become a major concern. This means we must treat all the information we have from clients with care to protect their privacy. We must assure that the information does not travel outside our firm. Not only do our clients deserve this out of respect, but we could become liable if this information is distributed inappropriately through our studio. Emphasis must be made with all outside contractors who are working on a project that your firm requires this privacy. Careful processing of documents should be in place. The way you store your records and the way you destroy your records is very important.

CLIENT RETENTION

On any residential or contract project, the designer and the client develop an intense relationship built on daily contact. When the project is finished, the intensity must be reduced so the designer can go on to the next assignment. Clients must be weaned away from the constant support and affirmation of the designer in a way that does not diminish their regard for the designer.

This takes special handling. If the project was an office building with 800 rooms, the designer and the project liaison worked together daily, and the designer may have practically lived at the job site. In residential work, the designer has often been privy to the client's innermost thoughts and feelings. Either way, the relationship has been very close and intense. The closest comparison is the relationship between patient and psychiatrist. To be abruptly dropped from this relationship can be devastating, and dropping a client cold is asking for a lot of problems.

When clients feel rejected, the designer loses them as a potential source for referrals and all chances of designing new projects for those clients. A planned withdrawal is strategic.

After the installation, assist clients in adjusting to the new space. Contact them weekly, at the same time of day as your previous calls, for the first one to three months, depending on the extent of the project. Do not wait for the clients to complain; call them first and ask if there is any way your firm can offer help. Later, call once a month for three to six months, and then try to call again three and six months later, so you have checked for possible problems during the entire year after the installation.

By extending the rapport with someone with whom you have worked closely, you reap the full potential of any marketing effort. After all, referrals from past clients make up the majority of new business in most firms. They know what you do and can explain it to appropriate potential clients. So spend some time on client retention. Too many design firms have this great untapped reservoir of former clients, and this can work against them.

CLIENT LOYALTY

Earning a client's loyalty is one of the most sought-after and emotionally rewarding accomplishments any design practice can achieve. Look through your list of successful jobs. You will find many of the outstanding ones have been jobs developed out of other successful projects. The original project may have been one or two rooms, or one building; then you went on to design the client's next 4 or 5, or 30 or 40, buildings. This is a loyal client. Still, clients must be happy with every project you do, or they will not hire you for the next project.

One of the best things to do is to maintain quality interaction with your client throughout the project. This will ensure every movement on the job is helping to develop the next phase of that job or the next project with that client or the client's friends or associates.

CONSIDERATIONS

Whatever your discipline, projects must be handled with skill and speed. You will find people installing jobs within three to seven days. This is the kind of work clients are looking for. If a job is managed properly, it can be done quickly with great skill and artistry. As we move forward, designers will need to understand much more about the process of getting the job done. If they don't understand all the aspects of construction, they must hire someone who does. Professionalism, care, and artistry are key.

CHAPTER 8

Charging for Your Services

Before you even think about estimating a project, make sure you understand exactly what the project involves. Many designers send out estimates or proposals too soon, before they have completely evaluated a project or understand what the client expects. The more time that you take up front to get to know the client and the project, the better able you will be to offer a contract that enables you to complete the job successfully.

JOB PRICING

Some very successful designers refuse to give a quotation or presentation unless the client first agrees to spend several hours with them to spell out the overall design requirements. The design service outline form is set up for this purpose (see page 255). A detailed project evaluation, documented at the precontract phase, can often help clients understand just what your design services encompass and what the costs entail. This form also clearly defines the job outline, services to be rendered, and scheduling. It stays with the project throughout the job. It is important to have the project manager and others working on the project assist in preparing this outline and the pricing of the project to ensure that everyone understands the project goals and the firm's responsibilities. Another excellent way to define a project is to do an up-front analysis for the client for a small fee. This will enable you to carefully examine the total project. You will then know how to determine whether it is an appropriate job for you and how to quote it.

Before You Give an Estimate: The 80-20 Rule

Choosing the right projects affects your firm's success and profit picture. When you are considering whether to take on a project, 80 percent of the project should be something so familiar that there is very little margin for error. You can be creative with the other 20 percent—learning, experimenting, or taking chances—but if you do not know 80 percent of the job thoroughly, experience shows this project will not be profitable. It will take too much time, be too risky, and cause too many problems.

Job Pricing

When pricing a job, there are four things to consider:

- Scope of the job
- Services to be rendered
- Staff required, including their time and cost
- Schedule

Obviously, the schedule can affect the cost of the project. The way your proposal is written strongly dictates the management style for the project. If your proposal states all of the processes to be done, then your project management list is almost complete. You know exactly who is going to do what, as well as the approximate time and outline of the project.

Without the project plan in place, it is almost impossible to make an appropriate estimate. As you do your estimates and your proposal, try to write them in a fashion that makes it easy for later programming.

A design firm must have the right work to build and maintain a reputation for quality. We all love to do new things and be creative, but we have to remember that we are running a business. We have a responsibility first to the client, staff, contractors, and vendors to do a successful and profitable project. Experience has shown that whenever this principle is violated, the project will not be profitable.

You may decide that you want to move into a new area of design, and that the project you are considering is a great opportunity. Consider the investment: Can you afford to produce this project at a loss? When design firms take on a new specialty, they plan to dedicate a certain amount of money from their marketing fund to position themselves in the new market. You need to consider the dollar potential of the specialty, the time it will take to become proficient (sometimes years!), and the probability that unforeseen risks will emerge.

Carefully defining and qualifying a project is the best way to determine the appropriate charging methods. Design firms usually invest large amounts of time in these efforts; a week or more is not unusual for a larger project; and it might even take months. It is much better to invest a week's labor to ensure that the job is right for the firm and priced correctly than it is to take the wrong job and risk losing six months of unpaid fees.

The Design Service Outline

The design service outline, shown in Table 8.1 below, not only helps me define the job but it also is a good reference, both for the staff members who help with the quotation as well as for those who are working on the project. Information is provided in the same format no matter what the project, so staff will know exactly where to look on the form for specific information.

Through a list of questions, the design service outline explains to clients the many aspects of doing a design project. There are usually other parts of the project they may not have considered. The outline also explains the complexity of interior design. This is a very involved discipline; we don't just select colors.

The design service outline was devised primarily for contract work. It covers some of the very basic issues: which staff people will be involved in the project; systems of communication with the client and other professionals; basic design requirements; and scheduling. It defines the management of the project.

It is common for a client to call in a designer to work on two or three specific areas and then try to work in additional areas at no extra charge. The design service outline defines the spaces to be done, the areas you have to include in your contract.

DESIGN SERVICE OUTLINE		**Date:**
Client:	Contact Person:	
	Position:	
Address:	Phone No.:	
Project:		
Decision-making Process:		
Presentation Form:	Floor plans:	
	Boards:	
	Renderings:	
	Models:	
Stages of Decisions:		
Client's Representatives:		
Staff Involved:		
Consultants:		
Contractors:		
Scheduled Contact Time:		

Table 8.1 Design service outline. This outline can help clients understand what your design services encompass and what is involved in doing a project. Process and complete this form before turning a job over to the project manager.

© *Design Business Monthly*, 1988.

Table 8.2   Determining requirements: Functional and organizational. This page refers to the space and the way it is used. This form will state clearly what the client's priorities are. It also helps the designer understand what financial investment the client is willing to make.

Determining Requirements: Functional and Organizational
Space Analysis:
Traffic Flow:
Workflow:
Personnel—Expected Growth:
Individual Space:
Visitors:
Flow:
Equipment:
Storage: Records:
Supplies:
Other:
Lighting:
Acoustical:
Audiovisual:
Security:
Handicapped

© *Design Business Monthly*, 1988.

This interview process helps to define the interior design process to the client and more clearly define the project to the design firm. Time invested at this point is so valuable to the overall project.

Estimating is probably the most difficult thing we do. Being able to put together good proposals and estimates is something of an art, and the only way it can be done properly is with very good up-front review and coordination. Before beginning estimations on any project, you need to:

1. **Define the scope of the work.** Determine exactly what is going to be done on this project and what position you will play: What kind of project is it? Is there a high-liability issue involved? Is the project one that will require a lot of research, or one you can manage comfortably because you have done it many times before? How prepared is your firm for this project? If it is a bank project and you have just designed 14 other banks, certain procedures will go much faster. If you have not designed a bank for a year or more, the project

Table 8.3 Scheduling. This page will show the expected time of completion of project. It allows the client to understand, prior to any work being performed, the approximate length of the project.

Scheduling

Owner's Projected Goals:

Design Schedule:

Work Schedule:

Other Issues:

Notes:

_____

_____

_____

_____

_____

_____

_____

_____

_____

_____

_____

_____

_____

_____

_____

_____

_____

_____

© *Design Business Monthly,* 1988.

is going to be a bit more difficult. Check out a job to see if it is the kind of project you really want to handle. If it is not the type of job you want, do not waste your time writing a proposal.

2. **Determine the expected quality of the project.** What is the client's past experience with interior design? Make note of the quality of furniture the clients are currently using and the quality of projects they are familiar with or use for reference.

3. **Evaluate the design team.** Who are the other people working on the project? How will the architect and other selected design professionals affect you and your team?

4. **Consider the schedule.** Is the project a fast-track job or one that will be done over several years? Review your proposal with the different design people

Table 8.4 Design concept. This form is used to identify what is anticipated for the various segments of the project.

Design Concept		
Architectural:	Changes:	
	Details:	
	Finishes:	
Floor Plans:		
Wall Elevations:		
Special Details:		
Cabinet/Built-in Work:		
Furniture:		
Special Equipment:		
Window Treatments:		
Lighting:		
Acoustical:		
Security:		
Audiovisual:		

© *Design Business Monthly*, 1988.

who are going to work on the project to get their feedback and time estimates. If they are committed to the project, they will feel a much greater sense of responsibility to complete it within the time period they specify. Ask your staff who are going to work on the job to estimate their time requirements. Compare their estimates with past records of similar jobs. Some staff members tend to underestimate, while others are more accurate.

5. **Investigate the regulations and codes that apply to the project.** Are there a lot of requirements necessary to meet either city or state codes or corporate standards? Are there extraordinary requirements?

6. **Assess your competition.** How does your firm compare to other firms bidding for the job?

7. **Predict what you will gain from the project.** What is your potential for making a profit on this project? How much risk is there? Will the time commitments or other restrictions on this project jeopardize your firm's profit opportunities on other projects? As you consider each job, look at it in terms of the benefits you can expect to accrue from it. Balance your financial expectations and

Table 8.5 Project documentation. This is a checklist of documentaton required for working with the various vendors and contractors.

Project Documentation
Floor Plans: (areas or rooms involved)
Furniture Plans:
Lighting Plan:
Elevations: (areas or rooms involved)
Finish Schedule: (special notes to be included)
Hardware Schedule:
Window Treatments:
Special Conditions:
Specifications:
Bidding:
Purchase Orders:
Maintenance Manual: (companies or products involved)
Moving Plan:
Schedule:

© *Design Business Monthly,* 1988.

the amount of time you expect to invest in the job. Also consider the marketing value of the job. We have all done jobs that were not overly profitable but brought us several other jobs that were. Determine just what this job means to your studio. Every now and then it is worth taking a job without much profit, because it brings other benefits. It may offer an introduction to a specialty—giving you an opportunity to test the waters. If you want to change your specialty, you may find that you have to do a few projects to earn credentials within that field. That may mean taking a project at a lower fee or even at no fee to get background and experience within this specialty. You go in knowing you will incur a loss; it is a planned loss.

8. **Evaluate the client. Is the client accustomed to working with an interior designer?** Has the client had experience with your firm or with other firms? What kind of decision maker is the client? How many meetings do you

Project Management

Coordination: Client:
                       Consultants:
                       Contractors:

Scheduling:

Shop Drawing Approval:

Supervision:

Revisions:

Change Orders:

Negotiations: Prebid Quotes:
                       Contractors:

Payment Authorization:

Occupancy Evaluation:

Postoccupancy Review:

Others:

© *Design Business Monthly*, 1988.

expect to have? How many revisions are going to be required? What kind of rapport do you have with the client? Will you get along very easily, or will it be difficult for you?

HOW TO CHARGE

Determining the appropriate fee structure for a job is of primary importance for your firm's reputation and profitability. The standard set by the proposal either gives the firm an opportunity for quality design work and profit or creates a losing situation. If the project is not priced and structured properly, it can turn out to be a disaster, both from the design and profit viewpoints. Everyone loses. The firm and the staff lose because it is not exciting or interesting to work on a job that is not a winner; the job loses them money and could cost the firm future jobs; and, obviously, the big loser is the client, who misses out on getting a first-rate design.

Jobs That Usually Lose Money

There are certain jobs on which you usually lose money because they take a great deal of time. Generally, they are for clients who are overly interested in the project but don't know a lot about interior design services. These clients often want to become totally consumed with the project, which requires you to spend considerable extra time with them. This can cause a great deal of unexpected expense.

Community buildings also can lose money for your firm. These projects require you to make multiple presentations to get the approval of every segment of the community that is involved. This can become very time-consuming and expensive. Country clubs and other buildings, in which there is an overwhelming sense of ownership among a large group of people, can also be money losers. Even if you restrict the project, too many people generally want to have a say in what's going on, which can make handling the phone calls and other interactions difficult and time-consuming.

Your client should be made aware of the way you charge and the way you handle finances. When you present a fee schedule or a quotation to a client, it is important to have an outline of all the services that you are going to include. Then, if the client says the quotation is too high, you can simply point to the areas that can be eliminated.

At this time, there are no official sources for standard fee scales for design work. Magazines occasionally publish lists of what has been charged, but these lists are not always accurate. Laws prohibit trade associations and other professional organizations from suggesting price or fee structures (this is considered price-fixing), so there is no official reference. This makes it important to keep a history of your past jobs. Comparing similar projects makes it easier to establish the appropriate price structure for the new project.

It may also be helpful to talk to other design firms that produce similar projects to learn about their experiences and the type of pricing structures that work best for them. Spell everything out, because every firm has different standard services or processes. Simply looking at the name of the project and the cost can be misleading. A good business consultant, especially one familiar with the design field and someone who knows how to grow businesses, could also be very helpful.

When estimating or creating a quotation, you should use several different methods to arrive at these figures—hours estimated versus square-foot price versus a percentage of the cost of furniture and finishes required—and then compare them.

Basic Methods of Compensation

There are many ways to charge. The interior design field is different from the architectural field in the methods that are appropriate and profitable. Normally, architectural projects have a higher-dollar volume than interior design projects, whereas labor and detailing on interior design projects are far more extensive. Many interior designers charge a straight hourly rate. Others charge an additional percentage on

Retainers or Down Payments

Asking for a retainer or deposit is important; it is part of the professional contract. It is safer to call the advance a "retainer" or "down payment" rather than a "deposit." The latter term is most appropriately used in real estate, where a deposit must be kept in an escrow account and cannot be used except for that transaction. Legally a deposit must be placed in a separate escrow account for a client and cannot be mixed with funds of other projects.

Can a client demand his or her deposit back? The Federal Trade Commission's (FTC) Fair Credit Billing Act's "cooling-off" rule gives the customer three days to cancel any purchase over $25. This rule gives the client the right to a full refund until midnight of the third business day after the sale. This rule affects any item purchased in the client's house, workplace or dormitory, or at a facility rented by the seller on a temporary or short-term basis, such as a hotel or motel, convention center or property, another location of an event, or any official store or place of business of the company selling the item.

The cooling-off rule requires the salesperson to inform the client of these rights at the time of purchase. There are some exceptions to this rule, such as purchases made by telephone or mail or at certain types of craft and art shows. The correct use of the term "deposit" is important in protecting the design. Every business is different. It is important that you discuss the issue of retainers with your attorney when setting up the standards for your practice.

If you have any questions about the Fair Credit Billing Act, visit the Federal Trade Commission Web site at www.ftc.gov.

each item purchased, or they keep a percentage of the cost of the total purchases. Some discount the retail price; others add to it. There are so many equations for charging that it is almost impossible to give anyone a guideline without reviewing that designer's own requirements and expenses. In my experience, the most profitable projects are generally those that use mixed methods of charging.

Have your accountant determine exactly what it will cost to run your company for the next year. Then figure your per-employee cost, library cost, and general production costs, and have your accountant review these figures. Your accountant should come up with an overall budget and suggested markup or multiplier.

Overhead Expenses

Today, overhead expenses generally equal at least one-and-a-half to two times an employee's expenses. This varies considerably, depending on the size of the firm, the overhead, and the amount of equipment. When calculating hourly fees, this expense is usually billed at two-and-a-half to three-and-a-half times the salary costs. This is separate from any direct expenses, which are also billed to the client. Direct expenses normally include blueprints; reproductions; illustrated drawings; models; all of your travel expenses; shipping, freight, and handling costs; and any expenses incurred during procurement and installation of furnishings. It is always wise to keep management overhead expenses as low as possible without sacrificing future business opportunities or quality of work.

Establishing Your Overhead Costs

Review all overhead costs, or fixed, expenses, such as:
- Advertising
- Automobiles
- Consulting
- Dues and subscriptions
- Education
- Insurance
- Loan payments
- Personnel whose time is devoted to business development or management
- Marketing
- Nonbillable support staff
- Office expenses
- Professional fees
- Rent
- Resource library
- Taxes and licenses
- Telephone
- Utilities

Calculating Hourly Rates

Hourly rates in the interior design field in the year 2005 ranged between $50 and $700. In many situations, the hourly rates have not really increased because of competition both within the field and many other sources. Clients question some traditional charges. Technology has changed, and they think the computer can do everything. I find interior designers very often cannot successfully charge more than

Establishing a Designer's Hourly Billing Rate* Example

Salary per year	$35,000
Fringe benefits** (30% of salary)	$10,500
Direct personnel expense (DPE)	$45,500 ÷ 49 weeks = $928.57 per week

Using a $2^1/_2$ to $3^1/_2$ percent multiplier, you can establish an appropriate billing rate, as follows:

$2^1/_2$: $77.38 per hour
3: $92.85 per hour
$3^1/_2$: $108.33 per hourv.

*If a designer works an average of 40 hours per week, the usual number of chargeable hours is 30.
**When calculating fringe benefits, include holidays, sick leave, vacation, company-paid payroll taxes, FICA, workmen's compensation, any company-paid health, dental, or vision insurance, and company-paid retirement plans.

psychiatrists do in the same city. I do not know why, but it seems a good rule of thumb to follow in setting hourly rates.

The way you charge affects the opportunities you are offered, the quality of your company and its longevity, and of course the profit you earn. If your rates cover only time and expenses and you are paid by the hour, you have not risked much; because you know that your profit is built into your multiplier and you will be reimbursed for all expenses. This is a safe system and one that can earn profit, if you calculate a good profit margin in your multiplier.

FEE BASES

Today, most clients are aware of the standard fees designers charge. They vary from area to area, but generally clients in any one area know what to expect. There are some basic methods of compensation.

The Design Concept Fee

This is a fee for developing a basic design concept (see Table 8.4, page 258). It is also called the "design study fee," and it encompasses studying the project to determine what must be done. At one time, the design study fee was considered the lead-in to the project, an opportunity for designers to demonstrate how they would handle it. If you were asked to provide a concept, you were almost assured of being awarded the rest of the project to develop and complete. Today, clients value the design concept but often feel that they can do the rest of the job themselves, that they know how to buy. And often they do. As a result, designers invest large quantities of time developing the design without proper compensation. Therefore, the trend today is for the design concept fee to be one of the larger charges. At one time, this was called "programming." Today, you will find that the system of design work varies from firm to firm and often goes by different names.

The Straight Design Fee

Compensation for design is on an hourly, per-diem, or fixed-fee basis. When the design fee is calculated on an hourly basis, the rate is usually two-and-a-half to three-

If It Works, Don't Fix It

After one of my seminars on design professionalism, a woman in the audience confided to me that a number of her fellow designers had criticized her for not charging a design fee. "I've never done it, and I don't think my clients would be comfortable with it," she said. This designer has children, works out of her home, and arranges her schedule to suit them. Her overhead for telephone, postage, and supplies was about $15,000 annually. Her clients paid all freight and delivery expenses, and her husband paid the rent. She did $350,000 in business each year—$170,000 to $175,000 in gross profit. No matter how you looked at it, she had to be making between $150,000 to $160,000 a year, which is rather good for five hours of work a day. Her method worked for her, and I suggested she continue it.

and-a-half times the cost of the employee (see page 263). You should quote a fixed fee only after you have had enough experience with certain types of jobs to provide a solid basis for estimating their costs. There is a strong trend today for design fees to be much larger then they were, since there is less and less opportunity for designers to earn profit on selling merchandise. Clients know that the creative part of a project is something they cannot do themselves, but often feel they can buy merchandise themselves at excellent prices.

Time and Expenses

Many designers bill their time and expenses. If you use this method, you bill either on a per-diem basis or an hourly basis. You build your profit into your multiplier. Generally, the multiplier is from three to three-and-a-half times the cost of the designer, to which expenses are added. The multiplier varies according to the size of the firm, its overhead, and the services rendered. Expenses can be calculated by the actual cost or a percentage of the fee.

Time and Expenses with Upset Limit. Charging for your time and expenses with a "not to exceed" price limit is a very difficult billing method. It is based on time and expenses with an "upset limit," or a guaranteed maximum. This is really the worst of all formats because it offers no room for extra profit and a tremendous potential for loss. Only very experienced firms can be confident of making a profit using this method of charging. The firm must be very familiar with the client and all of the demands and details of the project.

Time and Expenses: Estimated Amount. A safer way to charge is for your time and expenses based on a scheduled estimate of time. This method can work well and be more profitable because there is a basis for covering your extra charges.

Fee Plus Percentage of Savings. This billing method is based on hourly fees, plus a percentage of what you might save the client on the amount of the project. For example, if the project cost is estimated at $500,000, and you are able to bring it in for $240,000, the owner may agree to split the difference with you on a fifty-fifty basis. More of these types of incentive programs are being developed, because clients can see and understand their value. This method makes it worthwhile for the interior designer to try to plan the project in a price-effective way.

For example, designers may put the project out to bid among contractors who may not be familiar with their style of work. Or the designers may bring in an experienced team of craftspeople who have worked with them many times before. This can save a lot of time and money.

Time-Based Fee: Open-Ended. For the designer, this is the best way to charge and, often, the fairest if the designer is developing a project with the client and has no idea how long it will take. With this method, however, there is a need for good communication, trust, and ethics, so that clients understand your fees.

Value-Oriented Fees

The best way of charging, if you are very experienced and a specialist, is on the basis of value-oriented fees. This method is high risk, but it also offers excellent opportunities for profit. If you understand the project and you run an efficient design firm, this method can be controllable and profitable. If, however, the project is in an unfamiliar area, it can be disastrous.

This is a fee based on a lump sum for a particular project. Lump-sum fees are profitable. It can be the best way to charge when your firm has done a lot of similar projects, knows the client, and has a good idea of the anticipated time expenditures. Generally, specialist designers work on this basis, because they have certain elements predesigned and can therefore complete a job very cost-effectively. They may actually complete the job in one-half or one-fourth of the time of an inexperienced firm and still produce a higher-quality project. They have spent many years developing this expertise and deserve to be paid for it. Value-based fees are perfect for this situation. If the fees were based on an hourly rate, it would be unfair to an experienced firm.

Per-Square-Foot Charge

Charging per square foot is another system that can be profitable if you have a good rate and are experienced within a specialty. Otherwise, you can either make or lose a lot of money, depending on how well you have defined the project. This method has now become very popular in certain specialties. To calculate this charge, take the square footage of a space and multiply it by the per-square-foot cost. Years ago, we used to have nickel prints. Developers paid designers five cents a square foot for doing basic layouts for their buildings. Presently, there are design/build projects in which design fees, as well as all other costs on a building, are calculated in this manner. The per-square-foot charges are often worked out as a comparison with other charging methods.

Retail Sales–Based Methods

Many clients want to buy a product. Many design firms act as retail organizations responding to that need in many different ways. Today, many traditional furniture stores have closed and are gradually being replaced by specialty companies or design gallery operations. Good design services make these businesses outstanding. Some designers use a retail shop as a marketing tool; it is a comfortable way for a new client to get to know the designer and identify with that individual's style. The retail method enables a client to know exactly what the project is going to cost. Many residential clients understand product costs rather than fees. To the client who enjoys buying, this method will always remain attractive.

Retail or specialty companies usually have better buying methods and, therefore, can produce an item with their specifications at a better price, faster, and with fewer delivery problems than a typical design firm. They have chosen their preferred vendors, given them a large quantity of business, and therefore can expect certain considerations.

Earlier in my career, I thought the only professional way to work was on a fee or hourly basis. At that time, some designers earned a living by working for furniture stores; they received a commission or a percentage of the sales. I was told that being a professional interior designer and selling furniture were poles apart. Now I see the advantages of combining these disciplines. Many design firms have found it difficult to maintain the expenses of their firms on just an hourly fee. Either they need a very high rate and a constantly busy office, or they need additional forms of income, such as a percentage of the items contracted by the client. Markup and pricing methods vary according to the format of the business. The retail sales-based method has many advantages and opportunities for profitability.

Some professional design organizations, as well as many consultants, recommend that designers not sell merchandise. I can understand why. It is so important that a firm be prepared to handle whatever part or parts of the project it takes on, easily. It is also important that the firm be fully aware of the responsibilities that go with each of these phases. So often companies—especially young ones—feel that they can do it all, and this is where they get into trouble.

A firm that takes on the responsibility of retail sales or furnishing the merchandise for a project must be aware that doing so also requires installation, repair, and maintenance. Be sure you have a system in place to handle these tasks.

Contract Price

In many respects, contract price is similar to retail, in that you are charging clients for a project delivered to their house or place of business. The firm covers all overhead expenses, fees, delivery, handling expenses, and so on. The major difference between a retail and contract price is that in the case of the latter, the firm looks at the overall project, considers exactly what it will cost to deliver and install all the products, and then calculates exactly what is needed to complete the project appropriately. Firms know they must price competitively on certain items. Where large quantities of products are needed, a higher markup may not be as necessary as with other items. Some items can be delivered without problem; other products are so perishable or fragile you pray you do not break too many before you deliver one in good condition. Therefore, the cost of delivery and the markup are different. This is a reality of the field. Some things are easy to do, and some things are incredibly difficult.

When a design project incorporates several rooms or entire buildings, there are ways to buy products advantageously. If we can put a project together and price it in total, we can bring it in at a lower price. I like the term "contract price," because it tells the client that the firm will agree to deliver this project within this price range. I normally suggest that firms quote within a range of 10 percent if it is a more standard project. If it is very original, highly creative, and very risky, then the range could be broader—say 20 to 25 percent. In most instances, clients really appreciate knowing what the project is going to cost; there are no surprises. I feel that offering a range is fair, because with creative work, there are always variables. If, say, you are bidding a project that includes several hundred chairs, you will know exactly what each chair is going to cost. But if a special item must be constructed for the client, it is almost impossible to price it exactly, because there may be changes or additions needed down the road. It is the designer's job to make these adjustments or additions. This is why the clients hire designers.

After I explained our system to a client who was an attorney, he said, "This seems to be a very honest way of doing it. We want your judgment and your design expertise throughout the job and therefore this seems very fair."

Design Concept Fee Plus Percentage. On residential work and small contract jobs, many designers work for a design concept fee plus a percentage of the cost of the items that are to be purchased or supervised. This percentage applies to construction items, furniture, and accessories. The percentage varies, depending on the location and experience of the design firm.

Hourly Fee Plus Percentage. Another popular method of pricing is the time-based or hourly fee, plus a percentage of the merchandise that is specified. On smaller jobs,

Table 8.7 Gross profit percent formula. There is a great deal of confusion between markup and profit. This form compares markup to gross profit. The gross profit has nothing to do with your overhead expenses; it is the amount of money earned before you take into consideration anything other than items directly related to the sale. This means the price of the item plus the freight, handling, and delivery charges, if those are to be included in the amount you have charged. If these items are to be billed separately, they would not be included in this formula.

GROSS PROFIT PERCENT FORMULA

Item Cost × (1 + markup % = Sale Price $
Sale Price $ − Item Cost $ = Gross Profit $
Gross Profit $/ Sale Price $ = Gross Profit %

Sale Price − Item Cost = Gross Profit

OR, as one formula
$$((\text{Item cost} \times (1 + \% \text{ markup}) - \text{Item Cost}) / ((\text{Item cost} \times (1 + \% \text{ markup}))$$

ITEM COST $	% MARKUP	GROSS PROFIT %	SALE PRICE $	GROSS PROFIT $
100	10	9.1	110	10
100	15	13.0	115	15
100	20	16.7	120	20
100	25	20.0	125	25
100	30	23.1	130	30
100	35	25.9	135	35
100	40	28.6	140	40
100	50	33.3	150	50
100	60	37.5	160	60
100	70	41.2	170	70
100	80	44.4	180	80
100	90	47.4	190	90
100	100	50.0	200	100

this is often necessary. As jobs develop into high-level, large-quantity projects (such as large-contract projects), then the fee plus percentage method is not normally possible.

Percentage of Cost. An interior designer can also provide complete services, including furnishings and labor, at cost, adding a fee based on a percentage of the total cost. With this method, the design firm makes all purchases and passes on to the client all discounts, commissions, and savings. The client thus obtains merchandise at wholesale price, plus the designer's fee. This fee will vary considerably depending on the type of work being performed. Obviously, the larger the job, the smaller the percentage of the fee must be. When firms charge an hourly fee plus a percentage of cost, the client must be clearly informed that project management and follow-up on problems usually represent a large portion of the fee—from one-third to one-half of the total.

Percentage of Costs

Cost of Items	$1,000.00
Freight	100.00
Receiving, warehousing, and delivery	120.00
+ 25% fee	305.00
Subtotal:	$1,525.00
+ State Sales Tax @ 6%	91.50
TOTAL	$1,616.50

Another billing method is to charge for the cost plus a percentage of profit on the furnishings you are handling.

Percentage of List Price. If you act as a buying agent, you can often receive a percentage of the cost of items purchased by your client from your suppliers.

Percentage off List Price

List Price	$2,000.00
Less 20%	400.00
Subtotal:	$1,600.00
+ State Sales Tax @ 6%	96.00
TOTAL	$1,696.00

Many firms will include the freight, warehousing, and delivery charges in their estimates. Others will make an additional charge in their billing.

Procurement or Expediting Companies

There are specialized firms that will purchase and handle the complete installation of a project for designers. This arrangement has been standard for many years in the hospitality field but was not popular in many other specialties. In some cases, a group of designers will jointly own a procurement company. This permits them to buy at large volume, often at better prices. It also enables them to procure lines on a dealership basis—lines that may not be available to them as individuals in their given area.

Master Builders. These designers create very unusual things; they build or have their own products built and so have their own unique pricing structures. There are many more designers of this type in business today than there were in the past, because people now want very unusual products. Designers are finding the creativity of master builders very exciting and rewarding.

The Designer as Retail Employee. Designers employed by retail or specialty stores are usually paid either salary plus commission or straight commission. When a client purchases items from that store, the design services are either included in the cost of the item or can be featured for an extra fee. Today, an increasing number of these stores are charging professional fees in addition to their typical retail or list price; however, the fee will vary according to the type of store, location, and sales structure of the company.

The Designer as Agent. The designer, as an agent for the client, will prepare specifications, orders, and contracts, and place orders on the client's behalf—using funds that are either advanced by the client or have been paid directly by the client to the resources.

When working in this kind of arrangement, it is important that the designer inform all resources that the purchasing agreements and payments will be made by the client. The designer is acting as an agent only; the client has all financial responsibilities. On some larger projects, the manufacturers often prefer this arrangement; on others, it can present complications. Therefore, this fee arrangement must be made known up front on the original purchase orders.

In these situations, too, the design firm needs to clearly specify the financial and management responsibilities. If the client is purchasing directly, the client is also responsible for dealing with the manufacturers directly on follow-up issues. If the design firm is handling the purchasing, the client is charged a fee for management.

METHODS OF CHARGING TO IMPROVE PROFITS

If you are not satisfied with your firm's earnings at year-end, perhaps you should study some techniques to improve your profits.

Reducing Bookkeeping

Additional expenses have become a very cumbersome issue. For example, if you quote charges for prints and supplies at cost, plus 15 or 20 percent, each of these items must be documented. This can be very time-consuming and expensive. It is easier to quote costs for supplies for a fixed figure or for 5 or 10 percent of the fee. This eliminates an extensive bookkeeping process.

Factoring in a Margin for Cost Increases

One year, our accountant brought to our attention the fact that the cost of merchandise had increased 11 percent during that year. In the past, there had been very few increases on the prices of merchandise, so we had always given our clients a firm quotation on all the merchandise they were purchasing from us. After this announcement, we found that we had quoted below our normal markup procedures, while our cost of merchandise and delivery had increased 11 percent. (We included freight and delivery in the cost of our products to our client.) This, coupled with some additional increases in our office and overhead expenses, caused us to lose money. When you buy merchandise, you do not pay the listed price, but the price for the item on the day it is shipped to you. Because this can vary considerably from the amount you originally estimated, you should try to allow a 10 percent variance in your estimates. For example, when you expect something to cost $4,600, you should quote from $4,600 to $5,200 so you have some cushion in case there is a price increase.

DETERMINING THE FEE STRUCTURE

No matter how you estimate your projects, the only way to be accurate is to make a comparison to your own past work. If you don't have a similar project for comparison purposes, you need to speak with several other designers who have done similar jobs. For this purpose, it is a good idea to figure the fees for the job several different ways and compare them—for example, per-square-foot versus hourly rate. This can often reveal an error in your calculations.

Getting Higher Fees

Calculating fees is both an art and a science. Knowing your costs, your studio's working style, and your clients is important, but it may be equally important to understand the market values of our profession. Sometimes, raising the price can increase sales because the client may not feel a project is valuable unless it has a higher price tag.

You need to understand your market and the competition. For years, certain design processes may have brought good income to firms; then all of a sudden another competitor eliminated that income source. The point is, we must keep up with the market. We must understand our competition. We must understand what our clients want and what they value.

The strength of a practice lies in the ability of its principals to create desire and demand, which definitely affects how you charge and what your profit will be. Can you ask for a higher fee? Yes, if your office is very busy or if you are the leader in your specialty at the time. If you are very busy, it is a good time to raise your fees. Often, design firms get high fees and great jobs when they are most busy and don't need the work. That is because people like to follow the person who is successful. If you are successful within a given area, it is usually easier to get additional jobs.

Relating to the Client. Some people are just more comfortable than others asking for higher fees—and know how to get them. The range of fees in the interior design field is extremely broad, and many times the fee can depend on the client and on the designer's presentation. Most clients know what fees are being charged within their particular area. They have a pretty good basis for comparison when they make their proposal.

In order to demand, and get, top fees, you must have a good relationship with your clients. Clients must feel the design team understands their needs. Successful, talented designers are those who know how to make clients feel they are getting exactly what they want.

Repackaging Your Services. There are three ways to get to the top of the heap. You can be truly innovative, which is the most difficult way. The second way is to copy someone else at the top of the heap, which is also difficult. The third way is to repackage your present types of services and give them a different name. By creating a new category of service, you make the fee scale more flexible; no one knows what the appropriate charge should be. For instance, almost everyone knows what the square-footage prices are for space planning, but for certain types of design business analysis, none have been established. Therefore, they can bring in a higher fee.

Showing a Strong Portfolio. Having an excellent portfolio is another method for gaining top fees. The value of good photography cannot be overestimated. I have seen many designers walk away with major projects just because they had good photographs. They did not necessarily have an excellent background for the job, but they were able to present themselves well and sell the project appropriately. Also, if you have a specialty, and your portfolio represents that specialty adequately, you have a great entree to quality work within that specialty.

Offering Something Different. The competition is fierce on larger projects, and most people will bid on a square-foot or a percentage basis. If you can plan a presentation that is different from everyone else's, you have a better chance of winning a larger fee.

Offering Better Services. By offering a better or more all-encompassing service, firms can get the competitive edge. Some clients are looking for a multidisciplinary firm—a firm that consists of an interior designer, an architect, engineer, landscape architect, and other design professionals who work cooperatively to complete the total project. I have found that, in these firms, the person who brings in a project is usually the one who controls it. At one time, interior designers waited for architects to

In his lectures and books, Frank Stasiowski, FAIA, author of Architect's Essentials of Winning Proposals (John Wiley & Sons, 2003), claims that some jobs with the highest profit are the most innovative and the most unusual, the ones other people are not doing. To get the projects that permit innovation, a firm will often have to do a great deal of marketing research. This means that, in the beginning, jobs will principally be research-oriented, not necessarily profitable. Then, when the firm develops skill in that unusual specialty, the profits increase. When competition enters the field, the profits start to drop, until they reach the competitive bidding or cut-throat stage.

team with them. Today, however, interior designers want to be the ones who write the job, so that they can have control of the project, including the budget.

Many successful design firms are multidisciplinary and able to take care of all the design needs of the client. They are able to keep the competition at bay because they have built a strong team structure. Obviously, it takes a lot of organizational effort to coordinate a team that works well together; it also requires a tremendous amount of support and charisma on the part of the principals.

Adding services used to mean adding more staff. Today, we can form teams or joint ventures or blend our company with another company that is a specialist in the discipline we need.

Having a Good Reputation. The reputation of designers has a great deal to do with the rates they are able to charge. If someone is well known within a specialty or within a certain social circle, that individual will often be able to charge considerably higher fees than a lesser-known designer.

The charisma of the principals of a design firm also has a great deal to do with the size of the fee the firm can command. The value of charisma and ease of social interaction cannot be overestimated. Clients want their projects controlled by a person with whom they feel comfortable. If the design principal or the person selling the project has the ability to gain the confidence of the client, the quality and types of jobs that can be secured will be amazing.

CONSIDERATIONS

How to charge is one of the major questions people ask during the workshops, courses, and programs I have led. Fee assessment is an area in which many people have problems. Some of the systems detailed here will work for your practice. You should test several, and compare them to make sure you are on target. I have also found that this is an area in which you must be careful whom you ask for help or advice. Often, other designers will see you as potential competition, or just won't want you to know how they really charge.

You should review your charging system on a yearly basis, to accommodate any changes in the services you perform. Our practices change constantly. Sometimes we are unaware how much the little additions or subtractions may affect our bottom line.

Establish a policy to have a professional who specializes in charging systems review your system every year to be sure it is up to date. The market changes; our clients are often very willing to pay higher fees if they are presented and supported in a vocabulary that is suitable for the times and market.

Fees will be based on responsibility. The firm or professional who gives value and is willing to take on the responsibility can be well compensated. The two must be coordinated. Designers will be able to earn at a much higher level than before, but there will be greater requirements of professionalism and quality of work, tied in with sensitivity to the client's issues and needs. An understanding of and rapport with the different artists and craftspeople on the project also are essential. Working together gives designers an opportunity to make an excellent income in the future. We can command good fees as long as the clients know what they can expect in advance, with no surprises.

CHAPTER 9

Working with Sources and Contractors

Interior designers coordinate many different products, suppliers, and outside workers in the course of a project. The sources we engage—the contractors and craftspeople—make up our palette. We have to know how to choose and work with these resources.

The success of our practices depends on the quality of the contractors and suppliers we work with and the quality of our relationship with them. The goal is to have a small group of carefully selected vendors and contractors. If you have a specialty, you may be able to work with that same group of people on a continuing basis. In many practices, this is not possible. Different craftspeople and specialists are required, which means we have to search out and find the right people to form our palette. This is one of the major challenges in any design practice.

SELECTING SOURCES

There are many ways of learning which manufacturers want your business. If you become active in your local American Society of Interior Designers (ASID) or International Interior Design Association (IIDA) chapter's Industry Foundation programs, you will meet individuals from companies who are interested in doing interior design work. There are other professional organizations for designers, all of which provide opportunities to meet and work with manufacturers who want our business. They are often willing to adapt and adjust their products for you. Some firms are too big to do this; they simply want furniture store business or major contract projects.

Investigating Source Companies

Know your sources, and know them well. Before you consider specifying any material for a project, investigate the company from which you intend to purchase. If it is a new account, talk to other designers to find out what they know about the company. Do not use a firm you have not thoroughly investigated.

Choosing Appropriate Products. When a new catalog comes across your desk, examine it. Be sure it is an appropriate line for your work. Is it the type of material you would use on a job? For example, if a catalog lists only products for inexpensive contract use, and your firm designs very exclusive offices, this catalog probably has no place in your library. If you decide to keep it, you should store it in a section apart from your usual sources. If you are doing residential work, you should probably not keep contract catalogs, which require quantity purchases.

Review each company's line. If it is appropriate to your work, consider some basic ground rules. Do the products meet your quality standards? Are they products you as a designer would be pleased to recommend? Find out as much as you can about the product quality, either by personally visiting the company's showrooms or factories, or by visiting an installation that uses the company's products. The company's sales representatives can give you a list of places where you can see its products in use. You should also try to discuss the products with other designers.

Learn whether the company can handle special-product work. Many production lines are not in a position to change products as a designer requires. If you want something special, you may need to go to a smaller, more flexible company. Investigate your options carefully when considering changing any product or doing any special design work with an existing product. These variations can be not only expensive but disastrous as well if the companies you use are not set up to do special design work.

Geographic Convenience. Is the product manufactured within a reasonable distance from your studio or jobs? Freight and administration logistics can make long-distance deliveries expensive. Products that are available from your geographic area, or an area nearby, help a project move much more smoothly. Interior design firms are increasingly using neighborhood sources, especially for custom projects.

Jobber versus Manufacturer. Is the source a jobber or a manufacturer? A jobber is a wholesaler that buys in job lots from the manufacturer or importer and sells on a wholesale basis to interior designers. A number of fabric and accessory lines are sold through jobbers. Generally designers do not buy fabrics directly from mills, because, in most cases, they do not buy in large enough quantities. Many mills will not sell to interior designers unless the order is for very large lots—hundreds or thousands of yards per item. Jobbers generally charge more than manufacturers, but they provide a method of distribution on a smaller basis that meets the needs of the interior designer.

Web Resources. Most of our sources now have online catalogs. This gives us the opportunity to review a line and determine the feasibility of it for our project. Many design studios are eliminating a large number of their paper catalogs and substituting them either with catalogs on disk or on the Web. Fortunately, a lot of pricing and specifications are kept online, so they can be updated by the manufacturer on a daily basis. This is a preferred source for this type of information, as it permits us to have updated information anytime, day or night. Certain companies have their price lists protected in a confidential way for designers' use only.

It is important to determine exactly the way resources use the Internet. Some use it to sell directly to clients. For others, it is a reserved catalog resource only for professionals. Many designers go online to see what is available to consumers, so they know what *not* to specify on their projects. Their clients want unusual or special merchandise, so these designers consider items available online as too common or typical, hence not appropriate for an exclusive design practice.

Most designers find they still need samples of items, especially finishes and fabrics—those that have a tactile quality. Often, however, online catalogs serve us better than some of the traditional catalogs, as they give us the flexibility to determine the size of the illustrations we want to present to our clients. We can often, for example, enlarge the object and present four or five different items in the same size or the same type of visual presentation—which can make for a much more professional-looking presentation. This service is very efficient; however, it does not replace some of the traditional catalogs. We still find these a convenient source for locating certain items.

Whether you can do everything over the Internet or need a particular type of library depends on the way you work and the type of practice you have.

Working Arrangements. Once you have decided a product is suitable, find out who your contact person at the factory will be. You need a person whom you can contact anytime during working hours to answer your questions about the new product. This person should probably not be the company salesperson. Very often, salespeople are hard to reach except in the evenings or on Saturdays. The more familiar you are with the product, the easier it will be for you to talk to the factory staff about it.

Credit Arrangements. Most interior designers prefer to deal with their suppliers on an open-account basis. If your company has achieved a good credit standing, you should be able to establish open accounts. Most showrooms and design centers work on a cash before delivery (CBD) basis. Interior designers who have established businesses and deal with manufacturers directly in larger volume have the opportunity of having standard open accounts. This also means the designer must give that company a certain amount of work per year to maintain this account. It is important to establish your credit at the beginning of a relationship. If you wait until you place an order, it could delay delivery.

Making Sales Reps' Visits Worthwhile

Can designers profit from sales representatives' calls? If you learn to use the time you spend with salespeople properly, they can become a valuable resource. On the other hand, if you do not plan for their visits, sales reps can waste your time and cause chaos in your schedule. There are times when you need certain products and times when you don't. How can you control the situation?

In my firm, we have instituted a few policies that have helped us and that might work for you as well. First, we look on sales representatives as important contributors to our education about sources and the marketplace. We expect them to have information. If they want to sell us something, we expect them to have the information or know where to get it. In this day and age, with so many liability lawsuits, we must have the details; we can't afford to take chances. We must be sure we are selecting the right product for the correct situation.

Setting Aside Space. Our key to controlling the time we spend with sales representatives is never to permit them in our work area. First, they disrupt the work schedule. Second, we see no reason for them to see our projects. These representatives visit many other studios in the community. We do not want them discussing our work, much of which is confidential. Today, privacy issues have become primary, not just discretionary.

We have several rooms on our lower level where we see sales representatives. We make it convenient for them to come right in the door with their sample cases and set up their display for us to see. As soon as they are set up, they let us know, and we all come down and look at the line.

Setting a Schedule. Try to schedule sales rep meetings so they do not interrupt time that is scheduled for clients.

We schedule our sales reps' visits either early in the day (from 8:30 to 9:00 A.M.), right before lunch (from 11:30 to 12:00 noon), or late in the day (from 4:30 to 5:00 P.M.). This keeps interruptions to a minimum. Generally, we can see three or four sales rep in each half-hour period. We have found that almost every major fabric line can be reviewed in less than 15 minutes, and salespeople with other products can almost always be seen in three to five minutes if we know the line. A new line will take longer. There is absolutely nothing wrong with saying, "I do not have anything major for which I can use your line at this time. Keep our catalog up to date, and when I do have something, I will call you."

I have found that if you make a point never to keep sales reps waiting more than a few minutes, they will also respect your schedule. I am not saying we never run late; we do. But we try to have it happen only occasionally.

We pay attention to the reps and try to keep them abreast of what we are doing. If a line is not appropriate for us, we do not take the literature. There is no point in cluttering library shelves with hospital equipment brochures if your firm designs only offices.

Knowing the Line and the Rep. When we take on a new line, we want to know more than just what the brochure says. We want to know the salespeople, their background in the field, and how and when it is best to reach them. We also want to know the history of the company that produces the line. We want to know which designers have used that line, what they think of it, and how they feel about the company offering the line. We ask the sales rep for the names of three designers whom we can call to discuss the product.

Then, if at all possible, I like to visit the factory so I can understand the many processes that go into producing the company's products. So often, the price of a product depends on the way it is constructed, the vendor location, and many other small issues. One company can turn a product out easily and inexpensively, while another company will find it laborious and difficult—and then charge three or four times the price. If you can match the right vendors with the right projects, you will find you can run far more price-effective projects.

Get to know your sales representatives. Show them respect, but demand the same from them. I am very straightforward with our sales representatives. I tell them if I like something or not. This frankness saves me from having to see a product I do not like more than once.

Not all designers can see every line, but you should try to make sure you and your staff see what is exceptional. Our staff tries to meet and review new products at least once or twice a week, usually over lunch. Everyone trades information about new catalogs and products and about what we have learned from any of the sales reps or from material received through the mail.

When we buy, we also try to ensure that we know how to reach the reps or a reliable liaison at the factory at all times. When a problem occurs, we need to have immediate access to them. We always ask, "If something comes up during the day, evening, or on the weekend, how can we reach you?"

Using Design Centers. Design centers are an increasingly important part of the furniture industry (see the list on pages 281–283). These building complexes, where manufacturers of furniture and furnishings show their products, became part of the industry in the late 1960s, initially only in New York, Boston, Philadelphia, Atlanta, Miami, Chicago, Dallas, Houston, San Francisco, and Los Angeles. Many more are in operation today; smaller centers are being built, while others are growing.

Some design centers are closed to the public, which means a consumer cannot enter the building unless accompanied by the designer, an architect, or a letter from a design firm. Others permit the individual showrooms to set their own policies, and still others admit the public. In the latter case, a dual pricing system is in effect: interior designers and architects receive a discount, and consumers pay full price. Where the public is allowed free access to the design centers, the center is said to have an "open showroom" policy, as opposed to a "to the trade only" or "closed showroom" policy.

From the advertisements in consumer shelter magazines lately, it seems that even centers with closed showroom policies seek to attract the consumer. Does an open showroom help or hurt the designer? It depends on your methods of fee structuring. For example, most designers who use design centers work on a straight-fee or percentage basis. Their fee structure is protected, so it doesn't matter if their clients see two prices on each furniture hangtag. The designer who is hired on a professional-fee basis doesn't have to worry about the client having pricing information.

To get the best use of a design center, preshop it to determine exactly what you want to show your clients. Otherwise, you can spend weeks taking a client shopping. Letting your client see the merchandise you have specified is a good idea, because most people cannot visualize effectively; but first prepare your client for your visit to the design center. Explain that the purpose of the visit is to see two or three conference tables for the client's new office building, for example. The client can sit in several chairs to see if they are appropriate for the executive offices. This keeps the client from becoming overwhelmed by the variety and quantity of other merchandise.

Keeping a Research Sheet

When researching the possible suppliers for a client's project, you can sometimes go through dozens of catalogs or Web sites. If the subject and goal are not defined, it is easy to get off track. One way to prevent this is to keep a research sheet listing the client's name, the date on which the project was assigned, the date by which you need the information, and the person to whom the research is assigned. A sample research sheet is shown in Table 9.1 (see page 284).

Define the subject or the product. Perhaps it is a secretarial desk no longer than 60 inches or a table that must be viewed from a specific angle. Perhaps it is chairs with casters.

State your goals; list the price range, materials, or type of design you need. List the contacts you have made. Document all the companies you have researched, whether by telephone or showroom visit. If you have located a suitable product, list the price range. Also state the dates on which phone calls were made and how long they lasted. At the bottom of the sheet, write your final decision. If, at a later date, either you or another person picks up this sheet, your research has been documented, and the results are clearly marked.

Research sheets should be kept in the client's file until the product is ready for processing. You can refer to the sheets to refresh your memory on a project, or if you need to change something in the project. For example, if a client's price range changes, you can look at this sheet and quickly see, for example, that a particular sofa you had earmarked is going to be too expensive and that one of the sofas you had originally rejected may be a good choice instead. The research sheet provides a

Design Centers & Trade Marts

Arizona
Arizona Design Center
7350 North Dobson Road
Scottsdale, AZ 85256
888-830-2680

California
Design Pavilion at 200 Kansas
200 Kansas Street
San Francisco, CA 94103
415-558-9925

Galleria Design Center
101 Henry Adams Street
San Francisco, CA 94103
415-626-3037

Laguna Design Center
23811 Aliso Creek Road
Laguna Niguel, CA 92656
949-643-2929

LA Home Furnishings Mart
1933 South Broadway
Los Angeles, CA 90007
213-763-5881

Pacific Design Center
8687 Melrose Avenue
Los Angeles, CA 90069
310-657-0800

The San Francisco Mart
1355 Market Street
San Francisco, CA 94103
415-241-7958

Showplace Square Group
Two Henry Adams Street
San Francisco, CA 94103
415-490-5800

Showplace Square West
550 15th Street
San Francisco, CA 94103
415-626-8257

Sobel Design Building
680 Eighth Street
San Francisco, CA 94103
415-861-4443

Colorado
Denver Design Center
595 South Broadway
Denver, CO 80209-4001
303-733-2455

Denver Merchandise Mart
451 East 58th Street
Denver, CO 80216
303-292-6278

Design Center at the Ice House
1801 Wynkoop Street
Denver, CO 80202
303-298-9191

Florida
Dacra
3930 NE Second Avenue
Miami Beach, FL 33137
305-573-8116

Design Center of the Americas
(DCOTA)
1855 Griffin Road
Dania, FL 33004
954-920-7997

Miami Decorating & Design Center
180 NW 40th Avenue
Miami, FL 33137
305-575-7511

Miami Decorating & Design
District, Plaza II
180 NE 39th Avenue
Miami, FL 33137
305-573-8116

Miami Decorating & Design
District, Plaza III
3939 NE Second Avenue
Miami, FL 33137
305-573-8116

Miami Decorating & Design
District, Plaza IV
3901 NE Second Avenue
Miami, FL 33137
305-573-8116

Miami International Design
Center
4100 NE Second Avenue
Miami, FL 33137
305-576-7571

Miami International Design
Center II
4141 NE Second Avenue
Miami, FL 33137
305-576-5515

Miami International Merchandise
Mart
777 NW 72nd Avenue
Miami, FL 33126
305-261-2900

Georgia
Atlanta Decorative Arts Center
(ADAC)
351 Peachtree Hills Avenue
Atlanta, GA 30305
404-231-1720

Atlanta Merchandise Mart
240 Peachtree Street NW
Atlanta, GA 30303
404-220-3000

(continued)

Design Centers & Trade Marts *(continued)*

Illinois
The Merchandise Mart
200 World Trade Center
Chicago, IL 60054
800-677-6278

Massachusetts
Boston Design Center
One Design Center Place
Boston, MA 02210
617-338-5062

Michigan
Michigan Design Center
1700 Stutz Drive
Troy, MI 48084
248-649-4772

Minnesota
International Market Square
275 Market Street
Minneapolis, MN 55405
612-338-6250

Nevada
World Market Center
Las Vegas Design Center
495 Grand Central Parkway
Las Vegas, NV 89106
888-416-8600

New York
Architects & Designers (A&D)
   Building
150 East 58th Street
New York, NY 10155
212-644-6555

Design & Decoration (D&D)
   Building
979 Third Avenue
New York, NY 10022
212-759-5408

Interior Design Building
306 East 61st Street
New York, NY 10021
212-838-7042

International Showcase
24 East 64th Street
New York, NY 10021
212-838-0157

Manhattan Art & Antiques Center
1050 Second Avenue
New York, NY 10022
212-355-4400

The Marketcenter at 230 Fifth Ave.
230 Fifth Avenue
New York, NY 10001
212-689-4721

New York Design Center
200 Lexington Avenue
New York, NY 10016
212-679-9500

New York Merchandise Mart
41 Madison Avenue
New York, NY 10010
212-686-1203

North Carolina
Hamilton Wrenn Community of
   Showrooms
200 North Hamilton Street
High Point, NC 27260
336-884-1884

International Home Furnishings
   Center
210 East Commerce Street
High Point, NC 27260
336-888-3700

Market Square
305 West High Street
High Point, NC 27260
336-821-1500

Ohio
Longworth Hall Design Center
700 West Pete Rose Way
Cincinnati, OH 45203
513-721-1000

Pendleton Square Design
   Complex
118 Pendleton Street
Cincinnati, OH 45210
513-621-7619

Pennsylvania
Marketplace Design Center
2400 Market Street
Philadelphia, PA 19103
215-561-5000

Texas
Dallas Design Center
1025 North Stemmons Freeway
Dallas, TX 75207
214-747-2411

Dallas Market Center
2100 North Stemmons Freeway
Dallas, TX 55207
214-655-6100

(continued)

Design Centers & Trade Marts *(continued)*

Decorative Center Dallas
1400 Turtle Creek Blvd.
Dallas, TX 75207
214-698-1300

Decorative Center of
  Houston
5120 Woodway at Sage
Houston, TX 77056
713-961-9292

The Resource Center
7026 Old Katy Road
Houston, TX 77024
713-864-2760

Washington, DC
The Washington Design Center
300 D Street SW
Washington, DC 20024
202-554-5053

Washington State
Lenora Square Professional
1000 Lenora Street
Seattle, WA 98121
206-762-1200

Design Showrooms Seattle Gift
  Center
6100 4th Avenue South
Seattle, WA 98101
206-767-6800

system for documenting all the research we do for each individual item that goes into a project. The research process may require dozens or even hundreds of source checks and can extend over a long period. We record each source and the results. Even after the project is over, we may keep the records to serve as a basis for similar projects.

Keeping Up to Date with Your Sources

Review your sources at least once a year. New companies are forming, older companies are closing or their owners are retiring. Design centers are in a state of constant change because everything from environmental issues to international issues affects our sources. Not only do we have to make sure we have the right sources, but we have to make sure those sources are still in business.

WORKING WITH YOUR SUPPLIERS

Make each firm you deal with your ally, not just on exceptionally large projects but on every project.

When a project has specific needs, enlist your resource company to help find solutions. Define the problem, type of client, and probable maintenance, as well as the budget and design requirements. With this rundown, together, the resource company and you can usually come up with a product recommendation to work for the specific situation.

Some firms have laboratories and testing equipment that can help you analyze functional problems or do chemical analyses. The knowledge of your resource

Table 9.1 Research sheet. In researching information that is required for clients, document all the companies you have reviewed, whether by catalog, telephone, or showroom visit. If, at a later date, either you or another person picks up the file, this research is documented and the result is clearly indicated.

RESEARCH SHEET			
Client:	Date Assigned:	Due Date:	Staff Person:
Subject:			
Goal:			
Contacts:	Results:		Date/Time:
Final Decision:			

© *Design Business Monthly,* 1988.

company is an asset, something you could not supply in your own studio that helps make your presentations professional and your designs long-lasting.

Quality Control

Interior designers can be leaders in quality control. It is part of an interior designer's job to monitor quality. We know what clients want. We generally are very good judges of quality. We have researched the product; we know who makes similar products and what the product price should be. We are in a great position of control.

First, report all problems, even if your clients have not complained. If you see something is wrong with a product, report it to the company that supplied it. Let them know you are sensitive to quality.

Second, if you receive something that needs a simple repair, take care of it so you do not have to return it. Let companies know that you are willing to make small repairs and touch-ups as required. However, also alert companies when you have had to make repairs.

One of the best ways of maintaining your clients is to demand good-quality products from your resources. Quality is a commodity. We are producing better products for the price, but we also have more discriminating clients than ever before. Quality exists at all price levels, from the costly to the less expensive. Many excellent designs use products from top-quality sources, but these can be costly. On occasion, budget compels designers to use mass-market products, which discriminating clients will sometimes refuse to accept with even the slightest imperfection. If you must use mass-market products, make a point of having someone from your firm look over these pieces—checking the finish, upholstery details, and overall quality. Many times, even the finished piece needs work before you can deliver it to your client.

At times, every interior designer has been caught with expensive repair bills for mass-produced furniture. Try to build a safety cushion into each project for which you use mass-market or less-expensive products. We had one project for which we needed 12 reproduction chairs. One source offered the chairs at $4,100 each, and another source had similar chairs for about $1,500. We quoted the client a price for the less expensive chairs but added about 20 percent to the actual price to cover any adjustments or refinements that might have to be done when the chairs reached our studio. Quoting the client a variable price—that the chairs would cost about $1,800—gave us enough leeway within our budget to pay for any necessary refinements and repairs. The client received an excellent-quality product, because we refined it and addressed any shortcomings. Clients have no idea what happens behind the scenes. We want the job to run smoothly; we want our clients to have the best products possible for the investment they have made. We want them to enjoy the process of doing their interiors.

Project Management. There are many specialists and companies that only handle project management. Often, these specialists have a list of contractors they will use on the job and be totally responsible for completing the project. This can be a valuable service especially if a designer is working in an unfamiliar town or city. The project management specialist knows all the permits and licenses required to complete the job.

Project management is becoming a major specialty in many geographic areas. It is advantageous to have experience with a firm so they understand the nuances of your design style. Using these skilled professionals can be of great value, as it assures you and the client that the project will be handled with a high level of professionalism.

Maintenance Programs. Have your sources provide maintenance recommendations. This information is available from the companies supplying the products you purchase. Since factory guarantees are based on maintenance procedures, review these procedures with your resource companies. Find out in advance how the manufacturer wants problems handled; then make appropriate recommendations to your client.

Government Regulations. The government has instituted a lot of new regulations on the products interior designers handle. Your best source of regulation information is your suppliers. They are required to provide you with flameproofing certificates and other necessary papers to indicate they meet relevant requirements. You, as the designer, are responsible for every product you specify, so be sure to keep abreast of state and federal regulations.

Confidential Work. With today's privacy requirements, confidentiality is becoming a much more serious issue in the interior design discipline. It is best to keep our work confidential, and be sure everything is marked "confidential." We must be sure our vendors and resources understand the level of responsibility we have in this regard. Clients have a right to demand confidentiality of us, and we must respect their privacy. We must be assured that our various vendors do not use projects for reference or promotion without our and the client's permission. If your work is confidential, mark it so, and explain the reason for this confidentiality to the shop from the beginning, so all of the workers will understand the situation. (See also, pages 334–336).

Getting the Best-Quality Performance from Your Suppliers. Interior designers rely heavily on the performance of their craftspeople and suppliers to ensure the overall quality of a job. There are ways of improving the quality of this performance. Here are a few methods that have worked for some designers:

1. When you are designing a new project that you expect a shop to build, review the design with the shop before presenting it for pricing or to the client. Give the shop a chance to determine whether there are any ways of improving the design, reducing the cost, or upgrading the quality of the product.
2. As you review the project with the craftspeople, determine what their capabilities are and if there are any areas with which they may have difficulty. If so, ask yourself: Is there another resource you could use for that part of the job? Giving a project to a supplier that is uncomfortable with it will only delay the project and can cause problems in the quality of production. Talk the project over together, carefully. Maybe it would be better to take this project someplace else and bring this shop another project more suited to its equipment and capabilities. So often, problems in design work are due to the fact that the shops are not appropriate for the work to be done. I have found, for example, that giving a woodworking project to a company that specializes in laminates is usually a disaster because that company does not want to handle woodworking. Conversely, giving a laminate job to someone who is a master woodworker is probably equally foolhardy. Find out what each shop does best and use it for that. Before a shop starts working on a product, make sure everything is in good condition. Check all the components that go into the product with the shop. If there are problems with some aspect, help solve the problems before production begins.
3. Use as few suppliers as you possibly can. As long as they produce what you want and are competitive, it is better to work with suppliers you know. Giving

suppliers priority and letting them know you are really interested in using and supporting them is an excellent way of having people perform at a high level for you. If they do a good job for you, reward them. If they do an excellent job for you, show them some form of appreciation: pay them a little extra money or send them an arrangement of flowers or a little gift. It's amazing what a small gift, especially with a handwritten note, will do to improve the quality of that next job. When you thank your suppliers, send them a letter they will appreciate, one that they can proudly display on their bulletin board.

If you find sources that are not up to standard, replace them. Unfortunately, shops and sources do change for many reasons. Do not put up with a bad situation; look for a new source. They are out there.

Not all craft resources are located conveniently to your practice. You may need to travel a distance to find some of the specialists. Sometimes it is just not possible to have every craft you want, in which case you have to find another way to solve the design problem. Through the years, designers have had to make many adjustments because certain resources are just not practical or readily available.

Attending Markets. When you go to markets, make sure you meet the people from the factory. Ask them about their products. Try the products. Let the factory people tell you what the strengths and weaknesses are of the individual items—where they should be used, where they should not be used; and what the problems and limitations are. Factory people are very good at explaining just how these items should be treated. Often, quality is jeopardized by misuse. Remember, everything you put into a project that does not work, or presents a problem, reflects directly on your *designs*.

Visiting Factories. One of the best learning experiences designers can have is to visit the factory of a resource that is important to them. This not only provides information but also builds rapport. Here are a few guidelines that can help you get the most from your visit.

- Before you go, review the company's online catalog and any of its products you have used before. Make sure you have a general outline of what your past experiences were and what your future interests and uses might be.
- Make a list of questions you have about various products. Arriving with a list can help you make this trip much more productive. It will let the company know you are knowledgeable about the product, and you will leave with your questions answered.
- Ask to go through the production line to see just how the work is processed.
- Try to see all the components that go into the product. This will help you to better explain the product to contractors and clients.
- Talk to the people doing the production scheduling, so you can better understand their methods.

- Discuss any documentation you could provide that would be particularly helpful, such as information they would need for processing special orders, with factory personnel.
- Check with the factory to find out whether it is willing to do special orders. Find out what is practical and impractical for them.
- Meet the people in the factories. Find out which people are your best contacts. Then, when you phone for your next request (keeping your outline of whom you talked to about the functions at hand), you can ask for the right person for the situation and save yourself a lot of time and aggravation. Say hello to workers you might be speaking with later, so when you call, they will remember you. Building this rapport is immeasurably valuable.
- Follow up your visit with a thank-you letter to make sure the people at the factory will remember that you appreciated their hospitality.

Due Diligence

Due diligence is an area that deserves great consideration. Considering the litigious world we work in today, you need to ask the question, "Who is responsible for the quality of their work?" in any project for which you are recommending a resource or contractor. If it is a source you know very well, and so you are willing to accept responsibility or make corrections if there is a problem on the project, you will be the one performing due diligence. On larger projects, or for projects for which you do not want to take full responsibility, have an outside consultant perform the due diligence of the contractor or vendor to ensure your client directly of their credibility. This is now their responsibility, not yours. The procurement company can do this for you.

Our clients feel we are responsible for the work that is done. We know that in many cases it is impossible for us to take total responsibility. There are sources with whom we are comfortable sharing that responsibility, because the nature of the job is not too risky and we also know our team.

There are contract projects that become very sizable and involve a group of various vendors and craftspeople. Some of them we do not know as well as we would like. We also are dealing with very large dollar amounts and do not want to jeopardize our studio's position because of the performance of the various vendors. It is advisable for you to have someone else handle that responsibility and the due diligence.

There are specialty companies that handle the expediting of projects from the specification stage through ordering to the installation. In the case of larger projects, there are various consultants or companies that will take on that responsibility, review the vendor, and guarantee their position for your client. This will remove the liability from you and place it on someone who has the means and knowledge to handle it.

What Suppliers Want

From a source viewpoint, here are several suggested ways to improve communication between designers and sources.

1. Most orders are faxed today, but should you have a question regarding a particular product, you may want to actually speak with a person. Once your question is answered that person may not take your order by telephone. Check to be sure of your suppliers' preferences and procedures and that you are not duplicating an order. Suppliers handle hundreds of faxes and calls per day and cannot be responsible for spotting identical orders coming to them through different methods of communication. If you have faxed an order and later decide to call it in, make this clear to the person you are speaking with, to avoid duplication.

2. When ordering, provide complete identification or full specifications. Omissions or abbreviations may lead to misunderstandings about what you want.

3. When inquiring about an order you have already placed, always mention which products the order called for, rather than just giving an order number. This helps to expedite the order in the event the original order was never received by the supplier.

4. It is wise to give your client a range, or add a percentage, as a protection against price increases. (Your clients will think you are a hero if you are able to bill less than the quote. If you must increase it, they will not be happy.) Most suppliers bill at the price prevailing at the time of shipment if their products are selling and their inventory is turning over quickly. If you are ordering a substantial quantity of a product, it is important to get a firm quotation from the source.

5. When requesting a fabric sample of present stock from a supplier, advise as to the yardage that may be needed. Without knowing your requirements, the source cannot guarantee the same stock will be available when the final order is received, but most sources will reserve specific yardage for a reasonable length of time if they know your requirements.

6. When attempting to match fabric to paint, or vice versa, always obtain the fabric before painting. A small cutting from present stock can be deceptive. In a large piece, the intensity of color may look entirely different. The safe practice is to have the needed fabric yardage on hand and to work from it in determining the paint color.

7. When ordering fabrics for draperies, indicate the size and number of cut lengths needed. For many reasons, suppliers cannot always ship a specific requirement completely free of defects in one length. However, if the sources have your detailed requirements, it is often possible for them to expedite the shipment.

8. When you need to match a fabric, submit a cutting. Even though you may be ordering a small amount of yardage to supplement a recent shipment, the supplier may not be able to furnish this yardage from the same piece or dye lot as the first shipment. Few suppliers keep cuttings of what was shipped, so your sample is a safeguard.

9. When using a reversible fabric for Customer's Own Material (COM) orders, carefully instruct the manufacturer or fabricator as to which is the face side—

the side you want used. It is commonly assumed that the face side is the side that is rolled or folded to the inside, but this is not always the case. So many fabrics made today are reversible that it is easy to make a mistake. Send your manufacturer or fabricator a sample of the fabric showing the face side.

10. When suppliers drop-ship to a destination other than your studio address, ask them to attach a cutting to the invoice sent to you to show what has been shipped. You are responsible for checking that cutting for accuracy. Do it promptly, before any fabrication can be started.

11. Identify COM goods sent to a processor. Write to tell your processor what to expect, who is sending the goods, what processing is to be done, and to whom the goods should be shipped when completed. You would be surprised how many times COM goods sent to a workroom for quilting, flame-proofing, or fabrication sit for days because no one has bothered to say what should be done with them.

12. When you have a fabric flameproofed, request a certificate of the process in the name of your client, and make a photocopy for your files. If a claim is made later, it will be handled between the client and the manufacturer. Certificates can be issued only at the time that the flameproofing is done.

13. When requesting memo samples by phone, give as much information as possible—including a broad description and the ultimate end use. This helps the person selecting the samples give you the most satisfactory response.

14. When making a remittance, list your account number and the invoices being paid. This helps to maintain a mutual understanding of accounts.

15. If there is cause for merchandise to be returned, advise your supplier why you are making the return, and make the return promptly. This will avoid aggravation, confusion, and possible further inconvenience to you.

16. Keep the lines of communication open with your suppliers' credit departments. If you are unable to pay within their terms, notify them. Do not neglect to do this. Credit managers are generally very reasonable people who are anxious to help you in every way they can. Keeping them informed of your situation and intentions is the best way to gain their cooperation.

BUYING METHODS

There is much discussion about whether or not designers should buy for their clients. In some practices, it is appropriate for designers to specify; then procurement companies handle the purchasing and installation. In specialized or smaller practices, buying may be a requirement. Clients want the job finished. Your renderings and specification sheets are less important to them than having the room or building completed. Buying is a key part of many design practices today; it can make or break a practice.

Today, whom you buy from and how you buy is more involved and more complex than ever. Many companies sell directly to interior designers. Other companies sell only through dealerships or have minimum requirements (usually an annual dollar volume), so not all lines are available. Some of these amounts are substantial yearly expenditures. This, in effect, limits the range of products that can be used.

Since designers like to use different products on each project, so that every job does not look alike, it is important to establish buying methods for a project before you actually do the design. The purchasing method needs to be incorporated into the design process.

> You must consider your buying system carefully. First determine who is responsible for the problems that may arise either during the procurement process or later. In many situations, the designer is responsible for everything and does not have the appropriate backup support. In addition, we are dealing with product liability issues that can continue for years, since most states place no limit on the length of time one can be sued for a product if it fails. As a result, we must be very cautious where we purchase from and the conditions of the purchase, so we can "spread" the liability, if needed. Many firms today are simply not large enough to handle the amount of liability they may incur in certain situations. Be very cautious about the procedures you use for purchasing so you appear appropriately professional and are able to ensure you have the necessary backup to support you in the long term.

How can we be sure the client can secure merchandise within the appropriate price range? Only through research. Every project has a different budget and different social, cultural, and logistics issues. Thanks to technology, a great deal of merchandise is more readily available to us, but it cannot replace that great craftsperson who adds the special detail we need. Location affects the availability of products. In a large city, a designer has ready access to a wide variety of products; but in a very small community, the designer may be limited to purchasing paint in gallon cans, for example.

When designing a project, review the purchasing circumstances and consider this part of the budget. Determine which is the most appropriate way for your client to complete the project, and then recommend this method to your client.

Consider the different possibilities. First of all, if your firm can purchase merchandise, that puts the firm in the business of merchandising. Your design firm may not be organized for this. In that case, it is better to let someone else do the purchasing, someone who is willing to exert the extra management effort and to take on any risks involved.

In-house purchasing requires a purchasing specialist with good expediting policies. The way this purchasing is handled can add profits or bankrupt the firm.

Co-Op and Buying Services
Today, many designers buy as a co-op, forming organizations to buy together. The volume of purchases gives them access to more varied product choices and the collective clout to demand and get desirable quality and prices.

Strengths of Co-Op and Buying Services

A co-op or buying service can:

- Provide better buying management, leaving designers free to design, while someone else handles the negotiating, purchasing, and expediting.
- Reduce the cost of running a small independent studio.
- Give small studios more buying power.
- Give firms better prices and better quality control.
- Give small studios access to more lines.
- Educate designers about quality of products by sharing information.
- Give small firms a better chance to compete with large firms.
- Save time. Jobs can be processed faster, because the large volume permits management to use the latest equipment.
- Present fewer problems, since orders are checked and reviewed by another person—one familiar with companies and their ordering procedures.
- Make quicker substitutions. When the desired product is unavailable, the service can suggest suitable alternatives.

A designer can also use an outside buying service firm to expedite purchasing. If you take this option, choose the firm just as carefully as you do your clients and sources. Will this company give you the items you specify? Will it notify you if any changes are necessary? It should be the designer's decision to make any changes, not the purchasing company's.

Methods of handling the project can either enhance or hurt a design. When designers turn projects over to dealerships or expediting companies, some of the latter become competitors of the designer and end up taking over the client. The designer never sees the client again. Does the purchasing company have a record of this? Can you trust the head of the firm?

Traditional Buying Methods

Interior designers have three traditional ways of buying: through showrooms, from a dealer, and directly from the manufacturer.

Showroom. Showrooms can be a designer's greatest asset or greatest problem. Once you get to know the showroom, and you know it is a good source, stick with it. Loyalty is a big issue today. Building good rapport with a showroom is just like building good rapport with a craftsperson: it takes time. The showroom fees are included in the prices. For those fees, the designer gets a wide variety in furniture and furnishings. But there are also some well-known disadvantages. Often, these designer showrooms are run or staffed by former designers who no longer want to deal directly with clients. As a result, some orders are not relayed to the manufacturers as

A designer who had just opened her own firm told me an all-too-common tale of woe. She had gone into business for herself because she lived in a small community where there was little opportunity for her to test the waters by working for someone else. Within her first month in business, she believed she was a victim of fraud. A salesman in a showroom had taken her order for a sofa, along with her $2,000 deposit, but there had been no action. She found out eight months later that he had never ordered the sofa.

quickly as they might be, and the follow-up is not done on a regular basis. I have found that if you do not badger these showroom managers or staff people, you hear nothing from them, and there are often great delays in delivery.

Dealer. You may decide to buy through another firm, one that is preferably not in your immediate area, so your direct competition does not have the lines you like and can use in your practice. Such dealers are usually delighted to have you order through them, because your orders contribute additional volume. This is something every dealer has to consider. They will not be able to keep the line if they do not produce the volume. This can become a very workable relationship: dealers know the product and how to support it, and they have the facilities to make repairs and adjustments when needed.

Direct. If you are doing a lot of business with a specific line and know you can more than meet the line's volume requirements, it may be appropriate for you to establish a direct purchase agreement. The discount structure often varies with the amount of volume. It should also be a line you can do business with for many years. There is no point establishing an account for a one-time situation. Some companies limit the number of accounts they will service. One furniture company states, for example, that it will not accept more than 150 dealers nationwide; the company wants its line to be very exclusive. Other companies may have a limit of one dealer per city or community. But everything is subject to changes. If there is a line you think is good for you, it may be worth talking with the company about the possibility of buying directly.

VOLUME-BUYING SERVICE: A PROPOSAL FOR PROFITABILITY

Most of us do not have access to all the right lines at the right prices. Many of the lines we would like to use are available only to dealerships. Others are available only in quantity. We cannot buy enough per year to maintain all the lines, nor do we want to stock the inventory required to do this. Interior designers, unlike furniture dealers, do not want to have every job look alike; therefore, we need many resources and manufacturers.

Each new resource requires us to establish an account for proper pricing and account positioning. All this takes time, and many interior designers can't afford the time—or expense—required to run a top-notch purchasing division, as well as sell jobs. Usually, only large design firms have an official purchasing agent who handles these negotiations exclusively and makes sure the firm is buying the right items at the right price. In my own small firm, running a purchasing division costs over $100,000 per year. We know the status of our orders on a weekly basis, and we can negotiate for pricing—but it is quite expensive to do so.

Let's face it, most of us are designers because we enjoy designing and want to design, not to chase papers. We need a streamlined method of dealing with manufacturers—one that will give us access to diversity in sources without drowning us in credit references and negotiations.

Manufacturers find it very costly to service small accounts. Their sales staff find it unprofitable—credit checks, individual billings, and establishing accounts are all expensive. With small accounts, manufacturers often must wait long periods for payment. When they deal with larger firms, dealerships, or showrooms, they are assured of a certain dollar volume and know the payment habits of the account.

The Proposal

What if each designer had one main account? An account for which only one credit reference is needed and through which the designer could purchase anything that was needed? What if thousands of interior designers established a buying umbrella with manufacturers selected for quality products, at a wide range of prices?

Full-Service Interior Design Procurement and Installation Companies

These companies will buy everything for you. They will consolidate it, deluxe it, and make sure everything is cleaned, polished, and refined, and in perfect order. They will even install it for you, so the designer is merely responsible for creating the design. They will do all the pricing for you. They will make suggestions on how the project could be handled in a more efficient manner. They handle everything except the design and the selling of the project. They serve as a total assistant for your projects.

In this respect, these companies permit the designer to focus on design work. They have a laboratory of resources available to them, in some cases more than 50 or 100 people with different refined disciplines to support them. The billing can be done either by the expediting company or the design studio. That way all the responsibility of adjustments, repairs, or any problems that come up can be handled in a very professional, high-level manner. For example, two very expensive sofas were ordered by a designer for a new home. They cost over $40,000. When the home was completed, unfortunately, the room was not the size that had been shown on the drawing. To solve the dilemma, the procurement company simply cut 18 inches off the sofas. They were finished beautifully, so the adjustment in no way jeopardized the quality of the pieces of furniture. No one could tell they had been resized. The pieces were then delivered. The client had no idea there had been a problem and was very happy with the products. The designer was incredibly relieved.

In this ideal situation, the buying umbrella and purchasing firm and the vendors would have cooperative contracts requiring the vendors to send the participating designers first-quality merchandise, keep them informed on the status of an order, and agree to adjust and handle problems that occur. Designers would receive regular follow-up reports, so they could keep their clients well informed. The vendors would have the advantage of dealing with a single purchasing department and maintaining contact with a single individual rather than being harassed by several thousand calls. And there would be only one credit check to be done—on the purchasing firm itself. All orders would be shipped directly to the designers or to the receiving warehouses of the designers.

I believe the purchasing process as we know it is a "dinosaur"—its years are numbered. As professional designers, we need to be professional businesspeople as we relate to vendors. And I believe we are trained to design, not to track orders. Designers need to band together to make our jobs easier.

Purchase Orders

How precise is your purchase order? Today, we can be sued for almost anything, so it is advisable to review your purchase orders and include statements that offer protection from common problems. Freight claims are a time-consuming issue in any office. If a purchase order states the design firm is responsible for the merchandise *only* after it is received and inspected in the firm's studio, any freight claim is the responsibility of the shipper or resource. This simple declaration on your purchase order can save you a tremendous amount of time and aggravation.

I reviewed a large number of purchase orders with several consulting attorneys, and we found that very large firms and firms with high profits have extensive documentation on their purchase orders. Some have qualifying statements of seven pages or more. Is this appropriate or needed? These are big-name firms, and product resources are delighted to service them. I doubt whether small design firms could get away with that number of disclaimers, but at least some are in order. As a field, we need to join together and establish appropriate purchasing standards. By working with our resources on this, we can help them realize that designers—their repeat customers—need to be protected. In so many instances, the interior designer is the one left holding the bag.

Are your purchase orders easy to understand? Review purchase order procedures, either with another design firm or with some of your sources. Remember when writing your orders that you are not dealing with another designer, but with a contractor or manufacturer that may not be familiar with your vocabulary. It is easy to say that a firm that wants your business should learn your language, but you must also recognize that the talents that go into production scheduling and manufacturing are not the same talents interior designers must have. Try to find out what your suppliers need to know from you in order to give you what you want.

Learn to be very careful, to recheck that everything is properly side-marked and identified. In our firm, purchase order numbers relate to our individual order numbers and in-house communications and are as simple as we can make them. We also have a required follow-up procedure. If we have not heard from a company within 10 days with an acknowledgment or some comment, we either call or write to the company again. No purchase order simply sits in the files waiting for something to happen. Although we have a set day each week to review purchase orders, any problem regarding any order is handled on the day it is received.

Purchase orders for certain specialties require different conditions or products and, therefore, more extensive documentation.

When designing your purchase orders, be sure they include the terms and conditions shown in the sample in Figure 9.1 (see pages 297–299). The style and layout may vary according to your system. Many firms require three copies: one for the company from which merchandise is being purchased, one for your merchandise-on-order file (this may not be needed if your purchasing documents are computerized), and one for your client's file.

The following are the suggested details, terms, and conditions that should be listed on a purchase order from a general design firm.

- Name of the firm responsible for the purchasing documents. This should include your name, address, fax, and telephone number.
- Any special information, such as the name of a reference person with whom the supplier should speak if there are any questions.
- Your purchase order number. Ask that this number appear on all packages shipped for this order and on all statements and correspondence.
- Any special shipping instructions regarding your warehouse (time of receipt, particular location, or directions).
- Vendor's listing: the name, address, and any special details. Also note if the item should be addressed to anyone's attention.
- Shipping and billing addresses.
- Date of the order.
- Name of person placing the order and the person responsible for ordering.
- Any particular payment information and special terms.
- Direction for the freight bill: whether it is to be prepaid or if freight is to be charged to the bill.
- Quantity, unit, and description; the unit and total price. It is advisable to provide clear definitions of all details of items. Usually, a bit of extra information is far better than too little.
- Any other standards or other requirements of your firm. When you put statements on the back of your purchase order or on a second sheet, indicate clearly on the front of the order that the supplier should refer to the back or second sheet for performance information regarding the purchase order.
- Signatures of your purchasing agent or other person responsible for approving the order.

Clearly print terms and conditions on the copy of the purchase order sent to the vendor so they will not be missed. If you are printing terms on the back of the order

Figure 9.1 Purchase order terms and conditions. Review this list to determine which terms and conditions are the most important to your practice.

TERMS AND CONDITIONS

1. This order expressly limits acceptance to the terms stated herein. Any addition or different terms proposed by the Seller (this term is intended to include providers of services) are objected to and hereby rejected, notwithstanding any terms and conditions that may be contained in any acknowledgement, invoice, or other form of Seller, notwithstanding Buyer accepting or paying for any shipment or similar act of Buyer. Shipment of any goods or performance of any services ordered hereunder shall be considered an acceptance of this entire order, including all terms and conditions specified herein.

2. Time and shipping instructions are each of the essence to this contract.

3. It is understood that the cash discount period will date from the receipt of the goods or from the date of the invoice, whichever is later.

4. All goods shall be received subject to Buyer's right of inspection and rejection. Defective goods, or goods not in accordance with Buyer's specifications, will be held for Seller's instructions at Seller's risk and if Seller so directs will be returned at Seller's expense. If inspection discloses that part of the goods received are not in accordance with Buyer's specifications, Buyer shall have the right to cancel any unshipped portion of the order. The Buyer may reject and return at Seller's expense deliveries which exceed or substantially fail to meet the quantity ordered, or deliveries made more than fifteen (15) days in advance of the date required. Our time to inspect the goods and give appropriate notices under the Uniform Commercial Code is hereby extended by sixty (60) days.

5. In addition to any warranty implied in fact or law, Seller expressly warrants all items to be free from defects in design, workmanship, and materials, to conform strictly to applicable specifications, drawings, and approved samples, if any, and to be fit and sufficient for the purpose intended, and to be merchantable. Such warranties, together with all other service warranties of Seller, shall run to Buyer, its successors, assigns, and customers. All warranties shall survive delivery to, inspection test, acceptance, and payment by Buyer.

6. In the event of breach of this agreement, in addition to the remedies provided by the Uniform Commercial Code, Buyer may either alternatively or cumulatively:
   (a) Return all nonconforming merchandise at Seller's expense for repair or replacement at Buyer's option;
   (b) Repair all nonconforming merchandise at Seller's expense;
   (c) Cover and receive payment therefore at the time Buyer finally learns that seller will not satisfactorily cure the nonconforming tender;
   (d) Return for credit;
   (e) Terminate this agreement and accordingly reject all further deliveries of goods.

(continued)

Figure 9.1   *Continued*

7. No limits may be placed on damages resulting from Seller's breach of this agreement, other than as specified and accepted in writing by us.

8. Seller agrees to indemnify and hold Buyer harmless against any claims or suits arising in connection with the items purchased hereunder for defects in material or workmanship, and for infringement of patent, trademark, or copyright, or other intellectual property rights. Seller will pay, including without limitation, the claim, settlement or judgment, court costs, counsel fees and expenses, and interest; and will refund the price of the goods if Buyer is enjoined from using the same. Buyer shall notify Seller promptly of the initiation of any suit or proceeding, and Buyer may defend or otherwise deal with such matters, if Seller fails to do so after notice, with all costs ultimately paid by Seller.

9. The signature of our receiving clerk is for count of original packages only, and not for correct weight or count, quantity, or condition of contents. Net delivered weight, count, and actual fare shall govern settlement.

10. This purchase order is not valid unless signed by Buyer's authorized representative.

11. Seller agrees to return all physical and intellectual property (whether or not secret or confidential) furnished to him by Buyer or its agents in connection with the execution and billing of this order, and Seller further agrees not to disclose or use such property for the benefit of anyone else. All plans, drawings, specifications, memoranda, or other similar documents prepared by the Buyer, its employees, or its agents, shall be the sole and exclusive property of Buyer, and shall be delivered to Buyer at Buyer's request at any time.

12. If Buyer terminates or breaches this agreement for any reason at any time, Seller must submit an itemized list of all claims within fourteen (14) days.

13. No single or repeated waiver of any default for any period of time shall be construed as a continuing waiver by Buyer, and Buyer's right of termination under this agreement shall remain enforceable at any time any default may exist, no matter how long or how many times that default may have existed.

14. This agreement shall be binding upon and inure to the benefit of the parties hereto, and their respective successors, assigns, heirs, and legal representatives, provided that Seller shall not assign rights arising, nor delegate performance required herein, except to a successor in ownership of substantially the whole of its business.

15. This instrument contains the entire agreement between the parties hereto with respect to the transactions contemplated herein, and may be modified only by a duly executed purchase order change form signed by our authorized representative.

Figure 9.1 *Continued*

16. This contract shall be interpreted according to the laws of the Commonwealth of Pennsylvania.

17. Seller agrees to provide and maintain comprehensive general liability insurance, including products liability coverage, in an amount not less than $500,000.00 per occurrence for bodily injury or property damage. In addition, Seller shall provide errors and omissions coverage, when applicable, covering contractor's professional liability for any services and/or goods provided for herein with limits of liability which shall not be less than a combined single limit of $500,000.00. Such insurance will apply to all goods supplied under this order. Seller shall furnish Buyer with a certificate of insurance evidencing such coverage prior to shipment of goods. The certificate will provide that ten (10) days prior written notice of cancellation be furnished to Buyer at address listed on this order.

18. Seller shall pay all taxes imposed by the federal or any state or local government on payrolls or compensation of its employees, or any other taxes, fees, or charges on account of this order, the sale of the goods, or the performance of the services.

19. No partial invalidity of this order shall affect the remainder hereof.

20. The price stated in this purchase order shall include the freight costs, unless otherwise stated, however shipment is f.o.b. for delivery to job or to the nearest rail or truck terminal. Title of the goods shall pass from the shipper to the Buyer on receipt by Buyer, or its authorized representatives, subject to any defects or nonconformance as stated above. Buyer shall not be liable for any loss, damage, detention, or delay caused by freight damages, shortages, defective or incorrect material, or by circumstances beyond their control.

21. Buyer does not intend to be bound to Seller based upon any contract which Seller may have with another party. This purchase order is given in good faith for the materials listed on the reverse side, which must be acceptable to Buyer.

or on other sheets, make sure to provide a clear reference. Review the list of terms and conditions given in Figure 9.1 (pages 297–299) to determine which are the most important to your practice. A larger firm will have no problem including all these terms, because it has buying clout; smaller firms may be forced to modify their terms. If we all work together, however, we could make them a standard of the field.

Note: The terms in Figure 9.1 were written by an attorney. Before you include them in your purchase orders, have your attorney review them. He or she will explain their meaning and assist you in determining their value in your practice.

WORKING WITH YOUR CONTRACTORS

As designers, we do a lot of work with contractors on projects ranging from the very small to those costing many millions of dollars. In some instances, consulting architects and engineers work with us. By supervising the installation, to make jobs run more smoothly, you become a valuable asset to your clients, craftspeople, architects, and engineers. When designers assume this responsibility, some states may require a contractor's license. Many designers are qualified to assume it, but before you decide to do so, speak with your advisors. Be sure you know the extent of your additional responsibilities, that you will be properly compensated, and that you have the right insurance coverage.

Obviously, we can get into a lot of trouble here. It is so much better to take a smaller part of a project you can control rather than something larger that may become unmanageable.

Finding the Right Contractor

We build our team of contractors through a great deal of experience. Often, we lose a contractor because that person moves away, changes careers, or retires. Finding a new contractor can be one of the most difficult things we do. It is a good idea to talk to the contractor you are losing or to other craftspeople on projects: you can get suggestions from them for other contractors. Someone who does cabinetry will recognize good carpentry. Painters will know where they have seen a really clean, well-crafted job.

When you interview contractors, be sure to take the time to see some of their work. Frequently, contractors will show you photographs, but these often tell very little. Ask any contractor you are seriously considering where you may go to visit one of their projects. If the contractors are hesitant and do not have ready referrals, think twice about hiring them.

In smaller communities, contractors are sometimes not familiar with new processes and techniques. They will often say, "I can do it!" because they do not fully understand what you have in mind. If you are concerned, ask to see a similar project or have them prepare a sample for you before you hire them. You do not want to pay for unqualified contractors to learn on the job.

Designers usually like to be responsible for jobs, and when given the authority, *want* to be responsible. The benefit in hiring a designer is to obtain not only the best-quality design but to have it completed by the best-quality craftspeople.

In small communities, you often must design within the range of what the available craftspeople can handle. You may even have to educate many of them in special techniques to get the results you want, or find components for them they have never seen before. If all else fails, you may have to bring in someone from out of town. Sometimes you may feel like a teacher, but the time you spend educating your craftspeople will give you a better-quality project in the end.

I was raised with the philosophy that you do something right or you do not do it at all. Designers need a great deal of training and exposure to understand all the components of the design craft. The more you understand about the contracting field, the better designs you will be able to create.

Know the size of your contractor's organization, as well as the type and size of projects this individual handles best—both physically and financially. Giving a small contractor too large a job, although the contractor may really want it, is a mistake. If contractors do not have the ability to perform a job profitably, their organization—and your job—will be destroyed.

In my experience with contractors, it is best to give them work they know. A contractor who does good commercial work is usually not likely to understand the requirements of historical restoration, for example. For the restoration of a lovely 150-year-old house, when we knew the client wanted fine-quality craftsmanship, we took nine months to find someone appropriate for the project—and that person took a year to complete the project. We had previously done a large, fast-track office building project for this client. Now we had to make the client understand that the restoration project required a contractor with different abilities and a completely different mind-set. We had to explain to the client that the particular contractor we selected could not be rushed and that imposing a schedule on him would affect the quality of the project.

When to Use a General Contractor. When should you use a general contractor? It makes sense to use a general contractor on projects that require management of a number of disciplines. When the designer must provide every detail of supervision, it is usually easier and simpler to deal directly with subcontractors.

This depends on the type and size of the job and the amount of responsibility you as a firm want to take on. In most instances, when a project is large, you do not want the liability or the responsibility; and in many states, you cannot act as a general contractor without proper licensing. All of these conditions must be taken into consideration. Designers who do very unusual and artistic work and have spent a great deal of effort training their contractors will make one of the conditions of their projects that they select only contractors accustomed to working with them.

If the project is something you are very familiar with, and you are comfortable taking on the total responsibility, this often gives you a chance to develop your artistry, since you and the contractor are acting as a joint venture. In such a situation, the client will pay you directly, and you will be responsible for the various aspects of the project.

At my firm, we require our contractors to bill us and our clients to pay us. We feel this gives us authority. If we do not handle the money, we assume responsibility for approving all bills and instruct the client not to pay any bill without our approval. Designers often get into difficulties when they are given the responsibility for a job, but not the authority. Without the proper authority, a designer cannot maintain the quality control that is so important in our profession.

Business Arrangements

It is essential to clarify all legal and financial arrangements with contractors right from the start.

Quotations. Every contractor should understand you are getting two or three quotations on a job. That keeps them from inflating costs. It is not appropriate to get 10 quotations for an average-size job, nor is there time to do so. However, on large projects, you benefit by obtaining as many qualified quotations as possible. On smaller or medium-size projects, ask contractors to quote within 10 percent of their estimated figure. This gives you leeway for adjustments as you get into a project. On highly customized items that a contractor has never done before, it helps to keep estimates more reasonable if the contractor knows there is a 10 percent play. If you deal with your contractors on a regular basis, and they understand you, you will find that sometimes they use that extra money, and sometimes they do not. But everyone feels more comfortable knowing it is there. On special projects, clients usually consider estimates within 10 percent as reasonable.

Time Schedules. As part of every design, make a time schedule. Sometimes you develop this with the contractor; other times you do so before meeting the contractor. Coordinate the contractor's schedule and your schedule, your time estimates and the contractor's. Then go over the schedule with the client to see how much this work will interfere with the client's personal or business plans. The time factor can affect the cost of a job considerably. With proper preparation, fast-tracking to complete a job in a short period is probably the most economical way to schedule in the long run. When you fast-track a job, you can usually afford to have excellent supervision there for several days, which is generally not possible for longer periods.

On every letter, agreement, or contract you send out, include a time schedule. One designer I know writes his schedule on his deposit check alongside the following sentence: "By accepting this deposit, you have agreed to maintain this schedule." When the contractor signs the agreement, the contractor agrees to meet that schedule. There are many ways of handling this; what is important is that the schedule is in writing and the contractor understands it is an essential part of your contract.

Written Agreement. Have a written agreement with your contractor (see Independent Contractors Agreement on page 101). Be sure the contractor has outlined each and every detail of the project. If anything is missing on the contract, send it back. Be sure the contractor acknowledges and initials your drawings, and furnishes you with appropriate shop drawings. Our office has an agreement with each and every craftsperson who works for us relating to our standards, payment procedures, insurance, and guarantee requirements. For contractors we use frequently, such as paperhangers and carpenters, we simply get a quotation each time we use them, because we keep their statements of conditions in our files.

Financial Arrangements. At our firm, the contractors we use understand our standard structure for financial arrangements. We normally control the money, which means we have a retainer from the client that provides the monies for us to pay the subcontractors as the project progresses. As soon as the project has been approved by our design staff and the client, we see that the contractor receives a check, sometimes within 24 hours, sometimes within two or three days. Contractors are very concerned about cash flow. We handle this by seeing they are paid promptly. We will often withhold a certain amount as security until the project is complete, just in case there are any adjustments to be made. When contractors realize they will have their money when the project is completed and approved, they are more inclined to do the project in a high-quality, timely fashion.

Contractors see that projects are finished to our satisfaction and handle all our complaints, because they know we are going to generate more business for them. When a client pays the contractor directly, the designer loses this control.

Supervision

To what degree should you supervise a job? This depends on the project and the contractors or craftspeople with whom you are working. If the project is well defined, and you know the workers assigned to it, your job may be easy. If that is not the case, you may be required to assign a full-time supervisory person or visit the site several times a day.

It is important to be there to prevent errors, not to require someone to change something that has already been done wrong. There is nothing that destroys the morale of a good craftsperson more than having to redo work to please a client. If changes are required, it is good for you to be there to make sure the changes are made appropriately and in the least amount of time. Your goal is to have as few change orders as possible on your project.

Do not check a job when it is finished; check it as it goes along. For example, if a plumber has completed work, check to see that the drain is in the appropriate location before the tiling is started. If you wait until the end of the project, you may discover one of the subcontractors had mismeasured. Check all craftspeople and workers as the project progresses to control the quality of their work. If an electrical outlet is missing, you want to know it before workers start plastering the wall.

Clarify with the company you have hired who is in charge of the project and with which person you should communicate. In many cases, companies prefer you to talk to the foreperson on the project, but there are certain times they want all information in writing and put directly through the office. Be sure to clarify this first to determine the process for documentation.

There are many situations in which the office does not communicate well with those in the field. If you have permission, it may be advisable for you to review your drawings with the electrician or the plumber on the job. You may find that the person who understands the project is, say, away on vacation, and you need to explain the project again to be sure it is properly executed.

Review insurance coverage. Have your clients notify their insurance companies that the building will be under construction for a given amount of time. They should explain to the insurance company the extent of the project. Where possible, ask to be identified as an "additional insured" on the client's policy during the construction period. Since there is additional liability during this period, it is important that it be appropriately covered. Although each vendor working on the job has given you certificates of insurance, it is still difficult to cover all the client's personal possessions during construction. The least-expensive way of covering these situations is to have the clients request additional coverage from their insurance companies.

Be available. Do not start a project when you will not be around. At my firm, we have an understanding with contractors that they may call us anytime. We are readily available from 6:00 A.M. through 7:30 A.M. so they can reach us if they have any problems before starting the project. It is also our policy that, while we will not interrupt a designer to talk to a client or sales rep, we *will* interrupt if a contractor is on a project and has a problem. There are always two or more people in our studio familiar with the project who can answer contractors' questions. We do not want the client paying for lost time on a project, so we make sure we are available to cover any situation at any point.

Ways to Make the Job Easier

To ensure that a job is well completed, it is important to have a good relationship with your contractors. There are many facets to the relationship, all of which must be carefully considered.

1. **Perfect your drawings and specifications.** Be sure your drawings are well done. Include all the fine details you want to be part of the final project. Your drawings are as much a part of your contract as any other written form. If you miss a line or misdocument a detail, this is a breach-of-contract responsibility. If your drawings are clear, your communication with your client and your contractor will be much easier.

   Take the time and effort to make your specifications as detailed as possible. Effort spent at this point will pay off later in the project. The contractor will understand the project more easily and will know better how to price it, so you will not have discrepancies throughout the project. Too often, when communication problems occur, it is because the drawings and specifications have not been properly detailed. Before giving your drawings and specifications to your contractors, check to be sure they are easy to understand. Then go over them with the various contractors to be sure nothing is missing and that they fully understand your format.

2. **Check the availability of all specified items.** Be sure the items that you are selecting are available—and determine from which sources you should order them. Many wonderful products pictured in magazines are either not yet available or are unavailable in your area. Check to be sure you know where a contractor can get an item, and find out the cost. This information will help you to negotiate the project better for your client. If a project involves appliances or similar equipment, investigate who handles repairs and what kind of a maintenance program the client needs. It is much easier to do this research before specifying an item than it is to specify a product the client cannot have repaired or will complicate the project.

3. **Be sure your client understands the job to be done.** This is crucial. So often, misunderstandings occur because most clients cannot read blueprints. Take the time to go through the details of a job with clients so they understand what is involved in constructing your design.

   Do not create a false impression by downplaying the extent of a project. Forewarn clients about what will be involved, especially on complex projects. Discuss what kind of project it will be, what the time schedule will be, and whether the installation will be dirty. When the installation will be long and involved, suggest the client move out of an office space or a residence, or that person will hate you by the time the project is finished. If a project can be done without major inconvenience to the clients, let them know which contractors will arrive when. Warn the client about noise and the hours contractors work. If you surprise a client who sleeps until 9:00 A.M. with a contractor arriving at 5:45 A.M., this can create such hard feelings that it will harm the project. When clients understand in advance that contractors will begin work at a certain time, they will be prepared—and the likelihood of maintaining a good relationship with your clients will be greater.

4. **Be sure all supplies are available before a job starts.** To avoid disrupting time schedules, do not let any contractor begin until you have verified that each item needed for the job is in. At my firm, we send our representative to the suppliers' warehouses to be sure all the fixtures and items for the job are what we ordered—the correct sizes and the proper quantities. This step helps ensure the job will run smoothly. If you tear up a bathroom or kitchen before your work is ready to begin, hard feelings may develop that can undermine the design project. Often you may have to advance the contractor money to cover the costs of supplies just to be sure they are there.

5. **Organize permits.** Make permits the responsibility of the contractor, and include this in your agreement. In some states, the way designers work has been defined as "contracting." In our firm, we consider ourselves coordinators, not contractors. We use a general contractor who is responsible for the liabilities that come under his jurisdiction. All contractors who work for us must provide us with a certificate of insurance, which we keep in our files, or documentation that they carry insurance for the workers they are using for a project, as well as for the client's project itself. Depending on the situation, we will very often require certain craftspeople to be bonded. These issues must be clarified through our office before we start a project.

6. **Instill pride.** If you know your products and craftspeople and put together the right combination for the job, you will ensure quality control. Problems arise when you inappropriately place contractors on a project they cannot handle. If you choose your contractors properly and generate a special pride in projects, you will come up with some of the best-quality work you can imagine. Contractors like to work on our projects because they know when the projects are finished, they will see something they can be proud of.

It is important that your clients and contractors understand the objectives of your project. You may have to take contractors to other projects you have done so they can understand the quality you want. If you have seen a contractor's projects, and that person has seen yours, standards can be more easily communicated.

7. **Structure communications.** Set a communications structure for your clients and subcontractors. For example, in some projects, especially fast-track ones, you may have to say to your clients, "Please do not talk to the workers or contractors. You may say 'good morning' and that's all. Any communication regarding the project must come through our office. We are on an extremely tight time schedule, and it is up to our office to make the decisions if any changes should be considered." There is no way to maintain control of a project if your client makes changes every 10 minutes. Make sure your client understands that the contractor cannot do anything not in the written agreement because the contractor is not being paid for it. The contractor is working for you—the designer—and you are responsible for the project.

   Instruct the contractor to ensure that workers do not discuss the project with the client. There are always problems on a job, and there are ways of solving them if the team works together. There is no point in alarming the client over something you can easily remedy. Once a client feels there are flaws and problems on a project, the client can lose confidence in you, making the whole project more difficult for everyone. Let contractors understand you are always available to discuss the project or any problem, and that they should come directly to you.

8. **Delegate responsibility.** Do not let a contractor put the blame on someone else. For example, make sure the painting contractor covers having the carpenter putty holes so they will be ready for painting. If you do not cover these details, the contractor may not remember them. Address all the fine details, and you will save yourself a lot of headaches.

CONSIDERATIONS

Because we use so many individual artisans on projects we need to be confident that all of them are able to perform at the required level. There are many agents who can assist with this management process. But make sure the structure is in place to protect you, since you, the designer, can be considered responsible.

CHAPTER 10

Managing Your Office

Good management involves coordinating your client's goals and those of your design firm, then developing a method to reach these goals. Both long and short-term issues must be taken into consideration.

Management cannot replace leadership. Too many firms are overmanaged and do not have the direction only a qualified leader can give. In many of his books and articles, Peter Drucker stresses that the leader sets the tone for a business. The leader must establish the goals and identify their order of importance. And, perhaps even more critical to the future success of the business, the leader must be able to make the vision clear so others in the organization can help make the vision a reality. I believe that the leadership of an organization is the most underestimated role in the organization. The responsibility of designing a firm to meet the needs of the day is a continuous one.

MANAGEMENT

In a small firm, one of the principals usually acts as the manager. After a business starts to grow, however, the principals will often hire another person to handle the general management structures so they can be free to concentrate on marketing and design issues. Normally, managers can be hired more easily than designers or marketing specialists. For this reason, interior designers usually hire managers quite early in the process of setting up their firms.

The day-to-day office management of a small firm may be handled by a person with general administrative skills, including office procedures such as scheduling, bookkeeping, and other paperwork. As your firm grows larger or expands its line of services, you will need to establish other management structures. A firm dealing only in professional fees and hourly billings will require less management than one that provides both professional services and sale of products.

The minute a firm starts selling products, it requires a complete expediting and processing structure for proper management of purchasing and installation processes (see pages 238–248).

All management processes are overhead items; they are expenses, not billable items. Management forms a structure for many of the other design processes. In interior design and architecture, we are not working alone; we are working with many other people, including vendors, craftspeople, other consultants, and businesspeople. We are required to communicate in many ways with numerous other types of systems, including government, taxes, other regulatory organizations, and the list goes on. The management system we establish takes care of most of these processes for us. It assures us they are done in an appropriate and timely fashion.

Once the direction of the firm is established and the various requirements are defined for the management system, we can determine who the right people are to take care of these different processes. In some cases, the leader may be a person of great design talent, the person who really should be dedicating time to the design process and the client. In other instances, the leader may be a master administrator. It makes sense to look at the abilities of each of the players, then place them in their right positions. The most important task is to ensure that every administrative process we put in place has a definite purpose. Fortunately, today we have technology to help us do that. Many of the bookkeeping and other laborious processes can be done very easily, in far more detailed fashion and more accurately than ever before. This often means a company that formerly required a full-time bookkeeper may now need someone only part-time.

When a firm increases in size, it requires a better-qualified leader, one who knows the difference between profits that are generated from one base versus another base, their cost of acquisition, and some of the other components that lead to bottom-line profits.

Every firm needs to have a good financial management program in place. It is important for management to understand just what the resources and expenses are within a given design firm. For a good understanding of the business, management must be kept current on these financial issues.

How many management or administrative people does a design firm need? Generally, a firm must have at least five people with billable work to one administrative person. The better the equipment within an office, the fewer administrative people are required. Good equipment can enable the firm to reduce numbers of support staff or move them to other income-earning tasks.

The business manager can be billable in some instances. If your firm is handling project management, supervising installation, or purchasing, under some programs you may be able to charge your clients for your business management division's services. More design firms are adopting this policy, as it enables them to have better-qualified personnel in management divisions because these professionals bring in revenue.

The salary for an office or business manager will vary considerably, depending on whether the principals maintain most of the responsibilities and controls or the business manager is totally responsible for the firm's management. In the latter case, the business manager is usually paid as well as any of the other vice presidents or principals and has perks and advantages similar to those of the other principals in the firm.

Interior design firms are finding that if they want to grow and compete effectively in the mass market, they need to have an excellent business management structure. This normally requires administration by a professional with a business background, who is interested in business management and the financial development of the firm. This person also brings a different viewpoint to the firm. The key is to find someone who appreciates the interior design firm's objectives and can assist in creating a blend of good design and good financial management. It is often difficult to find the right person, but when you do, this coordinated effort can prove most profitable.

MANAGEMENT TOOLS

There are many different styles of management. Some design firms work in a cooperative team method, others are very autocratic, and still others are very patriarchal. Your particular style of work determines the type of people you will attract. Every interior designer should look at what it takes to be an effective manager or leader. Helping develop the other people within your firm usually creates a stronger firm.

If you want to develop a larger firm, find yourself good consultants who will assist you with the business management aspects. These outside people can review your firm and see just where you are going. Knowing your objectives, they will consider ways you can improve your management structure and style.

Management must be based on customer service. In order for design firms to have repeat business, they must provide excellent services. Businesses have learned that it costs five times as much to find a new client as it does to keep an old one. Design firms cannot afford to be constantly getting new clients; they must retain their present client base.

The main objective of management today is to give the customer what the customer wants: good service. The interior design field is very competitive; if one firm doesn't service its customers well, there are many other firms out there ready to do it.

Providing Leadership
Leading a company involves knowing the market and what the company can do and having a design for the future. I like to use the term "design" because the plan is not cast in stone but allows for changes and alterations. It is management with a vision.

The management must motivate staff to do quality work, both for their own benefit and that of their clients. If you are the leader, here are some ways this can be done:

1. **Emphasize to your staff that clients are the firm's most important asset.** There must be a constant effort to please the clients and give them the best possible product.

2. **Ensure management has the support of the staff.** The employees should like and respect their supervisors. To earn this respect, you must be interested in your employees as well as your clients. This is a message you should constantly broadcast and promote within every area of management.

3. **Give your employees good information.** They need to know the goals of the firm and their roles in reaching these goals. They need to recognize their strengths and weaknesses, which areas need improvement and which do not. Employees should feel they are in control, that they understand just what is going on. Employees who are not properly informed can be very destructive in a firm.

4. **Adequately compensate your employees.** They must be paid a reasonable amount. Although many surveys report that financial compensation is not nearly as important to interior designers as the opportunity to do excellent work in an appropriate professional setting, these people still need to support themselves—usually with their salary or income from the design firm. In small firms, where everyone usually knows one another's approximate salaries, offering a reasonable degree of shared profits usually promotes good company morale.

5. **Assemble a staff of high-quality individuals.** Select individuals who know how to handle their assigned tasks. Also, be sure any new team member shares your firm's attitude toward clients.

6. **Create a written job description for each staff member.** As a firm changes, so do the duties and responsibilities of its employees. Ask each staff member to write a job description. Compare your description of each job to the employees' descriptions, to determine if changes should be made. Perhaps an employee is spending 80 percent of his or her time performing a task that could be handled by another person in the firm. Maybe there are tasks a person could be performing that would be more valuable to the firm and would give the person the opportunity of advancing to a better position. Most people like to have a written job description. It helps them know whether what they are doing is on target.

7. **Make a commitment to educate management and staff.** Let your employees see that you are interested in learning, as well as in educating them. Do not just send staff to a seminar—go yourself. Try to pick up pointers you can share with your staff.

8. **Audit constantly.** Make your staff feel important. Make them aware of what is an excellent job, a medium-quality job, or a less-than-quality job through con-

stant evaluation. Document in writing measures of performance within each given area; this gives you a record you can reference next year to determine whether you and your staff met expectations or not. Could performance have been improved? You can use these audits when reviewing your next project to see whether your firm has improved.

9. **When there are problems, discuss performance.** Let your staff realize there are proper ways of dealing with problems. Do not just put them aside or forget them. Bring them out, discuss them, and consider how you are going to prevent them on the next project.

10. **Institute a reward system.** Make your employees feel valuable. Design firms have found that receiving a bonus or some kind of a reward periodically is worth much more to an employee than being paid a larger salary on a weekly basis. Let your employees know that when they do a good job, they will receive a reward. It is good to both compliment them on the process and give them some reward, monetary or otherwise, to show your pleasure.

11. **Measure customer satisfaction.** Talk to your clients and evaluate your firm's performance levels as you go through a project and upon its completion. Determine whether your clients are satisfied. If they are not satisfied, find out why. This is a job for you, not a member of your staff. It is up to you to be aware of what the clients need.

12. **Be aware of staff interactions.** Talk with your staff to see how they are interacting. If you do not have a good team effort within the studio, every client is going to be aware of it. The team must work smoothly. If there are problems with the staff's interaction, there are going to be problems with the projects. Find a way to evaluate staff interaction regularly—both in discussions with individual employees and in group meetings. Sometimes, management has to put extra effort into finding out just what is happening. Many times employees will try hard to cover up problems and difficulties.

13. **Always be on the scene.** Management cannot hide in an ivory tower. Your staff needs to know that you are in there with them working and developing projects. The only way you can determine how well your firm is being managed is to stay close to what is going on.

14. **When you lose a client, call that individual and conduct an exit interview.** Ask the client what you did wrong—why the client is going to another firm. Very often, clients who leave you will teach you more about your firm than you can learn in any other way. Use that former client to find out what you can do to prevent other clients from leaving in the future.

15. **Set high standards.** Keep your standards as high as possible, and let everyone know that this effort is ongoing. The quality of management must be set by the chief executive officer. This is not something middle management or support staff can do. It is totally up to the principals to set the firm's standards and construct and implement management systems to provide necessary support.

As designers, we must understand what excellence is and keep striving for it. What is excellent today has to be improved on tomorrow. The same is true of leadership.

TIME MANAGEMENT

Time is our most valuable commodity, but it is the hardest thing to account for. Good time management can make the difference between a profitable year and an unprofitable one. The perception of passing time is subjective. When we like the job we're working on, time evaporates. If we do not like the job, it seems to take ages. A good time management schedule and cost accounting system help distinguish reality from fantasy.

A creative person can deal with many things at once. Geniuses can successfully ignore everything but what they are working on at the moment. Interior designers who also own or manage small businesses must juggle many things at once. It helps to put these items into categories.

First, try to identify each project. Describe it, and break it down into its various components. Then determine how much time you expect each part of the project to take and what efforts or additional staff will be needed. Make sure you know what your goals are; write them down and keep them in the project folder so that every time you work on the project you can go back to your initial description and remind yourself of the expected results. Often, as you get involved in a job you had intended to be profitable or good for marketing, you find that it falls into another category. At that point, reevaluate the job and determine whether it is still worthwhile to pursue, should be dropped, or tied into another project.

Each time you accept a new project, you should either be finishing another one or adjusting your priorities. You just cannot keep adding, or you will get nothing done. Scheduling is easier when you limit the number of projects you are working on at any one time, although sometimes it is possible to incorporate several projects for more efficient handling. Setting up a good time management system takes time, but the payoff is tremendous.

Organizing Your Time

Time management must be planned on a regular basis, at a regular time, each and every week and each and every day. If you do not plan, your time may slip away.

To create an appropriate schedule for your personal or business goals, first outline what you have to accomplish. In order to create any kind of a to-do list, you need to prioritize your work. Ask yourself what it will take to accomplish each priority and what the chief priorities are within these priorities. Then determine how much time each of these activities will require.

It is usually difficult for executives to preschedule more than 50 percent of the day, because they need to reserve some time for talking with staff, clients, and other people who call with unexpected needs, causing a shift in their priorities. If you schedule your day too tightly, nothing works—there's just not enough time to accomplish everything. For major projects, you will need to block out a sizable amount of time and plan a definite change in your schedule.

Establish priority time within the studio schedule. However, recognize that most project work is done in bits and pieces. It is almost impossible to schedule or accomplish any major project within one straight block of time.

Interruptions during creative periods are very disturbing; the exact moment of creativity can never be replaced. However, interior designers also service clients and contractors, so you must expect interruptions and learn to work around them. Some studios schedule a quiet time each day for two or three hours when the staff will not be interrupted and can work on a certain project intensely for that block of time. You definitely need careful planning to have the luxury of time such as this.

Creative people often do not believe in time management. In a matter of three or four minutes, interior designers create an idea that can carry the studio for a year. The sad part is that many designers sit and wait for that next burst of creativity without doing anything productive in the interim. They rely on their creativity to the exclusion of everything else. Wasting time is destructive to morale and long-term profits. Studios that maintain a regular, disciplined, continuing working structure tend to come up with the most ideas and are the most productive over the years.

The Time Management Chart

What should a time management chart include? The chart should state the goal for billings for the week. It's a good idea to let your staff know just what kind of work they must produce in order to make the company profitable. At the top of the weekly time sheet (see Table 10.1, page 314) write the billable amount of work each staff person must do per week for the firm to be profitable. This must be done on a weekly basis; a daily basis is confusing; and any time period longer than a week becomes difficult to recall in detail.

System for Creative People

I had an interesting experience working with training specialists, which helped me to understand how creative brains work. With this knowledge as a base, we developed a technique at my firm that works well for creative people.

Look at your day as if you were designing a room. Is it a living room or a conference room? First, decide which design you want to give your day. What is the result you want? Just like doing a room, we decide what we want the day to be, then we collect the items needed. For example, we do not spend our time looking at kitchen appliances if we are doing a living room. The process takes about a day to really learn, but once you understand it, it is really fun and very productive.

Table 10.1 Weekly chargeable hours sheet. Each staff member needs to keep his or her billable work logged on a sheet such as this. The amount of work that needs to be done by the staff member to be profitable should be listed at the top of the sheet. These sheets are usually kept separate from nonchargeable, or in-house assignments.

WEEKLY CHARGEABLE HOURS			Staff:	
			Week Ending:	
Day:	**Client:**	**Project:**	**Code:**	**Hours:**
M O N				
T U E				
W E D				
T H U				
F R I				
S A T				

Refer to time-log categories sheet for job codes.

© *Design Business Monthly*, 1988.

When you take a job, you must budget your time as carefully as you budget the cost of materials, even if you earn your income from percentages or markups from furniture. Calculate the time you plan to spend on the job as if you were selling your hours on a basic hourly rate. You can then compare the money earned from commissions or markups against the time you spent and what your hourly rate would have been.

For each new project, you need to estimate how much time you expect each staff member to spend on the job. Some design firms pay their staff for only the amount of time the firm has allowed for a particular project. Other design firms try for more balance, and adjust their charges according to their experience documented on past time sheets.

When judging the pricing of a new project, you must separate fact from fantasy. If you do not have time and cost sheets on past projects, you have no way to estimate a new job accurately. In my firm, we have found many surprises on time sheets. Some of the jobs we had considered the least glamorous, exciting, and interesting turned out to be the jobs that earned the greatest profits in the shortest periods of time. They made a lot of difference in our end-of-the-year profit statements.

An example of "fact versus fantasy" is a luxury co-op complex project a firm I know undertook. The job appeared to be a glamorous project full of opportunities. In fact, it was really not worth it from a profit-and-loss viewpoint. The firm was called constantly by co-op members who were interested in what was happening or were involved in committees concerned about the project. This, along with the public relations and local publicity requirements, meant the firm spent many non-chargeable hours on this project. The firm was paid for professional services; however, the hours spent on the process were so far in excess of what had been planned that the project was really difficult and expensive. The project also prevented the firm from doing other projects that year because of all the time required for this one.

Though the project turned out beautifully, and the co-op members loved it, it was financially, physically, and emotionally taxing for the firm.

In contrast, another project this same firm did last year, which went almost unnoticed, turned out to be very financially profitable. It was for a previous client, and it involved replacing major textiles. Most of the furniture was vintage—some of it antique. The creative demands on the project were minimal; it was a restoration project. However, the textiles the client wanted were of good quality and provided a reasonable markup. The client had had previous experience with the firm and was easy to work with. When comparing the amount of hours the firm spent on the job and the size of the job, the profit was outstanding. The job was completed in less than 3 percent of the time that was spent on the co-op complex project, and the gross profit was similar.

This may sound like an extreme example, but it really isn't. When comparing jobs, you will find major contrasts in the amounts of time, effort, and emotional stress. At the end of the year, these factors all influence whether or not a designer is looking forward to continuing next year in the design field.

Time-Saving Methods and Ideas

The following list suggests ways you can save time on the job:

1. **Realize you are valuable.** When designers recognize they are valuable people whose time needs to be treated like a precious commodity, their whole attitude about time management changes. Time is such an intangible commodity that sometimes one forgets what it means to the profit structure of a business.

2. **Use consultants.** There are many specialists who can show you how to do something in one-tenth the time you would need to do it yourself. Using these people when it is appropriate can add professionalism to a job, as well as permit you to complete the project much more quickly.

3. **Design your studio as carefully as you would a client's office.** Have you thought out all of the details of your office? Does it really function as time-effectively as it should? After all, each time you have to move away from your work at hand to complete another phase of the project, it is a distraction. Review your office, and see that its design incorporates the latest time-and-motion studies.

4. **Do a time analysis for two weeks, approximately once a year.** Include for each 24-hour time period how long you sleep, how much time you put into daily maintenance issues, and how much time you spend on fun and relaxation. See that your week is appropriately balanced. This is important in your being highly productive and effective as a designer and as a person. It is amazing what you can learn from this intense time-motion study. It is usually well worth the effort.

5. **Learn new techniques.** There are many classes offered on special techniques to help designers do work simpler and faster. Keeping up with your education usually helps save time over time. Almost every good seminar can teach you something that pays many times over for the time it takes to attend.

6. **Stay abreast of new equipment and technology.** Every design studio needs to understand how to use the latest equipment, which often can save considerable time. Remember, when introducing new equipment or new processes to the studio, it is best to do it at a time when the studio is not under a lot of pressure. Technology can help us in many ways, but we must consider the fact that we now have such an overload of information that we have to be very discriminating to determine what is important and what is not. Look at all the information coming in and decide what you really need to know and what you can ignore; decide how you can simplify the information coming in so it is manageable for yourself, your staff, your resources, and your clients. Giving people too much information can be confusing and destructive to both your projects and your overall lifestyle.

7. **Take a time management course.** You can usually pick up a tip or two that will help save you some time or money. Because both good and bad habits develop over time, attending a time management course every few years is

usually worthwhile. If there is anyone in your studio who has not attended one recently, you should send that person. If you are a creative person, you may want to consider the "System for Creative People," suggested on page 313.

8. **Realize that other people's time is valuable.** By spending time talking to other workers in the office, you are interrupting and frustrating their work schedules, as well as detracting from your own. Be friendly, but understand that a staff member's most important objective is to work.

9. **Review your work habits.** Developing good work habits is a great way to improve your time management. Habits are subconscious and have been developed over a long period of time. They need careful review. Ask yourself: "Why do I do this first thing in the morning? Should I be opening my mail at this time, or is there a better time to do it?" You need to be willing to review your work habits and see if you can find more time-effective ways of working.

10. **Keep time logs.** Although not every hour in the day is chargeable, for many designers just understanding where and how you spend your time helps you to understand how your time will need to be adjusted when taking on a new project. Realize that anytime you take on a new project, you have to eliminate an activity you were doing in the past. If you have your activities logged, you can easily select which ones should be dropped for more important issues. Table 10.2 (page 318) shows a sample time log, and Table 10.3 (page 319) shows a sample project time sheet.

11. **Plan telephone calls.** Telephone calls mean business. Allow yourself the time you need to make telephone calls, and plan your calls so that they will not disturb the whole studio. Planning your telephone calls and letting people know when you can receive calls can save an amazing amount of time. Often, shorter calls can be more effective than longer ones. Learn to make your telephone calls brief; see if you can keep each call down to three minutes. Outline your agenda before making a phone call.

12. **Prepare for visitors.** Drop-in visitors can disrupt any day. Although you must see some of these visitors, do not see them in your office. See them in another part of the studio, so you have better control over the time you are spending with them. And, remember, though drop-in visitors can be inconvenient, they are your clients and, therefore, important.

13. **Learn to dictate.** Dictating is an excellent way to save a lot of time. It can help you manage your overall design practice much more time effectively. See pages 320–322 for an extensive review of dictating techniques.

14. **Reduce paperwork.** When you receive a piece of paper, determine its appropriate value. If it should be kept as a record in the client's file, put it there. If it is a paper that you should refer to until a certain time, date it so that you will throw it away at an appropriate time. Having a copy of every piece of paper does not always encourage better management; in fact, sometimes it can add confusion to management system.

TIME-LOG CATEGORIES	
Code:	**Client-related Activities:**
Tr.	Travel—actual time going to/from a client's project or to a location directly associated with a client's project
D.	Design—conceptual work in development of a design project; time spent with a client
DCo.	Design Coordination—planning sequences or scope of activities related to a project staff-meeting time reviewing a project
R/D.	Research/Development—preparing information for presentation, i.e., gathering samples, product research, pricing, requesting information from supplier
G/D.	Graphic/Drafting—time spent preparing floor plans, renderings, color boards, and other visual-presentation items for a project
DC.	Data Collection—measuring, photographing a client's project, interviewing, reviewing blueprints for measurements, etc.
I.	Installation—activities related to delivering and installing merchandise, including preparation of that merchandise for delivery
M.	Management—writing orders for a specific client; expediting or problem-solving activities for a specific client
Code:	**General Operations Activities:**
B.	Bookkeeping—all activities related to processing financial records
DS.	Design Support Services—filing samples, catalog information; reviewing new product information and other nonspecific activities related to the design process; meeting with sales representatives and on general product review
MS.	Management Support Services—activities related to the general operation of the company, i.e., maintenance, general administrative duties
MSS.	Merchandise Support Services—upkeep of inventory items, including preparation of items for stock, movement of artwork, etc.
M/P.	Marketing and Promotion—prospecting, interviews with prospective clients, advertising activities, public-relations functions, attendance at community functions
OP.	Order Processing—calls and paperwork associated with clients as a group with minimal time spent on a specific client
P.	Personnel—interviewing, staff evaluation meetings, etc.
T.	Training—attendance at seminars or in-house training sessions

© *Design Business Monthly,* 1988

15. **Instead of writing, make a telephone call.** Usually, it is a lot faster to exchange information by telephone. If the call requires some documentation, you can dictate it on your machine and follow it up with an e-mail or written memo.

16. **Do it yourself.** Review items you are handling or passing on. Determine whether an issue can be addressed with a quick note on a copy of a letter or requires formal correspondence. If there is a way you can handle something quickly and save the time of other people in the office, obviously this is more time-productive.

Table 10.3 Project time sheet. Having your staff members keep time logs such as these for each project not only helps you calculate billing but also helps you keep track of how your staff is spending their time.

PROJECT TIME SHEET

Project:		Staff:	
Date:	Activity:		Time:

Recap:

Design Time:	Research & Development:	Drafting & Rendering:	Data Collection:

© *Design Business Monthly,* 1988

17. **Limit forms and procedures.** Only use forms that help you be productive and make sense to your studio. Some forms are worthwhile, others are not. Designers can spend more time filling out forms than they are spending on designing. Determine just what is necessary.

18. **Simplify documentation.** Documentation is a requirement of the design field. Find a way to do it simply. Organization of your documentation can be a major time-saver.

19. **Plan sales reps' visits.** Sales reps can take up a lot of time, or their visits can be useful and efficient. See pages 278–279 for specific ways to get the most from sales reps' visits.

20. **Use travel time.** When considering taking an out-of-town job, realize it will take you time to get to and from the job. This time should be factored into every costing procedure. The least expensive and most effective design jobs are close to home, but these jobs are not always available. When you are traveling between your office and a job, try to use that time effectively. Two good ways to use this time are dictating or listening to tapes for learning.

21. **Organize your office.** How much time do you spend looking for things? Is everything where you expect it to be? What is the condition of your library and your files? In surveying design studios, we have found that the time designers spend trying to find what they need when they need it is the single largest time-waster. The organization of your library and your files is primary

to your time-effectiveness. Make the investment in time to organize your office, and then require everyone to follow set rules to keep it in order.

22. **Systematize your mail handling.** Many designers spend their most valuable part of the day handling the mail. Review how you handle the mail and determine how you can better manage this time-consuming task. Plan specific times of day to read and respond to e-mail. Being online all day can distract you and take up an amazing amount of time. Sign in and out a few times a day to handle e-mail communication.

23. **Organize reading and studying.** Designers need to exchange information that can only be learned through reading magazines and other written material. Develop a method of organizing and reviewing this material. Perhaps you might give material to other members of your studio and have each person report back on a particular article at a weekly meeting. This can save a lot of time and bring most pertinent items to the full review of your staff. Anyone who is particularly interested in a subject can then spend time further analyzing the material. This method is a great way to give other members of the studio an opportunity to explain what they know and become specialists on certain subjects.

24. **Control crises.** In any design studio there will be crises and problems. However, with proper scheduling, many crises can be averted. See what you can do with your schedule to prevent most of the crises during any week. This will save you from spending your time dealing with such difficult issues.

25. **Learn to delegate.** Delegation can be a time-saver or a time-waster, depending on how it is handled. See pages 327–328 for information on effective delegation methods.

26. **Eliminate indecision.** Many decisions cannot be made until future research is done. However, there are some items that demand immediate decisions. Determine which item belongs in which category, and make decisions appropriately. During the design process, there are many decisions that must be made to keep the job moving. Procrastination can interfere with any schedule.

Dictation

Learning to dictate into a tape recorder is one of the easiest ways to save time. You can "write" letters, memos, and staff instructions at any odd moment, saving many hours of laborious writing. I do a lot of dictating every day, all through the day. I am never without a tape recorder or a dictating machine. I carry a small tape recorder with me practically everywhere I go, whether I am in the car or on a project. I even carry one in the evening, just in case an opportunity to use it arises.

Here are a few tips to make your dictating go more smoothly:

1. **Buy a good machine.** Today, they are inexpensive and portable. There are simple voice-dictation programs for your computer that will type, fax, or e-mail your messages. You can work without support staff if necessary.

2. **Become comfortable with your machine.** You must learn how to talk to it. You want to sound natural and relaxed.

3. **Organize whatever you want to dictate.** Work from a list or outline; this also helps whoever does the transcribing. At our firm, we list the letters or subjects on a tape, number the tape, and, in some cases, code it. For example, a letter can start at 001 and finish at 073. The next item, a memo, starts at 074 and finishes at 110. This system allows our administrative assistant to know how long each item will be and how long it should take to type it.

4. **Try to conclude your dictation with instructions.** Tell your typist whether a letter is a rough draft or a final version. If there is punctuation, say how it should appear. Spell out unusual words like "Naugahyde," which are common to those in our field but often unfamiliar to other people. Explain what format you want for the letter. Is it a note? A formal letter? How do you want these notes typed? Do you want space left for additional notations? You may even want to set up a book of samples.

5. **Always spell out a person's name.** There is nothing worse than sending a letter with the addressee's name misspelled. And if the person's address might be misspelled, spell it out as well.

6. **Learn to enunciate.** Speak clearly so your secretary can understand what you are saying and will be able to transcribe it properly.

7. **Develop a speaking pace, and learn to pause.** When you stop to think, stop the recorder, too. A long silence will make the typist think you are finished.

8. **Be very short and to the point.** Do not give a long dissertation that will take seven pages to type when you could accomplish the same objective in one paragraph.

9. **Do not discard or reuse tapes unless you are certain everything on the tape has been completed.** Keep a good library of tapes, if necessary, to make sure your jobs are thoroughly documented. Table 10.4 (page 322) shows a sample dictation log.

When you are on the telephone with a client, and the client is giving extensive details or complaining, tell him or her you would like to record the call to make sure your staff has all the details. Also, take good notes, and at the end of the conversation review your notes with the client to confirm the issues.

At the end of meetings or interviews with clients, take your tape recorder out and dictate the items you have covered. Then go down the list and give details and instructions to your staff members while the client is there, so the client will be aware of the exact instructions regarding that stage of the project. Often, clients find little points to add or correct. This procedure works very well in preventing little misunderstandings that can grow into complaints. Instruct your staff to send your clients a copy of the transcript as part of the documentation for the project. The transcripts clarify the issues as you go along, helping to avoid legal difficulties.

Table 10.4 Dictation log. A dictation log similar to this one will assist you and your secretary with the management of your dictation.

DICTATION LOG					
Date:			Tape:	Side:	
Addressed to:			Subject:		Inst.:
Instruction Code:					
P = Priority	M = Mail	R = Return		D = Rough Draft	E = Edit/Complete
Delivery Method *Phone, E-mail, Fax, Mail, Overnight*					

© *Design Business Monthly*, 1988.

You may also want to record an entire interview with a client. In our firm, we often make tapes as we interview support staff for large business projects. We keep a tape of the entire conversation, summarize the contents, and prepare a written summary. Sometimes we give both tape and summary to the workers' manager to review for any discrepancies or unresolved issues.

You may be able to program your telephone voice mail to handle long-distance dictation simply by setting no time limit on the length of messages it can record. This lets you call in a quotation or any details you need typed and mailed in a hurry. You can dictate when phone rates are lowest or during hours that are nonproductive for sales work. Your typist can transcribe your message the next morning, and it can be on its way before you get back to the office.

MEETINGS

Your business day is a series of meetings—with your banker, your clients, your staff, your suppliers. Not all meetings are vital interactions, but any meeting that goes on your calendar should have one or more reasons for being there. There are five good reasons to hold meetings: to inform, to solve problems, to brainstorm, to plan, and to motivate. Cancel any meeting that has no clearly stated goal or purpose. There is nothing more tedious than sitting in an aimless meeting.

Managing Meetings

Here are some points to consider in managing meetings:

1. **Meet regularly.** Setting a regular time for staff meetings encourages your staff to hold nonurgent topics for discussion at that time, rather than interrupting your day to solve them. Obviously, some issues must be dealt with as they occur, but many issues do not merit minute-by-minute handling.

2. **Why are we here today?** A good meeting starts with a stated reason and an agenda (see Table 10.5, page 324). If possible, write out your agenda and distribute it before the meeting. Send an agenda to a client the day before you get together, or review it with the client's secretary the day before meeting. This gives both parties time to prepare.

Sometimes when I dictate, I listen to my tape and then redo what I've recorded, just to clean it up and make it easier for the typist to follow. Most often, I ask for a rough draft, which I simply edit and rearrange as required. I have all draft copies typed double- or triple-spaced so they are easy to edit.

I use a voice-dictation program so I can see the text printed; then I make the necessary corrections before sending it out. I also leave taped instructions for my staff when business takes me away from the office. That way they do not have to wonder what to do. Usually, they can listen to these taped instructions in a matter of a few minutes. I encourage my staff to leave me notes on tape; I find their notations on tape are usually better than their written ones. This not only saves time: it also eliminates procrastination. Very often, before leaving a project and returning to the office, my staff and I put our notes on tape. If we wait until we get back to the office to tape notes, we sometimes forget certain details. After our notes are transcribed and edited, we make a copy of them to send to the client. We ask if these notes agree with the client's understanding of the project and if there is anything the client would like to add.

I even dictate to myself. This is a great way of keeping notes when you cannot write something down, as when you are driving a car.

3. **Establish the duration of the meeting in advance and include it on the agenda.** Any meeting that takes two hours when you had allotted 15 minutes impacts your next appointment, and probably the rest of the day's schedule. When a problem is uncovered during a short meeting and the participants cannot stay to deal with it, set a date and time for a new meeting. If all issues are resolved before the meeting is scheduled to end, break up the meeting and use the extra time for some other activity.

4. **Who's in charge?** Someone must take control of the meeting, but select the leader by issue, not by rank. When the purpose for a meeting is to inform, the person with the information holds the floor. In a planning session, the project director is in charge. The person with the problem directs

Table 10.5 Meeting agenda. This sheet can greatly assist in the proper management of meetings.

MEETING AGENDA

							Date Scheduled:		
							Time:		

Client/Subject: Location:

Purpose:

Results Desired:

Scheduled:			Actual:			Meeting Cost:		
Start:	Stop:	Total Hours:	Start:	Stop:	Total Hours:	Billing Rate:	Value Per Hour:	Total:

Persons Attending:

Agenda:

Items Required for Meeting:	Person Responsible:

Meeting Notes:	Decisions:

© *Design Business Monthly*, 1988.

the problem-solving meeting, and the person who wants and needs ideas directs the brainstorming session. Motivation has to come from the top.

5. **Stick to the issue.** This is a good ground rule for all meetings. Be frank and open, and encourage the others to do the same; after all, what goes on at meetings is confidential. Beating around the bush instead of dealing directly with problems only takes up time, and time is money.

6. **Keep the meeting moving.** When the discussion gets bogged down or strays too far from the issue at hand, the leader should take control and stay focused on the stated purpose. Sometimes this is best achieved by interrupting the meeting briefly to serve snacks or pass around copies of relevant documents. Reintroducing the main topic can also help.

7. **Let participants contribute.** If you bring eight people together for a meeting, make sure all eight have an opportunity to speak and to comment. At a project meeting, it is most effective to include only the staff members directly involved with the project. Not every employee needs to attend every meeting, but if a person is valuable enough for you to hire, that person should attend some meetings.

8. **Take notes.** Three days after a meeting, details tend to fade from memory. Names, dates, decisions, financial details, who made what suggestion, and the resulting agreements all need to be recorded for future reference. I recap my meetings by summarizing into a tape recorder as the meeting is about to end. This firms up the issues discussed and gives people a chance to add anything that may have been left out. Later, these dictated notes are transcribed and distributed to the participants. This reinforces the importance of the meeting; the transcript is a written reminder of the decisions that were made and what must be done before the next meeting.

9. **Make the most of unplanned meetings.** You may encounter a prospective client or a current client anywhere—on a jogging trail, in a locker room, in a ticket line, or at a party. If you discuss business, follow up the discussion with a written note. It seals the contact.

10. **Include some humor in each meeting.** It helps everyone relax and keeps things moving.

11. **At the end, summarize.** Define results; list each person's to-dos and schedule the next meeting.

Corporate Board Meetings. All business owners who are part of corporations must have regular meetings, at least once a year. Any change in office, salary, or fringe benefits for one of the business owners must be made as part of this board meeting process. Board meetings must be formalized, which means records must be kept of any decisions. These records should be reviewed occasionally by your corporate lawyer.

All stockholders and board members must be present at a board meeting. If something happens and you cannot have an official board meeting in person, then an agreement may be reached by letter or telephone. However, to meet the regulations of a corporate structure, the agreement must be documented afterward (see Figure 10.1, page 326).

Figure 10.1 Corporate minutes form. This form can be used as an official minutes document, as required by law, by dating it and affixing your corporate seal to it after you have filled in the details of the meeting.

(corporation's name)

I, _____ (secretary's name) _____ , Secretary of _____ (corporation's name) _____ , do hereby certify that at a duly constituted meeting of the Directors and/or Stockholders of the Corporation held at on _____ , 20 ___ , it was upon motion duly made and seconded, that it be VOTED: (describe approved corporate action)

It was upon motion made and seconded that it be further VOTED: That (individual) _____ as _____ (officer) _____ of the Corporation be empowered and directed to execute, deliver, and accept any and all documents reasonably required to accomplish the foregoing vote, all on such terms and conditions as he or she in his or her discretion deems to be in best interest of the Corporation.

I further certify that the foregoing votes are in full force without rescission, as modification or amendment.

Signed this _____ day of _____ , 20____ .

A TRUE RECORD

ATTEST

Secretary of Corporation

(corporate seal)

It is important to keep good minutes of board meetings. Should the IRS examine your minutes and find any failure of your company to abide by the bylaws or hold regular meetings, this can be used against you. For example, in setting compensation levels, fringe-benefit programs as well as other employee and owner transactions must be a part of the documentation of board minutes. Ask your lawyer and financial advisor to check your documents to see that they all conform to standard, especially if any self-interest transactions are covered.

Minutes should be kept on a corporate minutes form (see Figure 10.1, page 326). Corporations must, by law, keep minutes, but the appropriate format is not explicitly spelled out. The form provided here can be photocopied. You can fill in the necessary decisions and the names of people who authorized the decisions. By dating the form and affixing your corporate seal, you have an official minutes document that can be filed in your book.

DELEGATION

Whether you work for a large or small company, for your own firm, or are part of a large corporation, your productivity depends on your ability to use support staff. Delegation is one of the processes by which you should coordinate your projects with other staff members.

Becoming a skillful delegator will allow you both to save time and to develop the abilities of your staff. To be an effective delegator you need to define:

- Your goals
- Your expected results
- Your needs
- The specific time by which you need the information
- The general outline of the subject
- The item you are covering

Your goal may be to locate an item that can be worked into a fast-track project or a product that requires very specialized design detail. Whatever your goals are, make them clear.

Make sure your staff understands your priorities and knows which items are important to complete first. We all want to do easy projects first, but that may not be wise. Keep your schedules coordinated.

Clearly spell out any hidden issues. Often, there are certain details about a project, or a client's preferences, your staff would not know unless you told them. Be very straightforward with your fellow workers. Tell them if the client is truly color-blind or cannot see farther than two feet.

As you present the projects or items you are going to delegate, ask your staff members how long they think the assignment will take and how they intend to handle it. A quick explanation from each worker will tell you whether that person understands your aim. The worker's method of handling the project may be off track or inappropriate. This is the time to set the parameters.

Keep in mind your staff's strengths and weaknesses. People are better at some projects than others. You should try to assign projects suited to each individual's strengths. When you must delegate tasks in areas where your staff is weak, tell them to let you know if they are having problems as they proceed and offer to help them develop a solution.

Regardless of the abilities of your staff, once you have delegated a task to an employee, suggest that he or she check back with you with a progress report in a set amount of time. There is no point having someone spend months working in the wrong direction.

Allow for problems. Let your staff know you are aware everything does not always run smoothly and that, if there is a problem, you are willing to be part of the problem-solving process. This does not mean employees can simply dump the project back on your desk; they are to tell you what the problem is and their recommendations for handling it. If your staff members run into trouble, they can come back and check with you.

There are certain situations you should never delegate. They include:

- **Any project that is not clearly defined.** To be able to pass on creative assignments to others, you must be able to define the project. If the criteria or specifications have not been determined by the client, wait until they have been set before you delegate the project.
- **Crisis situations.** These are difficult to delegate. If there is a crisis, the top management must take care of it.
- **Sorting out personality problems.** These should be worked out by the chief executive or management director. That is why so many chief executives and management people spend most of their time dealing with personality problems of either staff or clients and not doing interior design.
- **Making major changes.** Any change that requires an adjustment of procedures must first be developed by management. You are only going to cause chaos within the organization if you do not make these adjustments yourself.
- **Policymaking.** This is the responsibility of management. Policies should be made only by the chief executive officer or chief management director.
- **Making major decisions.** It is your job and responsibility to make decisions, such as whether to accept a project.
- **Giving congratulations.** Awards and praise are appreciated more when they come from top management. If you can keep the spirits high among your fellow workers, whether they are your own staff or various contractors, this will be one of the most valuable services you can perform.

HANDLING MAIL

Even in a small firm, handling mail can take a tremendous amount of time. Opening the mail and bringing it to the attention of the right people is not a job for your newest staff member. The person opening the mail must understand what is happening within the corporate structure. In some firms, the principal opens all the mail first thing in the morning, before anyone else is in the office, or the general manager has this responsibility. It is best to route mail to the person who needs to look at it, and to review any other mail details either by meeting or by note, as required.

When should mail be opened? As soon as it arrives. But not all mail needs the immediate attention of the addressee. Any items that are critical and need immediate attention should get it, but usually critical issues are brought to your attention by telephone or messenger. Schedule a time in your day for reviewing mail; mail should not disrupt the main part of your day.

E-Mail

Today e-mail has become an important part of most offices. Many companies e-mail their orders and use it for correspondence to vendors and for most of their communication. Others use the Internet only for research. Whether or not this works for you depends on your particular preference and ability to use these systems. There are still many of us who prefer to work by paper standards and are doing a very good job; however, e-mail does give us the advantage of partnering with other people throughout the world in an immediate and inexpensive way. E-mail programs allow us to send detailed drawings, photographs, and wonderful illustrations, which can be printed out in excellent photo quality at another location, easily. This was never possible with a fax or other systems. E-mail will continue to be a major player in our industry.

Personal Digital Assistant (PDA)

PDAs are very prominent in many design offices and can be used for all types of tasks. Some designers cannot live without their PDA to organize their calendars, maintain their phone lists, photograph rooms, find directions, and so forth, while others use it strictly as a calculator and address book. Some designers do their project management and other detailing right on their PDA and receive immediate replies. I personally have more than 3,500 names, addresses, phone numbers, fax numbers, and so on, on my PDA and do not know how I would manage without it. Still, I use my PDA in a more limited manner than other people use theirs. It is incredible to realize we can have this much support with us in such a miniaturized form.

RECORDKEEPING

Design firms get paid for designing. They do not get paid for bookkeeping. Of course, they need a bookkeeping system to document their design efforts. Make a list of the information you must have at your fingertips. Analyze it. Can someone with good administrative skills, rather than a designer, do certain processes? What do you really want to know? Try to streamline this information so you are getting just the pertinent information, the information you need to make decisions, and not a lot of the peripheral details that may or may not be of use to you. The key today is simplicity. Keep these processes as easy and simple as you can, so they do not distract from your design practice.

Every business today needs to keep good records. Interior design businesses especially need a simple and accurate recordkeeping system. It is easy to run one job out of a shopping bag. However, it is very difficult to continue to run job after job, year after year, in this fashion. As businesses grow and change, old methods of recordkeeping often become inappropriate. You must review new systems of recordkeeping on a continuing basis.

The computer is a standard tool for every firm today, especially for the record-processing part of the business. Computers enable us to retrieve records and keep documentation in an inexpensive and easy-to-use way.

If you are not computer-oriented, there are other basic recordkeeping systems that are simple and efficient to use. Any recordkeeping system you set up should be designed, or at least approved, by your accountant. It must also be a system you understand and is easy for everyone in the studio to use. Make sure you understand the reason for each particular aspect of the recordkeeping system. Your recordkeeping system also must be accurate and have some type of double-checking program to make sure errors are not being made in various categories.

Design firms need good documentation for day-to-day business, and in case of an audit. However, there is a lot of information you do not have time to use or review. There is no point in spending time documenting this type of information. Store and keep only essential information.

Make sure your system is well defined and functional. You can always add to it later on. Each year, review your system and see how much you use each part of it. Is it possible to delete certain sections? Would this save time?

You must keep your records up to date, and review files on a regular basis. I believe in good documentation. I have found so many times that having records of a past project or knowing what a client did in another situation prevents problems at a later date. Keep documents throughout every project, and make them part of your permanent record. Documentation is a necessary part of every design firm, particularly in these litigious times.

Keep records on a daily basis so you do not have to worry about documenting orders and other information at a later date, when you often cannot remember them entirely. At my firm, we make a point of documenting our projects while the clients are there so they have a chance to go over every detail with us. We review every part of the various contracts so clients understand our procedures and know the part they play in our relationship. Good records impress everyone who sees them. Sloppy records are inappropriate in a field that is based on organization.

How long must you keep business records? It depends on your type of business and style of management, as well as state and other regulatory requirements. For financial records, it is best to check with your accountant or lawyer for specific scheduling. The length of time you should keep project management records will vary as well, depending on your continued interaction with the client or project.

What kind of records should a designer keep as support in case of a lawsuit? My lawyer says that if you keep extremely complete records of the sort he really likes, you would probably get nothing else done. But it is practical to keep a record of all business transactions and copies of all purchase orders and requisitions.

While a job is going on, keep all the correspondence with suppliers and anything written to your client. If you do run into trouble, at that point, write a memorandum of every detail you recall about the job. Months later, you will not remember as well. Keep the documents in an orderly file, and keep the file for six years unless you think the situation involves fraud, which is usually tax-related. Your accountant can also advise you as to which records to keep and how long to keep them. There are many other legal issues designers should be aware of: state laws, federal laws, and city laws pertaining to the practice of design, for instance. An attorney can tell you about these; but a better source might be trade or professional associations. Very often, legal issues are brought to my attention by the American Society of Interior Designers (ASID) or by the Chamber of Commerce. I later discuss them with my attorney to see how much importance I should attach to them.

Areas That Require Recordkeeping
You are legally required to keep the following for three to seven years:

- Sales records of contracts acquired
- Cash receipts for all monies received from all sources
- All cash disbursements, which are the monies paid out by your business
- Accounts receivable and accounts payable
- Tax and payroll records

Daily Diary
A daily diary is a useful addition to the appointment books most of us keep. Here you can record not only appointments but the actual time spent on each project during the day, phone calls and their outcomes, business that requires follow-through, and anything else that comes up during the day. This saves time when you actually sit down to calculate direct billable hours. Because the records are kept daily and often hourly, the diary is a good method of documentation.

There are designers who find it useful to keep lists of all their phone conversations, client meetings, and other interactions throughout the day.

The range and variety of diaries available is quite broad, so you should be able to find one that suits your personal style. More and more designers use them, not just because they are a professional aid and good management tool but because they simply save time. You do not have to wonder whether you discussed Mrs. A's baroque lamp, because the conversation details are right there on the page. If you prefer using a computer, there are programs available to meet your needs.

INVENTORY

Some design firms have no inventory; others need a warehouse. It is a matter of business preference and convenience. Whether maintaining an inventory of furniture and furnishings is practical depends on a number of other factors.

When evaluating inventory, determine how it fits into the cash flow of your business. Having a product available when your client wants it means you can sometimes service a client when another designer cannot. If you have a good turnover, maintaining an inventory can be advantageous in marketing and selling. Any job that can be done quickly generally has a higher profit margin than one stretched out over a long period of time. Sometimes a certain amount of inventory is required for a particular type of project. But is keeping inventory really necessary? Quick-ship programs are becoming increasingly available.

Warehousing is expensive. You pay for using the warehouse and for the energy required to heat, air condition, and ventilate it. Furniture is relatively fragile and must be kept in a warehouse of reasonable quality or it does not hold up, especially in extreme climates.

Handling inventory can be cost-consuming. It requires good supervision, otherwise the breakage and damage rate can be tremendous. Although most of the furnishings you are apt to carry will require considerable care, you cannot always get well-trained labor.

You need to insure against fire and theft for every piece of inventory you have. This can be quite expensive. Also, extensive burglar-alarm systems may be required, depending on your location.

Holding inventory of interior design furnishings today usually costs around 30 to 35 percent of their worth per year, depending on such factors as your individual insurance rates and real estate costs. This is expensive. Consider how many projects you have won because you maintain an inventory, and determine whether you have made a wise investment. Every item in your warehouse or showroom shows up on your tax bill. Is it worth it?

There are designers I know who claim most of their income is derived from tremendous markups on antiques they have acquired and later sold. This may be true, but I wonder if the profit margin is as high as they believe. Some pieces sit at a warehouse for 8 or 10 years before being sold. When you factor in the cost of the repairs and alterations required to make the antiques saleable, the actual cost of the antique becomes quite high.

If you intend to hold inventory, check through it each year and ask your accountant to help you understand what the costs are. Some inventory does appreciate, but

Radio Frequency Identification Technology (RFID)

RFID is the next generation of the bar code used for inventory control and for collecting information on the use of a product. This technology has been used for paying tolls with EZ pass for several years. This type of device could be put in furniture to track the durability of the piece or to measure its usage.

The information you gather using RFID could be very valuable, but it raises privacy issues you must consider.

interior design is still a fashion industry in which a certain amount of stock will not be as appealing next year as it was this year.

FREIGHT CLAIMS

Freight damages are one of an interior designer's greatest problems—or, perhaps, greatest aggravations. At one time, if you took the normal precautions of documenting your claims with a photograph of the item, and followed shippers' instructions, you would generally get paid for your claim. Sometimes it took several months to a year, but at some point you got paid. Now, with the changes in trucking regulations, designers are finding it very difficult to collect payment for freight claims. The freight companies use every minor technicality they can to get out of paying them.

Some of our sources now include phrases in their invoices saying they are not responsible for any merchandise once it leaves the factory. But they pack similar merchandise all the time; they should know how to pack the merchandise to survive the freight process. They also should know which carriers will handle their merchandise carefully. It is neither appropriate nor fair for designers to be responsible for items over which they have no control.

Fair or not, design studios now have to take a new approach to the problem of freight damage. First of all, you must be sure any receiving warehouse or studio has the proper procedures for receiving, inspecting, and documenting anything they receive in your name. Whether the warehouse handlers are a third party or not, you, as the buyer, are responsible for the merchandise even if it is being shipped to them. The address may be in care of that warehouse, but it is your name on the invoice.

Our managing director and I spent many weeks researching this problem with our sources. They have recommended that we make sure anyone who receives merchandise goes through the standard and appropriate method of inspecting the boxes, looking for crushed corners or other signals that a package may be damaged. If a problem is noticed by our receiver or warehouse person, they are instructed to request the driver to let them open the package at that point to check to see if the materials are in good condition. If they are in good condition, the package or shipment will be accepted. If they are not in good condition, it will be refused. Accept delivery of damaged material only from a freight company with which you have experience and you know will handle the claim.

Suppose you check an item and it is not in good condition. Some suppliers advise us to simply refuse it, because the company that picked up that freight signed a bill of lading with the manufacturer, saying the company agreed to deliver the item to you in good condition. If you accept the item and decide you are going to deal with the freight claim, because perhaps only 20 percent of the merchandise needs replacement, remember that this will require a great amount of documentation.

If freight damage to an item is minor, take care of it in your studio. When the damage is less than 10 percent of the cost of the item, and it is something you can handle, it pays you to do so. The merchandise can be repaired in a matter of days and forwarded to your clients. If you return the merchandise, there might be a delay of three to six months before you get it replaced.

With any damage, it is important that you notify the shipper so the manufacturer knows whether it is a shipping problem or a manufacturing problem. That way they can do something to prevent this damage the next time. You are their best quality-control engineer.

When you make the decision as to whether or not you are going to accept a shipment, consider how much effort will go into making a freight claim. Photographs are absolutely necessary. Every receiving department and every warehouse must have a camera and facilities to take duplicate (or triplicate) photographs of damaged material. Send a photograph to whomever is handling the claim, and keep one as a record for yourself. You must also keep all packing materials and be able to show the exact condition in which the merchandise arrived. Storing damaged crates can take up a lot of warehouse space.

Anytime you make a freight claim, notify the manufacturer and shipper of all the details. Many suppliers realize how difficult freight claims are for receivers to handle and will offer to help handle these claims for you. These are the kind of resources designers need.

Similar merchandise is usually available from several sources. Find companies that will handle your freight claims appropriately, and give them your business. They take a lot of the pressure and freight management problems out of your hands. These companies are sometimes also willing to reship any damaged items within seven days at no additional cost to the designer.

As designers, we must demand the support and help of our resources in handling freight claims, and there is only one way to do that: by all working together. One- and two-day seminars are given on this topic. There are also agents who will handle your freight claims for a fee. Attorneys will also handle major freight claims.

Receiving Instructions

The receiving instructions should be posted in your warehouse, made part of your contract with the warehouse serving your firm, or included with purchasing documents when the client or other agent is handling the receiving. See the instructions given in Figure 10.2 (page 335).

PROTECTING CONFIDENTIAL MATERIAL

Confidentiality maintenance is a major concern these days. Unfair as it may sound, if you do not get a handle on the confidentiality aspect of your business, it may become a runaway train, with all fingers pointing to you in the caboose. This can become the foremost occupational hazard of your business. Establish boundaries and take control of that action.

How do you protect the confidential material you have in your studio? It is human nature to talk about one's work, and when your staff talks, they could

Figure 10.2 Receiving instructions. These instructions should be posted in your warehouse, be made part of your contract with the warehouse serving your firm, and/or be included with purchasing documents when the client or other agent is handling the receiving. This information has been provided by the Shippers National Freight Claim Council (SNFCC).

RECEIVING INSTRUCTIONS

1. Make sure you are signing for the same number of packages and piece count as on the delivery slip. Note amount received on delivery slip and have the driver sign and date it. *Count all pieces.*

2. Do not accept deliveries without inspection. Writing "subject to inspection" on the delivery receipt does not protect you.

3. Open and inspect packages during delivery. Insist on opening any package with evidence of damage in the driver's presence.

4. Note any damages on the delivery slip and have the driver sign and date it.

5. If you are not able to open packages at the time of delivery, note any visible damage to the cartons on the delivery slip. Be precise when noting these. (Example: one carton crushed on corners.) Do not give opinions as to possible causes of damage; report only the facts. Do not sign on the line "received in good condition," sign and date just above it.

6. Open package as soon as possible and within the freight carriers' claim for more complete inspection of goods (generally within 15 days for reporting concealed damage). After 15 days it may be presumed that you caused the damage.

7. If damage is discovered after the driver leaves, call the carrier immediately for inspection and *confirm in writing* your request for inspection.

8. Keep concealed damaged goods in original packing and set aside.

9. Do not reject the shipment to the carrier unless:
    • The shipment is "practically worthless," considering the cost of repair or salvaging.
    • You take pictures.
    • You get the driver to acknowledge and confirm the damage.
    • The shipment may contaminate or damage other freight in your place of business.

10. If carrier does not inspect within 30 days of your request, make a detailed inspection report, with *pictures*.

11. If carrier does inspect, request a copy of *all* inspection reports made.

inadvertently give away many secrets or confidential information that could hurt your project or your business.

To begin to address this important issue, the first step is to explain to your employees, in an overall review of staff policies, the reasons for confidentiality rules. At that point, you might even ask your employees to sign a nondisclosure statement. It is also often valuable to have your vendors, bankers, and consultants sign these statements.

On certain corporate projects, you must sign disclosure statements before you begin the project. More and more companies are requiring this, not just mega-firms such as IBM.

A copyright attorney explained to me that confidential materials must be treated as confidential throughout the design process. They also must be treated as confidential within the office, which means you should not display them on the wall. All confidential drawings must be locked in a special cabinet within the office when they are not in use. They cannot be shown to anyone unless you make a point of first saying the material is confidential. When items go out for quotation, you must mark them accordingly, and explain to anyone who touches them that confidentiality is required.

Which materials are confidential? Plans and drawings that show an exclusive design or technique should be labeled "confidential" and kept locked in a safe area. Your customer lists and marketing plans should also be kept confidential; there is nothing of more value to your competitors. Discuss this information only with people you can trust.

Computer software needs to be guarded with caution, too, as it often holds some of the top secrets of any business. Generally, your computer software packages provide sequential codes or passwords that must be entered before confidential data can be displayed or printed.

COPYRIGHTS

Every now and then, something you design for a project is not only original, but adaptable to quantity production for limited distribution. When you send such a design out to be maintained, you do not want the manufacturer or shop to copy the item and then sell it all over town. How can you protect the design?

There are very few items interior designers create that are patentable, but if you have developed something that is really that innovative, it deserves protection. Copyrighting is usually the best safeguard. It is easy, relatively inexpensive, and can be done without incurring legal fees.

What types of works can you copyright? Anything that is an original work "fixed in a tangible form of expression," such as pictorial, graphic, and sculptural works, as well as architectural works. You do not have to register to obtain a copyright, but there are some advantages to registration, as you will see later.

To copyright your work, mark each and every design or drawing with the copyright information. At the bottom of every drawing you should affix the copyright symbol (©), the year, and the owner of the copyright, which generally means the name of the design firm. For example, your drawing would read at the bottom: "© 2005 Business Design, Inc." That is the only way you can protect your design from being copied by other people who might see it.

When an employee of your firm produces an original work eligible for copyright protection while in the course of working with your firm, the firm, not the employee, is considered to be the originator. If you want the designer to hold the copyright, prepare a simple written document stating that he or she is the copyright owner. Have an authorized representative of the firm and the designer both sign and date the document.

There are a few reasons to register your copyright with the U.S. Copyright Office. First, it makes your design a matter of public record. Second, registration is necessary if you are going to defend any suits for infringements that might be filed in court. Copyrighting is very inexpensive. You can do it directly, without an attorney. All you need to do is submit a completed application form, your fee for the application, and two complete copies of the work being registered. The copy requirements vary, depending on the type of item you are registering. To obtain additional copyright information or forms, go to the Copyright Office Web site, www.copyright.gov; or call 202-707-3000; or write to the Library of Congress, Copyright Office, 101 Independence Ave. SE, Washington DC 20559-6000.

Copyrighting is good for the duration of the author's life, plus an additional 70 years after the author's death. If a copyright is registered under a company's auspices, the copyright duration would be 95 years from the date of publication, or 120 years from the date of creation, whichever is shorter. These units are based on laws that came into effect on January 1, 1978.

Design firms have hundreds of copyrights on various items. I know design firms that have made more money defending their copyrights than they have on doing design. Obviously, it does not pay to copyright something unless it is really an original work and has copyright value. But it does pay to put the copyright symbol and your name on each and every drawing. It keeps people from copying you without discretion.

USING OFFICE TOOLS

How you use your office tools—the library and telephone in particular—can often be as important as the systems you select.

Managing the Library

Libraries need constant management. They grow continuously, and if not regularly reviewed, can outgrow their space. In most cases, when a library outgrows its space, it is time to review and purge, to get rid of items that have been discontinued or you no longer use in your practice. Evaluate your library annually. If you do not have the right information, there is no point in having a library.

A library must be organized. It is not professional to have to look through 16 feet of catalogs to find two product specifications. At the prices designers charge, all time should be spent designing, not searching.

How extensively organized a library is really depends on its size and the number of people working with it. The larger the library and the greater the number of people with access to it, the more structured your categorizing-and-use regulations must be. Even a small library needs structure. Items must be returned to their positions after being used so they can be easily retrieved the next time they are needed.

Every collection that goes into your library needs an assigned position. Catalogs should be kept together, as should samples. You need open shelving for books, magazines, and catalogs. You need standard drawer files for smaller catalogs not in binders, articles, and pages torn from magazines. Product samples come in all shapes and sizes and should be filed according to their physical properties. Lucite trays and drawers are invaluable for some carpet samples, as are standard metal file drawers.

Within your catalog section, catalogs of furniture for contract-office spaces should be kept together, apart from catalogs for lighting fixtures or residential furniture.

Magazines. How much are you spending on design books and magazines? This expenditure can run into several thousands of dollars annually. Take the time once a year to review the value of each publication you receive. Are your designers and staff people reviewing copies, or do they simply fill up shelves in the studio? If you buy magazines, make sure you use them to keep up to date on current products and issues. If they are just cluttering your office, cancel those subscriptions, whether they are free or paid.

For every publication you decide to keep, ask yourself the following questions:

- Who reads it first?
- How long should we keep it?
- How often must the subscription be renewed?
- How often does it come—weekly, monthly, bimonthly, quarterly, or semiannually?
- Where will it be stored?
- Can you donate old copies to a design school?

Many magazines and newspapers can be read online. This permits designers to look at the articles they are interested in at their convenience. Articles can be printed for reference, filing, or passing on to associates or clients. This has become a major trend in magazine publishing. Newsletters for many of our professional organizations are now available exclusively online.

To effectively control the circulation and storage of magazines, consider using a form similar to the one shown in Table 10.6 (page 340). Consult this form to evaluate your magazine buying. Review it once a year and add to it as needed, and you will probably find it helps you to eliminate some of the clutter and confusion magazines can create in a studio.

Managing the Telephone

Make call handling a top priority in your company. When you look at the time you spend on the phone and the value the phone can bring to your company, it is worth the effort.

The Phone Receptionist. Who should answer the telephone? Should the principal or head designer do this? Probably not. After all, they are among the more expensive people on the payroll, so it really does not pay to have them answering the telephone. But it should be someone who has a good voice, is friendly, and is good at building rapport with people on the other end of the line. Enthusiasm helps. Make sure the person answering the phone sounds happy to receive the call, not that it is an annoyance or an inconvenience.

Probably the best person to answer your telephone is someone who has been with your firm for a very long time, or an experienced employee who does not enjoy the stress of a fieldwork schedule but who can be hospitable and knows a great deal about the firm.

It is a good idea to have the members of your staff take turns answering the phones so that everyone in the studio becomes familiar with client interests and desires. However, you should not let anyone who is not reasonably well informed answer the telephone, if you can possibly avoid it. When the person who answers the phone can handle a situation, there is no need to refer to a second or even third person. This saves a lot of staff time and helps develop better rapport with clients.

Structure your office so that the person who answers the phone is always pleasant. Any person answering the phone should do so in a polite and professional manner and not put the client through the third degree. You need information from your clients, but there are good ways and bad ways to get this information. I have heard of potential clients who decided against a firm because they did not like the way they had been treated over the phone.

Telephone Protocol. Anyone who answers your business telephones must build rapport with your clients. In doing so, they must also get basic information and get it accurately. Sometimes people do not pronounce their names clearly over the telephone. Your phone receptionist must be sure to get the caller's name correctly spelled—even if this requires spelling the name back to the caller to double-check. The receptionist should not put a call through without verifying who the caller is—even if the voice sounds like a familiar person.

It is critical for a caller's name to be spelled correctly in the record of each phone call. So often you will have three or four clients with a similar name. There is nothing more embarrassing and nothing that puts a client off more than if you address the person by the wrong name or cite incorrect information. Your phone

Table 10.6 Magazine management sheet. Using a form similar to this one can help you control the circulation and storage of magazines in your firm. It can also help you to evaluate which magazine subscriptions should be continued, discontinued, or added.

MAGAZINE MANAGEMENT SHEET							
MAGAZINES	LOCATION	STORED	LENGTH OF TIME	GIVEN TO	CIRCULATION OF STAFF	COST	EXPIRES

© *Design Business Monthly,* 1988.

receptionist should have a list of clients and their telephone numbers. If the receptionist recognizes the client's voice, the receptionist can then say, for example, "Yes, Mrs. Jones, are you going to be at your home number?" and read Mrs. Jones that number. If Mrs. Jones gives another number, the receptionist should write that number down. The receptionist should make sure before the call is completed that the return number is documented on the message, to speed up returning calls.

What is the subject of a call? To whom should a call be directed? It is a courtesy not to waste a caller's time. If the call should be returned, the receptionist should find out when the caller is going to be available. If the caller has several telephone numbers, the receptionist needs to get the correct number.

When you are training your receptionist or anyone else in telephone protocol, instruct the person to answer each call within two or three rings. When the phone rings forever it is very annoying to the caller. The receptionist must focus on telephone calls; no one can read a magazine or eat lunch and answer the telephone effectively at the same time.

If you can, hire a person whose primary job is to answer the telephones; do not expect that person to do 40 other things. Put receptionists where they can concentrate on the telephone and will not be distracted by people passing by.

Not everyone is a good telephone person. If someone does not have good diction or does not speak clearly, perhaps he or she will need some additional training. It is important that your receptionist's choice of words be appropriate to your business.

Handling Telephone Calls. Many designers tell me they are constantly harassed by the telephone. It is no different in our office. However, I contend that over 50 percent of telephone calls—especially the harassing ones—can be eliminated by good phone manners and by checking in regularly with clients and suppliers when you are handling a project. The other 50 percent are very important, because they are sales and marketing tools that need to be properly developed.

Every phone call you receive has taken someone time and effort to sit down and make. Yes, there are clients who call constantly. There are ways of handling this without aggravating them. Let them know the specific time when you will return their call and assure them you will have the proper information when you call them back. Most of our clients are so busy they do not want me to waste their time, but they do want the information. We find if we respond by gathering the information together and getting back to them at a set time, rather than reacting to their moods, we have a better-managed and happier office and better-informed and happier clients.

At one point, we had three Mrs. Moores as clients. Each one spelled her name slightly differently, and all had very different projects. They also did not like each other. In a small community, this was a problem. Two of their voices were not that distinctive from one another. When a phone call came in from one of the Mrs. Moores, it was very difficult to tell which it was unless we compared telephone numbers.

On another occasion, I received a message to return a call to a person whose name I did not quite recognize but at a number that seemed familiar. I called and got a business office. After getting through to the third secretary with a name that was not quite right, I finally realized who I was supposed to be calling. I was embarrassed because this was one of my largest clients, whom I obviously should have known well. Fortunately, the incident just caused embarrassment to me and was a big joke among the client's secretaries; however, it could have been far worse had my call gone directly to the client.

Prepare an outline for all of your calls, and document everything that is said. Many of us have clients who seem to be lying in wait for us to make a mistake. You should research and prepare solutions for problems before presenting them to a client. You can tell clients about almost any kind of problem if you do it in a controlled, organized manner. If you just present them with the problem, without offering any solution, you will soon have a bigger problem.

When you realize a caller is rambling, ask for that person's agenda outline. I am always prepared to give my outline. Callers must be kept on track. Many people like to talk about everything under the sun; if you are designing their boardroom, keep the conversation about the boardroom.

Some days, you may feel as if you are playing telephone tag with clients. You call them, they call you, you call back, and on it goes. How can you avoid wasting time this way? If you plan your time so everyone in your firm knows when you are making phone calls and clients learn when they can reach you, you will save an immeasurable amount of time and keep your dialing to a minimum. I know many designers who refuse to accept telephone calls except during certain hours. If they are interrupted, they cannot accomplish objectives. I think it is a good idea not to accept phone calls you are unprepared to handle.

When leaving messages, do not treat administrative assistants like second-class citizens. Frequently, they can help you more than any other person to reach the person you want. Leave a message that can easily be answered—say what you want and why— so when the person returns your call, the person can be ready with the appropriate information.

If you want a person to call you back, suggest a convenient time. There is no point in having a person call you back when you know you are going to be out on other projects during the day. Your messages should state when you will be available, such as, between 4:00 and 5:00 this evening. Usually, the assistant knows the schedule of the person you are trying to reach and can help you coordinate this.

When people call you, how do you screen those calls? There are a lot of calls that should never go through to you as they would just waste your time. You also want to be sure you have the right file in hand and are ready to give good information when you take certain calls.

In our office, we work as a team. Our clients know they can speak with four or five of us and they are going to get excellent information. I feel this develops far more respect for our staff among my clients than if only I gave the answers. (In my firm, clients are aware that several other members of our staff know a lot more about scheduling than I do.) When it comes to some of the design details, again, someone else can give them better information. Therefore, not every call is directed to me, which is a tremendous relief when it comes time to return calls at the end of the day.

Almost all calls can be divided into three groups: those from people you really want to talk to; those from people you surely do not want to talk to; and those you are not sure about. It is great if someone can screen these calls for you before you pick up the telephone. We try to keep a list in our office of those people we really want to

I make a special schedule for calls. For example, contractors know they may reach me between 6:30 and 7:30 every morning. They understand this is a good time to call me, because if I am not there, I will call them back very shortly. This is also the time I will have my files in front of me and will be prepared to answer any of their questions. There are other times during the day when I recommend sources or clients to call, depending on my schedule. When I am finished with a phone call with a client, I send the client a written review of any changes or items discussed during that phone call that would affect our original design or documents. When a client realizes what you have discussed on the phone will be sent in writing for verification, with the date of the phone call referred to on the transcript, it is much easier to support billing for phone time.

How to End a Call

Sometimes we have great difficulty getting off the phone. We do not want to insult the caller, but there are other projects to be done. The trick is to convey that you have other obligations but are ever so ready to give the client prime attention. The basic story in selling and marketing remains: Give clients attention, and they will ordinarily be very happy. Reduce that attention and you will have complaints and problems.

If a telephone call goes on too long, there are ways of cutting it off. Ask your secretary to ring so the caller hears a buzz. Or simply say, "I'm wanted on another phone. Would you hold the line a moment?" Or, better yet, "Let me get the rest of this information, and I'll call you back at four o'clock." Learn to break off calls if they are not productive. Sometimes this can be done by summarizing what you think has been covered and saying you are going to get back to the caller after you check on the points you discussed.

hear from to make sure they are put through every time. We also keep a list of the pests. My attitude is that certain people should be kept away from me; I want the freedom of not talking to them if at all possible.

Do not let people abuse you with telephone calls. I find it is much better to return a telephone call when it's convenient for me than to have people call and interrupt me at inappropriate times.

Telephone Record. Every phone call that comes into the office should be recorded in a daily phone log (see Table 10.7, page 344). You should post a phone log by every phone, and list each call, the day and time it came in, and the subject. This log should be written legibly enough for anyone to be able to pick it up and read it. The log should also include the name of the person to whom the message was given, so there is a record of who is following up on each message. If, three or four days after a call, you wonder whether a situation was remedied, you can look up the details of the call in the phone log.

Voice Mail. I used to hate voice mail. Now I think it's one of the greatest things in the world, because at least I can leave a message and let someone know I have responded to a call. In your voice mail message, do not apologize to your callers for receiving your voice mail. Do make your voice mail message short. It is boring for callers to sit through a 60-second message they have heard 90 times before. Conversely, it's best to use a service that allows callers to leave long messages, and encourage them to do so.

When you are expecting a call but may not be in, instruct your caller to leave details on the voice mail so you can take care of them immediately. Encouraging clients to do this will save you a lot of time.

Table 10.7 Telephone record. Every phone call that comes into your office should be recorded on a daily phone log such as this. Be sure all handwriting on the log is legible.

TELEPHONE RECORD				Date:
				Staff:
Time:	Person:	Purpose of Call:		Results:

© *Design Business Monthly,* 1988.

The Telephone as a Sales Tool. A telephone can be a great sales tool—though I must admit I would hate to make my living from cold calls; I am not polished at it. But I have learned a few ways to use the telephone effectively.

1. **Establish rapport with the secretaries.** Ask them questions such as, "Who is in charge of the office planning division of the company, and to whom does that person report?" If possible, try to get to this person; you can say the secretary referred you to them. This gives you a much better chance of getting their attention.

2. **If you are not sure how to pronounce a name, ask the company's telephone operator.** Or ask the secretary. They are usually happy to tell you, and it saves a lot of embarrassment later. Make sure you thank them, and try to develop some common interest with them so when you call back, you can say, "I spoke with you the other day about such and such and you were kind enough to refer me to Mr. Smith. Is Mr. Smith available now? May I speak with him now, or do you suggest I call back at another time when he might not be so busy?" If someone is not in, schedule a repeat call, and be careful to follow through on it. One little trick that often works is to call before 9:00 A.M. or after 5:00 P.M. Very often the staff is not there at those times but the principal is, and that individual will answer the phone personally. This is also a strategic time to talk with executives, because usually they are less pressured than during the day, and they often do not mind taking a few moments to discuss your marketing objectives.

Our policy is that if clients ask for absolutely anything, we try to handle it. If a client calls our design studio and asks about a lampshade, we will help locate it, although we do not really provide this service. We have clients we have been taking care of for over 30 years. I even help my father's clients—some of whom are now in their nineties—if they call me with a problem. I just take care of it, because I feel that if I were 90, I would be happy for someone to take care of me. I treat them the way I would like to be treated.

If someone who is not a client calls us for a service we do not provide, we try to find out how the person found out about us and why the person is calling us. We can learn from these calls. If people think we are a lamp shop and that is not correct, we are projecting the wrong image in our marketing. We try to determine why they do not understand what kind of services we really do render.

3. **When you make phone calls, ask the people you are calling if they have a few minutes to talk with you.** When you are calling someone at home, you never know in what condition you are going to find that person. There is no worse time to try to make a sale than when, for example, a person has stepped out of the bathtub dripping wet to answer the phone. Even at the office, there may be six people in front of the person, making it a very difficult time to talk over the phone.

4. **Keep a daily log of all phone calls and notes in an individual client's file.** I cannot tell you how valuable this can be for designers. In fact, on several occasions, when designers I knew had to appear in court to verify certain communications, the judges were very impressed when they saw the record of time and details of phone calls. It was obvious the logs were accurate, because they had been kept on a regular basis in the designer's handwriting.

5. **Make weekly reports by telephone.** One of the most successful sales and marketing techniques is to create good client rapport through frequent telephone communication (see page 234). Make a weekly report on every design project. At the beginning of a project confirm with your client the appropriate times for this interaction; then, at that time each week, have a member of your design team call the client with a full report on the status of the design project.

By scheduling your calls, you can be prepared, which makes you appear professional. Scheduling also can add considerably to the overall sales on a project because it encourages clients to add to the project.

Thank people for their kindness. When you make a thank-you telephone call to a factory foreman who has been abused by everybody else that week, he will never forget you. All you have to say is, "Congratulations! You've made a beautiful product for us. We're happy we used you and hope to use you again." The time you spend giving verbal rewards is not just good manners; you are ensuring you will be remembered in a favorable context.

Phone Call Process

A phone call process structures your calls for professionalism and maximum productivity. You need to organize to get the most out of your time on the phone, no matter with whom you are speaking. Here are some tips:

- **Make a written agenda before you make a call.** Skip socializing unless you feel it is necessary for smoothing something over.
- **Make sure the time you are spending in making this call now is important.** Consider whether you could wait and coordinate it with some other issues you need to discuss tomorrow or the next day.
- **Avoid being left on hold.** If you do have to wait, have another project on hand to review while you wait.
- **Group similar calls.** Make all calls once or twice during the day, and the rest of your day will be more productive. Keep a list handy of the people you are calling so you do not have to look up numbers.
- **Direct-dial your calls.** Very often it is faster and easier to dial yourself than to have an assistant dial for you.
- **Plan the time you are going to make your calls.** Consider when the most convenient times are for both you and the other party.
- **Be sure the call is necessary.** Do you need this information now or could it wait for another meeting?
- **Get to the point.** Before you start your business talk, allow some time to establish rapport, because most people do appreciate it, then get to the point; stay focused and concentrate on the subject.
- **Learn how to break in, if it is required.** Do not interrupt unless it is absolutely necessary. Then do it in an appropriate manner.
- **When you are transferring calls, make sure the person to whom you are referring the call is ready to take it.** If not, tell the caller you will have the person call back in just a few minutes.
- **Thank people.** Remember to use the person's name, because people like to hear their names.

Using Your Voice to Control a Conversation. On the telephone, your voice tells people who you are. You make a very strong impression within 15 seconds. Do you sound weak? Hesitant? Wishy-washy? Disorganized? And, remember, you can change the impression you make.

To come across as businesslike, professional, and strong, speak slowly. The normal telephone conversation pace is about 150 words per minute. If you can reduce this to just about 100 words per minute, you will definitely improve your communication level.

The volume and pace of a conversation are very important in winning a person's confidence. Listen to how the other person is speaking. If you are talking to someone who speaks very slowly, perhaps you need to reduce your pace. Or, if you are talking to someone who speaks very loudly and rapidly, you may want to reduce the other person's pace. When people start screaming at you on the telephone, slow down your pace; speak very quietly and very, very slowly. Many times, this calms them down. If you speak loudly and rapidly, it will make these people even more emotional. Your diction and enunciation are very important. Over the phone, we are judged strictly by our voices.

How can you tell what you sound like? Tape yourself making a call so you can analyze how you sound in different situations. That tape has two purposes: it is both a record of client interaction and a tool for improving your effectiveness on the telephone. If you are going to tape a phone conversation, let the client know you are taping it. Then pay attention to what the client says, and to what you say in reply. Is what you are saying really appropriate?

Talk with your whole body. Your posture, expression, and the shape of your mouth affect the way you sound. Your voice is like a window; it expresses everything inside of you. Some people stand when they talk on the phone. If you really want to be in control, standing may help.

Remember your facial expressions. I once accused a psychologist of being vain for having a very large mirror right across from his desk. Later on I thought it might be a good idea. If we saw how we looked when we talk on the telephone, perhaps we would change our ways.

There are many signals people listen for in your voice. They want to know that you are in control of the situation, that you are managing your own reactions. Do not respond emotionally, but reply to the issues at hand.

More than anything, check your attitude. If you are in a bad mood one day, perhaps you should not answer your own telephone. If you have had a really bad day, perhaps you should have someone hold your calls so you do not accidentally sabotage your relationship with your clients. Your secretary might handle this by saying, "I'm sorry, but she's in a meeting. Would you please let me have her return your call when she has time to go over these details with you?" Give your callers a little positive response when you ask for a delay.

Attitude is really important. We have all had experiences when we are talking with a supplier, arguing over a delivery date, and then the next person on the line is one of our very mild-mannered clients. You must answer the phone in the right tone of voice. Take time to restore yourself; poise yourself for that good client.

Many times, we are not able to give people the answers they want to hear. But there are ways of presenting negative news in positive terms. For example, you might say to a client, "How would you like it if we arranged to deliver your furnishings next Friday? We will have our best furniture installers available that day to handle your project." That sounds so much better than saying, "The furniture cannot be delivered until next Friday." The first statement makes Friday into a special day.

The goal of any call you make is to establish a true and positive agreement. You want to express feelings at the same time you are covering the facts. Rapport is very important. Use the person's name as you speak. Refer to various experiences you have had together. Expressing visual and emotional issues verbally is difficult. Creating visual pictures can be helpful.

Say what you mean. Review what you have to do each day so you know what is possible to schedule. Do not say, "I'll take care of it tomorrow," if you know you cannot. It is better to say, "I'll look that over in the morning with my associate to see just what it involves and how soon we can do the final detailing."

The Complaint Call. There is at least one way to handle complaints to ensure that angry clients remain clients. Irate clients love to call, full of anger and issuing unreasonable demands. What should you do? Do not ignore these calls; if clients cannot reach you with a complaint, they will go to another designer. Encourage people to tell you about their problems, and then help them find solutions. But prepare yourself: have your paper in hand ready for note-taking. Check: Are you're in control? Make sure your posture and everything else about you is perfect, because you are going to need all your ammunition.

Learn to separate facts from emotions. This is hard to do when somebody is screaming at you on the other end of the phone. Usually, you hear much more emotion than facts.

Think of it this way: If there were no problems, the whole design process could be handled by a computer, and clients would not need me.

Let angry clients talk. After all, that is why they called. They want to blow off steam. Let them do it, but encourage them to give you the details and define the problem. Ask them what you can do *together* to solve their problem. Try to involve a client in the solution; if you are successful, you will have developed a partner and great client for the future.

Try to win back clients you've lost by using only positive statements. Make notes of what you will say, and change any negatives to positives before you respond.

Long-Distance Savvy. When you are making long-distance phone calls, watch your time zones. They can often work to your advantage, because there are places you can call between 5:00 and 6:00 in the morning and even 6:00 and 7:00 in the evening.

You would be surprised how many mistakes there are in phone bills. We have had as many as four different long-distance services in our offices at one time. Sometimes it's difficult to get lines out of a small community. Check out the services in your area to be sure you will not have a problem getting long-distance lines at primary times.

Conference Calls. The quality of conference calls can vary greatly. You may have a mechanism on your phone that permits you to make conference calls, but you should test it to be sure the communication comes through clearly for everyone involved in the call.

A few years ago, a client we had worked with extensively called me about a fee on a project. We had billed him a considerable amount of money for the furnishings for his project. He had already paid our initial design fee; but, in addition, we had done a great deal of cabinetry and detailing. The client was told he would be billed for the time involved in these areas at our standard rates. This was clearly stated in writing, but the exact amount was left open; he was not sure what the exact bill would be. When he got the bill, he called, irate.

At this point, I said to him, "Here is our story: The furnishings we did, in a sense, sell you, so there is some profit and our design fee in those charges. However, the rest of this project was done by various contractors. We do not receive any compensation, except this billing for this part of the job, nor do we accept any kickbacks from any of the contractors. We bill only for our fee. We also negotiated with several contractors to get you the best-quality workers, as well as the best price possible. I think you'll agree we did a good job. How do you think I should have handled billing for this? You've been a client of ours for probably 15 years at this point, and we've done a lot of work together. Obviously, you feel I've done something wrong. You run a business a lot larger than mine, and if you do not think I did this in the right way, would you explain to me how I could do it better? After all, I can learn a lot from you. You know more about running a business than I do. Most of my career has been spent doing design work."

The client thought about what I had said a little bit, and then said, "No, Mary, I think what you did was exactly right." He thanked me for explaining it to him. When we finished talking, he was very calm. I have done several major jobs for him since.

I used this complaint to build confidence rather than to lose a client. In handling a complaint, make sure you confirm exactly what the client expects from you—what the solution is and what will be done. Then be sure your staff follows through. Do not promise something you cannot do.

Have a plan or outline for every conference call, just as you would for any staff meeting or other kind of conference. A conference call must be well orchestrated, or you will get into trouble.

Moderate your conference calls. As the moderator, introduce all the participants, including yourself. Give their backgrounds, and let each of them make a brief statement. Address the others by name, and ask each speaker for identification so you are sure exactly who is speaking. When you get four or five people from a factory on a call, you are sometimes not sure if you are talking to the sales manager or the production chief. On a conference call, usually you cannot hear as well as you can on a standard two-party call. Speak slowly and clearly.

Cellular or Mobile Phones. Today we are able to use our cell phones to do many masterful things. It is not just a communications tool to keep in touch with our offices or clients. It has become a system for learning. Your cell phone can permit you to be in control of your office and your project no matter where you are. You can manage a project with great detail and skill, even off-site. Listed are some of the advantages our cell phones provide:

- We can be a part of tele- or videoconferencing program that can be part of a Continuing Education Unit (CEU) or other learning program.
- We can view the person we are speaking to.
- We can receive e-mail directly and have instant video imaging.
- We can do banking, check stocks, and have total financial control.
- We can track our projects and the services that are required.
- We can shop and place orders.
- We can pay our bills.
- We can browse the Internet.
- We can take and forward photos instantly.
- We can watch television programs or anything on video.
- We can remotely turn on security systems, appliances, air conditioning, and other systems in our homes or businesses before we arrive.
- We can use the spycam to check on our projects and the individuals doing the work to make sure they are developing as we would like.

How you use this tool effectively depends on your good judgment; it can be the best or worst thing we own. Cellular telephones permit us to run our business and interact with clients whether we are in the studio, on our boat, or in our car. Clients now know we are accessible at all times, and this technology does permit broader use of that valuable commodity called "time"; however, cellular phones do require proper management.

Electronic Faxing. This is especially valuable, because it permits us to immediately distribute the information to everyone in the office through the networking system. It also keeps client files in a very easy-to-manage and readily accessible system through each individual computer, or even your PDA, when you are on a project.

Internet Telephones. Telephone service is now available over the Internet, and it has many advantages. First, you can be at any location; you do not have to have an address. You can work from anywhere, and people will not know where you are. You can set up a conference call online by entering the numbers and clicking your mouse a few times. It is much simpler than doing this with a typical phone system.

This Internet system is called Voice Over Internet Protocol (VOIP). Phone calls are treated the same as any other form of communication—that is, e-mails, instant messages, and digital pictures. Service will work anywhere, and the installation is very easy. This type of service is fierce competition for traditional telephone companies, since it has so many advantages and can be used anywhere in the country. At present, some of the voice quality is not as clear as over a typical telephone line, but this is expected to improve very soon. A telephone on a computer line is one of the hot new technologies that will be affecting many parts of our communication systems.

CONSIDERATIONS

In the future, the creative aspect of our work will be the primary focus of our work, with our management processes designed to complement this focus. The designer who has the ability to build rapport between the business and financial end of the firm and the client will be incredibly valuable to any design firm. Examine all your processes to make sure they are creativity-friendly as well as client- and staff-friendly.

CHAPTER 11

Mastering Financial Management

Good financial management and systems are a requirement for every design firm. More than a few design firms that are excellent at promoting themselves and getting new business later lose their profit for avoidable reasons. It is hard enough to get profitable projects today; let us find ways to keep that profit.

Profit is a measure of success in every form of business, including the design business. No one wants to deal with an unprofitable company. Clients instinctively feel unprofitability jeopardizes their interests. To have a strong business, you need to understand current financial and business ethics and procedures and make sure your relationships with all other companies and people, whether resources or clients, are based on them. No business can continue without a good financial profit structure.

YOUR PROFIT FORECAST

At the beginning of each year, or just before, prepare a profit forecast. Consider where your firm is going—what business you expect to acquire during the next year, how your firm will grow, and what monies will be required.

Then work out the necessary methods to handle your growth or change of focus. This is a prerequisite to preparing your budget and preliminary financial plan for the year. Every firm needs a budget, whether the company is new or has been in operation for years. A profit forecast will enable you to budget in the right areas. It also gives you a basis for comparing where you are actually going as compared with what your expectations are.

CASH MANAGEMENT

The basics of cash management for any interior design firm fall into two areas: cash flow and accounts receivable. Your cash flow projection predicts your expenses for the next several months to a year.

1. Have your accountant work out the details of your general expenses, including overhead, payroll, and any long-term loans on which you make payments. These will vary from week to week and month to month. With this general figure, you will be able to estimate your overall projected expenses.
2. Next, review your accounts receivable, accounts payable, and aging schedules regularly. Each month your bookkeeper or financial manager should give you a list of your accounts receivable and accounts payable and review the payment schedules. Obviously, the closer and tighter control you have over both these issues and the better informed you are, the easier it will be to run your interior design firm. There will be no surprises or emergencies.

Financial management in a firm with fewer than 10 members is generally handled by a part-time bookkeeper, office manager, or administrative assistant who also does the bookkeeping. When the firm grows beyond 10, usually it will require an experienced, full-time bookkeeper. If your firm grows beyond 25, you will also need a business manager. Computer systems have reduced the staffing required by a firm, but the firm must have an individual in charge of making the financial decisions and managing the overall practice. Once a firm becomes larger, a person with a strong financial background is needed to be the financial manager. Firms of every size need to have a certified public accounting firm available as a consultant and advisor.

The general formats of financial management structures are similar in all firms. Larger firms usually will require more extensive accounting than small firms, not only because of their higher volume of business but also because there is usually less immediate involvement of the principals in each and every project.

Your accountant will give you a year-end statement; however, it is generally advisable also to have a monthly financial report or statement showing your financial direction similar to the one illustrated on page 383, Table 11.4 which includes your cash flow projections and your cash planning for the month. These can be done by your bookkeeper on an in-house basis. If you have a financial manager, that person will want to set up appropriate documents suitable for your firm. With different practices, some of the requirements on these statements may vary slightly, but the ones included here show the basics.

Rules of Recordkeeping

Here are a few guidelines for maintaining a worry-free financial system:

1. **Always pay your bills by check or through your petty cash fund.** Do not pay for anything out of pocket; try to keep payments restricted to these two individual funds. Restrict petty cash payments to incidental expenses.
2. **Never pay any form of disbursement in cash.** If you happen to take in cash, do not make any disbursement out of it; deposit the cash and write a check for the disbursement.
3. **Be sure all money that is taken in is properly reported.** This applies to both cash and checks.
4. **Never take any money out of the company for your personal use.** Pay yourself a salary instead. A lot of small businesses run very loosely, which can be quite a problem, especially during an IRS audit. Use separate banking accounts for your design firm and your other businesses or personal funds.
5. **Have your accountant create your recordkeeping system.** A system runs most smoothly when your accountant is comfortable with it.

Cash Flow

Cash flow is critical in managing a business. When you have enough money to pay your bills on a regular basis, obviously it makes things a lot less stressful. Whether you are a new company or have been in business a long time, this is an everyday concern. Many projects take a long time to complete. Some clients pay quickly, whereas others can take six to nine months or even a year.

Many firms doing government work or work for certain corporations need a lot of cash to be able to accept this type of business. Government and these corporations are great clients! They will pay, but not quickly. Often, it takes six months to a year to receive payment for their work. So, consider what your operational expenses are and what you will need to keep things moving in a positive direction. Money is expensive, and, of course, you are in business to use money in an appropriate way. Accounts receivable is such a major factor in cash flow it is treated separately on pages 355–361.

Inventory. Inventory ties up cash. Are all the items you have in stock and those you are buying for inventory really worth having? The cost of maintaining inventory each year is approximately 33 to 38 percent of the cost of the item, based on the costs of insurance, maintenance, and money. It may be better for you to keep a cash reserve for use in other parts of your business than to maintain a large inventory.

Project Completion Times. Slow project completion times are costly. The sooner you complete a project, the faster you will get paid and the better your cash flow will be. Even though you have retainers for every project you start, you still incur additional costs in doing a job. So the faster you wrap it up, the better.

Buying Policies. Interior designers tend to be cautious about buying policies. There are ways of buying effectively and saving large sums of money. The most successful interior design firms I have seen are those with very shrewd buying policies. You may want to consider using a service that will negotiate prices for you and make sure you are getting the best possible prices.

Some firms buy a lot of products, others simply design and charge fees, and still others build products. The more you buy, the more concern you have with your buying procedures. There is a great dollar volume being purchased through interior designers today.

Other fields have been forced to take on more stringent buying policies. The interior design field needs to do the same. Most design firms are not buying as wisely as they could. Look at your practice and its charges. There are firms that purchase in groups; they form cooperatives and buy together, with someone managing it. There are many other interesting approaches to buying today. Our clients expect us to know how to buy products in the most effective way—not just the best price but also the best quality with the least trouble.

Aim to retain use of the funds you have for as long as possible. Ask for extended credit from your major resources so you can keep these monies invested and make a profit from them. This is a shrewd use of available funds.

Investments. Any money taken in as retainers on projects should be put into some type of interest-bearing account, such as a money market fund.

In addition, most firms charge interest on overdue accounts receivable. This helps encourage clients to pay promptly; it also reimburses the firm for extending credit. Some firms earn enough on their money market funds and the interest they charge on overdue accounts receivable to give their employees a very large bonus.

A few years ago, I reviewed the books of an interior design firm that was available for purchase. I was amazed as I examined the company's financial statement to find its major profits came from the interest clients were charged for installment payments. The company's accounts receivable were very large, but the profits from this division were well managed. The company extended a lot of credit, but it was paid well for it.

Accounts Receivable

Accounts receivable are the monies owed to you for services or furnishings you supplied to your clients. Good control of accounts receivable is extremely important to the financial profitability of a company. The profit objective is to speed up the whole process of design management. This means the faster you can process any job through the studio—no matter what kind of service is rendered—the faster it can be billed and the more profitable the project will be. Generally, billings in design firms are done either in advance, immediately after the project is completed, when the merchandise is delivered, or within a 30-day period. Designers who are lax in this area may have no idea how much slow billings cost them on a day-to-day basis.

When establishing and managing accounts receivable, keep in mind that the fewer dollars you have tied up in accounts receivable, the easier it is to manage the cash flow of your business and the smaller your losses will be. The longer an account remains unpaid, the greater the chances are it will become uncollectible. The sooner you bring money in, the more you have to work with or reinvest. Often, clients will avoid doing business with a firm to which they owe money. Therefore, the sooner a client's account is paid, the faster the client will start another project.

Maintaining accounts receivable costs at least 1.5 percent a month. This can take a tremendous bite out of your profits. A company whose accounts receivable are current is usually very profitable. Sometimes this requires that you adopt a tougher payment policy. If clients do not pay on time, you should consider stopping work. I know interior designers are reluctant to do this, but it may be your best leverage in getting payment. Many designers require payment before, rather than after, delivery. Obviously, whether this is suitable depends on the standards in your part of the country. Progress payments or staged payments are becoming the norm in most billing systems. The faster payments are received, the more profitable the job.

Sadly, many companies with a string of great design jobs have been forced into bankruptcy because they did not properly handle their accounts receivable. It is extremely disheartening to see designers forced out of business because their clients did not pay their bills.

Credit Checks. Before accepting a job, carefully investigate and analyze the client's ability to pay for the job. Determine exactly what the costs will be and ask what the client's position is in handling this expenditure.

Often, projects grow as they develop, and the initial budget is not enough to meet the costs. Clients who expected a project to cost perhaps $300,000 may find that, with the additions they requested, the work ends up costing $450,000 to $500,000. The client may need to get financing for the additional amount. I recommend making a credit check of the client in the initial or early interview stages, while your financial involvement in the project is relatively small. Do not wait until you are into a second or third contracting phase when a lot of money is at stake; it will be too late. If you find the client does not have the cash available, you can attempt to get it for the client through your sources.

The information you have collected regarding your client's credit should remain with the project file so the person responsible for collecting accounts receivable will have it available.

Terms. To establish your accounts receivable terms, you will need to have your accountant, financial advisor, attorney, and marketing consultant make a careful study, since these terms affect every part of your business. If you extend credit, you must have the capital available to support this investment. Every dollar invested must fit into your profit structure. Collection policies affect your future collection and legal costs. Your terms affect your ability to get jobs.

In most instances, designers will ask for a retainer or deposit on a project. The term "retainer," rather than "deposit," is used because certain states require deposits to be kept in a special account for that particular client's project. These funds cannot be put in your company's general account or used for any other purposes.

The amount of the retainer depends on the type of work being done. If the project is for professional services, excluding purchasing, for a small, private corporation, a normal retainer is half the estimated cost of the first phase of the project. For a larger project, the retainer is related to the details of the contract. Sometimes a contract alone is considered sufficient, and no retainer is required. In other instances, the retainer required could be from one-tenth to one-half of the total fee, depending on the size of the project. For a very large project, the retainer is often as low as 10 percent of the total estimated fee. Retainers for smaller projects range from one-third to one-half of the estimated fee. In situations when the billing is based on furnishings, retainers are usually one-third to one-half of the expected invoice total.

Scheduled Payments. In dealing with accounts receivable, it is obviously to the advantage of the design firm to get a retainer, followed by scheduled payments throughout the project. If you are billing just for professional service fees, it is best to have a payment schedule outlining the stages and amounts of payments.

The standard method of presenting a payment schedule is to list the stages of completion and state the percentage of payments due at these times.

Stage of Completion	*Amount Due*
Design	40%
Documentation	40%
Administration	20%

Although more than 20 percent may be spent for administration and supervision, it is always an advantage to collect as much of the fee up front, or at a set point, rather than at the end of the project. Billing on completion requires a considerable amount of bookkeeping and time spent evaluating your hours.

As you define the project to be done, work out a payment schedule and submit it to the client with your initial agreement, so that the client knows exactly when monies are expected and how much to pay.

Most design firms take from two weeks to 30 days to invoice clients after work is completed. Then it takes the client another 30 days to pay the invoice. With a payment schedule, you can often get your payments in much faster. Knowing ahead of time that there is a certain amount due in January, March, and June, for example, the client can then arrange to have funds available.

Extending Credit. Most businesses, including interior design firms, must extend credit. It is important to establish the terms of credit before starting a project. These should be stated at the time of the proposal. Often, your company needs to establish a credit policy. It can be changed at any time, but you must start somewhere. Your policy concept could state that you will receive a retainer of a certain amount or percentage up front, that there will be progressive payments due as the project continues, and that the balance is due 10 to 30 days after delivery. You can offer extended terms by use of a bank or other lending institution, or you can make financing available through the firm at a certain cost rate, depending what state law allows.

New Credit Card Regulations

Most interior design firms accept credit cards. Today, we must be concerned about the privacy of our customers' credit card information.

Visa and MasterCard enacted regulations to provide cardholders with greater security when they use their cards. This initiative is called "Cardholder Account Number Truncation" and is intended to eliminate pieces of the cardholder's account on the customer copy of the sales slip.

The guidelines are:

- No more than the last four digits of a credit card number can be printed on customers' receipts generated by electronic terminals.
- The expiration date must be blocked.
- Only the merchant copy of the receipt may display the entire card number and expiration date.

To be in compliance with these rules, call your credit processor, who should be able to assist you in downloading applications to update your software or instruct you on how to upgrade your equipment.

Invoicing Methods. At the time the client places the orders for work, before delivering merchandise, firms notify the client of the date and time you expect to make the delivery and the dollar value of the furnishings. They state when the payment will be due. This paves the way for prompt payment because the client knows in advance what you expect. Invoicing is normally done on the day items are shipped or on a weekly or a monthly basis.

The location of your firm and business customs of the area will determine your invoicing methods somewhat. In larger cities, payment is often expected in advance on delivery. A week prior to the day of a delivery, a firm will send a note saying, for example, "We are going to deliver the furnishings for your facility next Thursday. Enclosed is an invoice for $65,000 for the furnishings we will be installing. We will appreciate having your check available on the day of delivery." In some areas, however, this is not considered proper business courtesy.

When you are preparing the billing and dealing with accounts receivable, it is definitely to your advantage to get invoices out as soon as possible. In some design firms, it takes 30 days to process a bill, which can be self-defeating to the cash flow situation. At my firm, we aim to send out our invoices within three days of delivery. This requires us to have our data organized. Obviously, there are times when certain items are being shipped or delivered faster than your invoicing procedures can keep up with them, but the sooner you are able to generate your billings, the better your cash position will be.

If you do not bill in advance or send an invoice with the delivery, then invoices should go out within 72 hours of the time merchandise is delivered so clients can easily identify what they are being asked to pay for. If they receive billings a month later, they might not recall what arrived on specific days of the month.

A delay in billing also signals to your client your firm is not efficiently run or you do not need the money. Do not delay. It is a foolishly lax business habit. Billing is best done on a daily or weekly basis. Waiting for the end of the month can be too confusing and too expensive.

Insist any client invoice be checked thoroughly before it is sent out to ensure there are no mistakes. If a client finds errors in the billing, the client will often question the whole costing procedure. A bit of care in this area can prevent a lot of complaints. If clients find you are careless in finances, they will worry you may be careless in other areas, too.

Often, designers have difficulty collecting bills because they have not properly documented items or stayed in regular contact with their clients. This is absolutely necessary. Regularly scheduled reports by telephone with proper written documentation build rapport.

Check with your bookkeeping department to be sure your invoices are going out regularly. Do not accept excuses. Determine how quickly all of your orders can be processed and shipped. Tightening this lead time can give a boost to your cash flow.

Billing Sheets. When you are preparing to send out bills, a billing sheet is helpful. A sample of a simple billing sheet is shown for reference in Table 11.1 (page 360). If you use an accounting and project management software package, it should be able to provide you with similar data. Ask your bookkeeper to present all the items to be billed. The designer or project manager can then compare the amounts that were quoted against the actual costs and determine the appropriate prices to charge. This is an excellent billing method for both professional services and products, even if fees are based on value rather than actual time spent. The data on your billing sheet will give you a basis for determining the costing for your next project.

Require a monthly status report from your bookkeeper, outlining all client accounts and exactly what position they are in. (See Table 11.4, page 383, for a sample "monthly financial report.") Be sure the designer or the client coordinator is aware of exactly how these accounts stand.

Delinquent Payments. You must outline your firm's policy for delinquent payments at the beginning of a relationship. Spell out to your client how much and how often you expect to be paid. There are some clients who feel it is acceptable to pay an invoice within 90 or 120 days; other suppliers have extended them such credit to create loyalty. An integrated accounting system will help you see exactly where you stand and keep you up to date on the position of your clients' accounts.

Sometimes, the only way to control payments on a project is to have an assertive

Table 11.1 Billing sheet. The data on your billing sheet will give you a basis for determining appropriate prices and fees to charge. It will also help you to cost your next project.

BILLING SHEET								
Client:		Salesperson:			Date:			
Order No.:	Item:	Quote:		Unit:		Price:		
		Unit:	Total:	Unit:	Total:	Unit:	Total:	
Totals:								
Deposit Balance on Hand:				Sales Tax:				
				Total Billing:				
Orders in Process:				Less Deposit:				
				Amount Due:				

© *Design Business Monthly,* 1988.

business manner. Stop-work clauses are now becoming common in design contracts. These clauses state that the design firm has the right to stop work on a project if the client is in any way delinquent in making payments. The right to stop work on a design project must be clearly stated in the initial contract.

It is important to have your bookkeeper continuously follow up with clients regarding the status of their open accounts. This will identify clients who are paying promptly as well as uncover any problems or situations you may need to address.

Collections. Enforcing your accounts receivable procedures requires strict follow-up. You do not want to harass people, but you do want to find out why they have not paid their bills and how they intend to handle them. In my firm, we will normally make other terms available to clients if they cannot pay us promptly. And we do so with tact, explaining we cannot afford to carry large amounts in our accounts receivable. We also have a delinquency charge. In Pennsylvania, we are permitted to charge 1.5 percent of the balance due after 30 days.

Understanding a person's credit situation can help in collecting a payment. It is often useful to have a discussion about the client's payment habits with the other people working on the project.

Collection costs for accounts receivable are very high. Therefore, it is important to find ways to get your monies in ahead of time so you do not have to worry about collections. Although collection agencies can help collect bills, they charge from 25 to 50 percent, and their success rate is not as great as one would like. Often, you can also collect your delinquent accounts through the small claims court and other legal means. The legal force you can apply will vary, depending on the size of the claim and the type of legal recourse you have. Keep in mind, however, if you are forced to turn over a bill to a collection agency or an attorney, that is usually the last time you will ever see that client.

> Some clients are habitually late in paying, even though they are good credit risks. In my firm, we ask for payment within 30 days, and we encourage prompt payment by explaining to our clients that the pricing on their job is dependent on our being paid within 30 days. We ask to be notified if they cannot pay us within 30 days, so we can make arrangements accordingly.

Accounts Payable

Accounts payable is the system wherein you record all the expenses of the firm: materials, wages, rent, utilities, taxes, and so on. There are many ways to set up an accounts payable system. The standard ledger system is one.

Accounts Payable Systems. Before we had so many user-friendly accounting software programs available, I recommended the one-write check disbursement system for small design firms. When the bookkeeper wrote a check, the amount was automatically duplicated onto the disbursement journal so there was no chance for numbers to be transposed; they were automatically entered into the journal and then onto the ledger page. This system is still very useful for the smaller firm or for someone who does not want to use a computer.

Project Management and Accounting Software. Today there are many computerized software systems that work well for an interior design practice. The best systems integrate project management and accounting into one package to help you efficiently and effectively manage your projects as well as your office. Some systems are dedicated specifically to the interior design profession, such as Studio IT and Design Manager. There are also more general products, such as QuickBooks Professional Services Edition or QuickBooks Contractor Edition, which many interior designers find work well for their firms. Since QuickBooks is a commonly used program, most accounting firms are very familiar with it. And compared to a design-specific program, they are less expensive.

All of the packages have similarities. They all can do the following:

- Maintain lists of clients, vendors, and employees. This information can be retrieved readily when you need it.
- Maintain project information, including the various items that comprise a project.

- Create and maintain proposals and estimates.
- Create and maintain purchase orders.
- Create invoices for clients and enter payments received for those invoices, as well as retainers on account.
- Enter invoices and write checks.
- Enter employee time, to generate client billings as well as process payroll.

As similar as the systems may seem, however, they have almost as many differences. These differences are primarily:

- The user interface—that is, the appearance of the data screens.
- The way data is organized in the program.
- The amount of detailed information you can retrieve and how you can retrieve it.
- The types and content of the reports that can be produced by the software and whether you can easily sort, filter, or otherwise manipulate the information to generate custom reports.
- The ease of use of the programs, based on the user's knowledge or comfort level with computer software.
- Whether the data can be easily exported to other software, such as Excel or Word, or sent to output, such as e-mail.
- Price and scale of the software. The QuickBooks programs can be purchased at many office supply stores for around $500. Studio Designer and Design Manager programs must be purchased directly from the manufacturers, and they start at approximately $500 for a basic program. Modules can be added to the two designer-specific programs to accommodate networking, multiple users, and features such as inventory and time management.

Before selecting a specific program, I suggest you carefully look at the way you work. It is fine to make some adjustments to fit a computerized system, but it is often disastrous if you have to change everything you do just because this is the way the system does it. You have a management system. You have a familiar charging system. If these are working well for you, try to find a computer program as close to your present style as possible.

Another consideration when selecting a software package is who will actually be using the system and what is their skill level. Is training readily available for the system? If you rely on your accountant to provide you with interim financial reports or to support your office, does the accountant have the software expertise to assist you with this? Your accountant or computer software advisor can help you sort through the various software packages to identify the best match between your work structure and the capabilities of the systems.

You may find as you move into an integrated software program for your project management and accounting needs that your staffing may change. If you use all of the functions of the program, you may no longer need a full-time bookkeeper for your accounting functions or a full-time design assistant to track the projects. The software may be able to quickly and accurately provide you with the information you need without as much effort. You may find these staff members can now provide you with more information in a more timely manner to help you build your business.

In conclusion, there are two primary needs to consider: your management and your accountant. Each requires quality information from the program. Your design team needs information to run a professional business. Your accountant is responsible for presenting accurate information about your firm to various government and tax entities. Use of the appropriate computer software can help you meet both these needs with relative ease.

Suggestions for Selecting Computerized Accounting Systems

1. Define your management and charging systems.
2. Review several systems before determining which one is most appropriate to your way of working.
3. Work with your bookkeeper or accountant to set up the accounting system to ensure it will meet their reporting needs. Have your design team define the project management system to provide a smooth workflow of project documents and reports.
4. Obtain training on the software program through the software manufacturer, a local computer school, or other software professional.
5. Have your accountant review the general ledger on a regular basis—at least quarterly in the first year—to be sure the accounting system is working correctly and capturing the correct data. Find and make all necessary corrections early in the cycle.
6. Use the software in a completely integrated system for all accounts receivable, accounts payable, payroll, and job costing. Using an automated accounting system will enable you to keep accurate, valuable information in an extremely efficient manner.

Establishing Credit with Your Accounts. Today, there are several approaches to handling accounts payable that vary from those of the past. For most small design firms, the top priority is to keep a good credit rating and remain in good standing with their resources.

Establish credit with your resource companies; do not expect them to extend it. Before you start placing orders with a resource company, ask what amount of credit the resource is willing to extend to you. If you wait until you place an order, a credit check can delay your project by at least 30 days. This can cause a lot of problems if you have already quoted your client from the price list and you cannot buy directly from the company but have to go through a dealership or another resource. Ask the company what the discounting procedures are, and verify buying requirements before you attempt to sell the merchandise. If you only specify merchandise and do not get involved in any purchasing, understanding the credit policies of resource companies lets you judge reasonably how well the dealerships are handling your client accounts.

Many of our resources do not like working with small accounts, which is the typical designer account. They prefer dealerships and large-volume accounts, because these are less expensive to manage and are safer financial risks.

Unfortunately, because the economy has been changing and credit has been tightening, many resource companies require interior design firms to work on a cash-before-delivery (CBD) or cash-on-delivery (COD) basis. Generally, the larger established firms do not work in this manner. Many of them will not accept any CBD or COD shipments, but many will be happy to accept your credit cards.

COD

The U.S. Post Office permits any recipients to pay a COD bill with a check made out to the mailer. The reasoning is that if there is a problem with the merchandise, the recipient may stop payment on the check if the merchandise was damaged.

To be issued credit by a resource company, you must be a viable and valuable account. Manufacturers and dealers will not bother doing the necessary credit checks and establishing the bookkeeping process for an account that means a few hundred dollars' worth of business every now and then. That simply does not pay. It costs companies too much to investigate your company, determine how much credit they should give you, and maintain this relationship.

Credit checks and ongoing evaluations are affordable only for larger-volume accounts. When a design firm decides to buy for clients, the firm needs to position itself. A careful review of your financial and corporate position must be made by your financial advisor, lawyer, and marketing manager. The firm needs to establish an appropriate financial structure for obtaining credit and handling the required capital investment.

There are many other ways design firms can handle the purchasing part of the job; some of these are proving to be easier to manage and more profitable. Cooperatives or buying organizations are becoming increasingly popular, since they can negotiate from a position of strength.

Obviously, you want to be able to go back to a company and say, "We have a problem and what can we do about it?" and have some clout. This must be worked out in the process of establishing your accounts.

Resource companies also have financial management requirements. They have based their profits on time schedules and turnaround schedules. If design firms do not pay their bills on time, the resources have to protect themselves, which is why they must have strict terms. Companies are constantly notifying us, or even threatening us, with changes in their credit policies. For example:

Effective January 1, 2005, we are establishing new credit policies. Any account that is not paid within 30 days of the invoice date will be handled on a CBD basis with future purchases.

Figure 11.1 Sample proposal form from Design Manager Professional. Note the ability to show a picture of the product on the proposal.

PRO VERSION SAMPLE FORMS
Your Company Name and Address
Your City, PA 18901
Phone: (215) 345-0844 Fax: (215) 345-7243

Proposal
ROBE / Kenneth L. Roberts
No.: 0001
May 13, 2004
Page 1 of 1

To: Kenneth L Roberts
       7142 Church School Road
       Jordantown, PA 19853

Quantity	Description	Unit Price	Extended Price

Home Office

1	**Bookcase** - 58 5/8" wide x 15 3/8" deep x 58/58" high. Max load/shelf: 29 lbs. The fixed shelf and main frame are made of oak, printed and embossed lacquer, and clear lacquer. The suspension rail is steel and powder coating. A saftey anchoring device is included. *Please Note*: The baskets are not included but can be purchased separately. *Ref. #: 0002*	748.50	748.50
1	*Swivel Chair* - 24 3/4" wide x 24 3/4" deep x 38 5/8" high. Designed for heavy use with steel frame. Cover consists of cotton, wool, and nylon and is not removable. The foam interior consists of high resilient polyurethane foam (cold foam). The seat is adjustable starting at 16 1/2" and can be raised to 20 1/2". A lockable tilter tension is designed for safe change of position. The star base consists of aluminum and powder coating. *Ref. #: 0003*	583.50	583.50

Item Total	1,332.00
Freight	57.50
Sales Tax	83.37
Grand Total	1,472.87

Designer _____ Date _____

Approved _____ Date _____

Requested Deposit	**$736.44**

This is a sample Proposal printed from Design Manager Professional.
You can use this space to enter remarks, terms, and conditions.
You can type up to 64,000 characters in this area.
The text may be **in bold**, in color, *in italics*, underlined ***and any combination***.

Figure 11.2 Sample purchase order form from Design Manager Professional.

PRO VERSION SAMPLE FORMS
Your Company Name and Address
Your City, PA 18901
Phone: (215) 345-0844 Fax: (215) 345-7243

Purchase Order
PO No.: **ROBE-0001**
Date: 5/13/2004
Page 1 of 1

To: The Elegant Furniture Store
        234 Main Street
        Smalltown, PA 16532

        Contact: John
        Phone: (215) 555-5555 Fax: (215) 555-5556

Ship To: Kenneth L Roberts
          7142 Church School Road
          Jordantown, PA 19853

          Contact: Ken
          Phone: (888) 233-4455

Ship By	Ship Via	Account	Terms

Quantity	Description	Unit Cost	Extended Cost
1	**Bookcase** - 58 5/8" wide x 15 3/8" deep x 58/58" high. Max load/shelf: 29 lbs. The fixed shelf is made of particleboard, ABS plastic, printed and embossed lacquer, and clear lacquer. The main parts are particleboard fiberboard, ABS plastic, printed and embossed lacquer and clear lacquer. The suspension rail is steel and powder coating. A saftey anchoring device is included. *Ref#: 0002/001* **Catalog No.:** BC-107-002	499.00	499.00
1	***Swivel Chair*** - 24 3/4" wide x 24 3/4" deep x 38 5/8" high. Designed for heavy use with steel frame. Cover consists of cotton, wool, and nylon and is not removable. The foam interior consists of high resilient polyurethane foam (cold foam). The seat is adjustable starting at 16 1/2" and can be raised to 20 1/2". A lockable tilter tension is designed for safe change of position. The star base consists of aluminum and powder coating. *Ref#: 0003/001* **Catalog No.:** CH-047-003	389.00	389.00

Deposit Enclosed: **$444.00**

Authorized Signature: _____   Date: _____

Item Total	888.00
Freight	50.00
Grand Total	938.00

Figure 11.3 Sample invoice from Design Manager Professional.

PRO VERSION SAMPLE FORMS
Your Company Name and Address
Your City, PA 18901
Phone: (215) 345-0844 Fax: (215) 345-7243

INVOICE
No. 10004 / ROBE
Kenneth L. Roberts
5/13/2004
Page 1 of 1

Net Due Upon Receipt

Bill To: Kenneth L Roberts
7142 Church School Road
Jordantown, PA 19853

Ship To: Kenneth L Roberts
7142 Church School Road
Jordantown, PA 19853

Quantity	Description	Unit Price	Extended Price
Home Office			
1	**Bookcase** - 58 5/8" wide x 15 3/8" deep x 58/58" high. Max load/shelf: 29 lbs. The fixed shelf and main frame are made of oak, printed and embossed lacquer, and clear lacquer. The suspension rail is steel and powder coating. A saftey anchoring device is included.	748.50	748.50
	Please Note: The baskets are not included but can be purchased separately. *Ref. #: 0002*		
1	*Swivel Chair* - 24 3/4" wide x 24 3/4" deep x 38 5/8" high. Designed for heavy use with steel frame. Cover consists of cotton, wool, and nylon and is not removable. The foam interior consists of high resilient polyurethane foam (cold foam). The seat is adjustable starting at 16 1/2" and can be raised to 20 1/2". A lockable tilter tension is designed for safe change of position. The star base consists of aluminum and powder coating. *Ref. #: 0003*	583.50	583.50

Item Total	1,332.00
Freight	57.50
Sales Tax	83.37
Invoice Total	1,472.87
Less Deposit	-736.44
Balance Due	736.43

* *Denotes nontaxable*

All sales are final. Please contact our billing department if you have any questions.

Thank you for your business!

Figure 11.4 Sample report, "Profit Analysis—Project Summary," from Design Manager Professional. Note the ability to sort data in a variety of ways.

Profit Analysis—Project Summary

Franklin-Potter Associates

Ranges: All Projects. All Sales Categories.
All Locations. All Managers.
All Proposals. All Invoices.

Printed: 9/9/2004 at 11:02:08AM
Page: 1

Project	Cost		Price		Profit		Gross Profit %		Mark-Up %	
	Estimate	Actual	Estimate	Actual	Estimate	Actual	Estimate	Actual	Estimate	Actual
2124 / Lot 10 - Allenworth	108,314.81	34,588.44	124,746.07	45,366.14	16,431.26	10,777.70	13.17	23.76	15.17	31.16
2217 / The Ridings Model Townhome	249,696.88	115,601.23	296,001.88	11,808.03	46,305.00	-103,793.20	15.64	-879.01	18.54	-89.79
Total All Projects:	358,011.69	150,189.67	420,747.95	57,174.17	62,736.26	-93,015.50	14.91	-162.69	17.52	-61.93

2 Projects Listed

Figure 11.5 Sample proposal form from Studio Designer. Note the ability to show a picture of the product on the proposal.

Studio Interiors, Ltd.
49 West 11th Avenue
Denver, Colorado 80204

Mr. and Mrs. Brian Douglas
44005 Pacific Coast Highway
Los Angeles, CA 90069

Proposal
001
03/06/2003

Dining Room

Quantity:	1
Unit:	Each
Description:	Panache Designs 1115 Goya Center Table
	52 X 29 (WxDxH)
	Light Barcelona, Iron stretcher in aged rust
	Walnut with iron stretchers
	Top planked in banded border
	Custom cadroned edge detail

Unit Price: $0.00
Total Price: $0.00

Quantity:	1
Unit:	Each
Description:	Panache Designs 1800 La Scala Chandelier (16 Arm)
	43 x 46 (DxH)
	48 Distress Bronze Gold
	Iron in aged rust finish

Unit Price: $0.00
Total Price: $0.00

Sub Total:	$0.00
Freight:	$0.00
Crating:	$0.00
Installation:	$0.00
Other:	$0.00
Sales Tax:	$0.00
Total:	$0.00

Accepted and Approved

Deposit Requested: $0.00

Mr. and Mrs. Brian Douglas   Date

Figure 11.6 Sample purchase order form from Studio Designer.

Studio I.T., Inc.
49 West 11th Avenue
Denver, CO 80204

Phone 720-932-1235   Fax: 720-932-1285

Purchase Order

23
5/27/2004

To:
Max Furniture
800 Lexington Avenue, Suite 2300
New York, NY 10021

Phone: 212-440-8841   **Fax:** 212-440-8842

Ship To:
Canyon Designer's Warehouse
608 East Ridge Park Highway
Vail, CO 80446

Phone: 720-530-5200   **Fax:** 720-530-5200

Client: DOUGLAS
Project:
Proposal #: 0001
Ship Via: Best Way
Terms: 50% Deposit
FOB:

Account #:
Attention:
Date Req:
Sidemark: STUDIO I.T. / DOUGLAS / ENTRY / Marble Top for Ven

Quantity	Unit	Description	Unit Cost	Total Cost
1	Each	Venetian Console with Marble Top Console Finish: Natural Wheat	$3,470.00	$3,470.00
1	Each	Marble Top for Venetian Console	$910.00	$910.00

Sub Total:	$4,380.00
Freight:	$0.00
Crating:	$0.00
Installation:	$0.00
Other:	$0.00
Sales Tax:	$0.00
Total:	$4,380.00
Deposit Payment:	$2,190.00

Figure 11.7   Sample product invoice from Studio Designer.

Studio I.T., Inc.				**Invoice**
49 West 11th Avenue				1
Denver, CO 80204				5/27/2004

Phone 720-932-1235   Fax: 720-932-1285

Mr. & Mrs. Brian Douglas
44005 Pacific Coast Highway
Laguna Beach, CA 94401

Project:

Quantity	Unit	Description	Unit Price	Total Price
		Entry		
1	Each	Venetian Console with Marble Top	$4,511.00	$4,511.00
			Sub Total:	$4,511.00
			Freight:	$0.00
			Crating:	$0.00
			Installation:	$0.00
			Other:	$0.00
			Sales Tax:	$372.15
			Total:	$4,883.15
			Payments Received:	$4,883.15
			Balance Due:	$0.00

Figure 11.8 Sample time billing invoice from Studio Designer.

Studio I.T., Inc.
49 West 11th Avenue
Denver, CO 80204

Time Billing Invoice

29

5/27/2004

Phone 720-932-1235   Fax: 720-932-1285

Mr. & Mrs. Brian Douglas
44005 Pacific Coast Highway
Laguna Beach, CA 94401

Date	Description	Hours	Rate	Amount
5/27/2004	Client meeting regarding floor plans and furniture proposal.	2.5	$120.00	$300.00
5/27/2004	Shopping with client at design center for guest bedroom fabric selection.	2.5	$120.00	$300.00
			Sub Total:	$600.00
			Sales Tax:	$0.00
			Total:	$600.00
			Payments:	$0.00
			Balance Due:	$600.00

Figure 11.9 Sample report, "Project Worksheet Summary by Client," from Studio Designer. Note how concisely the financial status of a project, both purchases and sales, are presented.

Project Worksheet Summary by Client

Client	Project	Purchase	Payments	Balance	Selling	Payments	Balance
DOUGLAS		$22,636.00	$4,217.00	$18,419.00	$31,176.32	$11,722.16	$19,454.16
DOUGLAS	PARADISE	$9,115.50	$0.00	$9,115.50	$12,713.30	$7,861.10	$4,852.20
GOLDMAN		$12,548.00	$4,310.00	$8,238.00	$17,441.45	$17,441.45	$0.00
NICHOLS		$9,335.00	$2,212.50	$7,122.50	$12,874.06	$12,874.06	$0.00
SMITH		$9,528.00	$3,540.00	$5,988.00	$13,123.50	$11,614.20	$1,509.30
TAYLOR		$5,636.00	$2,037.50	$3,598.50	$7,811.38	$6,575.24	$1,236.14
		$68,798.50	**$16,317.00**	**$52,481.50**	**$95,140.01**	**$68,088.21**	**$27,051.80**

9/8/2004
9:51 AM

Page 1 of 1

Figure 11.10 Sample report, "Project Profit Analysis by Client," from Studio Designer. The report summarizes time and product data for each client.

Project Profit Analysis by Client

Client	Time Billing	Time Cost	Time Profit	Selling	Purchase	Item Profit	Total Profit
DOUGLAS	$1,165.00	$0.00	$1,165.00	$40,860.95	$31,751.50	$9,109.45	$10,274.45
GOLDMAN	$503.50	$0.00	$503.50	$16,312.40	$12,548.00	$3,764.40	$4,267.90
NICHOLS	$462.00	$0.00	$462.00	$12,135.50	$9,335.00	$2,800.50	$3,262.50
SMITH	$1,945.00	$0.00	$1,945.00	$12,386.40	$9,528.00	$2,858.40	$4,803.40
TAYLOR	$1,782.50	$0.00	$1,782.50	$7,326.80	$5,636.00	$1,690.80	$3,473.30

Project Profit Analysis by Proposal

Client DOUGLAS   Mr. & Mrs. Brian Douglas
Project

Item	Vendor	Description	Proposal	P.O. #	Invoice #	Budget	Actual	Variance	Selling	Purchase	Profit
019 004 A	EUROFAB	Queen Duvet Cover				$0.00	$455.00	$455.00	$455.00	$350.00	$105.00
						$0.00	**$455.00**	**$455.00**	**$455.00**	**$360.00**	**$105.00**
001 001 A	MAX	Venetian Console with Ma	0001	23	1	$0.00	$4,883.15	$4,883.15	$4,511.00	$3,470.00	$1,041.00
001 001 B	MAX	Marble Top for Venetian C	0001	23	2	$0.00	$1,280.60	$1,280.60	$1,183.00	$910.00	$273.00
001 002 A	STAR	Tulip Iron Sconces	0001	27	3	$0.00	$1,266.53	$1,266.53	$1,170.00	$900.00	$270.00
001 003 A	GOLDEN	Reupholster Side Chair	0001	1	4	$0.00	$527.72	$527.72	$487.50	$375.00	$112.50
001 003 B	EUROFAB	Fabric for Side Chair	0001	24	5	$0.00	$499.20	$499.20	$499.20	$384.00	$115.20
						$0.00	**$8,457.20**	**$8,457.20**	**$7,850.70**	**$6,039.00**	**$1,811.70**
023 001 A	MAX	Venetian Pedestal Sink	0002	3	9	$0.00	$1,927.93	$1,927.93	$1,781.00	$1,370.00	$411.00
023 002 A	GOLDEN	Reupholster Vanity Chair	0002			$0.00	$499.58	$499.58	$461.50	$355.00	$106.50
023 002 B	EUROFAB	Vanity Chair Fabric	0002			$0.00	$450.45	$450.45	$450.45	$346.50	$103.95
023 003 A	MAX	18th Century Venetian Wa	0002	2	9	$0.00	$2,420.47	$2,420.47	$2,236.00	$2,040.00	$196.00
						$0.00	**$5,298.43**	**$5,298.43**	**$4,928.95**	**$4,111.50**	**$817.45**
015 001 A	MAX	Mahagony Desk with Marl	0004			$0.00	$5,066.10	$5,066.10	$4,680.00	$3,600.00	$1,080.00
015 001 B	STELLA	Natural Wax Finish for Ma	0004	26	6	$0.00	$387.00	$387.00	$357.50	$275.00	$82.50
						$0.00	**$5,463.10**	**$6,463.10**	**$5,037.50**	**$3,876.00**	**$1,162.50**
015 002 A	MAX	Venice Open Armchair	0005	29	7	$0.00	$1,175.06	$1,175.06	$1,085.50	$835.50	$250.50
015 002 B	EUROFAB	Fabric for Venice Armchai	0005	28	8	$0.00	$403.00	$403.00	$403.00	$310.00	$93.00
015 002 C	STELLA	Stained Finish for Venice	0005			$0.00	$267.38	$267.38	$247.00	$190.00	$57.00
						$0.00	**$1,845.44**	**$1,845.44**	**$1,735.50**	**$1,335.00**	**$400.50**
015 003 A	STAR	Regency Candlestick Lam	0006			$0.00	$2,068.66	$2,068.66	$1,911.00	$1,470.00	$441.00
015 004 A	MAX	Custom Area Rug	0006			$0.00	$2,077.10	$2,077.10	$1,918.80	$1,476.00	$442.80
						$0.00	**$4,145.76**	**$4,145.76**	**$3,829.80**	**$2,946.00**	**$883.80**
019 001 A	MAX	Moonshadow Queen Uph	0007			$0.00	$1,618.34	$1,618.34	$1,495.00	$1,150.00	$345.00
019 001 B	EUROFAB	Fabric for Headboard	0007			$0.00	$568.10	$568.10	$568.10	$437.00	$131.10

9/8/2004
9:54 AM

Figure 11.11 Sample report, "Project Profit Analysis by Proposal," from Studio Designer. This report summarizes the components of a proposal to show its profitability.

The Expeditor by Action Date

Employee	Action	Action Date	Completed	Description	Company	EMail	Date EMail	Entered	Item
LANCE	CFA	5/27/2004		Request Cutting for Approval				7/7/2002	Fabric for Oxford Sofa
LANCE	CFA	5/27/2004		Request Cutting for Approval				7/7/2002	Fabric for Custom Sofa
LANCE	CFA APROV	5/27/2004	5/27/2004	CFA Approved				7/7/2002	Vanity Chair Fabric
LANCE	CFA APROV	5/27/2004	5/27/2004	CFA Approved				7/7/2002	Fabric for Headboard
LANCE	COM	5/27/2004		Check to see if COM arrived				7/7/2002	Fabric for Chaise Lounge
LANCE	COM ARRIV	5/27/2004	5/27/2004	COM Arrived				7/7/2002	Club Chair with Linen Fabric
LANCE	COM ARRIV	5/27/2004	5/27/2004	COM Arrived				7/7/2002	Fabric for Chaise Lounge
LANCE	EMAIL C	5/27/2004		Email Client regarding finish		GOLDMAN		7/7/2002	Marble Wall Sconces
LANCE	EMAIL C	5/27/2004		Email Client regarding delivery date		TAYLOR		7/7/2002	Club Chair with Linen Fabric
LANCE	EMAIL V	5/27/2004		Email Vendor regarding marble color		MAX		7/7/2002	Venetian Console with Marbl
LANCE	EMAIL V	5/27/2004		Email Vendor regarding electrical wiring		STAR		7/7/2002	Iron Floor Lamps
LANCE	EMAIL V	5/27/2004		Email Vendor regarding chintz selection		GOLDEN		7/7/2002	King Headboard Upholstereq
LANCE	NOTE	5/27/2004		Note - Fabric will ship on 7/20/2002				7/7/2002	Fabric for Headboard
LANCE	NOTE	5/27/2004		Note - Finish sample approved.				7/7/2002	Finish for Custom Slatted Si
LANCE	PHONE	5/27/2004		Phone client to verify finish sample				7/7/2002	Oak Dining Room Table
LANCE	PHONE	5/27/2004	5/27/2004	Phone - Client called regarding install				7/7/2002	Custom Area Rug
LANCE	PHONE	5/27/2004	5/27/2004	Phone - Client called regarding measurements				7/7/2002	Custom Area Rug

9/8/2004
9:57 AM

Figure 11.12 Sample report, "The Expeditor by Action Date," from Studio Designer. The report is a "to do" list for all items to be acted upon on a specified date.

The way you handle your finances should take into account major changes in the credit requirements of your suppliers. Do not jeopardize your credit rating by ignoring notices of this kind.

Negotiating Good Credit Terms. The amount of credit you can get from resources greatly extends the capital you have to run your business. If a supplier wants your business and realizes you are important in acquiring the contract, that supplier will very often extend better terms than would otherwise be available. The terms you are able to negotiate with your resources greatly affect your cash management. When design firms decide to sell merchandise or handle purchases for clients, the dollar amounts are often very large, and the terms and buying conditions the firms establish have a great deal to do with their profits. Paying your accounts and keeping them up to date makes it easier to get merchandise.

You can become a prime account by working closely with a particular resource. A resource may extend large amounts of credit to you if that source understands the way you work and the types of projects you handle. The first rule in establishing a good relationship with your resources is to inform the companies you buy from about your operation: the type of business you do, how you pay your bills, and how your company is financially structured. Do not expect to get credit without giving valid information and maintaining a standard bill-paying procedure.

Bill-Paying Procedures. Let your resources know your company's procedure for paying bills—whether you pay once a month, twice a month, every week, or 10 days after receipt of merchandise.

In our company, to keep bookkeeping simple, we try to handle invoices only once. That means if merchandise arrives in good condition, we issue the check for it before the end of the week. Now that we have adapted to using a computer, it is easier for us to extend the period before we pay to the 30 days most invoices require. This gives us use of this money for two or three additional weeks, and the interest it adds to our bank account enhances our profit picture.

Our company policy is to pay bills promptly even if it means borrowing. We have a line of credit at the bank that permits us to borrow on a weekly basis, if we must. We feel it is very important to keep accounts payable up to date so we can expect performance from our resources. Instead of check writing, we take advantage of the direct transfer many of our sources offer. Monies from our account can be directly deposited into theirs, and an immediate transaction takes place.

With proper controls in place, it may be expedient to give someone other than yourself the power to sign checks or commit your company to purchasing contracts. Introduce this staff member to your banker, your accountant, and your customers and suppliers. Should this person leave your employ, make sure these individuals know about it. This can be done tactfully, while introducing the new staff person.

Do not pay for any merchandise until the item is received and inspected. Your purchase orders should explain your payment policy right on them (see pages 297–298).

This ensures that resources know your terms when they receive the orders and that when they accept your order, they have accepted it under these conditions.

If problems prevent prompt payment of your bills, or you find you need more time to pay, call the companies that have billed you and let them know your situation before the bills are due. When resources do not hear from you and do not receive payments or any kind of action, they become concerned, and you cannot blame them. Keep your suppliers informed, and you will find they will work with you in most instances.

Cash Discounts. A number of companies still offer cash discounts. It is amazing how much an interior design firm can earn per year just on the 2 or 5 percent discounts allowed them by certain suppliers. Many carpet manufacturers allow us a 5 percent discount if the invoice is paid within 30 days, with the balance due in 60 days. For just a 30-day period, we could lose a 5 percent discount. It has paid us to borrow money to be able to pay in time to receive this 5 percent discount. By taking dis-

Credit Terms

5/10: If you pay this invoice within 10 days, you may take a 5 percent discount.

2/10: If you pay this invoice within 10 days, you make take a 2 percent discount.

2/30: If you pay this invoice within 30 days, you may take a 2 percent discount.

Net 30: This bill is due at the end of 30 days.

MOM (middle of month): The billing will be sent out on the fifteenth of the month. This includes all purchases made from the middle of the previous month to the date of billing.

EOM (end of month): The billing will be sent out at the end of the month. This includes all purchases made during the month.

CWO (cash with orders): Orders that are received will not be processed until payment is made.

CIA (cash in advance): The same as CWO.

CBD (cash before delivery): The merchandise will be prepared and packaged, but the shipper will not make shipment until the payment is received.

COD (cash on delivery): The amount of the total billing will be collected on the delivery of the merchandise.

SDBL (Sight Draft-Bill of Lading): A bill of lading will accompany the invoice, and a sight draft will be drawn on the buyer, which is forwarded to the seller by the customer's bank. The bill of lading is released by the bank to the customer only when the customer honors the draft.

2/10/N/30 ROG (receipt of goods): If you pay this invoice within 10 days, you may take a 2 percent discount; the bill is due at the end of 30 days and the discount period starts at the date of receipt of the goods, not the date of shipping or the date of the sale.

2/10/N/30 MOM (middle of the month): If you pay this invoice within 10 days, you may take a 2 percent discount; the bill is due at the end of 30 days, and both periods start from the fifteenth or the middle of the month following the date of the sale.

2/10/N/30 EOM (end of the month): If you pay this invoice within 10 days, you may take a 2 percent discount; the bill is due at the end of 30 days; and both periods start from the end of the month of sale.

counts, we can also keep ourselves in an excellent credit position. But can we afford to offer them to our clients?

A 2 percent/10-day cash discount is worth approximately 37 percent on an annual basis. (When you offer discounts it is very difficult to make 37 percent on your money.) Take that into consideration if you offer discounts to your clients. Giving cash discounts usually speeds up your receiving payment; however, there may be other, less expensive ways of doing this.

Keep in mind that discounts add up. For example, if you take advantage of a 2 percent 10-day discount, when the net is due in 30 days, this is worth 36.5 percent per year.

Petty Cash or Imprest Petty Cash Fund. Every company needs to have some cash on hand. Even a straight professional service business has to pay cash for some items occasionally. It is not appropriate, for example, to be without the money to pay for postage or shipping. Most design firms maintain a small petty cash fund.

Try to keep your petty cash fund documented and in order. The fewer people who handle petty cash, the better the chance of keeping it organized; if you put one individual in charge of this fund, it will run much more smoothly. Documentation of petty cash is required, so the payments can be properly classified for your financial statement. And a review of petty cash is standard when you are audited by the IRS—it is always interested in how cash is handled.

Petty cash is a simple fund created by drawing a check for a certain amount—$100.00 for example. All the items paid for out of that $100 are logged, and the money is replaced at the end of a given period, possibly on a weekly basis. For example, if receipts paid out add up to $88.14, there should be $11.86 left in the petty cash box. A check is written in the amount of $88.14 to cover expenses paid out and deposited in the petty cash box, bringing the balance to $100. Here's how it looks:

Petty Cash Fund	$100.00
Receipts	$88.14
Balance in Petty Cash Fund	$11.86
Reimburse Petty Cash Fund	$88.14
Balance on hand	$100.00

Staff Monthly Expenses. In our firm, we have our staff submit their expenses for reimbursement on a regular basis. It is important to keep track of these expenses for many reasons. Not only do they help you calculate the costs of your staff, they also provide important information for the IRS. An example of this form is shown in Table 11.2 (page 380).

We have separate envelopes for travel expenses, as shown in Table 11.3 (page 381). The travel expense envelope is a practical way to document travel expenses. When a staff member is given an advance, this is clearly noted, with the date. The staff member then keeps a record of all types and amounts of expenses, listing food separately, since meals are only 50 percent deductible for tax purposes.

Table 11.2 Staff monthly expense form. This form can be used to itemize the monthly expenses of your staff. It is a simple way of documenting expenses for reimbursement.

STAFF MONTHLY EXPENSE FORM					
Staff:			Month:		
Date:	Activity:			No. of Miles:	Other Expenses
Staff Signature:		Total Miles:			
		Allowance:	@		
Approved by:		Date Paid:	Subtotals:		
		Check No.:	Total Amount:		

© *Design Business Monthly*, 1988.

The staff member then turns in the envelope to the bookkeeper, and it becomes a permanent record for the files. The envelope shows the total reimbursement of expenses, less the advance, the amount due, and the check number that was issued. Any recalculation can be stated on the bottom. This simple envelope form makes management of travel expenses or any kind of expenses for job projects considerably easier to manage.

Financial Indicators

A number of years ago, I decided I did not want to spend all my time doing business management, and I knew I could hire good people to do this. We now have an excellent managing director in our office who does a great job. I still keep on top of what is happening at all times, however. I want to know where we are going, what I need to worry about, and what I do not need to worry about.

Through the years I have found a way to monitor our company and its direction so I do not have financial surprises. I can look ahead to see where trouble spots are likely to occur or when cash is needed. This is a system so simple our bookkeeper can extrapolate the necessary numbers and put the information on my desk any day

Table 11.3 Travel expenses form. This envelope is a practical way for staff members to document travel expenses. It is turned in to the bookkeeper when the staff member returns from a trip.

TRAVEL EXPENSES

Staff:	Date:	Advance Amount:

Summary of Expenses

Type: (excluding food)	Amount:

Total $_____

Food:	Amount:

Total Reimbursement of Expenses $_____

Less Advancement $_____

Due $_____

Reimbursement $_____

Check No. _____

of the week I want it. Usually, I get my report on Tuesday mornings, but you decide what day you want it, and I am sure your bookkeeper can accommodate you. From the copy of our monthly financial report shown in Table 11.4 (page 383) and detailed below, you can see how simple it is for me to keep abreast of most issues.

- **Accounts receivable.** Some data I like to review on a weekly basis, particularly our accounts receivable numbers. I am interested in whether they are for under 30 days, 30 days, or for over 60 days, because I want to know how well we are doing at keeping our accounts current.
- **Client retainer balances.** I want to know exactly how much money we are

holding against purchases or professional fees. Money being held for others is a liability.

- **Checking money market balance.** With the current banking arrangements, many of you probably do as we do: We deposit most of our money into our money market account and transfer from it to our regular checking account as required.

- **Accounts payable.** I want to see which vendors are for under 30 days and for over 30 days. Right now we pay our accounts promptly, so anything that is in the over 30-day category indicates a problem. Usually, if we are having a problem with a company and are not paying them, a client's project is also being affected. Seeing a figure in the over 30-day category is a double alert for me.

- **Monthly billings.** I also want to know what our total billings for the month are and how much of them are for product sales and how much for fees. Then I want to know the exact billing of each person within the studio. Every designer is responsible for various billings or sales, and I want to know what their numbers are.

- **Gross profit.** Gross profit is the difference between sales and cost of sales. We have our accountant do an expense estimate for us on an annual basis, and we always compare it to our actual. This lets us know what our expenses are per month. Because this does not vary a great deal from month to month in our firm, if I see the gross profit figure, I have a good idea exactly how we are doing.

- **Future work.** After I have seen the total billings for the month, I look toward the future. What are our sales for the month? What have we written in new contracts? In products or professional services fees? What exactly are our numbers, and how does this vary per person? Then I want to know the total dollar value of work in progress—and how much of it will be completed within 30 days, 60 days, or over 60 days—because obviously that will bring in revenues.

Decide what financial information you need to run your business on a day-to-day basis, and use computer accounting systems to produce your reports. But be careful: I have seen accounting programs that give designers a flood of unnecessary information—and they have no idea what it means. The information they need is there if they can find it, but it is not easily accessible. Have your software consultant review the materials and demonstrate to you exactly how to access the information you need from these programs.

Although you may not be the person inputting the data, it is very important that you be able to access the information you need whenever you need it. There may be times no one else is in the studio or perhaps others are busy when you need information on a regular basis. The system is designed to perform with great accuracy and speed, but be sure it is working for you.

Table 11.4 Monthly financial report. This form will help you evaluate how your firm is doing and where it is going.

MONTHLY FINANCIAL REPORT _____, 20____

CASH

Accounts Receivable—Total	$_____
Under 30 Days	$_____
30 to 60 Days	$_____
Over 60 Days	$_____
Customer's Retainer Balance	$_____
Checking Account Balance	$_____
Special Holding Account Balance	$_____
Vendor Deposits	$_____
Accounts Payable—Total	$_____
Under 30 Days	$_____
Over 30 Days	$_____

BILLING

This Month	Total Billings	Total Gross Profit
Products	$_____	$_____
Fees	$_____	$_____
	Billing	Gross Profit
Staff No. 1 Products	$_____	
Fees	$_____	
	Billing	Gross Profit
Staff No. 2 Products	$_____	
Fees	$_____	
	Billing	Gross Profit
Staff No. 3 Products	$_____	
Fees	$_____	
	Billing	Gross Profit
Staff No. 4 Products	$_____	
Fees	$_____	

SALES

Total Sales Written This Month	$_____	Products Total
	FEE	
Staff No. 1	$_____	$_____
Staff No. 2	$_____	$_____
Staff No. 3	$_____	$_____
Staff No. 4	$_____	$_____

WORK

Total Work in Process	FEE	Products Total
		$_____
Expected Completion		
30 Days	$_____	$_____
60 Days	$_____	$_____
Over 60 Days	$_____	$_____

© *Design Business Monthly*, 1988.

While this information gives me a forecast of financial issues, I need something more. I want to know exactly what we have sold in new jobs—either professional fees or product sales, for the week, and I like that figure to be ongoing throughout the month. Then I can look at the first, second, and third week and see what we have sold to date.

By looking at the monthly financial report, sales projections, and inquiries, I can tell not just what the financial picture is but also what the production schedule is and how we are handling our professional service direction. It is fascinating what these reports will tell you. If I receive these on my desk on a regular basis, I know where we are going, and I can quickly see which areas need polishing. Even though I might not know exactly why these areas need attention, I can spot them and know to focus on some of the details to see whether we can make improvements before a problem develops.

We also make sure that our bankers are kept properly up to date on all of our financial issues, so if we are going to need to borrow money, it will be there waiting for us.

I do not like surprises, so I make sure that I'm never in a position to be surprised. Give me these numbers, and I can tell you where any company is going. You can do the same. Forget about all the rest of the numbers that come off of the computer; just look at the important ones, and keep them current and regular. Then you will have an accurate reading on the status of your business.

How to Use a Financial Statement

On occasion, you will need to read a financial statement, either your own or someone else's. There are many different formulas for interpreting the information in a financial statement. The following lists some of the information that can be derived from a financial statement.

1. **Working capital ratio (also referred to as "current ratio").** Working capital is the excess of current assets over current liabilities. The working capital ratio expresses the relation of the amount of current assets to current liabilities and is determined by the following formula:

   Total Current Assets ÷ Total Current Liabilities = Working Capital Ratio

   This ratio is a measure of short-term solvency. While no current ratio standard can be applied indiscriminately to all types of businesses, it is generally recognized that for a retail-type business, a ratio of 1.5 to 1, or 2 to 1, is desirable.

2. **Acid-test ratio (sometimes called "quick ratio").** Because inventories must be sold and the proceeds collected before such proceeds can be used to pay current liabilities, many analysts supplement the working capital ratio by the so-called acid-test ratio. This ratio measures how well a company is able to cover

its short-term obligations, since it considers only cash or "near cash" assets. This ratio is determined by the following formula:

$$\text{Cash + Accounts Receivable + Marketable Securities} \div \text{Total Current Liabilities = Acid-Test Ratio}$$

An acid-test ratio of at least 1 to 1 is usually regarded as desirable.

3. **Working capital turnover.** This can indicate the adequacy of the working capital and the number of times it is replenished during a period. The working capital turnover is determined as follows:

$$\text{Sales for Period} \div \text{Average Working Capital During Period} = \text{Working Capital Turnover}$$

In my opinion, working capital turnover in and of itself is of practically no significance, because an increase in turnovers may be caused by an increase in current liabilities, which certainly represents no improvement. A much more meaningful statistic would be the *profitability* per turnover of *current assets*. This is determined by means of two computations:

$$\text{Cost of Sales and Expenses (excluding depreciation charges)} \div \text{Total Current Assets = Number of Current Asset Turnovers}$$

and

$$\text{Net Profit} \div \text{Number of Current Asset Turnovers = Profit per Turnover}$$

4. **Merchandise inventory turnover.** This is the number of times the inventory, on average, was sold, or "turned over," during a period. It is determined as follows:

$$\text{Cost of Goods Sold} \div \text{Average Merchandise Inventory} = \text{Merchandise Inventory Turnover}$$

Because the inventory quantity may vary substantially throughout the year, a monthly average will produce a more representative statistic. This ratio indicates the tendency to overstock or understock. For this reason, a high turnover is not necessarily good; it may really mean you do not carry sufficient inventory on hand.

5. **Accounts receivable turnover.** This measures the efficiency of collection, which is computed as follows:

$$\text{Net Credit Sales} \div \text{Average Trade Receivables} = \text{Accounts Receivable Turnover}$$

6. **Age of accounts receivable.** This item represents the average number of days credit sales are in the receivables. Assuming the business is in operation 300 days per year, this would be computed as follows:

300 Days in Accounts Receivable ÷ Accounts Receivable Turnover
= Number of days credit sales uncollected on average,
or age of accounts receivable

Sometimes, it may be useful to know the number of days credit sales are in the accounts receivable at the end of a period. In these cases, the accounts receivable at the end of the period would be used instead of the average receivables in computing the turnover. Either way, you can gauge the performance of your collection practices. If the number of days sales go uncollected is 90, and your credit terms are 30 days, it is obvious that something is wrong. Your collection practices may be at fault, or some of your clients may be in trouble, which means you, too, may be in trouble.

Ratio of Earnings

Ratios that measure operations and operating results are important management tools. By dividing net sales into each item in the income statement, you can determine exactly what percentage of sales has been spent for each item of cost and expense. By comparing such percentages with those in prior income statements, you can be alerted to your business's trends, both favorable and unfavorable. This comparison enables you to pinpoint weak areas in your operations (such as excessive payroll expenses or out-of-control office or travel expenses). If your percentage of gross profit on sales is 45 percent and your operating expenses total 65 percent, it is obvious you must reduce expenses somehow or increase your sale prices (assuming, as is usually the case, you cannot do much to reduce the cost of sales). For example:

Income	Dollar Amount	Percentage
Sales	100,000	100
Cost of Sales	40,000	40
Gross Profit	60,000	60
Operating Expenses		
Advertising	6,000	6
Rent	12,000	12
Salaries	40,000	40
Miscellaneous	500	.5
Total Operating Expense	58,500	58.5
Net Profit	1,500	1.5

There are a number of other ratios that can be useful, such as the following:

Ratio: Return on owner's equity
Formula for Computation: Net Income ÷ Owner's Equity
Result: Measures earnings on resources provided by the owners.

Ratio: Return on total assets
Formula for Computation: Net Income + Interest Expense ÷ Total Assets
Result: Measures earnings on all resources available (both from owners and creditors).

Ratio: Owner's equity to total liabilities
Formula for Computation: Owner's Equity ÷ Total Liabilities
Result: Indicates strengths and weaknesses of the financial structure.

Ratio: Fixed assets to total equities
Formula for Computation: Fixed Assets (book value) ÷ Total Owner's Equity and Liabilities
Result: May indicate excessive real estate and equipment for a retail operation.

Ratio: Sales to fixed assets
Formula for Computation: Net Sales ÷ Fixed Assets (book value)
Result: May cast additional light on possible excessive investment in fixed assets.

Break-Even Analysis

This tool is used to determine the relationship between your revenue and your costs. Your profit is the difference between the two.

Break-even analysis was developed about 40 years ago to help translate very complicated economic theories into a useful management technique. It tells management what it can expect in profits from a company's various levels of productivity. Whether evaluating the acquisition of a new piece of equipment or adding a new staff member, it is a good idea to do a break-even analysis before making a decision.

Begin by adding up all the fixed expenses related to the project. Fixed expenses are costs that continue even if there is no production. This includes rent, real estate occupancy costs, equipment, salaries, and general overhead.

Next, determine the variable costs, or production costs, that come into play when the item is in production. For example, if you buy a new piece of equipment, it will cost you the price of paying for the equipment, the space it takes in the office, and perhaps the salary for an additional person to run it. In some instances, you can simply reassign a person from somewhere else in your firm to work the equipment, so this is a variable.

After using fixed and variable expenses to determine the total cost per year, estimate what revenue you can expect as a result of adding that person or piece of equipment. Compare the two, and you will be able to determine where the break-even point is.

The true definition of "break even" is actually cost versus revenue. In any well-run business, one considers the profit figure. Therefore, profit should be added to the total costs when establishing the break-even point. Any average investment can make 8 to 10 percent, so there is no point in putting money at risk unless there is an opportunity for higher profits.

Figure 11.13 Break-even chart. A break-even chart illustrates the relationship between your revenue and your costs. Your profit is the difference between the two.

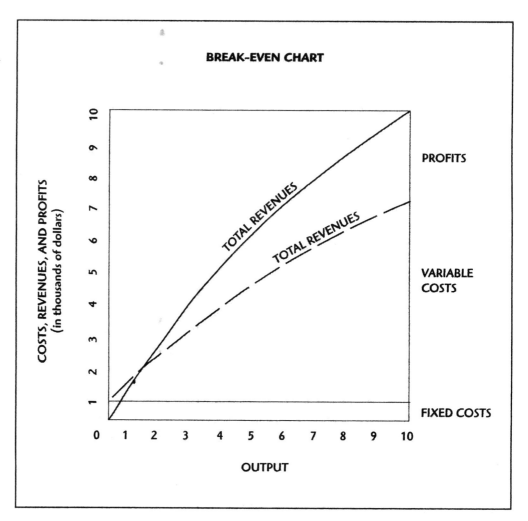

It is a good idea to create a break-even point for every major expenditure, to determine how long it will take for the item or the person to pay for itself. When making management decisions, this analysis can be helpful in choosing which venture you should do first. Obviously, the more quickly the break-even point can be reached, the more attractive the investment. However, there may be other factors that need to be taken into consideration. Every expenditure does not stand alone, so you need to make comparisons. This visual comparison is a beneficial tool in helping to make that decision.

OVERHEAD COSTS

Each year, have your accountant review your overhead costs, including items such as mortgage payments or rent and insurances—life and others, all the overhead expenses you have. Include the people on your staff who are considered nonbillable, as well as any other expenses, such as auto, utilities, maintenance of grounds and property, the general list.

You usually pay insurance premiums, taxes, and so on once a year. Some other expenses are paid at various intervals. Still, there is an over-amount that needs to be assigned to each month's overhead expenses. Once you have determined this amount, divide it by 12. You now know your overhead figures, and you should know exactly how much gross profit or fees you must bring in per month to cover your overhead first, and then what is necessary to generate profit.

When adding a staff member—if you have taken on additional work and see there is an opportunity for additional billable hours—you need to review exactly what will go into the next project. Will this be an ongoing project? Or will it just be a short-term project, for the next few months?

OVERHEAD COSTS

- Rent
- Taxes and licenses
- Insurance
- Utilities
- Telephone
- Advertising
- Marketing
- Office expenses
- Resource library

- Professional fees
- Transportation (e.g., automobile)
- Dues and subscriptions
- Loan payments
- Nonbillable management time
- Nonbillable support staff
- Consulting
- Education
- Other

BANKING RELATIONS

Today more than ever, you should consider your banker your advisor. With a good partnership, your banker should provide insight into strategic planning for your bottom line—including your long-term credit needs, proper cash management, time-saving tools, and long-term investment strategies. Handling money is an essential part of any business. The interior design business in particular depends a great deal on the ability to handle considerable sums. A solid, supportive relationship with a strong banking institution is crucial. Your bank is a partner you should be able to trust to keep your information confidential. Your relationship with your banker should be one in which, for example, the banker tells you candidly you really can't afford a particular transaction or you are borrowing too much money for your business. You should feel confident that such advice is valid. It is much more difficult to establish credit today than it was even five years ago, since money is expensive and banks are more cautious in making loans.

The best way to set up a working relationship with your banking institution is to make that bank part of your business. Banks are interested in doing business only with companies they know and whose purpose and management structure they understand.

Make your banker and banking institution a part of your company, and you will find they will be far more interested in you than you might expect. They will help you find ways to finance your business today and in the future.

When you make the initial contact, give your banker the type of information necessary to make a proper evaluation of your firm. Here is a checklist of the information your banker will need:

1. The type of ownership of your firm: corporation, partnership, S Corporation, limited liability corporation (LLC), or limited partnership.
2. The product or type of service you offer.
3. The competition in your area.
4. The market available to you.
5. Your sales and service facilities, including any special or unusual services you provide to your customers.
6. Your employees: number, qualifications (including length of service with your company), and their contributions to your company.
7. Your financial administration: who your certified public accountant is and what your general business administrative structure is.
8. Your current financial statements.
9. A history of your business and financial background.
10. The conditions and details of any outstanding loans.
11. A list of the clients or companies you have worked for and the jobs you have done for them, including dates and approximate sizes of the jobs.
12. A list of your sources.
13. A list of any banks or lending institutions you have worked with in the past.
14. The goals and objectives of your company. Carefully review these with your banker, and update them regularly.
15. Your management succession. If something happens to the principal or major officer, who will take over, and how will this be handled? What is that person's expertise? Is this person really capable of sustaining the business? What are the legal methods available to ensure business continuity?
16. Your insurance. Which insurance do you have to cover your company in general and in transition? The bank may require insurance not just as collateral but to pay off loans. The bank may also want to know if you have insurance to handle any other problems that might arise.

Selecting a Bank

I suggest you consider not the cheapest but the most appropriate bank for your needs. Sometimes the provider of low-cost services in banking is not the best long-term advisor. Many banking services reserved for middle-market and higher-level clients in the 1980s and early 1990s are available today to even the smallest business. There were about 14,500 commercial banks in 1989; today there are roughly 10,000 to 10,500. The industry continues to consolidate; but it is not just the big banks taking over the smaller banks that has resulted in such reduced numbers. What the numbers do not reflect are the "boutique" banks that have started up by executives from the large banks who were displaced by the mergers.

As a small business owner in an interior design business shopping for an institution, keep in mind:

- You bank with the banker, not the bank.
- Consider what the bank is offering.

Be comfortable with your banker first, because when you have a really good banker, you will hear from that person once in a while and he or she will help you with your needs.

For example, you might consider looking for the following offerings while shopping:

- Remember your time is money. Sometimes it makes more sense to look at *how* you do your banking. If your banker or your advisor knows your business, your relationship will offer no surprises and will become a key element in your wisely managed business.
- Ask your prospective bankers about convenient banking channels, such as nearby branches, online cash management and bill payment, and after-hours access, including telephone and Internet banking. Will your bank be there when you need it to offer the services you need to grow your business?
- Does your institution have business credit and purchasing card options? How about credit card and merchant services offering?
- Consider the alternative services your bank offers, such as online banking and cash management and Internet-based merchant services. Some institutions offer Internet shop "faces" and human resources services through third-party vendors. Why? Because bankers might know that by offering products that take care of tasks that would otherwise consume your client-focused time, they can save you considerable time.
- Pricing, such as balance requirements and transaction fees, is important, but it is not paramount to finding the right fit for your business. Your bank, if chosen wisely, will surely pay dividends for your business over the long term.

How Many Banks Should You Use? Most banks today will provide relationship pricing as long as you maintain your primary accounts with them. This is different from just a few years ago, when it might have made more sense to bank at more than one institution. Before the days of service charges, many of us dealt with four or five different banks. Today, it is too expensive to establish a relationship with a second bank unless you need to borrow large sums of money. Then you might find that you need to use two or three banks to get that amount. But it is probably better, from both a business as well as a financial viewpoint, to give one bank at least the majority, if not all, of your business; then you can have the clout to request and get certain privileges.

The Bank as a Resource

Your bank can be an excellent resource for services, investment opportunities, and loans. Reexamine your banking services and needs on an annual basis. The banking system changes so rapidly today that your bank may offer new services you had not explored previously.

You will notice when you are using a bank that you are now charged for certain services you were not charged for in the past. Banks no longer make their money on the amount of money you have invested with them; they earn a significant portion of their income from service fees.

You should get to know your business development officer at the bank. (This person may also be referred to as an account executive or relationship manager.) You might not necessarily meet this person when you are opening your account(s), but you should meet this manager later when your relationship with the bank has been established and the bank knows whom to assign to your account.

Your business development officer should review your accounts periodically to determine the suitability of the different investment accounts or other services the bank offers. This person will know your accounts, their size, and your general type of operation.

Payroll Services. Banks have direct-deposit payroll services that issue checks by preparing an automatic computer file that debits and credits accounts. When a payroll file is prepared and goes through, the employees' pay is automatically deposited into the banks they choose; an account does not have to be with the bank where the payroll account is established. The funds are debited from the employer's payroll account in that particular bank and issued to the employees' accounts. The bank (or data processing company the bank uses) writes the withholding checks for the IRS and for any other taxes. The bank then debits the employer's account, and it also does all of the tax reports. You can buy these services from the bank or from an outside source such as Automatic Data Processing (ADP) or Paychex.

The advantage of using direct deposit is that the bank deposits the money directly into the employees' checking accounts, eliminating in-house paycheck disbursement. A second advantage is that you do not have to run to the bank before noon on the dates the various taxes or withholding payments are due. The bank automatically takes care of those transactions, so your payments are made both accurately and on time. Check with your bank to see what the costs of this service would be and whether the bank requires you to have a minimum number of employees.

Your Checking Account. Most banks require that a minimum balance or an average minimum balance be maintained. Some require as little as $300; others may require thousands of dollars. This minimum balance is usually based on an average balance per month, since your balance might go down to $300 at one point and up to $10,000 at another.

According to federal law, corporations may not have interest-bearing checking accounts; only personal checking accounts can bear interest. Therefore, you should invest funds in excess of everyday business reimbursements in a money market account or savings account and transfer, as needed, to a checking account.

Banks tried to diversify their service offerings to be like a department store. Some have worked; some have not. When we look at what works, it is the core financial services such as online banking, which is a natural extension to a checkbook. The only difference is that you are clicking a mouse instead of writing a check.

Money can move industry, but some processes do take longer. Automatic clearing house (ACH) transactions can wire money within minutes or seconds from one institution to another. Many companies run their business that way. You can use online banking the way you would write a check, but you can set up the system so the check will not actually get to the vendor for a set number of days. That way you know when you write an online check that four days later, for example, your vendor will get paid. You do not have to worry whether a paper check went out to them or, if they accept electronic payments, whether they were paid on the fourth day via an electronic payment. The same thing works for business bank checking: If you would like to expedite a payment, you can call your banker, and your banker can wire the payment. If a bill is due on the fifteenth or the thirtieth of the month and you want to pay electronically, you can set up the system so the check will be received at a certain time. This is a similar system to what we use in personal banking, when there is about a four-day lag time.

You can ask your vendors which system they prefer—paper or automatic check. If, for example, a company is ready to deliver goods you ordered, but not until it receives a check from you, you can send the check automatically or put a delay on the check so it does not clear for three or four days. You can specify the payment date by using an automated check, which gives you financial control.

Regardless of what path a check takes, the goal is for it to arrive at the vendor at the desired time—and that you'll know it does. That way you will never hear yourself saying, "Why did I pay this bill two days ago, and it has already arrived, whereas I paid this bill four days ago with a paper check, and it has not yet arrived?" It is just a matter of being consistent. Regarding electronic checks, if you make a mistake and send someone a check that was incorrect, you have a two- or three-day window of time, possibly more, during which the link is still live on your computer screen, and you can delete it. You have more, rather than less, control.

There is also better recordkeeping. It is important to be able to monitor the amount of money in your account. Designers handle large amounts of money, compared to what they actually get to keep. It is easy to get into trouble if they do not understand the transaction time within the bank. They can mail checks thinking the money is in the bank because they deposited the check in the morning, but it actually isn't in your account according to the bank's terms. This could get a designer into trouble. This type of monitoring helps prevent that.

Check Clearing for the 21st Century Act (Check 21)

The Check Clearing for the 21st Century Act (Check 21) came about as a result of the terrorist action of September 11, 2001, when the financial world was thrown into turmoil. When commerce was physically halted, the exchange of paper to back financial transactions was stopped or delayed. Electronic commerce was seen as the solution.

A law that went into effect October 28, 2004, permits banks to create digitized copies of checks or to create substitute checks to facilitate the exchange of funds among banks. This process enables banks to eliminate the actual exchange of checks. Substitute checks are known as Image Replacement Documents (IRD). They have the same legal standing as your original check for all legal purposes and proof of payment.

The Check 21 Act may increase the availability of funds deposited, since the clearing can occur within hours rather than days. The recipient of the check may find this a tremendous aid to cash flow. On the other hand, it becomes more important to manage outgoing funds carefully, so checks are written only on funds that are truly available: no more float.

Other implications of Check 21 are:

- No more cancelled checks.
- You are less likely to be able to issue a stop payment due to the faster turn-around time on check clearing.
- Your deposits will not be processed any faster. Check 21 does not shorten the amount of time checks are held.
- Understand the terms of "voluntary check truncation": your bank will not return copies of substitute checks to you.

Today, with the new banking procedures, a check is often cleared the day a person receives it. So it may be difficult to stop payment. The usual procedure for stopping payment on a check is to call the bank and complete a written stop-payment request within 14 days. Many banks also have online procedures for stopping payments. Stop payment notices are usually good for six months and then need to be renewed if your bank will accept payments for checks that are more than six months old. Usually, banks have limits. A sample stop payment notice is shown in Figure 11.14 (page 395).

Your Employees' Financial Benefits. Some institutions extend free, or reduced, pricing on banking services to your employees. You, as an employer, can add this to your list of employee benefits. For example, banks prefer to sell as many checking accounts to consumers as possible. Through offers made to business owners that extend to employees of your business, you can create a win-win situation. In a majority of cases, you can add a benefit like this to your benefits package for no additional fee.

Figure 11.14 Stop payment notice. A letter such as this should be sent to your bank if you wish it to stop payment on a check.

Date:

TO: (bank name)

Gentlemen:

You are directed to stop payment on the following check:

Name of Payee:

Date of Check:

Amount:

Check Number:

This stop order shall remain in effect until further written notice.

(name of account)

(account number)

By: _____

Figure 11.14 Stop payment notice. A letter such as this should be sent to your bank if you wish it to stop payment on a check.

Credit Cards. We issue credit cards to various members of our staff so they can purchase gas and necessities while traveling for the firm. Keep a record of who has which cards and the card numbers. An easy way to do this is to make a copy of the credit cards on your copying machine. If a credit card is lost, you have a record. This can save you a lot of aggravation.

Money Market Account. A money market account has a daily rate of interest. You can make as many deposits as you want in a money market account. However, federal regulations limit withdrawal transactions, such as telephone transfers or automatic payments, to a maximum of six per month. Normally these six per month will be tracked on a per-statement cycle, rather than by calendar month. You can phone the bank from your office up to six times per month and withdraw any amount. If you find you are withdrawing funds from your money market account at the limit of six each month, you should consider talking to your banker about cash management services. Overnight investments of your checking balances might be a better option.

Short-Term Certificates of Deposit. Another way to handle your investment money is through short-term certificates of deposit, which are deposits for 14 days or longer. These usually give you a slightly higher interest rate than the money market accounts. Their disadvantage is that they often require visiting the bank in person to open and to close the certificate. However, your bank may permit you to make other arrangements to open or close certificates of deposit, such as a letter of instruction bearing your signature or a special setup in which you can phone in your instructions. Balance requirements vary from bank to bank but normally start at $1,000 to $5,000.

Cash Management Services. Corporate cash management services usually require a minimum investment of $100,000. This service invests your available funds by zero-balancing your account to invest every dollar in an overnight repurchase agreement. Although there is a minimum fee, plus transaction costs for managing this account, your company earns more than it would splitting your funds between a checking account and a money market account because all the money is invested together. Once you have reached the corporate level where you have excess cash on a consistent basis, you should consider investing in cash management services instead of money markets.

IRAs. An IRA is an excellent vehicle for employees to increase their retirement funds. There are currently two primary types of IRAs: the Traditional IRA and the Roth IRA. Both of these are established by individuals with their own contributions, up to a maximum dollar amount each year. Traditional IRA contributions may be tax-deductible. Roth IRA contributions are not tax-deductible. The most significant difference between a traditional IRA and a Roth IRA is that qualified distributions from a Roth IRA are never taxable, whereas qualified distributions from a traditional IRAs are treated as ordinary income and may be taxable.

Keogh Plans. Also known as an H.R. 10 plan, a Keogh plan is a retirement plan available only to a self-employed person or partnerships for the owners of the business and their employees. As with all employer-sponsored plans, there is a limit for contributions made to the plan for the benefit of the owners. Keoghs, nevertheless, may be worthwhile in certain situations and should be looked into if a retirement plan or fringe benefits for employees are under consideration.

As with all employer-sponsored plans, the details of Keogh plans are too complex to discuss adequately here. If you are interested, you should discuss the matter with your accountant or other financial advisor.

401(k) Plans. 401(k) plans, if established by the employer, allow the employee or participant tax benefits that include:

- **Pretax contributions.** The salary you contribute is not subject to income taxes until withdrawn from the plan.
- **Tax-deferred account earnings.** Your contributions would be invested on a pre-tax overhead basis. The IRS does not tax your earnings until distributed.

Therefore, your investment can grow faster than if taxes were paid each year.

Bank Loans

A banker will want specific information when you are negotiating a loan. I suggest you keep a summary of these points available:

1. The size of the loan required
2. The purpose of the loan
3. When the funds will be needed and for how long
4. The collateral available to secure the loan
5. How the loan will be repaid
6. A cash flow forecast, prepared by your accountant, covering the period of the loan
7. Personal credit data of the owner, partners, or associates of the business
8. Any life insurance available as collateral for the loan
9. Any outstanding loans you may have
10. A history of your business
11. Your financial statements and tax returns (both business and personal) for this year and for the three to five previous years
12. Some evidence of your reputation for paying your obligations
13. A consideration of the leases you have that may affect your business

Credit today seems to be based less on people's professions and industries and more on their individual qualifications. The dot-com experience of the late 1990s reinforced that it is not so much the type of business one is in that a bank looks at. Yes, there are still credit underwriting guidelines for specific types of businesses, but credit underwriters also look at whether or not a company is making money and, if so, how. Does it have good prospects for the future? Is the business important today?

If you look back, banks at one time would not lend money to women because they were not considered creditworthy. Now underwriters look at whether a company is well managed. Does it have a strategic plan? A strategic marketing direction? Is it creditworthy? Are the principals involved in an equity sense—putting their own capital on the line, their friends' and family's, or other small-venture capital that would indicate to the underwriter that the principals have their heart and soul in the business? If you take out a loan, you should understand that the bank does not want to own your business. Banks are in business to get their money back with profit, whether it be from loans, fees, or other transactions, and the services they provide.

Your relationship with your banker is a symbiotic one. You should never be afraid to share information with a banker. Lending institutions can provide you with information and advice that will confirm your plans or show them to be impractical.

Lines of Credit. When a bank extends a line of credit, the bank makes an advance commitment that it is willing to loan the design firm money under certain conditions, often on a revolving basis. Designers usually find this type of financing advantageous because it is flexible according to their needs. Financing is on a short-term basis and can be more easily controlled according to design projects. Lines of credit are normally reviewed annually. You must submit an audited financial statement for the review.

Today, most banks offering lines of credit are charging an annual maintenance fee to maintain it. By policy, when you have a line of credit from a bank, the bank is required to review your account and your financial status, usually on a quarterly or annual basis, and this costs money. So when you make your request for a line of credit, make it realistic. If you feel you occasionally might need something out of the ordinary, handle that more as a term loan rather than a line of credit, or make certain you have a sufficient credit line. That is why most of us need both a line of a credit and various term loans.

Term Loans. Term loans are usually for a specific period, such as 5, 10, or 15 years. Short-term loans are normally for less than a year, sometimes only 30 to 60 days. If a short-term loan goes beyond a year, it is considered a long-term loan. A short-term loan is usually desirable, because even though the interest may be higher, it must be paid over a short period. In most cases, a short-term loan can be paid off in advance if the project is completed and the monies are available. This type of loan is used for major expenditures. The rates of a long-term loan will vary according to the term of the loan.

Other Sources of Capital

Businesses constantly need money. Whether your firm is a new business or a well-established one, the boundaries of its development are strongly linked to the amount of money available.

There are a number of sources for capital. First of all, borrowing: Where can you borrow money, and what are the best sources? Naturally, your own money is the first source to consider. You must be ready to invest your monies in your business; otherwise, why should you expect someone else to do so? This is obviously the easiest source of revenue, so if you plan to start a business or to grow your business, try to accumulate some funds to give yourself a base from which to begin.

Your friends or relatives are also a good source of money—probably the second fastest—and they are usually inexpensive. If you borrow from a friend or a relative, however, be cautious. You do not want to give away the control of your business or

Get to Know Your Bank

It is good to learn something about your bank. Some of the opportunities for getting to know your bank include the following:

1. Attend your bank's seminars. Often banks hold seminars on taxes, lending, and other topics that relate to your business. When you attend these seminars, you will find out what your bank's attitudes are toward these issues.
2. Read your bank's annual report so you know how well the bank is managed. And, if you can, buy some of its stock.
3. Read the literature the bank puts out, whether it is in the form of articles in the newspaper (either advertising or news items) or brochures. These publications will advise you of any changes in direction and attitude at the bank.
4. Invite your banker to your Christmas party or other social event held at your studio. This familiarizes your banker with your firm and some of your jobs. If there is a new project opening that might be of interest to your banker, invite that individual. This gives your banker a feel for how a design firm runs. By giving your banker first-hand experience with design, you foster better understanding, which can work in your favor the next time you approach the bank for service.

cause problems within the family. If you do not want the person you borrow from to participate in your business, set up a loan structure whereby you retain control, and the lender does not automatically become a partner.

Banks are usually the best and, therefore, preferable, sources of capital, because a good banking relationship can fill continuing needs. However, there are other sources of capital.

Government-Sponsored Loans. The Small Business Administration (SBA) is a good source for information as well as loans. To qualify for an SBA loan, you must have good documentation and be ready to meet SBA standards. In general, the SBA's rates are favorable and comparable to traditional financing. The SBA will also extend loans in some situations when banks cannot. Generally, SBA loans are administered through banks, so be comfortable with the bank the SBA uses. Working with the SBA does take long-term planning, however. Other government-sponsored programs at the state level may provide attractive financial options for your business. Contact your banker or local economic development agency about these programs.

Factoring. Factoring involves selling your accounts receivable to another company or party. You get paid on delivery of your product or services, and your customer then pays the factoring company. This is not the same as accounts receivable loans, which are available through banks. Usually, factoring companies will buy your accounts receivable for less than their value, such as 80 or 90 percent of their worth; you get the additional 20 or 10 percent when the company pays. The factoring firm is responsible for checking each client's credit and determining whether it will be willing to assume the responsibility of that client. Service charges vary.

This type of service was set up primarily for large manufacturers in the 1950s through 1970s; but in the 1980s, numerous design firms used this type of borrowing. Today, because of lending programs, use of factoring has dropped dramatically.

Finance Companies. If you have a large debt or are not able to get financing from a bank, a finance company may be your only source. As a rule, this is the least-desirable source for money, because you pay a much higher interest rate. Commercial finance companies will make loans for items such as equipment and will also act as factors. Although interest rates are high, these loans are usually available faster than other loans. Sometimes you can obtain a loan within a few days or several weeks, whereas a bank loan or other types of loans will take considerably longer.

Suppliers as a Source for Additional Working Capital. Your suppliers will usually grant you terms of either 30, 60, or 90 days, but they may extend these terms for a longer time. If you are planning to do a large job and are not able to carry the financing for it, ask your suppliers what they might do to help. Perhaps they will give you additional terms, knowing it is for a particular project.

It is a good idea to review all your suppliers regularly: determine the amount of credit they are extending to you presently and what you feel you will need over the next six months. By identifying your requirements ahead of time and negotiating with your suppliers, you can often obtain much more credit than you might expect. Do not wait until the project is sold; it is then often too late to negotiate. If your sources are aware of your business potential or upcoming objectives, they are usually more than happy to cooperate by extending additional credit. It is amazing how much this can help a design firm develop its business potential.

Credit Card Loans. This is an easy and increasingly popular way to obtain money up to a specific dollar amount. There are now corporate credit cards, through which, if you do not have an account with a certain company, you can charge the money you owe the company through your corporate credit card. Through a corporate credit card, the credit card issuer might extend to you $50,000 or a $100,000 worth of credit, permitting you to pay off all of your creditors immediately to get cash discounts from creditors for early payment. You simply pay the credit card issuer at the end of 30 or 60 days, as agreed on, and the card issuer charges you interest for the amount of time your account is outstanding. If you do not have a corporate credit card, perhaps you should consider getting one. The card usually does not cost you anything until you use it. However, be sure to watch the rates of interest repayment terms, late fees, and other penalties because card issuers vary considerably.

Equity Capital Financing. You can sell a portion of your business to another person. If you have a corporation, you would have a stockholder's agreement, whereby you would not have to pay back that particular loan with the person making you the loan, but instead you would agree to share a certain portion of your profits. This can be a good method of acquiring capital; however, the relationship with the lender must be carefully considered. If the lender owns the business and plans to start controlling it, you may have a problem. In some cases, you may have to relinquish the majority of control. If you are confident of the personal relationship, then discuss this business agreement with your attorney to determine the value of the equity capital. In large corporations, selling stock is an impersonal relationship, so these considerations obviously do not apply.

Venture Capital, or Angel, Funds. Venture capital firms or individuals—so-called angel funds—lend their own capital to new businesses. They are usually interested in owning a portion of the business; many insist on owning over 50 percent. There are a lot of venture capitalists, and there are firms that put investors and businesses together. But they see a lot of proposals and probably reject 95 percent of them. Customarily, venture capitalists seek a return of three to five times their investment in five to seven years. Usually, they are interested in larger projects, from about $500,000 to many millions. This is a good source of capital for certain larger projects, but it is rarely suitable for the beginning design firm.

SBICs and MESBICs. Small Business Investment Companies (SBICs) and Minority Enterprise Small Business Investment Companies (MESBICs) are both regulated under the Small Business Administration. The government is putting a great deal of capital into these firms. They invest only in young companies or those managed by minorities, and they relax many of the rules in order to accommodate these types of business. SBICs and MESBICs are a great source of long-term loans, which are usually very difficult for a small business to acquire. They often give loans for five to seven years, or even as long as 20 years. It usually takes several months for loans to be approved by these types of organizations.

There are also small business development companies, called SBDCs, which are run in a similar fashion but are not government-owned. They are independently owned. Many times, SBDCs are run by a local chamber of commerce or regional development groups attempting to bring businesses into their area. Since these are supported locally, SBDCs will make special terms available for the businesses they want to attract into the area. Information on these companies can usually be obtained through local chambers of commerce.

Loan Finders. There are many financial consultants or professionals who act as loan finders. They usually charge you a fee, which can be from as low as 1 percent to as high as 15 or 20 percent. These finders are often advertised in the financial part of your local newspaper or in the *Wall Street Journal*. If you are going to use a loan finder, make sure you have clarified the fee amount up front and have included this amount within the loan scheduling you are planning.

Deciding Which Type of Funding to Use

When looking for a loan, to determine which type of resource is best for you, ask yourself these questions.

- How much will it cost?
- What are the projections?
- Am I sure that by borrowing this amount of money I can make money with it and repay the loan under the proposed terms?
- How much time will the loan take to get? Developing a loan and working on acquiring it takes a considerable amount of time—months, or even years. Usually, small design firms do not have a staff person they can assign solely to this task. Therefore, the process takes the principal's time, and the principal should be out selling or marketing instead of using time for this particular purpose. Simple bank loans may take less time if you have an established relationship or a regular line of credit.
- What is the risk my business is assuming by taking on this obligation? How will it affect me this year, next year, and in the future?
- Review the conditions of each individual resource, and determine how it will affect your ability to move, grow, or gain additional capital. Can you make changes within your company? Can you progress with your goals for next year? Will you be able to acquire more capital, if needed, or are you giving up flexibility?
- Will the control of your business be affected? By taking on that extra investor or partner, are you jeopardizing your position in the management of the company? Would this person's contribution be valuable? Weigh the value of the resources against the amount of interaction and control this person will want.
- What sources are available? What are the options? What needs to be done to broaden these options? Determine whether you can use the very best options available or need to consider some that are less advantageous. Look at the value of the overall accomplishment of your project and determine whether it really pays for you to borrow.

ESTABLISHING CREDIT

Your credit has a great deal to do with the success of your company. Unfortunately, there are too many interior design firms with bad credit ratings. Their stigma extends to all designers, whether or not our firms are run well. It takes extra effort to establish a financial structure to overcome this stigma.

Caution when planning financial requirements and obligations protects us from being hit with financial demands we cannot meet. Allow for the worst. You will usually be able to do better, which will make you look good to your creditors. If you always plan for the best and you cannot meet your obligations, you will be in trouble.

Financial planning and forecasting is something every small business owner must learn to do; I have included a form for projecting profits from financial indicators on page 383. The information on the Monthly Financial Report shows expected income and cash flow for the next three months.

Your Credit Rating

Once you receive a bad credit report, it is very difficult to work out of that position. It will save you a lot of trouble and add to the success and growth of your company if you can avoid getting a bad rating in the first place.

Know what your personal and business credit ratings are, and learn where you stand with all credit reporting agencies. What are they saying about you? Get your listing from them and verify the information; if it is not correct, furnish the correct information, and be sure they make the corrections.

Establish good rapport with your local bank; your bank is always asked for credit information. Make it a high priority to keep your banker up to date with your firm to maintain a good standing.

Forward your financial statements regularly to your bank, Lyons Mercantile Group, Dun & Bradstreet, and any other credit-related organization that regularly rates you in your geographic area. These organizations will be expecting these statements on an annual basis, so be sure they get them as quickly as possible. If there are issues you feel these organizations should know about that are not normally on the statements, ask your accountant to add a note explaining these specific issues. This is a better way to provide additional information than sending it directly from the accounting firm. Also, if you are changing your company's financial priorities, it may be a good idea to let the credit organizations know your objectives.

Ways to Establish Credit

Even if you do not need the money, it is a good idea to borrow from a bank or lending institution so that you can get a good credit record. Make sure the loan is paid off in advance of its due date. By doing this, you will become familiar to the lending institution and be recognized as a good credit risk.

Decide which companies and resources are going to be important for your company and build rapport with them. Learn which companies give credit reports on you and which do not. There are a number of large companies in our field that make a special point of not giving reports because they are called on too often. Find out which companies give good reports and attempt to develop rapport with them.

When you have established the companies you feel will be most important to you, talk to them about your payment schedule. Because companies want to develop rapport with you, they are often willing to extend terms beyond the norm. If this information is established up front, and they agree to carry you for 30, 60, or 90

Personal Credit Tips

- Obtain a copy of your personal credit report from your local credit bureau or one of the following agencies:

  Equifax:1-800-685-1111; www.equifax.com
  Experian: 1-800-397-3742; www.experian.com
  TransUnion: 1-800-916-8800; www.transunion.com

- Review your credit report to ensure it contains accurate information about you.
- Close old, unused credit accounts to reduce your risk of credit and identity theft.
- Know your Fair Isaac Corp. (FICO) score: It ranges between 300–900. The higher the score, the lower the credit risk. FICO is now used to determine your credit capability, as well as for insurance and employment purposes.

days, your credit report will be excellent if you pay within these terms. If, however, their statement says: "payable within 10 days" and you do not pay for 30 days, you are overdue, and your credit will be jeopardized.

Sometimes you may not be able to meet a payment because merchandise has been shipped to you too early. Early shipments can create real problems. Often, you must store the merchandise in a warehouse for several months before it can be delivered. You may have asked the company to ship the merchandise three months from now, but it came in early, so the company wants immediate payment. If this situation comes up, call your resource immediately and explain the situation. You have the right to refuse delivery of these items at this time or to make payment at the appropriate date, as previously scheduled.

Identity Theft

Identity theft losses were $48 billion in 2003. Check fraud has doubled in the last few years. This has now become a major issue all of us must deal with. The offshore work being done for insurance claims, accounting, and banking processing is really questionable, since there are no laws protecting the privacy of these documents once they leave our country. The Fair Credit Reporting Act was amended in 2005 to permit us to get our credit report each year at no cost, allowing us to see if any problems are developing. It will also protect information going to offshore contractors. In most instances, this new law will stop all offshore processing of documents that could affect our privacy. At this point, take these precautions:

- Shred everything: insurance forms, bank statements, client documents that may include money amounts, and so on.
- Do not give your Social Security number to just anyone. Be very careful.
- Never put your Social Security number on a check.
- Do not put any outgoing mail in your personal mailbox or an area where others

have access to it. Leave it either in a post office mailbox or a place where you are assured only the mailperson has access to it.

■ Check your credit rating regularly. That way, if you have any problems, you can be made aware of them as soon as possible.

Credit Reporting Agencies

Interior designers need to use credit reporting agencies regularly to check on prospective clients and to investigate resources.

The more you can find out about your clients, the better you are able to protect your business. Therefore, it is wise to check the credit history of prospective clients, whether you sought them out as part of your business development or marketing efforts or the prospective client approached you. The information gained from credit reports can help you tailor contracts and agreements to the individual client, provided you believe the client is a good risk. Checking the credit backgrounds of clients can save you many headaches.

The second reason to use credit organizations is to check out suppliers and resources. Other designers have given large retainers or deposits to companies, only to find, when the merchandise was long overdue, that the firm had gone out of business. If the supplier's credit had been checked in advance, these designers would never have extended deposits or retainers. In most instances, the designer is in a responsible position; if the resource defaults, it is up to the designer to make good to the client.

All credit bureaus have regular reporting services, such as newsletters, but these are beneficial only if you need constant up-to-date input. Most design services prefer to check credit on an as-needed basis, rather than using regular weekly or monthly reporting.

Many of these credit bureaus also have collection divisions, which can be very effective. To ensure appropriately professional handling of collections, you should make sure the bureaus are certified by the American Collector's Association and that they abide by all federal and state regulations. Collection bureaus generally have a pretty good recovery rate, which they classify as about 50 percent. You should use a collection agency only as a last resort, but it is available if all of your other methods fail. Fees generally run 30 percent or more for this type of service.

Local Credit Organizations. Most communities have a local credit bureau. There is usually a membership fee. As a member, you can make credit inquiries by telephone at the cost of a few dollars per inquiry, depending on the type of account you have and the frequency with which you use the service. In this type of report you get a person's name, account number, company codes, credit limits, types of accounts, mortgages, revolving charges, reasons for financing, salary, company balance owing, monthly payments, and the number of times the person has been late on payments during the past few years.

These reports will give you information on individual clients or companies working within the area. This information includes: some background and history; where they were born; how long they have lived in the community; their approximate age; salaries; marital status; number of dependents; and, in some cases, whether they have alimony payments or other obligations. Local credit organizations also report mortgages and other debts a person might have incurred. With this information, it is easier to tell whether a client will be able to meet the financial requirements of the contract the person is negotiating. Many designers like to review this information before they go for an initial interview or immediately thereafter. Do not wait to ask for credit information. Get it as early as possible.

A good credit report, however, is not an absolute guarantee that a new account will be satisfactory. It is an indicator, based on the theory that past experience does usually repeat itself.

Dun & Bradstreet. This company specializes in all types of corporate reporting and is a prime source for information on your resources and tradespeople, as well as business clients. Dun & Bradstreet gathers information regularly from all businesses and rates them according to size and payment activities. A Dun & Bradstreet report is an analysis of a commercial establishment: its operations, legal structure, payment records, banking relations, financial condition, management history, and business trends.

Dun & Bradstreet is available online at www.dnb.com and has offices in major towns and cities throughout the United States. Manufacturers, wholesalers, retailers, and many businesses and professional services use this organization for their reports. Dun & Bradstreet calls on businesses on a regular basis, and interviews the owners and their accountants.

If you requested a large purchase from a vendor, and Dun & Bradstreet was consulted by the vendor but did not have your records, Dun & Bradstreet would then arrange an interview with you. It is often necessary to refer their investigator to your accountant for detailed information. However, some of the information regarding the functioning and history of the firm needs to come directly from the managing officers. The type of information D & B publishes includes:

- **Your D-U-N-S number.** A nine-digit code that identifies your business name and location in their files.
- **A summary.** A quick reference analysis of the detailed information contained in the report. It includes the business "SIC" (standard industrial classification) code and function, your product line, the principal executive of your firm, and the D&B capital and credit rating (data as to payment habits, sales, worth, number of employees, history, financing, and general conditions and trends).
- **Your payment record.** Your firm's payment record, including the amount you owe or the amount that is past due. The settling terms and time of your last sales are also included.
- **Your financial record.** A statement of assets, liabilities, sales, expenses, and profits, along with a description of sales and profit trends.

- **Your banking record.** Your firm's average balances, previous and current loan activities, lengths of banking relationships, and statement of account satisfaction.
- **Your history.** The names, years of birth, and past business experience of the principals or owners of the firm, and the legal structure of the business.
- **Your operation.** The nature of your business, its premises, products or services, price ranges, classifications of customers, percentages of cash and credit sales, number of accounts, seasonal aspects, and number of employees.
- **Special events.** Any recent changes of chief executives, the legal structure, partners' control or location; business discontinuances; criminal proceedings; burglaries; embezzlements; fires; and other events.
- **Public filings.** Any public record filing, such as suits or judgments, uniform commercial code filings, tax liens, and record item update and releases.
- **D&B capital and credit ratings.** An indicator of estimated strength; a composed credit rating. This information is in the Dun & Bradstreet Records Book, published every two months, with a standard industrial classification, the name of the business, the starting year of the operation, and the D&B capital and credit rating.

The Allied Board of Trade. Many designers belong to the Allied Board of Trade (ABT) and are issued a card identifying them as members of the professional design community. Membership suggests to wholesalers and manufacturers that these are designers who should be purchasing from them on a wholesale basis. Designers who wish to be registered with this board must show proof they meet minimum professional standards for education and practical experience and actually are in business.

The Allied Board of Trade has been in business since 1925, predating the precursor organization of ASID, the American Institute of Designers. The ABT issues an annual directory with information about design-related businesses. ABT constantly investigates designers and registers newly formed companies. It has a considerable amount of information on specific design companies, not all of it published. ABT also tries to put designers in touch with appropriate resources and trades. It publishes a comprehensive reference called *The Green Book,* for members' use. The book contains lists and ratings of all recognized designers and design-related specialists.

Smaller design firms that might not be listed with Dun & Bradstreet usually would be included in *The Green Book* or in the *Lyon Credit Reference Book,* known as the *Lyon Red Book.*

The Lyon Mercantile Group, Ltd. Founded in 1876, the Lyon Mercantile Group Ltd. has had a major impact on the furniture industry. Interior designers and decorators are listed in the semiannual *Lyon Red Book,* but it is dealers, jobbers, furniture manufacturers, and allied tradespeople who maintain service contracts with Lyon.

Designers are contacted by Lyon in response to requests from showrooms and manufacturers. They are asked to furnish current credit and general information, usually by letter.

Lyon also offers validated registration cards for designers. For an annual fee, designers who supply current information are furnished with this card, which can be used as an entree to the major market buildings and showrooms. You need not purchase the card to be listed in the *Red Book*.

To find out what your Lyon credit rating is, you may use the services provided on the organization's web site, found at www.lyoncredit.com.

Do you know what credit organizations are saying about you? There is a law that requires them to provide you with all of the information they are releasing to their clients. Therefore, your credit rating and credit information are available to you at any time. I suggest you contact each of the organizations that have you rated on a regular basis and check out your classification. If you have any questions, speak with them. Some interior designers find themselves with very bad ratings they were unaware of. Take the time and check out just what your position is. If it is not what you think it should be, see what you can do to update it.

Construction Law

Many designers do a tremendous number of projects with other professionals and contractors. As designers, we may recommend the architects, engineers, and other professionals we have worked with in the past. This pleases our clients, because they know we have had prior experience with these professionals.

Any relationship you have with an architect or other design professional should be in writing. You will then have the option of including provisions that help protect you legally. In the complex relationships involved in construction cases, there is no way to absolutely avoid the possibility of being sued and of costs associated with defending a suit. But there are several ways to protect against these suits:

- **Indemnification clause.** Provisions of a contract that require the other party to indemnify your business—requiring the other party to pay your legal expenses or incur the cost of any claim or expense for actions brought by third parties against you because of a design professional's negligence or other liability. These clauses have been upheld fairly broadly. If the indemnification is based on the negligence of the other professionals, the court will require them to pay your defense, whether they are ultimately found liable or not.
- **Insurance clause.** Professional insurance is necessary, but this is extra insurance listing you as an additional insured under the architect or contractor's insurance policy. That way, if a suit is brought against them or you, you would be covered under their policy. The architect or contractor will provide you with an insurance certificate that verifies the addition of your company under this policy.
- **Arbitration clauses.** These provide alternate mediums for resolution of disputes, through which you meet in an informal environment and present your claims to a neutral board of arbitrators who make a decision about the claim presented. When you are talking about liability to an owner, it would be to your advantage to have these clauses. Arbitration is usually faster and less expensive than a law-

suit. Owners may be resistant to arbitration clauses, because the arbitration forum is often very beneficial to design professionals and contractors.

Most qualified designers take the National Council for Interior Design Qualification (NCIDQ) exam for admission to professional organizations, such as ASID, IIDA, and others. You should consider the manner in which the designer's design impacts life-safety codes—codes dealing with wiring, fire protection, ingress and egress from a building, emergency lighting, smoke alarm placement, and the like. These design elements could impact potentially on safety codes. It is a good idea to seek advice from a consulting engineer to share the responsibility. In this situation, the consulting engineer would become your subcontractor, so be sure to have the previously mentioned agreements in place.

What is the value of professional liability insurance for errors and omissions? All of us have insurance, but it's complicated and, in some areas, not well defined. It is prudent to shop around for the different policies and get specific information as to what is covered before you settle on a particular company or policy. Seek answers as to whether the policy will cover these areas of liability adequately; if not, shop around for another provider. Professional liability issues are based on state laws, even when these cases are filed in federal court. They also vary from state to state.

You may want to include in your contract that your firm is not responsible for anything above a specific amount. Have clients advise their insurance company to insure their project while it is under construction.

As discussed earlier, the risks involved in the work we do are often quite substantial. Request verification that the owner's insurance company is aware of the project and the potential liability that can be caused by the construction. Be sure that the company adjusts the policy to cover potential liability, not only for the owner but for you as well.

Universal Construction Code

All states were requested to put the Universal Construction Code (UCC) into effect as of August 2004, and each city, township, and borough in a state must then adopt it individually. Many large cities have requirements more stringent than those of the UCC; therefore, these cities' codes would be enforced before the UCC.

By implementing the Universal Construction Code, it has become easier for designers to understand construction codes, since they are based on one system. You should understand the UCC requirements for the area you are working in to determine how that area follows the code.

Codes vary in our field even within a single building. For example, in a nursing home, you may have one type of code in a certain area; but in assisted care, which is a hospital area, there is a completely different set of codes. Moreover, the UCC has a provision that deals specifically with nursing home-managed care facilities. So anyone working in this environment needs to consult the particular subdivisions of the regulations.

The work of many building designers does not comply with the UCC. If they are not making major changes, they are not required to comply. But it is our responsibility as professionals to verify that the projects we are working on meet the appropriate codes and that all related issues are covered in the best way possible.

Designers need someone specializing in construction law to review the types of projects they are working on to make sure they are properly positioned with regard to other professionals, clients, and the laws of the areas in which they work.

INSURANCE

No design firm can afford to be without a good insurance program.

Insurance Advisor

Your insurance consultant is an important member of your financial advisory group, working with your accountant and your attorney. Therefore, it's important to select someone who will be available you at all times and is compatible with the rest of the group. This working rapport is just as important as the insurance consultant's ability and knowledge.

How do you select an insurance advisor? It is important to find someone you can work with. Another businessperson or one of the financial professionals in your advisory group might be able to help you select a competent and capable professional. A very large corporation would hire an advisor or an independent insurance consultant. A small company, like many interior design firms, would use an agent or broker.

An independent insurance agent has contracts with multiple insurance companies to represent them. A broker is entitled to do business with a number of companies but does not have a contract with the insurance companies. Regardless of whether you use an agent or broker, your insurance advisor should understand the needs of your business and seek the most appropriate fit between your firm and an insurance carrier.

Unless insurance agents understand the interior design field, it will be very hard for them to define your needs. They should speak with your accountant and attorney; together, they will define the particular needs of your company so the agents can match you with an appropriate coverage package.

In today's world, it is sometimes necessary to go to several difference sources to get the coverage you need. Use your insurance advisor as a coordinator so the advisor can review the policies and prevent overlap of coverage. By combining various policies, you often reduce the expense of coverage and get an all-encompassing package. But for certain forms of insurance, such as errors and omissions and other special liabilities (which can be obtained through professional associations such as ASID), you may need to go to a specialist. I have found it is more valuable to keep my insurance advisor on a local basis, if I can, even though I must use several out-of-town resources for specialties. A local advisor is more aware of what is happening in the area and what my needs are.

Selecting Insurance

Several companies offer an insurance package that includes coverage for "comprehensive perils": special property, comprehensive general liability, and professional liability or errors and omissions in design. Because this is packaged, this insurance may be less expensive and more encompassing than when policies are purchased individually. If you are a member of ASID or another professional organization, you need to evaluate the policies offered by your organization. In some cases, these organizations may offer better coverage than you can purchase from your own insurance agents.

Ask your agent or broker to provide information on the financial condition of the companies they are using. A. M. Best publishes an annual rating of each insurer, based on overall financial strength and performance. An "A" rating or better is recommended. Exercise every caution you can to make sure the company (or companies) you select will be in business to pay your long-term claims, such as those arising from product liability. An illustration of this is the billions of dollars being paid by insurance companies on asbestos claims for exposures that occurred over 30 years ago.

Remember: The obligation is the designer's, not the insurance company's, according to law. The designer uses insurance to transfer the risk to the insurance company. The transfer of risk ceases to exist when an insurance company goes bankrupt. Insurance demands differ considerably from state to state and from area to area because of the attitudes of the local people. In some areas, people are far more litigious on certain issues, and therefore you may require additional insurance of a particular type because you are in, say, New York State and not Ohio. Your local advisor will know the state laws as well as the social issues of your community.

In the interior design business, you are often exposed to possible litigation. There are four methods of handling the various exposures you face:

1. **Eliminate the exposure.** This is done by limiting the responsibilities you choose to accept and the way you write your contracts with both clients and vendors.
2. **Assume the exposure yourself.** This method can be selected only after you have measured the financial impact of a loss to your business.
3. **Reduce the exposure.** This method allows you to establish a loss prevention program. Such a program helps your organization identify and reduce the hazards that cause losses.
4. **Transfer the exposure.** This method allows you and your organization to transfer the risk to an insurance company.

There are three essentials to remember in buying proper insurance:

1. Never risk more than you can afford to lose.
2. Do not risk too much for too little.
3. Know the odds of sustaining loss.

Clarify the way your policy is written. Replacement value is almost universally worded the same way. Individual circumstances dictate how it is interpreted.

I have had several experiences in which replacement value was interpreted in different ways by the adjusters. In one case—a country club project—the claim was adjusted before we started the project. Part of the claim involved chairs and stacking chairs, which were stored on the third floor. Although they had not been used for many years, they were evaluated at today's current replacement value, and the club was given this full value in cash.

In the second case—a church project—the evaluation also was based on replacement value but was interpreted differently. In this case, the insurance adjuster decided that since the church had, for example, wool carpeting worth about $60 a yard, we were permitted to buy carpeting priced at up to $60 a yard. However, we could not buy carpeting for $30 a yard and then spend the rest of the money on lighting fixtures. The replacement money was to be spent only on the particular items specified in the church's claim.

It is a good idea to clarify this value in advance, if you can. Most designers are interested in making changes and updating at the time of a disaster; they do not always want to replace exactly the same items. This can be a problem at the time of a claim.

If you are assisting a client in handling a claim, check the individual company's practice with regard to replacement costs. The General Adjustment Bureau gives guidelines; however, claim practices vary. Be sure you know the ground rules for repair or replacement procedures. It would be unwise for you to make a commitment before having solid information about the specific insurance company's settlement procedures.

Definition of loss: The insured considers a loss to be the amount paid for the repair of a fire-damaged building. The policy includes depreciation in determining the amount to be paid to the insured. For example, the contractor's bill of $50,000 could be considered the amount of loss by the insured. However, the policy determination of the loss would be $50,000 less $10,000, or $40,000. The depreciation value used would be determined by various factors, such as age and condition of the building, and, in some cases, use and type of structure.

Use of the replacement basis of loss settlement eliminates the foregoing, in that the insured is paid the actual cost of replacement or repair (if possible), whichever is lower.

Types of Insurance

There are a number of types of insurance you should consider:

Building Property Insurance. Property coverage insures against many risks to your buildings and premises. Very often, a company will write a package policy that saves you money. The package policy works best when it is custom-designed for your particular needs, rather than a standard prepackaged policy.

The two general ways in which this type of coverage is set up are: (1) insuring for reimbursement losses due to specific perils such as fire, and (2) insuring on a special or comprehensive basis whereby reimbursement is made for all losses except those excluded under the policy. If the special or comprehensive basis is available in your coverage, the small additional premium required for this more complete protection is usually well worth spending.

You will probably need insurance in some of the following areas:

1. **Building.** This insurance applies to the described structures and permanent fixtures belonging to and constituting a part of your building. Machinery used in your building—such as air conditioning systems, boilers, and elevators—is covered under the policy. The location of your building will affect the premium of this particular policy. If you desire specific coverage for a sudden breakdown in boiler or air conditioning equipment, you may wish to consider a boiler or energy equipment policy, where available.

2. **Contents and personal property.** Insurance should be carried on all furniture, fixtures, and inventory. General coverage is similar to building property coverage.

3. **Replacement costs endorsement.** This insurance provides for the full reimbursement of the actual costs of repair or replacement of the insured building, without any deduction for depreciation.

4. **Removal of coinsurance.** It is essential that coinsurance be removed from your policy on both your building and contents. Coinsurance in property and casualty coverage is far different than under medical insurance. For your buildings and contents policy, coinsurance is, in essence, a guarantee by you, the policyholder, that your property was insured to 80 percent of the full value on the day of the loss. This is very dangerous, because even an appraisal may be in error or become dated over time.

   Approximately 75 percent of policies will be business owner policies, which do not include coinsurance clauses; but one solution is to have coinsurance waived, which the insurer will do routinely for the asking. The additional premium to waive is minimal. Failure to have coinsurance waived can result in a (1) coinsurance penalty for being underinsured, and (2) a much longer time period before your claim is settled and you receive your claim check.

5. **Comprehensive perils.** The special causes form places your policy on a comprehensive basis; that is, there is coverage for you under the property form for all causes of loss unless the policy specifically excludes it. This means all issues are covered, unless specifically stated in the policy.

6. **Flood insurance.** This protects the owner of a dwelling and contents against financial loss in catastrophic floods; it includes coverage against inundation from mudslides. Flood insurance is available in declared areas; coverage can be obtained from your local broker through the National Flood Insurance Program. Because the cost of this policy is partially covered by the federal government, it is still economical. A small number of insurance companies now write this type of coverage.

Business Operations Insurance. You can also purchase insurance to help protect your business operations.

1. **Accounts receivable policy.** This policy protects the insured against loss related to the inability to collect accounts receivable when books and records have been destroyed, lost, or damaged. Coverage can be extended to cover losses off the premises of your business.
2. **Valuable papers.** The policy covers the loss or destruction of valuable papers such as mortgages, records, financial data, product specifications, merchandise records, customer lists, blueprints, and plans and specifications.
3. **Transportation floater.** This floater provides an "all-risk" coverage for the designer's property while it is in transit—while being delivered to your customer or en route from your source to the client. Coverage is usually written on a per-vehicle basis. Make certain your coverage is truly adequate to handle all limited situations.
4. **Bailee customer floater.** This floater insures against the loss of a customer's property from fire, burglary, holdup, and windstorms. It covers any articles or materials you have accepted from your client for renovation, repair, or any other reason. This floater covers the client's property while in the possession of the interior designer or craftspeople. It does not cover damage to articles while they are being repaired.
5. **Transportation damage insurance.** This insurance is offered by many resources and is popular with companies providing breakable or fragile merchandise. It can be well worth the cost. Different types of coverage are offered by various vendors. Under one plan, you do not file a claim with the carrier for merchandise damaged in transit. For an additional charge of 2 percent of the net invoice, any covered merchandise that is damaged in transit will be replaced at no charge, or credited to your account, as you prefer. Certain restrictions do apply. This insurance is available from vendors only.
6. **Business interruption.** This policy reimburses designers for the profits they would have earned if a fire or other hazard had not occurred. It includes reimbursement for continuing expenses, such as payroll, for a specific time or number of days.
7. **Earnings insurance.** This is a simplified business-interruption policy. It is suitable for small businesses whose earnings are not regular and are difficult to forecast. It is based on a predetermined expected profit amount. Extra expenses, earnings, and business interruption coverage are now often included under the policy provision termed "Business Income."
8. **Comprehensive general liability insurance.** Interior designers and other professionals are subject to the threat of third-party claims. Injury exists as long as there is a client on the premises. It does not terminate when the doors are closed. The designer and the manufacturer are often named jointly in suits alleging injuries caused by defective products. There are policies designed to cover the interior designer in most situations where protection is required

against injury or property damage. It is extremely important to use the same insurance company for both worker's compensation insurance and general liability insurance. This prevents litigation between two different carriers if a person is injured. It frequently occurs that, when different companies are used, you, as both the insured party and the employer, are caught in litigation that can take years to be resolved.

Comprehensive general liability insurance also includes:

- ❏ **Commercial general liability.** This insures against all declared existing hazards subject to policy exclusions, plus unknown hazards occurring during the policy term—subject to the policy text—that might come from the designer's offices or business operations.
- ❏ **Personal injury.** This insures against libel, slander, or defamation of character against the designer or an employee.
- ❏ **Medical payments.** This policy pays up to a certain amount, with specified limits, to customers and other members of the public injured on the premises as a result of the insured party's business operations. Payments are made to the injured party on a voluntary basis, regardless of the insured's liability.
- ❏ **Product liability and completed operations liability insurance.** This is designed to provide coverage against claims resulting from misuse or use of products installed by interior designers. Product liability insurance addresses claims for accidents arising after the insured has completed repairs or installations and has departed from the client's premises.

9. **Worker's compensation.** This insures all employees, including officers active in the business operations, for the statutory liability resulting from bodily injury or death suffered in the course of employment. This coverage is mandatory in most states. Benefits are payable in accordance with the program of each state. Employers' liability coverage is usually offered in conjunction with worker's compensation. Coverage can be endorsed for employees living and operating in all states, except Ohio, North Dakota, Washington, West Virginia, and Wyoming. The states excepted operate monopolistic funds, and coverage can be obtained only through the state funds. (Note: In some states, the employer is responsible not only for occupational disabilities but also nonoccupational disabilities. In addition, sole proprietors, partners, and shareholders of LLCs are not generally considered employees and are not covered by worker's compensation.)

10. **Motor vehicle insurance.** If you provide delivery service, you must insure your trucks and other delivery vehicles against damage or loss. The same is true of any passenger cars your company uses. It is most important to have high liability coverage for all vehicles used in the interest of business. (See also, "Comprehensive general liability insurance," pages 414–415.)

11. **Automobile liability.** This insures you against loss or damages for reason of liability or bodily injury; it also provides property damage coverage to members of the public for any operation of business autos or delivery trucks. Claims

arising out of the use, ownership, and maintenance of company-owned vehicles are covered. Defense costs are paid on behalf of the insured by the insurance company, without limit. Some states have mandatory (compulsory) liability regulations. Insurance requirements vary from state to state. Special conditions also exist for operation of your vehicles in Mexico. The type or form of business under which you operate dictates the use of various provisions to provide proper coverage.

12. **Employer's nonownership liability.** This covers your business against claims in situations when employees are using their own cars for business purposes.

13. **Hired car insurance.** This covers the use of any hired cars, such as additional delivery trucks that are rented or leased. A minimum premium is usually required under this policy. Coverage is available for both liability and physical damage.

14. **Collision insurance.** This insures you against loss due to collision or upset of your motor vehicle while in use for your business.

15. **Comprehensive automobile insurance.** This insures the interior designer's own business automobiles against loss, fire, or theft, or other physical-damage hazards, including glass breakage. This coverage reimburses you for loss or damage to owned vehicles—regardless of fault—for such claims as fire, flood, theft, vandalism, windstorm, tornado, glass damage, and similar losses.

16. **Professional liability insurance.** This insurance is available for interior designers through your insurance carrier or ASID. It covers liability for claims resulting from the commission or omission of professional acts. Such claims are often without merit; nevertheless, they are troublesome and expensive to defend. This policy protects you against such claims.

17. **Employment-related practice (ERP) liability.** This protects you as an employer against allegations of improper acts in hiring, firing, and treatment of your employees. Coverage is included for wrongful termination, employment-related discrimination, and sexual harassment. In past years, this coverage has been most expensive. However, since 1996, the annual premium for ERP liability coverage has dropped dramatically.

18. **Group life insurance.** This may be purchased by businesses for the benefit of their employees.

19. **Disability insurance.** Most interior designers work on their own or with small firms and need good disability insurance. In my own situation, it has proved very helpful. I recommend all designers have some sort of disability policy to provide a form of income during any time that they may be disabled by illness or accident. Benefits are available on both an occupational and nonoccupational basis. The noncancelable or guaranteed renewable policies are the most desirable ones to have, although their premiums are somewhat higher. With these policies, restrictive endorsements cannot be issued later to prevent reimbursement for claims recurring from the same cause or unusual claim activity. The noncancelable premiums at issuance cannot be increased.

Premium increases can be made under a guaranteed renewable policy for various reasons but are normally on a class rather than an individual basis.

20. **Group medical insurance.** Group medical coverage can provide you and your employees with coverage for hospitalization, surgery, physician visits, tests, and prescription drugs other than those caused by worker's compensation injuries. So-called managed care plans—including the Preferred Provider Organization (PPO) and Health Maintenance Organization (HMO) plan formats—may provide premium reduction from traditional indemnity coverage in return for your use of a published network of physicians and hospitals. Generally, this coverage responds to nonoccupational injuries.

21. **Pensions.** Employees value pension benefits. Only group hospitalization, life, and disability benefits are valued more. There are so many types of financial programs available it is difficult to decide which, if any, is the best for your employees. In providing pension benefits, you make a long-term commitment. In most cases, it is against the law to change the basic elements of your pension program. If your business in later years cannot make the required contributions to the plan, and you plead your inability to continue to the government, your pleas will fall on deaf ears. Unless you are going out of business or filing for bankruptcy, you will find it very difficult to make such a change. Profit-sharing plans used for pension purposes provide the employer relief, in that the amount of profits determines the employer's contribution. Thus, in a year in which no profits were made, the plan would not require a contribution from the employer.

22. **Key personnel life insurance.** This is commonly used to enable a business to offset the financial loss of a person vital to its continued profitable operation. Owners also use life insurance to finance buy-sell agreements involving the business. Corporations can accumulate money on a tax-deferred basis to provide for retirement for themselves, as well as for key personnel.

Many interior designers serve on volunteer boards. Check with the volunteer organization to see if they carry directors and officers liability coverage, and with your insurance agent, to see if you are covered for any liability you might incur when serving on volunteer boards. This coverage may be included under your homeowner's umbrella policy. This insurance would not cover your liability on boards for which you are financially compensated.

Care, Custody, and Control

We need insurance today for things we could never have dreamed would become an issue. Almost every designer I know has liability insurance and daily policies on items handled for clients, and most have a variety of other liability insurances. I thought my firm was very well covered until a broken chandelier showed us otherwise.

One of our designers was decorating a chandelier when it fell from a 30-foot ceiling. It hit a marble floor, and a number of other accessories, and did considerable damage along the way. The designer immediately called the office. Our managing director instructed him to clean up the damage and take care of everything he could. We then notified our insurance company, as we were sure that we had very good coverage.

But, as we soon learned, there was a small, but very important, clause in our insurance policy called "Care, Custody, and Control," which means any item designers or staff people have in their hands is not in any way covered. According to our policy, the marble floor and other items that were damaged by the chandelier were covered but the item our designer was working on—the chandelier—was not. It was considered under our "care, custody, and control."

When I heard this, I became very concerned. Not just about this $15,000 fixture, for which we had to pay, but about all of our projects. I thought of the many costly items we handled on an everyday basis. When clients move, we are always there assisting. In some cases, we take the complete responsibility for the move. Our staff people are on location the day the furniture is transferred. When the furniture arrives, they see it is arranged properly, so when the client arrives at the new location, everything is in place.

When I think of the hundreds of thousands of dollars of merchandise our firm handles in a year, I find the prospect of being held liable for it chilling. I know enough about art and porcelain to tell the difference between a $50 vase and a $500 vase, but I have no way of knowing the value of rare and unusual antiques or art objects.

After the incident with the chandelier, and in trying to diminish our future liability, my eyes were opened to a number of risks. I consulted with our attorney and insurance broker and with two other attorneys who handle nothing but insurance work for large companies such as Equitable. I checked with the brokers and agents who handle Lloyd's of London and found there is no way we, as designers, can insure our clients' furniture or art objects—simply because we do not know their value. If you, as an individual, wanted to insure a piece of jewelry or furniture, the procedure would be simple. You would have the item appraised and present the appraisal to your insurance company, and the company in turn would insure it for you. But they could not possibly sell you insurance on an unknown item of undetermined value.

My solution was to require our clients, at the start of a project, to sign a "Release of Liens." This document states that since we do not know the value of the objects on a client's property, our firm can only be responsible for items valued at $500 or less.

You may put a "waiver of subrogation" clause in your contract with the owner of the item. Or, as we do, you may ask the client to notify our staff of all items worth more than $500, so that they will not touch or handle these items. We also ask clients to notify their insurance companies to list our interior design firm as an "additional insured" on their policy and to have a copy of this sent directly to us. Most policies do include this coverage.

It is sad to realize that doing something kind for a client—many times without charge—makes me legally liable for damages way beyond my ability to afford. In self-protection, we now notify the clients so they can see to it that their policies cover these items; or they can remove these items from the area while our staff is working. We feel this is the only safe way to handle the situation.

Ways of Saving Money

It is not practical for interior designers to carry all the insurance they might like to have. It is important that your insurance advisor, accountant, and attorney, as well as your business advisor, give you some advice as to which areas present your greatest loss potential, which losses you should insure, and which losses should be covered by self-insurance. If the maximum amount of loss potential is a small, calculable number, it is usually preferable to self-insure. Your business can self-insure small claims less expensively than the cost of insurance company premiums. Where the probability of loss is not great, but the potential loss cannot be calculated or controlled (such as liability claims), the risk should be transferred to your insurance company.

Taking Higher Deductibles. By taking higher deductibles on certain insurance policies and doing some self-insuring, you can reduce premiums. The amount of the deductible or the uninsured loss is considered an income tax deduction.

Using high deductibles is advisable on property insurance of all types, in bonding employees, and on automobile insurance, but *not* on anything that involves liability insurance because of third-party involvement.

Look over all your insurance policies for the last five years. See which policies you normally do not have claims on. Check with your company to see whether you can save yourself a considerable amount of money by raising the deductible on these policies.

Lower Your Insurance Rates. In a roundtable discussion at our Harrisburg Chamber of Commerce, representatives from the Pennsylvania Insurance Department recommended ways interior designers can lower insurance rates:

1. **First, reexamine the coverage you have now to see if it includes the full scope of your business.** If you make changes in your business, discuss them with your insurance advisor. Many people are not going into certain businesses or are limiting their areas of work because they cannot get good insurance coverage. In my own business, I have stopped extending certain services, or am requiring signed releases from clients, because I cannot get proper coverage.
2. **How well trained your employees are affects your insurance rates.** If you cannot get well-trained employees, do not take the job. You are better off to hire the job out and let someone else be liable, rather than jeopardize the relationship you have with your client and, in turn, your financial position. If you subcontract work to others, require a proper, current Certificate of Insurance—including commercial general liability, auto liability, and worker's compen-

sation coverage. Your firm should be listed as "additional insured" on both the Commercial General Liability and Auto Liability sections. If necessary, send your employees to school or require them to have extra training that might help them do the job well.

3. **Is your firm safety-conscious?** Hold training sessions for safety. I know one firm that holds Saturday training sessions in safety awareness for its management. Anyone who does not show up does not have a job. Do whatever is necessary to be sure that your people understand what they can do to prevent accidents and avoid claims.

4. **Make your staff responsible for any damages they do.** For example, a number of firms now make staff members responsible for the first $100 on an auto claim. That way, the employees are much more careful in the way they handle a company vehicle—and save the firm a lot of expense.

5. **Give a bonus at the end of the year if there have been no damages or suits.** Have a party. Celebrate. Make your staff aware that avoiding suits is a very important issue.

Insurance Claims

If you do have to use your insurance, these guidelines may help you in handling your claims.

Calculating Losses. Calculate your losses accurately. Many businesspeople cannot determine the extent of their losses because their accounting system and record-keeping procedures are not in order. Interior designers have a better opportunity than most professionals to calculate losses. At most times, we do know the cost of replacing or restoring whatever property losses we might have.

If you overstate your loss, you automatically raise many questions and delay get-

Product Liability Bills

In the past few years, there have been many product liability bills before the Senate, on both the national and state levels. Interior designers should support these bills, since most of them attempt to ease the product liability situation. In other words, the bills propose that, if a company manufactures an item and it fails, the company alone could be sued. The designer, architect, contractors, distributors, or other intermediate people could not be named in the suits. This would reduce malpractice insurance rates considerably, since responsibility would be assigned automatically.

These bills would also give statute-of-limitation rights, which currently do not exist in some states. Whether designers sell or specify merchandise, they are still liable. Liability insurance is required for each situation. Therefore, interior designers need to define the services they offer to a given client when purchasing the appropriate amount of liability insurance, as well as of errors and omissions insurance.

ting the claim settled. Be careful also not to understate value; this is just as inappropriate as an overstatement.

Present the claim properly. Review your claim with your accountant and insurance agent before presenting it to the adjuster. If it is not presented properly, you will not get the results you seek.

Coordination. Be sure the coordination between your office and the insurance company is handled by one person. Have this person follow through carefully to be sure there is a record of all of the necessary details and that all interaction between you and the insurance company is documented for future reference.

As designers, we know which contractors we want to use in restoring a project or who the merchandise came from initially. Present this to your insurance adjuster. Normally, you will be able to use the person you want.

Use your insurance consultant or agent as a member of your negotiating group. The consultant plays a very strong role with the insurance company, since the consultant is purchasing the insurance in your name. Let the consultant or agent take your stand. Be sure they are aware of each and every detail of the negotiation. This is an excellent opportunity to find out the value of an insurance agent.

It is just amazing: You do not have to do anything to get sued, which is one of the reasons that liability insurance and proper documentation of projects are really critical.

What can we do to protect ourselves? First, we must have reasonable contracts and documents. Compare yours with those other firms are using. This is something

You cannot live without liability insurance. I never thought I would have to worry about being sued for events that had nothing to do with my interior design performance. My eyes were opened a few years ago when I was involved in a small country club project. The club had been destroyed through arson, and our design team designed, built, furnished, and completed the new club within a year. We more than tripled its size and certainly made it more efficient to run, as well as more attractive. The club opened in June, in good time for its season.

That winter was very cold. I recall that on Christmas Day everyone's car battery was dead, including mine. You could not go anywhere because you could not get your car fixed. Over that particular holiday, the country club decided to close and, for some reason, no one walked into the club for over 30 days.

During that time, the water pipes in the building froze. The sprinkler system broke, flooding both levels of the clubhouse. The water in the lower level then froze, creating over four feet of ice. Doors had to be broken down in order to get into the office.

I was not the specifier of the sprinkler system. I may have suggested moving a head or two because of interference with a lighting fixture, but that was all I had to do with the sprinkler system. Nevertheless, I was one of the design consultants, so our firm was included in the suit. Our attorney found a way to remove me from the claim; however, it cost me a good bit of money, time, anguish, and aggravation.

for you to discuss with your attorney. But this is only part of the process. The kind of relationship you have with your client is crucial. Ideally, your relationship is one in which you work together with mutual respect. If that respect is lost, or if clients feel they are not getting enough attention, very often that is when problems begin.

In lawsuits, what it boils down to is not whether you made a mistake or were careless, but if you can be held responsible for the problem. Proper documentation of each stage of the project can help greatly in establishing your position.

On a project like the country club, designers probably cannot avoid a suit, because when people are going to sue one design professional, they will sue all those who are on the team. However, there are many individual suits against interior designers, and your chances of winning are not very good. There are states, I am told by an experienced source, in which there has never been a case against an interior designer won by the interior designer. When I hear statistics like this, I realize we must assume that juries and judges are not on our side. Few understand what we do. The simplest way to protect yourself is to have positive rapport with your client. As I mentioned earlier, if you find someone who is litigious, probably you are going to be the next person to be sued. So look for another client.

TAXES

One of the primary reasons for keeping records is to support our tax documents. There are basically four types of federal taxes: income taxes, FICA taxes, unemployment taxes, and excise taxes.

Interior designers are usually involved with the first three. Income taxes depend completely on the earnings of your company, or you as an individual. The amounts vary according to the type of organizational structure you choose—a sole proprietorship, a partnership, a limited liability company, or a corporation. Your documentation of all exemptions, nonbusiness deductions, and any credits will play an important part in the amount of taxes you must pay. If you are involved in a corporation, regular income tax will be paid on your salary and any other income you receive as an employee of the corporation. The corporation will file a Form 1120, Corporation Income Tax Return.

If your company is a sole proprietorship, your taxes will be paid based on the earnings of the business, instead of from a salary. You file an annual Form 1040 like any individual taxpayer would file, but you also file additional forms that identify the expenses and income of your business. Schedule C shows the profit and loss from your business or profession. This federal tax is reported on Schedule SE, which is a part of the individual income tax return.

If you are in a partnership, you must file a return showing the income and expenses from the business (Form 1065, Return of Partnership Income). You will report only your share of the profit on your own return, as reported on the Schedule K-1, Partner's Share of Income, credits, deductions, and so on, issued to you.

As an individual proprietor or a partner in a partnership, you are required to pay the federal self-employment tax as you receive the income. The self-employment tax is the FICA tax (Social Security and Medicare), both the employee and matching employer rate paid by people who work for themselves. You must file a declaration of estimated tax (Form 1040 ES) on or before April 15 of each year. A partner is subject to self-employment taxes in the same way as a sole proprietor.

This declaration is an estimate of the income and self-employment taxes that you expect to owe during this coming year. You then make estimated payments each quarter—April 15, June 15, September 15, and January 15. At these times, you can adjust each of your estimates according to your income.

If you have a regular corporation, not an S Corporation, the corporation pays taxes on its profits, and the owner of the corporation pays income taxes on the salary the owner received or the dividends the corporation paid the owner. Similar to a sole proprietorship, limited liability companies are taxed to the individual owners.

The federal corporation income tax is due two-and-a-half months after the end of your fiscal year. This return is filed just once a year; most corporations pay quarterly. It is important that you make allowances in your money management to be sure that you are prepared to pay these taxes. The Small Business Administration has worksheets for meeting tax obligations, which can help you in this documentation if your accountant is not taking care of it for you.

Federal Taxes

There are a number of federal taxes every business needs to consider, in addition to "entity" taxes. These are discussed on page 54.

Withholding Income Taxes. If you have employees, you must, by law, withhold federal income tax. These taxes are deposited with the government on a regular basis. The process begins the minute you hire any employee. Your employees must sign a W4 form, an Employee Withholding Allowance Certificate, on which they list their exemptions and any additional withholding allowances they claim. The W4 certificate is your authorization to withhold tax in accordance with the tables the Internal Revenue Service has issued. At the end of the year, you must complete a W2 form, which is a statement showing income paid to the employees and taxes withheld. This must be in the employees' hands before January 31 of each year. The employees then submit this form as part of their personal income tax returns. Send a copy of the W2s to the IRS, using Form W3 as a transmittal.

FICA. As an employer, you must withhold FICA taxes (Social Security and Medicare) for both your employees and yourself. You must then match the amount for each employee. The taxes are deposited with the government at the same time the withholding taxes are made. Form 941, Employer's Quarterly Federal Tax Return, is due for each calendar quarter on the last day of the month following the end of the quarter: April 30, July 31, October 31, and January 31.

Federal Unemployment Taxes. If you pay wages of more than $1,500 in any calendar quarter, or have more than one employee, you must pay federal unemployment taxes. Just as with withholding and FICA taxes, these payments generally are deposited with either a commercial bank or a federal reserve bank. This must be done by the end of the month following the quarter. File a Form 940, Employer's Annual Federal Unemployment (FUTA) Tax Return, at the end of each calendar year.

Form 1099. Form 1099 is an "Information Return" on which certain business payments are required to be disclosed to the government. Every business enterprise, corporate or otherwise, that makes payments of $600 or more in a calendar year to a nonemployee who is not a corporation—for rents, prizes and awards, fees, commissions, or other compensation—must report the payment. All payments of interest or dividends in the amount of $10 or more in a calendar year must also be reported. A copy of Form 1099 must be issued to the payee no later than January 31 for the preceding calendar year. The original must be filed with the IRS no later than February 28, using Form 1096 as a transmittal slip.

Remitting Taxes. Make deposits with Form 501, a Federal Tax Deposit Form, for withholding income, FICA, and taxes. You send this form with your check to a commercial bank authorized to accept these tax deposits. The due dates for these deposits will vary, depending on the type of tax and amount due.

State Taxes

Although these taxes vary from state to state, each state usually requires unemployment tax, income tax, and sales tax. It is important to know what the taxes are within your state.

State Unemployment Taxes. These are required by every state, though the rates vary. They are based on the amount of wages your employees are paid and on the employee turnover in your business.

State Employee Income Taxes. These are also imposed by most states, although the amounts and ways they are collected vary from state to state. As with federal income taxes, the employer is usually required to collect this tax from the employee through payroll withholdings.

Sales Tax. Any retailer is required to collect and pay state and local sales taxes when goods are sold to the end consumer. You must obtain a sales tax identification, license number, or resale permit, as required from the state or local agency, in order to collect the taxes.

Sales tax is collected from your client and usually has to be separately stated on your invoice. Use tax is paid by you and cannot be charged as a tax to your client. A careful review of these state sales tax laws is necessary to avoid problems later on. If you, as a consumer, purchase a taxable item from an out-of-state source that does not collect the tax, it is your responsibility to report and pay a use tax on the purchase.

Some other considerations for sales and use tax are:

- Designers generally must charge sales tax on anything that is "movable," which would include all furniture or any movable unit that goes into a project.
- If an item is "attached" to the building and the design firm is responsible for installing it, then the firm is generally required to charge use tax. For example, if you sell wallcovering to a client and the client has a paperhanger install it, you must charge the client sales tax on the wallpaper. If you have a paperhanger install the wallcovering, then you must pay the use tax on the price of the wallpaper.
- In most states, designers do not charge sales tax on their design fees. Designers who break down their charges and charge a set amount for a product plus a percentage, only charge sales tax on the base price of the material. If charges are invoiced as a total price, then sales tax is charged on the complete item.
- Usually, a firm is not responsible for charging taxes on items shipped out of state. The client receiving the merchandise is responsible for paying the tax. If you work in more than one state on a regular basis, you will be required to pay sales tax in each state. At this time, states frequently audit designers to be sure all taxes are paid on all items. This issue should be reviewed with your tax advisor according to the specific project or installation.

Taxes vary considerably from state to state. However, most interior designers, whether practicing on a professional service basis or acting as selling agents or retailers, are responsible for some form of tax. This needs to be reviewed on a regular basis with your tax advisor, since the laws change often.

Penalties for Nonpayment of Taxes

These penalties are severe and stringently enforced. The corporate officers or business owner may be held personally liable for withholding or not remitting payroll taxes.

Special Tax Notes

Consult with your accountant to avoid the following pitfalls:

- Be sure to record every portion of your income; the IRS has no tolerance for unreported or underreported income. Of course, try to take every deduction you possibly can, but be prepared to support them with thorough documentation.
- Check with your accountant to make sure you are taking every possible deduction into account. Interior designers can deduct expenditures, but the accepted deductions vary considerably according to your location and the standards in your individual practice.

Interest on Overpaid or Underpaid Taxes. The Internal Revenue Service pays interest on any amount of taxes you have overpaid and charges interest on underpaid taxes. The rate of interest fluctuates and is set by the IRS on a quarterly basis. The rate for underpayments (interest charged to you) is generally higher than the rate for overpayments (interest paid by the IRS to you). What this really means is that it does not pay to play games with tax issues. You are better off to pay on time. Even if you overpay, today you are not losing interest as you would have in the past.

It is a good idea to review your tax projections with your accountant at the beginning of the year, not at tax time. Let accountants spell out what they think your deductions are, and compare their list with your own. A number of designers I know have been able to deduct their clothing expenses; their accountants received permission from the IRS to do this. On the whole, however, deducting for clothing is not appropriate. The IRS contends we are not wearing a uniform, since we usually wear standard clothing that could be worn somewhere else. Therefore, clothing is not deductible. But clothing damaged on a construction job can be deducted, if details and costs are documented.

Travel Expenses. Beginning in 1987, the IRS instituted stringent requirements for travel and entertainment expenses. In general, you may deduct only 50 percent of meals and entertainment expenses. The records must be specific for both the employer and the employee.

Receipts are necessary for all lodging and for daily meals and incidentals over $30. For daily meals and incidentals under $30, you do not need a receipt, but you must keep a record in your diary. When you are traveling, keep track of each and every expense. I find if I do this on a daily basis, I am accurate. If I wait until the end of the week, I can never remember how much I spent for what or when. So I do my recordkeeping religiously, several times a day. When I am in a taxi, or waiting for someone, I will mark down exactly what I have spent. I have an envelope in which I keep my receipts and an account of everything I have spent on that particular trip. The IRS requires that records be maintained as the expenses are incurred.

A most important IRS requirement concerns business-connected expenditures. For every meal or entertainment expense you list, you must be able to document the person you were with and the business subject you discussed. A goodwill dinner with a long-standing customer is not deductible, unless current business is discussed either before, during, or after the meal. However, if this meal is one during which business is discussed, the 50 percent rule applies.

If money is advanced, or expenses reimbursed, to an employee who is a stockholder, and the transaction is not clearly documented, the IRS may declare this payment to be a dividend—taxable to the employee but not deductible by the employer. If you give an employee a flat expense allowance and do not require the employee to account for those expenses, you must include it on the employee's W-2 form; otherwise, the company will lose the tax deduction.

The IRS looks at owners' expense accounts carefully and requires that all travel and entertainment expenses be itemized. An owner may no longer declare a per diem amount on meals or lodging. This law also applies to any other family member, owner, or stockholder of the business. If you give your employees a flat rate for expenses, the IRS has limits on this standard rate. (Note: There are some special cities to which the IRS has assigned higher standard rates, such as New York City and Los Angeles.) The standard rate covers all lodging, meals, and incidental expenses. Transportation is a separate deduction.

There are two ways you may reimburse employees for travel in their own car: (1) repayment of all expenses incurred, which means that the company would pay for the gas, oil, and maintenance of the car; (2) a flat-rate method based on miles traveled.

The IRS resets a standard mileage reimbursement rate regularly. If you reimburse employees more than the allowance per mile, the entire amount of the reimbursement must be shown on their W-2 forms, and taxes must be paid on that amount.

Automobile expenses and receipts must be kept to verify all prices and costs (the base cost of the automobile, plus cost for maintenance, gas, oil, and so forth). You must also keep a detailed mileage log, which records all usage of the company car—including the driver's name, purpose of the trip, miles driven, and the date of each trip. A mileage log also must record any personal use of the car.

It is important to see that all expense records are turned in on a regular basis and are not permitted to accumulate, because there is no way accurate documentation can be done on a long-term basis; it must be kept current. In our firm, we have had great success using travel expense envelopes (see page 381). We give our employees their traveling expense advances in these envelopes and have them document their expenses on the outside of the envelope and put in all their receipts. We think this envelope is much easier to use for the person who makes an occasional trip and perhaps does not keep a weekly or daily account. It also makes our recordkeeping much simpler, by having all the receipts in one envelope.

Tax Audits

What should you do if you are being audited by the IRS or any other tax agency? First, notify your tax advisor. Then, ask the agent conducting the audit to get in touch with your tax advisor. Do not answer any questions relating to the audit, and do not discuss anything with the agent. Leave it to your tax advisor to handle. It is best, in fact, if you are absent during the conduct of the audit.

If you have followed your tax advisor's direction, you will have good records and will be prepared for this kind of audit. Your tax advisor will let you know exactly how to present the required information.

Ask your tax advisor to control the audit. I find it is important for one person to be in charge, and it is usually best if that person is your tax advisor. Let your advisor select the location, as well.

After the audit is completed, you and your tax advisor should discuss the audit and make notes of any weak spots in your records. Ask your tax advisor how these can be remedied for the future. Review all the disallowed items to determine the reason for disallowance. If you find your records were inadequate, now is the time to edit and revise your recordkeeping system. What adjustments can be made on future schedules? After this review, file all your documents again properly so you are ready for the next audit.

Recently, a design firm I know had a state sales tax audit, which took a considerable amount of time. The auditor arrived with two other men, whom he was training, He asked for certain papers, which the firm's tax advisor had reviewed and had ready. The auditors established themselves in the conference room, which is a very pleasant room, with coffee and refreshments convenient to it. They came each day for approximately five weeks, during which time they continually asked for additional materials and items. This kept two, and sometimes three, staff members busy reviewing or pulling records and information for them. When the auditor and his men were finished, they found the records were in reasonably good order. The only tax they were able to collect was one inadvertently not paid on items purchased for office use. The company from which the items had been purchased had not charged sales tax; therefore, the design firm was responsible for the use tax. The auditors' total tax collection was less than $2,000 after reviewing six years of taxes over a five-week period.

Sales and use taxes are not clearly defined in many states. Another designer told me of a similar situation he had had a few weeks earlier, when auditors had asked to see his records for the past two years. He related the following:

"As you can probably guess, our records are not very well kept, because bookkeeping is not one of our specialties. Our bookkeeper had just left, and I had no idea where things were, so my tax advisor gave me the following instructions: He told me to take an enormous cardboard box and put all of our records in it—everything we could find to fill the box with as many papers as possible— to put this box in our station wagon, and deliver it to the tax auditor's office. We did exactly as he said, and when we arrived, the auditors looked at the box and said, 'Sorry, I think we've changed our minds; we do not want to audit you'—and we weren't audited."

So, whereas the first firm went through considerable expense and harassment, the second individual was able to get out of his audit completely because of his method of presentation. The first firm was very cooperative, but sometimes I wonder which approach is the most effective.

It is now the practice of the IRS to examine the tax returns of all related parties. For example, in the examination of a partnership, the returns of all of the partners will be examined. If there are related corporations (subsidiaries or brother-sister corporations, for example), their returns, too, will be examined. In an examination of a corporation, the returns of the principals will be at least scanned.

In an independent contractor relationship, the IRS will look very carefully into the working relationship to determine whether it is a bona fide independent contractor's situation or, in reality, an employer-employee relationship and thus subject to employee payroll tax requirements.

If the IRS agent is a special agent, as opposed to a revenue agent, you are involved in a criminal investigation and need to hire a lawyer immediately. Let your lawyer work with your tax advisor, or let the lawyer hire a tax advisor to properly defend you. A tax advisor who works for a lawyer is legally protected by the lawyer-client privilege. If your tax advisor is working for you directly, the advisor is not protected by this privilege.

A final cautionary word: Keep in mind that taxes are subject to frequent changes. Accordingly, it is most important, whenever the tax effect of a contemplated transaction will be significant for you and your advisors, to be aware of the tax laws currently in force.

CONSIDERATIONS

We need to know where our money is at all times so we can make the appropriate decisions and move quickly when necessary. We also need to be cautious about how we manage our money so we are assured we won't get caught in problem situations. With global resources we do not have a way of knowing all the companies or professionals we are dealing with, so we must be sure to have good control. There is opportunity for profit in this field, but it includes risk and responsibility. There are many systems by which we can outsource or share the risks—perhaps resulting in better projects and better profits.

CHAPTER 12

Growing Your Firm and Your Professional Skills

EVALUATION

Designers are not happy unless they see their practices growing. They become bored if there is not some constructive change. To that end, we can learn so much by looking at the people we work with, our sources, and our final projects. We are the best critics of our own work.

We must improve if we are to succeed with the present competition. If you feel you can do more work and would like to work at a higher level, this can be accomplished through many of the skills you already use in design. Start with a review of where you are, then consider where and how you would like to see your design practice grow.

Interior design is a growing and changing field, which means designers must evaluate their firms and their professional skills as part of an ongoing process to be sure they are in tune with current requirements. It is important to review your firm's position and your professional skills on a regular basis. Take an inventory of your past year according to the following checklist:

- Types of projects
- Your staff and their ability
- Your list of consultants

- Time invested in your projects
- Income
- Profit
- Marketing value
- Referrals

Compare the various projects you worked on to determine where you are progressing and where you need to change or improve based on the projects you see developing.

Next, look at your cash flow and consider where you stand financially:

- Do you have investments?
- Do you have funds set aside for your future?
- Were you able to give bonuses this past year?

Look at the amount of money you have in your checking account, money markets, investments, future funds dedicated to future development, retirement fund, and bonuses paid.

System of Charging

Review the income generated by fees and sale of merchandise and other sources over the past three years. Were there any major changes? Are you doing different work? Have you lost income in certain areas? Are there services you could add that would generate additional income? Are you earning at the level that is appropriate to your talent and efforts?

For the past three years, review the following criteria to assist you in determining your personal position:

Gross Income
Product
Fees
Others
Net profit from each area

Working Capital
Cash
Checking account
Money market
Future fund
Retirement account

Investments
Inventory
Equipment

Now consider next year: What needs and challenges must you meet? Evaluate each person on your team, staff members, other professionals, and artisans you work with:

- Do they work at your level?
- Do they have the skills required to contribute to your projects?
- Are they people you are proud to work with?

Consider the work you will be doing in the next year. After you review your position, consider where you should be working considering your skills. What is needed? You are a designer; you know how to design the preferred situation. Now position your firm to be the best it can be in this market.

Use this form as a guide to review your status today. Keep these forms on file to assist you in your evaluations in the years to come. They will give you a perspective on your team, your staff, and other people you work with. Your notes today will provide an interesting comparison for the future—helping you to evaluate future growth.

TEAM

Your Staff

Person	Skills	Relationship
_____	_____	_____
_____	_____	_____
_____	_____	_____

Other Professionals

Person	Skills	Relationship
_____	_____	_____
_____	_____	_____
_____	_____	_____

Contractors

Vendor	Product or Skill	Relationship
_____	_____	_____
_____	_____	_____
_____	_____	_____

Do you have the right contractors and resources for the type of work you are doing?

Look where you are and what you have to work with in taking your firm into the future. What do you need to meet the requirements of your market? Is it something you can buy, or will you need to develop new or better skills?

DEVELOPING YOURSELF AND YOUR STAFF

Education

Success and advancement in interior design are closely related to continuing education. Often, it is not what you do while at work, but what you do on your own time that affects your future positioning in a field. This applies especially to interior design. This is a field that continues to grow and change. When you enter interior design, you embark on a continuing-education process—just as other professionals do. Since most design programs do not provide sufficient business training, seeking additional education in the form of business courses can have a major positive impact on your firm, especially if you are new to the design field. As one matures, in age and position, you may want to consider the use of consultants when needed, so you can use your own time more effectively.

Continuing Education

Tuition is tax-deductible if it is for education within your professional discipline. This includes professional seminars, conventions, and formal university curricula. Though the IRS does not allow deductions of expenses incurred in learning about a new field, you can deduct anything related to maintaining or improving your skills in your current field. You may also deduct your automobile expenses in traveling to seminars, based on IRS guidelines. Aside from attending seminars and going back to school, there is a lot you can do to keep yourself up to date on current issues affecting your business.

Learning on the Job

Formal education is necessary, but so is practical experience. There is no better way to learn than to watch another successful person work. We all learn so much and prevent so many expensive mistakes by working for other companies before starting our own businesses.

If you are a business owner, hire knowledgeable people. You will learn from them, and they will help you develop your business. You do not have the time or energy to train everyone, and it is far too expensive. Be willing to pay for skill and talent instead.

Lunch is sometimes the most valuable time I spend with my staff. During a shared meal, we talk about the problems of the day and what we can do to make things better. We try to use mealtime as a creative problem-solving period, and we learn a lot from each other in this casual atmosphere.

Form a board of advisors. Most people are hesitant to be on a board of directors unless they are provided with good liability insurance coverage, and this gets very involved for a small company. But they *will* sit on your board of advisors. A number of past clients and several outstanding businesspeople in the community sit with my firm and review our progress and goals. We learn a great deal from having this outside point of view.

Surround yourself with innovative people. Talk to your suppliers. Find out what they are doing. They will also be able to tell you what other similar design firms are doing. It is amazing what you can learn from your suppliers. They will show you what is selling and help you understand why.

Bring in experts. Every time someone is visiting our area who knows something about our business, if possible, we invite the person to have lunch with the whole staff. If a designer is visiting from another community, we invite that person to our office. We ask these designers to show us what they are doing. This is a great way of keeping everybody on our staff on top of changes in our field.

Prepare a list of consultants to advise on every major design issue you might encounter, so that when a project comes up you do not have to scramble to gather a design team.

For those who are studying interior design or are new in the field: business education is an important part of your training. The business process should be a major emphasis in all design programs. And after you have been in practice for a while, you will find that your business needs revisions. The language of business is always growing and changing and technology has accelerated the process. One of the best ways to develop your firm is to hire a consultant, who will define your specific needs and find an appropriate system to meet them.

Additional business education is very good. However, after you reach a certain age and position, you are probably far better off using consultants. You can get much more out of your time, and the lessons will be directed to your particular needs.

Learning from Friends and Acquaintances

Anytime you meet someone from whom you would like to learn more, offer to take the person to breakfast, lunch, or dinner. (I usually make it either breakfast or dinner because I have a hard time getting away from my office for lunch in the middle of the day.) You share ideas with another professional, and the feedback you receive is often very valuable.

Your family members and friends can also be very valuable. People are all "experts" in their own lives and lifestyles. Usually, friends and family are more than willing to give you information. In exchange for reasonable courtesies you can obtain information of great value.

For the last 30 years, one night a week, I have been inviting a group of my friends in to talk about business issues. I cook for them at my house, and we talk about what is progressive and new in business. Some of the same people come almost every week, others only occasionally. These days this practice is called *networking* (see pages 133–135).

Join any club that is of value to you. Of course, ASID, IFDA (International Furnishings and Design Association), IIDA, and IDS (Interior Design Society), and some of the major design associations are very worthwhile. The Chamber of Commerce is a must, as is any group in which you can find people in a similar position to yours. Social service clubs, such as the Lions and Rotary, often provide good opportunities to make new contacts with other professionals.

Business Courses

While many colleges offer business courses, often designers do not have the time to attend. But this does not mean you cannot learn about business. Technology today provides us with tools to continue learning how to accomplish our goals. Many courses in business or related subjects are available on the Internet, television, or videos. These resources are at your fingertips, and you do not have to leave your home to take advantage of them.

Listen to tapes. In an average week, I listen to 12 to 30 hours of tapes. I drive over 40,000 miles a year, which gives me a great deal of tape-listening time. By listening to tapes, you can hear a lot of relevant information with minimal effort on your part.

ASID, IIDA, IFDA, IDS chapters, and other associations often present courses on business. Review the speakers' credentials carefully to determine that they understand the way interior designers do business. There are many consultants today who know about business but may not have a thorough understanding of what really works in the interior design field. Interior designers are creative individuals. Business procedure must complement that creativity. Check out what the Small Business Administration (SBA) is doing in your geographic area. The SBA sponsors business courses, sometimes through colleges, and will keep you attuned to economic developments.

Reading

I believe in reading, I read more than 150 publications a month, plus four newspapers a day. I do not read every word, but I find that even a cursory read is critical for keeping abreast of issues. Learn which publications are really useful to you, and then try to follow them on a regular basis. You may not choose to do that much reading, in which case you should find a way of exposing yourself to someone who does keep up with the new issues. Use this consultant to fill you in on the points that are critical to your firm.

I have friends and consultants who search information for me. This gives me exposure to a lot of material. We pass this information on to other members of the business, so they will be informed about pertinent issues in a concise, easy-to-follow manner.

Getting Other Points of View

Retired people who are experienced in their fields have a lot to offer. They are not in competition with you, and they are often curious about your firm. They often come up with good tips, problem-solving ideas, information, and methods that can be very beneficial.

Observe what other people are doing, and find a way to do it better. It is so much easier than starting from scratch. Look around when you visit places. Visit other design firms and see what they are doing. There's always some idea you can adapt to fit your needs.

Asking questions is the single best way to learn, and do not worry about whether a question seems silly or irrelevant. If you want to know something, ask. The more you learn, the better equipped you are to evaluate the information you have already received.

EDUCATING YOUR STAFF

Help your employees become better informed. Growing your employees' expertise is essential. Their increased knowledge can impact performance and contribute to the success of your firm. Educate them, develop them, polish them. Through your interest and concern, they will develop into ideal employees—and friends.

ATTENDING SEMINARS

A designer's education is never really complete, and attending seminars is a relatively fun way to take in new information or to earn continuing education units (CEUs). Most professional organizations or licensing entities today require their members to complete a certain number of CEU credits each year. In the design profession, CEUs are increasingly important and need to be scheduled into every designer's life. Doctors and attorneys reserve several days a month for attending seminars, and designers must do the same.

Usually, a day spent in a seminar is more rewarding than a day of independent study, because you are with people whose interests are similar to your own. It is an efficient use of time, in that you learn the latest information and you see how other people solve problems you face. It is also often fun. Attending a seminar can lend a new perspective to some of your day-to-day activities. Interior design is a constantly changing field. You need to update your knowledge, evaluate your position in the field, and determine where you are going. The results of a seminar can be reassuring, or they might well be an incentive to go home and do better.

Selecting the Right Seminars

Seminars are an excellent way to keep you apprised of new trends and interests. You must take responsibility for your own career development, whether you are working alone or with a firm. The attitude of many firms is, "Take your career in your own hands, and we will provide training to help you accomplish this." Identify the seminars you wish to attend. Seminars are an investment. You measure the worth of a seminar by this guideline: You should make from 6 to 10 times the price of the seminar from the information you gain. Sometimes the company pays for these seminars. If so, place in writing requests to your firm for each seminar you wish to attend, and do it well ahead of time. Try to work out how many days you can devote to seminars and continuing education throughout the year, then determine which areas of information are important to you and gear your seminar choices accordingly.

Brochure write-ups are so glowing it is often hard to tell good programs from bad ones until after you have spent your money and sat through the seminar. Make sure it is a good program by checking references. Contact the sponsor and ask for some names and addresses of people who attended past seminars. Ask for their telephone numbers as well, so you can check with them personally. Then go on their recommendations. It is highly unlikely the sponsors would refuse to give you past references, but if they do, ask for a copy of the evaluations of this seminar. There is no point in wasting your time in a seminar that is not worthwhile.

Paying for Seminars

Seminars cost more than just the admission fee. Each day you are away from the office, even at an inexpensive seminar, costs the firm at least $1,000. If your employer pays for you to attend a seminar, send him or her a copy of your summary, and highlight what you feel you learned by attending. If there is evidence that the seminar was useful, your employer will be more likely to send you and other employees to other programs.

Preparing for Seminars

Before you go to a seminar, list your goals. Outline exactly what you would like to get out of a particular seminar when you first sign up for it.

Plan ahead for the seminar. Make sure you know where it is and how much time it will take you to get there. It is best to arrive about 20 minutes to a half-hour early so you can select your seat and meet other participants. It is also a good time to introduce yourself to the speaker and mention some of your primary reasons for coming to the seminar.

Benefiting from the Seminar

During the seminar, assess its value to you. What are the good ideas coming from this program, and how can you use them? Make note of several good points. If you find, in reviewing your notes, that you have 30 or 40 ideas, select the one, two, or three that are the best, and try out those ideas within 24 hours. If you do this, statistics tell us that you will probably make these changes a part of your life, and they will continue to be of value to you. If you try to do too many things, however, you will find you accomplish nothing. After you have incorporated the first few ideas into your practice, you can always refer to your notes to see which other ideas might be profitable in other situations.

Buy the books or tapes that relate to the seminar. Normally, we forget about 90 percent of anything we learn within two weeks; books and tapes are good reference materials. Tapes are especially good, because you can play them in your car or while you are doing something else.

Do not call the office while you are at a seminar. Devote your energies to the topic at hand and get all you possibly can from it. It is most likely that your call to the office will not really do any good anyhow. Program yourself and your staff to understand that you will just not be available for that seven- or eight-hour period.

Participate in the seminar. Do not be afraid to ask questions. This is your chance to try things out. It is much better to make a mistake in the seminar atmosphere than it is out there on the job. Take good notes that you can read later; most of us never have time to rewrite seminar notes, but we may need to refer to them later on.

A seminar is also an opportunity to make contacts. I always try to meet at least one new person during a seminar who may be important to me later on. This is a chance to expand your networking circle. Mingle. Exchange cards with the people you meet. You will later be able to call them and review other issues of concern.

Summarize what you got out of the day. Keep a copy of this summary for yourself in your CEU file. I recommend you maintain a reference book or a file on any continuing education courses you attend. These may become necessary documentation of professional standing. In addition, it is useful to know which seminars you have attended and what you got from them as you consider what to attend in the future. This summary will help you evaluate the worth of each event.

ADDITIONAL DESIGN EDUCATION

Designers often like to further their education beyond the required CEUs. Perhaps your prior education had a certain focus that is different from what you are presently doing. Many schools haves a special program designed to update their graduates. Or you may just wish to be with other creative people who are studying and have the luxury of thinking only about design. As you consider this, find an institution of quality; often they are accredited by the Foundation for Interior Design Education Research (FIDER). Many of these schools offer continuing education classes designed for practicing professionals. Some of their courses meet current needs, while others are designed to simulate interest in new directions. Use the Design School listing in the back of this book, pages 462–471, to determine one that meets your needs and fits your schedule in a convenient way.

Use consultants. One of the most valuable things we can do is to expose ourselves to consultants. Keep in mind that a consultant is automatically responsible to see that you are acquiring the information required for your practice. This is an inexpensive way to educate yourself and your staff. We have talked about this in other chapters.

Become part of a design forum led by a professional. Through this process, the professional shows you how to grow and keep your firm up to date on the pertinent issues in your practice. This is an exceptionally valuable way of staying current and gaining exposure to other practices similar to yours throughout the country.

Education Online
Many courses on business, as well as design, are offered over the World Wide Web. There are CEUs as well as college courses. This is an excellent way for many professionals, who may not have the time for full-time study, to acquire additional knowledge.

Many subjects are taught online, some perhaps even better than in person. For other subjects, personal instruction is very valuable. I believe a combination of both personal and online instruction is beneficial. The point is, education is at our fingertips, when we want it, any time of day or night or any day of the year.

CONSIDERATIONS

We are creative people; we love to grow and change. This profession is excellent because it always encourages growth.

It's important to understand our personal abilities and those of our team, if we want to make the interior design profession exciting, creative, and interesting for as long as we choose to work in it.

As long as we practice, education should be a continuing requirement, to keep up with the demands of the market. Our original education is only a starting point.

Appendix:
AIA Document B171 ID

AIA® Document B171™ID – 2003

Standard Form of Agreement Between Owner and Architect for Architectural Interior Design Services

AGREEMENT made as of the   day of   in the year of
(In words, indicate day, month and year)

BETWEEN the Owner
(Name, address and other information):

This document has important legal consequences. Consultation with an attorney is encouraged with respect to its completion or modification.

and the Architect
(Name, address and other information):

For the following Project
(Include detailed description of Project, location, address, scope and any applicable client/tenant/landlord relationships):

The Owner and Architect agree as follows:

TABLE OF ARTICLES

ARTICLE 1 ARCHITECT'S RESPONSIBILITIES

§ 1.1 Architect's Services

§ 1.1.1 The Architect's services consist of those services performed by the Architect, Architect's employees and Architect's consultants as enumerated in Articles 2 and 3 of this Agreement and any other services included in Article 13.

§ 1.1.2 The Architect's services shall be performed as expeditiously as is consistent with professional skill and care and the orderly progress of the Work. Upon request of the Owner, the Architect shall submit for the Owner's approval a schedule for the performance of the Architect's services which may be adjusted as the Project proceeds, and shall include allowances for periods of time required for the Owner's review and for approvals of submissions by authorities with jurisdiction over the Project. The Architect or Owner shall not, except for reasonable cause, exceed time limits established by the schedule approved by the Owner.

§ 1.1.3 The services covered by this Agreement are subject to the time limitations contained in Section 11.7.

§ 1.1.4 Except with the Owner's knowledge and consent, the Architect shall not (1) accept trade discounts; (2) have a significant financial interest; or (3) undertake any activity or employment or accept any contribution if any such activity, employment, interest or contribution could reasonably appear to compromise the Architect's professional judgment.

§ 1.1.5 The Architect shall provide information to, and incorporate information received from, those separate consultants retained by the Owner and identified in Article 13 whose activities directly relate to the Project.

§ 1.1.6 The Architect shall have the right to rely upon the accuracy of the information provided by the Owner.

ARTICLE 2 SCOPE OF ARCHITECT'S BASIC SERVICES

§ 2.1 Programming Phase

§ 2.1.1 The Architect shall consult with representatives of the Owner to review the applicable requirements of the Project in order to understand the goals and objectives of the Owner with respect to their impact on the Owner's space requirements.

§ 2.1.2 The Architect shall review the requirements necessary for the various Project functions, relationships or operations, such as those for existing and projected personnel, space, furniture, furnishings and equipment, operating procedures and communications.

§ 2.1.3 The Architect shall assist the Owner in the preparation of a budget for the Work and a project schedule.

§ 2.1.4 The Architect shall gather information furnished by the Owner's designated representatives to aid the Architect in understanding the Owner's present, short-term and long-term personnel and space requirements, including special equipment needs, organizational structure, adjacencies and workflow.

§ 2.1.5 The Architect shall conduct interviews with the Owner's designated representatives and shall observe existing conditions at the Owner's facilities.

§ 2.1.6 The Architect shall develop personnel space standards based upon an evaluation of the functional requirements and standards of the Owner. Personnel space standards shall take into consideration the design and layout of furniture system workstation environments, if applicable. The proposed space standards shall be submitted for the Owner's review and approval.

§ 2.1.7 The Architect shall develop a general understanding of the Owner's equipment requirements, including data and telecommunications equipment, reproduction equipment and the corresponding environmental conditions required to maintain such equipment.

§ 2.1.8 The Architect shall prepare a written summary of observations and make recommendations with respect to the planning of the facility. The Architect shall prepare a written space program for the Owner's review and approval.

§ 2.2 Pre-lease Analysis and Feasibility Services Phase

§ 2.2.1 At the request of the Owner, the Architect shall evaluate alternative buildings with respect to the Owner's programmatic requirements. The number of alternative buildings shall be specified in Section 11.2.3.

§ 2.2.2 The Architect shall review the alternative buildings with respect to gross, usable or rentable area; building configuration; and architectural features.

§ 2.2.3 The Architect shall prepare one test floor plan in each alternative building.

§ 2.2.4 The Architect shall review the quality and quantity of the building standards being offered in the landlord's workletter.

§ 2.2.5 The Architect shall report to the Owner observations and recommendations based on the evaluation of the alternative buildings.

§ 2.3 Schematic Design Phase

§ 2.3.1 Based on the approved written program, the Architect shall prepare for the Owner's approval adjacency diagrams showing the general functional relationships for both personnel and operations.

§ 2.3.2 The Architect shall review with the Owner alternative designs and methods for procurement of the furniture, furnishings and equipment, and shall notify the Owner of anticipated impacts that such designs and methods may have on the Owner's program, financial and time requirements and on the scope of the Project.

§ 2.3.3 Upon approval of the adjacency diagrams, the Architect shall prepare a space plan that delineates the location of walls, doors, rooms, offices, workstation areas and special-use areas to conform to program requirements. The Architect shall submit the space plan for the Owner's review and approval.

§ 2.3.4 The Architect shall prepare the design concept for the Project, indicating the types and quality of finishes and materials and furniture, furnishings and equipment.

§ 2.3.5 The Architect shall assist the Owner in the preparation of a preliminary project schedule and estimate of the Cost of the Work.

§ 2.4 Design Development Phase
§ 2.4.1 Based on the approved Schematic Design, the Architect shall prepare and present, for approval by the Owner, Design Development drawings and other documents describing the size and character of the interior construction of the Project.

§ 2.4.2 The Architect shall obtain product data and prepare illustrations for furniture, furnishings and equipment as may be appropriate for the Project, including specially designed items or elements, to indicate finished appearance and functional operation.

§ 2.4.3 The Architect shall illustrate the architectural and decorative character of the Project. Such illustrations may include drawings, plans, elevations, sections, renderings and photographs, as well as samples of actual materials, colors and finishes.

§ 2.4.4 The Architect shall assist the Owner in the preparation of adjustments to the preliminary schedule and estimate of the Cost of the Work.

§ 2.5 Contract Documents Phase
§ 2.5.1 Based on the approved Design Development drawings and other documents including schedule and Cost of the Work, the Architect shall prepare Drawings, Specifications and other documents, required to describe the interior construction necessary for the Project.

§ 2.5.2 The Contract Documents shall include plans, elevations, sections, details and specifications required to describe the interior construction work.

§ 2.5.3 The Architect shall prepare, for the Owner's approval, documents describing the requirements for the procurement, fabrication, shipment, delivery and installation of furniture, furnishings and equipment for the Project.

§ 2.5.4 The Architect shall assist the Owner in the preparation of the necessary Quotation and Bidding Documents.

§ 2.5.5 The Architect shall assist the Owner in connection with the Owner's responsibility for filing documents required for the approval of governmental authorities having jurisdiction over the Project.

§ 2.6 Bidding and Quotation Phase
§ 2.6.1 The Architect shall assist the Owner in establishing a list of prospective contractors for construction and vendors for furniture, furnishings and equipment.

§ 2.6.2 The Architect shall assist the Owner in obtaining competitive bids for construction and quotations for furniture, furnishings and equipment.

§ 2.6.3 Bidding Documents shall consist of bidding requirements, proposed contract forms, General Conditions and Supplementary Conditions, Drawings and Specifications.

§ 2.6.4 Quotation Documents include the Quotation Requirements, the proposed Contract Documents and any Reference Documents.

§ 2.6.5 The Architect shall prepare written responses to questions from prospective contractors and vendors and provide written clarifications and interpretations of the Bidding and Quotation Documents in the form of addenda.

§ 2.6.6 The Architect shall assist the Owner in reviewing bids and quotations. The Architect shall assist the Owner in awarding and preparing agreements for the Project.

§ 2.7 Construction Contract Administration Phase
§ 2.7.1 General Administration
§ 2.7.1.1 The Architect shall provide administration of the Contract between the Owner and Contractor as set forth below and in the edition of AIA® Document A201™, *General Conditions of the Contract for Construction,* current as of the date of this Agreement. Modifications made to the General Conditions, when adopted as part of the Contract Documents, shall be enforceable under this Agreement only to the extent that they are consistent with this Agreement or approved in writing by the Architect.

§ 2.7.1.2 The Architect's responsibility to provide services for the Construction Contract Administration Phase under this Agreement commences with the award of the initial Contract for Construction and terminates at the issuance to the Owner of the final Certificate for Payment.

§ 2.7.1.3 The Architect shall be a representative of and shall advise and consult with the Owner during the provision of the Construction Contract Administration Phase. The Architect shall have authority to act on behalf of the Owner only to the extent provided in this Agreement unless otherwise modified by written amendment.

§ 2.7.1.4 The Architect shall review properly prepared, timely requests by the Contractor for additional information about the Contract Documents. A properly prepared request for additional information about the Contract Documents shall be in a form prepared or approved by the Architect and shall include a detailed written statement that indicates the specific Drawings or Specifications in need of clarification and the nature of the clarification requested.

§ 2.7.1.5 If deemed appropriate by the Architect, the Architect shall on the Owner's behalf prepare, reproduce and distribute supplemental Drawings and Specifications in response to requests for information by the Contractor.

§ 2.7.1.6 The Architect shall interpret and decide matters concerning performance of the Owner and Contractor under, and requirements of, the Contract Documents on written request of either the Owner or Contractor. The Architect's response to such requests shall be made in writing within any time limits agreed upon or otherwise with reasonable promptness.

§ 2.7.1.7 Interpretations and decisions of the Architect shall be consistent with the intent of and reasonably inferable from the Contract Documents and shall be in writing or in the form of Drawings. When making such interpretations and initial decisions, the Architect shall endeavor to secure faithful performance by both the Owner and Contractor, shall not show partiality to either, and shall not be liable for the results of interpretations or decisions so rendered in good faith.

§ 2.7.1.8 The Architect shall render initial decisions on claims, disputes or other matters in question between the Owner and Contractor as provided in the Contract Documents. However, the Architect's decisions on matters relating to aesthetic effect shall be final if consistent with the intent expressed in the Contract Documents.

§ 2.7.2 Evaluations of the Work
§ 2.7.2.1 The Architect, as a representative of the Owner, shall visit the site at intervals appropriate to the stage of the Contractor's operations, or as otherwise agreed by the Owner and Architect (1) to become generally familiar with and to keep the Owner informed about the progress and quality of the portion of the Work completed; (2) to endeavor to guard the Owner against defects and deficiencies in the Work; and (3) to determine in general if the Work is being performed in a manner indicating that the Work, when fully completed, will be in accordance with the Contract Documents. However, the Architect shall not be required to make exhaustive or continuous on-site inspections to check the quality or quantity of the Work. The Architect shall neither have control over or charge of, nor be responsible for, the construction means, methods, techniques, sequences or procedures, fabrication, procurement, shipment, delivery or installation, or for safety precautions and programs in connection with the Work, since these are solely the Contractor's rights and responsibilities under the Contract Documents.

§ 2.7.2.2 The Architect shall report to the Owner known deviations from the Contract Documents and from the most recent construction schedule submitted by the Contractor. However, the Architect shall not be responsible for the Contractor's failure to perform the Work in accordance with the requirements of the Contract Documents. The Architect shall be responsible for the Architect's negligent acts or omissions but shall neither have control over or charge of, nor be responsible for, acts or omissions of the Contractor, subcontractors, or their agents or employees, or of any other persons or entities performing portions of the Work.

§ 2.7.2.3 The Architect shall at all times have access to the Work wherever it is in preparation or progress.

§ 2.7.2.4 Except as otherwise provided in this Agreement or when direct communications have been specially authorized, the Owner shall endeavor to communicate with the Contractor through the Architect about matters arising out of or relating to the Contract Documents. Communications by and with the Architect's consultants shall be through the Architect.

§ 2.7.2.5 The Architect shall have authority to reject construction Work that does not conform to the Contract Documents. Whenever the Architect considers it necessary or advisable, the Architect shall have authority to require inspection or testing of the Work in accordance with the provisions of the Contract Documents, whether or not such Work is fabricated, installed or completed. However, neither this authority of the Architect nor a decision made in good faith either to exercise or not to exercise such authority shall give rise to a duty or responsibility of the Architect to the Contractor, subcontractors, material and equipment suppliers, their agents or employees, or other persons or entities performing portions of the Work.

§ 2.7.3 Certification of Payments to the Contractor
§ 2.7.3.1 The Architect shall review and certify the amounts due the Contractor and shall issue Certificates for Payment in such amounts. The Architect's certification for payment shall constitute a representation to the Owner, based on the Architect's evaluation of the Work as provided in Section 2.7.2 and on the data comprising the Contractor's Application for Payment, that the Work has progressed to the point indicated and that, to the best of the Architect's knowledge, information and belief, the quality of the Work is in accordance with the Contract Documents. The foregoing representations are subject to (1) an evaluation of the Work for conformance with the Contract Documents upon Substantial Completion; (2) the results of subsequent tests and inspections; (3) the correction of minor deviations from the Contract Documents prior to final completion; and (4) specific qualifications expressed by the Architect.

§ 2.7.3.2 The issuance of a Certificate for Payment shall not be a representation that the Architect has (1) made exhaustive or continuous on-site inspections to check the quality or quantity of the Work; (2) reviewed construction means, methods, techniques, sequences or procedures of construction, fabrication, procurement, shipment, delivery or installation; (3) reviewed copies of requisitions received from subcontractors and material suppliers and other data requested by the Owner to substantiate the Contractor's right to payment; or (4) ascertained how or for what purpose the Contractor has used money previously paid on account of the Contract Sum.

§ 2.7.3.3 The Architect shall maintain a record of the Contractor's Applications for Payment.

§ 2.7.4 Submittals
§ 2.7.4.1 The Architect shall review and approve or take other appropriate action upon the Contractor's Submittals such as Shop Drawings, Product Data and Samples, but only for the limited purpose of checking for conformance with information given and the design concept expressed in the Contract Documents. The Architect's action shall be taken with such reasonable promptness as to cause no delay in the Work or in the activities of the Owner, Contractor or separate contractors, while allowing sufficient time in the Architect's professional judgment to permit adequate review. Review of such Submittals is not conducted for the purpose of determining the accuracy and completeness of other details such as dimensions and quantities, or for substantiating instructions for installation or performance of equipment or systems, all of which remain the responsibility of the Contractor as required by the Contract Documents. The Architect's review shall not constitute approval of safety precautions or, unless otherwise specifically stated by the Architect, of any construction means, methods, techniques, sequences or procedures of construction, fabrication, transportation or installation. The Architect's approval of a specific item shall not indicate approval of an assembly of which the item is a component.

§ 2.7.4.2 The Architect shall maintain a record of Submittals and copies of Submittals supplied by the Contractor in accordance with the requirements of the Contract Documents.

§ 2.7.4.3 If professional design services or certifications by a design professional related to systems, materials or equipment are specifically required of the Contractor by the Contract Documents, the Architect shall specify appropriate performance and design criteria that such services must satisfy. Shop Drawings and other Submittals related to the Work designed or certified by the design professional retained by the Contractor shall bear such professional's written approval when submitted to the Architect. The Architect shall be entitled to rely upon the adequacy, accuracy and completeness of the services, certifications or approvals performed by such design professionals.

§ 2.7.5 Changes in the Work
§ 2.7.5.1 The Architect shall prepare Change Orders and Construction Change Directives for the Owner's approval and execution in accordance with the Contract Documents. The Architect may authorize minor changes in the Work not involving an adjustment in Contract Sum or an extension of the Contract Time that are not inconsistent with the intent of the Contract Documents. If necessary, the Architect shall prepare, reproduce and distribute Drawings and Specifications to describe Work to be added, deleted or modified.

§ 2.7.5.2 The Architect shall review properly prepared, timely requests by the Owner or Contractor for changes in the Work, including adjustments to the Contract Sum or Contract Time. A properly prepared request for a change in the Work shall be accompanied by sufficient supporting data and information to permit the Architect to make a reasonable determination without extensive investigation or preparation of additional drawings or specifications. If the Architect determines that requested changes in the Work are not materially different from the requirements of the Contract Documents, the Architect may issue an order for a minor change in the Work or recommend to the Owner that the requested change be denied.

§ 2.7.5.3 If the Architect determines that implementation of the requested changes would result in a material change to the Contract or may cause an adjustment in the Contract Time or Contract Sum, the Architect shall make a recommendation to the Owner, who may authorize further investigation of such change. Upon such authorization, and based upon information furnished by the Contractor, if any, the Architect shall estimate the additional cost and time that might result from such change, including any additional costs attributable to a Change in Services of the Architect. With the Owner's approval, the Architect shall incorporate those estimates into a Change Order or other appropriate documentation for the Owner's execution or negotiation with the Contractor.

§ 2.7.5.4 The Architect shall maintain records relative to Changes in the Work.

§ 2.7.6 Project Completion
§ 2.7.6.1 The Architect shall conduct inspections to determine the date or dates of Substantial Completion and the date of final completion; shall receive from the Contractor and forward to the Owner, for the Owner's review and records, written warranties and related documents required by the Contract Documents and assembled by the Contractor; and shall issue a final Certificate for Payment based upon a final inspection indicating that the Work complies with the requirements of the Contract Documents.

§ 2.7.6.2 The Architect's inspection shall be conducted with the Owner's Designated Representative to check conformance of the Work with the requirements of the Contract Documents and to verify the accuracy and completeness of the list submitted by the Contractor of Work to be completed or corrected.

§ 2.7.6.3 When the Work is found to be substantially complete, the Architect shall inform the Owner about the balance of the Contract Sum remaining to be paid the Contractor, including any amounts to be withheld for final completion or correction of the Work.

§ 2.7.6.4 The Architect shall receive from the Contractor and forward to the Owner (1) consent of surety or sureties, if any, to reduction in or partial release of retainage or the making of final payment; and (2) affidavits, receipts, releases and waivers of liens or bonds indemnifying the Owner against liens.

§ 2.8 Furniture, Furnishings and Equipment Contract Administration Phase

§ 2.8.1 The Architect shall provide administration of the contracts for furniture, furnishings and equipment only as set forth below and in AIA® Document A275™ID-2003, *General Conditions of the Contract for Furniture, Furnishings and Equipment.*

§ 2.8.2 The Architect shall assist the Owner in coordinating schedules for fabrication, delivery and installation of the Work, but shall not be responsible for any failure of a Vendor to meet schedules for completion or to perform its duties and responsibilities in conformance with such schedules.

§ 2.8.3 The Architect shall review and approve or take other appropriate action upon a Vendor's Submittals such as Shop Drawings, Product Data and Samples, but only for the limited purpose of checking for conformance with information given and the design concept expressed in the Contract Documents.

§ 2.8.4 As the buyer of goods, the Owner shall receive, inspect and accept or reject furniture, furnishings and equipment at the time of their delivery to the premises and installation unless otherwise provided. The Architect is not authorized to act as the Owner's agent in contractual matters.

§ 2.8.5 The Architect shall review final placement and inspect for damage, quality, assembly and function in order to determine that furniture, furnishings and equipment are in accordance with the requirements of the Contract Documents. The Architect may recommend to the Owner acceptance or rejection of furniture, furnishings and equipment.

§ 2.8.6 The Architect, as a representative of the Owner, shall visit the Project premises at intervals appropriate to the stage of the Vendor's installation to (1) become generally familiar with and to keep the Owner informed about the progress and quality of the portion of the Work completed; (2) endeavor to guard the Owner against defects and deficiencies in the Work; and (3) determine in general if the Work is being performed in a manner indicating that the Work, when fully completed, will be in accordance with the Contract Documents. The Architect shall neither have control over or charge of, nor be responsible for, the means, methods, techniques, sequences or procedures of fabrication, shipment, delivery or installation, or for the safety precautions and programs in connection with the Work, since these are solely the Vendor's rights and responsibilities under the Contract Documents.

ARTICLE 3   CHANGE IN SERVICES

§ 3.1 General

§ 3.1.1 The services described in this Article 3 are not included in compensation for Basic Services and shall be provided only if authorized or confirmed in writing by the Owner.

§ 3.2 Project Representation Beyond Basic Services

§ 3.2.1 If more extensive representation at the Project premises than is described in Section 2.7.2.1 is required, the Architect shall provide one or more Project Representatives to assist in carrying out such responsibilities at the Project premises.

§ 3.2.2 The Architect shall select, employ and direct its Project Representatives, and the Architect shall be compensated therefore as agreed by the Owner and Architect. The duties, responsibilities and limitations of authority of Project Representatives shall be as described in the edition of AIA® Document B352™ –2000, *Duties, Responsibilities and Limitations of Authority of the Architect's Project Representative,* current as of the date of this Agreement, unless otherwise agreed.

§ 3.2.3 Through the observations by such Project Representatives, the Architect shall endeavor to provide further protection for the Owner against defects and deficiencies in the Work, but the furnishing of such project representation shall not modify the rights, responsibilities or obligations of the Architect as described elsewhere in this Agreement.

§ 3.3 Purchasing of Furniture, Furnishings and Equipment by the Architect

§ 3.3.1 If the Owner and Architect agree that the Architect will purchase furniture, furnishings and equipment on behalf of the Owner with funds provided by the Owner, the duties and compensation related to such additional services shall be set forth in a separate agreement.

§ 3.4 Additional Services

§ 3.4.1 Providing services or making revisions to Drawings, Specifications and other documents when such revisions are:

.1 inconsistent with approvals or instructions previously given by the Owner, including revisions made necessary by adjustments in the Owner's program, Project budget or schedule;

.2 required by the enactment or revision of codes, laws or regulations subsequent to the preparation of such documents;

.3 due to change in the procurement method, Change Orders or Change Directives; or

.4 due to proposed substitutions from contractors or vendors.

§ 3.4.2 Providing services to investigate existing conditions or facilities or to make measured drawings thereof.

§ 3.4.3 Making investigations or inventories of materials or furniture, furnishings and equipment, or valuations and detailed appraisals of existing facilities, furniture, furnishings and equipment, and the relocation thereof.

§ 3.4.4 Providing services to verify the accuracy information furnished by the Owner.

§ 3.4.5 Providing assistance to the Owner in contracting for special surveys, environmental studies and submissions required for approvals of governmental authorities or others having jurisdiction over the Project.

§ 3.4.6 Providing services for the design or selection of graphics and signage.

§ 3.4.7 Providing services in connection with the selection and procurement of works of art.

§ 3.4.8 Providing services involving travel for the purpose of evaluating materials, furniture, furnishings and equipment proposed for the Project.

§ 3.4.9 Providing services of engineering consultants not enumerated in Article 13.

§ 3.4.10 Providing special studies or services in connection with special consultants for the design of information technology, security or acoustic systems.

§ 3.4.11 Providing services relative to future requirements for facilities, systems, furniture, furnishings and equipment.

§ 3.4.12 Providing detailed estimates of the Cost of the Work.

§ 3.4.13 If requested by the Owner, organizing and participating in selection interviews with prospective contractors.

§ 3.4.14 Providing a detailed analysis of parts and components to verify the accuracy of quotations provided by the furniture, furnishings and equipment Vendor.

§ 3.4.15 Receiving, inspecting and accepting or rejecting, on behalf of the Owner, furniture, furnishings and equipment at the time of their delivery to the premises and installation.

§ 3.4.16 Providing services in evaluating an extensive number of claims submitted by contractors or others in connection with the Work.

§ 3.4.17 Providing post-occupancy evaluations.

§ 3.4.18 Providing assistance in the utilization of equipment or systems such as testing, adjusting and balancing, preparation of operation and maintenance manuals, training personnel for operation and maintenance, and consultation during operation.

§ 3.4.19 Providing analyses of maintenance and operating costs.

§ 3.4.20 Preparing a set of reproducible record drawings or specifications showing significant changes in the Work made during the performance thereof based on marked-up prints, drawings and other data furnished by the Contractors to the Architect.

§ 3.4.21 Providing services relating to the Work of a contractor after issuance to the Owner of the final Certificate for Payment for such contractor's Work, or in the absence of a final Certificate for Payment, more than 60 days after the date of Substantial Completion of the Work.

§ 3.4.22 Providing services made necessary by the default of a Contractor or Vendor, by major defects or deficiencies in their Work, or by failure of performance of the Owner, an independent contractor or independent vendor.

§ 3.4.23 Providing consultation concerning replacement of Work damaged by fire or other cause, and furnishing services required in connection with the replacement of such Work.

§ 3.4.24 Providing services in connection with a public hearing, mediation, arbitration or legal proceeding, except where the Architect is party thereto.

ARTICLE 4 OWNER'S RESPONSIBILITIES

§ 4.1 The Owner shall provide full information regarding requirements for the Project, including notification of incorporation, ownership, tenancy or nonprofit status.

§ 4.2 The Owner shall establish and update an overall budget for the Project, including the Cost of the Work, the Owner's other costs and reasonable contingencies related to all of these costs.

§ 4.3 If requested by the Architect, the Owner shall furnish evidence that financial arrangements have been made to fulfill the Owner's obligations under this Agreement.

§ 4.4 Prior to commencement of services, the Owner shall designate a representative authorized to act on the Owner's behalf with respect to the Project. The Owner's authorized representative shall render decisions in a timely manner pertaining to documents submitted by the Architect in order to avoid unreasonable delay in the orderly and sequential progress of the Architect's services.

§ 4.5 The Owner shall furnish structural, mechanical, chemical, air and water pollution tests, tests for hazardous materials and other laboratory and environmental tests, inspections, reports and mitigation required by law or the Contract Documents.

§ 4.6 The Owner shall furnish all legal, accounting and insurance counseling services as may be necessary at any time for the Project, including auditing services the Owner may require to verify the Contractors' or Vendors' applications for payment or to ascertain how or for what purposes the Contractors or Vendors have used the money paid by or on behalf of the Owner.

§ 4.7 The Drawings, Specifications, services, information, surveys and reports provided by the Owner pertaining to the Project shall be furnished at the Owner's expense, and the Architect shall be entitled to rely upon the accuracy and completeness thereof.

§ 4.8 Execution of this Agreement is an affirmation that the Owner has disclosed, to the extent known to the Owner, the results and reports of prior tests, inspections or investigations, if any, conducted for the Project involving structural and mechanical systems; chemical, air and water pollution; hazardous materials; or other environmental and subsurface conditions. The Owner shall disclose all information known to the Owner regarding the presence of pollutants at the Project site.

§ 4.9 Prompt written notice shall be given by the Owner to the Architect if the Owner becomes aware of any fault or defect in the Project or nonconformance with the Contract Documents.

§ 4.10 The proposed language of certificates or certifications requested of the Architect or Architect's consultants shall be submitted to the Architect for review and approval at least 14 days prior to execution. The Owner shall not request certifications that would require knowledge or services beyond the scope of this Agreement.

§ 4.11 The Owner shall be responsible for negotiations and obligations of the lease, if any, and shall serve as the contact with the landlord. The Owner shall provide information contained in the lease or landlord correspondence relevant to the Project.

§ 4.12 The Owner shall be responsible for the relocation or removal of existing facilities, furniture, furnishings equipment and the contents thereof, unless otherwise provided by this Agreement.

ARTICLE 5 COST OF THE WORK
§ 5.1 Definition
§ 5.1.1 The Cost of the Work shall be the total cost including applicable taxes, or to the extent the Project is not completed, the estimated cost to the Owner of all elements of the Project designed or specified by the Architect. A reasonable allowance for contingencies shall be included for market conditions at the time of bidding and for changes in the Work.

§ 5.1.2 The Cost of Work does not include the compensation of the Architect and Architect's consultants, the cost of financing or other costs that are the responsibility of the Owner.

§ 5.2 Evaluation of Budget and Cost of the Work
§ 5.2.1 When the Project requirements have been sufficiently identified, the Architect shall prepare a preliminary estimate of the Cost of the Work. This estimate may be based on current area, volume or similar conceptual estimating techniques. As the design process progresses through the end of the preparation of the Construction Documents, the Architect shall update and refine the preliminary estimate of the Cost of the Work. The Architect shall advise the Owner of any adjustments to previous estimates of the Cost of the Work indicated by changes in Project requirements or general market conditions. If at any time the Architect's estimate of the Cost of the Work exceeds the Owner's budget, the Architect shall make appropriate recommendations to the Owner to adjust the Project's size, quality or budget, and the Owner shall cooperate with the Architect in making such adjustments.

§ 5.2.2 Evaluations of the Owner's budget for the Project, the preliminary estimate of the Cost of the Work and updated estimates of the Cost of the Work prepared by the Architect represent the Architect's judgment as a design professional familiar with interior design. It is recognized, however, that neither the Architect nor Owner has control over the cost of labor, materials, furniture, furnishings or equipment; over the Contractors' methods of determining bid prices; or over competitive bidding, market or negotiating conditions. Accordingly, the Architect cannot and does not warrant or represent that bids or negotiated prices will not vary from the Owner's budget for the Project or from any estimate of the Cost of the Work or evaluation prepared or agreed to by the Architect.

§ 5.2.3 In preparing estimates of the Cost of the Work, the Architect shall be permitted to include contingencies for design, bidding and price escalation; to determine what materials, furniture, furnishings and equipment, finishes, component systems and types of construction are to be included in the Contract Documents; to make reasonable adjustments in the scope of the Project; and to include in the Contract Documents alternate bids as may be necessary to adjust the estimated Cost of the Work to meet the Owner's budget for the Cost of the Work. If an increase in the Contract Sum occurring after execution of the Contract between the Owner and the Contractor causes the budget for the Cost of the Work to be exceeded, that budget shall be increased accordingly.

§ 5.2.4 If bidding or negotiating has not commenced within 90 days after the Architect submits the Contract Documents to the Owner, the budget for the Cost of the Work shall be adjusted to reflect changes in the general level of prices in the interiors industry.

§ 5.2.5 If the budget for the Cost of the Work is exceeded by the lowest bona fide bids or negotiated proposal, the Owner shall:
  .1   give written approval of an increase in the budget for the Cost of the Work;
  .2   authorize rebidding or renegotiating of the Project within a reasonable time;
  .3   terminate in accordance with Section 9.5; or

.4   cooperate in revising the Project scope and quality as required to reduce the Cost of the Work.

§ 5.2.6 If the Owner chooses to proceed under Section 5.2.5.4, the Architect, without additional compensation, shall modify the documents for which the Architect is responsible under this Agreement as necessary to comply with the budget for the Cost of the Work. The modification of such documents shall be the limit of the Architect's responsibility under this Section 5.2. The Architect shall be entitled to compensation in accordance with this Agreement for all services performed whether or not construction is commenced.

ARTICLE 6 INSTRUMENTS OF SERVICE

§ 6.1 Drawings, Specifications and other documents, including those in electronic form, prepared by the Architect and the Architect's consultants are Instruments of Service for use solely with respect to this Project. The Architect and the Architect's consultants shall be deemed the authors and owners of their respective Instruments of Service and shall retain all common law, statutory and other reserved rights, including copyrights.

§ 6.2 Upon execution of this Agreement, the Architect grants to the Owner a nonexclusive license to reproduce the Architect's Instruments of Service solely for purposes of constructing, using and maintaining the Project, provided that the Owner shall comply with all obligations, including prompt payment of all sums when due, under this Agreement. The Architect shall obtain similar nonexclusive licenses from the Architect's consultants consistent with this Agreement. Any termination of this Agreement prior to completion of the Project shall terminate this license. Upon such termination, the Owner shall refrain from making further reproductions of Instruments of Service and shall return to the Architect, within seven days, all originals and reproductions in the Owner's possession or control. If and upon the date the Architect is adjudged in default of this Agreement, the foregoing license shall be deemed terminated and replaced by a second, nonexclusive license permitting the Owner to authorize other similarly credentialed design professionals to reproduce and, where permitted by law, to make changes, corrections or additions to the Instruments of Service solely for purposes of completing, using and maintaining the Project.

§ 6.3 Except for the licenses granted in Section 6.2, no other license or right shall be deemed granted or implied under this Agreement. The Owner shall not assign, delegate, sublicense, pledge or otherwise transfer any license granted herein to another party without the prior written agreement of the Architect. However, the Owner shall be permitted to authorize the Contractor, Vendors and material or equipment suppliers to reproduce applicable portions of the Instruments of Service appropriate to and for use in their execution of the Work by license granted in Section 6.2. Submission or distribution of Instruments of Service to meet official regulatory requirements or for similar purposes in connection with the Project is not to be construed as publication in derogation of the reserved rights of the Architect and the Architect's consultants. The Owner shall not use the Instruments of Service for future additions or alterations to this Project or for other projects, unless the Owner obtains the prior written agreement of the Architect and the Architect's consultants. Any unauthorized use of the Instruments of Service shall be at the Owner's sole risk and without liability to the Architect and the Architect's consultants.

§ 6.4 Prior to the Architect providing to the Owner any Instruments of Service in electronic form or the Owner providing to the Architect any electronic data for incorporation into the Instruments of Service, the Owner and the Architect shall by separate written agreement set forth the specific conditions governing the format of such Instruments of Service or electronic data, including any special limitations or licenses not otherwise provided in this Agreement.

ARTICLE 7 MEDIATION

§ 7.1 Any claim, dispute or other matter in question arising out of or related to this Agreement shall be subject to mediation as a condition precedent to arbitration or the institution of legal or equitable proceedings by either party. If such matter relates to or is the subject of a lien arising out of the Architect's services, the Architect may proceed in accordance with applicable law to comply with the lien notice or filing deadlines prior to resolution of the matter by mediation or arbitration.

§ 7.2 The Owner and Architect shall endeavor to resolve claims, disputes and other matters in question between them by mediation, which unless the parties mutually agree otherwise, shall be in accordance with the Construction Industry Mediation Rules of the American Arbitration Association in effect at the time of the mediation. Request for mediation shall be filed in writing with the other party to this Agreement and with the American Arbitration Association. The request may be made concurrently with the filing of a demand for arbitration, but in such event, mediation shall proceed in advance of arbitration or legal or equitable proceedings, which shall be stayed pending mediation for a period of 60 days from the date of filing, unless stayed for a longer period by agreement of the parties or court order.

§ 7.3 The parties shall share the mediator's fee and any filing fees equally. The mediation shall be held in the place where the Project is located, unless another location is mutually agreed upon. Agreements reached in mediation shall be enforceable as settlement agreements in any court having jurisdiction thereof.

ARTICLE 8   ARBITRATION

§ 8.1 Any claim, dispute or other matter in question arising out of or related to this Agreement shall be subject to arbitration. Prior to arbitration, the parties shall endeavor to resolve claims and disputes by mediation in accordance with Article 7.

§ 8.2 Claims, disputes and other matters in question between the parties that are not resolved by mediation shall be decided by arbitration, which unless the parties mutually agree otherwise, shall be in accordance with the Construction Industry Arbitration Rules of the American Arbitration Association currently in effect at the time of the arbitration. The demand for arbitration shall be filed in writing with the other party to this Agreement and with the American Arbitration Association.

§ 8.3 A demand for arbitration shall be made within a reasonable time after the claim, dispute or other matter in question has arisen. In no event shall the demand for arbitration be made after the date when institution of legal or equitable proceedings based on such claim, dispute or other matter in question would be barred by the applicable statute of limitations.

§ 8.4 No arbitration arising out of or relating to this Agreement shall include, by consolidation or joinder or in any other manner, an additional person or entity not a party to this Agreement, except by written consent containing a specific reference to this Agreement and signed by the Owner, Architect and any other person or entity sought to be joined. Consent to arbitration involving an additional person or entity shall not constitute consent to arbitration of any claim, dispute or other matter in question not described in the written consent or with a person or entity not named or described therein. The foregoing agreement to arbitrate and other agreements to arbitrate with an additional person or entity duly consented to by the parties to this Agreement shall be specifically enforceable in accordance with applicable law in any court having jurisdiction thereof.

§ 8.5 The award rendered by the arbitrator or arbitrators shall be final, and judgment may be entered upon it in accordance with applicable law in any court having jurisdiction thereof.

ARTICLE 9   TERMINATION OR SUSPENSION

§ 9.1 If the Owner fails to make payments to the Architect in accordance with this Agreement, such failure shall be considered substantial nonperformance and cause for termination, or at the Architect's option, cause for suspension of performance of services under this Agreement. If the Architect elects to suspend services, prior to suspension of services, the Architect shall give seven days' written notice to the Owner. In the event of a suspension of services, the Architect shall have no liability to the Owner for delay or damage caused the Owner because of such suspension of services. Before resuming services, the Architect shall be paid all sums due prior to suspension and any expenses incurred in the interruption and resumption of the Architect's services. The Architect's fees for the remaining services and the time schedules shall be equitably adjusted.

§ 9.2 If the Project is suspended by the Owner for more than 30 consecutive days, the Architect shall be compensated for services performed prior to notice of such suspension. When the Project is resumed, the Architect shall be compensated for expenses incurred in the interruption and resumption of the Architect's services. The Architect's fees for the remaining services and the time schedules shall be equitably adjusted.

§ 9.3 If the Project is suspended or the Architect's services are suspended for more than 90 consecutive days, the Architect may terminate this Agreement by giving not less than seven days' written notice.

§ 9.4 This Agreement may be terminated by either party upon not less than seven days' written notice should the other party fail substantially to perform in accordance with the terms of this Agreement through no fault of the party initiating the termination.

§ 9.5 This Agreement may be terminated by the Owner upon not less than seven days' written notice to the Architect for the Owner's convenience and without cause.

§ 9.6 In the event of termination not the fault of the Architect, the Architect shall be compensated for services performed prior to termination, together with Reimbursable Expenses then due and all Termination Expenses as defined in Section 9.7.

§ 9.7 Termination Expenses are in addition to compensation for the services of the Agreement and include expenses directly attributable to termination for which the Architect is not otherwise compensated, plus an amount for the Architect's anticipated profit on the value of the services not performed by the Architect.

ARTICLE 10   PAYMENTS TO THE ARCHITECT

§ 10.1 Payments on account of services rendered and for Reimbursable Expenses incurred shall be made monthly upon presentation of the Architect's statement of services. No deductions shall be made from the Architect's compensation on account of penalty, liquidated damages or other sums withheld from payments to contractors or vendors or on account of the cost of changes in the Work other than those for which the Architect has been found to be liable.

§ 10.2 Reimbursable Expenses are in addition to compensation for the Architect's services and include expenses incurred by the Architect and Architect's employees and consultants directly related to the Project, as follows:

.1   transportation in connection with the Project, authorized out-of-town travel and subsistence, and electronic communications;

.2   fees paid for securing approval of authorities having jurisdiction over the Project;

.3   reproductions, plots, CAD translations, standard form documents, postage, handling and delivery of Instruments of Service;

.4   expense of overtime work requiring higher than regular rates, if authorized in advance by the Owner;

.5   renderings, models, materials and mock-ups requested by the Owner;

.6   expense of professional liability insurance dedicated exclusively to this Project or the expense of additional insurance coverage or limits requested by the Owner in excess of that normally carried by the Architect and the Architect's consultants;

.7   reimbursable expenses as designated in Section 11.5; and

.8   other similar direct Project-related expenditures.

§ 10.3 Records of Reimbursable Expenses, of expenses pertaining to Additional Services and of services performed on the basis of hourly rates or a multiple of Direct Personnel Expense shall be available to the Owner or the Owner's authorized representative at mutually convenient times.

§ 10.4 Direct Personnel Expense is defined as the direct salaries of the Architect's personnel engaged on the Project and the portion of the cost of their mandatory and customary contributions and benefits related thereto, such as employment taxes and other statutory employee benefits, insurance, sick leave, holidays, vacations, employee retirement plans and similar contributions.

ARTICLE 11   BASIS OF COMPENSATION

The Owner shall compensate the Architect as follows:

§ 11.1 AN INITIAL PAYMENT of   Dollars ($) shall be made upon execution of this Agreement and credited to the Owner's account as follows:
(Indicate whether initial payment will be credited to the first, to the last or proportionately to all payments on the Owner's account.)

§ 11.2 BASIC COMPENSATION

§ 11.2.1 FOR BASIC SERVICES, as described in Article 2, and any other services included in Article 13 as part of Basic Services, Basic Compensation shall be computed as follows:
(Insert basis of compensation, including stipulated sums, multiples or percentages, and identify phases to which particular methods of compensation apply, if necessary.)

§ 11.2.2 Where compensation is based on a stipulated sum or percentage of the Cost of the Work, progress payments for Basic Services in each phase shall total the following percentages of the total Basic Compensation payable:
(Insert additional phases as appropriate.)

Programming Phase	percent (%)
Pre-lease Analysis and Feasibility Services Phase	percent (%)
Schematic Design Phase	percent (%)
Design Development Phase	percent (%)
Contract Documents Phase	percent (%)
Bidding and Quotation Phase	percent (%)
Construction Contract Administration Phase	percent (%)
Furniture, Furnishings and Equipment	percent (%)
Contract Administration Phase	percent (%)

Total Basic Compensation	one hundred	percent (100 %)

§ 11.2.3 Basic Services compensation for the Pre-Lease Analysis and Feasibility Services Phase is based upon   (   ) alternative buildings.

§ 11.3 FOR PROJECT REPRESENTATION BEYOND BASIC SERVICES, as described in Section 3.2, compensation shall be computed as follows:

§ 11.4 COMPENSATION FOR ADDITIONAL SERVICES

§ 11.4.1 FOR ADDITIONAL SERVICES OF THE ARCHITECT, as described in Articles 3 and 13, other than (1) Additional Project Representation as described in Section 3.2 and (2) services included in Article 13 as part of Basic Services, but excluding services of consultants, compensation shall be computed as follows:
(Insert basis of compensation, including rates and/or multiples of Direct Personnel Expense for Principals and employees, and identify Principals and classify employees, if required. Identify specific services to which particular methods of compensation apply, if necessary.)

§ 11.4.2 FOR SERVICES OF CONSULTANTS identified in Article 13, a multiple of   (   ) times the amount billed to the Architect for such services.

§ 11.5 FOR REIMBURSABLE EXPENSES, as described in Section 10.2, and any other items included in Article 13 as Reimbursable Expenses, a multiple of   (   ) times the expenses incurred by the Architect, Architect's employees and consultants in the interest of the Project.

§ 11.6 Payments are due and payable   (   ) days from the date of the Architect's invoice. Amounts unpaid   (   ) days after the invoice date shall bear interest at the rate entered below, or in the absence thereof at the legal rate prevailing from time to time at the principal place of business of the Architect.
(Insert rate of interest agreed upon.)

(Usury laws and requirements under the Federal Truth in Lending Act, similar state and local consumer credit laws and other regulations at the Owner's and Architect's principal places of business, the location of the Project and elsewhere may affect the validity of this provision. Specific legal advice should be obtained with respect to deletions or modifications, and also regarding requirements such as written disclosures or waivers.)

§ 11.7 IF THE BASIC SERVICES covered by this Agreement have not been completed within   (   ) months of the date hereof, through no fault of the Architect, extension of the Architect's services beyond that time shall be compensated as provided in Section 11.4.1.

ARTICLE 12   MISCELLANEOUS PROVISIONS

§ 12.1 Unless otherwise provided, this Agreement shall be governed by the law in the principal place of business of the Architect.

§ 12.2 Terms in this Agreement shall have the same meanings as those in the edition of AIA Document A201™, *General Conditions of the Contract for Construction*, current as of the date of this Agreement and A175™ID-2003, *General Conditions of the Contract for Furniture, Furnishings and Equipment*, as appropriate.

§ 12.3 The Owner and Architect, respectively, bind themselves, their partners, successors, assigns and legal representatives to the other party to this Agreement and to the partners, successors, assigns and legal representatives of such other party with respect to all covenants of this Agreement. Neither the Owner nor Architect shall assign this Agreement without the written consent of the other.

§ 12.4 This Agreement represents the entire and integrated agreement between the Owner and Architect and supersedes all prior negotiations, representations or agreements, either written or oral. This Agreement may be amended only by written instrument signed by both Owner and Architect.

§ 12.5 Nothing contained in this Agreement shall create a contractual relationship with or a cause of action in favor of a third party against either the Owner or Architect.

§ 12.6 Unless otherwise provided in this Agreement, the Architect and Architect's consultants shall have no responsibility for the discovery, presence, handling, removal or disposal of or exposure of persons to hazardous materials in any form at the Project premises, including but not limited to pollutants, asbestos, asbestos products, polychlorinated biphenyl (PCB), mold or other toxic substances.

§ 12.7 The Architect shall have the right to include representations of the design of the Project, including photographs of the exterior and interior, among the Architect's promotional and professional materials. The Architect's materials shall not include the Owner's confidential or proprietary information if the Owner has previously advised the Architect in writing of the specific information considered by the Owner to be confidential or proprietary. The Owner shall provide professional credit for the Architect on the construction sign and in the promotional materials for the Project.

§ 12.8 The Architect and Owner waive consequential damages for claims, disputes or other matters in question arising out of or relating to this Agreement. This mutual waiver is applicable, without limitation, to all consequential damages due to either party's termination in accordance with Article 9 (including incidental, indirect to or punitive damage).

ARTICLE 13   OTHER CONDITIONS OR SERVICES

(Insert descriptions of other services included within Basic Compensation and modifications to the payment and compensation terms included in this Agreement.)

This Agreement entered into as of the day and year first written above.

OWNER   **ARCHITECT**

_____   _____
(Signature)   *(Signature)*

_____   _____
(Printed name and title)   *(Printed name and title)*

Professional Associations

American Furniture Manufacturers
  Association (AFMA)
P.O. Box HP 7
High Point, NC 27261
Phone: 336-884-5000
Web site: www.afma4u.org

American Hardware Manufacturers
801 N. Plaza Dr.
Schaumburg, IL 60173
Phone: 708-605-1025

American Hospital Association
1 N. Franklin St.
Chicago, IL 60606
Phone: 312-895-2500

American Hotel & Motel Association
1201 New York Ave., NW
Suite 600
Washington, DC 20005
Phone: 202-289-3100

American Institute of Architects (AIA)
1735 New York Ave., NW
Washington, DC 20006
Phone: 202-626-7300
Web site: www.aia.org

American National Standards Institute
  (ANSI)
24 W. 43rd St.
4th Floor
New York, NY 10036
Phone: 212-642-4900
Web site: www.ansi.org

American Society of Civil Engineers
1801 Alexander Bell Cr.
Reston, VA 20191
Phone: 703-295-6300

American Society of Furniture Designers
  (ASFD)
P.O. Box 2688
High Point, NC 27261
Phone: 910-576-1273
Web site: www.asfd.com

American Society of Interior Designers
  (ASID)
608 Massachusetts Ave., NE
Washington, DC 20002
Phone: 202-546-3480
Web site: www.asid.org

American Society of Landscape Architects
636 Eye St., NW
Washington, DC 20001
Phone: 202-898-2444
Web site: www.asla.org

American Textile Manufacturers Institute
1130 Connecticut Ave., NW
Suite 1200
Washington, DC 20036
Phone: 202-862-0500

Associated Builders and Contractors
4250 N. Fairfax Dr.
9th Floor
Arlington, VA 22203
Phone: 703-812-2000
Web site: www.abc.org

Association for Project Managers
1227 W. Wrightwood Ave.
Chicago, IL 60614
Phone: 773-472-1777
Web site: www.constructioneduction.com

Association of Registered Interior
  Designers of Ontario
717 Church St.
Toronto, Ontario, Canada M4W 2M5
Phone: 416-921-2127
Web site: www.arido.on.ca

Carpet and Rug Institute
P.O. Box 2048
Dalton, GA 30722
Phone: 706-278-3176
Web site: www.carpet-rug.com

Center for Universal Design/Center
  for Accessible Housing
North Carolina State University
Box 8613
Raleigh, NC 27695
Phone: 919-515-3082

Color Association of the United
  States
315 W. 39th St.
Studio 507
New York, NY 10018
Phone: 212-947-7774
Web site: www.colorassociation.com

Color Marketing Group (CMG)
5904 Richmond Hwy.
Suite 408
Alexandria, VA 22303
Phone: 703-329-8500
Web site: www.colormarketing.org

EnvironDesign
840 U.S. Hwy. One
Suite 330
North Palm Beach, FL 33408
Phone: 531-627-3393
Web site: www.environdesign.com

Foundation for Design Integrity
1950 N. Main St.
No. 139
Salinas, CA 93906
Phone: 650-326-1867
Web site: www.ffdi.org

Foundation for Interior Design
  Education Research (FIDER)
146 Monroe Ctr., NW
Suite 1318
Grand Rapids, MI 49503
Phone: 616-458-0400
Web site: www.fider.org

Human Factors & Ergonomics
  Society (HFES)
P.O. Box 1369
Santa Monica, CA 90406
Phone: 310-394-1811
Web site: www.hfes.org

Illuminating Engineering Society
  of North America
120 Wall St.
17th Floor
New York, NY 10005
Phone: 212-248-5000
Web site: www.iesna.org

Industrial Designers Society
  of America (IDSA)
45195 Business Ct.
Suite 250
Dulles, VA 20166
Phone: 703-707-6000
Web site: www.idsa.org

Interior Design Legislative Coalition
  of Pennsylvania
P.O. Box 44144
Pittsburgh, PA 15205
Phone: 215-561-0751
Web site: www.idlcpa.org

Interior Design Society (IDS)
3910 Tinsley Dr.
Suite 101
High Point, NC 27265
Phone: 336-886-6100
Web site: www.interiordesignsociety.org

Interior Designers of Canada (IDC)
Ontario Design Center
260 King St. E.
No. 414
Toronto, Ontario, Canada M5A 1K3

Phone: 416-564-9310
Web site:
  www.interiordesigncanada.org

International Association of Lighting
  Designers
200 World Trade Center
Merchandise Mart
Suite 9-104
Chicago, IL 60654
Phone: 312-527-3677
Web site: www.iald.org

International Facility Management
  Association (IFMA)
1 E. Greenway Plaza
Suite 1100
Houston, TX 77046
Phone: 713-623-4362
Web site: www.ifma.org and
  www.worldworkplace.org

International Furnishings and Design
  Association (IFDA)
191 Clarksville Rd.
Princeton Junction, NJ 08550
Phone: 609-799-3423
Web site: www.ifda.com

International Interior Design
  Association (IIDA)
13-122 Merchandise Mart
Chicago, IL 60654
Phone: 312-467-1950
Web site: www.iida.org

National Association of Home
  Builders (NAHB)
15th and M Sts., NW
Washington, DC 20005
Phone: 202-822-0200

National Council for Interior Design
  Qualification (NCIDQ)
1200 18th St., NW
Suite 1001
Washington, DC 20036
Phone: 202-721-0220
Web site: www.ncidq.org

National Council of Acoustical
   Consultants
66 Morris Ave.
Suite 1A
Springfield, NJ 07081
Phone: 201-564-5959

National Fire Protection Association
   (NFPA)
1 Battery March Park
Quincy, MA 02169
Phone: 617-770-3000
Web site: www.nfpa.org

National Home Furnishings
   Association (NHFA)
3910 Tinsley Dr.
Suite 101
High Point, NC 27265
Phone: 336-886-6100

National Kitchen & Bath Association
   (NKBA)
687 Willow Grove St.
Hackettstown, NJ 07840
Phone: 908-852-0033

National Restaurant Association
1200 17th St., NW
Washington, DC 20036
Phone: 202-331-5900
Web site: www.restaurant.org

National Trust for Historic
   Preservation
1785 Massachusetts Ave., NW
Washington, DC 20036
Phone: 202-588-6000
Web site: www.nationaltrust.org

Occupational Safety & Health
   Administration (OSHA)
200 Constitution Ave., NW
Washington, DC 20210
Phone: 202-219-8148

Organization of Black Designers
   (OBD)
300 M St., SW
Suite N-110
Washington, DC 20024
Phone: 202-659-3918

Rocky Mountain Institute
1739 Snowmass Creek Rd.
Snowmass, CO 81654
Phone: 970-927-3851
Web site: www.rmi.org

U.S. Green Building Council
1015 18th St., NW
Suite 805
Washington, DC 20036
Phone: 202-828-7422
Web site: www.usgbc.org

Wallcoverings Association (WA)
401 N. Michigan Ave.
Chicago, IL 60611
Phone: 312-644-6610
Web site: www.wallcoverings.org

Design Schools

ALABAMA

Auburn University Interior Design Program
College of Human Sciences
*Bachelor of Science, Interior Design
(2002, 2008)*
160 Spidle Hall
Auburn, AL 36849
Phone: 334-844-1334
Web site: www.humsci.auburn.edu

Samford University, Birmingham
Department of Interior Design
School of Education and Professional
Studies
Bachelor of Arts (2003, 2009)
800 Lakeshore Dr.
Birmingham, AL 35229-2239
Phone: 205-726-2843
Web site: www.samford.edu

University of Alabama, Tuscaloosa
Interior Design Program
Clothing, Textiles, and Interior Design
Human Environmental Sciences
*Bachelor of Science-Human Environmental
Sciences (2001, 2007)*
Box 870158
Tuscaloosa, AL 35487-0158
Phone: 205-348-6176
Web site: www.ches.ua.edu

ARIZONA

Arizona State University, Tempe
Interior Design Program
School of Design
College of Architecture and Environmental
Design
Bachelor of Science in Design (2002, 2008)
College of Architecture and Environment
Design
Tempe, AZ 85287
Phone: 480-965-4135
Web site:
www.asu.edu/caed/SOD/index.htm

The Art Center Design College, Tucson
Interior Design Program
Bachelor of Arts (2004, 2010)
2525 N. Country Club Rd.
Tucson, AZ 85716
Phone: 520-325-0123
Web site: www. theartcenter.edu

ARKANSAS

University of Arkansas, Fayetteville
Interior Design Program
School of Human Environmental Sciences
*Bachelor of Interior Design (BID)
(1999, 2005)*
118 HOEC Building
Fayetteville, AR 72701-1201
Phone: 501-575-2578
Web site: www.uark.edu

CALIFORNIA

Academy of Art University, San Francisco
Interior Architecture and Design
*Bachelor of Fine Arts, Interior Design
(2002, 2008)*
79 New Montgomery St., 6th Floor
San Francisco, CA 94105
Phone: 415-274-2209
Web site: www.academyart.edu

American InterContinental
   University, Los Angeles
Interior Design Department
Bachelor of Fine Arts (2000, 2006)
12655 W. Jefferson Blvd.
Los Angeles, CA 90066
Phone: 310-302-2515
Web site: www.qiuniv.edu

California College of the Arts,
   San Francisco
Interior Design Program
*BFA, Interior Design Major
   (2003, 2009)*
450 Irwin St.
San Francisco, CA 94107
Phone: 415-551-9288
Web site: www.cca.edu

California State University, Fresno
Interior Design Program
Department of Art and Design
*Bachelor of Arts in Interior Design
   (2003, 2009)*
5225 N. Backer Ave., MS 65
Fresno, CA 94107
Phone: 559-278-2046
Web site:
   www.csufresno.edu/artanddesign

California State University,
   Northridge
Department of Family and Consumer
   Sciences
Bachelor of Science (1998, 2004)
18111 Nordhoff St.
Northridge, CA 91330
Phone: 818-677-3051
Web site: www.fcs.csun.edu

California State University,
   Sacramento
Interior Design, Department of
   Design
*Bachelor of Arts Interior Design
   (1998, 2004)*
6000 J St.
Sacramento, CA 95819
Phone: 916-278-6375
Web site: www.csus.edu/design

Design Institute of San Diego
Interior Design Program
*Bachelor of Fine Arts in Interior Design
   (1998, 2004)*
8555 Commerce Ave.
San Diego, CA 92121
Phone: 858-566-1200
Web site: www.disd.edu

Interior Designers Institute,
   Newport Beach
Interior Design Program
*Bachelor of Arts Degree in Interior
   Design (2001, 2004)*
1061 Camelback Rd.
Newport Beach, CA 92660
Phone: 949-675-4451
Web site: www.idi.edu

San Diego Mesa College
Interior Design Program
7250 Mesa College Dr.
San Diego, CA 92111
Phone: 858-627-2941
Web site:
   www.sandiegomesacollege.net

UCLA Extension, Los Angeles
Interior Design Program
*Professional Designation in Interior
   Design (2001, 2007)*
10995 Le Conte Ave., No. 414
Los Angeles, CA 90024
Phone: 310-825-9061
Web site: www.uclaextension.edu

University of California,
   Berkeley Extension
Interior Design and Interior
   Architecture
*Certificate in Interior Design and
   Interior Architecture (1997, 2003)*
1995 University Ave.
Berkeley, CA 94720
Phone: 510-643-6949
Web site: www.unex.berkeley.edu

West Valley College, Saratoga
Interior Design Department
*FIDER Advanced Certificate
   (2000, 2006)*
1400 Fruitvale Ave.
Saratoga, CA 95070
Phone: 408-741-2406
Web site: www.westvalley.edu/wvc/id

Woodbury University, Burbank
Department of Interior Architecture
Bachelor of Science (2001, 2007)
7500 Glenoaks Blvd.
Burbank, CA 91510
Phone: 818-767-0888
Web site: www.woodbury.edu

COLORADO

Colorado State University, Fort Collins
Interior Design Program
Bachelor of Science (2002, 2008)
154 Aylesworth S.E.
Fort Collins, CO 80523
Phone: 970-491-1629
Web site: www.cahs.colostate.edu/dm

Rocky Mountain College of Art
   and Design, Denver
Interior Design Program
Bachelor of Fine Arts (2001, 2007)
1600 Pierce St.
Lakewood, CO 80214
Phone: 303-753-6046
Web site: www.rmcad.edu

DISTRICT OF COLUMBIA

The George Washington University
Interior Design Program
*Bachelor of Fine Arts and Master
   of Fine Arts (2002, 2008)*
2100 Foxhall Rd. NW
Washington, DC 20007
Phone: 202-242-6700
Web site:
   www.gwu.edu/~art/PRG_id.html

FLORIDA

Florida State University, Tallahassee
Department of Interior Design
BS and BA, Interior Design
(2002, 2008)
105 Fine Arts Annex
Tallahassee, FL 32306
Phone: 904-644-1436
Web site: www.fsu.edu

International Academy of Design,
Tampa
Interior Design Program
Bachelor of Fine Arts in Interior Design
(2002, 2008)
5225 Memorial Hwy.
Tampa, FL 33634
Phone: 813-881-0007
Web site: www.academy.edu

Ringling School of Art and Design,
Sarasota
Interior Design Department
Bachelor of Fine Arts, Interior Design
(2002, 2008)
2700 N. Tamiami Trail
Sarasota, FL 34234
Phone: 941-351-5100
Web site: www.rsad.edu

Seminole Community College
Interior Design Technology
100 Weldon Blvd.
Sanford, FL 32773
Phone: 407-328-2267
Web site: www.scc-fl.edu

University of Florida
Department of Interior Design
Bachelor of Fine Arts in Interior Design
(2003, 2009)
Box 115705
Gainesville, FL 32611
Phone: 352-392-0252
Web site:
www.sitedcp.ufl.edu/interior

GEORGIA

American International University,
Atlanta
Interior Design Program
Bachelor of Fine Arts in Interior Design
(2003, 2009)
3330 Peachtree Rd. NE
Atlanta, GA 30326
Phone: 404-965-5847
Web site: www.aiuniv.edu

Art Institute of Atlanta
Interior Design Program
Bachelor of Fine Arts in Interior Design
(2003, 2009)
6600 Peachtree Dunwoody Rd.
Atlanta, GA 30328
Phone: 770-394-8300
Web site: www.aia.artinstitues.edu

Atlanta College of Art
Interior Design Program
1280 Peachtree St. NE
Atlanta, GA 30309
Phone: 404-733-5160
Web site: www.aca.edu

Bauder College, Atlanta
Interior Design Department
Associate of Arts in Interior Design
3500 Peachtree Rd. NE
Atlanta, GA 30326
Phone: 404-237-7573
Web site: www.bauder.edu

Brenau University, Gainesville
Interior Design Program
Bachelor of Fine Arts (2000, 2006)
One Centennial Circle
Gainesville, GA 305001
Phone: 770-718-5319
Web site: www.brenau.edu

Georgia Southern University,
Statesboro
Interior Design Program
Bachelor of Science in Interior Design
(2004, 2010)
P.O. Box 8024
Statesboro, GA 30460
Phone: 912-681-0584
Web site:
www.chhs.georgiasourthern.edu/
rasm/id.html

University of Georgia, Athens
Interior Design Program
Bachelor of Fine Arts/Interior Design
(2000, 2006)
Jackson St.
Athens, GA 30602
Phone: 706-425-2917
Web site: www.art.uga.edu

IDAHO

**Brigham Young University-Idaho
(Formerly Ricks College)**, Rexburg
Interior Design Program
Bachelor of Science in Interior Design
(2001, 2007)
525 S. Center St.
Rexburg, ID 83460
Phone: 208-496-1368
Web site:
www.byui.edu/interiordesign

ILLINOIS

**Harrington Institute of Interior
Design**, Chicago
Bachelor of Fine Arts in Interior Design
(2001, 2007)
410 S. Michigan Ave.
Chicago, IL 60605
Phone: 877-939-4975
Web site: www.interiordesign.edu

Illinois Institute of Art at Chicago
Interior Design Department
Bachelor of Fine Arts in Interior Design
(2001, 2007)
350 N. Orleans St., No. 136
Chicago, IL 60654
Phone: 312-280-3500
Web site: www.ilia.aii.edu

Illinois Institute of Art
   at Schaumburg
Interior Design Department
Bachelor of Fine Arts in Interior Design
(2002, 2004)
1000 Plaza Drive
Schaumburg, IL 60173
Phone: 847-619-3450
Web site: www.ilis.artinstitute.edu

Illinois State University, Normal
Interior and Environmental Design
   Program
BA or BS in Family and Consumer
Sciences (2002, 2008)
Illinois State University Interior and
   Environmental Design Program
Normal, IL 61790
Phone: 309-438-8007
Web site: www.ilstu.edu

International Academy of Design
   and Technology, Chicago
Interior Design Department
Bachelor of Fine Arts in Interior Design
(2003, 2009)
One N. State St., Suite 400
Chicago, IL 60602
Phone: 312-980-9236
Web site: www.iadtchicago.com

Southern Illinois University,
   Carbondale
Interior Design
Bachelor of Science in Interior Design
(2001, 2004)
410 Quigley Hall
Carbondale, IL 62901-4337
Phone: 618-453-3734
Web site: www.siu.edu/

INDIANA

Indiana University, Bloomington
Interior Design Program
Bachelor of Science in Interior Design
(1998, 2004)
232 Memorial Hall East
Bloomington, IN 47405
Phone: 812-855-5497
Web site: www.indiana.edu

Purdue University, West Lafayette
Interior Design Program
Bachelor of Arts (2004, 2010)
1352 Creative Arts Bldg., No. 1 West
Lafayette, IN 47907
Phone: 765-494-3055
Web site: www.sla.purdue.edu

IOWA

Iowa State University of
   Science/Tech, Ames
Interior Design Program
Bachelor of Science in Interior Design
(2003, 2009)
158 College of Design
Ames, IA 50011
Phone: 515-294-8898
Web site: www.iastate.edu

KANSAS

Kansas State University, Manhattan
Interior Design Program
Bachelor of Science in Interior Design
(2003, 2009)
206 Anderson Hall
Manhattan, KS 66506
Phone: 785-532-1304
Web site: www.ksu.edu

KENTUCKY

University of Kentucky, Lexington
Interior Design Program
Bachelor of Interior Architecture
(2000, 2006)
113 Funkhouser Building
Lexington, KY 40506
Phone: 859-257-3106
Web site: www.uky.edu/design

University of Louisville
Interior Architecture Program
Bachelor of Fine Arts in Interior
   Architecture (2002, 2008)
Schneider Hall
2302 S. 3rd St.
Louisville, KY 40292
Phone: 502-852-6794
Web site: www.art.louisville.edu

LOUISIANA

Louisiana State University,
   Baton Rouge
Department of Interior Design
Bachelor of Interior Design (B.I.D)
(2001, 2007)
402 Design Bldg.
Baton Rouge, LA 70803-7030
Phone: 225-578-8422
Web site: www.www.id.lsu.edu

Louisiana Tech University, Ruston
Interior Design Program
Bachelor of Interior Design
(2002, 2008)
Box 3175 Tech Station
Ruston, LA 71272
Phone: 318-257-2816
Web site: www.latech.edu

University of Louisiana at Lafayette
Interior Design Program
Bachelor of Interior Design
(1998, 2004)
P.O. Box 43850
Lafayette, LA 70504
Phone: 337-482-6225
Web site: www.arts.louisiana.edu

MASSACHUSETTS

Boston Architectural Center
Interior Design Program
Bachelor or Master of Interior Design
(2002, 2008)
320 Newbury St.
Boston, MA 02115
Phone: 617-262-5000
Web site: www.the-bac.edu

Endicott College, Beverly
Interior Design Program
Bachelor of Science in Interior Design
 (2004, 2010)
376 Hale St.
Beverly, MA 01915
Phone: 978-232-2202
Web site: www.endicott.edu

Mount Ida College, Newton
Interior Design Program
Bachelor or Science in Interior Design
 (2001, 2007)
777 Dedham St.
Newton, MA 02159
Phone: 617-928-4500
Web site: www.mountida.edu

Newbury College, Brookline
Interior Design Program
Bachelor of Science (2003, 2005)
129 Fisher Avenue
Brookline, MA 02445
Phone: 617-730-7068
Web site: www.newbury.edu

The New England School of Art and
 Design at Suffolk University,
 Boston
Interior Design Program
Diploma: Bachelor of Fine Arts, Interior
 Design and Master in Interior Design
 (2002, 2008)
75 Arlington St.
Boston, MA 02116
Phone: 617-994-4250
Web site: www.suffolk.edu/nesad

Wentworth Institute of Technology,
 Boston
Interior Design Program
Bachelor of Science, Interior Design
 (1998, 2004)
550 Huntington Ave.
Boston, MA 02115
Phone: 617-989-4051
Web site: www.wit.edu

MICHIGAN

Eastern Michigan University,
 Ypsilanti
Interior Design Program
Bachelor of Science in Interior Design
 (1998, 2004)
206 Roosevelt Hall
Ypsilanti, MI 48197
Phone: 734-487-1299
Web site: www.emich.edu

Kendall College of Art and Design
 of Ferris State University,
 Grand Rapids
Interior Design Program
Bachelor of Fine Arts in Interior Design
 (2003, 2009)
111 Division Ave. North
Grand Rapids, MI 49503
Phone: 616-451-2787
Web site: www.kcad.edu

Lawrence Technological University,
 Southfield
Interior Architecture
Bachelor of Interior Architecture
 (2002, 2008)
21000 W. 10 Mile Rd.
Southfield, MI 48075
Phone: 248-204-2848
Web site: www.ltu.edu

Michigan State University,
 East Lansing
Interior Design Program
Bachelor of Arts (1998, 2004)
204 Human Ecology
East Lansing, MI 48824
Phone: 517-355-7712
Web site: www-msu-edu

Western Michigan University,
 Kalamazoo
Interior Design Program
Bachelor of Science (2004, 2010)
1903 W. Michigan Ave.
Kalamazoo, MI 49008
Phone: 269-387-3727
Web site: www.wmich.edu

MINNESOTA

Dakota County Technical College,
 Rosemount
Interior Design and Sales Program
AAS Degree (2003, 2009)
1300 145th St. East
Rosemount, MN 55068
Phone: 651-423-8261
Web site: www.dctc.mnscu.edu

University of Minnesota, St. Paul
Interior Design Program
Bachelor of Science (1999, 2005)
1985 Buford Ave.
St. Paul, MN 55108
Phone: 612-624-1717
Web site: www.che.umn.edu

MISSISSIPPI

Mississippi State University
Interior Design Program
Bachelor of Science (2000, 2006)
128 Lloyd-Ricks, Box 9745
Mississippi State, MS 39762
Phone: 662-325-2950
Web site: www.msstate.edu

University of Southern Mississippi,
 Hattiesburg
Interior Design Program
Bachelor of Science (1998, 2004)
Box 5035
Hattiesburg, MS 3406
Phone: 601-266-5988
Web site: www.usm.edu

MISSOURI

Maryville University of St. Louis
Interior Design Program
Bachelor of Fine Arts in Interior Design
 (2003, 2009)
13550 Conway Rd.
St. Louis, MO 63141
Phone: 314-529-9381
Web site: maryville.edu

University of Missouri, Columbia
Interior Design Program
Bachelor of Science (1999, 2005)
137 Stanley Hall
Columbia, MO 65211
Phone: 573-882-7224
Web site: www.missouri.edu/

NEBRASKA

University of Nebraska, Lincoln
Interior Design Program
*Bachelor of Science in Design
  (2001, 2007)*
232 Arch Hall
Lincoln, NE 68588
Phone: 402-472-9245
Web site: www.archsite.unl.edu

NEVADA

University of Nevada, Las Vegas
Interior Architecture and Design
  Program
*Bachelor of Science in Interior
  Architecture (2001, 2007)*
4505 Maryland Parkway
Las Vegas, NV 89154
Phone: 702-895-3031
Web site: www.unr.edu

NEW JERSEY

Kean University, Union
Interior Design Program
*Bachelor of Fine Arts in Interior
  Design (1999, 2005)*
100 Morris Ave.
Union, NJ 07083
Phone: 908-737-4434
Web site: www.kean.edu

NEW YORK

Buffalo State
Interior Design Program
Bachelor of Fine Arts (2004, 2010)
1300 Elmwood Ave.
Buffalo, NY 14222
Phone: 716-878-4209
Web site: www.buffalostate.edu

Cornell University, Ithaca
Interior Design Program
Bachelor of Science (2002, 2008)
E106 Van Rensselaer Hall
Ithaca, NY 14853-4401
Phone: 607-255-2168
Web site: www.dea.human.cornell.edu

Fashion Institute of Technology
State University of New York
Interior Design Department
Bachelor of Fine Arts (2000, 2006)
7th Ave at 27th St.
New York, NY 1001-5992
Phone: 212-217-7800
Web site: www.fitnyc.suny.edu

New York Institute of Technology,
  Old Westbury
Interior Design Department
*Bachelor of Fine Arts in Interior Design
  (2000, 2006)*
Box 8000, Northern Blvd.
Old Westbury, NY 11568
Phone: 516-686-7786
Web site: www.nyit.edu

New York School of Interior Design,
  Manhattan
Interior Design Program
Bachelor of Fine Arts (2000, 2006)
170 E 70th St.
New York, NY 10021
Phone: 212-472-1500
Web site: www.nysid.edu

Pratt Institute, Brooklyn
Interior Design Department
*Bachelor of Fine Arts, Interior Design
  (2003, 2009)*
200 Willoughby Ave.
Brooklyn, NY 11205
Phone: 718-636-3630
Web site: www.pratt.edu

Rochester Institute of Technology,
  Rochester
Professional Level Program
Bachelor of Fine Arts (2001, 2007)
73 Lamb Memorial Dr.
Rochester, NY 14623-6357
Phone: 716-475-6357
Web site: www.rit.edu

School of Visual Arts, Manhattan
Interior Design Department
*Bachelor of Fine Arts in Interior Design
  (1998, 2004)*
209 E. 23rd St.
New York, NY 10010
Phone: 212-592-2572
Web site: www.schoolofvisualarts.edu

Syracuse University
Interior Design Program
*Bachelor of Fine Arts in Interior Design
  (2002, 2008)*
334 Smith Hall
Syracuse, NY 13244
Phone: 315-443-2455
Web site: www.syr.edu

NORTH CAROLINA

East Carolina University, Greenville
Interior Design Program
Bachelor of Science (2002, 2008)
East Fifth St.
Greenville, NC 278581
Phone: 252-328-6929
Web site: www.ecu.edu

Meredith College, Raleigh
Interior Design Program
Bachelor of Science (2001, 2007)
3800 Hillsborough St.
Raleigh, NC 27607-5298
Phone: 919-760-8550
Web site: www.meredith.edu

University of North Carolina at Greensboro
Department of Interior Architecture
Bachelor of Science in Interior Architecture (2000, 2006)
259 Stone Bldg., Box 26170
Greensboro, NC 27402
Phone: 336-334-5320
Web site: www.uncg.edu/iarc

Western Carolina University, Cullowhee
Interior Design Program
Bachelor of Science (2002, 2005)
308F Belk Building
Cullowhee, NC 28723
Phone: 828-227-2155
Web site: www.ides.wcu.edu

NORTH DAKOTA

North Dakota State University, Fargo
Department of Apparel, Design, Facility, and Hospitality Management
BA or BS in Interior Design (2003, 2009)
EMLI 178
Fargo, ND 58105
Phone: 701-231-8604
Web site: www.ndsu.nodak.edu

OHIO

Columbus College Art and Design
Interior Design Program
Bachelor of Fine Arts (2003, 2009)
107 N. 9th St.
Columbus, OH 43215
Phone: 614-224-3156
Web site: www.ccad.edu

Kent State University
Interior Design Program
Bachelor of Arts in Interior Design (1999, 2005)
100 Nixson Hall
Kent, OH 44242
Phone: 330-672-5833
Web site: www.saed.kent.edu

Miami University, Oxford
Interior Design Program
Bachelor of Fine Arts (2002, 2008)
301 S. Patterson Ave.
Oxford, OH 45056
Phone: 513-529-7210
Web site: www.muohio.edu

Ohio University, Athens1
Interior Architecture Program
Bachelor of Science (2001, 2007)
108 Tupper Hall
Athens, OH 45701-2979
Phone: 740-593-2869
Web site: www.ohiou.edu

Ohio State University, Columbus
Interior Design
Bachelor of Science in Design (2002, 2008)
380 Hopkins Hall
Columbus, OH 43210
Phone: 614-292-6746
www.osu.edu

University of Akron
Interior Design Studies
Bachelor of Arts in Interior Design (2002, 2008)
215 Schrank Hall South
Akron, OH 44325-6103
Phone: 330-972-7864
Web site: www.uakron.edu

University of Cincinnati
School of Architecture and Interior Design
Bachelor of Science in Interior Design (2003, 2009)
Box 210016
Cincinnati, OH 45221
Phone: 513-556-0222
Web site: www.said.uc.edu

OKLAHOMA

Oklahoma State University, Stillwater
Interior Design Program
Bachelor of Science (2002, 2008)
431 Human Environmental Sciences
Stillwater, OK 74078-6142
Phone: 405-744-5035
Web site: www.okstate.edu

University of Central Oklahoma, Edmond
Department of Design
Bachelor of Fine Arts (2004, 2010)
100 N. University Dr.
Edmond, OK 73034
Phone: 405-974-5212
Web site: www.ucok.edu

University of Oklahoma, Norman
Interior Design Division
Bachelor of Interior Design (2004, 2010)
830 Van Vleet Oval, Room 1621
Norman, OK 73019-0265
Phone: 405-325-6764
Web site: www.ou.edu

OREGON

University of Oregon, Eugene
Interior Architecture Program
Bachelor or Master of Interior Architecture (1999, 2005)
1206 University of Oregon
Eugene, OR 97403-1206
Phone: 541-346-3656
Web site: architecture.uoregon.edu

PENNSYLVANIA

Bradley Academy of Visual Arts, York
Interior Design Program
Associate of Specialized Technology
1409 Williams Rd.
York, PA 17402
Phone: 800-864-7725
Web site: www.bradleyacademy.edu

Drexel University, Philadelphia
Interior Design Program
Bachelor of Science (1999, 2005)
33rd and Market St.
Philadelphia, PA 19104
Phone: 215-895-2390
Web site: www.drexel.edu

La Roche College, Pittsburgh
Interior Design Department
*Bachelor of Science in Interior Design
   (1999, 2005)*
9000 Babcock Blvd.
Pittsburgh, PA 15237
Phone: 412-536-1024
Web site: www.laroche.edu

Moore College of Art and Design,
   Philadelphia
Interior Design Department
Bachelor of Fine Arts (2001, 2007)
20th St. and the Parkway
Philadelphia, PA 19103
Phone: 215-568-4515
Web site: www.moore.edu

Philadelphia University
Interior Design Program
*Bachelor of Science in Interior Design
   (2001, 2007)*
School House Lane and Henry Ave.
Philadelphia, PA 19144
Phone: 215-951-6882
Web site: www.philau.edu

SOUTH CAROLINA

Winthrop University, Rock Hill
Interior Design Program
*Bachelor of Fine Arts in Interior Design
   (2003, 2006)*
Rock Hill, SC 29733
Phone: 803-323-2689
Web site: www.winthrop.edu/

TENNESSEE

Middle Tennessee State University,
   Murfreesboro
Interior Design Program
Bachelor of Science (2003, 2009)
Box 86
Murfreesboro, TN 37132
Phone: 615-898-2884
Web site: www.mtsu.edu

O'More College of Design, Franklin
Interior Design Program
*Bachelor of Fine Arts Majoring in
   Interior Design (2003, 2009)*
Box 908
Franklin, TN 37065
Phone: 615-794-4254
Web site: www.omorecollege.edu

The University of Memphis
Interior Design Program
*Bachelor of Fine Arts in Interior Design
   (2002, 2008)*
101 Wilder Tower
Memphis, TN 38152
Phone: 901-678-2980
Web site: www.memphis.edu

**University of Tennessee
   at Chattanooga**
Department of Human Ecology
*Bachelor of Science in Human
   Ecology/Interior Design (2002, 2008)*
615 McCallie Ave.
Chattanooga, TN 37403
Phone: 423-425-4550
Web site: www.utc.edu

University of Tennessee, Knoxville
Interior Design Program
*Bachelor of Science in Interior Design
   (1998, 2004)*
224 Art and Architecture Bldg.
Knoxville, TN 37996-2400
Phone: 865-974-3269
Web site: www.arch.utk.edu

Watkins College of Art and Design,
   Nashville
Division of Interior Design
Bachelor of Fine Arts (2004, 2010)
100 Powell Place
Nashville, TN 37204
Phone: 615-383-4848
Web site: www.watkins.edu

TEXAS

The Art Institute of Dallas
Interior Design Program
*Bachelor of Fine Arts in Interior
   Design (2003, 2009)*
Two North Park East
8080 Park Lane, Suite 100
Dallas, TX 75231
Phone: 469-587-1243
Web site: www.aid.edu

El Centro College, Dallas
Interior Design Department
*Advanced Technical Certificate in
   Interior Design (2002, 2008)*
Main at Lamar St.
Dallas, TX 75202
Phone: 214-860-2353
Web site: www.dcccd.edu

Stephen F. Austin State University,
   Nacogdoches
Interior Design Program
Bachelor of Science (2002, 2008)
Box 13014 SFA Station
Nacogdoches, TX 75962
Phone: 936-468-4502
Web site: www.sfasu.edu/hms

Texas Christian University,
   Fort Worth
Interior Design Program
Bachelor of Science (1998, 2004)
Box 298360
Fort Worth, TX 76129
Phone: 817-257-7499
Web site: www.demt.tcu.edu

Texas State University, San Marcos
Interior Design Program
*Bachelor of Science in Family and
Consumer Sciences (2002, 2008)*
601 University Dr.
San Marcos, TX 78666
Phone: 512-245-2155
Web site: www.fcs.txstate.edu

Texas Tech University, Lubbock
Interior Design Program
*Bachelor of Interior Design
(1999, 2005)*
Box 41162
Lubbock, TX 79409
Phone: 806-742-3050
Web site: www.hs.ttu.edu

University of North Texas
School of Visual Arts
Interior Design Program
Bachelor of Fine Arts (2002, 2008)
Box 305100
Denton, TX 76203
Phone: 940-565-4010
Web site: www.art.unt.edu

University of Texas at Arlington
Interior Design Program
*Bachelor of Science in Interior Design
(2002, 2008)*
701 S. Nedderman Dr.
Arlington, TX 76019
Phone: 817-272-2801
Web site: www.uta.edu

The University of Texas at Austin
Interior Design Program
*Bachelor of Science in Interior Design
(2001, 2007)*
115 Gearing Hall
Austin, TX 78712
Phone: 512-471-6249
Web site: www.ar.utexas.edu

**The University of Texas
at San Antonio**
Interior Design Program
*Bachelor of Science in Interior Design
(2003, 2009)*
501 W. Durango Blvd.
San Antonio, TX 78207
Phone: 210-458-3010
Web site: www.utsa.edu/architecture

UTAH

Utah State University, Logan
Interior Design Program
*BS and BA in Interior Design
(2002, 2008)*
Family Life College
Logan, UT 84322-2910
Phone: 435-797-8245
Web site: www.usu.edu

VIRGINIA

James Madison University,
Harrisonburg
Interior Design Program
Bachelor of Fine Arts (2002, 2008)
Harrisonburg, VA 22807
Phone: 540-568-6216
Web site: www.jmu.edu

Marymount University, Arlington
Interior Design Department
Bachelor of Arts (2001, 2007)
2807 Glebe Rd.
Arlington, VA 22207
Phone: 703-284-1671
Web site: www.marymount.edu

Virginia Commonwealth University,
Richmond
Department of Interior Design
Bachelor of Fine Arts (1998, 2004)
111 W. Broad St.
Richmond, VA, 23284
Phone: 804-828-1713
Web site: www.vcu.edu

**Virginia Polytechnic Institute
and State University**, Blacksburg
Interior Design Program
Bachelor of Science (1999, 2005)
201 Cowgill Hall
Blacksburg, VA 24061
Phone: 540-231-2438
Web site:
www.interiordesign.caus.vt.edu

WASHINGTON

Washington State University,
Pullman
Interior Design Program
Bachelor of Arts in Interior Design
White Hall 202
Box 642020
Pullman, WA 99164
Phone: 509-358-7513
Web site: www.idi.spokane.wsu.edu

WEST VIRGINIA

West Virginia University,
Morgantown
Interior Design
*Bachelor of Science in Family and
Consumer Sciences/Interior Design
(2003, 2009)*
704-L Allen Hall
Box 6124
Morgantown, WV 26506-6124
Phone: 304-293-3402
Web site: www.cafcs.wvu.edu

WISCONSIN

Mount Mary College
Interior Design Program
*Bachelor of Arts/Interior Design
(2003, 2009)*
2900 N. Menomonee River Pkwy.
Milwaukee, WI 53222
Phone: 414-256-1213
Web site: www.mtmary.edu

University of Wisconsin, Madison
Interior Design Major
BS, Environment Textiles and Design-
Interior Design (1998, 2004)
1300 Linden Dr.
Room 234
Madison, WI 53706
Phone: 608-262-2651
Web site: www.sohe.wisc.edu

University of Wisconsin,
    Stevens Point
Interior Architecture Program
Bachelor of Science and Bachelor
of Arts (1999, 2005)
101 College of Professional Studies
Stevens Point, WI 54481
Phone: 715-346-4600
Web site: www.uwsp.edu

University of Wisconsin–Stout,
    Menomonie
Interior Design Program
Bachelor of Fine Arts, Art/Interior
Design (2000, 2006)
325 Applied Arts Bldg.
Menomonie, WI 54751
Phone: 715-232-1477
Web site: www.uwstout.edu

CANADA

Algonquin College, Ottawa
Interior Design Program
Diploma in Interior Design
(2001, 2007)
1385 Woodroffe Ave.
Ottawa, Ontario Canada K2G 1V8
Phone: 613-727-4723
Web site: www.algonquincollege.com

Dawson College, Montreal
Interior Design Department
Diplome d'Etudes Collegiales
(2001, 2007)
3040 Sherbrooke St. West
Montreal, Quebec H3ZIA4
Phone: 514-931-8731, ext. 3211
Web site: www.dawsoncollege.qc.ca

Humber Institute of Advanced
    Learning and Technology, Toronto
Interior Design Program
Diploma of Interior Design
(2002, 2006)
205 Humber College Blvd.
Toronto, Ontario, Canada M9W 5L7
Phone: 416-675-6622
Web site: www.humber.ca

International Academy of Design
    and Technology
Interior Design Program, Toronto
Diploma in Interior Design
(2003, 2009)
31 Wellesley Street E.
Toronto, Ontario M4Y 1G7
Phone: 416-922-0308
Web site: www.www.iadttoronto.com

Kawantlen University College,
    Richmond
Professional Level Interior Design
    Program
Bachelor of Applied Design in Interior
Design (2000, 2006)
8771 Lansdowne Rd.
Richmond, British Columbia V6X 3Vi
Phone: 604-599-2542
Web site: www.kwantlen.bc.ca

Ryerson University, Toronto
The School of Interior Design
Bachelor of Interior Design
(1998, 2004)
350 Victoria St.
Toronto, Ontario Canada M5B 2K3
Phone: 416-979-5188
Web site: www.ryerson.ca

University of Manitoba
Department of Interior Design
Master of Interior Design (2001, 2007)
Winnipeg, Manitoba, Canada R3T 2N2
Phone: 204-474-9458
Web site: www.umanitoba.ca

Glossary

This glossary includes many business terms and designer terms that people use on a regular basis. We recommend you refer to more extensive resources for others. This will give you an overview of the terminology that is currently being used in the interior design business. The language used in this glossary is that used in official business, and these are official business terms you will need in your vocabulary.

Amortize
Reduce debt by installments; to reduce a debt by making payments against the principal balance in installments or regular transfers.

Arbitration
The process of resolving disputes between people or groups by referring them to a third party, either agreed to by them or provided by law, who makes a judgment.

As-built drawings
Drawings done after projects are completed, showing exactly how the building was constructed.

Assets
(a) A property to which a value can be assigned; (b) somebody or something that is useful.

Back orders
Orders placed that have not yet been received or not currently in stock or available. A back order is held until it is available.

Balance sheet
A financial report showing the assets, liabilities, and owners' equity of a business as of a specific date.

Bar chart
A method used to display related data visually in reference to each other; uses an x and y axis and bars of varying heights and widths.

Barrier-free
A design standard to make buildings accessible to the physically limited or handicapped, enforced by law in most public and some residential spaces.

Benefit
A payment made to a claimant or entitled person by an employer, insurance company, or other institution.

Bid
The amount a prospective buyer is willing to pay, negotiated on at an auction.

Bid bond
Purchased by the designer, contractor, or vendor and presented to the buyer or client to guarantee work will be completed.

Bid opening
Date, time, and place offers are opened and winning proposal is announced.

Bill of lading
Shipping document used by freight companies; identifies what is being shipped, from where to where, and when.

Billable hours
Hours worked that can be actually charged to the client and project.

Billing rate
The hourly rate charged by the design firm to a client for work performed by an owner, designer, or other associate.

Bonus plan
An incentive structure for associates of a firm to earn monetary rewards when set targets are met or exceeded.

Break-even point
The financial point at which total income equals total expenses; there is zero profit.

Building codes
The specific set of standards by which construction must conform; they are generally set by each locality but governed by each state's uniform set of codes.

Building permit
Issued by local governing body, giving permission to build or alter a structure.

Build-out
Finishing the construction on a building, often to meet tenant requirements.

Buyer
A person who makes a purchase.

Capital
Material wealth in the form of money or property; cash for investment; finance money that can be used to produce further wealth; economic resource, any resource or resources that can be used to generate economic wealth.

Case study
A written analysis of a situation outlining the facts, possible solutions, and actual outcome.

Cash

Money used in the form of coins and bills, as distinct from money orders or credit.

Cash-basis accounting

A method of accounting where profit and loss is determined by the amount of cash actually received or actually spent during the period; it does not include any accruals.

Cash discount

A reduced price to be paid for a product when cash is used to buy the product.

C Corporation

State-chartered entity with limited liability, taxed at a corporate rate.

Certificate of occupancy

An official document showing that a building conforms to government regulations and can be occupied.

Certificate of substantial completion

A document stating and certifying the construction project has almost reached the conclusion.

Change order

A written document that revises the work to be performed on a project: either additional or deleted. Generally includes the work to be performed, price, time frame. and signatures of all parties are included.

Codes

A system of accepted laws and regulations that govern procedure or behavior in particular circumstances or within a particular profession.

Cold calling

A sales technique used to call on potential clients without giving the customers advance notice.

Commission

A fee paid to an agent for providing a service, especially a percentage of the total amount of business transacted.

Compensation

Money paid to an employee or by a client for work performed.

Compensatory time

Time off given to an employee in lieu of overtime or holiday work.

Competitive bidding

Asking several providers of products or services to submit a quote; generally the provider with the lowest price and/or best quality will be awarded the project or purchase.

Concealed damage

Damage to product that cannot be seen until the shipping package is opened.

Conditions, covenants, and restrictions (CCRs)

Particular specifications for planned communities such as condos, townhouses, and so on.

Construction documents

Official legal documents, including working drawings, specifications, schedule and bid documents, required for doing a project.

Construction drawings

Includes plans, elevations, and details for constructing a project.

Contract

A formal or legally binding agreement, such as one for the sale of products or services or one setting out terms of employment; a document that records an agreement. Sets requirements and standards of performance and can be legally enforced.

Contract documents

Paperwork used to support the agreement between buyers and sellers.

Co-op advertising

Used by manufacturers and retailers to share the cost of advertising products; that is, cooperative advertising.

Copyright

The legal right of creative artists or publishers to control the use and reproduction of their original works.

Corporation

A company recognized by law as a single body with its own powers and liabilities, separate from those of individual members.

Customer Relationship Manager (CRM)

A person who designs the system by which business relationships between the clients and the various disciplines of the firm are developed and maintained, and the person who renews and supports this system.

Debt capital

Financing by use of loans or other instruments that must be repaid over a period of time or at a set point in time, generally with interest.

Direct labor

The time a designer or employee spends that is specifically involved in working on a given client's project.

Direct personnel expense (DPE)

Salary plus employee benefits, such as taxes, medical insurance, holidays, and so on.

Drop ship

When one requests a manufacturer to ship goods to an address other than the designer's general location; for example, it could be "drop shipped" to a warehouse in another city or, perhaps, the client's location.

Earned income

Money realized by providing goods or services, such as through wages, salaries, or net profit to a business, in contrast to dividend income.

Earnings before taxes

Total revenue less cost of sales, operating expenses, and interest. Net income before taxes have been calculated and/or paid.

Electronic bulletin board

A computer program that permits readers to post and receive messages.

Electronic filing

Transmitting tax returns to the IRS or other government entities via the Internet. This has become a common way for tax reports to be remitted.

Electronic mail or e-mail

A system by which messages are sent from one computer and received on another computer. This system has become a standard for both text and graphic communications.

Eminent domain

Information whose source is available to anyone and is not subject to copyright.

Employee

A person who works under the direction and control of a company and receives compensation from the company.

Employer

A person or business that hires staff, pays wages, and is responsible for providing a structured income and environment in which the staff are working. The employer pays Social Security and other taxes for the employee.

Employment at will

Arrangement whereby employees may quit their job at any time because they are not under contract; conversely, the employer may dismiss an employee at any time without prior notice or explanation. Neither is bound by a contract.

End user

The consumer that uses the products or the services.

Enterprise zone

A geographic area in which a business may have favorable tax credits or other advantages granted by a government body. This may include reduced state sales tax on all purchases made by clients in that area.

Entrepreneur

A person who creates an opportunity and develops his or her own business; this is usually someone very adventuresome and creative.

Equity capital

Money from stock sales; funds for a business raised by selling stock or by retaining earnings.

Ergonomics

The study and science of the way people move within their work areas.

Errors and omissions insurance

Protection against anything that is nonintentionally or nonfraudulently neglected or overlooked, resulting in any form of property damage or liability to a client.

Escape clause

A provision in a contract permitting either party to cancel part or all of a contract in the event of certain situations.

Escrow

Money or property kept in an individual depository account with a neutral party until a contract is completed or certain conditions are met.

Estimate

Expresses the approximate parameters of a project. This may include the items, the time schedule, as well as the financial commitment.

Ethics

Moral or professional principles. In business, work is performed in a diligent, honest, and scrupulous fashion.

Exclusion

Part of a contract or a bid not to be included in the quote or contract.

Executive

A person in a top management position who is responsible for major decision making.

Exit interview

An interview, conducted as an employee is leaving an organization, for the purpose of getting feedback and information regarding the general issues of employment.

Expeditor

A person within the company who is responsible for handling the paperwork from the time an item is ordered to the time it is delivered. The role is directed at providing a professional speedy process.

Expense account

Costs, such as travel, meals, lodging, and entertainment, incurred by an employee in the course of business and that will be reimbursed by the company. These costs generally are itemized, and receipts are provided to the company by the employee to substantiate the reimbursement.

Expenses

The costs incurred in operating and maintaining a business. These are generally deductible.

Exposure

The risk of loss a company or person is willing to assume, usually as related to cash or types of payables. Exposure can also be the amount of publicity one gets in a marketing situation, such as the television, newspapers, and other media.

Fabricator

A person or a company that takes raw materials and turns them into a product, such as the manufacturer.

Face time

Time spent face to face with a person, usually a client.

Facsimile or fax

A document that can be transmitted electronically to another party via a machine that scans the original document.

Factoring

A service whereby a company sells its accounts receivable to a financial company for an amount less than the face value of the receivable. The customer then pays the financial company, rather than the company from which he or she bought the merchandise.

Factory representatives
Salespeople, usually employed by a manufacturer, who sell product lines of the manufacturer to business. Today, many reps may represent more than one manufacturer, but they work under the same professional obligations as if they were employed exclusively by the company.

Fair market value
An economic term, meaning a price for an item or service that both the seller and the purchaser agree is the most appropriate at a set point in time.

Feasibility study
Research and analysis performed to determine the value of a proposed project. This usually includes use issues, the estimated costs, legal considerations, break-even points, and other types of consideration that may affect the decision to go forward.

Features
A list of the various aspects of a product, usually used in the presentation of a project.

Federal Express
An overnight courier company that provides fast pickup and delivery service of letters and parcels.

Federal Insurance Contributions Act (FICA)
A federal payroll tax comprised of Social Security and Medicare components and based on earned income. The Social Security portion has an earned income limit whereby employees don't pay on earnings over the annual limit. The Medicare component has no annual limit; all earnings are subject to the tax.

Fee
The cost of professional services.

Fiduciary
A person, company, or association that holds assets in trust for a beneficiary and is often responsible for investing money appropriately for the best interest of the beneficiary.

Finance charge
A fee made for extending credit or the interest on a credit transaction.

Finance company
An enterprise that makes loans to businesses or individuals. Unlike a bank, a finance company does not receive deposits but obtains its money by borrowing funds from other institutions or market sources.

Financial advisor
A professional who offers financial counseling, usually for a fee.

Financial management
The structure, review, analysis, forecasts, and operation of the financial part of a company.

Financial statement
A record of the financial position of an individual, a company, or an association. It includes a balance sheet, income statement, and statement of cash flows.

Finder's fee
A sum paid to an individual or company for bringing together two or more parties or individuals for a business project.

Finished goods
Products that have been completed and are ready for delivery.

Fire
To terminate or discharge an employee.

Fire code
Regulations generally enacted by the federal, state, or local government for the safety of people in buildings.

Firewall
Software or hardware that limits access to a computer system from an outside network.

Firm
A term used colloquially to refer to a business in general but legally refers to a nonincorporated business.

Firm offer
When a company states in writing that an offer to purchase an item or service is irrevocable for a certain period of time.

First mortgage
The lender for this type of financing (mortgage) has priority over all other lenders or liens that may be against the property.

First right of refusal
The right to match the offer and the terms of the contract before the contract is "firmed."

Fiscal year
A 12-month period used by a business as an accounting year; this may be the same or different from the calendar year.

Fixed asset
Property or items used in a business, such as machinery and equipment that is intended to be kept for a long period of time.

Fixture
An item once attached to a building that, if removed, could damage the property.

Flex time
A work plan by which an employee can select his or her starting and ending times for each day, generally within a range set by the employer.

Flood insurance
An insurance that is subsidized by the federal government to cover property damage due to a natural flood.

Floodplain

An area of land subject to periodic flooding. The standard is set by the Army Corp of Engineers.

Floor-area ratio

The mathematical relationship between the total square footage of a building to the total land area.

Flowchart

A diagram consisting of symbols, words, and descriptions and often used to show how a project is being developed or a product is being manufactured.

Follow-up letter

A letter sent to a prospective client after the initial meeting or product purchase.

Forced sale

When a seller must sell product or property immediately, without the benefit of finding a buyer who will pay the best price.

Foreclosure

The legal termination of all the conditions regarding a mortgage. For example, the bank will foreclose when the owner is not maintaining his or her financial obligation with the bank.

Foreign corporation

A corporation chartered in a state other than the one in which it is conducting its business. This is often confused with a corporation from a foreign country, which is more properly called an "alien corporation."

Forensic accounting

A specialized type of accounting and auditing used to define facts in a legal dispute. This situation may be used in cases of divorces, criminal fraud, or when companies feel accounting procedures may have been presented inappropriately.

Forgery

An object, writing, or painting with the intention of prejudicing the rights of others.

"For-profit" corporation

A corporation formed for the purpose of earning a profit and subject to federal, state, and local income taxes.

Fortuitous loss

A loss by chance or accident, not by anyone's intention. Insurance policies provide coverage against losses that are by chance or not under the control of the policyholder.

Forward buying

A retail term meaning to purchase more than is needed currently to obtain a special discount or opportunity; buying in advance of the need or for the future due to special circumstances.

Four Ps

The four components of a marketing plan: product, price, place, promotion.

Franchise

A company that gives the right to market or sell the company's services or goods to others in a certain territory.

Fraud

To intentionally deceive someone, resulting in some injury.

Free and clear

A legal term meaning there are no liens against the property. Example: the title is "free and clear."

Freedom of Information Act (FOIA)

The federal law requiring particular information to be made available to the public. There are guidelines for the disclosure.

Free enterprise

The ability to conduct business without direct government interference.

Free on board (FOB)

A transportation term identifying the point from which the purchaser assumes responsibility (risk) for the item or product. Example: FOB New York, means the purchaser is

responsible for the safety, liability, insuring, and so on from the time the item leaves the New York dock or storage facility.

Freight bill

An invoice that comes from the shipping company to the designer or the client for the transportation of products.

Freight insurance

Insurance on items while they are in the process of being shipped by a common carrier.

Frivolous lawsuit

An insufficient claim, not supported by the facts. When the courts consider a claim or suit a waste of time and money.

Front money

The necessary cash to start a project.

Front office

Offices of the major executives in the company.

Frozen account

A bank account from which you cannot take money until certain court liens have been satisfied.

Fulfillment

The process necessary to service and track orders.

Full disclosure

The requirement to disclose all the facts and issues relevant to a transaction.

Fully depreciated

When the value of a fixed asset has been completely written down to zero.

Functional authority

When the staff has been empowered to make decisions and implement them in areas in which they are experts. Most design specialists have this power within a firm: they act with full authority in their area of expertise.

Functional organization

An organization created for functions, such as a design firm that has divisions and different departments comprising, in this case, a design company.

Functional resume

A resume that presents the qualifications and skills of the person, not necessarily in chronological order.

Funded retirement or pension plan

Funds that are put aside by an employer to purchase retirement benefits for employees. An employee is guaranteed to receive those payments even if the company is no longer in business at the time the employee retires.

Furniture, fixtures, & equipment (FF&E)

Term used in the interior design field to include all movable items involved in a project. FF&E does not include the building or construction on the project.

General conditions

Part of a bid document stating the legal responsibilities, procedures, rights, and duties of all parties involved in a construction project.

General contractor

A person or company that constructs a building and is responsible for the overall project, including hiring the subcontractors. This is the person or company with which the contract is made.

General expense

An expense that is for the operations, other than selling, administration, and the cost of goods.

General ledger

The accounting "books" of the business, showing all of the transactions, including debts and credits.

General partnership

A form of business organization where people join together to form a business entity. All are responsible for the liabilities and gain from the profits of the business.

Golden handcuffs

A colloquial term referring to the method companies use to retain key employees, often through stock options, incentives, or noncompete agreements.

Golden parachute

A colloquial term referring to a lucrative contract given to an executive of a company, which may include severance pay, stock options, or other such bonuses that will be made available to the person if the company is acquired and the contract is terminated.

Goods

Property, other than real estate, that can be moved.

Goodwill

An intangible asset of a company generated by a positive reputation of the company.

Gross profit

The difference between the net sales and cost of sales, including administrative, marketing, and selling expenses, of a business.

Gross receipts

Total amount the company takes in during the year, including fees and product sales.

Gross revenue

Income prior to any deductions.

Gross salary

Total amount of pay before any deductions are taken.

Guarantee

A promise by a company to replace or repair a product should it become defective, such as under warranty.

Guarantor

A person who takes responsibility by endorsing or guaranteeing the payment of a debt on a financial obligation of another person.

Guide

A manual outlining policies and procedures used in a certain situation.

Handling allowance

A special fee or price offered by a manufacturer to a distributor or retailer to enable them to handle the manufactured product in a special way.

Headhunter

A person or firm specializing in recruiting management or professional personnel. Headhunters charge a fee to the company that is searching to fill the position.

Hearing

A formal procedure, like a trial, in which both parties present their cases, after which a final decision is made.

Hidden agenda

An undeclared objective or expectation or need. Certain strategies a person may have but is not admitting to. Something kept secret.

Hidden asset

A value that is understated on the balance sheet, done deliberately as an action by management.

Hidden tax

An indirect tax paid by the consumer he or she is unaware of paying. Many times these taxes are levied at different points in the process of production or distribution.

Hierarchy

The structure of importance of the various responsibilities and roles in organizations, typically shown as a pyramid. Example: The president or chief executive officer holds the highest position in the hierarchy of management.

Highest and best use

A real estate term meaning the best use for the building, property, or site, both physically and legally at the time of appraisal.

Highly leveraged

A business financed to a very high degree using borrowed money.

Hobby

An activity one does primarily for enjoyment.

Home office

(a) In a business having several locations, the primary site, where most administrative and management functions are preformed. (b) Having your office in your residence. It could be your primary location or a work space that you use in addition to another.

Home page

The first page that appears when you access a Web site.

Homestead

A house and land owned and used as a primary dwelling. In many states, the homestead is exempt for the execution and sale by creditors in the case of bankruptcy.

Honorarium

A fee paid by an organization to a professional who provides a speaking or other type of services.

Horatio Alger

An author of novels that featured poor, honest people who were successful in our country due to persistence and hard work: they ucceeded against very difficult odds. There is a Horatio Alger society that awards people who have this type of background.

Hospitalization insurance

Health insurance covering hospital expenses and related medical costs.

Hostile takeover

Taking control of a company against the wishes of the management and the board of directors.

Hourly fee

A charge based on the amount of hours a person spends on a project. The fee can vary depending on the professional level of people working on the project and their expense to the firm.

House

In the context of interior design, a company or firm, such as a fabric design house.

House account

When credit is extended to a business directly from the main office of the firm. This is often done because of special needs and past relationships.

Housing code or ordinance

Decreed by the government, city, or state to review regulations for all types of residential buildings. Often these include safety and minimum sanitation standards for existing residential buildings. These differ from building codes, which address new construction.

Human factor

A term relating to how humans work within spaces: how we use equipment, move, and perform various tasks effectively and with ease. The human factor refers to all the human physical properties that relate to a space.

Human relations

A system of management that looks at humans in the workplace and what motivates them, how they are affected by the various parts of business, including the way they are recognized, encouraged, or rewarded for their efforts.

Implied contract

An agreement that is not written but is taken from the actions that occurred.

Import

A product brought into a country from another country.

Import quota

A limit of the quantity of goods that may be brought into a country or an economy within a certain period of time.

Impound

When an officer or government official takes and retains merchandise, records, or money into the custody of the law.

Improvement

Where money and effort are put into upgrading a property, not just as a repair but for the purpose of increasing its value.

Incentive pay

Wages paid for special productivity or performance in addition to an employee's regular income.

Income property

A property purchased for the purpose of long-term investment, where the buyer hopes to gain capital income or a capital gain when the property is sold.

Income statement

A financial report showing the operating position for a stated period of time. It is often referred to as a profit and loss statement.

Income stream

A regular flow of money generated by a business or investment.

Incorporate

A legal procedure required to establish a business as a unique entity.

Incorporation

A process by which the company is given a state charter allowing it to operate in that state as a corporation. It also acknowledges the company's legal name: A company that is incorporated must use "Inc." as part of the company title.

Independent contractor

A self-employed person who works independently and is not subject to the restrictions of the person or company for which they are working. This person pays his or her own Social Security and other taxes.

Independent representative
A salesperson who is not an employee of the manufacturer and may represent more than one product line.

Industry
A segment of the business world, such as the furniture industry.

Inflation
A rise in prices that occurs when there is an increased need or demand for certain products on the market.

Infringement
Using another's protected rights or materials, such as a copyright, without approval of the owner.

In-house
When work is performed within the company rather than by an outside source.

Initiate
To start, create, or begin a project.

Injunction
A restraining order given by the courts to stop an activity.

Insolvent
Being unable to meet one's financial obligations.

Inspection
To physically check documents, goods, or property.

Installation
The delivery to a property or a space of the interior furnishings, details, and finishes of a project.

Installment
Payment in increments over a period of time of an agreed amount for each increment.

Insurance
Protection against potential hazards or losses available from authorized companies.

Insurance claim
A request made by the policyholder to his or her insurance company when an incident of covered damage has occurred.

Insurance coverage
Total amount or limit of an insurance policy.

Insurance policy
A document written by an insurance company stating, in the event of loss: items covered; the costs, limits, and time period of coverage; any exclusions; and the details relating to the contract with policyholders.

Intangible asset
Items of value that cannot be physically touched or held, including design patents, trademarks, goodwill, licenses, and issues belonging to a company that are not physical goods. Includes all intellectual property.

Integrity
Honesty, reliability, faithfulness. The character of a relationship that has developed through experience and over time.

Intellectual property
Designs, written material, artistic, and other creative work that can be defined has a proprietary value and can be sold.

Interest
The cost of using money. A percentage is the rate of interest.

Interest income
The money derived from investments upon which interest is paid.

Interest-only loan
A loan for which only the interest is payable on a regular basis; the principal amount is due upon maturity.

Interest rate
A percentage figure applied to the principal amount of a loan or asset base, generally due or payable annually.

Intermediary
A liaison between two people or organizations.

Internal audit
A comprehensive review of an organization's business systems and/or financial operations or reports done within the company by an employee or someone associated with the company.

Internal control
Systems used within the firm to properly manage and control the financial assets of the business.

Internal Revenue Service (IRS)
A U.S. federal government agency that administers and collects federal income tax.

International law
Laws governing the relationships and activities of countries globally.

Internet
An electronic network allowing computers to communicate with other computers throughout the world.

Inventory
The amount of stock or material a company has on hand, available for sale.

Inventory control
A system that manages and protects the inventory of a company, including purchasing reorder points, release of goods, and loss prevention measures.

Inventory turnover
The ratio of inventory to sales, showing how quickly the merchandise is sold and replaced.

Investment portfolio
A method of diversifying one's investment to maximize the opportunity and reduce the risk.

Investor
A person or company that purchases financial assets of a company and expects financial reward.

Invitation to bid
A proposal stating a project's parameters, the process of bidding, and other information required

regarding the details of a project to inform the proposed bidders.

Invoice
A bill prepared by the seller of the goods or services and sent to the purchaser for payment.

Involuntary lien
A lien put against property without the consent of the owner.

Jobber
A company that buys from a manufacturer and sells to a retailer. Many fabric companies are jobbers: They purchase in bolts and sell to designers by the yard.

Job evaluation
A review to analyze a job function and responsibilities within a corporation, including the level of pay and performance expected.

Job sharing
Dividing the functions, responsibilities, and hours worked between two or more employees for one position.

Joint venture
A work arrangement whereby two or more professionals or organizations come together to act as one, sharing the responsibilities, rewards, and risks. This is often done in the field of architecture for work on a particular project.

Journal
(a) A record of all accounting transactions; (b) a diary recording the details of a job or business or serving as a record of daily activities; (c) a professional periodical.

Jury
A group of impartial parties who review the facts and issues presented at a trial.

Just-in-time inventory control
Purchases made at the time needed, rather than maintaining a large stock of the product.

Keogh plan
A tax-deferred pension plan for self-employed people, subject to limitations.

Kickback
When money or gifts are given to purchasers inappropriately or illegally.

Kinesthetics
The study of body movements and positions. This is a major component of the human factor and is key to interior design.

Knockoff
An illegal copy made of a fine design and offered for sale at a much lower price than the original. This is significant in the design field because designers are taught to believe in the integrity of copyrights and patents.

Labor agreement
An agreement made between management and labor listing terms of employment.

Labor pool
A group of trained personnel, with similar types of skills, who work together.

Labor union
An organization that bargains on behalf of its members and offers them benefits such as health insurance and retirement plans.

Landlord
One who collects rent from a tenant.

Last in/first out (LIFO)
A method of inventory valuation whereby the most recent items purchased are considered to be the first ones sold.

Late charge
A fee charged when the borrower fails to pay on time.

Law of supply and demand
A position of a market at any one time regarding the products available and the cost of those particular products.

Lay off
To remove a person from employment either on a temporary or permanent basis, usually because of lack of work.

Lead time
The time between when an order is placed and when the merchandise is received.

Learning curve
The amount of time it takes to master a skill.

Leasehold improvement
Fixtures or items attached to the piece of real estate that are installed by an owner.

Lease with option to purchase
When a tenant is given the right to purchase the property from the owner under certain conditions.

Leave of absence
Time taken off from work with approval, without the loss of the position; may be with or without pay.

Ledger
A book of accounts where transactions are recorded.

Legal age
The age at which a person can enter into a lawful contract or agreement, usually 18 years of age.

Legal name
The name a person uses for official purposes, not a nickname.

Legal notice
A notice that is published when required by law.

Legal representative
A person or firm you have authorized to represent you, such as an attorney or another individual.

Lemon
Slang term given to a product that, after purchase, provides consistently poor performance.

Lender
A person or company that extends credit or loans money to a borrower.

Letter of agreement
Similar to a contract but in a simpler form. The agreement is between the designer and client and states the work to be done and the obligations of both parties.

Letter of credit
A letter issued by a bank guaranteeing payment from a customer's account to the vendor, listing the exact amount and the time limit. This eliminates the risk the seller may have. It is used frequently on items coming to the United States from foreign countries.

Letter of intent
A letter written stating the basic terms of an agreement between two or more parties. The letter can be an authorization to begin work on a project.

Leverage
To use borrowed money for a particular purchase, such as a company.

Liability
A debt, an obligation to repay or do something.

Liability insurance
A policy that insures you if anyone is injured on your property.

Lien
A document against a property that secures the property until the debt, such as mortgage or taxes, has been paid.

Life cycle
The process by which a product or company begins, develops, matures, and declines.

Life insurance
A policy that pays at the death of the insured.

Lifestyle business
A business designed or built around a person's way of life. It is intended to make income, sufficient to properly support the lifestyle of the person.

Limited liability company (LLC)
A form of business organization in which all of the shareholders have limited the ability of creditors to look only to the company for repayment of debt, rather than to the individual shareholders. LLCs are usually taxed as partnerships, but look like corporations.

Limited partnership
A form of business organization in which one or more general partners manage the business and are personally responsible for the debts of the business; limited partners do not participate in the management of the company, but they contribute capital, share in the profits, and are not liable for the debts of the company beyond their contribution.

Limited warranty
A guarantee made by a manufacturer that limits the items it will repair or replace if broken.

Line item
A particular entry taken from a list of products that may be part of an order.

Line of credit
A loan agreement with a bank or financial institution for a specified amount of preapproved money that you can access on an as-needed basis.

Liquid asset
An asset easily converted to cash.

Liquidate
Pay off, as in a debt, or convert to cash.

Liquidity
The rate at which assets are convertible into cash. Investments and certain money market funds can be easily converted into cash, for example, whereas real estate would take a longer time.

List price
Generally, the same as retail price, or the price from which discounts are taken.

Litigation
The legal process to determine the outcome of a case.

Loan
To borrow money from a lender.

Loan application
Information required by a lender from the borrower to determine if a loan should be extended.

Loan commitment
An agreement stating a specific amount and the term of the loan given by the institution lending the money.

Loan value
Determination of what a loan is worth.

Logo
A graphic design or symbol that represents a firm.

Long-range planning
Strategizing into the future, from three to five years or more.

Long-term contract
A contract that goes beyond one year or more.

Lump-sum purchase
Buying two or more items for a total price, as opposed to individually.

Mail fraud
Using the mail to disseminate illegal promotional materials designed to deceive the purchaser.

Mail-order firms
Companies that use catalogs sent directly to customers as their method to present their product lines. Orders are taken and shipped to the customer.

Maintenance
The necessary care and management of equipment and products that we use and sell.

Maintenance fee

(a) A fee accessed from homeowners in a cooperative; (b) a charge made by a bank or broker to maintain an open account.

Malicious mischief

To intentionally destroy the properties of others. Insurance can be purchased to protect against this.

Malpractice

Unprofessional or inappropriate conduct of professionals while in the practice of their work.

Malpractice insurance

Insurance available to professionals, such as designers and architects, to protect them against claims alleging injury, negligence, or improper practice.

Management

The process of directing of the personnel, finances, and all physical properties of a business in order to accomplish the goals of that business.

Management by objective (MBO)

A business technique whereby the goals and objectives are defined and then a management structure is created to achieve the goals.

Management by walking around (MBWA)

Management that takes place where work is being done rather than by sitting in an office. Points out the importance of interpersonal relations.

Management consultants

An individual or organization that advises management, often assisting in handling problems and establishing systems and procedures to complement the company's direction.

Management fee

A charge made for managing assets, usually in an investment portfolio. This could also be a charge for managing other items such as real estate, business processes, or even design processes.

Management ratio

The number of management people versus other personnel.

Management style

The style of leadership and administration a person uses within an organization.

Manager

The person responsible for administering and directing the company's activities.

Man-hour

The amount of productivity one person produces in one hour.

Manual

A reference book containing instruction and information needed for a specific situation.

Manual skill

The hand labor one puts into a task.

Manufacturer's inventory

The materials and parts held on hand in order to keep the manufacturing process running smoothly.

Manufacturer's suggested retail price (MSRP)

The price the manufacturer recommends the product be sold for.

Manufacturer's dealer

A dealership that represents one manufacturer exclusively and usually sells retail.

Manufacturing cost

The cost a company incurs in producing a product: direct materials, labor, and overhead.

Margin of profit

The difference between the gross profit and net sales.

Markdown

A reduction from the selling price, done for a particular reason, such as an end-of-season clearance.

Market

(a) An area in which products and services are sold; (b) a place or location where products and sources are displayed for sale, such as High Point or NeoCon.

Marketability

How well a particular product can sell.

Market analysis

Research directed at defining the potential market for a particular product or service.

Market area

The geographic region in which a company's products or services are sold.

Market center

An area supporting many trade sources.

Market demand

(a) Willingness and ability of consumers to purchase a commodity or service; (b) the quantity of a commodity or service wanted at a specified price and time.

Market economy

An economy in which most goods and services are produced and distributed through free markets.

Marketing

The many activities it takes to promote, develop, and sell services and products.

Market plan

A detailed approach to a firm's marketing objective, includes a budget and schedule.

Market research

Gathering information and analyzing it to position a firm within its market.

Market segment

A specialty area of work, which could include one or two areas.

Market share

The amount of the industry a particular firm can capture and service.

Markup

The percentage added to the net cost in order to cover overhead expenses, personnel costs, as well as profit.

Mass appeal

Marketing directed to the general population of buyers, not to a particular subgroup.

Mass production

Manufacturing identical products in large quantities.

Master plan

A document describing the overall strategy of a project.

Masthead

The printed matter in a newspaper or periodical that gives the title and details of ownership, advertising rates, and subscription rates.

Maturity

The legal date on which something is due or is official.

Meals and entertainment expenses

Costs for meals and entertainment, which are deductible at the rate of 50 percent for tax purposes when they are a business expense.

Mechanics lien

A lien against buildings, initiated by contractors, suppliers, or laborers to assure payment is made in full for all work performed by them.

Media

Forms of communication that address the masses, such as newspapers, radio and television, the Internet, and any form of advertising.

Mediation

The practice of bringing conflicting groups or people together with a third party, whose job it is to assist in reaching a settlement.

Memorandum

A brief note.

Memo sample

A sample that is loaned to a designer with the understanding it will be returned within a given length of time.

Mercantile agency

An organization that defines businesses with credit ratings and reports obtained from firms the business is purchasing from or selling to, such as Dun & Bradstreet.

Mercantile law

Often called commercial law, focusing on commercial transactions.

Merchandise

Materials sold at a retail or wholesale level.

Merchant

One who sells merchandise.

Merger

When one organization acquires another, usually through a buyout. This process liquidates the company that is being acquired.

Merit increase

An increase in a person's wage awarded in recognition of outstanding performance.

Metered mail

Letters or packages stamped by a postage machine.

Metric system

A decimal system of measures and weights.

Metropolitan area

The region surrounding a larger city center.

Middle management

The level of management that falls above the first-line management and below executive management.

Milestone chart

A schedule that outlines the activity and dates of completion; it can be considered benchmarking.

Millage rate

The tax applied to real property.

Millionaire on paper

A person worth $1 million or more in the form of assets, not cash.

Minimum payment

The least amount one can pay on an account.

Minor

A person under the legal age in a state; usually 18, but in some cases 21.

Minority business

A business owned by a person of a race or gender different from the majority of business owners in the industry.

Mission statement

A written pronouncement incorporating the vision and value, as well as the direction, of a company.

Mistake

Omission or error.

Mock-up

A sample model of a project.

Modification

An adjustment or change made to a contract or another given agreement.

Modular housing

Units or buildings constructed in a factory and then moved to the building site.

Monetary

Relating to money.

Money order

A financial instrument that can be purchased to make secure payment to a vendor or creditor. Payment is guaranteed by the issuer of the instrument.

Monitor

To keep track of things.

Moonlighting

Working a second or additional job outside of one's primary employment.

Morale

The mental and emotional condition of an individual or group, including their principles, attitudes, and standards.

Moral law

A behavior structure that exists in most civilizations, usually unwritten.

Moratorium

A period of time in which certain activities are held in abeyance.

Mortgage

Name given to a loan made to purchase real estate.

Mortgage banker
A person or company that sells or services the mortgage.

Mortgage broker
A person or company that finds mortgages for clients and generally charges a fee.

Mortgage commitment
The written agreement between the person borrowing the money and the person lending the money.

Mortgage insurance
Insurance required by lenders to guarantee repayment of the loan in the event of the borrower's death. This is used most frequently on loans with less than 20 percent down payment.

Mortgage life
Term life insurance that is intended to pay off the loan in the case of death.

Mortgage Real Estate Investment Trust (REIT)
REITs lend capital to builders and buyers.

Mortgaging servicing
The management of a mortgage, often done by a company other than the one that originated the mortgage.

Motion study
Research performed on individual job functions to determine more efficient ways of working to make jobs easier.

Motor freight
Shipping by truck.

Movable equipment
All furnishings and items not attached to a building.

Multilevel marketing (MLM)
A system of selling directly to a client by independent business-people of a manufacturer. MLM includes a structure whereby upper-tier individuals gain income from the sales of those under them.

Multimedia
Using more than one form of media to present an idea or launch an advertising campaign.

Multiplier
A system used to multiply something times a certain percentage to equal the selling amount, as in professional fees or certain other product sales.

Multitasking
Doing more than one thing at a time.

Murphy's Law
An axiom that states: "Whatever can go wrong, will go wrong."

National bank
A bank chartered by the Controller of Currency and a member of the FDIC.

Negative cash flow
When a business spends more than it takes in during an accounting period.

Negligence
When something is not handled appropriately, potentially resulting in injury to a person or property.

Negotiable
When something can be sold or transferred to another party for money or to settle a business obligation.

Negotiate
To work with another person or company to reach an agreement that benefits both parties.

Net cost
The purchase price of an item, after discounts or rebates.

Net income or net profit
The income remaining after all expenses have been paid.

Net lease
Arrangement whereby, in addition to the rent, the tenant pays the other expenses of the property, such as utilities and taxes.

Net price
The price paid for something, taking into account any discounts or benefits.

Networking
To connect with other individuals for professional contacts and marketing purposes.

Net worth
Assets minus liabilities.

Niche
An area of specialty.

No fault
A type of insurance whereby people insure themselves; it does not matter who is at fault because the loss will be covered.

Noncompete clause
A clause in a legal agreement that states the undersigned agrees not to work for a competitor while working with the contracted company or upon leaving the firm, for a stated period of time.

Nonconforming use
Land or building not being used for what it is zoned for.

Nondisclosure agreement
Agreement often signed by contractors before beginning a project, promising to retain confidentiality regarding information gained through association on the project.

Nondurable goods
Goods that must be continuously replaced.

Nonsufficient funds check (NSF)
A check drawn on a bank without adequate funds to honor the check.

Norm
A standard or a rule.

Normal price
The price one would expect to pay in the market.

Normal profit
Profit that sufficiently supports a business, enabling it to continue to function.

Normal wear and tear
Ordinary physical wear from expected use of a product.

Notarize
To attest that something is correct

by signing it in front of a notary public.

Notary public
A person authorized by the government to witness signatures on official documents.

Note
In the legal sense, a document acknowledging the amount of debt and conditions of payment, defining the relationship between the borrower and the lender.

Not-for-profit
An organization designed as a charity, not a profit-making entity.

Objective
A goal of a project or a company. What one is aiming for.

Observation test
Visual review and physical inspection of an item to make sure it meets the expected standards.

Occupancy level
The percentage of units sold or rented in an apartment building, hotel, or a neighborhood.

Occupation
An individual's job, business, trade, or vocation.

Occupational hazard
A situation in the workplace that could be dangerous, potentially causing disability, illness, or a fatality to workers.

Occupational Safety and Health Administration (OSHA)
A U.S. government agency formed to enforce the laws of health and safety in the workplace.

Occupational taxes
Local or state taxes applied to various business activities or permits.

Offer
An agreement or contract that one makes with another person or company, stating all issues, provisions, and financial properties required.

Offeree
The person receiving the offer.

Offerer
The person making the offer.

Office management
The organizational system by which a firm handles its day-to-day business activities.

Office manager
The person who administers and handles office management responsibilities.

Off-the-books
Payment that is not listed in the accounting records or reported to the IRS. Payment off-the-books is often done to avoid paying taxes.

On demand
Due upon presentation and payment.

Online
When a computer is connected to a digital network and the network has been accessed.

On order
An order that has been placed but not yet delivered.

On record
The state or fact of being recorded, such as an official document.

Open
In a financial context, the unpaid balance of an account.

Open account
Credit is available to the buyer.

Open bid
The policy that allows any person or firm to make an offer on a product or job.

Open-door policy
In an office, policy that encourages staff to discuss issues with an owner or manager at any time.

Open-end credit
Credit approved by a financial entity for a certain amount of time. The funds can be accessed via phone, credit card, check, or other method.

Open house
When a home for sale or lease is available for viewing; usually for a limited time.

Open shop
A business that employs workers who are not members of a labor union.

Open specifications
When unspecified products can be used for a project; no named product is required.

Open stock
Items kept in stock and that can be ordered on a regular basis.

Open to buy
A retail system used to replace items and to continue to buy as items are sold.

Operating expense
The cost required to maintain a business.

Operating ratio
A ratio between income and expenses and the amount of profit generated from a business.

Option
(a) An additional feature one might add to a purchased product; (b) an alternate choice; (c) an opportunity to buy or sell property for a given time and under certain conditions.

Oral contract
An agreement made verbally, not in writing.

Order
A request to purchase certain goods or services.

Ordinance
A law that applies to certain functions and permits.

Ordinary income
Income subject to ordinary income tax.

Ordinary interest
Simple interest, as opposed to compound interest.

Or equal
A term used on specification sheets to indicate it is acceptable to use the product of another manufacturer as long as the item is equal to the original one specified.

Organization

A group of people working together for a common purpose with particular functions and responsibilities.

Organizational chart

A chart showing the relationships of the people working within an organization and their responsibilities and activities.

Orientation

The process of introducing individuals to a subject.

Other income

Income earned from activities not normal to a company or income individuals receive from jobs or projects other than their regular employment.

Outbid

To place a higher bid.

Outlet store

A retail operation, owned by a manufacturer to sell overruns or irregular items.

Out-of-pocket expenses

Items or services paid for out of personal funds will be reimbursed by the company.

Outplacement

A program that assists people who lost their jobs, often as a result of downsizing a company, to find new work.

Output

The production of a factory or company.

Outside directors

Corporate managers who are not direct employees of a company.

Outsourcing

Having an item or service produced or conducted outside of your company.

Outstanding

When referring to money, an invoice, bill, or debt that is unpaid.

Outstanding balance

The amount presently owed on your account.

Overimprovements

When a property improves far beyond what is appropriate to the appraised value of the neighborhood or situation.

Overrun

When too much of a product is manufactured; in excess of a quantity ordered by a customer.

Overage

Surplus; excess.

Overbooked

When a business accepts orders beyond what it is able to handle.

Overbuilding

When there is too much real estate (buildings) available for sale, for the conditions and needs of the economy.

Overdraft

A system of honoring a check by the bank when the account holder has insufficient funds. The check writer will have a loan account or deduction taken from another bank account to pay for the overdraft amount.

Overhead

Expenses not directly associated with a product; the general expenses of running a business.

Overpayment

When more payment is received than what is due.

Oversold

When a company sells beyond what it has in inventory or in scheduled production.

Overtime

Hours worked by an employee beyond what he or she has contracted.

Owner

The person who holds the title of a given property.

Owner equity

The amount of a company's assets that belong to the owner.

Owner/operator

A person who owns and operates a business.

Ownership

The right of possessing and having control of an item.

Ownership form

A type of company, such as a corporation or partnership, under which employees work.

Packing slip

A detailed list of what is included in a container that comes with a shipment.

Padding

In a financial context, the addition of unnecessary costs or expenses.

Paid-up policy

A policy for which the entire premium has been paid at one time.

Paradigm shift

A change in the model or the usual. It is no longer a standard.

Paralegal

A person who is employed by a law office and is responsible for doing various court tasks to support a lawyer; a paralegal is not a licensed lawyer.

Parcel

(a) A property; (b) a package sent through a common carrier; (c) to separate or divide, such as to distribute.

Parcel post

A U.S. mail service.

Parent company

A company that owns and controls another company or a subsidiary.

Partner

A member of a partnership.

Partnership

An organization of two or more people who put their money and abilities into a business and divide the profit and losses proportionately.

Part-time employee

An employee who works less than full-time hours and who often does not qualify for benefits. Fewer than 1,000 hours of service in a 12-month period.

Passbook

A document issued by a bank to record bank activity.

Passive income generator

A form of investment that generates income without requiring any effort.

Passport

Official document given by a country to citizens of that country allowing them to travel outside of their home country.

Patent

An official document given to the inventor or owner of a product, giving that person exclusive right to sell it.

Patent infringement

When someone trespasses on the right of a patent.

Pay

Compensation received for services.

Payable

The amount owed.

Pay as you go

Paying for services as they are used.

Payback period

The time in which you have to pay back a debt.

Paycheck

Wages or salary received by an employee for work performed; includes details of the remuneration, including deductions.

Payday

The day on which employees receive their paycheck.

Payee

The person to whom a check is paid.

Payment

Paying what is due or paying on account.

Payroll

The system a business uses to pay its employees.

Payroll deductions

The amount of money required to be deducted from a payroll check for taxes, insurances, and so on.

Payroll period

The period during which wages are paid.

Pecking order

Colloquial term for the hierarchy of an organization.

Penalty of fine

A payment that must be made after failing to comply with some rule or regulation.

Pension fund

Monies put aside by a company to be paid out in retirement benefits at a later date; must be secured.

People-intensive

Requiring a lot of labor power.

Per capita

Equally to each individual.

Percentage

A proportion of something.

Percentage of completion

The method of reporting income or collecting income based at the level at which the project is completed.

Per diem

By the day; daily allowance.

Per forma

A statement or invoice that comes prior to standard invoices.

Performance

In a legal context, part of the law that requires you to do the work you have been contracted to do.

Performance bond

A bond purchased by the winning bidder on a project to guarantee that the vendor or designer will meet the specifications of the project. The monies are held to reimburse the client.

Performance evaluation

The review of an employee's work to determine if he or she should be promoted, get a raise in pay, or have disciplinary action.

Perishable

An item that spoils or decays.

Permit

A document issued by a govern-ment entity authorizing a person to do something.

Personal financial statement

An accounting statement, showing the financial position of an individual, listing the assets, liabilities, and net worth.

Personal identification number (PIN)

A unique number assigned for security purposes and used by individuals to access ATMs or other software programs.

Personal injury

An invasion of property or slander of character; injury against a person, in contrast to property damage.

Personal liability

An obligation that exposes one's personal assets to potential danger.

Personal property

Items that belong to an individual and that are movable; does not include items such as real estate or things that are attached to a building.

Personal residence

The place a person claims as his or her legal residence.

Personnel

The employees or working staff of a company or organization.

Persuasion

Effort to influence the attitude or belief of a certain group of people or market.

Petition

A formal written request.

Petty cash

A small amount of cash retained in a company for incidental purchases. A voucher accompanies each with-drawal.

Physical examination

A visual accounting to ensure every-thing is in place.

Physical inventory

A detailed accounting of all stock items, listing type, quantity, and other detailed information.

Piecework

Work done by the piece and paid for at a set rate per unit.

Pie chart

A type of graph wherein a circle representing the whole amount is divided into different categories, as slices of pie.

Planning commission

A group of citizens appointed by local government to review and recommend the appropriateness of buildings or building plans within a community.

Plan review

The process of examining plans before a building permit is issued by the local government building department or others who have jurisdiction over the issuance of the permit.

Plant

Building and machinery used to manufacture products.

Policy

A statement or procedure stating the direction and actions of a company.

Pollution

Contamination, especially of the environment by man-made waste.

Portfolio

A case containing an overview of a designer's work, including drawings, photographs, slides, or Web graphics, for the purpose of demonstrating the quality of the designer's work.

Post

To enter figures in a journal or an accounting book.

Postdated check

A check dated into the future, which is not usable until that date.

Postoccupancy evaluation (POE)

A site visit performed by the designer just after construction is completed to evaluate the construction to determine if there are any problems or issues.

Poverty

Condition in which an individual's income is too low to support his or her health and lifestyle at a reasonable level.

Power of attorney (POA)

A legal document giving another person the ability to act on behalf of the person initiating the document.

Practical capacity

The maximum level at which a factory can operate and still be efficient.

Practice acts

The laws that govern professionals in certain fields, such as design, and require them to meet specific educational and business standards and be registered by the state.

Prefabrication

To prebuild components in a factory to ease the final on-site construction.

Premium

The amount one is charged for an insurance policy.

Prepaid income

Advance income compensated to an individual.

Prepaid interest

Interest paid in advance of when it is due.

Prepayment

An amount paid before it is due, such as expenses paid in advance for one year.

Prepayment clause

Allows the privilege of paying before a debt is due.

Prepayment penalty

Penalty for paying in advance.

Prerogative

An exclusive right of an individual or entity.

Presale

Selling in advance.

Presentation

Giving an overview through verbal and visual means of a perspective project.

President

The highest-ranking officer in a corporation.

Press kit

Materials prepared and compiled in advance to distribute to the media to give them a reference for understanding your firm.

Price

The amount charged for a given service or product.

Price fixing

Setting a price and stating it cannot be raised or lowered in a certain situation.

Primary resources

Familiar and preferred resources of an individual or firm.

Prime rate

The lowest interest rate charged by a bank.

Principal amount

The value of an obligation such as a loan.

Principal place of business

The headquarters of a business.

Principle

A standard or rule.

Priority mail

A system of first-class mail, which is given special treatment.

Priority of tax lien

The order in which tax liens take precedence.

Privacy laws

Laws requiring information held by a company to be kept secure and not shared with others.

Private accountant

An accountant who is employed by an individual or organization.

Private corporations

Companies owned by individuals, as opposed to publicly traded stock entities.

Privatization

The process of making something private.

Privilege

A right.

Probability

The chance something will happen.

Probationary employee

A person hired on a trial basis in consideration for a permanent job.

Proceeds

Money received after commissions and other deductions are made.

Process division

A management system wherein different procedures are reviewed to determine the most efficient way to divide the requisite work.

Procurement

The acquisition of merchandise.

Produce

To manufacture a product or provide a service.

Product liability

A manufacturer's responsibility to bring safe products to market.

Product liability insurance

Insurance bought by a manufacturer or service provider to protect against losses from product failures, misuses, or negligence.

Product life cycle

The entire process of developing a product, from introduction through development and end use.

Product line

A group of items a company produces and is prepared to market.

Production

The activity of manufacturing something.

Productivity

A measure of labor efficiency, between the quantity of an item manufactured and the amount of time it takes.

Profession

Specialized area of work, generally requiring a high level of education and standards; includes professional ethics.

Professional corporation

A form of business entity formed for the purposes of supporting professionals, such as accountants, attorneys, and so on.

Professional liability

Legal responsibility of firms or professional individuals for damage or injury caused to purchasers of their services.

Professional service firm (PSF)

A firm dedicated to providing a professional service and usually does not sell products.

Profit

The excess of returns over expenditure in a transaction or transactions, usually for a given period of time.

Profit and loss statement

A financial statement reporting a company's accounting position over a period of time.

Profit center

An area of a business that consistently generates income.

Profit-sharing plan

A financial arrangement between a company and its employees, whereby the employees receive financial rewards based on the profit of the company.

Programming stage

In project management, the information-gathering stage; the first part of a project.

Progress payment

Systematic payments made during the process of a project, based on the satisfactory completion of each phase.

Project completion

The point at which a project is completed and all final inspections and reviews are made.

Project file

A file kept on all the details of a project; also includes samples.

Project forecasting

Estimating what future production might be.

Project management

The whole process of handling the administrative work of a project from the beginning to completion.

Project manager

The person responsible for handling a job.

Project report

Document containing all correspondence referencing a project that is given to the client and other administrative parties to track the progress of the project.

Promotion

A personal advancement in position, pay, or level of responsibility.

Prompt

On time; meeting obligations on time and on schedule.

Proof of claim

A document supporting a claim or assertion made, especially, in the case of an insurance loss.

Property

Possessions one owns, such as real estate.

Property tax

A tax placed by municipalities on a local property.

Proposal

A statement or document outlining the work or services to be provided.

Proprietor

The owner of a building or business.

Prorate

To proportionately share an obligation.

Pros and cons

Advantages and disadvantages of a situation, an undertaking, a process, an activity, and so on.

Prospect

(a) A potential client; (b) to go out and find clients.

Prosperity

Success; growth, usually financial.

Protect

To care for.

Protest
To demonstrate against or object.

Protocol
Rules of formal etiquette.

Proxemics
The study of the physical, psychological, and cultural impact of space on people.

Proxy
To act on behalf of another.

Public adjuster
Representative of insurance companies, who negotiates with the owners when there is property damage.

Public corporation
A corporation providing a public service, such as a post office.

Public interest
An interest shared by the public at large.

Public record
A court document that is available to everyone.

Public relations (PR)
The business of inducing the public to be favorably inclined toward a person, firm, or institution. In the interior design field, a public relations professional is paid to solicit the media and other interested parties to promote a designer's work.

Public sales notification
A notice stating that something will be sold to the public at a certain time and date; anyone from the public may bid on the listed item(s).

Public use area
A piece of property available for use by the public at large.

Public utility
A company that supplies gas, electricity, and phone services; a for-profit company.

Puffing
Overstating; to give exaggerated praise not supported by the facts.

Punch list
Items that need to be completed or corrected before a job is considered 100 percent complete.

Punctuality
The act of being on time.

Punitive damage
Money awarded in excess of the actual damage as a punishment.

Purchase order
Written authorization to a vendor to buy specific goods at a specific price.

Purchasing power
The value of the amount of buying ability of a consumer.

Qualifying a prospect
Reviewing a client's interest in, and financial capability to pay for, the services of a firm, according to established criteria.

Qualifying opinion
An independent financial auditor's opinion that accompanies the financial statement.

Quality
A degree of excellence.

Quality assurance
A system of guaranteeing the high quality of a product or service.

Quality control
The process of ensuring the standard for manufacturing a product or providing a service remains consistent.

Quality engineering
A management system designed to maintain the production standards set by a company.

Quantity discount
A discount given to buyers who purchase large amounts of a single item or a variety of different items.

Quarterly
Every three months.

Quota
A proportional part or share; in the context of production or sales, the established amount of an item or service an employee is responsible for producing or selling within a set period of time.

Quotation
In the context of business, the bid, offer, or price for a project, product, or service; included as part of a proposal.

Quote
To give an estimate of cost or of the price of providing a product or service.

Rainmaker
A person who brings opportunities to a business or company.

Rapport
Relationship marked by goodwill and accord. In a business environment, a positive working relationship that is supportive and harmonious to those who participate in it.

Raw materials
The products that go into the manufacture of other items or products.

Real earnings
Earnings that have been corrected for inflation, taking into consideration the changes in purchasing power.

Real estate agent or broker
Someone who arranges for a sale of a property. An agent works directly below a broker; they are licensed within the state.

Real income
The income of an individual, adjusted for inflation.

Realtor
A professional who deals in real estate.

Reasonable care
The care taken under usual circumstances.

Reasonable time
A standard amount of time an effort should take under certain circumstances.

Rebate
A refund.

Recall
When a manufacturer asks for the

return of faulty merchandise so it can be replaced or repaired and brought up to standards.

Receivables

The amount of money owed to a company.

Receivables turnover

The average time it takes to collect money due.

Receiving clerk

The person who receives merchandise for a company.

Receiving department

The area where merchandise is received by a receiving clerk.

Recession

A marked drop in the economic activity in a country or industry over a period of time.

Reciprocal buying

An arrangement under which two people buy from each other, rather than one person servicing another.

Reciprocity

A relationship between people or companies wherein privileges are granted to meet both parties' criteria: I work for you, you work for me.

Recognition

A formal acknowledgment given in some form of public method.

Reconciliation

The act of bringing people together to resolve their differences; also, in a financial context, to check an account for accuracy.

Record

A collection or a file of information, times, and schedules to be used for future reference.

Recording

The process of documenting a transaction in an appropriate formal fashion, usually as part of permanent record.

Recourse

In finance, the ability of a lender to get money from another source if a payment is not paid appropriately by the debtor.

Recourse loan

A loan in which the endorser is liable for the payment in case another borrower defaults.

Recruitment

A formal effort of seeking employees.

Redemption

A coupon or receipt of partial payment for something that was purchased.

Redlining

To review prints and mark them with red where there are changes or errors. This is done before the final prints go out or before seeking a building permit.

Redundancy

Duplication; superfluous; of effort, in a record, of production.

Reengineering

Making changes to improve business operations.

Referee

In a legal environment, a person appointed by the court to take informational testimony and findings for the court.

Referral

A reference from a colleague or other source to to a perspective client.

Refinance

To revise the terms of a loan with the same or another financial institution to receive additional advantages.

Refund check

Money returned to a company or an individual for an overpayment.

Registered check

A check issued by a bank for a customer. The bank puts the funds in a special registry to provide a secure check to the payee.

Registered mail

A type of mail service providing proof of sending and delivery of a letter or parcel.

Registrar

A person who keeps the records for an organization or institution.

Registration

An enrollment process.

Registry of deeds

A governmental department that keeps the records of all the real estate transactions in a local area.

Reimbursement

Repayment for expenses.

Reinstatement

In the context of insurance, the reestablishment of a policy after it has lapsed due to lack of payment: once the payment has been made, the policy is reinstated.

Relevant

Something of significance and that has bearing on the matter at hand.

Reliability

Regarding accounting, describes information that is reasonably accurate.

Relief

In the context of construction, acknowledgment that a job or service is completed and therefore the contractor agreement is concluded.

Relocation management

The process of moving a client from one location to another.

Relocation specialist

A person who assists in helping people find housing and coordinating the move from one place to another.

Remittance

A payment.

Rent

Money paid for the use of property.

Replacement cost

The cost to rebuild or purchase a building or items based on the most current prices for goods.

Reputation

The overall quality or character by which one is known within a given environment.

Request for proposal (RFP)
A document sent to firms or other vendors to ask for their interest in providing services for a project. An RFP outlines the terms and conditions of work to be performed.

Requisition
A purchase order.

Reschedule
To change the timing arrangements from those originally set.

Rescind
To cancel an agreement or contract.

Research
To gather information into a structure or system for future use.

Research and development (R&D)
The process of reviewing and continuing to develop to produce a better-quality product or better design.

Reserve fund
Money set aside in a separate account or investment for future needs.

Residential interior design
The design of a residence, including the specifications, plans, and details.

Resident manager
A person who supervises or generally cares for a personal living complex, such as an apartment community.

Resolution
In an official or formal group context, an expression of intent, will, or opinion.

Resource
A source of supply or support; in business, the people or companies supplying materials or information.

Responsibility
The duties associated with one's profession or job assignment.

Restocking charges
A fee charged for returning products. It can be charged by the manufacturer or the design firm.

Restraining order
An order granted without notice or hearing, such as an injunction to prevent a person from taking an action against another.

Restraint of trade
The use of laws to restrain or interfere with free commerce.

Restrictive covenant
An agreement that limits performance, such as property rights, or employment where an employee is restricted from working with a competitor.

Retail price
A list or suggested price applied for sale to a client.

Retainage
Money held back from payment by a customer to assure the quality of work is as agreed. The money is released at the end of the job when both parties agree the work is as specified. Generally, this procedure is used in payment of contractors.

Retained earnings
Money earned by a business to be reinvested and not distributed as dividends. This money is kept within the business for future development of the company.

Retainer
An advance payment made for professional services to be performed, such as by interior designers and attorneys.

Retroactive
To go back to an earlier date.

Return
Merchandise sent back to a company for a refund or an exchange.

Revenue
The earnings of a company.

Revolving charge account
A credit account that has a set limit, fluctuates as purchases are made, and remains open as long as periodic payments are made.

Revolving credit
An agreement between a customer and a bank whereby the bank agrees to make loans up to a certain amount for a certain period of time and remains available as long as periodic payments are made. Similar to a line of credit.

Rezoning
A legal action that changes the approved use of a given property.

Right of first refusal
An opportunity given to a person to match a given amount, if he or she is bidding on something such as a property, before the second contract is accepted.

Right of refusal
The period of time given for a client to return items as described in a signed contract.

Right of return
The agreement that enables a purchaser to return an item for credit.

Right of way
In real estate, an easement.

Risk
In a financial context, the possibility of losing value.

Risk management
A system instituted to forestall financial loss by identifying the issues that might cause loss.

Rollover
To replace debt with another type of loan or investment.

Roth IRA
A type of individual retirement account that permits the owner to set aside, after tax income, a specified amount each year.

Royalty
A percentage paid to the creator of a product when the item is sold on the market.

Rubber Check
A colloquial term used to describe a check that has been written against insufficient funds—it bounces back.

Salary

Compensation an employee receives for work done, generally without regard to specific hours worked per pay period.

Sale

Exchanging services or materials for financial compensation or money.

Sales contract

An agreement in which the materials to be sold are defined and the prices agreed upon.

Sales journal

An accounting record book where sales are posted.

Salesperson

A person whose principal activity is selling a product or service.

Sales revenue

Income received from selling a service or product.

Sales tax

A tax imposed by a government entity based on the value of merchandise or services.

Sample

An example of an item to be sold.

Schedule

(a) A program that details times and events, included in project plans; (b) a tax form.

Schematic design phase

In a project timeline, when the preliminary designs and the supporting documents are prepared.

S Corporation

A form of business entity that "looks" like a corporation but permits each individual owner to pay his or her taxes on the personal tax return rather than on a standard corporate tax return.

Seasonal discount

Special discount typically offered as part of an annual or holiday sale.

Second mortgage

A loan on a property where the creditor takes a secondary position to the first loan or originator.

Secondary sources

Sources not coming from direct manufacturers.

Secured debt

A loan secured by collateral or some form of property.

Seed money

The initial funding for a project.

Self-employed

People who work for themselves and, therefore, have total responsibility for their business.

Self-employment tax

Social Security tax imposed on self-employed people; they pay both the employer and employee portion of this two-phase tax.

Self-insurance

Protection against loss through personal funding system.

Selling price

The price negotiated with the client.

Service

Work done on behalf of or to benefit another person.

Service department

A division in a company dedicated to servicing the customers.

Service fee

A charge for services rendered. In design firms, for example, there is a service fee for handling certain products.

Servicing

(a) The regular maintenance of a product; (b) management of the financial part of a business.

Setback

(a) Property line requirement; (b) problems or difficulties that can cause delays.

Settle

To pay or complete something in full.

Settlement

In real estate, for example, when the final papers have been signed and money has been exchanged between all parties to a transaction.

Severance pay

Compensation given to an employee on leaving a company, generally as part of downsizing or permanent layoff actions.

Sexual harassment

Inappropriate verbal or physical sexual advances made by one person toward another in the workplace.

Shareholder

A person or group of people who own shares of a company, corporation, or property.

Shop

A business location where production work is done.

Shopping service

A service provided by an independent person or designer who selects and purchases items on behalf of a client who pays a fee for the work.

Short list

A small group of individuals or businesses considered appropriate for bidding on a project.

Short run

A limited quantity of product manufactured, generally to accommodate a client.

Shrinkage

The difference between what is shown in the inventory and what is shown in the books.

Sick pay

Compensation given to a staff person when he or she is unable to work due to illness.

Sidemark

A notation made on a purchase order to identify the client for whom the fabric, furniture, accessory, or other item is being made or purchased. The vendor will then put the notation (client's name) on his or her paperwork to track the order through production and shipment.

Signature guarantee

Usually a required signature on legal documents.

Silent partner
A person who invests in a company but plays no direct management or other role in the company.

Simple interest
Interest calculated only on the original principal deposited or loaned.

Skimming
To remove or conceal monies or taxes in bookkeeping records to avoid paying taxes.

Slamming
An illegal practice of changing a customer's long-distance service without consent.

Slander
False charges made against a person, which damage that person's reputation.

Slush fund
An unregulated fund, often used for illicit purposes.

Small Business Administration (SBA)
A federal agency charged with helping to develop small businesses; among other services, the SBA provides low-interest loans to those small enterprises that qualify.

Small-claims court
A special court intended to simplify and expedite the handling of small claims or debts.

Social Security number
A government-issued number used to identify United States citizens.

Sole proprietorship
A business owned by an individual.

Spam
Electronic junk mail.

Special agent
One who acts for another, such as a real estate agent or an interior designer who purchases and handles projects for others.

Specialist
One with expert knowledge or skill in a particular area.

Specialty shop
A store with a small range of selected merchandise.

Special-use permit
A permit granted by the zoning authority in a community to undertake an activity not considered normal use.

Specifications
Detailed instructions provided with drawings or purchase orders.

Spendable income
The money left after taxes.

Spokesperson
A person who represents a product, company, or a service.

Spread
A banking term meaning the difference between the cost of a fund and the lending rate.

Staff
The personnel of an organization.

Standard
Established criteria detailing the quality and performance measures of a company.

Standard of living
A minimum of necessities, comforts, or luxuries held essential to maintaining a person or group in customary or proper status or circumstances.

Start-up
A new business venture.

Statement
A summary of an account showing the financial activity for a period of time.

Statute of fraud
Requires that certain contracts must be in writing to be enforceable; in the design field, usually anything over $500.

Stock
Shares in a corporation.

Stock option
The opportunity given to an employee to buy company stock at a certain price.

Stop payment
The process of canceling a payment to a payee after a check has been written and sent but before the check has cleared the bank.

Strategic planning
A process for defining a vision and putting it into a form that is workable for a project or a firm.

Strategy
A plan for accomplishing objectives.

Strike
An organized stoppage of work by employees to put pressure on company management to implement better working conditions.

Subcontractor
One who works under the general contractor on a project.

Subpoena
A legal document requiring one to appear in court.

Subsidiary
A business or company wholly controlled by another, the "parent," company.

Supplier
A company that or person who provides merchandise or services on a wholesale or retail basis.

Supply
To provide merchandise or service.

Survey
(a) The measurements of an area to determine exact size; (b) poll taken to determine supply and demand or opinion about a product, an idea, a trend, and so on.

Suspension
When a person is removed from a position for a specified time, usually as part of a disciplinary action.

Syndicate
A group of individuals or companies that come together in a joint venture.

Synergy
Mutually advantageous compatibility

of distinct business participants or elements (as resources or efforts).

Tactic

A method for resolving a problem.

Tag

To attach a document to an item to ensure it gets to the proper location.

Tangible asset

A physical piece of property, something you can touch.

Tangible personal property

A physical property that is not real estate.

Target market

A group of people a firm identifies as its primary purchasers, to which to direct its advertising to meet their particular needs.

Tax

An assessment on a person, property, or activity collected to support a government.

Tax credit

An allowed exemption against a tax bill.

Tax deduction

Items that reduce a tax bill.

Telemarketing

Using the telephone as a marketing tool.

Tenant

A person or business that leases property from a landlord.

Tenant improvements

Changes or upgrades made to a property, paid for by the tenant of the property.

Term

The period of time under which a contract will be carried out.

Testimonial

A letter or statement written by a respected person or company stating the value of a person or company's work or services.

Time card

A recording system to keep an accounting of the number of hours worked by each employee.

Time management

A system of scheduling various activities to increase productivity.

Title

All the elements constituting ownership to an asset.

Tort

A wrongful act other than breach of contract; relief from the liable person is in the form of damages or an injunction.

Trade

An occupation, business, or profession requiring a particular skill.

Trade discount

The privilege to purchase items at a discounted price within a profession.

Trade magazine

A publication targeted to the members of a particular profession.

Trademark

A legally registered proprietary name or symbol that indicates a product is made by a particular company; a distinctive characteristic associated with a particular person.

Trade show

An event at which the work, products, and people of a particular profession are gathered.

Trade sources

Sources that cater to a particular profession or discipline.

Transmittal letter

Document sent from a designer, architect, or other professional to those involved in a project.

Travel expenses

Costs incurred when traveling for business reasons, which are tax-deductible and refundable by the company to the employee.

Treasurer

The person who handles the financial funds of a company or corporation.

Trend

The direction things are moving; a fad or popular product or style at a given time.

Trunk show

Merchandise sent to a designer for the purposes of a special feature presentation intended to generate sales of that particular item, such as a linen show.

Trustee

A fiduciary relationship wherein the title to a property is held by one person for the benefit of another person.

Tuition

Fees paid for education expenses.

Turnkey

A project that is built, furnished, and installed and ready for occupancy.

Turnover

A ratio used to identify sales volume, inventory flow, accounts receivable collection, and so on.

Umbrella policy

An insurance policy that provides additional liability coverage over the basic insurance.

Unemployment compensation

Money paid by the state to an unemployed or disabled person under certain conditions.

Uniform Commercial Code (UCC)

A group of laws governing the sales of goods and promotional transactions, varying by state.

Union

An organization of craftspeople or workers formed to pursue a common purpose, such as to protect or improve rights and benefits.

Union shop

A business where all employees must be union members.

Use tax

A form of sales tax based on how the item is "used," not the fact of its sale.

Value

Relative worth; what someone is willing to pay for something.

Variable pricing

When different prices are charged to various clients for the same item.

Variable rate mortgage

A mortgage in which the interest rate changes at specific times in the duration of the loan, as outlined in the loan agreement.

Vendor

A seller of a product.

Venture

A business undertaking that involves some risks.

Venture capital

Money invested by a third party to start a business, with the goal of obtaining a high rate of return for the investor.

Vested

When an employee has been with a company long enough to become eligible for its retirement or pension program.

Vice president

In a leadership hierarchy, the position directly under the president.

Virus

In technology terms, a computer program, usually hidden within another computer program and transmitted over the Internet, designed to damage programs on the infected computer.

Voice-activated

A machine that recognizes and responds to a voice.

Voice recognition

Computer software that recognizes the human voice and is programmed to respond to commands to perform an activity, such as to type a document.

Void

Something that has no value; empty.

Volume

The amount of something.

W2

A form an employer must give an employee by January 31 of each year to verify the amount of income received and the amount of deducted taxes for the prior calendar year.

Wage

The amount of money paid to an employee for his or her services.

Wage bracket

A salary range; typical income paid for a certain occupation or position in a firm.

Wage rate

A rate of pay for a given job.

Waiver

Surrendering a known right, as to an agreement.

Warranty

A guarantee to a buyer from a provider.

Webmaster

A person in charge of managing a Web site.

Web page

A electronic document available for viewing on the World Wide Web.

Web site

A group of World Wide Web pages usually containing hyperlinks to each other and made available online by an individual, company, educational institution, government, or organization.

Wetlands

Land, such as marshes or swamps, covered intermittently with water. Protected wetlands cannot be developed. Usually controlled by the U.S. Army Corps of Engineers.

White elephant

Something of little or no value; in business, an extremely difficult product or service to sell.

Wholesale

The sale of merchandise in large quantities, usually for later distribution.

Will

A legal document that serves to transfer personal property and funds from the writer of the will to others at the time of his or her death.

Window

A period of time in which a person or company has the opportunity to act on something.

Withholding tax

Funds withheld from an employee's check for taxes.

Worker's compensation

An insurance paid by employers against job-related injuries.

Workforce

The total number of employees within a company.

Working capital

The total amount of cash, accounts receivable, inventory, and other assets a company has to run its business.

Working papers

A document a minor employee, generally a school-age person, must have in order to be allowed to perform a paid job.

Work-in-process

All the jobs a company is presently working on. Orders have been contracted but not yet delivered.

Workload

The amount of work being performed within a certain period of time.

Work order

A form requesting an individual or firm to fulfill a certain duty or request.

Work out

In a financial context, to come to an agreement between a borrower and a lender to avoid bankruptcy by the borrower.

Work permit

A document given by the government to a non-U.S. citizen, giving the individual permission to legally work in the United States.

Workstation

The area in which one performs his or her job.

Work stoppage

When employees of a company cease work for the purpose of compelling management to improve their working conditions.

Workweek

The number of hours and days a company requires an employee to work.

Work worth paying for (WWPF)

Valuable work more than worthy of the fee being charged.

World Wide Web

A part of the Internet accessed through a graphical user interface and containing documents often connected by hyperlinks; a system in use for the purposes of serving the Internet.

Worth

The value of a company or commodity measured in a specific term.

Year-end

An accounting term for the end of the business year. This could be the calendar or fiscal year.

Yield

Income generated from an investment.

Zero-based budgeting

A budgeting system used by businesses, starting from zero expenses, building to a new budget based on substantiated expenses.

Zip code

A numerical system defined by the United States Post Office to expedite mail distribution.

Zoning

The regulations for the use of property as declared by a governing body.

Recommended Reading

Here are books I have found of value to our business and hope you may enjoy them.

Abercrombie, Stanley. *A Philosophy of Interior Design*. New York: Harper and Row, 1990.

Alderman, Robert L. *How to Prosper as an Interior Designer: A Business and Legal Guide*. New York: John Wiley & Sons, Inc., 2000.

Autry, James A., and Mitchell, Stephen. *Real Power: Business Lessons from Tao Te Ching*. New York: Riverhead Books, 1998.

Baraban, Regina S., and Durocher, Joseph. *Successful Restaurant Design*. 2nd ed. New York: John Wiley & Sons, Inc., 2001

Beckwith, Harry. *Selling the Invisible*. New York: Warner Books, Inc., 1997.

Beckwith, Harry. *What Clients Love*. New York: Warner Books, Inc., 2003.

Bennis, Warren. *An Invented Life: Reflection of Leadership and Change*. Reading, MA: Addison-Wesley, 1993.

————. *Why Leaders Can't Lead*. New York: John Wiley & Sons, Inc., 2000.

Bennis, Warren, and Townsend, Robert. *Reinventing Leadership: Strategies to Empower the Organization*. New York: William Morrow and Company, Inc., 1995.

Berger, C. Jaye. *Interior Design Law and Business Practices*. New York: John Wiley & Sons, Inc., 1994.

Berman, Morris. *The Twilight of American Culture*. New York: W. W. Norton & Co., Inc., 2000.

Binggeli, Corky. *Building Systems for Interior Designers*. New York: John Wiley & Sons, Inc., 2002.

Block, Peter. *Stewardship—Choosing Service over Self-Interest*. San Francisco, CA: Berrett-Koelher Publishers, 1993.

Bradford's Directory of Marketing Research Agencies. *Bradford's Directory of Marketing Research Agencies and Management Consultants in the United States and the World*. 27th ed. Middleburg, VA: Bradford's Directory of Marketing Research Agencies, 1997–1998; orig 1965–1966.

Brooks, David. *Bobos in Paradise*. New York: Simon & Schuster, 2000.

Celente, Gerald. *Trend 2000*. New York: Warner Books, Inc., 1997.

Ching, Frank. *Illustrated Guide to Interior Architecture*. New York: Van Nostrand Reinhold, 1987.

Ching, Francis D. K., and Binggeli, Corky. *Interior Design Illustrated*. 2nd ed. New York: John Wiley & Sons, Inc., 2004.

Cochrane, Diane. *This Business of Art*. Revised ed. New York: Watson-Guptill, 1988.

Collins, James C., and Ponas, Jerry I. *Built to Last: Successful Habits of Visionary Companies*. New York: HarperBusiness, 1994

Coxe, Weld, Maister, David, and the Coxe Group. *Success Strategies for Design Professionals*. New York: McGraw-Hill, 1987.

Cramer, James P. *Design Plus Enterprise*. Washington, DC: AIA Press, 1994.

Crawford, Tad. *Legal Guide for the Visual Artist*. New York: Madison Square Press, 1987.

Curtis, Eleanor. *Hotel: Interior Design*. New York: John Wiley & Sons, Inc., 2003.

Danziger, Pamela N. *Why People Buy Things They Don't Need*. Chicago: Dearborn Trade Publishing, 2004.

Davis, Stan. *Lessons From the Future*. Oxford, UK: Capstone Publishing Ltd., 2001.

Dell'Isola, Alphonse, and Kirk, Stephen J. *Life Cycle Costing for Design Professionals*. New York: McGraw-Hill, 1981.

Dent, Harry S. Jr. *The Roaring 2000s*. New York: Simon & Schuster, 1998.

De Pree, Max. *Leading without Power*. New York: John Wiley & Sons, Inc., 1999.

Derlouza, Michael. *The Unfinished Resolution: Human-Centered Computers and What They Can Do for Us*. New York: HarperCollins, 2000.

Dilenschneider, Robert L. *On Power*. New York: HarperCollins, 1994.

Drucker, Peter F. *Management Challenges for the 21st Century*. New York: HarperCollins, 1999.

Drucker, Peter F., and Flaherty, John E. *Shaping the Managerial Mind*. New York: John Wiley & Sons, Inc., 2000.

Elliott, A. Larry, and Schroth, Richard J. *How Companies Lie*. New York. Crown Business, 2002.

Enriquez, Juan. *As the Future Catches You*. New York: Crown Business, 2001.

Farrelly, Lorraine. *Bar and Restaurant*. New York: John Wiley & Sons, Inc., 2004.

Florida, Richard. *The Rise of the Creative Class*. New York: Basic Books, 2002.

Fox, Jeffrey, J. *How to Become a Rainmaker*. New York: Hyperion, 2000.

Frick, Don M., and Spears, Larry C. *On Becoming a Servant Leader*. New York: John Wiley & Sons, Inc., 2000.

Friedman, Thomas L. *The Lexus and the Olive Tree: Understanding Globalization*. New York: Farrar, Straus and Giroux, 1999.

Getz, Lowell, and Stasiowski, Frank. *Financial Management for the Design Professional*. New York: Whitney Library of Design, 1982.

Gladwell, Malcolm. *The Tipping Point*. Boston: Little, Brown and Company, 2000.

Godin, Seth. *All Marketers are Liars*. New York: Penguin Group, Inc., 2005.

Godin, Seth. *Purple Cow*. New York: Penguin Group, Inc., 2003.

Gordon, Gary. *Interior Lighting for Designers*. 4th ed. New York: John Wiley & Sons, Inc., 2003.

Handy, Charles. *The Hungry Spirit*. New York: Broadway Books, 1998.

——————. *Ideas for Managers*. New York: John Wiley & Sons, Inc., 2000.

Hesselbein, Frances, and Cohen, Paul M. *Leader to Leader*. New York: John Wiley & Sons, Inc., 2000.

Hesslebein, Frances, Goldsmith, Marshall, and Beckhard, Richard. *The Leader of the Future*. New York: John Wiley & Sons, Inc., 2000.

Holtzschue, Linda, and Noriega, Edward. *Design Fundamentals for the Digital Age*. New York: John Wiley & Sons, Inc., 1997.

Jones, Gerre. *How to Market Professional Design Services*. New York: McGraw-Hill, 1983.

Josephson, Michael S., and Hanson, Wes. *The Power of Character*. New York: John Wiley & Sons, Inc., 2000.

Karlen, Mark, and Benya, James R. *Lighting Design Basics*. New York: John Wiley & Sons, Inc., 2004.

Karlen, Mark. *Space Planning Basics*. 2nd ed. New York: John Wiley & Sons, Inc., 2003.

Kennedy, Eugene, and Charles, Sara C., MD. *Authority: The Most Misunderstood Idea in America*. New York: The Free Press, 1997.

Kliment, Stephen A. *Writing for Design Professionals.* New York: W. W. Norton & Co., Inc. 1998.

Knackstedt, Mary V. *Interior Design for Profit.* New York: Kobro Publications, 1980.

————. *Interior Design and Beyond.* New York: John Wiley & Sons, Inc., 1995.

————. *The Interior Design Business Handbook.* 1st, 2nd, and 3rd eds. New York: John Wiley & Sons, Inc.1988, 1992, and 2002.

————. *Marketing and Selling Design Services: The Designer-Client Relationship.* New York: Van Nostrand Reinhold, 1993.

Knackstedt, Mary V., with Laura J. Haney. *Profitable Careers Options for Interior Designers.* New York: Kobro Publications, 1985.

Koomen, Sharon, and. Dennon, Katherine E. *The Codes Guidebook for Interiors.* 3rd ed. New York: John Wiley & Sons, Inc., 2005.

Krugman, Paul. *Peddling Prosperity.* New York: W. W. Norton & Co., Inc., 1994.

————. *The Return of Depression Economics.* New York: W. W. Norton & Co., 1999.

Levinson, Jay Conrad. *Guerilla Creativity.* New York: Houghton Mifflin Company, 2001.

Levy, Matthys, and Salvadori, Mario. *Why Buildings Fall Down.* New York: W. W. Norton & Co., 1992.

Loebelson. *How to Profit in Contract Design.* New York: Interior Design Books (distributed by Van Nostrand Reinhold), 1983.

Martin, Jane D. *Marketing Basics for Designers: A Sourcebook of Strategies.* New York: John Wiley & Sons, Inc., 1995.

Maslow, Abraham H. *The Maslow Business Reader.* New York: John Wiley & Sons, Inc., 2000.

————. *Maslow on Management.* New York: John Wiley & Sons, Inc., 2000.

Mattox, Robert F. *Financial Management for Architects.* Washington, DC: American Institute of Architects, 1980.

McGowan, Maryrose, and Kruse, Kelsey. *Interior Graphic Standards.* New York: John Wiley & Sons, Inc., 2003.

McGrath, Norman. *Photographing Buildings Inside and Out.* 2nd ed. New York: Whitney Library of Design, 1993; orig. 1987.

Mickelhwait, John, and Woodridge, Adrian. *The Witch Doctors.* New York: New York Times Books, 1996.

Mitton, Maureen. *Interior Design Visual Presentation: A Guide to Graphics, Models, and Presentation Techniques.* 2nd ed. New York. John Wiley & Sons, Inc., 2003.

Moore, James F. *The Death of Competition: Leadership and Strategy in the Age of Business Ecosystems.* New York: HarperCollins, 1996.

Morgan, Jim. *Marketing for the Small Design Firm.* New York: Whitney Library of Design, 1984.

Mudrick, MaryBeth, and Smith, Lawrence. *Federal Style Patterns.* New York. John Wiley & Sons, Inc.,2005.

O'Dell, Susan M., and Pajunen, Joan A. *The Butterfly Customer.* Ontario, Canada: John Wiley & Sons, Canada, Ltd., 1997.

Ogillvy, James. *Living without a Goal: Finding the Freedom to Have a Creative and Innovative Life.* New York: Doubleday, 1995.

Pegler, Martin M. *Dictionary of Interior Design.* New York: Fairchild, 1983.

Peppers, Don. *Life's a Pitch, Then You Buy.* New York: Currency, Doubleday, 1995.

Peters, Tom. *The Seminar: Crazy Times Call for Crazy Organizations.* New York: Vintage Books, 1994.

————. *Reinventing Work 50, The Brand 50, The Project 50, The Professional Service Firm 50.*

————. *Liberation Management: Necessary Disorganization for the Nanosecond Nineties.* New York: Alfred A. Knopf, 1992 (Also on tape).

Peters, Thomas J., and Waterman, Robert H. *In Search of Excellence: Lessons from America's Best-Run Companies.* New York: HarperBusiness Essentials, 2004.

————. *Re-Imagine!* London, UK: Dorling Kindersley Ltd., 2003.

Pile, John. *A History of Interior Design.* 2nd ed. New York: John Wiley & Sons, Inc., 2004.

Piotrowski, Christine. *Becoming an Interior Designer.* New York: John Wiley & Sons, Inc., 2003.

Piotrowski, Christine. *Professional Practice for Interior Designers.* 3rd ed. New York: John Wiley & Sons, Inc., 2001.

Postrel, Virginia. *The Substance of Style.* New York: Harper Collins, 2003.

Preiser, Wolfgang. *Universal Design Handbook.* New York: McGraw Hill, 2001.

Ries, Al. *Focus: The Future of Your Company Depends on It.* New York: Harper, Allens, 1996.

Rose, Stuart W. *Achieving Excellence in Your Design Practice.* New York: Whitney Library of Design, 1987.

Schlossberg, Edwin. *Interactive Excellence.* New York: The Ballantine Publishing Group, 1998.

Senge, Peter M., Roberts, Charlotte, Ross, Richard, Roth, George, Smith, Bryan, and Kleiner, Art. *The Dance of Change: The Challenges to Sustaining Momentum in a Learning Organization.* New York: Random House, 1999.

Siegel, Harry, and Siegel, Alan. *A Guide to Business Principles and Practices for Interior Designers.* Revised ed. New York: Whitney Library of Design, 1982.

————. *This Business of Interior Design.* New York: Whitney Library of Design, 1976.

Slywotzky, Adrian. *The Art of Profitability.* New York. Warner Books, Inc., 2002.

Stanley, Thomas J. *Selling to the Affluent.* Homewood, IL: Business One Irwin, 1991.

————. *Marketing to the Affluent.* Homewood, IL: Dow Jones-Irwin, 1988.

Stasiowski, Frank. *Negotiating Higher Design Fees.* New York: Whitney Library of Design, 1985.

Stasiowski, Frank, and Burstein, David. *Project Management for the Design Professional.* New York: Whitney Library of Design, 1984.

Stitt, Fred A., ed. *Design Office Management Handbook.* Santa Monica, CA: Art & Architecture Press, 1986.

Trout, Jack, with Steve Revlin. *The Power of Simplicity: A Management Guide to Cutting through the Nonsense and Doing Things Right.* New York: McGraw-Hill, 1999.

Wacher, Watts, and Taylor, Jim. *The Visionary's Handbook.* New York: HarperBusiness, 2000.

Whitehead, Randall. *Residential Lighting: A Practical Guide.* New York: John Wiley & Sons, Inc., 2003.

Designers' Business Forum

The Designers' Business Forum is a program developed to help designers, architects, and other creative professionals establish their best opportunities in today's business environment. These businesses are very much needed and valued today, but they require a special structure and process to make them successful.

The forum uses a design process, a system, that creative people find familiar and user-friendly. It considers each person's special abilities and works to develop the best opportunities for growth and success for that individual's firm.

The program is highly participatory and interactive. You meet with other designers to share experiences. You benefit from regular personal contact with other creative people. Regular support is available to assist you with daily problems and the process of growing your business. Whenever you have a question or problem, call us first. We will assist you or find support for you. You are not alone.

If you are interested in growing your firm, you will enjoy the forum. You will gain the opportunity to do better work, experience an easier process, earn better income, and have more time for the pleasures of life.

Our goal is to raise the level of the design profession. Join us. Let's make it happen.

For more information on this program or other issues contact:

Mary V. Knackstedt
2901 North Front Street
Harrisburg, PA 17110
Phone: 717-238-7548
Fax: 717-233-7374
E-mail: maryknackstedt@aol.com

Index

Page numbers in *italic* indicate forms and letters.

Paperwork, reducing, 317
Park design, 22
Partnerships
  advantages/disadvantages of, 49–50
  agreement in, 48–49
  attorney role in, 123
  taxes, 55, 422–423
  types of, 49
Party and ball design, 22–23
Patio design, 23
Payment. *See* Accounts payable; Accounts
    receivable; Billing and collection
Payroll services, bank, 392
Payroll taxes, 50, 54
Pennsylvania
  design center/trade mart in, 282
  design schools in, 468–469
Pension benefits, 111–113, 417
Percentage of cost charge, 269
Percentage of fee charge, 166, 167
Percentage off list price charge, 269
Performance evaluation. *See* Evaluation
Periodicals. *See* Magazines
Permits, 56, 305
Personal digital assistant (PDA), 329
Personal goals, 61–62
Personal injury insurance, 415
Personality
  for design firm start-up, 35–36
  for interior design career, 1–2
Personnel. *See* Staff
Per-square-foot charge, 266
Peters, Thomas, 95
Petty cash, 354, 379
Photographic set design, 23
Photographing Buildings Inside and Out
    (McGrath), 150
Photography, interior, 150–151
Photography stylists, 23
Planning, 60–73
  goal setting, 61–63
  of installation, 243–244
  mission statement, 63
  for profit, 65–67
  project analysis, 67–69
  for selling business, 70–72
  for staffing requirements, 92–93
  team evaluation, 69–70
  value of, 61
  See also Business plan
Plants, placement of, 17
Plumbing fixture design, 23
Portfolio, 140, 272
Postcards, promotional, 142
Postoccupancy evaluation, 248, 249, 250
Presentation, to prospective client,
    160–163, 235–236
President, corporate, 53
Price lists, in design studio library, 89
Pricing. *See* Costs; Fee; Fee structure

Prison design, 23
Privacy
  consultants, 23
  of credit card information, 358
  identity theft and, 404–405
Procurement companies, 269–270, 290,
    294
Product
  in business plan, 64
  catalogs, 88, 89, 276, 338
  design, 24
  display, 24
  evaluation of, 24
  government regulations, 285–286
  invoice, *367, 371*
  liability, 415, 420
  line
    dealerships, 57–58
    information sources, 279
    licensing of, 19
    samples, 88, 90, 91
    selecting, 276
  maintenance, 285
  marketing of, 24, 146–147
  proposal form, *365, 369*
  quality control, 284–285
  research, 227
  in show house displays, 145
  See also Furniture and furnishings;
      Manufacturers; Merchandise;
      Purchasing; Suppliers
Production, for business start-up, 37
Production costs, 387
Productive systems analysts, 127
Professional liability insurance, 409, 416
Professional organizations, 24
  educational opportunities in, 434,
      435
  insurance coverage through, 410, 411
  listed, 459–461
Professionals
  job referrals from, 133
  learning from, 435–436
Professional service corporations (PCs),
    51–52
Profitability
  accounts receivable and, 355–356
  on book, 72
  as business goal, 62
  of design associate work, 5–6
  factors affecting, 66
  fee structure and, 66, 254, 259, 260
  forecast, 65, 352–353
  gross profit, *268,* 382
  improving, 66–67, 270–271
  innovation related to, 273
  money-losing jobs, 261, 315
  planned loss, 259
  on project analysis form, 68
  specialization and, 7, 66

  time management and, 315
  valuation of business purchase for,
      45–46
Profitable Career Options for Designers, 32
Profit analysis, *368, 374, 375*
Profit-sharing plan, 112
Programming phase of project
    management, 225, 226–227
Project analysis, 67–69
Project completion time, 354
Project management, 24, 225–252
  accounting software for, 361–363
  client relations, 250–251
  contract administration phase, 226,
      233–241
  contract development phase, 226,
      232–233
  design development phase, 226,
      227–228, *229*
  design review, 247
  postoccupancy evaluation, 248, *249,*
      250
  programming phase, 225, 226–227
  schematic design phase, 225–226, 227,
      228, 231
  specialists, 285
  stages of, 225–226
  time organization, 312, 315, *319*
  See also Installation
Project manager, 98, 241–242
Project master sheet, 232–233, *232, 235,*
    239
Project schedule. *See* Schedule
Project time sheet, *319*
Promotion consultant, 125
Property taxes, 76
Proposal form, *365, 369*
Prospective client. *See* Client, prospective
Proxemics, 24
Psychiatric care facility design, 24
Publications. *See* Magazines
Publicists, 138, 146–147
Public relations, 25, 138–147
  activities in, 138–139
  client participation in, 69
  contests, 146
  entertaining, 143–145
  goals of, 138
  publication in consumer-oriented
      magazines, 148
  show houses, 145
  tools of, 139–142
  See also Advertising
Purchase order
  checking, 295–296
  number, 238
  in On Order file, 238
  sample form, *366, 370*
  terms and conditions on, 295, 299,
      297–299, 377–378